THE BLUE GUIDES

D1276124

Albania
Austria
Belgium and Luxembourg
China
Cyprus
Czechoslovakia
Denmark
Egypt

FRANCE
France
Paris and Versailles
Burgundy
Loire Valley
Midi-Pyrénées
Normandy
South West France
Corsica

GERMANY
Berlin and Eastern Germany
Western Germany

GREECE
Greece
Athens and environs
Crete

HOLLAND
Holland
Amsterdam

Hungary
Ireland

ITALY
Northern Italy
Southern Italy
Florence
Rome and environs
Sicily
Umbria
Venice

Mexico
Morocco
Moscow and Leningrad
Portugal

SPAIN
Spain
Barcelona
Madrid

Sweden
Switzerland

TURKEY
Turkey
Istanbul

UK
England
Scotland
Wales
London
Museums and Galleries
    of London
Oxford and Cambridge
Country Houses of England
Gardens of England
Literary Britain and Ireland
Victorian Architecture in
    Britain
Churches and Chapels of
    Northern England
Churches and Chapels of
    Southern England
Channel Islands

USA
New York
Boston and Cambridge

The ancient 'witch's olive tree' (Magliano in Toscana)

The publishers and the author welcome comments, suggestions and corrections for the next edition of Blue Guide Tuscany. Writers of the most informative letters will be awarded a free Blue Guide of their choice.

BLUE GUIDE

Tuscany

Alta Macadam

Maps and plans by John Flower

A & C Black
London

WW Norton
New York

Second edition August 1995

Published by A & C Black (Publishers) Limited
35 Bedford Row, London WC1R 4JH

A CIP catalogue record of this book
is available from the British Library.

ISBN 0-7136-4197-5

Published in the United States of America by
WW Norton and Company, Inc
500 Fifth Avenue, New York, NY 10110

Published simultaneously in Canada by
Penguin Books Canada Limited
10 Alcorn Avenue, Toronto, Ontario M4V 3B2

ISBN 0-393-31401-4   USA

The author and the publishers have done their best to ensure the accuracy of all the
information in Blue Guide Tuscany; however, they can accept no responsibility for any
loss, injury or inconvenience sustained by any traveller as a result of information or
advice contained in the guide.

Alta Macadam has been a writer of Blue Guides since 1970. She lives in Florence with
her family (the painter Francesco Colacicchi, and their children Giovanni and Lelia).
Combined with work on writing the guides she has also been associated in Florence
with the Bargello Museum and the Alinari photo archive. She is now involved in work
for Harvard Unviersity at the Villa I Tatti in Florence. As author of the Blue Guides to
Northern Italy, Rome, Venice, Sicily, Florence, Tuscany, and Umbria she travels
extensively in Italy every year in order to revise new editions of the books.

For permission to reproduce the photographs in this book the publishers would like
to thank **Joe Cornish** (pages 2, 142, 239, 280, 289, 298, 315, 329), Susan Benn (pages
46, 54, 172), Antonio Quattrone (page 86), APT Florence (pages 97, 106 and 388), APT
Siena (page 259), and Vincenzo Mencaglia, Cetona (page 334).

Printed in Great Britain by The Bath Press, Avon

CONTENTS

Maps and Plans

INTRODUCTION

Tuscany (in Italian *Toscana*) is the most famous of the twenty regions of Italy. It has an area of 22,991 square kilometres, and a population of about 3,473,000. It lies between the Apennines and the Tyrrhenian sea, bordered on the N by Emilia and Liguria, on the E by the Marches and Umbria, and on the S by Lazio. It includes the famous towns of Florence, Siena, and Pisa, as well as numerous beautiful and interesting small towns including Lucca, Cortona, Volterra, Massa Marittima, Pienza, Montepulciano, San Gimignano, and Montalcino.

It is well known for its splendid landscape, particularly that of the Chianti region between Florence and Siena with its charming low hills covered with olive groves, vineyards, woods, and isolated cypress trees, and dotted with beautiful old farmhouses. The region also includes the Apuan Alps, white with snow and marble, which form a dramatic background to the coastal plain of Versilia. The high Monte Amiata is almost always prominent in the southern Tuscan landscape. Other areas of particular natural beauty, and with their own special characteristics, include the Casentino with its country churches and castles (below the forest of Camaldoli), the Mugello, the hilly wooded area N of Florence with numerous villas and churches, and the remote areas around Pitigliano, near the southern border of Tuscany.

Although the sea coast of Versilia, which first became popular for its bathing resorts in the 18C, has lost much of its charm, beautiful stretches of coastline can still be found in the Maremma (notably the Monti dell'Uccellina) and on Monte Argentario. The island of Elba retains some unspoilt parts, and Capraia, another lovely island in the Tuscan archipelago, can now be visited.

Tuscany derives its name from the inhabitants of ancient Etruria, known as Tusci who probably landed at Tarquinia (now in Lazio) in the 8C BC. In *Etruria Propria* they formed themselves into a Confederation of twelve principal cities, of which Chiusi (Clevsins) was the most important in present-day Tuscany. Other member cities included Cortona, Vetulonia, Volterra (Velathri), Arezzo (Arretium), Populonia, Roselle (Rusellae), and Fiesole (Faesulae). There were also important Etruscan settlements in the Maremma, and around Pitigliano, and Saturnia. Numerous Etruscan remains, including tombs and walls, can still be seen in these places, and important finds from excavations are exhibited in museums all over the region.

In the Middle Ages Lucca was a powerful independent town, and Pisa, at the head of its Maritime Republic, was one of the most important cities in Europe in the 12C. Siena reached the height of its power in the 12–13C, and is still one of the most beautiful medieval towns in Italy. Numerous small hill towns survive in Tuscany as testimony to the rise of independent communes in the Middle Ages, the most famous of which is San Gimignano.

Many beautiful country churches can be seen all over the region, as well as the splendid 12C Romanesque abbey of Sant'Antimo and the 13C Gothic ruins of San Galgano. Important Tuscan monasteries and charter houses include Monte Oliveto Maggiore, La Verna, Camaldoli, Vallombrosa, the Certosa del Galluzzo (outside Florence) and the Certosa di Pisa (near Calci).

Siena, Lucca, and Pisa (as well as Florence) have some of the most beautiful Gothic and Romanesque buildings to be seen in Italy. The early

14C Sienese school of painting produced masters such as Duccio, Simone Martini and Pietro and Ambrogio Lorenzetti. In the 13C and early 14C the great sculptors Nicola Pisano and his son Giovanni were active in Pisa.

Florence is world famous for its Renaissance buildings, but other Renaissance monuments in Tuscany include the piazza in Pienza, Santa Maria del Calcinaio in Cortona, and Santa Maria delle Carceri in Prato. Delightful enamelled terracotta works by the Florentine Della Robbia family are to be found all over the region (Pistoia, Lucca, Impruneta, La Verna, the Valdarno, the Casentino, etc.). The great Florentine school of painting had a wide influence over local masters whose works are preserved in country churches and small towns. Luca Signorelli left some masterpieces in his native city of Cortona, and in Arezzo and Borgo San Sepolcro some of the best works of Piero della Francesca can be seen.

Apart from the fundamental importance to western civilisation of the Florentine Renaissance, Tuscany also produced some of the greatest artists and writers of all time: Giotto, Masaccio, Brunelleschi, Donatello, Leonardo da Vinci, Michelangelo; Dante, Boccaccio, Poliziano, and Petrarca.

Towns interesting for their 19C architecture include Viareggio and Livorno, and the spa of Montecatini has elaborate buildings dating from the beginning of this century.

Numerous travellers (including poets and writers) have come to Tuscany over the centuries, and Florence, Livorno, Pisa and Bagni di Lucca have particular Anglo-American associations. In the early 20C Aldous Huxley and D.H. Lawrence spent much of their time writing in Tuscany.

The inhabitants of some of the larger towns in Tuscany retain notable individual characteristics, and often rivalry is strong between them. Pisa has traditionally been the enemy of Florence, and Lucca proudly independent of the two. Carrara has been an active centre of the Anarchist movement throughout this century.

Tuscany has more museums than any other region in Italy, and more and more interesting small local museums are being opened, including those at San Casciano Val di Pesa, Empoli, Tavarnelle, Montelupo Fiorentino, and Cetona, to name but a few. Tuscany is known for its gardens and it is now becoming easier to visit those in private hands. In summer there are numerous music and theatre festivals in small villages throughout the region.

Note on the Second Edition

This new edition comes out just under two years after the publication of the first Blue Guide to Tuscany. Despite this short elapse of time, numerous changes have had to be recorded in the text, especially with regard to museums and new restorations.

In Florence the splendid Appartamenti Reali in Palazzo Pitti have been reopened after a meticulous restoration. The remarkable collection of Attic vases on the top floor of the Museo Archeologico are again on view. The chapel decorated by Benozzo Gozzoli in Palazzo Medici Riccardi has been restored and reopened. Severe structural damage was caused to the Uffizi gallery in 1993 when a car bomb exploded nearby (probably placed by the Mafia) and some ninety paintings were damaged. Repair work has been carried out efficiently and quickly, many works have already been restored and only some of the rooms in the West Corridor are still closed.

In Siena the famous Maestà by Simone Martini can again be seen on a wall of the Palazzo Pubblico after its restoration, and the beautiful frescoes in the Baptistery have been restored. The Museo Archeologico has been moved to a part of the Ospedale di Santa Maria della Scala. The Oratorio di San Bernardino is now open regularly. In Lucca the interesting churches of Santi Giovanni e Reparata, with their excavations, have been reopened after more than twenty years' closure, and the Museo della Cattedrale has reopened in a new display. Changes have been made in the arrangement of the Museo Guinigi.

At Volterra an underground car park has been constructed at the entrance to the town, and the Museo d'Arte Sacra and Roman Theatre reopened. The castle of Poppi in the Casentino is again open regularly. There have been changes in the Galleria e Museo Medioevale e Moderno and the Museo Archeologico in Arezzo, in the Museo dell'Accademia Etrusca in Cortona, and in the museums of San Gimignano. The Madonna del Parto by Piero della Francesca has been restored but moved from its chapel outside Monterchi to a more banal setting in an old school building in the little town on the hill.

As for the first edition of this guide I am indebted to **Françoise Pouncey Chiarini** who greatly assisted me in preparing the revised text of the Chianti area, the Maremma, and southern Tuscany. We received help from the Soprintendenze per i Beni Artistici e Storici of Siena (particular thanks to Bruno Santi) and of Florence (particular thanks to Rosanna Caterina Proto Pisani).

The offices of the APT of Prato, Pistoia, Arezzo, Massa Carrara, Grosseto, the Arcipelago Toscano, and Chianciano Terme Valdichiana were extremely helpful. Special thanks to Paolo Bacciotti of the Consorzio Turistico Mugello and Piero Fiumi of Volterra. I am also grateful to the APT of Versilia, Siena, Lucca, and Monte Amiata, and the Comunità Montana della Garfanana (Alberto Cresti).

How to use the Guide

As in other Blue Guides, the guide is divided into **routes** which describe the main towns, with their environs, certain areas of the region known for their distinctive landscape, often with numerous country churches, or itineraries between two important centres (such as Florence and Siena or Florence and Pisa). The routes dedicated to the major towns are organised into a number of walking itineraries; they include, at the end of the route, descriptions of places of particular interest which can be reached in less than a day. For the other routes, road itineraries are provided which describe the prettiest (and often the most direct) roads, off which diversions are sometimes suggested to see places of interest along the way. **Distances** are given cumulatively from the starting point in kilometres (km) and roads given with their official numbers (N3, etc.). For those without a car, details are given at the beginning of each of these routes about public transport.

An exhaustive section at the beginning of the book lists all the **practical information** a traveller is likely to need in preparation of a visit to Tuscany and while on the journey. This information, which includes public transport, is integrated with specific details at the beginning of each route and at the beginning of the description of each town. Information has been given both for those who visit the area by car and those who travel by public transport.

A small selection of **hotels** has been given throughout the text (the names emphasised in italics) with their official star rating in order to give an indication of price. In making the choice for inclusion, generally speaking the smaller hotels have been favoured, those in the centre of towns, or in particularly beautiful positions in the countryside. For further information, see under Accommodation in the Practical Information section. On the double page town plans of Siena and Pisa hotels have been marked with a number which corresponds to the key in the text (i.e. Pl.II;3;4, or Pl.3;5) given with the list of hotels at the beginning of the description of the town. Since there are two plans for Siena (called Siena I and Siena II) the first number in the key refers to the Plan (I or II), the second number to the square, and the third number to the number which marks the position of the hotel. For Pisa hotels the first number refers to the square on the Pisa plan and the second number to the number which marks the position of the hotel. On some of the single page plans hotels have been marked with a number (which corresponds to the key in the text; i.e. Pl.5).

Restaurants have also been indicated throughout the book (the names in italics), and these have been divided into three categories which reflect price ranges in 1995: 'LUXURY-CLASS' where the prices are likely to be over Lire 60,000 a head (and sometimes well over Lire 100,000 a head). These are the most famous restaurants in Tuscany and they usually offer international cusine. 'FIRST-CLASS RESTAURANTS' where the prices range from Lire 40,000 and above. These are generally comfortable, with good service, but are not cheap. The third category, called 'SIMPLE TRAT-TORIE AND PIZZERIE' indicates places where you can eat for around Lire 25,000 or 30,000 a head, or even less. Although simple, and by no means 'smart', the food in this category, which often includes local specialities, is usually the best value. For further information, see under Eating in Italy in the Practical Information section.

The **most important monuments or works of art** in Tuscany have been highlighted in bold capital letters or bold type throughout the text, and **asterisks** are used to indicate places or works of art which are particularly beautiful or interesting. The 'Highlights' section on pages 11–12 singles out the major monuments which should not be missed.

Small capital letters are used in **churches** to differentiate the various parts of the building (i.e. the façade, south side, east end, important chapels, etc.). All churches are taken as being orientated, with the entrance at the west end and the altar at the east end, and the south aisle on the right and the north aisle on the left.

In Florence, Pisa, and Siena all the main monuments have been keyed (i.e. Pl.2) against the double page **town plans** which are gridded with numbered squares. On the ground plans of museums and churches figures or letters have been given to correspond with the description in the text.

The **local tourist boards** (Azienda di Promozione Turistica, shortened to APT) are usually extremely helpful and are the only way of securing up-to-date information on the spot about opening times and accommoda-tion. They have all been listed with their telephone numbers on page 26, and the information offices are listed at the beginning of each route and in each town. On the town maps they are marked with **i**, the symbol which is used on local signposts throughout Italy.

Opening times of museums and monuments have been given throughout the text (i.e. 9–14; fest. 9–13), with the abbreviation *fest.* showing times for Sundays and holidays. The times vary and often change without warning, and it is best to consult the local APT on arrival about up to date times. For further information, see p 35. Almost all churches close at 12.00 and do not reopen again until 15.00, 16.00, or even 17.00.

Although detailed town plans are provided, every traveller to Tuscany whether driving or using public transport, will also need a large scale **map** of the region: the best are those produced by the TCI (details on p 28).

Abbreviations used in the guide:

ACI	Automobile Club Italiano
Adm.	admission
APT	Azienda di Promozione Turistica (official local tourist office)
b.	born
C	century
c	circa (about)
CAI	Club Alpino Italiano
d.	died
ENIT	Ente Nazionale per il Turismo
fest.	*festa*, or festival (i.e. holiday)
fl.	floruit (flourished)
FS	Ferrovie dello Stato (Italian State Railways)
IAT	Information office of APT
Pl.	plan
Rte	Route
St	Saint
TCI	Touring Club Italiano

Highlights of the Region

The **most famous towns** of Tuscany—Florence, Siena, Pisa, Lucca, Arezzo, and San Gimignano—have many of the most important buildings, works of art, and museums in the region. The Campo of Siena and the Piazza del Duomo of Pisa are unforgettable sights.

The region also has numerous **less well known small towns** which are extremely interesting and pleasant places to visit (and much less crowded in spring and summer than the more famous towns). These include Cortona, Pienza, Volterra, Massa Marittima, Montalcino, San Quirico d'Orcia, Pitigliano, Sansepolcro and Colle Val d'Elsa. Near Florence the towns of Prato and Pistoia, often overlooked, have much of interest.

Small **well preserved villages** in lovely countryside include (in the order they appear in the book): Uzzano, Barga, Bolgheri, Tirli, Caldana, Montepescali, Capalbio, Montefioralle, San Gusmé, Monteriggioni, Certaldo Alto, Torri, Bagno Vignoni, Castiglione d'Orcia, Cetona, Magliano in Toscana, Pereta, Sovana, Sorano, Poppi, Cennina, Anghiari, Civitella in Val di Chiana, and Lucignano.

Besides the large museums in the famous towns, there are often excellent **small museums** in lesser known places such as Cortona and Volterra. Other particularly fine museums include the Museo della Collegiata di Sant'Andrea at Empoli, the museum at San Casciano in Val di Pesa, the Pinacoteca Comunale at Castiglion Fiorentino, the Museo della Cattedrale di San Zeno in Pistoia and the Museo della Cattedrale in Pienza.

Numerous **masterpieces by great artists** are to be found all over the region, including the best works of Duccio, Simone Martini, Pietro and Ambrogio Lorenzetti, Fra Angelico, Filippo Lippi, Piero della Francesca, Luca Signorelli, and the sculptors Nicola and Giovanni Pisano, Donatello, and the Della Robbia family. These can easily be found by reference to the index of artists at the back of the book.

Some of the most **beautiful landscape** in Tuscany can be found in the Chianti region, the Casentino, the forest of Camaldoli, the Mugello, the Garfagnana (the Parco Naturale delle Alpi Apuane and the Parco dell' Orecchiella), Monte Amiata, the Maremma (particularly in the Parco dell'Uccellina, and near Capalbio and Pitigliano, at the nature reserve of Bolgheri, the Lago di Burano, and Cala Martina and Cala Violina on the coast near Follonica). Fine countryside can also be found in parts of Monte Argentario (and the Tombolo di Feniglia), Elba, and Capraia. For the **gardens** of Tuscany, see page 34.

Etruscan sites and tombs in interesting towns or lovely countryside include those at Chiusi, Cortona, Vetulonia, Volterra, Arezzo, Populonia, Roselle, Fiesole, Pitigliano, Saturnia, and Artimino. **Roman** monuments are to be found at Lucca, Arezzo, Fiesole, Volterra, Cosa and Roselle. **Archae-ological collections** with prehistoric, Etruscan and Roman material are kept in museums in the following towns or localities: Florence, Fiesole, Artimino, Pistoia, Pontremoli, Pisa, Siena, Volterra, Arezzo, Cetona, Cortona, and Chiusi.

The following are some of the most important **Romanesque churches** in Tuscany (apart from those in Florence, Pisa, Siena, and Lucca): Sant' Antimo, San Galgano, San Godenzo, the Duomo of Prato, the Duomo of Barga, San Piero a Grado, Abbadia Isola, the Pieve di Santa Maria a Chianni, the Collegiata of San Gimignano, the Pieve di Cellole, Mensano, the Pieve di San Lazzaro a Lucardo, the Duomo of Massa Marittima, the Collegiata of Sant'Agata at Asciano, the Collegiata of San Quirico d'Orcia, the Pieve di Romena, Gropina, the Pieve di Santa Maria in Arezzo, and San Pietro a Cedda.

Monasteries and charterhouses in Tuscany in beautiful natural settings, interesting also for their works of art, include: Monte Oliveto Maggiore, La Verna, Camaldoli, Vallombrosa, the Certosa del Galluzzo, the Certosa di Pisa, Montesenario, Sant'Anna in Camprena, Abbadia San Salvatore, Rosano, Badia a Passignano, and Lecceto.

Masterpieces of **Renaissance architecture** (apart from those in Florence) include Santa Maria delle Carceri in Prato, the Tempio di San Biagio at Montepulciano, Santa Maria del Calcinaio at Cortona, and the Renaissance town of Pienza.

TUSCANY: AN HISTORICAL INTRODUCTION

John Law

Tuscany has long fascinated foreign visitors. For this its cultural history provides a principal explanation. The region's contribution to the visual arts and architecture has been astounding in quantity and quality, in terms of technical mastery and innovation. The importance and influence of this contribution can also be gauged from the fact that Tuscany largely created the Renaissance as both a historical phenomenon and as an idea. A revealing figure here is the painter, architect and art historian Giorgio Vasari (1511–74). He came from Arezzo and his compendious and influential *Lives of the Artists*, first published in 1550, propagated the concept of the Renaissance, a period of rebirth.

Vasari shared in the belief that civilisation had reached a high point with the Roman Empire, only to decline with the barbarian invaders and the iconoclasm of early Christianity. Its eventual revival, or rebirth, Vasari located largely in Tuscany and attributed to a succession of gifted painters, sculptors and architects, most of whom were Tuscan. For Vasari, the process began with remarkable pioneers, Cimabue (c 1240–1302?) and Giotto (c 1267–1337). It reached further heights with artists like the painter Masaccio (1401–28), the sculptor Donatello (c 1386–1466) and the architect Filippo Brunelleschi (1377–1446). It attained its peak with Vasari's friend and hero, Michelangelo Buonarotti (1475–1564). And not only were most of the leading participants Tuscan; Vasari also assigned a key role in the recognition and support of talent to the Medici. Cosimo I, duke of Florence from 1537 and Grand-duke of Tuscany from 1569, was among Vasari's own patrons.

Vasari's work has had considerable bearing on the interpretation of European cultural history, and while the main focus of his attention was the fine arts and architecture, the concept of Renaissance was applied to other areas. For the poet and Latinist Francesco Petrarch (1304–74) and his humanist followers—of whom many of the leading lights were again Tuscan—literature, moral philosophy and the study of history also underwent a Renaissance, distancing the modern era in cultural terms from the Middle Ages. Moreover, the recovery of the values of ancient Rome and Greece was believed by those involved to be of more than academic or antiquarian interest. The Renaissance, and the study of the humanities, were thought to have a wider relevance for society as a whole.

But the cultural contribution of Tuscany goes beyond even the important and influential channels opened up by humanism and the Renaissance. Petrarch was a fine poet in the vernacular, and here again the Tuscan contribution was remarkable. The poets Dante Alighieri (1265–1321) and Petrarch, and the story-teller Giovanni Boccaccio (1313–75) not only raised Italian to a literary language of the highest level; they also had a profound effect on the literature of the rest of Europe. The prestige of Latin and Greek as the languages of scholarship somewhat eclipsed Italian in the 15C, but it continued as the expressive vehicle for a remarkable number of chroniclers, diarists and letter writers from the Tuscan political and mercantile elite. In the 16C the vernacular re-emerged as the language of another generation of influential writers of whom the Florentine historians and political thinkers Niccolò Machiavelli (1469–1527) and Francesco Guicciardini (1483–1540) are the most famous.

Of course, it would be misleading to suggest that the entire course of Tuscan history can match the achievements of the period c 1300 to c 1550. However the legacy of the Renaissance continued to inspire later generations of craftsmen, artists, architects, men of letters, and their patrons. It also encouraged salons, libraries, art collections and learned societies. The Accademia della Crusca of Florence is a good example; it was established in 1582 to champion the purity of the Italian language. The Accademia Etrusca was founded in Cortona in 1727 to study the pre-Roman civilisation of the region. In its turn, this tradition inspired generations of foreign artists, connoisseurs and scholars to visit Tuscany; in the 18C Florence became a principal stopping point for travellers on the Grand Tour, as Tobias Smollett vividly recalls in his *Travels through France and Italy* (1766). In the 19C and 20C the history and civilisation of Tuscany have been intensely studied. Moreover, research, curiosity and taste have not been satisfied with the major cities, the principal artists or the Renaissance period alone.

There are other reasons for foreign interest in Tuscany. Although generally a satellite of Habsburg power from 1530 to 1859, the region never sank to provincial status, like the provinces of the Papal States. This was largely due to the fact that the Medici ruled from Florence, as dukes and then grand-dukes; in 1737 they were succeeded by the House of Lorraine which lasted—with interruptions during the Revolutionary and Napoleonic periods—down to 1859. The survival of an active court preserved a source of patronage and attracted foreign visitors, diplomats, adventurers and political exiles; Prince Charles Edward Stuart resided in Florence from 1775 to 1788. And there were other autonomous states within the boundaries of Tuscany. The city of Lucca preserved its republican constitution from the end of the Middle Ages to 1805, when it became a principality ruled by various dynasties down to 1859. Minor principalities, which also changed hands, were centred at Massa and Piombino. More famously, Napoleon was ruler of Elba from May 1814 to February 1815.

To captains of industry, however, Elba was better known for its iron ore. Deposits on the island and the mainland had been worked from pre-Roman times; the name 'Elba' was often given to foundries in 19C Britain. This introduces the point that Tuscany remained of economic importance in the modern era, if its cities had lost the commercial, financial and industrial pre-eminence they had acquired in Europe between the 12C and 14C—a phenomenon to be discussed below. Marble and alabaster were quarried in its hills. Abroad the reputation of its olive oil preceded that of its wine. Luxury items were manufactured for export, ceramics and silk for example. From the 18C there was a growing international market for its works of art. Some of the grand-dukes actively encouraged the Tuscan economy, for example by draining the Maremma region to improve health and agricultural production, or by developing Livorno as an international port where Jewish and Protestant communities could trade and worship unmolested. The second commercial railway in Italy was built by Robert Stevenson between Livorno and Pisa (1841–44).

For a variety of reasons, therefore, Tuscany did not have to await the invention of 'Chiantishire' or the introduction of the summer school or the art trail to become familiar to foreign—often Anglo-Saxon—visitors and residents. Furthermore, the rich travel literature and—more poignantly—

the English cemetery in Florence suggest that a simple categorisation of such travellers is impossible. Some came to study art (John Ruskin, 1819–1900), others to develop the art market (Bernard Berenson, 1865–1959). The 'paradise of exiles' attracted bohemian rebels (Shelley and Byron in Pisa, 1821–22); others aimed for a more aristocratic life-style (the Sitwells at Montegufoni, 1909–74). If the relatively liberal policies of the Tuscan grand-dukes encouraged the arrival of merchants and engineers, they also gave hope to Protestant preachers and teachers who planted churches and schools in the principal resorts and cities of the region in the 19C. Health could be a motive. Ancient spas like Bagni di Lucca were revitalised. Viareggio was an early centre for sea bathing. While some visitors were consumed by the dangers, frustrations, opportunities and responsibilities of living abroad, others found them a source of inspiration. E.M. Forster's *Where Angels Fear to Tread* (1905) and *Room with a View* (1908) were set in Tuscany. In the 19C, the politics of the Risorgimento were a source of inspiration and excitement, encouraged when Florence became capital of Italy (1865–71). A later generation was introduced to Tuscany by the war against Fascism and German occupation, and the heavy battles on the Gothic Line (1943–45). The period is captured in the writings of Iris Origo (*War in Val d'Orcia*), Eric Newby (*Love and War in the Apennines*) and Stuart Hood (*Carlino*).

Tuscany (Toscana) is derived from the Roman and early medieval name Tuscia which in turn comes from Etruria, the land of the Etruscans (Tusci, Etrusci). Etruscan power and civilisation were at their height from the 8C to the 4C BC. Quite apart from being seafarers with trading connections across the Mediterranean, the Etruscans settled and influenced other peoples in the Italian peninsula well beyond the frontiers of the modern region. They settled north of the Apennines and deep into what is now Umbria. They also spread southwards, through Lazio to Rome and beyond; the Tarquin rulers of Rome for around 100 years from 616 BC were an Etruscan dynasty. Lars Porsena who beseiged Rome in 508 BC was an Etruscan chieftain from Chiusi.

But the Etruscans did not create a centralised state; their civilisation was a city-based federation whose unity lay more in language, customs and religion than in political power. Eventually this proved a weakness and exposed the Etruscans to Roman conquest in the 4C BC. But although there were battles and rebellions, and Roman colonies were established (e.g. Florence, Lucca, Pisa), the Etruscans were not displaced. Their religion was respected. Some of the southern cities (Arezzo, Cortona) had welcomed Rome as an ally and Etruscan communities were accorded rights of self-government. The region did not desert Rome for Hannibal during the darkest days of the Second Punic War (217 BC), and in 90 BC its inhabitants were granted Roman citizenship. In the 3C and 2C BC, links with the capital had been strengthened with improvements and extensions to the road system, but the surviving identity of the Etruscans resulted in Tuscany being recognised as the seventh region of Italy under the emperor Augustus. Diocletian united it with Umbria in the late 3C AD, with Florence as the capital.

Whatever its frontiers, Roman regional administration was overwhelmed by the barbarian invasions, though between 535 and 553 Byzantine armies had success in regaining imperial territory from the Ostrogoths. But these gains were swept aside in the late 6C by the Lombards who occupied all Tuscany and created a duchy with its capital at Lucca (568–774).

The next fundamental change in the balance of power was created by the entry of the Franks to Italy under Pepin III (751–68) and Charlemagne (768–814) as papal champions, eventually conquering the Lombard duchy of Tuscany in 774. In 800, Pope Leo III (795–816) tried to secure his ally by crowning Charlemagne as emperor in Rome. Tuscany became part of this new western empire, and a Frankish march, or frontier province, was established with its capital at Lucca. However, as in other parts of western Christendom in the age of feudalism, effective authority was wielded from the centre only fitfully and real power was exercised by lay and ecclesiastical landlords, great monastic houses and, increasingly, by the cities.

The rise of the cities to a position of prominence in late medieval and Renaissance Tuscany was a phenomenon of such importance that it demands some explanation. Of course, none of the major centres were purely medieval foundations; all proudly claimed a Roman past, but some went back to Etruscan times and even earlier (Volterra, Chiusi, Fiesole). Whenever their precise origins, towns and cities were founded for a variety of reasons: for security, on defensive sites (Volterra); on river crossings (Florence); near good anchorages (Pisa). In Tuscany, the continuity of urban life was never broken despite the instability following the fall of the Roman Empire and the Saracen raids that intensified with the break-up of Charlemagne's empire in the 9C. A fundamental reason for urban growth—and indeed survival—was the wealth of the countryside in terms of agricultural production and raw materials. The insanitary conditions of urban life, the readiness with which their inhabitants were afflicted by famine and disease, meant that such communities depended on a steady flow of immigrants from their hinterlands. But this did not depopulate the countryside, where the majority of the population continued to live until relatively modern times. The intensity, age and variety of rural settlement—from monastic houses to villas, from medium-size towns to isolated households—points to the wealth of much of the region.

But the principal cities of Tuscany developed in economic terms far beyond the role of local market towns and centres of industry. A lead in this process was taken by Pisa which turned defensive warfare against Saracen raiders into expansion overseas, settling colonies on Corsica, Sardinia and the Balearic Islands in the 10C and 11C, participating in the crusading movement in the eastern Mediterranean and becoming a commercial and naval power of international importance.

The population of Pisa rose from around 12,000 in the mid 12C to around 20,000 in the early 13C and to around 40,000 in the late 13C, small by modern standards but large in the context of medieval Europe. The other cities of Tuscany also expanded rapidly over the same period; the economic revolution in which Pisa took part caused, and was sustained by, the development of its neighbours, Florence, Lucca, Siena. The first two became industrial giants for the production of textiles (woollen cloth and silk). All three became centres of finance, and Tuscan bankers and money-changers operated on an international scale by the 12C and 13C. For example, on the security of royal customs receipts, the Riccardi bankers of Lucca lent vast sums to Edward I of England, financing, among much else, the construction of castles in Wales. Again, the remarkably rich commercial and personal archive left by Francesco Datini (1335–1410), the merchant of Prato so vividly evoked by Iris Origo, shows business acumen at work on a local and international scale.

However, the economic upswing demonstrated most dramatically by the leading Tuscan cities was not sustained. Natural disasters intervened gradually or suddenly. The port of Pisa began to silt up and the population became increasingly exposed to malaria from the 14C. The economies of all the Tuscan cities were disrupted by the Black Death of 1348–49; its arrival in Florence was graphically described by Boccaccio in his *Decameron*. Though precise statistics are lacking, it seems likely that the plague, which became endemic, was a major factor in reducing the populations of Tuscany by at least one third.

Other checks on the economy were man-made. As in the 20C so in the 13C and 14C, heavy advances to demanding foreign clients could place the lenders in the hands of their debtors, as relations between Florentine banking houses and Edward III of England demonstrate. The Tuscan cities also faced competition, first on an Italian and later on an international scale. The rivalry of Genoa, Venice and Florence seriously weakened the naval and commercial power of Pisa; the last rival subjected Pisa to its rule in 1406. Furthermore, the commercial revolution so linked to Tuscan enterprise encouraged the development of other centres of industry, commerce and finance in Europe (e.g. Barcelona, Flanders, the Rhineland). The Medici bank, the leading Florentine finance house of the 15C, counting the papacy among its clients, did not have the resources of its 14C predecessors, and political considerations and mismanagement at the centre and branch level gradually reduced the scope of its operations. Finally, the growth of the Atlantic powers and the Ottoman empire from the late 15C further reduced the relative importance of Tuscany in the economies of Europe and the Mediterranean. It was only in the 19C that Florence—the largest city in the region—saw its population pass the 100,000 mark, the level that it had reached c 1300.

The economic development of Tuscany earlier in the Middle Ages, its agricultural wealth and its relative accessibility by land and sea were principal reasons for the growing autonomy of its towns and cities, and their emergence in the 11C and 12C as self-governing communes. There were other factors. The authority of the emperor's representatives in the region, the marquisses of Tuscany, was only spasmodically effective and came to an end with the death of Matilda in 1115. The emperors themselves, though certainly capable of effective military and political intervention down to the 13C and even beyond, were generally distant overlords with many other preoccupations. Their struggles with the papacy, particularly intense in the late 11C and 12C, for control of the personnel and wealth of the Church proved very debilitating.

The communes that benefited from this conflict and the collapse of central authority could be represented, particularly by historians in the 19C, in a heroic and sometimes patriotic light. They could be seen in terms of a people fighting for freedom from alien rule, and also as devoted allies of the papacy and the cause of the Church. The communes could also be portrayed as breaking the repressive, reactionary, 'medieval' power of the feudal aristocracy with weapons and policies derived from more 'modern' economies and social attitudes.

However historians have now become more cautious, even sceptical, when discussing the phenomenon. It was only in 1859 that Tuscany ceased to be part of the Holy Roman Empire. In the medieval period some communes—Siena, Lucca, Pisa—could have pro-imperial, or Ghibelline, regimes that continued to look to the emperors for protection and privileges. The confrontation once seen between feudal aristocrats and bourgeois entrepreneurs is now regarded as overdrawn. Great landowners of ancient pedigree could also have interests in banking and commerce, like the

Piccolomini of Siena. Upwardly mobile bourgeois families enthusiastically adopted an aristocratic life-style and acquired titles, coats of arms, country estates and well-connected marriages. If the communes of Tuscany did try to control with force and legislation the political and military influence of noble clans, they could not end it as the castles of the Tuscan countryside show. Moreover, they often turned to such families for support, for example when in need of leaders and resources in time of war.

Furthermore, the communes were far from being democracies. The participation of such bodies as the *popolo* and guilds in the 13C and 14C may have widened government, but it did not end the ascendancy of a *de facto* oligarchy of the wealthier and longer-established families. In 14C Florence, for example, the *Arti Maggiori*, or greater guilds of bankers, merchants, lawyers maintained a predominance over the *Arti Minori* representing the much more numerous artisans and retailers. In none of the communes was the bulk of the rural or urban population ever admitted to government. In conditions of economic hardship this could result in violence; in July 1378 the unenfranchised day labourers of Florence, the Ciompi, tried and failed to win for themselves a place in government.

But violence was not confined to resentful workers and peasants. Within communal government there was little sense of 'loyal opposition'; a regime's enemies faced legal and fiscal penalties, fines, exile, imprisonment or death. Beyond the borders of a city state, exiles could gather in vengeful 'contrary commonwealths', though others could choose a more solitary path. Most famously, faction in Florence condemned Dante Alighieri to exile in 1302; the poet gradually distanced himself from other exiled Florentines and their allies, though his bitterness never left him.

Dante's career also points to other sources of instability in the political and social life of the communes of Tuscany. His family shared, and continued, his exile; a strong sense of kin, often intensified by local loyalties founded on the parish or quarter of a city, meant that patron-client relationships, a reliance on the clan, could undermine public authority. Secondly, internal faction could have a wider, even international, dimension as Guelfs (nominally pro-papal) fought Ghibellines (nominally pro-imperial) for control of the cities of Tuscany in the 13C and 14C.

Lastly, if communes were jealous of their own authority they were less prepared to recognise the liberties of others. For reasons of military and economic security, the towns and cities of Tuscany all sought to extend the area of their jurisdiction, or *contado*. The larger communes also sought to bring their rivals under their dominion. This was markedly the case with Florence whose self-centred belief in liberty encouraged rather than inhibited its expansion in Tuscany: Prato, 1350; Pistoia, 1351; Volterra, 1361; Arezzo, 1384; Pisa, 1406; Cortona, 1411; Livorno, 1421.

But it can be as anachronistic to belittle as to exaggerate the achievements of the communes. In a Europe largely dominated by monarchical forms of government and a hierarchic view of society, they did represent an alternative: a concept of popular sovereignty; republican constitutions; more open, answerable, forms of government; greater social mobility. Such an alternative view found expression in books of statutes and the resolutions and debates of governing councils. It shaped political thought, attitudes to history and forms of propaganda. It informed the astounding range of often vivid and detailed chronicles and diaries produced in the cities of late medieval Tuscany.

Even more tangibly, it was expressed in the construction of public buildings, the *palazzi*, where councils and courts met and archives and treasuries were stored. The communes also tried to improve the quality of life: establishing markets, building bridges, paving streets and squares, regulating private building, installing fountains, passing legislation on hygiene. They tried to encourage public education, the more enlightened communes supporting universities (Pisa from the 12C, Siena from the 13C). They tried to further security: fortifying the city with walls and gates; curbing powerful families who sought to build towers and castles for themselves in town and country; regulating the carrying of weapons; placing garrisons in strategic fortresses.

The sense of community could also be expressed in religious terms with the communes supporting the Church, charitable institutions and the cults associated with saints and relics. The main focus of attention was generally the cathedral, but the commune could also support hospitals and the churches associated with religious orders and local cults. The case of Siena can be taken to illustrate these general points: from ambitious plans to enlarge and embellish the cathedral, to support for the central hospital of Santa Maria della Scala; from the construction of the seat of government, the *Palazzo Pubblico*, to its decoration with frescoes expressing civic pride, piety and political beliefs; from the paving of the central *Piazza del Campo*, to the engineering feat of installing in it a public fountain, the *Fonte Gaia*.

It is in the *Campo* that the famous horse race, the *palio* between rival *contrade*, or districts, of the city is still run. This serves to introduce a further point. Loyalty to parish, family or guild was not necessarily incompatible with the common good of the wider community. Competition could be expressed in a civic context as the patronage of the guilds of Florence for the shrine of Or San Michele in the early 15C clearly demonstrates. The foundation (1495) of the beautiful Piccolomini library in the cathedral of Siena by cardinal Francesco Piccolomini (later Pius III, 1503) was in part intended to celebrate the family name and the achievements of his uncle Aeneas Sylvius (Pius II, 1458–64). It was also intended to enrich the church and contribute to learning.

As a form of government, republicanism failed to survive the Renaissance other than in Lucca. The political instability of the region had earlier seen communes come under the rule (*signoria*) of a native or foreign lord (*signore*). In some instances, such lordship could be largely nominal, like that of the Angevin kings of Naples over Florence in the early 14C. However, some *signori* were sustained by real economic and military power and the support of a faction or party of the population. This was the case with the military leader Castruccio Castracane (1281–1328) who, from a base in Lucca over which he was made duke (1327), extended his rule over a number of Tuscan cities.

But the strength of republicanism in the region and the jealousy of other families prevented signorial regimes from being more than interludes, though principalities did take root at Massa and Piombino. With the Renaissance the situation changed. In the course of the 15C, and particularly after 1434, the Medici established an ascendancy in Florence. This was not based on force, nor was the family's influence formalised in terms of office or title; they remained private citizens. Medici power was based on wealth, family alliances and patronage in the broadest sense. It depended crucially on the political and diplomatic skills of the Medici themselves, and more particularly the heads of the leading household: Cosimo (1389–68), Piero (1418–69), Lorenzo 'the Magnificent' (1449–92).

When these qualities were lacking, as happened after the death of Lorenzo, republicanism quickly re-established itself.

But however informal their hold on power in the 15C, abroad the Medici had established themselves as Italian princes, and two members of the dynasty became pope: Leo X (1513–21) and Clement VII (1523–34). Papal support helped sustain the family in its periods of exile and also contributed—along with the armies of the emperor Charles V—to its eventual return in 1530, first as lords of the city and then as dukes (1532). Not only was the Medici hold on power formalised and given some legitimacy; they also inherited the ascendancy Florence had achieved over Tuscany. Thanks again to Habsburg arms, the Medici state was enlarged by the Treaty of Cateau-Cambrésis (1559) with the addition of Siena and the commune of Montalcino, both of which had put up a heroic defence of Tuscan republicanism against superior forces. In 1569 Cosimo I was created Grand-duke of Tuscany.

But if the rule of the Medici, their transformation from private citizens to princes and the construction of fortresses and citadels in Florence and elsewhere brought about the end of republican government in most of Tuscany, the legacy of the republican past was not destroyed. The civic sense and cultural vitality generated in the Middle Ages survived in Florence and the other cities of Tuscany, informing and moderating the relatively enlightened and liberal grand dukes down to Tuscany's unification with the kingdom of Italy in 1860.

Further Reading

J. Bentley, *Italy: the Hill Towns* (London, 1990).

G. Brucker, *Renaissance Florence* (New York, 1969).

J.R. Hale, *Florence and the Medici* (London 1977).

J.R. Hale (ed.), *A Concise Encyclopedia of the Italian Renaissance* (London, 1981).

O. Hamilton, *The Divine Country* (London, 1982).

D. Hay (ed.), *The Longman History of Italy* (London, 1980–)

H. Hearder and D.P. Waley (eds), *A Short History of Italy* (Cambridge, 1962).

H. Hearder, *Italy: a Short History* (Cambridge, 1990).

J. Hook, *Siena* (London, 1979).

J. Keates, *Tuscany* (London, 1988).

I. Origo, *The Merchant of Prato*

J. Pemble, *The Mediterranean Passion* (Oxford, 1988).

M. Phillips, *The Memoir of Marco Parenti. A Life in Medici Florence* (London, 1990).

D.P. Waley, *The Italian City Republics* (London, 1978).

D.P. Waley, *Siena and the Sienese* (Cambridge, 1991).

Place names in Italian towns and cities

Many of the place names in Italian towns and cities have ancient origins; the names assigned to public buildings, market places, towers, bridges, gates and fountains frequently date to the Middle Ages. But the practice of formally naming all streets and squares began in the 19C. Frequently local—even parochial—patriotism determines the choice as the community celebrates its own history and its own political, literary, religious and scientific figures, as well as famous foreign visitors.

But the choice of place names can reflect wider issues, and events and figures from Italian national history are prominently represented. Thus a united republican Italy can be celebrated in terms of concepts (e.g. Via della Repubblica, della Libertà, della Vittoria), events (e.g. Via del Plebiscito recalling the vote that preceded a region uniting with the Kingdom of Italy in the 19C), or by drawing on the gazetteer of Italian rivers, mountains, seas and cities.

Broadly speaking the national figures and events chosen tend to be representative of four phases in recent Italian history. Probably the most emotive and frequently commemorated is the Risorgimento (the Resurgence), the movement that led to the unification and independence of Italy in the 19C; among the battles commemorated are: Custoza, Lissa, Solferino, Magenta, Montebello, Mentana. For some historians, Italy's entry to the First World War represents the final phase in the pursuit of national unity; the battles and campaigns between Italy, and her allies, and the Central Powers are also frequently recorded in place names: the Isonzo; Monte Pasubio; Caporetto; Monte Grappa, the Piave; Vittorio Veneto. Opposition to Fascism and the ending of the Second World War are also commemorated in this way, as are the statesmen and events associated with the country's reconstruction, economic development and membership of the EU. Casualties in Italy's successful struggle against political terrorism (Aldo Moro, murdered by the Red Brigades in 1978) and the less successful war with organised crime (Alberto della Chiesa, killed by the Mafia in 1982) are also being so honoured.

Largely censored and deleted from the record are the events and personalities closely linked to Fascism, Italy's empire and the reigns of the last two members of the House of Savoy, Vittorio Emanuele III (1900–46) and Umberto II (1946). However, the keen-eyed observer might be able to identify traces of Fascist insignia and the Fascist system of dating (1922, when Mussolini was invited to lead the government, is year 1) on public buildings and monuments, and some street names still recall territories once ruled from Rome (e.g. Istria, Dalmazia, Albania, Libia).

Below are listed a selection of the more prominent figures and events from recent Italian history the traveller is likely to encounter time and again.

People

Vittorio ALFIERI (1749–1803), poet and dramatist.

Cesare BATTISTI, Italian patriot executed by the Habsburg regime in Trent, 12 July 1916.

Giosuè CARDUCCI (1835–1907), patriotic poet and literary critic.

Camille CAVOUR (1810–61), statesman and cautious architect of Italian unification.

Francesco CRISPI (1818–1901), statesman.

Ugo FOSCOLO (1778–1827), poet and patriot.

Giuseppe GARIBALDI (1807–82), inspirational political and military leader in the Risorgimento.

Antonio GRAMSCI (1891–1937), political thinker, Marxist, opponent of Fascism.

Daniele MANIN (1804–57), Venetian patriot and statesman, defender of that city against Habsburg forces, 1848–49.

Guglielmo MARCONI (1874–37), electrical engineer and radio pioneer.

MARGHERITA of Savoy (1851–1926), wife of King Umberto I, noted for her piety, good works and cultural patronage.

MARTIRI DELLA RESISTENZA (or DELLA LIBERTÀ), opponents of Fascism and German occupation, 1943–45.

Giacomo MATTEOTTI (1885–1924), socialist politician, assassinated by Fascists.

Guiseppe MAZZINI (1805–82), leading republican figure of the Risorgimento.

Guglielmo OBERDAN (1858–82), Italian patriot, executed by the Habsburg regime in Trieste.

Bettino RICASOLI (1809–80), Florentine statesman, instrumental in securing Tuscany's adherence to the Kingdom of Italy in 1860.

Aurelio SAFFI (1819–1890), man of letters and hero of the Risorgimento.

UMBERTO I of Savoy, King of Italy, 1878–1900.

Giuseppe VERDI (1813–1901), prolific opera composer whose output was often associated with cause of a united Italy. His surname could be read as the initials of 'Vittorio Emanuele Re d'Italia'.

VITTORIO EMANUELE II of Savoy, King of Sardinia-Piedmont from 1849, King of Italy 1861–78.

Events

XI FEBBRAIO: 11 February 1929, formal reconciliation between the papacy and the kingdom of Italy.

XXIX MARZO: 29 March 1943, armistice between Italy and the Allies.

XXVII APRILE: 27 April 1945, Benito Mussolini captured by partisans in northern Italy. the Fascist leader was quickly 'tried' and executed on 28 April.

XI MAGGIO: 11 May 1860, Garibaldi landed with 1000 men at Marsala (Sicily) and launched the military campaign that led to the Unification of Italy.

XXIV MAGGIO: 24 May 1915, Italy enters the First World War.

II GIUGNIO: 2 June 1946, referendum designed to favour a republican constitution.

XX GIUGNO: 20 June 1859, papal forces and their supporters violently suppressed a pro-Unification rising in Perugia.

XIV SETTEMBRE: 14 September 1860, the forces of the Kingdom of Italy entered Perugia.

XX SETTEMBRE: 20 September 1870, Italian forces enter Rome, overthrowing papal rule.

IV NOVEMBRE: 4 November 1918, proclamation of the armistice between Italy and Austria.

PRACTICAL INFORMATION

Getting to Italy

Direct air services (scheduled flights as well as charter flights) operate between London (Heathrow, Gatwick, and Stansted) and Italy. Pisa, Florence, Bologna, Genoa, and Rome are the nearest airports to Tuscany. There are direct rail services from Calais and Boulogne via Paris to Florence and Rome. The easiest approaches by road are the motorways through the Mont Blanc, St Bernard, or Monte Cenis tunnels, over the Brenner pass, or along the S coast of France.

Among the numerous **Tour Operators** who sell tickets and book accommodation, and also organise inclusive tours to Tuscany are: Prospect Music and Art Tours Ltd, Martin Randall Travel, Page and Moy, Specialtours, Abercrombie and Kent, Italian Escapades, Italiatour, Citalia, and Magic of Italy. Chapter Travel (Tel. 0171-722 9560) specialise in self-catering accommodation in Italy.

Air Services between London and Italy are operated by British Airways (Tel. 0181-897 4000), Alitalia (Tel. 0171-602 7111), and (Florence only) Air UK (Tel. 01345 666777) and Meridiana (Tel. 0171-839 2222). Charter flights (often much cheaper) are also now run to most of the main cities in Italy; the fare often includes hotel accommodation. Scheduled services offer special fares which are available according to season. Youth fares are available. Car hire schemes in conjunction with flights can also be arranged.

Rail Services. The most direct routes from Calais and Boulogne via Paris and Dijon (with sleeping compartments) are via Modane to Turin, Genoa, and Pisa or via Lausanne and Domodossola to Milan, Bologna, and Florence. A service from London Victoria via Dover, Calais, Basel, and Chiasso runs to Milan, Florence, and Rome. The route via Ostend and Brussels may offer useful connections. Information on the Italian State Railways (and tickets and seat reservations) may be obtained in London from Citalia, Marco Polo House, 3–5 Lansdowne Road, Croydon, Surrey CR9 1LL (Tel. 0181/686 0677) and Wasteels Travel, adjacent to Platform 2, Victoria Station, London SW1V 1JT, who also issue Italian Rail passes.

Bus Service. A bus service operates in two days between London (Victoria Coach Station) and Rome (Piazza della Repubblica) via Dover, Calais, Paris, Turin, Milan, Bologna, and Florence, daily from June to September, and once or twice a week for the rest of the year. Youth fares are available. Information in London from the National Express office at Victoria Coach Station (Tel. 0171-730 0202), from local National Express Agents, and in Italy from SITA offices.

By Car. British drivers taking their own cars by any of the routes across France, Belgium, Luxembourg, Switzerland, Germany, and Austria need the vehicle registration book, a valid national driving licence (accompanied by a translation, issued free of charge by Wasteels and the Italian State Tourist Office), insurance cover, and a nationality plate attached to the car. If you are not the owner of the vehicle, you must have the owner's written permission for its use abroad. A Swiss Motorway Pass is needed for Switzerland, and can be obtained from the RAC, the AA or at the Swiss border.

The continental rule of the road is to drive on the right and overtake on the left. The provisions of the respective highway codes in the countries of transit, though similar, have important variations, especially with regard to priority, speed limits, and pedestrian crossings. Membership of the 'Auto-mobile Association' (Tel. 01256 20123), or the 'Royal Automobile Club' (membership enquiries and insurance, Tel. 0345 3331133; route informa-tion Tel. 0345 333222) entitles you to many of the facilities of affiliated societies on the Continent. They are represented at most of the sea and air ports.

Motorway routes to Italy from Europe. The main routes from France, Switzerland, and Austria are summarised below.

A. The direct motorway route from France, by-passing Geneva, enters Italy through the **Mont Blanc Tunnel**. The road from Courmayeur to Aosta has not yet been improved. At Aosta the A5 motorway begins: it follows the Val d'Aosta. Just beyond Ivrea is the junction with the A4/5 motorway: the A5 continues S to Turin, while the A4/5 diverges E. At Santhia the A4 motorway from Turin is joined for Milan via Novara, or the A26/4 can be followed S via Alessandria, reaching the coast at Voltri, just outside Genoa. For Tuscany there is a choice between the *Autostrada del Sole* (A1) from Milan or the Florence–Pisa motorway from Genoa. The latter route avoids the Apennine pass between Bologna and Florence which carries very heavy traffic and can be subject to delays.

B. The most direct approach to Turin from France is through the **Monte Cenis Tunnel** from Modane in France to Bardonecchia. A road continues to Oulx where a motorway is under construction via Susa to Turin parallel to the old road. From Turin a motorway (A6) descends direct to the coast at Savona, or the motorway (A21, A26) via Asti and Alessandria leads to Genoa; either one joins directly the coastal motorway for Pisa and Florence. Alternatively, the A4 motorway leads from Turin E to Milan for the *Autostrada del Sole*.

C. The **Coastal route from the South of France** follows the A10 motorway through the foothills with frequent long tunnels to enter Italy just before Ventimiglia. The motorway continues past Alassio, Albenga, and Savona (where the motorway from Turin comes in), to Voltri (where the A26 motorway from Alessandria comes in) and Genoa (with the junction of the the A7 motorway from Milan). The coastal motorway continues beyond Rapallo and La Spezia into Tuscany past the resorts of Versilia, and at Viareggio divides. The left branch (A11) continues via Lucca to Florence (and the *Autostrada del Sole*), while the coastal branch (A12) continues to Pisa and Livorno.

D. The approach to Italy from Switzerland (Lausanne) is usually through the **Great St Bernard Tunnel** (or by the pass in summer) which only becomes motorway at Aosta (see A, above).

E. Another motorway route from Switzerland is via the **St Gotthard Tunnel** (opened in 1980) and Lugano. The motorway (A9) enters Italy at Como and continues to Milan where the *Autostrada del Sole* (A1) begins for central Italy.

F. From Germany and Austria (Innsbruck) the direct approach to Italy is by the motorway over the **Brenner Pass**. The motorway (A22) continues down the Isarco valley to Bolzano and the Adige valley via Trento to Verona. Here motorways diverge W for Brescia and Milan, or E for Vicenza and Venice, or continue S via Mantua to join the A1 motorway just W of Modena for Florence and central Italy.

Car Sleeper Train services operate from Boulogne and Paris, Hamburg, Vienna, and Munich to Milan, Bologna, Rome, etc.

Passports or Visitors Cards are necessary for all British travellers entering Italy; American travellers must carry passports. British passports valid for ten years are issued, on the spot, at the Passport Office, Clive House, Petty France, London, SW1, or can be requested by post—forms available at post offices—although you should allow one month for this. A 'British Visitor's Passport' (valid one year) can be purchased at post offices in Britain. You are strongly advised to carry some means of identity with you at all times while in Italy, since you can be held at a police station if you are stopped and found to be without a document of identity. A stolen or lost passport can be replaced with little trouble by the British or US embassy in Rome, or the US consulate in Florence.

Money. The monetary unit is the Italian lira (plural; lire). There are coins of 10, 20, 50, 100, 200 and 500 lire, and notes of 1000, 2000, 5000, 10,000, 50,000, and 100,000 lire. Travellers' cheques and Eurocheques are the safest way of carrying money while travelling, and most credit cards are now generally accepted in shops and restaurants (and at some petrol stations). The commission on cashing travellers' cheques can be quite high. For banking hours, see under 'General Information', below. Money can be changed at exchange offices (cambio), in travel agencies, some post offices, and main stations. Exchange offices are usually open seven days a week at airports and some main railway stations. At some hotels, restaurants, and shops money can be exchanged (but usually at a lower rate). There are now some automatic machines for changing foreign bank notes outside banks in the main towns.

Police Registration is formally required within three days of entering Italy. If you are staying at a hotel the management takes care of this. The permit lasts three months, but can be extended on application.

Information Offices

Italian Tourist Boards. General information can be obtained abroad from the Italian State Tourist Office (ENIT; Ente Nazionale Italiano per il Turismo), who distribute free an excellent 'Traveller's handbook' (revised about every year), and provide detailed information about Italy.

In London their office is at 1 Princes Street, WIR 8AY (Tel. 0171-408 1254); in New York at 630 Fifth Avenue, Suite 1565 (Tel. 212 2454822); in Chicago at 500 North Michigan Avenue, Suite 1046 (Tel. 312 6440990).

In Tuscany the Regional State Tourist office is in Florence: Dipartimento Turismo della Regione Toscana, 26 Via di Novoli, Tel. 055-4382111. Tuscany is divided into sectors, each with a local tourist information office, the

Azienda di Promozione Turistica (APT) which provides invaluable help to travellers on arrival: they supply a free list of accommodation (revised annually), including hotels, youth hostels, and camping sites; up-to-date information on museum opening times and annual events; and information about local transport. They also usually distribute, free of charge, illustrated pamphlets about each town, sometimes with a good plan, etc. The head-quarters are normally open Monday–Saturday 8–14.00, but in the towns of particular interest there is sometimes a separate APT information office, which is often also open in the afternoon.

The APT of Tuscany are as follows:

APT Versilia, 10 Viale Carducci, Viareggio (Tel. 0584-48881).

APT Arcipelago Toscano, 26 Calata Italia, Portoferraio, Elba (Tel. 0565-914671).

APT Montecatini Terme-Valdinievole, 66 Viale Verdi, Montecatini Terme (Tel. 0572-772244).

APT Chianciano Terme-Valdichiana, 7 Via Sabatini, Chianciano Terme (Tel. 0578-63538).

APT Firenze, 16 Via Manzoni, Florence (Tel. 055-23320).

APT Grosseto, 206 Via Monterosa, Grosseto (Tel. 0564-454510).

APT Livorno, 6 Piazza Cavour, Livorno (Tel. 0586-898111).

APT Massa Carrara, 24 Lungomare Vespucci, Marina di Massa (Tel. 0585-240063).

APT Pisa, 26 Via Benedetto Croce, Pisa (Tel. 050-40096).

APT Siena, 43 Via di Città, Siena (Tel. 0577-42209).

APT Arezzo, 116 Piazza Risorgimento, Arezzo (Tel. 0575-23952).

APT Abetone-Pistoia-Montagna Pistoiese, 28 Via Marconi, San Marcello Pistoiese (Tel. 0573-630145).

APT Lucca, 2 Piazza Guidiccioni, Lucca (Tel. 0583-491205).

APT Prato, 51 Via Muzzi, Prato (Tel. 0574-35141).

APT Amiata, 97 Via Mentana, Abbadia San Salvatore (Tel. 0577-778608).

Getting to Tuscany from the rest of Italy

By Air. Pisa is the main international airport in Tuscany. From the airport a train service runs in 1hr via Pisa to Florence. There is also an international airport at Bologna, across the Apennines in Emilia-Romagna (trains from Bologna to Florence in just over 1 hr). The small airport near the centre of Florence (Peretola) has some flights from England (Stansted and Gatwick).

By Train. The main line from Milan and Bologna to Rome has stations at Prato, Florence and Arezzo (although not all trains stop at Prato and Arezzo). The coastal line from Turin and Genoa serves Massa Carrara and Versilia, Pisa, Livorno, and Grosseto.

By Car. The A1 motorway from Milan and Bologna to Rome runs through Tuscany from Prato to Florence, the Valdarno, Arezzo, Valdichiana, and Chiusi. The coastal motorway from the south of France and Genoa enters Tuscany at Massa Carrara and continues S through Versilia to Lucca and Pisa.

Driving in Italy

Temporary membership of the *Automobile Club d'Italia* (ACI) can be taken out on the frontier or in Italy. The headquarters of ACI are at 8 Via Marsala, Rome (branch offices in all the main towns). They provide a breakdown service (*Soccorso ACI*, Tel. 116).

Rules of the road. Italian law requires that you carry a valid driving licence when travelling. It is obligatory to keep a red triangle in the car in case of accident or breakdown. This serves as a warning to other traffic when placed on the road at a distance of 50 metres from the stationary car. It can be hired from ACI for a minimal charge, and returned at the frontier. It is now compulsory to wear seat-belts in the front seat of cars in Italy. Driving in Italy is generally faster (and often more aggressive) than driving in Britain or America. Road signs are now more or less standardised to the international codes, but certain habits differ radically from those in Britain or America. If a driver flashes his headlights, it means he is proceeding and not giving you precedence. In towns, Italian drivers are very lax about changing lanes without much warning. Unless otherwise indicated, cars entering a road from the right are given precedence. Italian drivers tend to ignore pedestrian crossings. In towns beware of motorbikes, mopeds, and Vespas, the drivers of which seem to consider that they always have the right of way.

Motorways (*Autostrade*). Italy probably has the finest motorways in Europe, although in the last ten years or so too many have been constructed to the detriment of the countryside. Tolls are charged according to the rating of the vehicle and the distance covered. There are service areas on all autostrade (open 24 hours), and, generally speaking, the FINI cafés and restaurants are usually the best. Most autostrade have SOS points every two kilometres. Unlike in France, motorways are indicated by green signs (and normal roads by blue signs). At the entrance to motorways, the two directions are indicated by the name of the most important town (and not by the nearest town) which can be momentarily confusing.

Superstrade are dual carriageway fast roads which do not charge tolls. They do not usually have service stations, SOS points, or emergency lanes. They are also usually indicated by green signs. In Tuscany the superstrada between Florence and Siena is particularly busy, and it is a poorly engineered road, and rather narrow.

Petrol stations are open 24 hours on motorways, but otherwise their opening times are: 7–12, 15–20; winter 7.30–12.30, 14.30–19. There are now quite a number of self-service petrol stations open 24hrs operated by bank notes (Lire 10,000), usually near the larger towns. Unleaded petrol has become easy to find in the last few years. Petrol in Italy costs more than in Britain, and a lot more than in America.

Car Parking. Almost every town in Tuscany (as in the rest of Italy) has taken the wise step of closing its historic centre to traffic (except for residents). This makes them much more pleasant to visit on foot. Access is allowed to hotels and for the disabled. It is always advisable to leave your car well outside the centre (places to park are usually indicated), and details have been given in the text below. Some car parks are free, while others charge an hourly tariff. In some towns mini-bus services connect car parks with the centre. With a bit of effort it is almost always possible to find a place to leave your car free of charge, away from the town centre. It is forbidden to park in front of a gate or doorway marked with a 'passo carrabile' (blue and red) sign. Always lock your car when parked, and never leave anything of value inside it.

Car Hire is available in most Italian cities. Arrangements for the hire of cars in Italy can be made through Alitalia or British Airways (at specially advantageous rates in conjunction with their flights) or through any of the principal car-hire firms (the best known include Maggiore, Avis, and Hertz).

Roads in Tuscany. Tuscany has an excellent network of roads, and drivers are strongly advised to avoid motorways and *superstrade* and use the secondary roads which are usually well engineered and provide fine views of the countryside. Buildings of historic interest are often indicated by yellow signposts (although there are long-term plans to change the colour to brown). White road signs sometimes indicate entry into a municipal area which is (confusingly) often a long way from the town of the same name.

Maps

Although detailed town plans have been included in this book, it has not been possible, because of the format, to provide an atlas of Tuscany adequate for those travelling by car. The maps at the end of the book are only intended to be used when planning an itinerary. The Italian Touring Club publishes several sets of excellent maps: these are constantly updated and are indispensable to anyone travelling by car in Italy. They include the 'Grande Carta Stradale d'Italia' on a scale of 1:200,000. This is divided into 15 sheets covering the regions of Italy: Tuscany is covered on the sheet (No. D39) entitled *Toscana*. These are also published in a handier form as an atlas (with a comprehensive index) called the *Atlante Stradale d'Italia* in three volumes (the one entitled 'Centro' covers Tuscany). These maps can be purchased from the Italian Touring Club offices and at many booksellers; in London they are obtainable from Stanfords, 12–14 Long Acre, WC2E 9LP.

The *Istituto Geografico Militare* of Italy has for long been famous for its map production (much of it done by aerial photography). Their head-quarters are in Florence (10 Via Cesare Battisti). Their maps are now available at numerous bookshops in the main towns of Italy. They publish a map of Italy on a scale of 1:100,000 in 277 sheets, and a field survey partly 1:50,000, partly 1:25,000, which are invaluable for the detailed exploration of the country, especially its more mountainous regions; the coverage is however, still far from complete at the larger scales, and some of the maps are out-of-date.

Public Transport

Railways. The Italian State Railways (FS—*Ferrovie dello Stato*) run various categories of trains. (1) EC (*Eurocity*), international express trains (with a special supplement, approximately 30 per cent of the normal single fare) running between the main Italian and European cities (seat reservation is sometimes obligatory). (2) IC (*Intercity*), express trains running between the main Italian towns, with a special supplement (on some of these seat reservation is obligatory, and some carry first-class only). (3) P (*Pendolino*; ETR 450) an extra fast service (first and second-class) which costs considerably more and advance booking is obligatory. The fastest *pendolino* service between Rome via Florence Rifredi and Bologna to Milan takes just 4 hours, reaching a maximum speed of 250km an hour. (4) *Espressi*, long-distance trains (both classes) not as fast as the 'Intercity' trains. (5) IR (*Interegionali*) local trains; and (6) *Diretti* stopping at all stations (usually only second-class).

Trains in Italy are usually crowded, especially on holidays and in summer, and it is now always advisable to book your seat when buying a ticket. There is a booking fee of Lire 4500 and the service is available from 2 months to 3 hrs before departure at station ticket offices or travel agents who are agents for Italian State Railways. The timetable of the train services changes on about 26 September and 31 May every year. Excellent timetables are published twice a year by the Italian State Railways (*Il Treno*; one volume for the whole of Italy) and by Pozzorario in several volumes (*Nord e Centro* covers Tuscany). These can be purchased at news-stands and railway stations.

Fares and Reductions. In Italy fares are still much lower than in Britain. Tickets must be bought at the station (or at agencies for Italian State Railways) before starting a journey, otherwise a fairly large supplement has to be paid to the ticket-collector on the train. It is always best, if possible, to buy tickets for journeys over 50km in advance so you can also book a seat (see above), also because there are often long queues at the station ticket offices. Some trains carry first-class only; some charge a special supplement; and on some seats must be booked in advance. It is therefore always necessary to specify which train you are intending to take as well as the destination when buying tickets. If you purchase a return ticket, you must stamp it at an automatic machine on the platform before starting the return journey. In the main stations the better known credit cards are now generally accepted (but there is a special ticket window which must be used when buying a ticket with a credit card). There are limitations on travelling short distances on some first-class Intercity trains. Tickets for journeys under 70km can now be bought in main cities at newsagents and tobacconists.

Children under the age of four travel free, and between the ages of four and 12 travel half price, and there are certain reductions for families. For travellers over the age of 60 (with Senior Citizen Railcards), the Rail Europ Senior card offers a 30 per cent reduction on rail fares to Italy. The Inter-rail card (valid one month), which can be purchased in Britain by young people up to the age of 26, is valid in Italy. In Italy the *Carta d'Argento* and the *Carta Verde* (both valid one year) allow a 20 per cent reduction on rail fares for those over 60, and between the ages of 12 and 26. The *Biglietto Turistico di libera circolazione* (Travel at Will ticket), available to those resident outside Italy, gives freedom of the Italian railways for 8, 15, 21, or 30 days (and another scheme of this type is offered by the Italy Flexy Railcard).

These tickets can be purchased in Britain or at main stations in Italy. A 'Chilometrico' ticket is valid for two months for 3000 kilometres (and can be used by up to five people at the same time). There is a 15 per cent discount on Day Return tickets (maximum distance, 50km) and on 3-Day Return tickets (maximum distance 250km). A *Carta Blu* is available for the disabled, and certain trains have special facilities for them (information from the main railway stations in Italy).

Left Luggage offices are usually open 24 hours at the main stations; at smaller stations they often close at night. **Porters** are entitled to a fixed amount (shown on notice boards at all stations) for each piece of baggage, but trollies are now usually available in the larger stations.

Restaurant Cars (sometimes self-service) are attached to most international and internal long-distance trains. Also, on most express trains, snacks, hot coffee and drinks are sold throughout the journey from a trolley wheeled down the train. At every large station good snacks are on sale from trolleys on the platform and you can buy them from the train window. These include carrier-bags with sandwiches, drink, and fruit (*cestini da viaggio*) or individual sandwiches (*panini*).

Sleeping Cars, with couchettes or first- and second-class cabins, are also carried on certain trains, as well as 'Sleeperette' compartments with reclining seats (first-class only).

Train services in Tuscany are generally good. All the towns which can be easily reached by train are indicated in the text below. The main line from Milan to Rome has stations at Prato, Florence, Arezzo, and Chiusi, as well as numerous smaller towns (slow trains only). The main line down the coast from Genoa to Rome has stations at Massa, Viareggio, Pisa, Livorno, and Grosseto, as well as the smaller towns (slow trains only). There is a line from Florence via Empoli to Pisa, and via Empoli to Siena, and a secondary line from Florence to Prato, Pistoia, and Lucca.

Country Buses. Local country buses abound between the main towns in Italy, and offer an excellent alternative to the railways. It is difficult to obtain accurate information about these local bus services outside Italy. Details have been given in the text. The main bus companies operating in Tuscany are: SITA, 15 Via Santa Caterina da Siena, Florence (Tel. 055-211487); *Lazzi*, 4 Piazza Stazione, Florence (Tel. 055-215154); CAP and COPIT, 9 Largo Alinari, Florence (Tel. 055-214637); LFI, 37 Via Guido Monaco, Arezzo (Tel. 0575-370687); TRA-IN, 33 Largo Gramsci, Poggibonsi (Tel. 0577-937207).

Town Buses. Now that most towns have been partially closed to private traffic, town bus services are usually fast and efficient. You buy a ticket before boarding (at tobacconists, bars, newspaper kiosks, information offices, etc.) and stamp it on board at automatic machines.

Taxis (yellow or white in colour) are provided with taximeters; make sure these are operational before hiring a taxi. They are hired from ranks or by telephone; there are no cruising taxis. A tip of about 1000 lire is expected. A supplement for night service, and for luggage is charged. There is a heavy surplus charge when the destination is outside the town limits (ask roughly how much the fare is likely to be).

Hotels

Hotels in Italy are classified by 'stars' as in the rest of Europe. Since 1985 the official category of Pensione has been abolished. There are five official categories of hotels from the most expensive luxury 5-star hotels to the cheapest and simplest 1-star hotels. *Hotels in Tuscany have been listed in the text, although only a small selection has been made. They have been given with their official star rating in order to give an indication of price. In making the selection for inclusion, smaller hotels have been favoured, and those in the centre of towns, or in particularly beautiful positions in the countryside.* They have been keyed with numbers on the town plans. Each local tourist board (APT, see above) issues a free list of hotels giving category, price, and facilities. Local tourist offices help you to find accommodation on the spot; it is however advisable to book well in advance, especially at Easter and in summer. To confirm the booking a deposit should be sent (you have the right to claim this back if you cancel the booking at least 72 hours in advance). Hotels equipped to offer hospitality to the disabled are indicated in the APT hotel lists.

Up-to-date information about hotels and restaurants can be found in numerous specialised guides to hotels and restaurants in Italy. These include the red guide to Italy published by Michelin (*Italia*, revised annually). In Italian, the Touring Club Italiano publish useful information about hotels in *Alberghi e Ristoranti in Italia* (published every year) and in the *Guida Rapida d'Italia* (four volumes, one of which covers Umbria, Tuscany and the Marches). Gambero Rosso publish a selection of 3-star hotels (*Alberghi d'Italia*) and another sound publication is the *Charming Small Hotel Guide: Italy* (Duncan Petersen). A complete list of hotels in Italy is published by Dossier (*Italy: Hotels*).

Charges vary according to class, season, services available, and locality. In all hotels the service charges are included in the rates. The total charge is exhibited on the back of the door of the hotel room. Breakfast (usually disappointing and costly) is by law an optional extra charge, although a lot of hotels try to include it in the price of the room. When booking a room, always specify if you want breakfast or not. It is usually well worthwhile going round the corner to the nearest bar for breakfast. Hotels are now obliged by law (for tax purposes) to issue an official receipt to customers: you should not leave the premises without this document.

A new type of hotel has been introduced into Italy, called a Residence. They are normally in a building, or group of houses, of historic interest, often a castle or monastery. They may have only a few rooms, and sometimes offer self-catering accommodation. They are listed separately in the APT hotel lists, with their prices.

Agriturism has recently been developed throughout Italy, which provides accommodation in farmhouses in the countryside. Terms vary greatly from bed-and-breakfast, to self-contained flats. These are highly recommended for travellers with their own transport, and for families, as an excellent (and usually cheap) way of visiting Tuscany. Some farms require a stay of a minimum number of days. Cultural or recreational activities are sometimes also provided, such as horse-back riding. Information about such holidays from Agriturist, Associazione Regionale Toscana, 3 Piazza San Firenze, Florence (Tel. 055-287838). Other associations which provide information are: Turismo Verde Regionale, 4 Viale Lavagnini, Florence (Tel. 055-489760) and Terranostra, 2 Via dei Magazzini, Florence (Tel. 055-280539).

Information is also given in the APT hotel lists, and by the local APT offices. Terranostra publish an annual list of Agriturism accommodation called *Vacanze Natura.*

Religious organisations sometimes run hostels or provide accommodation. Information from local APT offices.

Renting accommodation for short periods in Italy has recently become easier and better organised. Villas, farmhouses, etc., can be rented for holidays through specialised agencies. Information from ENIT in London, and APT offices in Italy.

Camping is now well organised throughout Italy. An international camping carnet is useful. In Tuscany, camping sites are listed in the local APT hotel lists, giving details of all services provided, size of the site, etc. In some sites caravans are allowed. The sites are divided into official categories by stars, from the most expensive 4-star sites, to the simplest and cheapest 1-star sites. Their classification and rates charged must be displayed at the camp site office. Some sites have been indicated in the text, with their star ratings. Full details of the sites in Italy are published annually by the Touring Club Italiano and Federcampeggio in *Campeggi e Villaggi turistici in Italia.* The Federazione Italiana del Campeggio have an information office and booking service at No. 11 Via Vittorio Emanuele, Calenzano, 50041 Florence (Tel. 055-882391).

Youth Hostels. The Italian Youth Hostels Association (Associazione Italiana Alberghi per la Gioventù, 44 Via Cavour, 00184 Rome (Tel. 06-4741256) has 52 hostels all over the country. They publish a free guide to them. A membership card of the AIG or the International Youth Hostel Federation is required for access to Italian Youth Hostels. Details from the Youth Hostels Association, Trevelyan House, 8 St Stephen's Hill, St Albans, Herts AL1 2DY, and the American Youth Hostel Inc, National Offices, PO Box 37613, Washington DC 20013-7613. The regional office in Tuscany is at the Ostello *Villa Camerata*, 2 Viale Augusto Righi, Florence (Tel. 055-600315). In Tuscany there are youth hostels at: Florence (see above); Marina di Massa: *Apuano*, 89 Viale delle Pinete, Partaccia; Abetone: *Renzo Bizzarri*; Lucca: *Il Serchio*, Via del Brennero, Salicchi; Livorno: *Villa Morazzana*; Tavarnelle Val di Pesa: *Ostello del Chianti*, Via Cassia; and Cortona: *San Marco*, 57 Via Maffei.

Eating in Italy

Restaurants in Italy are called *Ristoranti* or *Trattorie*; there is now no difference between the two. Italian food is usually good and not too expensive. The least pretentious restaurant almost invariably provides the best value. Almost every locality has a simple (often family run) restaurant which caters for the local residents; the decor is usually very simple and the food excellent value. This type of restaurant does not always offer a menu and the choice is usually limited to three or four first courses, and three or four second courses, with only fruit as a sweet. The more sophisticated restaurants are more attractive and comfortable and often larger and you can sometimes eat at tables outside. They display a menu outside, and are also usually considerably more expensive.

In the text below a small selection of restaurants open in Tuscany in 1995 has been given, which is by no means exhaustive. The restaurants have been divided into three categories to reflect price ranges in 1995: LUXURY-CLASS RESTAURANTS where the prices are likely to be over Lire 60,000 a head (and sometimes well over Lire 100,000 a head). These are the most famous restaurants in Tuscany and they usually offer international cuisine. FIRST-CLASS RESTAURANTS where the prices range from Lire 40,000 and above. These are generally comfortable, with good service, but are not cheap. The third category, called 'TRATTORIE AND PIZZERIE' indicates places where you can eat for around Lire 25,000–30,000 a head, or even less. Although simple, the food in this category is usually the best value.

Specialised guides to the restaurants in Italy (in the 'Luxury-class' and 'first-class' categories as described above) in Italy (revised annually) include the red guide published by Michelin (*Italia*), *I Ristoranti di Veronelli*, and *Alberghi e Ristoranti* (Touring Club Italiano). An excellent (annual) guide to cheaper eating is published by Slow Food: *Osterie d'Italia*. Gambero Rosso also produce sound advice on where to eat in '*Firenze e il Chianti Classico*' e *Toscana*.

Prices on the menu do not include a cover charge (*coperto*, shown separately on the menu) which is added to the bill. The service charge is now almost always automatically added at the end of the bill: tipping is therefore not strictly necessary, but a few thousand lire are appreciated. Restaurants are now obliged by law (for tax purposes) to issue an official receipt to customers; you should not leave the premises without this document (*ricevuta fiscale*). Fish is always the most expensive item on the menu in any restaurant.

Pizze (a popular and cheap food throughout Italy) and other excellent snacks are served in a *Pizzeria*, *Rosticceria* and *Tavola Calda*. Some of these have no seating accommodation and sell food to take away or eat on the spot. For **picnics**, sandwiches (*panini*) are made up on request (with ham, salami, cheese, anchovies, tuna fish, etc.) at *Pizzicherie* and *Alimentari* (grocery shops), and *Fornai* (bakeries) often sell delicious individual pizzas, bread with oil and salt (*focaccia* or *schiacciata*), cakes, etc. Some of the pleasantest places to picnic in towns or their environs have been indicated in the text below.

Bars (cafés) are open all day. Most customers eat the numerous excellent refreshments they serve standing up. You pay the cashier first, and show the receipt to the barman in order to get served. If you sit at a table the charge is considerably higher (at least double) and you will be given waiter service (and should not pay first). However, some simple bars have a few tables which can be used with no extra charge (it is always best to ask before sitting down). Black coffee (*caffè* or *espresso*) can be ordered diluted (*alto*, *lungo* or *americano*) or with hot milk (*cappuccino*) or with a liquor (*corretto*). In summer, cold coffee (*caffè freddo*) or cold coffee and milk (*caffè-latte freddo*) are served. Ice-creams are always best in a *Gelateria* where they are made on the spot: bars usually sell packaged ice-cream only.

Tuscan Food is traditionally excellent, but now good genuine cuisine is becoming less and less easy to find. The region is perhaps best known for its dishes stewed slowly in a tomato sauce, called *in umido*. *Minestrone* is a thick vegetable soup. In winter this is made in a richer version, called *ribollita* or *zuppa di pane*, with white beans, black cabbage, and bread. Another vegetable soup, often found in the Maremma (and the Casentino), is *acquacotta*, made with onions, basil, celery, and greens (first lightly fried) with the addition of tomatoes, toasted bread, pecorino cheese, and eggs. A summer salad (*panzanella*) has dry bread, tomatoes, fresh onions, cucumber, basil, and capers. *Pappa al pomodoro* is also made in summer, a thick tomato soup with bread, seasoned with basil, etc.

In the autumn *fettunta* or *bruschetta* is served: toasted bread with garlic and oil straight from the olive press; if it is topped with hot black cabbage it is called *cavolo con le fette*. Traditional Florentine dishes include *fagioli all'uccelletto*, haricot beans in a tomato sauce, and *trippa alla fiorentina*, tripe in a tomato sauce with parmesan cheese. Regional first course dishes include *tortelli di patate* (or *topini*), made with potatoes (found especially in the Casentino and Mugello), *pici*, handmade spaghetti (found in Siena), *tortelli maremmani*, fresh pasta filled with ricotta and spinach, *pappardelle alla lepre*, short pasta with a rich hare sauce.

The famous *bistecca alla fiorentina*, a T-bone steak cooked over charcoal can still be found in some restaurants which offer it as their speciality. In the Maremma, wild boar (*cinghiale*) is often served, sometimes with polenta. *Scottiglia* is a traditional dish of various meats (chicken, lamb, etc.) chopped up and cooked in oil, sage, hot pepper, and tomato, served on toast. *Rosticciana* is grilled spare ribs. Fresh mushrooms, especially *porcini*, are served all over Tuscany in season. Another good seasonal dish is *tortino di carciofi*, baked artichoke pie.

Fish dishes, for which Livorno is particularly famous, include *baccalà alla Livornese*, salt cod cooked in tomatoes, black olives, and pepper, and *cacciucco alla Livornese*, a stew of fish in a hot sauce. In Versilia *seppie in zimino* are often served, cuttlefish cooked with spinach.

Tuscany is not famous for its sweets, although two excellent puddings produced in the autumn are *castagnaccio*, a chestnut cake with pine nuts and sultanas, and *schiacciata all'uva*, black grapes cooked in the oven on a bready dough. *Frittelle di San Giuseppe* are fritters made with rice, eggs, milk, and lemon rind; *cenci* are simpler fritters. In Livorno *torta* is sold, a delicious thin pizza-like bread cooked with chick-peas. This is also found in Volterra, where it is called *cecina*.

Tuscan Wines. The best known Italian wine is *Chianti* produced in Tuscany. The name is protected by law and only those wines from a relatively small district which lies between Florence and Siena are entitled to the name *Chianti Classico* (for a fuller description, see the beginning of Rte 13). Chianti Classico *Gallo Nero* (distinguished by a black cock on the bottle) is usually considered the best, but Chianti *Putto* and Chianti *Grappolo* are also very good. Other Chianti wines from different parts of Tuscany are: *Chianti Montalbano*, *Chianti Rufina*, *Chianti Colli Fiorentini*, *Chianti Colli Senesi*, *Chianti Colli Aretini*, and *Chianti Colline Pisane*.

In Tuscany the red table wine is usually of better quality than the white. Excellent red wines (not cheap) are *Brunello di Montalcino* and *Vino Nobile di Montepulciano*. Good red wine is also produced at Carmignano near Florence, and around Lucca. The most famous white wine of Tuscany is the *Vernaccia di San Gimignano*, but other good white wines are produced around Pitigliano, Montecarlo, and in the Val d'Arbia. White and rosé wines are also found in the region of Bolgheri. Elba used to produce excellent wines (now hard to find), including *Aleatico*, a dessert wine.

More and more farms which produce wine are opening their cellars to the public, and allowing wine tasting. Some of the best known have been mentioned in the text. Information about those in the Chianti region from Consorzio Vino Chianti, 4 Lungarno Corsini, Florence (Tel. 055-210168) and Consorzio Chianti Classico, 155 Via Scopeti, Sant'Andrea in Percussina

(Tel. 055-8228245). There is a wine museum open in summer at Rufina, and *enoteche* open in the fortresses of Siena and Montalcino.

Opening Times of Museums, Sites, and Churches

The opening times of **museums and monuments** have been given in the text but they vary and often change without warning; when possible it is always advisable to consult the local tourist office (APT) on arrival about the up-to-date times. The opening times of State-owned museums and monuments are in the process of change: they are usually open 9–14, fest. 9–13; and closed on Monday, but in a few cases they are now also open in the afternoon. On Monday some local museums are now staying open. However, there is no standard timetable and you should take great care to allow enough time for variations in the hours shown in the text when planning a visit to a museum or monument. Some museums, etc., are closed on the main public holidays: 1 January, Easter, 1 May, 15 August, and Christmas Day (although there is now a policy to keep at least a few of them open on these days in the larger cities; information has to be obtained about this on the spot). Admission charges vary, but are usually between Lire 4000 and Lire 13,000. British citizens under the age of 18 and over the age of 60 are entitled to free admission to state-owned museums and monuments in Italy (because of reciprocal arrangements in Britain). The *Settimana per i Beni Culturali e Ambientali* is usually held early in December when for a week there is free entrance to all state-owned museums and others are specially opened, etc.

Churches, although they usually open very early in the morning (at 7 or 8), are normally closed for a considerable period during the middle of the day. Almost all churches close at 12.00 and do not reopen again until 15, 16, or even 17.00. Cathedrals and some of the larger churches (indicated in the text) may be open without a break during daylight hours. Smaller churches and oratories are often open only in the early morning, but it is sometimes possible to find the key by asking locally. The sacristan will also show closed chapels, crypts, etc., and sometimes expects a tip. Some churches now ask that sightseers do not enter during a service, but normally visitors not in a tour group may do so, provided you are silent and do not approach the altar in use. An entrance fee is becoming customary for admission to treasuries, cloisters, bell-towers, etc. Lights (operated by lire coins) have now been installed in many churches to illuminate frescoes and altarpieces, but a torch and binoculars are always useful. Sometimes you are not allowed to enter important churches wearing shorts or with bare shoulders.

Tuscan Gardens

Gardens are a special feature of Tuscany, and it is becoming possible to visit more and more private gardens, usually by previous appointment. Those described (with their opening times) in the general text below are included in the following list.

In and around Florence: Giardino di Boboli (where an entrance fee of Lire 4000 is now charged), Villa di Castello, Villa della Petraia, the botanical gardens (Giardino dei Semplici), and the Giardino dell'Orticoltura. In May and June the Giardino dell'Iris and the Giardino delle Rose are open. The Villa Medici in Fiesole and Villa della Gamberaia in Settignano charge an entrance fee. The private gardens of Villa I Tatti, Villa La Pietra, Villa Capponi, and Villa I Collazzi are only sometimes open with special permission. In the environs of Florence gardens surround the Villa di Poggio a Caiano and Villa Corsi Salviati (Sesto Fiorentino).

In the Mugello, the private garden of the Castello del Trebbio is only sometimes open by previous appointment. One of the most famous gardens in Tuscany is that of the Villa Garzoni at Collodi. In Lucca the Botanical Gardens are open regularly, and in the environs there are well-known private gardens open at the Villa Reale di Marlia, Villa Mansi, and Villa Torrigiani. In the Apuan Alps, there is an alpine garden at Pania di Corfina. The Botanical Gardens at Pisa are one of the most important in Tuscany, and between Pisa and Florence there are gardens at the Villa Medici of Cerreto Guidi, and private gardens which can sometimes be visited at Bibbiani and the Villa di Belvedere at Crespina. Siena has a Botanical Garden, and in the environs there are private gardens at Villa di Vicobello and Cetinale. The Horti Leonini at San Quirico d'Orcia are open as public gardens, and at Pienza the hanging garden of Palazzo Piccolomini may be visited. Lesser known gardens include Villa La Fratta (near Torrita di Siena), La Peschiera at Santa Fiora, the Villa Rinuccini di Torre a Cona near San Donato in Collina and Villa Chigi on the outskirts of Castelnuovo Berardenga.

Annual Festivals and Local Fairs in Tuscany

There are a number of traditional festivals in Tuscan towns which are of the greatest interest. At these times, the towns become extremely lively, and, apart from the central race or competition, numerous celebrations take place on the side, and local markets are usually held at the same time. The most important local festivals have been mentioned in the text, and described in detail, but a summary is given below, in case you are able to choose a period in which to visit Tuscany when some of them are taking place. They are particularly exciting events for children. Information from local APT offices.

Spring. Carnival celebrations at Viareggio, Cerreto Guidi, Borgo San Lorenzo. *Bello Ballo* on Shrove Tuesday at Bibbiena. Easter: *Scoppio del Carro* on Easter Day in Florence, Good Friday passion play at Grassina. Ascension Day: *Festa del Grillo* in Florence. Other festivals include: *Palio* at Fucecchio; *Balestro del Girifalco* at Massa Marittima; *Maggiolata* at Castiglione d'Orcia; *Palio dei Somari* at Torrita di Siena.

Summer. The *Palio* at Siena, the most splendid and exciting of all annual festivals in Italy (see Rte 14). *Calcio in Costume* in Florence; *Palio del Cerro* at Cerreto Guidi; Corpus Domini procession in Prato; *Giostra del Saracino* in Arezzo; *Balestro del Girifalco* at Massa Marittima. Marine festivities, with procession of boats at Porto Santo Stefano, Porto Ercole, Orbetello, Isola del Giglio, and Castiglione della Pescaia. Rodeo at Alberese; *Palio* at Piancastagnaio; *Fiera di Sant'Antonino* and *Palio Marinaro* in Livorno; *Palio degli Arcieri* in Piombino; *Disfida fra gli arcieri di Terra e Corte* at Fivizzano; *Festa* *di San Ranieri* and *Gioco del Ponte* at Pisa; *Giostra dell'Orso* at Pistoia; *Bravio delle Botti* at Montepulciano.

Autumn. *Festa della Rificolona* in Florence; *Diotto* at Scarperia; *Festa dell'uva* and *Fiera di San Luca* in Impruneta; *Sagra dei Marroni* at Marradi; Display of the *Sacro Cingolo* in Prato; *Palio della Balestra* in Sansepolcro; *Palio* at Castel del Piano; *Astiludio* at Volterra; *Sagra del Tordo* at Montalcino.

Street Markets take place once a week in country towns, and local fairs are held in Florence (*Festa dell'Annunziata*), Vicchio (*Fiera Calda*), Piancastagnaio, Sansepolcro, Monte San Savino, Carmignano, and Filetto (Villafranca Lunigiana). Specialist fairs include the antiques fair (*Fiera Antiquariato*) at Arezzo, the first Saturday and Sunday of the month, and the cattle market at Alberese in spring. Wine fairs are held all over Chianti in autumn.

Summer Music and Theatre Festivals in Tuscany include: *Maggio Musicale* in Florence; *Estate Fiesolana* in Fiesole; *Festival di Pentecoste* at Badia a Passignano; *Festival del Teatro* at Sorano; Puccini opera festival at Torre del Lago; *Settimana musicale senese* at the Accademia Musicale Chigiana, Siena; Music festival at Montepulciano; Theatre festival (*Teatro Povero di Monticchiello*) at Monticchiello; chamber music festival at La Foce (*Incontri in Terra di Siena*); Music and Theatre festival at Radicondoli; Buskers' festival (On the Road) at Pelago. Concerts are usually held at Sant'Antimo, Cennina, and Montalcino.

Walking in Tuscany

Hiking and walking has become more popular throughout Italy in recent years and more information is now available locally. Details have been given in the main text below. Specialist guides to walking in Tuscany are now published with detailed maps. The areas of Tuscany particularly adapted for walking are the Garfagnana, the Mugello, the Casentino (Monte Falterona, and the Foreste Casentinesi), and Monte Amiata. **Protected areas** in Tuscany include the *Parco Naturale delle Alpi Apuane*, the *Parco dell'Orecchiella*, the *Parco Naturale di Migliarino-San RossoreMassaciuccoli*, the *Parco Naturale della Maremma*, the *Parco Naturale di Cavriglia*, and the *Parco Nazionale dell'Archipelago Toscano*. **World Wildlife Fund oases** in the Maremma include Bolgheri, Lago di Burano, and Orbetello. Local offices of the Club Alpino Italiano (CAI), the Comunità Montana, the World Wildlife Fund, and the APT all provide information. The Tuscan Region and the WWF publish a guide to walking in Tuscany called *Cammina Toscana* (Arcadia). Walking tours of Tuscany are organised by Alternative Travel Group Ltd, 69–71 Banbury Road, Oxford, tel. 01865 310399.

Visiting Tuscany with Children

A holiday can often be marred for parents as well as children if too much serious sight-seeing is attempted in too short a time. Tuscany has a variety of sights which may be of special interest to children and may help to alleviate a day of undiluted 'Madonnas' and churches. A golden rule when allowing a 'break' for an ice-cream is to search for a 'Gelateria' (rather than a bar) where the locally produced ice-creams are generally excellent.

A few suggestions are given below of places that might have particular appeal to children, listed in the order of the routes by which the book is divided. These include some important monuments which are likely to give a clear impression of a particular period of art or architecture, a few museums, places of naturalistic interest, and the most exciting annual festivals. Detailed descriptions of all the places mentioned below are given in the main text (and can easily be found by reference to the index at the back of the book).

Rte 1. Florence: the Baptistery, the cupola of the Duomo (which can be climbed), Museo dell'Opera del Duomo, Palazzo Davanzati, Palazzo Vecchio, Ponte Vecchio, Boboli gardens, Museo dello Spedale degli Innocenti, Museo di San Marco, Palazzo Medici Riccardi, Cappellone degli Spagnuoli, Museo del Bargello, Anthropological Museum, Cappella dei Pazzi, Museo di Storia della Scienza, Brancacci chapel, Forte di Belvedere, San Miniato al Monte, Museo Stibbert, Giardino dell'Orticoltura. The markets of San Lorenzo and the Mercato Nuovo. Festivals, see above.

Rte 2. Fiesole (including the Roman theatre), Villa di Poggio a Caiano, Villa della Petraia, Villa di Castello.

Rte 3. Walks in the Mugello, Villa Demidoff at Pratolino, Ethnographical museum at Palazzuolo sul Senio, Casa d'Erci at Grezzano, Fortezza di San Martino at San Piero a Sieve, Palazzo dei Vicari and artisan's workshop at Scarperia, museum of mechanical tableaux at Sant'Agata, birthplace of Giotto near Vicchio. Buskers' festival (*On the Road*) at Pelago.

Rte 5. Zoo at Verginina (Pistoia), Abetone, Monsumanno Alto, Montecatini (funicular to Montecatini Alto), Pinocchio park at Collodi. *Giostro dell'Orso* at Pistoia.

Rte 6. In Lucca: the walls, Piazza San Michele, the piazza of the Roman amphitheatre, and the Guinigi tower (which can be climbed).

Rte 7. Walks and horse-back riding in the Garfagnana (Parco Naturale delle Alpi Apuane and the Parco dell'Orecchiella). Museum of figurines at Coreglia Antelminelli, the Grotta del Vento, the ethnographical museum at San Pellegrino in Alpe.

Rte 8. Seaside resorts of Viareggio and Versilia. The Lago di Massaciuccoli, and Roman remains at Massaciuccoli. The Castello Malaspina of Massa (when restored), marble quarries of Carrara, the castle of Fosdinovo, the ethnographical museums at Casola in Lunigiana and Villafranca in Lunigiana, and the Castello del Piagnaro in Pontremoli (with the Museo delle Statue-stele). Carnival at Viareggio.

Rte 9. Pisa: Campo dei Miracoli, Santo Stefano dei Cavalieri, Gioco del Ponte. The Parco Naturale di Migliarino-San Rossore-Massaciuccoli and the Marina di Vecchiano.

Rte 10. Seaside resorts near Livorno. In Livorno: Fortezza Nuova, Natural History Museum, Aquarium. The 'Mercatino' in Piazza XX Settembre, and the funicular to Montenero.

Rte 11. Museo Archeologico e della Ceramica at Montelupo Fiorentino, the Leonardo Museum at Vinci, dinosaur park at Peccioli, castle of Lari, Vicopisano, the Museo di Storia Naturale at the Certosa di Pisa (Calci).

Rte 12. Parco Naturale della Maremma; wildlife sanctuaries at Bolgheri, Orbetello, and Lago di Burano; ethnographical museum at Villa La Cinquantina; cypress avenue of Bolgheri; Etruscan necopolis of Populonia; Populonia (castle and museum); Rocca San Silvestro; beaches at Cala Martina and Cala Violina; seaside resort of Castiglione della Pescaia; Talamone; lagoon of Orbetello (tombolo di Feniglia); Monte Argentario; Isola del Giglio; Ansedonia (Tagliata Etrusca and ruins of Cosa); Capalbio.

Rte 13. Puppet theatre at Greve. Towns of Montefioralle and Monteriggioni. Castles in the Chianti, including Brolio and Meleto. Fairs at Impruneta and Greve.

Rte 14. Siena: the Campo, Palazzo Pubblico (the Torre del Mangia can be climbed), Cathedral (and Libreria Piccolomini), Museo dell'Opera del Duomo (Scala del Falciatore). The *Palio*.

Rte 15. Certaldo.

Rte 16. Volterra: Roman Theatre, Museo Etrusco, Parco Archeologico gardens, frescoes in the Cappella della Croce di Giorno in San Francesco, Le Balze. *Astiludio* festival.

Rte 17. San Gimignano.

Rte 18. Larderello museum. Massa Marittima: Duomo, Archeological museum, Museo della Miniera, Torre del Candeliere (which can be climbed), Museo di Storia e Arte delle Miniere, Lago dell'Accesa. 'Il Girifalco' cross-bow contest.

Rte 19. San Galgano (and the chapel on Monte Siepi); Bagni di Petriolo; ruins of Roselle.

Rte 20. Cuna, Monte Oliveto Maggiore, Montalcino (including the fortress), Sant'Antimo, Horti Leonini in San Quirico d'Orcia, Bagno Vignoni, Rocca d'Orcia, Bagni San Filippo. 'Sagra del Tordo' in Montalcino.

Rte 21. Pienza, Castelmuzio (with its museum), San Biagio at Montepulciano, the Museo Civico at Cetona, Parco Archeologico Naturalistico di Belverde on Monte Cetona. *Palio dei Somari* at Torrita di Siena, and 'Bravio delle Botti' at Montepulciano.

Rte 22. Monte Amiata. La Peschiera at Santa Fiora. Fair at Piancastagnaio.

Rte 23. Roccalbegna, Magliano in Toscana, San Bruzio, Terme di Saturnia, Pitigliano, Sovana.

Rte 24. Walks in the Casentino. Castel Castagnaio, Castello di Romena, Castello di Porciano, Monte Falterona, forest of Camaldoli, Ornithological museum near the monastery of Camaldoli, Poppi (Castello), Zoo at Poppi, La Verna.

Rte 25. Ethnographical museum at Pieve di San Romolo (Gaville), Parco Naturale di Cavriglia, paleontological museum at Montevarchi, Gropina, Castello di Sammezzano, Vallombrosa.

Rte 26. Arezzo: San Francesco, and the Roman amphitheatre and Museo Archeologico. 'Giostra del Saracino'.

Rte 27. Cortona: Santa Maria del Calcinaio, the *Passeggiata* public gardens, Museo dell'Accademia Etrusca, Museo Diocesano, Porta Colonia, Porta

Montanina, Fortezza Mediceo, Etruscan tombs in the environs. Monte Egidio, Abbazia di Farneta, castle of Montecchio Vesponi.

Rte 28. Piero della Francesca's Madonna del Parto at Monterchi; Museo di Palazzo Taglieschi and Museo della Misericordia at Anghiari; Museo Civico at Sansepolcro. *Palio della Balestra* and *Festa di San Rocco* at Sansepolcro.

Rte 29. Castle of Civitella in Val di Chiana, Gargonza, Lucignano (Museo Comunale). At Chiusi: Museo della Cattedrale, catacombs, Museo Nazionale Etrusco, and Etruscan tombs. Lago di Chiusi and Lago di Montepulciano. Fair at Monte San Savino.

Rte 30. Islands of Elba and Capraia.

General Information

Public Holidays. The Italian national holidays when offices, shops and schools are closed are as follows: 1 January, 25 April (Liberation Day), Easter Monday, 1 May (Labour Day), 15 August (Assumption), 1 November (All Saints' Day), 8 December (Immaculate Conception), Christmas Day and 26 December (St Stephen). Each town keeps its patron Saint's day as a holiday.

Italy for the disabled. Italy is at last catching up slowly with the rest of Europe in the provision of facilities for the disabled. All new public buildings are now obliged by law to provide access for the disabled, and specially designed facilities. In the annual list of hotels published by the local APT offices, hotels which are able to give hospitality to the disabled are indicated. Airports and railway stations provide assistance, and certain trains are equipped to transport wheelchairs. Access is allowed to the centre of towns (normally closed to traffic) for cars with disabled people, where parking places are reserved for them. For all other information, contact local APT offices.

Telephones and Postal Information. Stamps are sold at tobacconists (displaying a blue 'T' sign) and post offices (open 8.10–13.25, Monday–Saturday). Central offices in main towns are open 8.10–19.25. Correspondence can be addressed c/o the Post Office by adding *Fermo Posta* to the name of the locality. It is always advisable to post letters at post offices or railway stations; collection from letterboxes may be erratic. There are numerous public telephones all over Italy in bars, restaurants, kiosks, etc. These are now usually operated by coins or telephone cards. Telephone cards can be bought from tobacconists, bars, some newspaper stands, and post offices.

Working Hours. Government offices usually work from 8–13.30 or 14.00 six days a week. Shops (clothes, hardware, hairdressers, etc.) are generally open from 9–13, 16–19.30, including Saturday, and for most of the year are closed on Monday morning. Food shops usually open from 8–13, 17–19.30 or 20, and for most of the year are closed on Wednesday afternoon. From mid-June to mid-September all shops are closed instead on Saturday afternoon. Banks are usually open Monday–Friday 8.20–13.30, 14.30–15.45. They are closed on Saturday and holidays, and close early (about 11.00) on days preceding national holidays.

Public Toilets. There is a notable shortage of public toilets in Italy. All bars (cafés) should have toilets available to the public (generally speaking the larger the bar, the better the facilities). Nearly all museums now have toilets. There are also toilets at railway stations and bus stations.

Help is given to British and American travellers in Tuscany who are in difficulty by the British and American consulates in Florence. They will replace lost or stolen passports, and will give advice in emergencies. British Consulate, 2 Lungarno Corsini, Florence (Tel. 055-284133); US Consulate, 38 Lungarno Vespucci, Florence (Tel. 055-2398276).

Health Service. British citizens, as members of the EU, have the right to claim health services in Italy if they have the E111 form (issued by the Department of Health and Social Security). There are also a number of private holiday health insurance policies. First Aid services (Pronto Soccorso) are available at all hospitals, railway stations, and airports. **Chemist Shops** (farmacie) are usually open Monday–Friday 9–13, 16–19.30 or 20. On Saturdays and Sundays (and holidays) a few are open (listed on the door of every chemist). In all towns there is also at least one chemist shop open at night (also shown on the door of every chemist). For emergencies, dial 113.

Crime. Pick-pocketing is a widespread problem in towns all over Italy: it is always advisable not to carry valuables in handbags, and be particularly careful on public transport. Crime should be reported at once to the police, or the local carabinieri office (found in every town and small village). A detailed statement has to be given in order to get an official document confirming loss or damage (essential for insurance claims). Interpreters are provided. For all emergencies, dial 113.

Glossary

AEDICULE, small opening framed by two columns and a pediment, originally used in classical architecture.

AMPHORA, antique vase, usually of large dimensions, for oil and other liquids.

ANCONA, retable or large altarpiece (painted or sculpted) in an architectural frame.

ANTEFIX, ornament placed at the lower corners of the tiled roof of a temple to conceal the space between the tiles and the cornice.

ANTIPHONAL, choir-book containing a collection of *antiphonae*—verses sung in response by two choirs.

ARCA, wooden chest with a lid, for sacred or secular use. Also, monumental sarcophagus in stone, used by Christians and pagans.

ARCHITRAVE, lowest part of an entablature, horizontal frame above a door.

ARCHIVOLT, moulded architrave carried round an arch.

ATLANTES (or *Telamones*), male figures used as supporting columns.

ATRIUM, forecourt, usually of a Byzantine church or a classical Roman house.

ATTIC, topmost story of a classical building, hiding the spring of the roof.

BADIA, *Abbazia*, abbey.

BALDACCHINO, canopy supported by columns, usually over an altar.

BASILICA, originally a Roman building used for public administration; in Christian architecture, an aisled church with a clerestory and apse, and no transepts.

BORGO, a suburb; street leading away from the centre of a town.

BOTTEGA, the studio of an artist: the pupils who worked under his direction.

BOZZETTO, sketch, often used to describe a small model for a piece of sculpture.

BROCCATELLO, a clouded veined marble from Siena.

BUCCHERO, Etruscan black terracotta ware.

BUCRANIA, a form of classical decoration—heads of oxen garlanded with flowers.

CAMPANILE, bell-tower, often detached from the building to which it belongs.

CAMPOSANTO, cemetery.

CANEPHORA, figure bearing a basket, often used as a caryatid.

CANOPIC VASE, Egyptian or Etruscan vase enclosing the entrails of the dead.

CANTORIA, singing-gallery in a church.

CAPPELLA, chapel.

CARTOON, from *cartone,* meaning large sheet of paper. A full-size preparatory drawing for a painting or fresco.

CARYATID, female figure used as a supporting column.

CASSONE, a decorated chest, usually a dower chest.

CAVEA, the part of a theatre or amphitheatre occupied by the row of seats.

CELLA, sanctuary of a temple, usually in the centre of the building.

CENACOLO, scene of the Last Supper (often in the refectory of a convent).

CHALICE, wine cup used in the celebration of Mass.

CHIAROSCURO, distribution of light and shade, apart from colour in a painting.

CIBORIUM, casket or tabernacle containing the Host.

CIPOLLINO, onion-marble; a greyish marble with streaks of white or green.

CIPPUS, sepulchral monument in the form of an altar.

CISTA, casket, usually of bronze and cylindrical in shape, to hold jewels, toilet articles, etc., and decorated with mythological subjects.

CLOISONNÉ, type of enamel decoration.

COLUMBARIUM, a building (usually subterranean) with niches to hold urns containing the ashes of the dead.

COMMUNE, a town or city which adopted a form of independent self-government in the Middle Ages.

CONDOTTIERE, professional military commander.

CONFESSIO, crypt beneath the high altar and raised choir of a church, usually containing the relics of a saint.

CORBEL, a projecting block, usually of stone.

CORSO, main street of a town.

CRENELLATIONS, battlements.

CUPOLA, dome.

CYCLOPEAN, the term applied to walls of unmortared masonry, older than the Etruscan civilisation, and attributed by the ancients to the giant Cyclopes.

DIPTYCH, painting or ivory panel in two sections.

DOSSAL, altarpiece.

DOSSERET, a second block above the capital of a column.

DUOMO, cathedral.

EDICOLA, *see* aedicule.

EXEDRA, semicircular recess.

EX-VOTO, tablet or small painting expressing gratitude to a saint.

FRESCO (in Italian, *affresco*), painting executed on wet plaster. On the wall beneath is sketched the *sinopia*, and the *cartoon* (see above) is transferred onto the fresh plaster (*intonaco*) before the fresco is begun either by pricking the outline with small holes over which a powder is dusted, or by means of a stylus which leaves an incised line on the wet plaster. In recent years many frescoes have been detached from the walls on which they were executed.

GIALLO ANTICO, red-veined yellow marble from Numidia.

GONFALON, banner of a medieval guild or commune.

GRAFFITI, design on a wall made with an iron tool on a prepared surface, the design showing in white. Also used loosely to describe scratched designs or words on walls.

GREEK-CROSS, cross with the arms of equal length.

GRISAILLE, painting in various tones of grey.

GROTESQUE, painted or stucco decoration in the style of the ancient Romans (found during the Renaissance in Nero's Golden House in Rome, then underground, hence the name, from 'grotto'). The delicate ornamental decoration usually includes patterns of flowers, sphynxes, birds, human figures, etc., against a light ground.

HERM (pl. *Hermae*), quadrangular pillar decreasing in girth towards the ground surmounted by a bust.

HYPOGEUM, subterranean excavation for the interment of the dead (usually Etruscan).

ICONOSTASIS, high balustrade with figures of saints, guarding the sanctuary of a Byzantine church.

IMPASTO, early Etruscan ware made of inferior clay.

INTARSIA (or *Tarsia*), inlay of wood, marble, or metal.

INTONACO, plaster.

INTRADOS, underside or soffit of an arch.

KRATER, Antique mixing-bowl, conical in shape with rounded base.

KYLIX, wide shallow vase with two handles and short stem.

LATIN-CROSS, cross with a long vertical arm.

LAVABO, hand-basin usually outside a refectory or sacristy.

LOGGIA, covered gallery or balcony, usually preceding a larger building.

LUNETTE, semicircular space in a vault or ceiling, or above a door or window, often decorated with a painting or relief.

MAESTÀ, Madonna and Child enthroned in majesty.

MATRONEUM, gallery reserved for women in early Christian churches.

MEDALLION, large medal; loosely, a circular ornament.

META, turning-post at either end of a Roman circus.

MONOCHROME, painting or drawing in one colour only.

MONOLITH, single stone (usually a column).

NARTHEX, vestibule of a Christian basilica.

NIELLO, black substance used in an engraved design.

NIMBUS, luminous ring surrounding the heads of saints in paintings; a square nimbus denoted that the person was living at that time.

OCULUS, round window.

OPERA (DEL DUOMO), the office in charge of the fabric of a building (i.e. the Cathedral).

OPUS RETICULATUM, masonry arranged in squares or diamonds so that the mortar joints make a network pattern.

OPUS TESSELLATUM, mosaic formed entirely of square tesserae.

PALA, large altarpiece.

PALAZZO, any dignified and important building.

PALOMBINO, fine-grained white marble.

PAVONAZZETTO, yellow marble blotched with blue.

PAX, sacred object used by a priest for the blessing of peace, and offered for the kiss of the faithful. Usually circular, engraved enamelled or painted in a rich gold or silver frame.

PENDENTIVE, concave spandrel beneath a dome.

PERISTYLE, court or garden surrounded by a columned portico.

PIETÀ, group of the Virgin mourning the dead Christ.

PIETRE DURE, hard or semi-precious stones, often used in the form of mosaics to decorate cabinets, table-tops, etc.

PIEVE, parish church.

PISCINA, Roman tank; a basin for an officiating priest to wash his hands before Mass.

PLAQUETTE, small metal tablet with relief decoration.

PLUTEUS (pl. *plutei*), marble panel, usually decorated; a series of them used to form a parapet to precede the altar of a church.

POLYPTYCH, painting or panel in more than three sections.

PORTA, gate (or door).

PORTA DEL MORTO, in certain old mansions of Umbria and Tuscany, a narrow raised doorway, said to be for the passage of biers of the dead, but more probably for use in troubled times when the main gate would be barred.

PREDELLA, small painting or panel, usually in sections, attached below a large altarpiece, illustrating the story of a saint, the life of the Virgin, etc.

PRESEPIO, literally, crib or manger. A group of statuary of which the central subject is the Infant Jesus in the manger.

PRONAOS, porch in front of the cella of a temple.

PUTTO (pl. *putti*), figure of a boy sculpted or painted, usually nude.

QUADRATURA, painted architectural perspectives.

QUATREFOIL, four-lobed design.

REREDOS, decorated screen rising behind an altar.

RHYTON, drinking-horn usually ending in an animal's head.

ROOD-SCREEN, a screen below the Rood or Crucifix dividing the nave from the chancel of a church.

SCAGLIOLA, a material made from selenite and used to imitate marble or 'pietre dure', often used for altar frontals and columns.

SCENA, the stage of a Roman theatre.

SCHIACCIATO, term used to describe very low relief in sculpture, where there is an emphasis on the delicate line rather than the depth of the panel.

SCHOLA CANTORUM, enclosure for the choristers in the nave of an early Christian church, adjoining the sanctuary.

SINOPIA, large sketch for a fresco made on the rough wall in a red earth pigment called sinopia (because it originally came from Sinope on the Black Sea). By detaching a fresco it is now possible to see the sinopia beneath and detach it also.

SITULA, water-bucket.

SOFFIT, underside or intrados of an arch.

SPANDREL, surface between two arches in an arcade or the triangular space on either side of an arch.

STAMNOS, big-bellied vase with two small handles at the sides, closed by a lid.

STELE, upright stone bearing a monumental inscription.

STEMMA, coat of arms or heraldic device.

STEREOBATE, basement of a temple or other building.

STOUP, vessel for Holy Water, usually near the W door of a church.

STYLOBATE, basement of a columned temple or other building.

TABLINUM, room in a Roman house with one side opening onto the central courtyard.

TELAMONES, see *Atlantes.*

TESSERA, a small cube of marble, glass, etc., used in mosaic work.

THERMAE, Roman baths.

THOLOS, a circular building.

TONDO, round painting or bas-relief.

TRANSENNA, open grille or screen, usually of marble, in an early Christian church.

TRAVERTINE, tufa quarried near Tivoli.

TRICLINIUM, dining room and reception room of a Roman house.

TRIPTYCH, painting or panel in three sections.

TROMPE L'OEIL, literally, a deception of the eye. Used to describe illusion-ist decoration, painted architectural perspectives, etc.

VILLA, country house with its garden.

WESTWORK, W end of a Carolingian or Romanesque church with a massive central tower and, inside, a double story, with the upper room open to the nave.

The terms QUATTROCENTO, CINQUECENTO (abbreviated in Italy '400, '500), etc., refer not to the 14C and 15C, but to the 'fourteen-hundreds' and 'fifteen-hundreds', i.e. the 15C and 16C, etc.

Brunelleschi's cupola of the Duomo, Florence

1

Florence

FLORENCE, in Italian **Firenze**, is one of the most famous cities in Italy. As the birthplace of the Renaissance it preserves some of the greatest works of art and most beautiful buildings in the world. From the fifteenth century onwards it became a centre of learning in the arts and sciences unparalleled since the time of Athens. It is now a small city (457,000 inhabitants), the regional capital of Tuscany, with nearly all its beautiful buildings concentrated within a relatively small area beside the museums of the Uffizi, Pitti, and Bargello which contain the masterpieces of Florentine art. The delightful low hills which surround the city have been preserved from new buildings. The best time to visit Florence is in the winter: it can be unpleasantly crowded with tourists in the spring and unbearably hot in July and August. The river Arno, a special feature of the city, has caused disastrous floods throughout its history (last in 1966). **For a fuller description of the city, see** *Blue Guide Florence*.

Information Offices. APT, 1 (red) Via Cavour (Pl. 7; Tel. 055/290832). Hotel Booking Office (ITA) at the railway station and on the motorway approaches to Florence (Chianti Est and Peretola Sud).

Railway Stations. Santa Maria Novella (Pl. 6) for nearly all services. A few local trains, and fast trains to the S depart from Campo di Marte station (beyond Pl. 8), and Rifredi station (beyond Pl. 2) is used by local trains and by the *pendolino* train between Milan and Rome.

Airports. The nearest large airport is at **Pisa** (85km W; see Rte 9). Direct train service in 1 hour to Florence Santa Maria Novella station (which has an Air Terminal). There is a small airport at **Peretola**, a few kilometres N of Florence, with some flights from Europe (including Stansted and Gatwick in England). SITA bus service to 15 Via Santa Caterina da Siena (beside Santa Maria Novella railway station), c every hour in 15mins. **Bologna** airport also has international flights (airport bus every 30mins to Bologna station, and from there trains to Florence in 60–75mins).

Car parking. Most of the centre of Florence (within the *Viali*, and in the Oltrarno; see the Plan) has been closed to private cars (from 8.30–18.30), except for access (which includes hotels in the area). Car parks (with hourly tariff) at the Fortezza da Basso, Piazza Stazione (underground), Piazza Libertà, Parterre (underground), Piazza Beccaria, and Lungarno della Zecca Vecchia.

Hotels all over the city, but it is essential to book well in advance in summer and at Easter. 5-star: *Helvetia e Bristol*, 2 Via de' Pescioni. 4-star: *Lungarno* 14 Borgo San Jacopo, and *Monna Lisa*, 27 Borgo Pinti. 3-star: *Annalena*, 34 Via Romana; *Loggiato dei Serviti*, 3 Piazza Santissima Annunziata; *Porta Rossa*, 19 Via Porta Rossa; *Beacci Tornabuoni*, 3 Via Tornabuoni. 2-star: *Villani*, 11 Via delle Oche and *Boboli*, 63 Via Romana. Hotels outside the centre of Florence include the 4-star *Torre di Bellosguardo*, 2 Via Roti Michelozzi (for hotels in the environs, including Fiesole, see Rte 2).
YOUTH HOSTEL (*Ostello per la Gioventù*) at *Villa Camerata*, 2 Viale Righi. CAMPING SITE (2-star) *Italiani e Stranieri*, Viale Michelangelo (closed November to March).

Restaurants. Luxury-class: *Enoteca Pinchiorri*, 87 Via Ghibellina; *Bristol* in the Hotel Helvetia e Bristol, 2 Via de' Pescioni. First-class: *La Capannina di Sante*, Piazza Ravenna (specialising in fish); *Cibreo*, 118 Via dei Macci. Well-known trattorie: *Latini*, 6 Via Palchetti; *Cocco Lezzone*, 26 Via del Parioncino; *Il Troia* 29 Via Porcellana. Simple trattorie: *Acquacotta*, 51 Via dei Pilastri; *Benvenuto*, 16 Via Mosca; *Diladdarno*, 108 Via de' Serragli. *Alessi*, 24 Via di Mezzo (a club; membership by previous appointment;

annual subscription) is run by a scholar of Renaissance cuisine who produces excellent traditional Tuscan dishes (not expensive). Cheap eating places: *La Casalinga*, 9 Via Michelozzi; *Mario*, 2 Via Rosina.

Some of the most pleasant spots in the city to have a **Picnic** include: the Boboli gardens, Forte di Belvedere, the Giardino dell'Orticoltura, the park of Villa il Ventaglio, the park of Villa Stibbert, and in the gardens off Viale Machiavelli.

Buses to the environs, see Rte 2. **Country Buses**. A wide network of bus services in Tuscany is operated by *Lazzi*, 4 Piazza Stazione (Tel. 055/215154), SITA, 15 Via Santa Caterina da Siena (Tel. 055/211487), COPIT and CAP, 9 Largo Alinari (Tel. 055/214637).

British Consulate, 2 Lungarno Corsini (Pl. 10); **American Consulate**, 38 Lungarno Vespucci (Pl. 5). *Anglican Church*, St Mark's, 16 Via Maggio; *American Episcopalian*, St James, 9 Via Bernardo Rucellai.

Institutes. *British Institute*, 2 Via Tornabuoni (Italian language courses), with an excellent library and reading room at 9B Lungarno Guicciardini; *Institut Français*, 2 Piazza Ognissanti; *German Institute of Art History*, 44 Via Giuseppe Giusti, with the best art history library in Florence (post-graduate students); *Dutch Institute*, 5 Viale Torricelli; *Harvard University Center for Italian Renaissance Studies*, Villa I Tatti, Ponte a Mensola, Settignano (with a good library, open to post-graduate students); *Centro Linguistico Italiano 'Dante Alighieri'*, 12 Via de'Bardi (Italian language courses).

Concerts and Drama. *Teatro Comunale* (Pl. 5), 16 Corso Italia, symphony concerts and opera. Here is held the MAGGIO MUSICALE, an annual music festival (May–July). *La Pergola* (Pl. 7), 12 Via della Pergola (drama season, and chamber music concerts organised by the *Amici della Musica* in January–April and October–December). Concerts are often given by the *Orchestra Regionale Toscana* and the *Orchestra da Camera Fiorentina*.

Annual Festivals and exhibitions. The *Scoppio del Carro*, on Easter Day, is a traditional religious festival held in and outside the Duomo. On 24 June, St John's Day (St John is the patron saint of Florence), a local holiday is celebrated with fireworks at Piazzale Michelangelo. A 'football' game in 16C costume (Calcio in costume) is held in three heats during June. An Antiques Fair (the *Mostra Mercato Internazionale dell'Antiquariato*) is held biennially (next in 1995) in the autumn.

History. The Roman colony of *Florentia* was founded in 59 BC by Julius Caesar. The city was built on the Arno where the crossing is narrowest, and it flourished in the 2C and 3C AD. The commune of Florence came into being in the first decades of the 12C, and there followed a long drawn-out struggle between Guelfs and Ghibellines. By the middle of the 13C Florentine merchants, whose prosperity was largely based on the woollen cloth industry, were established in a privileged position in trade and commerce, and the florin, first minted in silver c 1235, and soon after in gold, was used as the standard gold coin in Europe. In the 14C Florence was one of the five largest cities in Europe. By this time Palazzo Vecchio had been built by Arnolfo di Cambio, and the two churches of Santa Maria Novella and Santa Croce were erected.

The city's greatest moment of splendour came in the 15C when a new conception of art and learning symbolised the birth of the Renaissance, under the brilliant leadership of Cosimo de' Medici and, later, under his famous grandson Lorenzo il Magnifico. The origins of Florentine art in the 14C had been marked by the works of Cimabue and Giotto, who led the way for the Renaissance, which found its highest expression in the works of Brunelleschi, Donatello, and Masaccio. Numerous great artists worked together in Florence in the 15C creating remarkably beautiful paintings, buildings, and statuary. Among them were Lorenzo Ghiberti, Luca della Robbia, Beato Angelico, Filippo Lippi, and Paolo Uccello. In the later 15C Pollaiolo, Verrocchio, and Sandro Botticelli produced splendid works, and they were followed by the 'universal' artist Leonardo da Vinci. The fame of Michelangelo, who was favoured by the patronage of Lorenzo il Magnifico, spread throughout Europe and he was recognised as the greatest artist of his time.

Despite opposition from Republican exiles, enlightened Medici rule continued into the 16C when they became grand-dukes of Tuscany. Andrea del Sarto, Pontormo, Giambologna, Benvenuto Cellini, and Bronzino represent the Mannerist era of art in the city. The Medici were succeeded in 1737 by Austrian grand-dukes. From 1861 to

1875 Florence was the capital of the Italian kingdom. All the bridges except Ponte Vecchio were blown up in the Second World War, and in 1966 a disastrous flood of the Arno caused severe damage to the city and its works of art.

A.   The Baptistery and the Duomo

The **Baptistery of San Giovanni** (Pl. 7; open 13–18; fest. 9.30–13) is one of the oldest and most revered buildings in the city, called by Dante his *bel San Giovanni*. It was probably built in the 6C or 7C, and in any case not later than the 9C. It is a domed octagonal building of centralised plan derived from Byzantine models. In the 11C–12C the EXTERIOR was entirely encased in white and green marble from Prato in a classical geometrical design, which became a prototype for numerous other Tuscan Romanesque religious buildings. The cupola was concealed by an unusual white pyramidal roof (and the 11C lantern placed on top), probably in the 13C. The building is famous for its three sets of gilded bronze doors. The two doors by Lorenzo Ghiberti were erected after he won a competition in 1401, often taken as a convenient point to mark the beginning of the Florentine Renaissance.

The *SOUTH DOOR (1336) is by Andrea Pisano with reliefs illustrating the history of St John the Baptist. The bronze frame was added by Vittorio Ghiberti (1452–64). Over the doorway are statues of the Baptist, the Executioner, and Salome, by Vincenzo Danti (1571). The *NORTH DOOR, by Lorenzo Ghiberti (1403–24) contains scenes of the Life of Christ, the Evangelists, and the Doctors of the Church. The beautiful frame is also by Ghiberti, and his self-portrait appears in a head on the left door. The sculptures above of St John the Baptist, the Levite, and the Pharisee are by Francesco Rustici (1506–11), from a design by Leonardo da Vinci.

The **EAST DOOR is the most celebrated work of Lorenzo Ghiberti, the completion of which took him most of his life (1425–52). It is said to have been called by Michelangelo the 'Gate of Paradise'. The pictorial reliefs, no longer restricted to a Gothic frame, depict each episode with great conciseness, and the workmanship of the carving is masterly. A copy of the door made from casts taken in 1948 was set up here in 1990, and the orignal panels will all be exhibited in the Museo dell'Opera del Duomo after their restoration. The subjects are: 1. The Creation and the Expulsion from Paradise; 2. Cain and Abel; 3. Noah's Sacrifice and Drunkenness; 4. Abraham and the Angels and the Sacrifice of Isaac; 5. Esau and Jacob; 6. Joseph sold and recognised by his Brethren; 7. Moses receiving the Tablets of Stone; 8. The Fall of Jericho; 9. Battle with the Philistines; 10. Solomon and the Queen of Sheba. The frame contains beautiful statuettes of Prophets and Sibyls, and medallions with portraits of Ghiberti himself and his contemporaries. The splendid bronze door-frame is by Ghiberti also. Above, the sculptural group of the Baptism of Christ, attributed to Andrea Sansovino and Vincenzo Danti, with an Angel added by Innocenzo Spinazzi (18C), has been removed and restored.

The harmonious INTERIOR is designed in two orders, of which the lower has huge granite columns from a Roman building, with gilded Corinthian capitals, and the upper, above a cornice, a gallery with divided windows. The walls are in panels of white marble divided by bands of black, in the dichromatic style of the exterior. The oldest part of the splendid mosaic

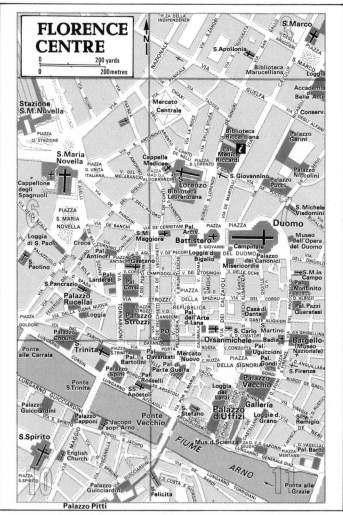

FLORENCE
CENTRE

0   200 yards
0   200 metres

*pavement in *opus tessellatum* (begun 1209) is near the Gothic font. Beside the 13C high altar is an elaborate paschal candlestick delicately carved by Agostino di Jacopo (1320). The *tomb of the antipope John XXIII (Baldassarre Coscia, who died in Florence in 1419) by Donatello and Michelozzo is one of the earliest Renaissance tombs in the city. This beautifully carved monument in no way disturbs the architectural harmony of the building. The *MOSAICS in the vault are remarkably well preserved. The earliest (c 1225) are in the 'scarsella' above the altar; they are signed by the monk 'Jacopo', who is also thought to have begun the main dome, the centre of which is decorated with paleo-Christian motifs. Above the apse is the Last

Judgement with a huge (8m) figure of Christ attributed to Coppo di Marcovaldo. The four bands of the cupola illustrate the Story of Genesis, the Story of Joseph (the design of some of the scenes is attributed to the Maestro della Maddalena), the Story of Christ, and the Story of St John the Baptist (some of the early episodes are attributed to Cimabue). Work on the mosaics was well advanced by 1271, but probably continued into the 14C.

The *Duomo (Pl. 7; open 10–17; fest. 7–12, 14.30–17), the cathedral dedicated to the Madonna of Florence, *Santa Maria del Fiore*, fills Piazza del Duomo; a comprehensive view of the huge building is difficult in the confined space. It produces a memorable effect of massive grandeur, especially seen from its southern flank, lightened by the colour and pattern of its beautiful marble walls (white from Carrara, green from Prato, and red from the Maremma). The famous dome, one of the masterpieces of the Renaissance, rising to the height of the surrounding hills (from which it is nearly always visible), holds sway over the whole city.

The paleo-Christian church, dedicated to the Palestinian saint Reparata, is thought to have been founded in the 6–7C, or possibly earlier. The Bishop's seat, formerly at San Lorenzo, was probably transferred here in the late 7C. By the 13C a new and larger cathedral was deemed necessary, and in 1294 Arnolfo di Cambio was appointed as architect. In 1355 Francesco Talenti continued work on the building, probably following Arnolfo's original design of a vaulted basilica with a domed octagon flanked by three polygonal tribunes. By 1417 the octagonal drum was substantially finished. The construction of the cupola had long been recognised as a major technical problem, and after a competition Brunelleschi was appointed to the task, and had erected the dome up to the base of the lantern by 1436 when Pope Eugenius IV consecrated the cathedral.

EXTERIOR. The majestic **CUPOLA, the greatest of all *Brunelleschi*'s works (1420–36), is a feat of engineering skill. It was the first dome to be projected without the need for a wooden supporting frame to sustain the vault during construction, and was the largest and highest of its time. The cupola has two concentric shells, the octagonal vaults of which are evident both on the exterior and the interior of the building; the upper section is built in bricks in consecutive rings in horizontal courses, bonded together in a herringbone pattern. The lantern was begun a few months before the architect's death in 1446, and carried on by his friend Michelozzo. In the late 1460s Verrocchio placed the bronze ball and cross on the summit. Brunelleschi also designed the four decorative little exedrae with niches which he placed around the octagonal drum between the three domed tribunes. The balcony at the base of the cupola added by Baccio d'Agnolo was never completed, according to Vasari, because of Michelangelo's stringent criticism. The dome has been under constant surveillance since 1980 when alarm was raised about its stability (the main problem seems to the weight of the dome which has caused fissures in the drum).

The building of the cathedral was begun on the S side where the decorative pattern of marble can be seen to full advantage. The PORTA DEI CANONICI has fine sculptural decoration (1395–99). On the N side, the *PORTA DELLA MANDORLA (1391–1405) is by Giovanni d'Ambrogio, Piero di Giovanni Tedesco, Jacopo di Piero Guidi, and Nicolò Lamberti. In the gable is an *Assumption of the Virgin in an almond-shaped frame by Nanni di Banco (c 1418–20) which had an important influence on early Renaissance sculpture. The FAÇADE, erected to a third of its projected height by 1420, was demolished in 1587–88; the present front in the Gothic style was designed by Emilio De Fabris and built in 1871–87.

The Gothic INTERIOR is somewhat bare and chilly after the warmth of the colour of the exterior, whose splendour it cannot match. The huge grey stone arches of the nave reach the clerestory beneath an elaborate sculptured balcony. The massive pilasters which support the stone vault have unusual composite capitals. Three dark tribunes with a Gothic coronet of chapels surround the huge dome. The beautiful marble pavement was designed by Baccio d'Agnolo, Francesco da Sangallo and others. WEST WALL. Mosaic of the Coronation of the Virgin, attributed to Gaddo Gaddi. Ghiberti designed the three stained glass windows. The huge clock was decorated with four heads of prophets by Paolo Uccello in 1443. The recomposed tomb of Antonio d'Orso, Bishop of Florence (died 1321) by Tino da Camaino includes a fine statue. SOUTH AISLE. In a tondo is a bust of Brunelleschi by Buggiano, his adopted son (1446). On the side altar, statue of a Prophet by Nanni di Banco. The bust of Giotto by Benedetto da Maiano bears an inscription by Poliziano. On the second altar, statue of Isaiah by Ciuffagni.

Steps lead down to the EXCAVATIONS OF SANTA REPARATA (open 10–17). Through a grille to the left at the bottom of the steps can be seen the simple tomb slab of Brunelleschi, found here in 1972. The architect of the cupola was the only Florentine granted the privilege of burial in the cathedral. The complicated remains of Santa Reparata (shown in a model), on various levels, include Roman edifices on which the early Christian church was built, a fine mosaic pavement of the paleo-Christian church, and remains of the pre-Romanesque and Romanesque reconstructions. Here are displayed finds from the excavations, fresco fragments, plutei, etc.

EAST END OF THE CHURCH (open to visitors only when services are not in progress). Above the octagon the great dome soars to a height of 91m. The fresco of the Last Judgement by Vasari and Federico Zuccari (1572–79) was restored in 1981–94. The stained glass in the roundels of the drum was designed in 1443–45 by Paolo Uccello, Andrea del Castagno, Donatello, and Ghiberti. Against the pillars stand 16C statues of Apostles by Jacopo Sansovino, Vincenzo de'Rossi, Andrea Ferrucci, Baccio Bandinelli, Benedetto da Rovezzano, Giovanni Bandini, and Vincenzo de'Rossi. The marble SANCTUARY by Bandinelli (1555), with bas-reliefs by himself and Bandini, encloses the high altar, also by Bandinelli, with a wood Crucifix by Benedetto da Maiano. Each of the three apses is divided into five chapels with stained glass windows designed by Lorenzo Ghiberti. Above the entrance to the SOUTH SACRISTY is a large lunette of the Ascension in enamelled terracotta by Luca Della Robbia. In the central Apse are two graceful kneeling angels, also by Luca, and a bronze reliquary *urn by Lorenzo Ghiberti with exquisite bas-reliefs. Over the door into the NORTH SACRISTY is another fine relief by Luca Della Robbia of the *Resurrection. This was his earliest important work (1442) in enamelled terracotta. The doors were his only work in bronze. It was in this sacristy that Lorenzo il Magnifico took refuge on the day of the Pazzi conspiracy in 1478 in order to escape the death which befell his brother, Giuliano. The *interior has beautiful intarsia cupboards dating from 1436–45 by artists including Lo Scheggia and Antonio Manetti. The end wall was continued by Giuliano da Maiano in 1463 (possibly on a cartoon by Antonio del Pollaiolo). The carved frieze of putti is by various artists probably including Benedetto da Maiano. On the entrance wall is a fine marble lavabo by Buggiano probably based on a design by Brunelleschi. In the pavement of the left apse is Toscanelli's huge Gnomon (1475) for solar observations.

The *ASCENT OF THE DOME (entrance in N aisle; adm. 10–17; closed fest.) is highly recommended. The climb (463 steps) is not specially arduous, and it follows a labyrinth of corridors, steps, and spiral staircases (used by the builders of the cupola) as far as the lantern at the top of the dome. During the ascent the structure of the dome can be examined, and the views of the inside of the cathedral from the balcony around the drum (45.5m in diameter), and of the city from the small windows and from the lantern, are remarkable. On the way down, there is a room with instruments used during the construction of the dome.

In the NORTH AISLE is a painting of Dante with the 'Divina Commedia' which illuminates Florence (1465) by Domenico Michelino. On the side altar, Bernardo Ciuffagni, King David. The two splendid frescoed *Equestrian memorials to the famous *condottieri*, the Englishman Sir John Hawkwood (*Giovanni Acuto*) who commanded the Florentine army from 1377 until his death in 1394, and Nicolò da Tolentino (died 1434), are by Paolo Uccello and Andrea del Castagno. The bust of the organist Antonio Squarcialupi is by Benedetto da Maiano. On the last altar, Donatello (attributed), the prophet Joshua (traditionally thought to be a portrait of the humanist friend of Cosimo il Vecchio, Poggio Bracciolini), originally on the façade of the Duomo.

The *Campanile (Pl. 7) (nearly 85m high) was begun by Giotto in 1334 when, as the most distinguished Florentine artist, he was appointed city architect. It was continued by Andrea Pisano (1343), and completed by Francesco Talenti in 1348–59. It is built of the same coloured marbles as the Duomo, in similar patterns, in a remarkably well-proportioned design. The original bas-reliefs and statues of Prophets and Sibyls in the niches have been removed to the Museo dell'Opera and have been replaced by copies. The ascent of the bell-tower (adm. daily 9–sunset) via 414 steps is interesting for its succession of views of the Duomo, the Baptistery, and the rest of the city. Although lower than the cupola, the climb is steeper.

Between the Baptistery and the Campanile is the little Gothic *LOGGIA DEL BIGALLO built in 1351–58 probably by Alberto Arnoldi, who carved the reliefs. Beneath the loggia lost and abandoned children were exposed for three days before being consigned to foster-mothers. The MUSEO DEL BIGALLO (usually closed) is the smallest museum in the city, but one of the most charming. It preserves most of the works of art commissioned over the centuries by the Misericordia and the Bigallo from Florentine artists, including a portable triptych by Bernardo Daddi.

Across Via dei Calzaiuoli is the MISERICORDIA, a charitable institution which gives help free to those in need, and runs an ambulance service. The lay confraternity, founded in 1244, continues its work through some 2000 volunteers who are a characteristic sight of Florence in their black capes and hoods. The Oratory contains an altarpiece by Andrea Della Robbia and a statue of St Sebastian by Benedetto da Maiano. Other works of art can sometimes be seen on request. At No. 9 Piazza del Duomo is the *Museo dell'Opera del Duomo (Pl. 7; adm. 9–18; summer 9–19.30; fest. closed), in a building which has been the seat of the Opera del Duomo (responsible for the maintenance of the cathedral) since the beginning of the 15C. One of the pleasantest museums in the city, it contains material from the Duomo, the Baptistery, and the Campanile, including important sculpture.

In the COURTYARD are two Roman sarcophagi (mid-3C) from the Baptistery. In the ENTRANCE HALL, marble bust of Brunelleschi attributed to Giovanni Bandini, and fine marble panels from the choir of the Duomo by

Baccio Bandinelli and Giovanni Bandini. On the left are two small rooms devoted to Brunelleschi, with the apparatus which may have been used in the construction of the cupola, together with the original brick moulds, and his death mask, and models in wood of the cupola (probably made by a contemporary of Brunelleschi), and of the lantern (thought to date from 1436 and to be by the architect himself). In the large hall beyond are displayed numerous *sculptures from the old façade by Arnolfo di Cambio, and four seated statues of the Evangelists added to the lower part of the façade by Nanni di Banco (St Luke), Donatello (*St John the Evangelist), Bernardo Ciuffagni (St Matthew), and Niccolò di Piero Lamberti (St Mark). The drawing of the old façade (never completed) of the Duomo designed by Arnolfo di Cambio was made shortly before its demolition in 1587 by Bernardino Poccetti. On the STAIR LANDING is the famous *Pietà of Michelangelo. A late work, it was intended for the sculptor's own tomb. According to Vasari, the head of Nicodemus is a self-portrait. Unsatisfied with his work, Michelangelo destroyed the arm and left leg of Christ, and his pupil Tiberio Calcagni restored the arm and finished the figure of Mary Magdalen.

FIRST FLOOR. Room I is dominated by the two famous *Cantorie made in the 1430s by Luca Della Robbia and Donatello for the Duomo. The original sculptured panels by Luca are displayed beneath the reconstructed

A carved panel from the Cantoria by Luca della Robbia, Museo dell'Opera del Duomo, Florence

Cantoria. The children (some of them drawn from Classical models), dancing, singing, or playing musical instruments, are exquisitely carved within a beautiful architectural framework. Donatello's Cantoria provides a striking contrast, with a frieze of running putti against a background of coloured inlay. Beneath it is displayed his expressive statue in wood of *St Mary Magdalen, thought to be a late work. Around the walls are the sixteen statues from the niches on the Campanile by Donatello (two Prophets, Abraham and Isaac, Geremiah, *Habbakuk), Nanni di Bartolo, and Andrea Pisano. Next door are the original *bas-reliefs from the Campanile. The lower row are charming works by Andrea Pisano (some perhaps designed by Giotto) illustrating the Creation of Man, and the Arts and Industries. The last five reliefs (on the right wall) were made in the following century by Luca Della Robbia. The upper row of smaller reliefs by pupils of Pisano illustrate the seven Planets, the Virtues, and the Liberal Arts. The Seven Sacraments are by Alberto Arnoldi. The lunette of the Madonna and Child is by Andrea Pisano.

In Room II are four gilded bronze *panels by Lorenzo Ghiberti, removed from the East Door of the Baptistery (described above), and displayed here since their restoration. The magnificent *altar of silver-gilt from the Baptistery, is a Gothic work by Florentine goldsmiths finished in the 15C. The statuette of the Baptist is by Michelozzo; the reliefs (at the sides) of the Beheading of the Saint, and of his birth are by Verrocchio and Antonio del Pollaiolo. The silver *Cross is the work of Betto di Francesco, Antonio del Pollaiolo, and others. Also displayed here are needlework *panels from a liturgical tapestry worked by the craftsmen of the *Arte di Calimala* and designed by Antonio del Pollaiolo; sculptures by Andrea Pisano and Tino da Camaino, and paintings of the 14–15C Florentine school.Beside the Baptistery is the *Pillar of St Zenobius*, erected in the 14C to commemorate an elm which came into leaf here when the body of the bishop saint (died c 430) was translated from San Lorenzo to Santa Reparata in the 9C.

B. Piazza del Duomo to Piazza della Signoria

VIA DE'CALZAIOLI (Pl. 7), on the line of a Roman road, was the main thoroughfare of the medieval city, linking the Duomo to Palazzo Vecchio and passing the guildhall of Orsanmichele. On the right is PIAZZA DELLA REPUBBLICA (Pl. 7), on the site of the Roman forum, and still in the centre of the city. It was laid out at the end of the 19C after the demolition of many medieval buildings. Much criticised at the time, it remains a disappointing intrusion into the historical centre of the city. It has several large cafés with tables outside.

The tall rectangular church of *Orsanmichele (Pl. 7) was built as a market by Francesco Talenti, Neri di Fioravante, and Benci di Cione in 1337. The arcades were enclosed by huge Gothic windows by Simone Talenti in 1380. The upper storey was intended to be used as a granary. The decoration of the exterior was undertaken by the Guilds (or *Arti*) who commissioned statues of their patron saints for the canopied niches. They competed with each other to command work from the best artists of the age, and the statues are an impressive testimony to the skill of Florentine sculptors over a period of some two hundred years. Since 1984 restoration of the statues and niches has been underway, and it has been decided for conservation reasons that

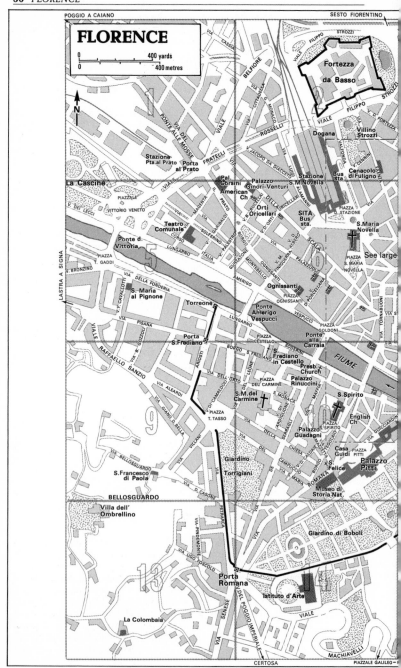

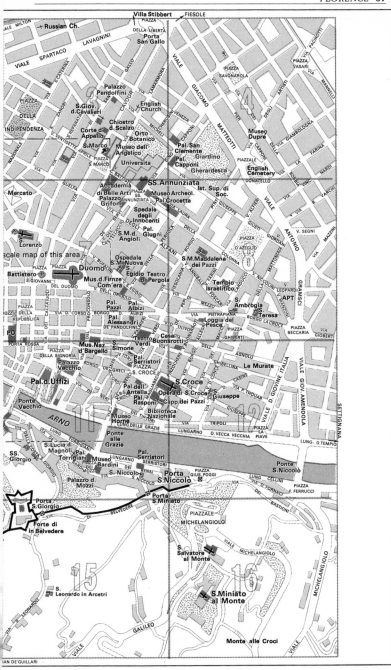

IAN DE'GUILLARI

the original statues cannot be replaced in situ (they may be exhibited after their restoration in rooms above).

The statues, beginning at Via de'Calzaioli (corner of Via de'Lamberti) and going round to the right are: St John the Baptist (1414–16), by Lorenzo Ghiberti, the first life-size statue of the Renaissance to be cast in bronze (removed); *Incredulity of St Thomas (1466–83), by Verrocchio (removed and restored), in a tabernacle by Donatello (the *stemma* above is by Luca Della Robbia); St Luke, by Giambologna (1601), in a tabernacle by Niccolò Lamberti; St Peter (1408–13) attributed to Donatello (removed); tabernacle and St Philip (c 1415) by Nanni di Banco (removed); tabernacle, relief, and statues of *four soldier saints (the *Quattro Santi Coronati*), modelled on Roman works, by Nanni di Banco (c 1415), and *stemma* above by Luca della Robbia; St George by Donatello (copies of the statue and relief removed to the Bargello); tabernacle and *St Matthew (1419–22) by Ghiberti; *St Stephen by Ghiberti (1428); St Eligius (removed and restored) and bas-relief by Nanni di Banco; *St Mark by Donatello (replaced by a cast); St James the Greater (removed and restored) and bas-relief attributed to Niccolò Lamberti; Gothic tabernacle attributed to Simone Talenti, with a *Madonna and Child attributed to Giovanni Tedesco, and *stemma* by Luca Della Robbia; St John the Evangelist by Baccio da Montelupo (1515).

The INTERIOR of the dark rectangular hall now serves as a church, and it contains interesting frescoes (14–16C), and fine Gothic stained glass windows. The Gothic *tabernacle by Andrea Orcagna (1349–59) is a masterpiece of all the decorative arts. A beautiful frame of carved angels encloses a painting on the altar of the *Madonna by Bernardo Daddi. On the other altar is a statue of the Madonna and Child with St Anne, by Francesco da Sangallo (1522). The two large Gothic halls on the upper floors are sometimes used for exhibitions.

An overhead passageway connects Orsanmichele to *Palazzo dell'Arte della Lana*, built in 1308 by the Guild of Wool Merchants but arbitrarily restored in 1905. At the base of the tower is the little 14C oratory of Santa Maria della Tromba, with a painting of the Madonna by Jacopo del Casentino. *Palazzo dell'Arte dei Beccai*, also facing Orsanmichele, the headquarters of the Butchers' Guild until 1534, is now the seat of the Accademia delle Arti del Disegno founded in 1563 by Vasari and his contemporaries.

On Via Porta Rossa is the 16C loggia of the MERCATO NUOVO (Pl. 11), the Florentine straw-market (with stalls also selling leather goods, cheap lace, and souvenirs). It is known to Florentines as *Il Porcellino* from the popular statue here of a bronze boar (a copy by Tacca from an antique statue in the Uffizi).

Via Porta Rossa continues to **Palazzo Davanzati** (Pl. 11), the MUSEO DELLA CASA FIORENTINA ANTICA (adm. 9–14; fest. 9–13; closed Monday), and the best surviving example of a medieval nobleman's house in Florence (despite numerous restorations). It is particularly interesting as an illustration of Florentine life in the Middle Ages. The typical 14C façade consists of three storeys above large arches on the ground floor. The INTERIOR, of great interest for its architecture and contemporary wall paintings (rare survivals of a decorative form typical of 14C houses) has been beautifully arranged with the furnishings of a Florentine house of 15–17C (including tapestries, lacework, ceramics, sculpture, paintings, decorative arts, domestic objects, etc.). The 16–17C furniture is a special feature of the house.

Via Pellicceria leads to *Palazzo di Parte Guelfa*, built as the official residence of the Captains of the Guelf party in the 13C. The palace was enlarged by Brunelleschi who added a hall. Nearby is *Palazzo dell'Arte della Seta*, with a beautiful 'stemma' in the style of Donatello.

VIA DELLE TERME, and the parallel BORGO SANTI APOSTOLI to the S, are both pretty medieval streets with numerous towers and old palaces. **Santi Apostoli** (Pl. 10), one of the oldest churches in the city, has a Romanesque stone façade. The basilican INTERIOR (open 15.30–18.30) has fine green marble columns and capitals. It contains a *sinopia of a fresco of the Madonna by Paolo Schiavo formerly on the façade; the Tomb of Prior Oddo Altoviti by Benedetto da Rovezzano; and a *tabernacle by Andrea Della Robbia.

Across Via Por Santa Maria (rebuilt since 1944) is the church of SANTO STEFANO AL PONTE (Pl. 11; closed for restoration), another very old church. The interior was altered by Ferdinando Tacca in 1649. The altar-steps are by Buontalenti, and the altarpieces by Santi di Tito, Matteo Rosselli, and others.

*Piazza della Signoria** (Pl. 11), dominated by Palazzo Vecchio, the town hall, has been the political centre of the city since the Middle Ages. Here, from the 13C onwards, the *popolo sovrano* met in *parlamento* to resolve crises of government. In the life of the city today, the piazza is still the focus of political manifestations. It is now a pedestrian precinct and usually crowded with tourists as well as Florentines. By 1385, when it was paved, the piazza had nearly reached its present dimensions. The 18C pavement was virtually destroyed when it was renewed in 1991. The huge *Loggia della Signoria** (Pl. 11; also known as *Loggia dei Lanzi* and *Loggia dell' Orcagna*), with three beautiful lofty arches, was built in 1376–82 by Benci di Cione and Simone Talenti (probably on a design by Orcagna) to be used by government officials during public ceremonies and as an ornament to the square. The exterior has recently been restored.

Since the end of the 18C the loggia has been used as an open-air museum of sculpture. The magnificent bronze *Perseus trampling Medusa and exhibiting her severed head was commissioned from Cellini by Cosimo I in 1545 (being restored). The original bas-relief and statuettes from the pedestal are now in the Bargello. The *Rape of the Sabine (1583), a three-figure group, is Giambologna's last work, and one of the most successful Mannerist sculptures. Also here are two lions, one a Greek work, the other a 16C copy; Hercules and the Centaur, by Giambologna; the Rape of Polyxena, by Pio Fedi; and Roman statues.

Michelangelo's famous DAVID was commissioned by the city of Florence in 1501 and set up here in 1504 as a political symbol representing the victory of Republicanism over tyranny. It was removed to the Accademia in 1873 and replaced here by a copy. The colossal statue of Hercules and Cacus, an unhappy imitation of the David, was sculpted in 1534 by Bandinelli. Donatello's statue of Judith and Holofernes has been replaced by a copy (original inside Palazzo Vecchio, see below). The NEPTUNE FOUNTAIN, by Ammannati, is dominated by a colossal flaccid figure of Neptune, known to Florentines as 'il Biancone'. The more successful elegant bronze groups on the basin were carved by Giambologna, Andrea Calamech, and others. The porphyry disk in the pavement in front of the fountain marks the spot where Savonarola was burnt at the stake as a heretic in 1498. The fine bronze equestrian monument to Cosimo I is by Giambologna. At the end of the piazza, towards Piazza San Firenze, is the *Tribunale di Mercanzia* (or

Merchants' Court), founded in 1308 and established in this building in 1359. *Palazzo Uguccioni* (No. 7) has an unusual but handsome façade attributed to Mariotto di Zanobi Folfi (1550), with a bust of Francesco I by Giovanni Bandini. Above a bank at No. 5 is displayed the COLLEZIONE DELLA RAGIONE (adm. 9–14 except Tuesday, and fest. 10–13), a representative collection of 20C Italian art left to the city in 1970 by Alberto Della Ragione.

*\ **Palazzo Vecchio** (Pl. 11; also known as *Palazzo della Signoria*), the medieval Palazzo del Popolo, is still the town hall of Florence. On a design traditionally attributed to Arnolfo di Cambio (1298–1302), it is an imposing fortress-palace built in pietra forte on a trapezoidal plan. The façade has remained virtually unchanged: it has graceful two-light windows and a battlemented gallery. It became the prototype of many other Palazzi Comunali in Tuscany. It was the tallest edifice in the city until the 15C; the tower (1310), asymmetrically placed, is 95m high. Many of the rooms on the upper floors are open to the public, or used for exhibitions. Adm. 9–19; fest. 8–13; closed Thursday.

The palace stands on part of the site of the Roman theatre of Florence built in the 1C AD. Here the *priori* lived during their two months' tenure of office in the government of the medieval city. Cosimo il Vecchio was imprisoned in the 'Alberghetto' in the tower in 1433 before being exiled. In 1540 Cosimo I moved here from the private Medici palace in Via Larga. It became known as Palazzo Vecchio after 1549 when the Medici grand-dukes took up residence in Palazzo Pitti. From 1865 to 1871 it housed the Chamber of Deputies and the Foreign Ministry when Florence was capital of the Kingdom of Italy.

Above the ENTRANCE is a frieze (1528) dedicated to *Cristo Re*. The CORTILE was reconstructed by Michelozzo (1453), and the elaborate decoration added in 1565 by Vasari on the occasion of the marriage between Francesco, son of Cosimo I, and Joanna of Austria. The fountain bears a copy of Verrocchio's putto, now inside the palace. The statue of Samson killing the Philistine is by Pierino da Vinci. In the 14C SALA D'ARME exhibitions are held. The rest of the ground floor is taken up with busy local government offices (and the ticket office). A monumental double GRAND STAIRCASE by Vasari ascends to the immense *\ **Salone dei Cinquecento**, built by Cronaca in 1495 for the meetings of the Consiglio Maggiore of the Republic. Leonardo da Vinci and Michelangelo were commissioned to paint huge murals of the battles of Anghiari and Cascina on the two long walls. Only the cartoons and a fragment by Leonardo were ever completed; these were copied and studied by contemporary painters before they were lost. The room was transformed by Vasari in 1563–65 when the present decoration was carried out in honour of Cosimo I, and the Florentine victories over Siena and Pisa, by Giovanni Stradano, Jacopo Zucchi, and Giovanni Battista Naldini. Michelangelo's *\ Victory, a strongly knit two-figure group, was intended for a niche in the tomb of Julius II in Rome. Giambologna's Virtue overcoming Vice was commissioned as a 'pendant' (the original plaster model is displayed here). The statues of the Labours of Hercules are Vincenzo de'Rossi's best works.

An inconspicuous door (opened on request) gives access to the charming *\ STUDIOLO OF FRANCESCO I. This tiny study is a masterpiece of Florentine Mannerist decoration created by Vasari and his school. It is entirely decorated with paintings and bronze statuettes celebrating Francesco's interest in the natural sciences and alchemy, by Il Poppi, Bronzino, Vincenzo Danti, Vasari, Santi di Tito, Giovanni Battista Naldini, Giovanni Battista Stradano, Alessandro Allori, Giovanni Bandini, Maso di San Friano, Giambologna,

Vincenzo de'Rossi, Giovanni Maria Butteri, Alessandro Fei, Bartolomeo Ammannati, and Jacopo Zucchi. The Town Council meets in the SALA DEI DUGENTO, reconstructed in 1472–77 by Benedetto and Giuliano da Maiano, who also executed the magnificent wood ceiling (with the help of Domenico, Marco and Giuliano del Tasso). The *tapestries made in Florence by Bronzino, Pontormo, Salviati, and Allori have been removed since 1983 for restoration.

The QUARTIERE DI LEONE X was decorated for Cosimo I by Vasari, Marco da Faenza, Giovanni Stradano, and others with paintings illustrating the political history of the Medici family. Only the Sala di Leone X is at present open. Stairs lead up to the QUARTIERE DEGLI ELEMENTI, also decorated by Vasari and assistants. The Terrazza di Saturno (closed for restoration) has a good view of Florence. In a little room here is displayed the original of Verrocchio's *putto with a dolphin, removed from the courtyard. In some of the rooms are fine cabinets in pietre dure. A balcony leads across the end of the Sala dei Cinquecento. The apartments of the wife of Cosimo I are known as the QUARTIERE DI ELEONORA DI TOLEDO. The *chapel was entirely decorated by Bronzino. In the Sala di Ester is a painting of 1557 which shows the lost fragment of the Battle of Anghiari by Leonardo, probably the best copy that has survived. Beyond the Cappella della Signoria decorated by Ridolfo del Ghirlandaio is the SALA D'UDIENZA with a superb *ceiling by Giuliano da Maiano and assistants. The *doorway crowned by a statue of Justice is by Benedetto and Giuliano da Maiano. The mural paintings (1545–48) are by Salviati. The SALA DEI GIGLI has another magnificent *ceiling and frescoes by Domenico Ghirlandaio. Here is displayed Donatello's bronze statue of *Judith and Holofernes, removed from Piazza della Signoria and recently restored. It is one of his last and most sophisticated works. The Cancelleria was Niccolò Machiavelli's office when he was government secretary. The Guardaroba contains 57 maps illustrating the entire known world by Fra Egnazio Danti and Stefano Bonsignori (1563–81). The COLLEZIONE LOESER in the Quartiere del Mezzanino is at present closed to the public. It includes a *portrait of Laura Battiferri, wife of Bartolomeo Ammannati, by Bronzino; a tondo of the Madonna and Child with St John, by Alfonso Berruguete; and a 16C bust of Machiavelli. Also here the musical instruments from the Conservatorio Cherubini have been arranged (stringed instruments by Stradivari, Guarneri, Arnati, and Ruggeri; a harpsichord by Cristofori, etc.) but they have not been open to the public for several years.

C. Galleria degli Uffizi

The massive *Palazzo degli Uffizi (Pl. 11) extends from Piazza della Signoria to the Arno. The unusual U-shaped building with a short 'façade' on the river front was begun in 1560 by Vasari, and completed according to his design by Alfonso Parigi the Elder and Bernardo Buontalenti. It was commissioned by Cosimo I to serve as government offices (*uffici*, hence 'uffizi'). Resting on unstable sandy ground, it is a feat of engineering skill. The use of iron to reinforce the building permitted extraordinary technical solutions during its construction, and allowed for the remarkably large number of apertures.

The **˙˙Galleria degli Uffizi** is the most important collection of paintings in Italy and one of the great art collections of the world. The origins of the collection go back to Cosimo I, and numerous members of the Medici dynasty continued to add works of art in the following centuries. The last of the Medici, Anna Maria Lodovica, settled her inheritance on the people of Florence in 1737. All the works are well labelled and the collection is arranged chronologically by school. In 1993 the west corridor of the gallery was severely damaged by a car bomb (placed by the Mafia). Rooms 26–33 and 41–45 are still closed and 90 paintings will have to be restored. (Admission 9–18.45; fest. 9–12.45; closed Monday.) The following description includes only some of the most important paintings and sculptures.

Ground Floor. In a room which incorporates the remains of the church of San Pier Scheraggio (founded c 1068) a series of ˙frescoes of illustrious Florentines by Andrea del Castagno are displayed. Nearby is a detached fresco of the ˙Annunciation by Botticelli. There is a LIFT for the picture galleries on the third floor (although it is now officially reserved for the use of the disabled and the gallery staff). The STAIRCASE, lined with antique busts and statues, leads up past the **Prints and Drawings Room**, with one of the finest collections in the world, particularly rich in Renaissance and Mannerist works (shown in ˙Exhibitions).

On the **Third Floor** the VESTIBULE (A) contains good antique sculpture. The long U-shaped gallery, once lined with tapestries by Bachiacca and the 16C Flemish school (now removed for conservation reasons) provides a fine setting for the superb collection of antique sculptures (mostly Hellenistic works). Room 1 (almost always closed) has fine antique reliefs. R. 2 contains three famous paintings of the ˙Maestà by **Cimabue, Duccio di Boninsegna** (both c 1285), and **Giotto** (painted some 25 years later). R. 3 displays works of the 14C Sienese school including, the Lorenzetti brothers, and an ˙Annunciation, one of Simone Martini's most famous works. R. 4. Florentine school of the 14C (Bernardo Daddi, Nardo di Cione, Giovanni da Milano, etc.). RR. 5 and 6. Works by Lorenzo Monaco and Gentile da Fabriano, including two charming representations of the ˙Adoration of the Magi.

R. 7 (Florentine School of the early 15C). Domenico Veneziano, ˙Madonna enthroned with saints; **Piero della Francesca**, ˙portraits of Federico di Montefeltro and Battista Sforza; **Paolo Uccello**, ˙Battle of San Romano. R. 8 contains some lovely ˙works by **Filippo Lippi** (Coronation of the Virgin, Madonna and Child with two angels, etc.). R. 9. Paintings by Piero and Antonio del Pollaiolo (Six Virtues, and Saints Vincent, James, and Eustace, from San Miniato) and Botticelli (Story of Holofernes). RR. 10–14 have been converted into one huge room to display the masterpieces of **Botticelli**, including the famous ˙PRIMAVERA and ˙BIRTH OF VENUS. The Primavera is an allegory of Spring, richly painted on poplar wood; the Birth of Venus illustrates a poem by Poliziano and is painted with a remarkable lightness of touch. Other works by Botticelli here include: ˙Adoration of the Magi, Calumny of Apelles, ˙Pallas and the Centaur, and ˙Madonna of the Magnificat. Also here, Hugo van der Goes, ˙Triptych commissioned by the Portinari family, Verrocchio, ˙Tobias and three archangels, and works by Domenico Ghirlandaio.

R. 15 displays the early Florentine works of **Leonardo da Vinci** (˙Annunciation, and the ˙Adoration of the Magi, an unfinished composition), together with paintings by his master Verrocchio (Baptism of Christ). Also works by Perugino, Luca Signorelli, Piero di Cosimo, and Lorenzo di Credi.

The beautiful octagonal ˙TRIBUNA (18) was designed by Buontalenti, and contains the most important ˙sculptures owned by the Medici (the famous

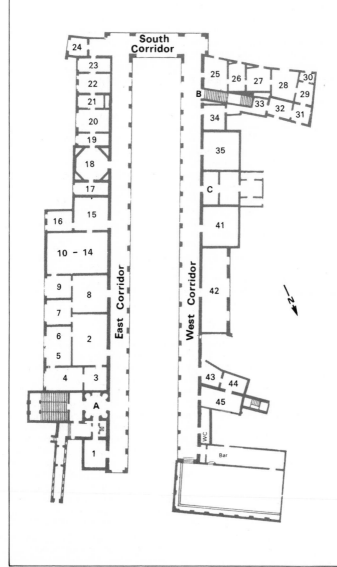

UFFIZI GALLERY

0 _____ 30 yards
0 _____ 30 metres

Medici Venus, a copy of the Praxitelean Aphrodite of Cnidos; the *Arrotino*; the Dancing Faun; and *Apollino*). Around the walls are a remarkable series of distinguished court *portraits, many of them of the family of Cosimo I commissioned from Bronzino.

Room 19. Signorelli, *tondi of the Madonna and Child and Holy Family. R. 20 is devoted to Dürer (Adoration of the Magi) and the German School, including Cranach (Adam and Eve). R. 21 (Venetian School): works by Giovanni Bellini, (*Sacred Allegory), Giorgione, Cima da Conegliano, etc. R. 22 contains German and Flemish works. *portraits by Holbein, and Joos van Cleve the Elder; and works by Albrecht Altdorfer, Gerard David (Adoration of the Magi), etc. R. 23: *triptych by Mantegna; and works by Bernardo Luini, Giovanni Antonio Boltraffio, etc.

The short SOUTH CORRIDOR (good view of the Arno) displays some more fine sculpture (Roman matron, Crouching Venus, etc.). R. 25 contains the famous *Tondo Doni of the Holy Family, the only finished oil painting by **Michelangelo**, and works by Mariotto Albertinelli. Rooms 26–33 are closed for restoration. In R. 26 are some famous works by **Raphael**: *Madonna del Cardellino, *Leo X with Cardinals Giulio de'Medici and Luigi de'Rossi, and a self-portrait; works by Andrea del Sarto. Fine portaits by Pontormo are displayed in R. 27, together with works by Bronzino, and Rosso Fiorentino. R. 28 is devoted to **Titian**: *Flora, *Venus of Urbino, *Knight of Malta, Venus and Cupid, etc. RR. 29–30 are devoted to the Emilian school. RR. 31 and 32 (Veneto School): Sebastiano del Piombo (*Death of Adonis). R. 33 (French School): François Clouet, equestrian portrait of Francis I. R. 34 (re-opened in 1994) Venetian School, including works by Paolo Veronese (*Annunciation, *Holy Family with St Barbara), and Giovanni Battista Moroni (*Count Pietro Secco Suardi).

The **Corridoio Vasariano** (B) is also closed after damage in 1993; it can usually be visited by previous appointment. It was built by Vasari in 1565 to connect Palazzo Vecchio via the Uffizi and Ponte Vecchio with Palazzo Pitti, in the form of a covered passageway. It affords unique views of the city, and is hung with notable paintings including a celebrated collection of *SELF-PORTRAITS (begun by Cardinal Leopoldo), by Vasari, Bronzino, Salvator Rosa, Rubens, Rembrandt, Van Dyck, Velazquez, Hogarth, Reynolds, David, Delacroix, Corot, Ingres, and many others.

R. 35 is temporarily used to display restored paintings; it usually contains fine works by Tintoretto (portraits, *Leda), Jacopo Bassano, and Federico Barocci (Noli me tangere, portraits). Rooms 41–45 are closed for repairs. R. 41. Rubens, huge canvases illustrating the history of Henri IV, Philip IV of Spain, *Isabella Brandt; Van Dyck, portraits, including an equestrian portrait of the Emperor Charles V; Sustermans, Galileo Galilei. The Niobe Room (R. 42) contains Roman statues of Niobe and her children and the neo-Attic Medici vase. R. 43: Works by Caravaggio (*Sacrifice of Isaac), Annibale Carracci (Bacchic scene), and Claude Lorrain (seascapes). R. 44 has three *portraits by Rembrandt (two of them self-portraits), and Dutch and Flemish works (Jan Steen, Jacob Ruysdael, etc.). R. 45 contains 18C works by Piazzetta, Giovanni Battista Tiepolo, Francesco Guardi, Canaletto, Alessandro Longhi; and portraits by Etiene Liotard, Francesco Xavier Fabre, Chardin, and Goya. On the landing by the STAIRS down to the exit is a sculptured boar (copy of a Hellenistic original).

D. Ponte Vecchio, Palazzo Pitti, and the Boboli Gardens

The fame of **Ponte Vecchio** (Pl. 11; open to pedestrians only), lined with quaint medieval-looking houses, saved it from damage in 1944. It was the only bridge over the Arno until 1218. The present bridge of three arches was reconstructed after a flood in 1345 probably by Taddeo Gaddi (also attributed to Neri di Fioravante). The jewellers' shops have pretty fronts with wood shutters and awnings; they overhang the river supported on brackets. The excellent jewellers here continue the traditional skill of Florentine goldsmiths whose work first became famous in the 15C. Above the shops on the left side can be seen the round windows of the Corridoio Vasariano. From the opening in the centre there is a view of Ponte Santa Trínita. In the Oltrarno, Via Guicciardini continues towards Piazza Pitti; on the left opens Piazza Santa Felicita with a granite column of 1381 marking the site of the first Christian cemetery in Florence. Here is **Santa Felicita** (Pl. 11), probably the oldest church in Florence after San Lorenzo. The paleo-Christian church, dedicated to the Roman martyr, St Felicity, was last rebuilt in 1736 by Ferdinando Ruggeri in a 15C style.

The fine INTERIOR is notable chiefly for the superb *works (1525–27) by Pontormo in the Cappella Capponi (an altarpiece of the Deposition, and frescoes of the Annunciation, and the Evangelists). The church also contains altarpieces by Antonio Ciseri and Simone Pignone. The high altarpiece is attributed to Francesco Brina. In the SACRISTY are works by Taddeo Gaddi, Niccolò di Pietro Gerini and Luca della Robbia.

*Palazzo Pitti** (Pl. 10) was built by the merchant Luca Pitti, an effective demonstration of his wealth and power to his rivals the Medici. The majestic golden-coloured palace is built in huge rough-hewn blocks of stone of different sizes. Its design is attributed to Brunelleschi although it was begun c 1457, after his death. Luca Fanelli is known to have been engaged on the building, but it is generally considered that another architect, whose name is unknown, was also involved. The palace remained incomplete on the death of Luca Pitti in 1472; by then it consisted of the central seven bays with three doorways. Bartolomeo Ammannati, and then Giulio and Alfonso Parigi the Younger completed the building, and the two 'rondò' were added in the 18C and 19C.

In 1549 the palace was bought by Eleonora di Toledo, wife of Cosimo I. It became the official seat of the Medici dynasty of grand-dukes after Cosimo I moved here from Palazzo Vecchio. The various ruling families of Florence continued to occupy the palace, or part of it, until 1919 when Victor Emmanuel III presented it to the State.

The splendid *COURTYARD by Ammannati serves as a garden façade to the palace. It is a masterpiece of Florentine Mannerist architecture, with bold rustication in three orders. Under the portico to the right is the entrance to the celebrated **Galleria di Palazzo Pitti** or **Galleria Palatina**, formed in the 17C by the Medici grand-dukes, and installed here in the 18C. The reception rooms on the piano nobile were decorated in the 17C by Pietro da Cortona for the Medici grand-dukes. They contain the masterpieces of the collection, including numerous famous works by Raphael and Titian. The arrangement of the pictures (most of them richly framed) still preserves to some extent the character of a private royal collection of the 17–18C, the aesthetic arrangement of the rooms being considered rather than the chronological placing of the paintings. This produces a remarkable effect of magnificence even though in some cases the pictures (all of which are well labelled) are difficult to see on the crowded walls.

Tickets for the **Galleria Palatina** (which include admission to the **Appartamenti Reali**) are purchased off the courtyard, left of the stairs up to the gallery. For the **Galleria d'Arte Moderna** tickets are purchased at the entrance on the second floor. The **Museo degli Argenti** is entered off the left side of the courtyard, and tickets (valid also for the **Galleria del Costume**) are purchased near the entrance to the Museo degli Argenti.

Admission 9–14; fest. 9–13; closed Monday. The rooms are unnumbered: the numbers given in the description below refer to the plan of Palazzo Pitti.

The grand staircase by Ammannati ascends to the entrance to the Galleria Palatina. Beyond three reception rooms (A, B, and C) is (left) the SALA DI VENERE (1), with the earliest ceiling (1641–42) of the fine group executed for the following four rooms by Pietro da Cortona for Ferdinand II. The paintings here include: **Titian**, *Concert (a famous work, also attributed to Giorgione); *Pietro Aretino, a splendid portrait; and *Portrait of a lady ('la bella'); **Rubens**, Ulysses in the Phaecian Isle, and *Return from the hayfields; seascapes by Salvator Rosa. The *'Venus Italica' was sculpted by Canova, and presented by Napoleon in exchange for the Medici Venus which he had carried off to Paris. SALA DI APOLLO (2): portraits by Van Dyck, Rubens, and Sustermans; Guido Reni, Cleopatra; Andrea del Sarto, *Holy Family, and *Deposition; Rosso Fiorentino, Madonna enthroned; **Titian**, *portrait of a gentleman, once thought to be the Duke of Norfolk, and *Mary Magdalen. SALA DI MARTE (3): portraits by Tintoretto (Luigi Cornaro), Van Dyck (Cardinal Bentivoglio), Paolo Veronese, and Titian (*Cardinal Ippolito de'Medici); **Rubens**, *Consequences of War, a huge allegorical painting, and *'The Four Philosophers' (Rubens, his brother Filippo, Justus Lipsius, and Jan van Wouwer). THE SALA DI GIOVE (4): Venetian School, *'Three Ages of Man' (attributed to Giorgione); **Raphael**, *Portrait of a lady ('la Velata'), one of his most beautiful paintings; works by Andrea del Sarto (including *Young St John the Baptist) and Fra Bartolomeo (*Deposition).

SALA DI SATURNO (5): **Raphael**, *Madonna 'della Seggiola', a beautifully composed tondo, among the artist's most mature and most popular paintings; *Maddalena Doni, and her husband; Vision of Ezekiel; Madonna 'del Baldacchino'; Cardinal Tommaso Inghirami; *Madonna 'del Granduca', an early work showing the influence of Leonardo; Perugino, *Deposition; and works by Ridolfo del Ghirlandaio, Annibale Carracci, etc. SALA DELL'ILIADE (6): Portraits by Sustermans, Francesco Pourbus the Younger, Ridolfo del Ghirlandaio, and Joos van Cleve; Andrea del Sarto, two large paintings of the *Assumption; **Titian**, *Philip II of Spain, *Diego de Mendoza; **Raphael**, *Portrait of a woman expecting a child.

The other rooms of the Galleria Palatina house the smaller works in the collection. The SALA DELL'EDUCAZIONE DI GIOVE (8): Judith with the head of Holofernes by Cristofano Allori, and the Sleeping Cupid, a late work by Caravaggio; also typical pious works by Carlo Dolci. The *SALA DELLA STUFA (left; 7) is beautifully frescoed by Pietro da Cortona (the four Ages of the World) and Matteo Rosselli. Beyond the delightful 'Empire' BATHROOM (9) is the SALA DI ULISSE (10) which contains fine portraits by Moroni and Tintoretto. Also, Filippino Lippi, *Death of Lucrezia; and Raphael, *Madonna dell'Impannata. The SALA DI PROMETEO (11): Baldassarre Peruzzi, Dance of Apollo with the Muses; Filippo Lippi, *Tondo of the Madonna and Child, one of his best works; Guido Reni, Young Bacchus; Botticelli (attributed), Portrait of a lady in profile; and works by Pontormo,

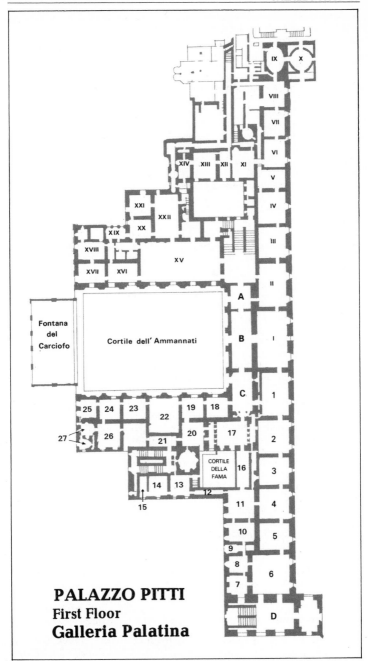

IX X

VIII

VII

VI

V

IV

III

XIV XIII XII XI

XXI

XXII

XX

XIX

XVIII

XVII XVI

XV

II

A

Fontana
del
Carciofo

Cortile dell' Ammannati

B

I

C

1

25 24 23

22

19 18

27 26

21

20

17

2

3

CORTILE
DELLA
FAMA

16

14 13

12

15

11

4

10

5

9

8

6

7

D

PALAZZO PITTI
First Floor
Galleria Palatina

Francesco Botticini, Luca Signorelli, Marco Palmezzano, etc. Beyond a CORRIDOR (12) with small Flemish paintings is the SALA DELLA GIUSTIZIA (13) with fine portraits by Titian (*Portrait of a man, once thought to be Vincenzo Mosti) and Tintoretto. R. 14 contains the Story of Joseph by Andrea del Sarto; and R. 15 the Three Graces by Rubens.

From the Sala di Prometeo (see above) is the entrance to the GALLERIA DEL POCCETTI (16) with portraits by Rubens, Pontormo, Peter Lely, and Niccolò Cassana. Beyond the SALA DI MUSICA (17) built in 1811–21, is the entrance (left) to another series of rooms (18–27). The SALA DELLE ALLE-GORIE (18) contains works by Volterrano and Giovanni da San Giovanni. Rooms 19–27 include works by Cigoli, Carlo Dolci, Empoli, Lorenzo Lippi, Cristoforo Allori, Jacopo Ligozzi, Jacopo Vignali, Giovanna Garzoni, Francesco Furini, Giovanni Bilivert, Francesco Curradi, Salvator Rosa, etc.

The other half of the piano nobile along the façade of the palace is occupied by the *Appartamenti Reali** (I–XV; usually open at the same time as the Galleria Palatina). These lavishly decorated rooms were used as state apartments from the 17C onwards by the Medici and Lorraine grand-dukes and later by the royal house of Savoy. They were beautifully restored in 1993 to their appearance in 1880–1911. The contents, which reflect the eclectic 'Victorian' taste of the Savoy rulers, as well as the neo-Baroque period of the 19C Lorraine grand-dukes, include splendid silk curtains, drapes, wall hangings and furnishings made in Florence and France; sumptuous gilded chandeliers, neo-classical mirrors and frames; early 19C carpets from Tournai, huge oriental vases; furniture decorated with pietre dure; and portraits of the Medici by Sustermans.

On the floor above the Galleria Palatina is the **Galleria d'Arte Moderna** (adm. see above). The collection is particularly representative of Tuscan art of the 19C, notably the *Macchiaioli* school (Giovanni Fattori, Silvestro Lega, Telemaco Signorini, etc.). Many of the rooms on this floor were decorated in the 19C by the last Grand-dukes Ferdinand III and Leopold II. In every room there is a detailed catalogue of the works displayed which cover the period from the mid-18C up to the end of the First World War. They are arranged chronologically and by schools. The collection of 20C works is particularly representative of the years between the two Wars.

The *Museo degli Argenti** (adm. see above), arranged in the summer apartments of the grand-dukes, is entered from the left side of the court-yard. The main room contains exuberant and colourful frescoes by Giovanni da San Giovanni. In the Sala Buia is displayed the magnificent *collection of vases in pietre dure which belonged to Lorenzo il Magnifico, most of which date from the late Imperial Roman era. The reception rooms are decorated with trompe l'oeil frescoes by Angelo Michele Colonna and Agostino Mitelli. The rooms towards the gardens were the living quarters of the grand-dukes. Here, and on the mezzanine floor, are displayed their eclectic collection of personal keepsakes, gifts presented by other ruling families, objets d'art made specially for them, and the *jewellery collection of the electress Anna Maria.

In the Palazzina della Meridiana, which was begun in 1776 by Gaspare Maria Paoletti, is the **Galleria del Costume** (adm. see above) which illus-trates the history of costume from the 18C to the early 20C. On the upper floor the COLLEZIONE CONTINI-BONACOSSI is awaiting removal to the Galleria degli Uffizi.

On the hillside behind Palazzo Pitti lie the magnificent *Boboli Gardens** (Pl.10, 14; open 9–sunset; except first and last Mon of the month), laid out for Cosimo I by Tribolo and extended in the early 17C. They are entered from the courtyard of Palazzo Pitti (ticket office in the atrium) or from the Annalena Gate in Via Romana. The biggest park in the centre of Florence, it is laid out on two main axes; the lower gardens, with 17C arboured walks on either side of a splendid long cypress avenue (the *Viottolone*) and the *Isolotto* with its fruit trees in pots, are the most attractive. The vegetation is predominantly evergreen with tall double hedges and ilex woods. About 170 statues decorate the walks, many of them restored Roman works and others dating from the 16C and 17C (some are removed for restoration or replaced by copies). The amphitheatre was designed by Ammannati in imitation of a Roman circus. At the top of the garden in the secluded Giardino del Cavaliere (charming views) is the Museo della Porcellana (closed) with 18C–19C porcelain. There is another exit to the gardens at the Porta Romana gate. Near the Piazza Pitti exit is the 16C *Grotta Grande (closed for restoration).

E.   The Galleria dell'Accademia, Santissima Annunziata, Museo di San Marco, Palazzo Medici-Riccardi, and San Lorenzo

At No. 60 Via Ricasoli is the entrance to the ***Galleria dell'Accademia** (Pl. 7; adm. 9–14; in summer 9–19; fest. 9–14; closed Monday), visited above all for its famous works by Michelangelo, but also containing an important collection of Florentine paintings. The collection was formed in 1784 with a group of paintings given, for study purposes, to the Academy by Pietro Leopoldo I. Since 1873 some important sculptures by Michelangelo have been housed here, including the David.

In the first room of the PINACOTECA: works by Fra Bartolomeo (*Madonna enthroned with Saints), Francesco Granacci, Mariotto Albertinelli, Filippino Lippi and Perugino (Descent from the Cross), etc. The GALLERIA contains **SCULPTURES BY MICHELANGELO. The four Slaves or Prisoners (c 1521–23) were begun for the ill-fated tomb of Julius II. The St Matthew (1504–08), one of the twelve apostles commissioned from the sculptor by the Opera del Duomo, was the only one he ever began. These are all magnificent examples of Michelangelo's unfinished works, some of them barely blocked out, the famous *non-finito*, much discussed by scholars. The Pietà from Santa Rosalia in Palestrina is an undocumented work, and is not now usually considered to be by Michelangelo's own hand.

To the right are three more rooms of the Pinacoteca: Lo Scheggia, *frontal of a *cassone* or marriage-chest of the Adimari family showing a wedding scene in front of the Baptistery; works by Mariotto di Cristofano, Botticelli (two *Madonnas), Alesso Baldovinetti (*Trinity and Saints), Lorenzo di Credi (Adoration of the Child), Raffaellino del Garbo, Cosimo Rosselli, etc.

The TRIBUNE was specially built in 1882 to exhibit the *DAVID by Michelangelo (1501–04) when it was removed from Piazza della Signoria. It is perhaps the most famous single work of art of western civilisation, and has become all too familiar through endless reproductions, although it is not the work by which Michelangelo is best judged. It was commissioned by the city of Florence to stand outside Palazzo Vecchio where its huge scale fits its setting. The figure of David, uncharacteristic of Michelangelo's works, stands in a classical pose suited to the shallow block of marble, 4.10m high. The hero, a young colossus, is shown in the moment before his victory over Goliath. A celebration of the nude, the statue established Michelangelo as the foremost sculptor of his time at the age of 29.

To the left are three more rooms containing early Tuscan works of the 13–14C, (including a Pietà by Giovanni da Milano). In the huge room at the end (not always open), 19C works by Academicians, including plaster models by Lorenzo Bartolini. On the first floor (not always open), Florentine paintings of the 14C and 15C.

At the crossing of Via Ricasoli with Via degli Alfani is the *Conservatorio Luigi Cherubini*. At No. 78 Via Alfani is the OPIFICIO DELLE PIETRE DURE, founded in 1588 by the grand-duke Ferdinando I. The craft of working hard or semi-precious stones (*pietre dure*) was perfected in Florence. Beautiful mosaics were made to decorate cabinets, table-tops, etc. some of which are exhibited in a small Museum here (closed for restoration). Nearby is the *Rotonda di Santa Maria degli Angeli* (now used by the university; no adm.), one of the first centralised buildings of the Renaissance begun by Brunelleschi in 1434 and left unfinished. Via dei Servi is lined with a number of handsome 16C palaces, including Palazzo dei Pucci attributed to Ammannati. The church of *San Michele Visdomini* (or San Michelino) contains a *Holy Family by Pontormo. The *Tabernacolo delle Cinque Lampade* encloses a fresco by Cosimo Rosselli.

*Piazza Santissima Annunziata** (Pl. 7), designed by Brunelleschi, is surrounded on three sides by porticoes. It is the most beautiful square in Florence. The equestrian statue of the grand-duke Ferdinando I is by Giambologna, and the two fountains by Tacca. The *Spedale degli Innocenti**, opened in 1445 as a foundling hospital, the first institution of its kind in Europe, is still operating as an orphanage and as an institute dedicated to the education and care of children. Brunelleschi began work on the building in 1419, and the *COLONNADE of nine arches is one of the first masterpieces of the Renaissance. It takes inspiration from classical antiquity as well as from local Romanesque buildings. In the spandrels are delightful *medallions, perhaps the best known work of Andrea Della Robbia (1487), each with a baby in swaddling-clothes against a blue background.

The CONVENT may be visited to see the **Museo dello Spedale degli Innocenti** (adm. 8.30–14; fest. 8.30–13; closed Wednesday). Among Brunelleschi's works are the Chiostro degli Uomini (with a lunette by Andrea Della Robbia), and the oblong *Chiostro delle Donne, with 24 slender Ionic columns beneath a low loggia. Stairs lead up to the Loggia, with detached frescoes. In the Long Gallery are Florentine paintings, including the splendid *Adoration of the Magi by Domenico Ghirlandaio. The *Madonna and Child is one of the most beautiful works by Luca Della Robbia.

The church of the *Santissima Annunziata** (Pl. 7), was founded by the seven original Florentine members of the Servite Order in 1250 and rebuilt, along with the cloister, by Michelozzo and others in 1444–81. The series of frescoes on the walls of the CHIOSTRINO DEI VOTI is particularly interesting since most of them were painted in the second decade of the 16C by the leading painters of the time: (right to left): Rosso Fiorentino, Assumption; Pontormo, Visitation; Franciabigio, Marriage of the Virgin; Andrea del Sarto, *Birth of the Virgin, Coming of the Magi. The frescoes by Alesso Baldovinetti (*Nativity) and Cosimo Rosselli (Vocation and Investiture of

San Filippo Benizzi) are earlier works. The last five frescoes (damaged) are works by Andrea del Sarto.

In the heavily decorated and dark INTERIOR is a highly venerated shrine of the Madonna. The huge *tabernacle was designed by Michelozzo and executed by Pagno di Lapo Portigiani. On the SOUTH SIDE, monument to Orlando de'Medici, by Bernardo Rossellino, and a Pietà by Bandinelli who is buried here. The fine organ is by Domenico di Lorenzo di Lucca (1521). The unusual circular TRIBUNE was begun by Michelozzo and completed in 1477 by Leon Battista Alberti. In the cupola is a fresco by Volterrano. The high altar dates from the 17C. Near the *tomb of Bishop Angelo Marzi Medici, signed by Francesco da Sangallo (1546), is the burial place of Andrea del Sarto. In the semicircular chapels which radiate from the SANCTUARY are paintings by Alessandro and Cristofano Allori, Bronzino (Resurrection), and a statue of St Roch by Veit Stoss. The E chapel is the burial place of Giambologna; it contains reliefs and a Crucifix by him, and statues by his pupils including Francavilla. The Madonna is attributed to Bernardo Daddi. The SACRISTY, with a fine vault, was built by Pagno di Lapo from Michelozzo's design. On the NORTH SIDE, statue of the Baptist by Michelozzo; an Assumption by Perugino; and a Crucifixion by Giovanni Stradano. The Last Judgement by Alessandro Allori is derived from Michelangelo's fresco. The last two chapels contain a *Holy Trinity with St Jerome, and *St Julian and the Saviour, two frescoes by Andrea del Castagno.

In the CHIOSTRO DEI MORTI, over a side door into the church, is the *Madonna del Sacco, one of Andrea del Sarto's best works. The other lunettes contain 17C frescoes by Andrea Mascagni, Bernardino Poccetti, Matteo Rosselli, and Ventura Salimbeni. The CAPPELLA DI SAN LUCA has belonged to the Accademia delle Arti del Disegno since 1565. It contains works by Vasari, Pontormo, Alessandro Allori, Luca Giordano, and Montorsoli.

At No. 4 Via Gino Capponi is the *Cloister of the ex-Compagnia della Santissima Annunziata* (or '*di San Pierino*') with a lunette by Santi Buglioni over the portal, and a delightful little cloister with frescoes (c 1585–90) by Bernardino Poccetti and others.

At No. 38 Via della Colonna is the *Museo Archeologico (Pl. 7; adm. 9–14; closed Monday), with one of the most important collections of Etruscan antiquities in existence (it has been undergoing rearrangement for years, and parts of the museum are often closed). On the GROUND FLOOR is displayed the famous *Chimera, an Etruscan ex-voto (late 5C or early 4C BC) and a silver *amphora (380–390 AD). On the FIRST FLOOR is the EGYPTIAN MUSEUM (being rearranged), with statues, bas-reliefs, sarcophagi, etc., and a Hittite Chariot in wood and bone from a Theban tomb of the 14C BC. The Etruscan, Greek, and Roman sections of the museum (also partially closed) contain urns and bronzes including Minerva (restored), the *Arringatore (late Republican), the *Idolino (probably a Roman copy of a Greek original), and a *horse's head (2C–1C BC). A collection of precious *gems is to be opened. On the ground floor of a new pavilion the first section of the Etruscan Topographical Museum has been reopened with the 'Mater Matuta', a canopic vase of c 440 and the tomb of Larthia Seianti. On the second floor are eleven rooms of *Attic vases including the famous *François Vase made in Athens c 570 BC.

PIAZZA SAN MARCO (Pl. 3) is one of the liveliest squares in the city. Here, beneath the Loggia dell'Ospedale di San Matteo, is the seat of the ACCADEMIA DI BELLE ARTI, an art school opened in 1784. Across Via Cesare

Battisti are the administrative offices of the University of Florence, and on Via La Pira is the *Giardino dei Semplici*, a botanical garden laid out in 1545–46 by Tribolo for Cosimo I. The N side of the square is occupied by the Dominican church and convent of San Marco, which contains the *Museo di San Marco (or 'dell'Angelico'; Pl. 3), famous for its works by the 'Blessed' Fra Angelico who was a friar here. Adm. 9–14; closed Monday.

Cosimo il Vecchio founded a public library here, the first of its kind in Europe. Antonino Pierozzo (1389–1459) and Girolamo Savonarola (1452–98) were famous priors of the convent. The beautiful CLOISTER OF ST ANTONINO was built by Michelozzo. The lunettes with scenes from the life of St Antonino are by Bernardino Poccetti. In the corners are frescoes by Fra Angelico. The PILGRIMS' HOSPICE, also by Michelozzo, contains a superb *collection of paintings by Fra Angelico, many of them from Florentine churches (all well labelled), including the *tabernacle of the Linaioli, with a marble frame designed by Ghiberti. The GREAT REFECTORY displays 16C and 17C works (Fra Bartolomeo, Giovanni Antonio Sogliani, etc.). The CHAPTER HOUSE contains a large *Crucifixion and Saints by Fra Angelico and assistants, and the SMALL REFECTORY a charming Last Supper by Domenico Ghirlandaio and his workshop.

FIRST FLOOR. The *DORMITORY consists of 44 small monastic cells beneath a huge wood roof, each with their own vault and adorned with a fresco by Fra Angelico or an assistant. The *Annunciation, at the head of the stairs, is justly one of the most famous works of the master. Among the most beautiful frescoes are those in Cells 1, 3, 6, and 9, and the Madonna enthroned in the corridor. Savonarola's cell contains two portraits by Fra Bartolomeo. The *LIBRARY, a light and delicate hall, is one of the most pleasing of all Michelozzo's works; it contains illuminated choirbooks and psalters.

The church of SAN MARCO (Pl. 3) contains a *Madonna and saints by Fra Bartolomeo; an 8C mosaic of the *Madonna in prayer; and the tomb slabs of Pico della Mirandola (1463–94) and his friend Poliziano (Angelo Ambrogini, 1454–94).

In Via Cavour (Pl. 7,3) is the Casino Mediceo, built by Buontalenti and now occupied by the law courts. This was the site of the Medici Garden where Cosimo il Vecchio and Lorenzo il Magnifico collected antique sculpture, and where Bertoldo held a school of art. At No. 69 is the **Chiostro dello Scalzo** (Pl. 3; open Mon & Thurs 9–13), with fine *frescoes in monochrome by Andrea del Sarto and Franciabigio.

A short way W of Piazza San Marco is the former convent of **Sant'Apollonia** (Pl. 3; open 9–14; closed Monday) which contains a *Last Supper, the masterpiece of Andrea del Castagno, and other works by him.

Via Cavour leads S from Piazza San Marco to *Palazzo Medici-Riccardi (Pl. 7), now the seat of the Prefect. This town mansion was built for Cosimo il Vecchio by Michelozzo after 1444, and was the residence of the Medici until 1540 when Cosimo I moved into Palazzo Vecchio. Its rusticated façade served as a model for other famous Florentine palaces. The COURTYARD is decorated with medallions ascribed to Bertoldo. A staircase leads up to the dark little *CHAPEL (open 9–13, 15–18; fest. 9–13; closed Wed) the only unaltered part of Michelozzo's work, with a beautiful ceiling and marble inlaid floor. The walls are entirely covered with decorative *frescoes, the masterpiece of Benozzo Gozzoli of the Procession of the Magi to Bethlehem, which includes portraits of the Medici (shown with their emblem of the three ostrich feathers). The decorative cavalcade is shown in a charming landscape with hunting scenes. The GALLERY (lift) has a vault fresco by Luca Giordano (1683), and a Madonna and Child by Filippo Lippi.

The back of Palazzo Medici-Riccardi stands on Via de' Ginori, with a number of fine palaces and the *Biblioteca Riccardiana* (1718). Here is PIAZZA SAN LORENZO (Pl. 7), filled with a busy street market (leather-goods, straw, clothing, etc.). The church of *San Lorenzo (Pl. 7) was intimately connected with the Medici after they commissioned Brunelleschi to rebuild it in 1425–46. It is the burial place of all the principal members of the family from Cosimo il Vecchio to Cosimo III. Thought to be the earliest church in Florence, a basilica on this site was consecrated by St Ambrose of Milan in 393. The grandiose façade designed by Michelangelo was never built; the exterior remains in rough-hewn brick.

The grey cruciform INTERIOR, built with pietra serena, with pulvins above the Corinthian columns in pietra forte, is one of the earliest and most harmonious architectural works of the Renaissance. It was completed on Brunelleschi's design by Antonio Manetti (1447–60) and Pagno di Lapo Portigiani (1463). In the SOUTH AISLE, *Marriage of the Virgin by Rosso Fiorentino, and *tabernacle by Desiderio da Settignano. The two bronze *pulpits in the nave are the last works of Donatello, finished by his pupils Bertoldo and Bartolomeo Bellano. Beneath the dome a simple inscription with the Medici arms marks the grave of Cosimo il Vecchio *Pater Patriae*. Off the N transept is the *OLD SACRISTY (1420–29; open Mon, Wed, Fri & Sat 10–12; Tues & Thurs 16–18) by Brunelleschi, one of the earliest and purest monuments of the Renaissance, with a charming vault. The decorative details are by Donatello (the *tondi in the pendentives and lunettes, the reliefs above the doors, and the doors themselves). In the centre is the sarcophagus of Giovanni di Bicci de'Medici and Piccarda Bueri, by Buggiano. Set into the wall is the magnificent porphyry and bronze sarcophagus of Giovanni and Piero de'Medici by Verrocchio. In a chapel in the N transept is an *Annunciation by Filippo Lippi, and a 19C monument marking the burial place of Donatello.

From the 15C CLOISTER a staircase ascends to the *Biblioteca Laurenziana (Pl. 7; adm. 9–13 except Sunday), begun by Michelangelo c 1524 to house the collection of MSS made by Cosimo il Vecchio and Lorenzo il Magnifico. The heavily decorated VESTIBULE, filled with an elaborate staircase was constructed by Vasari and Ammannati on Michelangelo's design. The peaceful READING ROOM provides an unexpected contrast. The collection is famous above all for its Greek and Latin MSS. *Exhibitions are held every year.

The entrance to the **Cappelle Medicee** (or Medici Chapels; Pl. 7; adm. 9–14; fest. 9–13; closed Monday) is from outside San Lorenzo, in Piazza Madonna degli Aldobrandini. From the crypt a staircase leads up to the *CAPPELLA DEI PRINCIPI, the opulent, if gloomy, mausoleum of the Medici grand-dukes begun by Matteo Nigetti (1604). Its minor details were completed only in the 20th century. It is a tour de force of craftsmanship in pietre dure. A passage to the left leads to the so-called *SAGRESTIA NUOVA (or New Sacristy), begun by Michelangelo and left unfinished when he departed from Florence in 1534. It is built in dark pietra serena and white marble in a severe and idiosyncratic style. Here are the famous **MEDICI TOMBS of Lorenzo, Duke of Urbino, and Giuliano, Duke of Nemours with statues of the dukes, and allegorical figures of Dawn and Dusk, Night and Day, all superb works by Michelangelo. On the entrance wall is the Madonna and Child, also by Michelangelo, intended for the monument to Lorenzo il Magnifico and his brother Giuliano.

On the walls behind the altar architectural graffiti have been uncovered, attributed to Michelangelo and his pupils including Tribolo. Nearby is a little room (adm. by appointment at the ticket office, 9.30–12) where charcoal *drawings of great interest were discovered on the walls in 1975, attributed by most scholars to Michelangelo himself.

The animated Via dell'Ariento behind San Lorenzo with numerous market stalls leads past the huge MERCATO CENTRALE (in a cast-iron market building by Giuseppe Mengoni, 1874), the biggest food market in Florence, to the busy Via Nazionale. In Via Faenza, just to the left, is the so-called **Cenacolo di Fuligno** (Pl. 2; adm. 9–12 when custodian available) with a fresco of the *Last Supper by Perugino.

F. Santa Maria Novella, Ognissanti, and Santa Trínita

*Santa Maria Novella** (Pl. 6) is the most important Gothic church in Tuscany. The Dominicans were given the property in 1221 and building was begun in 1246 at the E end. The Dominican friars Sisto and Ristoro are thought to have been the architects of the impressive nave, begun in 1279. The church was completed under the direction of Fra Jacopo Talenti in the mid–14C. The lower part of the beautiful marble *FAÇADE, in a typical Tuscan Romanesque style, is attributed to Fra Jacopo Talenti. In 1456–70 Leon Battista Alberti was commissioned by Giovanni di Paolo Rucellai to complete the upper part of the façade. Its classical lines are in perfect harmony with the earlier work. To the right of the façade are the Gothic *avelli* or family-vaults of Florentine nobles, which extend around the old cemetery. The CAMPANILE, also attributed to Fra Jacopo Talenti, was grafted onto an ancient watch tower.

INTERIOR (closed 11.30–15.30). The spacious nave has remarkably bold stone vaulting, its arches given prominence by bands of dark grey pietra serena. The stained glass in the rose window at the W end is thought to have been designed by Andrea di Bonaiuto (c 1365), and over the W door is a good fresco of the Nativity, thought to be an early work by Botticelli. In the SOUTH AISLE are 16C altarpieces by Girolamo Macchietti, Giovanni Battista Naldini, Jacopo del Meglio, and Jacopo Ligozzi. In the SOUTH TRANSEPT are Gothic tombs including that of Joseph, Patriarch of Constantinople (died in Florence in 1440), with a contemporary fresco of him. Steps lead up to the CAPPELLA RUCELLAI (light on left) which contains a marble *statuette of the Madonna and Child signed by Nino Pisano, and the bronze tomb slab of Francesco Leonardo Dati, by Ghiberti. The walls have traces of 14C frescoes. The CAPPELLA DEI BARDI has damaged frescoes in the lunettes attributed to Cimabue, and an altarpiece by Vasari. The CAPPELLA DI FILIPPO STROZZI has exuberant *frescoes by Filippino Lippi with stories from the life of St Philip the Apostle and St John the Evangelist. Behind the altar, *tomb of Filippo Strozzi, exquisitely carved by Benedetto da Maiano. Boccaccio in the 'Decameron' takes this chapel as the meeting-place of a group of young people during the Plague year of 1348.

On the MAIN ALTAR is a bronze Crucifix by Giambologna. In the SANCTUARY (light behind the altar) are delightful *frescoes commissioned by Giovanni Tornabuoni. They are the masterpiece of Domenico Ghirlandaio;

he was assisted by his brother Davide, his brother-in-law, Sebastiano Mainardi, and his pupils (including perhaps the young Michelangelo). In the scenes from the life of St John the Baptist, and of the Virgin, many of the figures are portraits of the artist's contemporaries, and the whole cycle mirrors Florentine life of the late 15C. On the end wall are the two kneeling figures of the donors, Giovanni Tornabuoni and his wife Francesca Pitti. NORTH TRANSEPT. The CAPPELLA GONDI with marble decoration by Giuliano da Sangallo contains the famous wood *Crucifix by Brunelleschi traditionally thought to have been carved to show Donatello how the Redeemer should be represented. The CAPPELLA GADDI has paintings by Alessandro Allori and Bronzino. At the end of the transept the *CAPPELLA STROZZI is a remarkably well-preserved example of a Tuscan chapel of the mid-14C. The *frescoes of the Last Judgement, Paradise, and Inferno are the most famous work of Nardo di Cione (c 1357). The fine *altarpiece is by his brother, Orcagna. The SACRISTY has a fine cross-vault by Fra Jacopo Talenti and stained glass windows dating from 1386. The lavabo is by Giovanni Della Robbia, and the *Crucifix (removed for restoration) is an early work by Giotto. The paintings are by Jacopo Ligozzi, Giovanni Stradano, Pietro Dandini, and Vasari. The altarpieces in the NORTH AISLE are by Alessandro Allori, Vasari, and Santi di Tito. Also here is the famous *fresco of the Trinity with the Virgin and St John the Evangelist and donors, a remarkable work by Masaccio. The pulpit was designed by Brunelleschi.

To the left of the church is the entrance to the ***Museo di Santa Maria Novella** (8–14; fest. 9–13; closed Friday). The Romanesque *CHIOSTRO VERDE has damaged *frescoes by Paolo Uccello (c 1446) painted in terraverde and illustrating stories from Genesis: (in the East walk) the Creation of Adam, and of the Animals, and the Creation and the Temptation of Eve, and the Flood and the *Recession of the Flood (with Noah's ark), and the Sacrifice and Drunkenness of Noah. The other frescoes in the cloisters also date from the first half of the 15C.

Off the cloister opens the *CAPPELLONE DEGLI SPAGNUOLI, or *Spanish Chapel*. It received its name in the 16C when it was assigned by Duchess Eleonora di Toledo to the Spanish members of her suite. It was originally the chapter house built by Jacopo Talenti in the mid-14C with a splendid cross-vault. It is entirely covered with colourful *frescoes by Andrea di Bonaiuto (Andrea da Firenze) dating from c 1365. They represent the Mission, Works, and Triumph of the Dominican Order (including the artist's vision of the completed Duomo), and the Triumph of Catholic doctrine personified in St Thomas Aquinas. In the CHIOSTRINO DEI MORTI are frescoes dating from the mid-14C. In the large REFECTORY with fine cross-vaulting a fresco by Alessandro Allori surrounds a good fresco attributed to a follower of Agnolo Gaddi. Here, and in the adjoining chapel, are displayed church silver, charming reliquary busts by the Sienese school, vestments, etc.

PIAZZA SANTA MARIA NOVELLA, with its irregular shape, was created by the Dominicans at the end of the 13C. The two obelisks were set up in 1608 (resting on bronze tortoises by Giambologna) as turning posts in the course of the annual Palio dei Cocchi. Beneath the 15C *Loggia di San Paolo* is a beautiful *lunette showing the Meeting of Saints Francis and Dominic by Andrea Della Robbia. In the house on the corner of Via della Scala Henry James wrote 'Roderick Hudson' in 1872. At No. 16 Via della Scala is the *Farmacia di Santa Maria Novella* (open 9–13, 15.30–19.30 except Saturday afternoon and Monday morning) of ancient foundation, decorated in neo-Gothic style in 1848. The charming old chemist's shop has 17C vases.

The church of **Ognissanti** (Pl. 6), reached by Via de'Fossi and Borgo Ognissanti, was founded in 1256 by the Umiliati, a Benedictine Order skilled in manufacturing wool. The church was rebuilt in the 17C; the façade incorporates a terracotta attributed to Benedetto Buglioni.

INTERIOR. On the S side are two frescoes by Domenico and Davide Ghirlandaio; the Madonna della Misericordia protects the Vespucci whose family tombstone (1471) is in the pavement. Between the third and fourth altars, on the N and S side are *St Jerome by Domenico Ghirlandaio, and *St Augustine's vision of St Jerome, by Botticelli, both painted c 1481. Elsewhere in the church are altarpieces by Santi di Tito, Matteo Rosselli, Maso di San Friano, and Jacopo Ligozzi. Botticelli (Filipepi) is buried in the S transept. The sacristy has late-13C wall paintings, and works by Taddeo and Agnolo Gaddi. From the CLOISTER with 17C frescoes by Jacopo Ligozzi, Giovanni da San Giovanni, and others, is the entrance (open Monday, Tuesday, and Saturday 9–12) to the REFECTORY with a *Last Supper by Domenico Ghirlandaio. In the piazza is Palazzo Lenzi (now the French Consulate and French Institute) built c 1470, with restored graffiti.

Ponte Santa Trínita (described in Rte 1;I) crosses the Arno at the beginning of **Via Tornabuoni** (Pl. 7), the most elegant street in Florence with fashionable shops. Here is *Palazzo Spini-Feroni* (1269; restored), one of the best preserved and largest private medieval palaces in the city. Opposite is the church of ***Santa Trínita** (Pl. 10), dating in its present Gothic form from the end of the 14C. The façade was added by Buontalenti in 1593.

In the fine INTERIOR the interior façade of the Romanesque building survives. SOUTH AISLE: third chapel, altarpiece by Neri di Bicci, and detached fresco and sinopia by Spinello Aretino; the fourth chapel is entirely frescoed by Lorenzo Monaco, who also painted the beautiful *altarpiece of the Annunciation (removed for restoration); fifth chapel, part of a monument to St John Gualberto by Benedetto da Rovezzano. Outside the choir chapels are remains of frescoes by Giovanni del Ponte. The *SASSETTI CHAPEL contains frescoes of the life of St Francis by Domenico Ghirlandaio. They include views of Florence and portraits of the Medici and personages of the Renaissance city. The *altarpiece of the Adoration of the Shepherds, also by Ghirlandaio, is flanked by the donors, Francesco Sassetti and his wife Nera Corsi. Their tombs are attributed to Giuliano da Sangallo. In the SANCTUARY is a triptych by Mariotto di Nardo and remains of vault frescoes by Alesso Baldovinetti. In the second chapel left of the altar, *tomb of Benozzo Federighi by Luca Della Robbia (1454–57). NORTH AISLE: fifth chapel, Mary Magdalen, a wood statue by Desiderio da Settignano (finished by Benedetto da Maiano); fourth chapel, frescoes by Neri di Bicci and Bicci di Lorenzo; second chapel, paintings by Ridolfo del Ghirlandaio.

In Piazza Santa Trínita, with the Column of Justice, a granite monolith from the Baths of Caracalla in Rome, are Palazzo Buondelmonti, with a façade attributed to Baccio d'Agnolo, and, perhaps, his best work, Palazzo Bartolini Salimbeni. Beyond several more handsome palaces rises the huge *Palazzo Strozzi* (Pl. 6; used for exhibitions), the last and grandest of the magnificent Renaissance palaces in Florence, built for Filippo Strozzi by Benedetto da Maiano in 1489 (and finished by Cronaca). Via della Vigna Nuova leads past the home (1614) of Sir Robert Dudley, and the house where George Eliot stayed while gathering material for Romola, to *Palazzo Rucellai* (Pl. 6). This was designed for Giovanni Rucellai by Leon

Battista Alberti and executed by Bernardo Rossellino (c 1446–51). In modernised rooms on the ground floor is the *Museo di Storia della Fotografia Fratelli Alinari*, illustrating the history of the firm of Alinari, famous in black-and-white photography. Photograph exhibitions are often held here.

Behind the palace the former church of *San Pancrazio*, has been converted into a gallery (open 10–13, 15–18 except Tuesday) to display sculptures by Marino Marini (1901–80), left to the city by him. The fine classical porch is by Alberti. At No. 18 Via della Spada is the entrance to the remarkable *Cappella di San Sepolcro* (usually closed) built in 1467 also by Alberti for Giovanni Rucellai. It contains a *model in inlaid marble of the Sanctuary of the Holy Sepulchre.

At No. 19 Via Tornabuoni *Palazzo Larderel*, attributed to Giovanni Antonio Dosio, is a model of High Renaissance architecture. Opposite is the huge church of **San Gaetano**, the most important 17C church in the city. The façade is by Pier Francesco Silvani, and the interior (closed for restoration) was built in pietra serena in 1604–49 by Matteo Nigetti and Gherardo Silvani. Nearly all the frescoes and altarpieces were painted in the 1630s and 1640s by Jacopo Vignali, Matteo Rosselli, Giovanni Bilivert, Lorenzo Lippi, and others. *Palazzo Antinori* (Pl. 6), attributed to Giuliano da Maiano (1461–69), is one of the most beautiful smaller Renaissance palaces in Florence. Nearby, on Via de'Cerretani is the Gothic Cistercian church of SANTA MARIA MAGGIORE. It contains frescoes by Mariotto di Nardo, a Byzantine relief in painted wood of the *Madonna enthroned attributed to Coppo di Marcovaldo (removed for restoration), and an effigy of Bruno Beccuti attributed to Tino da Camaino.

G. The Museo Nazionale del Bargello and the Badia Fiorentina

*Palazzo del Bargello** (Pl. 7,11), a massive battlemented medieval fortified building in pietra forte, was erected in 1250 as the 'Palazzo del Popolo'. Building was continued in the 14C and it was well restored in the 19C. At first the seat of the *Capitano del Popolo*, it became the residence of the 'Podestà', the governing magistrate of the city, at the end of the 13C. From the 16C, as the police headquarters, it became known as the *Bargello*. The palace now contains the **Museo Nazionale del Bargello**, famous for its superb collection of Florentine Renaissance sculpture, including numerous works by Donatello and the Della Robbia family. 16C Florentine sculpture is well represented by Michelangelo, Cellini, and Giambologna, among others, and an exquisite collection of small Mannerist bronzes. There is also a notable collection of decorative arts. (Adm. 9–14; fest. 9–13; closed Monday.)

GROUND FLOOR. The fine hall (right) contains 16C sculptures by Michelangelo and his Florentine contemporaries. Works by Michelangelo include: *Bacchus drunk (an early work; c 1497); *tondo of the Madonna and Child with the infant St John made for Bartolomeo Pitti; *bust of Brutus (c 1539–40); and *Apollo (or David). Other sculptors well represented here include Jacopo Sansovino (Bacchus), Bartolomeo Ammannati, Bandinelli (bust of Cosimo I, Adam and Eve), De'Rossi (*Dying Adonis), Cellini (Narcissus, Apollo and Hyacinthus, *bronzes from the pedestal of his statue of Perseus, bust of Cosimo I), and Giambologna (*Mercury). The Gothic

*CORTILE displays more 16C sculptures. A room off the courtyard displays 14C sculpture (Arnolfo di Cambio, Tino da Camaino).

FIRST FLOOR. The LOGGIA contains more works by Giambologna. The SALONE DEL CONSIGLIO GENERALE, a fine vaulted hall, displays superb sculptures by Donatello and his contemporaries. Works by Donatello include: *St George from Orsanmichele (in a reconstructed tabernacle), two statues of *David, one in bronze and one in marble, *Atys-Amorino, a bronze putto, the Marzocco (heraldic lion), a bust of a youth with a medallion at his neck, and *bust of Niccolò da Uzzano (the last two both attributed to Donatello). Also here: Desiderio da Settignano, *busts of a young woman and a boy; fine works by Giovanni di Bertoldo; Michelozzo, *reliefs of the Madonna; Luca Della Robbia, *Madonnas in enamelled terracotta, and two marble reliefs of St Peter; the two trial *reliefs of the Sacrifice of Isaac by Ghiberti and Brunelleschi made for the competition for the second bronze doors of the Baptistery; and a *reliquary urn by Ghiberti. The other rooms on this floor contain a beautifully displayed *collection of decorative arts (seals, glass, enamels, ecclesiastical ornaments, jewellery, goldsmiths' work, *ivories, and majolica). The CAPPELLA DEL PODESTÀ contains restored frescoes attributed to the school of Giotto.

SECOND FLOOR (sometimes closed for lack of staff). R. 13 contains a number of colourful enamelled terracottas by Giovanni Della Robbia and cases of plaquettes. R. 14 displays beautiful *works by Andrea Della Robbia. R. 15: sculptures by Verrocchio and a number of fine Renaissance portrait busts. Works by Verrocchio include his bronze *David, and a *bust of a lady holding flowers. Also here are works by: Antonio del Pollaiolo (*bust of a young cavalier, and *portrait-bust of a man); Mino da Fiesole (marble *portrait busts, and two Madonnas); Benedetto da Maiano (*Pietro Mellini); Antonio Rossellino; and Francesco Laurana (*bust of Battista Sforza). The Medagliere Mediceo (RR. 18 and 19) contains the collection of Italian medals begun by Lorenzo il Magnifico, including works by Pisanello, and busts by Bernini and Algardi. The SALONE DEL CAMINO (R. 16) contains a superb display of small Renaissance *bronzes, by Antonio Pollaiolo (*Hercules and Antaeus), Cellini, Giambologna, Tacca, Tribolo, Bandinelli, Il Riccio, Danese Cattaneo, etc. The fine *chimneypiece is by Benedetto da Rovezzano. The anatomical figure made in wax by Lodovico Cigoli was cast by Giovanni Battista Foggini. Also on this floor (not always open) is a magnificent collection of *arms and armour (well labelled).

In Piazza San Firenze is *Palazzo Gondi by Giuliano da Sangallo (c 1489), and San Firenze, a large building now occupied by the law courts, by Francesco Zanobi del Rosso (1772) next to the church of San Filippo Neri (1633) with an interior of 1712. Opposite the Bargello, in Via del Proconsolo, is the **Badia Fiorentina** (Pl. 7,11), the church of a Benedictine abbey founded in 978 by Willa, the widow of Uberto, Margrave of Tuscany. The graceful, slender CAMPANILE is Romanesque (1307) below and Gothic (after 1330) above. The 17C INTERIOR contains a painting of the *Madonna appearing to St Bernard by Filippino Lippi; a sculpted altarpiece, the tomb of Bernardo Giugni, and (N transept), *monument to Ugo, Margrave of Tuscany, all by Mino da Fiesole; and frescoes attributed to Nardo di Cione. The CHIOSTRO DEGLI ARANCI, by Bernardo Rossellino, has an interesting fresco cycle with scenes from the life of St Benedict by an artist known as the Maestro del Chiostro degli Aranci (c 1430).

Via Dante Alighieri leads left from Via del Proconsolo to Piazza San Martino with the splendid 13C Torre della Castagna, and the little chapel of SAN MARTINO DEL VESCOVO decorated with charming frescoes by the workshop of Ghirlandaio (Francesco d'Antonio del Chierico?) illustrating the life of St Martin and works of charity. The area is traditionally associated with the great Florentine poet Dante Alighieri, who was probably born on the street that now bears his name. The so-called *Casa di Dante* is in a group of houses restored in the 13C style in 1911. In the little church of *Santa Margherita de'Cerchi* Dante is supposed to have married Gemma Donati (it contains an altarpiece by Neri di Bicci).

At No. 10 Via del Proconsolo is the handsome *Palazzo Pazzi-Quaratesi* attributed to Giuliano da Maiano. Here begins *BORGO DEGLI ALBIZI, one of the most handsome streets in the city, lined with numerous fine palaces, including two (Nos 28 and 26) by Bartolomeo Ammannati. Across the borgo is *Palazzo Nonfinito*, begun in 1593 by Buontalenti. It now houses the MUSEO NAZIONALE DI ANTROPOLOGIA ED ETNOLOGIA (open Thursday, Friday, Saturday, and the third Sunday of the month, 9–12.30), founded in 1869 by Paolo Mantegazza, and probably the most important museum of its kind in Italy. The most interesting material comes from Africa, North Pakistan, South America, Mexico, Asia. The exhibits from the Pacific Ocean were probably acquired by Captain Cook on his last voyage.

At No. 24 Via dell'Oriuolo is the **Museo di Firenze com'era** (Pl. 7; adm. 10–13; closed Thursday), a topographical historical museum of the city. The maps, paintings, and prints displayed in several rooms of the old Convento delle Oblate illustrate the life of the city since the 15C. Nearby is the hospital of SANTA MARIA NUOVA founded in 1286 by Folco Portinari with a portico by Buontalenti, and the church of Sant'Egidio, both with a number of interesting works of art. In Via Sant'Egidio is the *Museo Fiorentino di Preistoria*.

H. Santa Croce and the Casa Buonarroti

PIAZZA SANTA CROCE (Pl. 11), an attractive and spacious square, is the centre of a distinctive district of the city. Some houses in the piazza have projecting upper storeys resting on *sporti*. *Palazzo dell'Antella*, built by Giulio Parigi, has a worn polychrome façade painted in 1619. *Palazzo Cocchi (Serristori)* at the end of the square has recently been attributed to Giuliano da Sangallo. ***Santa Croce** (Pl. 11,12), the Franciscan church of Florence, was rebuilt c 1294 possibly by Arnolfo di Cambio. The neo-Gothic façade dates from 1853.

The huge, wide INTERIOR (closed 12.30–15) has an open timber roof. The Gothic church was rearranged by Vasari in 1560. For five hundred years it has been the custom to bury or erect monuments to notable citizens of Florence in this church; it is the burial place of Ghiberti, Michelangelo, Machiavelli, and Galileo. SOUTH AISLE. First pillar, *Madonna del Latte a relief by Antonio Rossellino. The tomb of Michelangelo was designed by Vasari. The neo-classical cenotaph to Dante (buried in Ravenna) is by Stefano Ricci. The *pulpit is by Benedetto da Maiano. There follow monuments to Vittorio Alfieri (by Antonio Canova), and to Niccolò Machiavelli (by Innocenzo Spinazzi, 1787). The altarpieces in this aisle are by Vasari, Jacopo Coppi di Meglio, Alessandro del Barbiere (Flagellation of Christ), and Andrea del Minga (Agony in the Garden). By the side door is a *tabernacle with a beautiful high relief of the Annunciation by Donatello. The *tomb of Leonardo Bruni by Bernardo Rossellino (c 1446–47) is one of the most harmonious and influential sepulchral monuments of the Renaissance. SOUTH TRANSEPT. The Castellani Chapel contains decorative *frescoes by Agnolo Gaddi and assistants. The Baroncelli Chapel has *frescoes by Taddeo Gaddi (father of Agnolo), a pupil of Giotto. The restored altarpiece of the Coronation of the Virgin is by Giotto and his workshop. Also here is a 15C fresco of the Madonna by Sebastiano Mainardi, and a 16C statue of the Madonna and Child by Vincenzo Danti. The *SACRISTY has frescoes by Taddeo Gaddi, Spinello Aretino (attributed), and Nicolò di Pietro Gerini, and, in the Rinuccini Chapel, *frescoes by Giovanni da Milano, one of the most gifted followers of Giotto. The MEDICI CHAPEL by Michelozzo contains an *altarpiece by Andrea Della Robbia.

The small rectangular vaulted CHAPELS at the E end are famous for their frescoes by Giotto and his school. The two chapels right of the sanctuary were decorated by Giotto; the frescoes are damaged and in poor condition. The *PERUZZI CHAPEL contains scenes from the life of St John the Evangelist and of St John the Baptist painted in his maturity (the altarpiece is by Taddeo Gaddi); the frescoes illustrating the story of St Francis in the *BARDI CHAPEL were designed by Giotto, but some of them may have been executed by his pupils. The painting of St Francis on the altar dates from the 13C. The SANCTUARY is frescoed with the *Legend of the Cross by Agnolo Gaddi (c 1380), who also designed the fine stained glass lancet windows. The polyptych is by Nicolò Gerini and Giovanni del Biondo, and the Crucifix above by the Master of Figline. In the last two E chapels are frescoes of the lives of St Lawrence and St Stephen by Bernardo Daddi, and colourful and well-preserved frescoes of the *life of St Sylvester by Maso di Banco, perhaps the most original follower of Giotto, who also probably painted the Last Judgement in the Gothic tomb here.

NORTH TRANSEPT. The Niccolini Chapel designed by Giovanni Antonio Dosio, has frescoes by Volterrano, statues by Francavilla, and paintings by Alessandro Allori. The second Bardi Chapel contains a wooden *Crucifix by Donatello. The story told by Vasari of Brunelleschi's complaint that it was a mere 'peasant on the cross' is now thought to be apocryphal. In the Salviati Chapel is the *tomb of Princess Sofia Czartoryska (died 1837) with a Romantic effigy by Lorenzo Bartolini. NORTH AISLE. By the side door, *monument to Carlo Marsuppini (died 1453) by Desiderio da Settignano. The classical sarcophagus may be the work of Verrocchio. In the pavement between the fifth and fourth altars is the handsome tomb-slab with niello decoration of Lorenzo Ghiberti, and his son Vittorio. The monument to Galileo Galilei (1564–1642) was set up by Giovanni Battista Foggini in 1737 when the great scientist was allowed Christian burial inside the church. In the nave is the tomb-slab of his ancestor and namesake, a well-known physician in 15C Florence. The altarpieces in this aisle are by Giovanni Stradano, Santi di Tito (Supper at Emmaus and Resurrection), and Giovanni Battista Naldini.

On the right of the church is the entrance to the conventual buildings and the **Museo dell'Opera di Santa Croce** (Pl. 11,12; adm. 10–12.30, 14.30–18.30; winter, 10–12.30, 15–17; closed Wednesday). In the first cloister (14C) is the charming *Cappella dei Pazzi, one of the most famous works of Brunelleschi (1442–46). The portico may have been designed by Giuliano da Maiano; the shallow cupola bears delightful enamelled terracotta decoration by Luca Della Robbia, who also made the medallion with *St Andrew over the door. The beautiful calm interior is one of the masterpieces of the early Renaissance. The twelve *roundels of the seated Apostles are by Luca Della Robbia; the polychrome roundels of the Evangelists may have been designed by Donatello. The *SECOND CLOISTER is another beautiful work by Brunelleschi.

Off the First Cloister is the entrance to the MUSEO DELL'OPERA DI SANTA CROCE. In the fine Gothic REFECTORY is displayed Cimabue's great Crucifix which has been restored after it was almost completely destroyed in the flood of 1966. The huge *fresco on the end wall of the Last Supper below the Tree of the Cross is by Taddeo Gaddi. Also here are fragments of a large fresco by Orcagna of the Triumph of Death and Inferno detached from the nave of the church, and several other fine 14–15C frescoes (including one with a view of the Baptistery and Duomo). In a reconstructed tabernacle is Donatello's colossal gilded bronze *St Louis of Toulouse from Orsanmichele. The other rooms contain more frescoes (14–17C), Della Robbian terracottas, interesting large sketches detached from walls of the Cappella dei Pazzi, and sculptures by Tino da Camaino. Beneath the colonnade, just before the exit from the cloister, is a memorial to Florence Nightingale, named after the city where she was born.

To the right of Santa Croce is the huge BIBLIOTECA NAZIONALE (severely damaged in 1966). At the other end of Piazza Santa Croce VIA DEI BENCI, with its old rusticated houses, runs towards the Arno. The polygonal 13C *Torre degli Alberti* has a 15C loggia below. *Palazzo Bardi alle Grazie* (No. 5) is an early Renaissance palace attributed to Brunelleschi; No. 1, *Palazzo Malenchini* was reconstructed on the site of a 14C palace of the Alberti where the great architect Leon Battista died in 1472. Off the interesting old Via dei Neri a road (right) leads to the church of SAN REMIGIO, founded in the 11C. The fine Gothic interior (often closed) contains a *Madonna and Child by a follower of Cimabue known as the 'Master of San Remigio'. Nearby is the interesting medieval Piazza Peruzzi, and Via dei Bentaccordi which takes its shape from the curve of the Roman amphitheatre (2–3C AD). The church of SAN SIMONE, founded in 1192–93, has a fine interior by Gherardo Silvani (1630), and an altarpiece of St Peter enthroned (1307); opposite is *Palazzo da Cintoia* one of the best preserved medieval palaces in the city.

From the N side of Santa Croce Via delle Pinzochere leads to Via Ghibellina, where, at No. 70 is the ***Casa Buonarroti** (Pl. 7,12; adm. 9.30–13.30; closed Tuesday). Three houses on this site were purchased in 1508 by Michelangelo who left the property to his only descendant, his nephew Leonardo.

The GROUND FLOOR is used for interesting exhibitions. Also displayed here are: a statue of Venus attributed to Vincenzo Danti, and part of the eclectic collection of antiquities and Renaissance works made by Michelangelo's descendants, including a copy from Titian of a *love scene, Etruscan stelae, etc. FIRST FLOOR. Two early works by Michelangelo: *Madonna of the Steps, a marble bas-relief, carved at the age of 15 or 16, and a *battle relief, modelled on a Roman sarcophagus. The wood model for the façade of San Lorenzo was designed by Michelangelo (but never carried out). The *torso, a model in clay and wood for a river god, is also by Michelangelo. A selection of his *drawings owned by the museum are shown in rotation. The four rooms decorated in 1613 by Michelangelo Buonarroti the Younger in celebration of his great-uncle and his family, contain paintings by Cristofano Allori, Giovanni Bilivert, Empoli, Giovanni da San Giovanni, Matteo Rosselli, Jacopo Vignali, etc. Also here: portrait of Michelangelo attributed to Giuliano Bugiardini, a predella by Giovanni di Francesco, Roman and Etruscan sculpture and small bronzes, and bozzetti by Michelangelo (the allegorical model in terracotta in case 408), and his followers including Tribolo. The *Crucifix in painted poplar wood was found in Santo Spirito in 1963 and is now generally attributed to Michelangelo.

The church of **Sant'Ambrogio** (Pl. 8), to the N, was rebuilt in the late 13C. It contains a number of interesting frescoes including a *Madonna enthroned with saints, attributed to the school of Orcagna. In the chapel on the left of the high altar is an exquisite *tabernacle by Mino da Fiesole (who is buried here), and a large *fresco by Cosimo Rosselli of a procession with a miraculous chalice (preserved here) in front of the church. On the N side, *angels and Saints by Alesso Baldovinetti surrounding a Nativity by his pupil Graffione. The church is the burial place of Cronaca (died 1508) and Verrocchio (died 1488). Nearby is the produce market of Sant'Ambrogio and the Mercatino, a flea market in Piazza dei Ciompi, with Vasari's graceful Loggia del Pesce (removed from the Mercato Vecchio). Lorenzo Ghiberti lived here, and Cimabue lived in Borgo Allegri which was given this name, according to Vasari, after his painting of the Maestà (now in the Uffizi) left his studio in a joyous procession down the street.

To the N, beyond the huge SYNAGOGUE (1874–82) with a green dome (and a small museum), is the ex-convent of **Santa Maria Maddalena dei Pazzi** (Pl. 8), on Borgo Pinti (No. 56). The *cloister is by Giuliano da Sangallo. The church has a fine Baroque sanctuary (1675, by Ciro Ferri) and altarpieces by Carlo Portelli, Matteo Rosselli, Domenico Puligo, and Santi di Tito. In the CHAPTER HOUSE (open 9–12, 17–19; or ring at No. 58) is a beautiful and very well preserved *fresco of the Crucifixion and saints by Perugino, one of his masterpieces.

I. The Arno

Ponte alla Carraia (Pl. 6,10), first constructed in 1218–20, was the second bridge to be built over the Arno. It was several times rebuilt and repaired, and reconstructed after it was blown up in 1944. At the N end Lungarno Vespucci, opened in the 19C, leads away from the centre of the city towards the park of the Cascine past two modern bridges.

The **Cascine** (Pl. 5) is a huge public park (not as well maintained as it might be, and not safe at night) which skirts the Arno for 3.5km. It was used as a ducal chase by the Medici grand-dukes, and festivals were held here. It was first opened regularly to the public c 1811. In these gardens the Ode to the West Wind was 'conceived and chiefly written' by Shelley in 1819. At the far end is a monument to the Maharajah of Kolhapur who died in Florence in 1870. From here the view is dominated by a suspension bridge (1978) over the Arno.

Lungarno Corsini leads past the huge Palazzo Corsini built between 1656 and c 1737 in a grandiose Roman Baroque style. It contains the most important private art collection in Florence (adm. by appointment only at 11 Via Parione). In rooms frescoed by Alessandro Gherardini and Antonio Domenico Gabbiani it is particularly interesting for its paintings of the 17C Florentine school. It also contains a Madonna by Pontormo, a Crucifix by Giovanni Bellini, a cartoon attributed to Raphael of his portrait of Julius II, and works attributed to Signorelli and Filippino Lippi. Farther on is Palazzo Masetti (now the British Consulate) where the Countess of Albany, widow of Prince Charles Edward Stuart, lived from 1793 to her death. *Ponte Santa Trínita (Pl. 10) was first built in 1252. The present bridge is an exact replica of the bridge begun by Ammannati in 1567 and destroyed in 1944. The high flat arches which span the river are perfectly proportioned and the bridge provides a magnificent view of the city. The statue of Spring on the parapet is the best work of Pietro Francavilla (1593). Lungarno Acciaioli continues to Ponte Vecchio (described in Rte 1 D). The modern buildings on both banks of the river near the bridge replaced the medieval houses which were blown up in 1944 in order to render Ponte Vecchio impassable. Beyond the Uffizi opens Piazza dei Giudici with the medieval *Palazzo Castellani* which now contains the *Museo di Storia della Scienza (Pl. 11; adm. 9.30–13; Monday, Wednesday, and Friday also 14–17; closed fest.), a beautifully displayed and well maintained collection of scientific instruments.

A large part of the collection was owned by the Medici grand-dukes. Excellent hand-lists are lent to visitors. FIRST FLOOR. Room I: astrolabes, quadrants, solar clocks, and mathematical instruments. R.II: German instruments, and navigational instruments, including some invented by Sir Robert Dudley. R.III: scientifical instruments made for the Medici grand-dukes. R.IV: precious collection of instruments which belonged to Galileo, including his compass, the lens he used in discovering the four largest moons of Jupiter (cracked by him before he presented it to Ferdinando II), and the 'Giovilabio'; models of his inventions. R.V: astronomy, including Galileo's two wood telescopes. R.VI: lenses and prisms. R.VII: globes, including the armillary sphere made by Antonio Santucci in 1588. R.VIII: microscopes. R.IX: material relating to the Accademia del Cimento, an experimental academy founded by Cardinal Leopoldo in 1657 (including elaborate glass). R.X: barometers, thermometers, rain gauges, etc. R.XI: astronomy in the 18C and 19C (large telescopes). SECOND FLOOR. R.XII: mechanical clocks. R.XIII: mathematical instruments (18C–19C). R.XIV: magnetic and electrostatic machines. R.XV: pneumatic apparatus. RR.XVI–XVII: demonstration models made in 1775 illustrating mechanical principals. R.XVIII: surgical instruments and anatomical models. R.XIX: history of pharmaceutical research. R.XX: instruments concerning fluids and gases. R.XXI: weights and measures.

Farther on, at Ponte alle Grazie is Via dei Benci. Here at No. 6 *Palazzo Corsi*, attributed to Cronaca, contains the **Museo Horne** (Pl. 11; adm. 9–13, except fest.). The interesting collection of 14–16C paintings, sculptures, and decorative arts (notable furniture and majolica) was presented to the nation, along with his house, by the English art historian Herbert Percy Horne (1864–1916). A handlist is lent to visitors. FIRST FLOOR. Paintings by Masaccio (attributed), Pietro Lorenzetti, Bernardo Daddi, Benozzo Gozzoli, Giotto (*St Stephen), Filippino Lippi, Beccafumi (*tondo of the Holy Family), and Renaissance sculptures. SECOND FLOOR. 15C furniture, and paintings by the Master of the Horne Triptych, Neri di Bicci, Simone Martini (attributed), etc.

Ponte alle Grazie (Pl. 11), first built in 1237, was replaced after 1944 by a modern bridge. At the S end is Piazza dei Mozzi, with the large *Palazzo Bardini* (No. 1), built by the famous antiquarian and collector Stefano Bardini in 1883 to house his huge collection of works of art bequeathed to the city in 1923 as the **Museo Bardini** (Pl. 11; adm. 9–14; fest. 9–13; closed Wednesday). His eclectic collection includes architectural fragments, sculpture, paintings, the decorative arts, furniture, ceramics, carpets, arms and armour, musical instruments, etc. Many of the rooms were built specially to contain the fine doorways, staircases, and ceilings from demolished buildings. The rooms are crowded with a miscellany of works. GROUND FLOOR. Medieval and Renaissance architectural fragments; classical sculpture; medieval sculpture (statue of Charity attributed to Tino da Camaino); altarpiece attributed to Andrea Della Robbia. FIRST FLOOR.

Armour; sculpture (reliefs attributed to Donatello); paintings (St Michael by Antonio Pollaiolo); musical instruments, etc.

The Palazzi dei Mozzi built in the 13–14C are among the most noble private houses of medieval Florence. The severe façades in pietra forte have arches on the ground floor. The building, together with a huge collection of decorative arts, was left to the State in 1965 by Ugo, son of Stefano Bardini, and there are long-term plans to open it to the public.

*Via di San Niccolò, a narrow medieval street, leads left to the church of SAN NICCOLÒ SOPR'ARNO (Pl. 11), with several interesting 15C frescoes, including the *Madonna della Cintola (in the sacristy), attributed to Alesso Baldovinetti, and St Ansano, attributed to Francesco d'Antonio. The road continues past (right) the pretty 14C *Porta San Miniato* to the massive PORTA SAN NICCOLÒ with a high tower built c 1340.

The winding *Via de'Bardi leads right from Piazza dei Mozzi past a series of noble town houses to Ponte Vecchio.

J. The Oltrarno

In the characteristic district on the S bank of the Arno known as the *Oltrarno*, the two most important churches are Santo Spirito and Santa Maria del Carmine, and around them focuses the life of this part of the city. The church of *Santo Spirito (Pl. 10) was rebuilt by Brunelleschi in 1444. Building was continued after his death by Antonio Manetti and others. The slender campanile is by Baccio d'Agnolo (1503), and the modest façade dates from the 18C.

The *INTERIOR, designed by Brunelleschi, was executed mostly after his death and modified in the late 15C. It is remarkable for its harmonious proportions, its solemn colour, and the perspective of the colonnades and vaulted aisles. The plan is a Latin-cross with a dome over the crossing, and the columns with fine Corinthian capitals are carried round the transepts and E end forming an unbroken arcade with 38 chapels in semi-circular niches. The Baroque HIGH ALTAR by Giovanni Caccini disturbs the harmony of the architecture. The interior façade was designed by Salvi d'Andrea (1483–87), and the stained glass oculus is from a cartoon by Perugino. SOUTH AISLE CHAPELS. 2nd chapel, Pietà, a free copy of Michelangelo's famous sculpture in St Peter's by Nanni di Baccio Bigio; 4th chapel, Giovanni Stradano, Christ expelling the money-changers from the temple; 6th chapel, Passignano, Martyrdom of St Stephen. SOUTH TRANSEPT CHAPELS. 10th chapel, Madonna del Soccorso, a painting of the early 15C; 12th chapel, Filippino Lippi, *Madonna and Child, with the young St John, saints, and donors, one of his finest works; 13th chapel, Felice Ficherelli, copy of Perugino's Vision of St Bernard, now in Munich; 14th chapel, Giovanni Camillo Sagrestani, Marriage of the Virgin (1713), his best work.

CHAPELS AT THE EAST END. 15th chapel, Madonna and saints, a good painting in the style of Lorenzo di Credi; 16th chapel, Maso di Banco, polyptych; 17th chapel, Aurelio Lomi, Epiphany; 18th, 19th chapels, Alessandro Allori, martyred saints, *Christ and the adulteress; 21st, 22nd chapels, 15C Florentine paintings. NORTH TRANSEPT CHAPELS, 23rd chapel, Maestro di Santo Spirito, Madonna enthroned between saints; 24th chapel, *St Monica and Augustinian nuns in black habits, traditionally attributed to Botticini, but possibly by Verrocchio; 25th chapel, Cosimo Rosselli, Madonna enthroned between saints; 26th chapel, *altarpiece by Andrea Sansovino; 27th chapel, *Trinity with saints, a good painting of the late 15C, attributed to the Maestro di Santo Spirito; 28th chapel, Raffaellino dei Carli, *Madonna enthroned with saints. A door beneath the organ in the N aisle leads into a grandiose *VESTIBULE built by Cronaca in 1491. The *SACRISTY, taking its inspiration from Brunelleschi, was designed by Giuliano da Sangallo.

To the left of the church, at No. 29, is the entrance to the REFECTORY (adm. 10–13; closed Monday), the only part of the 14C convent to survive. Above a fresco of the Last Supper (almost totally ruined) is a huge *Crucifixion, both of them painted c 1360–65 and attributed to Andrea Orcagna and his bottega. Here is displayed the **Fondazione Salvatore Romano**, an interesting collection of sculpture notable for its Romanesque works, two statuettes by Tino da Camaino, and sculptures attributed to Jacopo della Quercia, Donatello, and Ammannati.

PIAZZA SANTO SPIRITO is one of the most attractive little squares in the city, the scene of a small daily market. *Palazzo Guadagni* (No. 10) was probably built by Cronaca c 1505. Via Sant'Agostino leads to Via de' Serragli, a long straight road with handsome 17–18C palaces. Via Santa Monica continues past a tabernacle by Lorenzo di Bicci into Piazza del Carmine. Here is the rough stone façade of the church of **Santa Maria del Carmine** (Pl. 10), famous for its frescoes by Masaccio in the Cappella Brancacci, which escaped destruction in a fire in 1771 that ruined the rest of the first church. The huge, broad INTERIOR was rebuilt in an undistinguished late Baroque style. At the end of the N transept is the sumptuous *CHAPEL OF SANT'ANDREA CORSINI by Pier Francesco Silvani, one of the best Baroque works in Florence. The ceiling is by Luca Giordano, and the marble and silver reliefs by Giovanni Battista Foggini. The Gothic SACRISTY has frescoes from the life of St Cecilia by the school of Bicci di Lorenzo.

The **Brancacci Chapel**, in the S transept, is now entered at No. 14 in the piazza through the early-17C cloisters. Adm. 10–17 (fest. 13–17) except Tuesday. The frescoes illustrating the life of St Peter were commissioned by Felice Brancacci c 1424 from Masolino and Masaccio. Seriously damaged in the 18C and 19C, they were restored in 1983–89, and many of the details formerly obscured by surface mould can now be seen. The design of the whole fresco cycle may be due to Masolino, but his pupil Masaccio seems to have continued work on them alone in 1428. Later that year Masaccio himself broke off work abruptly on the frescoes and left for Rome where, by the end of the year, he had died at the early age of 27. The frescoes were at once recognised as a masterpiece and profoundly influenced Florentine art of the Renaissance. All the major artists of the 15C came here to study the frescoes which combine a perfect application of the new rules of perspective with a remarkable use of chiaroscuro. The cycle was completed only some 50 years later by Filippino Lippi (c 1480–85) who carefully integrated his style with that of Masaccio, possibly following an earlier design. The frescoes are arranged in two registers. UPPER ROW (right to left): Masolino, Temptation of Adam and Eve; Masolino, St Peter, accompanied by St John, brings Tabitha to life and heals a lame man (the figures on the extreme left may be by Masaccio); Masaccio, *St Peter baptising; Masolino, St Peter preaching; Masaccio, *The Tribute money, perhaps the painter's masterpiece; Masaccio, *Expulsion from Paradise, one of his most

Detail from the fresco of St Peter and St John distributing alms by Masaccio, in the Brancacci Chapel, Santa Maria del Carmine, Florence

moving works. LOWER ROW (right to left): Filippino Lippi, *Release of St Peter from prison; Filippino Lippi, Saints Peter and Paul before the proconsul, and Crucifixion of St Peter; Masaccio, Saints Peter and John distributing alms; Masaccio, *St Peter, followed by St John, healing the sick with his shadow; Masaccio, *St Peter enthroned with portraits of friars, his last work, and St Peter bringing to life the Emperor's nephew, finished by Filippino; Filippino Lippi, St Peter in prison visited by St Paul. The altarpiece of the Madonna del Popolo is a Tuscan Byzantine work of the mid-13C attributed to Coppo di Marcovaldo.

The rooms off the Cloister have been closed since 1987. They contain works by Alessandro Allori, Starnina, Filippo Lippi (*Rule of the Order), Giovanni da Milano, Lippo Fiorentino, and Francesco Vanni.

BORGO SAN FREDIANO (Pl. 10,9), at the N end of the piazza, gives its name to a characteristic district with numerous artisans' houses and workshops. The large church of *San Frediano in Cestello* with its main entrance on the Arno was rebuilt with a fine dome in the 17C by Antonio Maria Ferri. It contains late-17C and early-18C paintings and frescoes by Francesco Curradi, Jacopo del Sellaio, Giovanni Camillo Sagrestani, Alessandro Gherardini, Antonio Domenico Gabbiani, and others. The fortified *Porta San Frediano* (Pl. 5,9) is the best preserved part of the last circle of walls built by the commune in 1284–1333. The gate, built in 1324, perhaps by Andrea Pisano, has a high tower and huge wooden doors.

VIA DI SANTO SPIRITO (Pl. 10) runs parallel to the Arno in the other direction, past the 17C *Palazzo Rinuccini, Palazzo Manetti* with a 15C façade (the home of Sir Horace Mann in 1740–86 while he was serving as English envoy to the Tuscan court), and *Palazzo Frescobaldi*. On Lungarno Guicciardini is *Palazzo Lanfredini* by Baccio d'Agnolo with bright (restored) graffiti decoration. From the foot of Ponte Santa Trìnita the handsome VIA MAGGIO leads away from the Arno. Its name (from *Maggiore*) is a reminder of its origin as the principal and widest street of the Oltrarno. *Palazzo Ricasoli* (No. 7) was built at the end of the 15C. *Palazzo di Bianca Cappello* (No. 26), with good graffiti decoration attributed to Bernardino Poccetti, was built by the Grand-Duke Francesco I for Bianca Cappello. *Palazzo Ridolfi* (No. 13) dates from the late 16C, and *Palazzo Commenda di Firenze* (No. 42), first built in the late 14C, was reconstructed in the 16C. Via Maggio ends in Piazza San Felice. No. 8 is the 15C *Casa Guidi*, where Robert and Elizabeth Barrett Browning rented a flat on the first floor and lived after their secret marriage in 1846 until Elizabeth's death in 1861. It is now owned by Eton College and is leased to the Landmark Trust (and may be reopened in 1995). SAN FELICE is a Gothic church with a Renaissance façade by Michelozzo. It contains a large *Crucifix attributed to Giotto or his workshop, a triptych by Neri di Bicci, and a triptych by a follower of Botticelli.

Via Romana continues SW to Porta Romana, a well-preserved gate built in 1327 on a design by Andrea Orcagna. No. 17, *Palazzo Torrigiani*, was built in 1775 as a natural history museum, known as *La Specola*. Here in 1814 Sir Humphry Davy and Michael Faraday used Galileo's 'great burning glass' to explode the diamond. It now contains a Zoological Museum (adm. 9–12; fest. 9–13; closed Wed) with a remarkable collection of anatomical models in wax, many of them by Clemente Susini (1775–1814).

In Piazza Pitti, dominated by the huge Palazzo Pitti (see Rte 1 D), the pretty row of houses facing the palace includes the home of Paolo dal Pozzo Toscanelli (1397–1482), the famous scientist and geographer. While staying at No. 21 in 1868 Dostoyevsky wrote *The Idiot*. Via Guicciardini continues to Ponte Vecchio; on the left is the ancient BORGO SAN JACOPO with the *Torre Marsili di Borgo*, a fine towerhouse, and the church of *San Jacopo sopr'Arno* with an 11C portico transported here in the 16C from a demolished church.

K. Forte di Belvedere and San Miniato al Monte

San Miniato can be reached directly from the Station by Bus 13, or on foot by the steps from Porta San Niccolò (Pl. 12). However, if you have time, the following route on foot is highly recommended (and Bus 13 can be taken back from San Miniato).

Near Ponte Vecchio the narrow COSTA SAN GIORGIO (Pl. 11) winds up the hill towards Forte di Belvedere past the pretty Costa Scarpuccia (left). The church of SAN GIORGIO SULLA COSTA has a good Baroque interior by Giovanni Battista Foggini, altarpieces by Tommaso Redi, Jacopo Vignali, and Passignano, and a *Madonna, an early work by Giotto (removed since its restoration). Beyond the house (No. 19) purchased by Galileo for his son Vincenzio, the road reaches *Porta San Giorgio* with a fresco by Bicci di Lorenzo. Built in 1260 this is the oldest gate in the city to have survived. Here is the entrance to *Forte di Belvedere (Pl. 11), a huge fortress designed by Buontalenti for Ferdinando I in 1590. From the ramparts (adm. 9–20) there is a splendid *view in every direction. The fine interior is used for important exhibitions.

*Via di San Leonardo (Pl. 15), one of the most beautiful country roads on the outskirts of the city, leads to the church of SAN LEONARDO IN ARCETRI which contains a *pulpit of the early 13C, and several 15C paintings.

*VIA DI BELVEDERE (Pl. 15), a picturesque country lane, follows the straight line of the city walls (first built in 1258) from Forte di Belvedere to Porta San Miniato. From here Via del Monte alle Croci or Via di San Salvatore al Monte return uphill. Across the busy Viale Galileo, a monumental flight of steps leads up past a cemetery (1839) to *San Miniato al Monte (Pl. 16). The finest of all Tuscan Romanesque basilicas, with a famous façade, it is one of the most beautiful churches in Italy. Its position on a green hill above the city is incomparable.

Deacon Minias is thought to have been martyred c 250 during the persecutions of Emperor Decius and buried on this hillside. The church was built in 1013 by Bishop Hildebrand on the site of Decius' tomb. The *FAÇADE, begun c 1090, is built of white and dark greenish marble in a beautiful geometrical design reminiscent of the Baptistery. The mosaic (restored) of Christ between the Virgin and St Minias dates from the 13C. The tympanum is crowned by an eagle, emblem of the 'Arte di Calimala' who looked after the fabric of the building. The fine *INTERIOR built in 1018–63, with a raised choir above a large hall crypt, is practically in its original state. In the centre of the pavement are seven superb marble intarsia *panels (1207) with signs of the zodiac and animal motifs. At the end of the nave is the *CAPPELLA DEL CROCIFISSO, an exquisite tabernacle by Michelozzo (1448). The painted panels are by Agnolo Gaddi, and the enamelled terracotta roof and ceiling by Luca Della Robbia. In the aisles are a number of 13–15C frescoes. On the N wall is the *CHAPEL OF THE CARDINAL OF PORTUGAL, begun by Antonio Manetti in 1460. The exquisitely carved *tomb is by Antonio Rossellino and the ceiling, with five *medallions, by Luca Della Robbia. The altarpiece of Three Saints by Antonio and Piero del Pollaiolo is a copy of the original in the Uffizi. The *Annunciation is by Alesso Baldovinetti.

Before the CHOIR is a beautiful marble *transenna dating from 1207, and *pulpit. The low columns in the choir have huge antique capitals. The large apse mosaic, representing Christ between the Virgin and St Minias (1297), was first restored in 1491 by Alesso Baldovinetti. The SACRISTY (S side) is entirely frescoed with scenes from the *life of St Benedict, one of the best works of Spinello Aretino (restored in 1840). The 11C CRYPT has slender columns with antique capitals. The original 11C altar contains the relics of St Minias. The frescoes are by Taddeo Gaddi.

The massive stone CAMPANILE was begun after 1523, but never finished. During the siege of Florence (1530) Michelangelo mounted two cannon here, and protected the bell-tower from hostile artillery by a screen of mattresses. The battlemented *Bishop's Palace* dates from 1295 (restored). There is a splendid view from the terrace in front of the church.

In a grove of cypresses on the side of the hill is the church of SAN SALVATORE AL MONTE, a building of gracious simplicity by Cronaca, called by Michelangelo his *bella villanella* (his pretty country maid). Steps lead down to PIAZZALE MICHELANGELO (Pl. 16), a celebrated viewpoint much visited by tourists. From the balustrade on the huge terrace is a remarkable panorama of the city. VIALE DEI COLLI (bus 13), a fine roadway 6km long, was laid out by Giuseppe Poggi in 1865–70. It is one of the most panoramic drives near Florence.

L. The Viali

The wide avenues (or *viali*) form a ring-road busy with traffic around the centre of the city N of the Arno. They were laid out in 1865–69 by Giuseppe Poggi after he had demolished the last circle of walls built in 1284–1333; he left some of the medieval gates as isolated monuments. Viale Filippo Strozzi skirts the huge FORTEZZA DA BASSO (Pl. 2).

This massive fortress, on a grand scale (with its exterior wall still intact), was built for Alessandro de'Medici in 1534 by Antonio da Sangallo. It became a symbol of Medici tyranny, and Alessandro was assassinated here by his cousin Lorenzino in 1537. It is now used partly as a restoration laboratory for paintings, by the Opificio delle Pietre Dure, one of the two official schools of restoration in Italy, and partly as an international exhibition centre. Public gardens have been laid out on the glacis.
    From the Fortezza a bus (No. 4 from near the Duomo and the Station) runs NE to the *Museo Stibbert (adm. 9–13; closed Thursday), created by Frederick Stibbert (1838–1906), born in Florence. His eclectic collection, with an extraordinary variety of objects, is crammed into 57 period rooms designed by him, producing a remarkably bizarre atmosphere. Stibbert was particularly interested in armour and costume, and the museum is famous for its armour (including a remarkable collection of Asiatic armour). The PARK, also created by Stibbert, is open daily (9–dusk).

Across Viale Strozzi is *Palazzo dei Congressi* (1964), an international conference centre. At No. 14 is the *Istituto Geografico Militare*, the most important cartographical institute in Italy. Viale Lavagnini continues towards Piazza della Libertà. In Via Leone X (left) is the delightful *Russian Church* built in 1904 by Russian architects. It is owned by the Russian Orthodox community of Florence and is open for services. In the arcaded PIAZZA DELLA LIBERTÀ is the medieval Porta San Gallo and a triumphal arch erected in 1739.

To the N of the square is Ponte Rosso near which is the entrance to the *Giardino dell'Orticoltura*, a horticultural garden created in 1859 (open daily) with an elaborate greenhouse (1880; by Giacomo Roster). Here begins VIA BOLOGNESE which leads uphill out of the city (bus 25) past a number of villas including (1.5km) *La Pietra* (No. 120), the former residence of the aesthete and historian Sir Harold Acton (1904–94) and left by him to New York University. The beautiful Italianate *garden (with topiary laid out in 1904) can only be seen with special permission (for information, Tel. 474448). The Villa contains one of the most interesting private collections of works of art in Florence.

The Viali continue to PIAZZA DONATELLO, in the centre of which is the disused *English Cemetery* (Pl. 4) on a mound shaded by cypresses. Here are buried Elizabeth Barrett Browning, Isa Blagden, Arthur Hugh Clough, Walter Savage Landor, Frances Trollope, Theodore Parker of Lexington, Robert Davidsohn, and Gian Pietro Vieusseux. From the next square, Piazza Beccaria, the ex-CONVENT OF SAN SALVI is reached (c 1.5km; bus 6 from Piazza San Marco). In the refectory (entrance at No. 16 Via San Salvi; open 9–14; closed Monday) is the celebrated *CENACOLO DI SAN SALVI by Andrea del Sarto (c 1520–25), a masterpiece of Florentine fresco, remarkable for its colouring, and one of the most famous frescoes of the Last Supper in Italy. 16C altarpieces and other works by Andrea del Sarto are displayed in the conventual buildings. Nearby is the sports ground of Campo di Marte with the *Stadio Comunale*, a remarkable building (1932) by Pier Luigi Nervi (enlarged in 1990).

2

Environs of Florence

For a full description of the places described below, see Blue Guide Florence.

A. Fiesole and San Domenico

Information Office. IAT, 36 Piazza Mino, Fiesole (Tel. 055/598720).

Bus No. 7. Frequent service in 30mins from Florence (the Station and Piazza San Marco) via San Domenico.

From Viale Alessandro Volta (with the park of *Villa il Ventaglio*, open daily) Via di San Domenico ascends the hillside with a beautiful view of Fiesole and its villas to (6.5km) **San Domenico di Fiesole**, a little hamlet (pizzeria *San Domenico*) with several handsome private villas. The 15C church of SAN DOMENICO has a 17C portico and campanile (by Matteo Nigetti). INTERIOR. First N chapel, Fra Angelico, *Madonna with angels and saints (c 1430). The architectural background was added by Lorenzo di Credi in 1501, when the frame was redesigned (the saints are by a follower of Lorenzo Monaco). The other altarpieces are by the school of Botticelli (Crucifixion), Lorenzo di Credi (Baptism of Christ), Giovanni Antonio Sogliani (Epiphany), and Jacopo da Empoli (Annunciation). In the Convent of San Domenico St Antoninus and Fra Angelico were friars. In the little

CHAPTER HOUSE (ring at No. 4) is a *Crucifixion and Madonna and Child by Fra Angelico.

Via della Badia descends (left; beware of traffic) from San Domenico to the *Badia Fiesolana, in a beautiful position, the cathedral of Fiesole until 1028. It was rebuilt in the 15C under the direction of Cosimo il Vecchio. In the conventual buildings the *European University Institute* was established in 1976. The rough stone front incorporates the charming *façade of the smaller Romanesque church with inlaid marble decoration. The simple cruciform *INTERIOR (open for services, or sometimes by request at the European University) is attributed to a close follower of Brunelleschi.

From San Domenico the ascent to Fiesole may be made either by the main road or by the shorter and prettier old road (Via Vecchia Fiesolana, very narrow and steep); both are lined with fine villas and beautiful trees and provide splendid views of Florence. 8km **FIESOLE** (295m) is a little town (14,000 inhab.) in a magnificent position on a thickly wooded hill over-looking the valleys of the Arno and the Mugnone. It has always been a fashionable residential district with fine villas and gardens and stately cypress groves. An Etruscan city, its foundation preceded that of Florence by many centuries, and, with its own local government, it is still proudly independent of the larger city. It is crowded with Florentines and visitors in summer when its position makes it one of the coolest places in the neighbourhood of the city.

Hotels. 4-star: *Villa San Michele*, 4 Via Doccia (with swimming pool) and *Villa Aurora*, 39 Piazza Mino. 3-star: *Villa Bonelli*, 1 Via F. Poeti. *Bencistà*, 4 Via Benedetto da Maiano. Rooms to let at the *Villa San Girolamo*, Via Vecchia Fiesolana. **Camping site**. *Panoramico*, 1 Via Peramonda (3-star).

Lovely places to **picnic** include the park below San Francesco; near the Roman theatre; near Maiano; and off the *Strada dei Bosconi* (particularly on the road to Vincigliata).

An **Annual Festival**, called the *Estate Fiesolana*, is held from the end of June to the end of August, with open-air performances of music, drama, and films in the Teatro Romano.

History. Excavations have proved that the hill was inhabited before the Bronze Age. The site of *Faesulae*, on a hilltop above a river valley, was typical of Etruscan settlements. Probably founded in the 6C or 5C BC from Arezzo, it became one of the chief cities of the Etruscan confederacy. With the Roman occupation it became the most important town in Etruria. After a decisive battle in 1125 the ascendancy of Florence over the older city was finally assured.

The bus from Florence (No. 7; see above) terminates in Piazza Mino da Fiesole, the main square, with the APT information office. The **Cathedral**, founded in 1028, was over-restored in the 19C. The tall battlemented bell-tower dates from 1213. The bare stone INTERIOR has a raised choir above a hall crypt. The massive columns have fine capitals (some of them Roman). Above the W door is a statue of St Romulus in a garlanded niche by Giovanni Della Robbia. In the CAPPELLA SALUTATI (right of the choir) are frescoes by Cosimo Rosselli, and the *tomb of Bishop Salutati with a fine portrait bust, and an *altar-frontal, both superb works by Mino da Fiesole. Over the high altar is a large *altarpiece by Bicci di Lorenzo. The CRYPT (restored in 1992) has interesting primitive capitals.

At the upper end of the piazza is the old *Palazzo Pretorio* next to the church of *Santa Maria Primerana* with a quaint porch. The equestrian monument (1906) in the square celebrates the meeting between Victor Emmanuel II and Garibaldi at Teano. Between the 17C Seminary and Bishop's Palace, Via San Francesco, a very steep paved lane, climbs up the hill past a terrace with a *view of Florence. The ancient church of **Sant'Ales-sandro** contains cipollino marble *columns with Ionic capitals and bases from a Roman building. At the top of the hill (345m), on the site of the Etruscan and later Roman acropolis are the convent buildings of **San Francesco**. The church contains altarpieces by Neri di Bicci, Piero di Cosimo, and Raffaellino del Garbo. A small missionary MUSEUM contains Eastern objets d'art. The wooded hillside is a public park.

From Piazza Mino the street behind the apse of the cathedral leads to the entrance to the ***Roman Theatre, Archaeological Excavations, and Museum** (adm. daily 9–dusk; closed Tues in winter). From the terrace there is a good comprehensive view of the excavations, which were begun in the 19C, in a plantation of olive trees. The ROMAN THEATRE (1C BC) held 3000 spectators (the seats on the right side are intact; the others have been restored). To the right are the ROMAN BATHS, reconstructed in 1892, probably built in the 1C AD and enlarged by Hadrian. A small terrace provides a fine view of a long stretch of ETRUSCAN WALLS which enclosed the city. NW of the theatre is a ROMAN TEMPLE (1C BC), and, on a lower level, remains of an ETRUSCAN TEMPLE (3C BC). The MUSEUM, built in 1912, contains a topographical collection (well labelled) from Fiesole and its territory ('she-wolf' in bronze, Bronze Age material, Etruscan stelai, urns, architectural fragments from the theatre and temples, and the *Stele Fieso-lana* (5C BC). The same ticket gives access to the *ANTIQUARIUM COSTAN-TINI nearby at No. 9 Via Portigiani, with a splendid collection of Greek vases. On the lower floor can be seen excavations of Roman structures made in 1988 and finds from them.

In Via Dupré is the small **Museo Bandini**, a collection of 13–15C Florentine paintings by Bernardo Daddi, Neri di Bicci, Taddeo Gaddi, Lorenzo Monaco, and Bicci di Lorenzo, etc. in a pretty little building built for the collection in 1913.

There are many beautiful old roads in the vicinity of Fiesole. Even though most of them are very narrow, they are still used by cars, and if you are on foot you should take great care of the traffic. From Piazza Mino *Via Santa Maria* and *Via Belvedere* climb up the hill with superb views to the wall along the E limit of the Etruscan city. Below are the beautiful woods of *Montececeri.* *Via Vecchia Fiesolana* descends steeply from the piazza and passes the *Villa Medici* built by Michelozzo for Cosimo il Vecchio. The beautiful garden on the steep hillside (adm. 9–15, Sat 9–12; closed Sun) stretches all the way up to Via Beato Angelico, the main road to Fiesole. A by-road leads to *Fontelucente* with a church built over a spring. It contains a triptych by Mariotto di Nardo. In Via Dupré is *Ville Le Coste* (No. 18) where the painter Primo Conti (1900–88) lived, and which contains a collection of his works (open 10–13 except Monday and fest.) The pretty *Via Benedetto da Maiano* diverges from the main Florence road below Fiesole for the hamlet of *Maiano* (2.5km; restaurants *La Graziella* and *Le Cave di Maiano*). The church contains a painting by Giovanni Battista Naldini. Nearby are disused quarries of pietra serena. Via del Salviatino returns down to Florence, while Via Benedetto da Maiano continues to Ponte a Mensola (see Rte 2B).

From Piazza Mino in Fiesole (see above) the main street continues uphill and, beyond Borgunto, the *Strada dei Bosconi* leads out of the town with increasingly beautiful views over the wide Mugnone valley to the N. It continues to (9km) L'Olmo where it joins Via Faentina which leads N for the Mugello valley (see Rte 3), while, soon after leaving Fiesole, a by-road diverges right for Montebeni and Settignano. It runs along a ridge round the the N shoulder of Monte Ceceri through magnificent woods. Just beyond Villa di Bosco there is a superb view of Florence. The road climbs to a fork; the road on the right continues past *Castel di Poggio* (restored in the 19C) and then descends, lined with magnificent cypresses, past (5km) the *Castello di Vincigliata*, the ruins of which were rebuilt in 1855 by John Temple Leader who planted the cypresses here. The road goes on downhill past Villa I Tatti for Settignano, see Rte 2B.

Longer trips may be taken to the N of Fiesole, to the Convento della Maddalena, Pratolino, and Montesenario, all described in Rte 3.

B.   Ponte a Mensola and Settignano

Bus No. 10 from Florence (Piazza San Marco) via Ponte a Mensola (frequent service in c 30min).

Rooms to let at the Benedictine convent *Villa Linda*, 5 Via Poggio Gherardo.

Restaurant (First-class) *Osvaldo*, Ponte a Mensola; trattoria *La Capponcina*, 17 Via San Romano, Settignano. Numerous places to **picnic** near Ponte a Mensola and Settignano.

At the foot of the hill of Settignano in the village of **Ponte a Mensola**, Via Poggio Gherardo branches left from the main road past the *Villa di Poggio Gherardo*, traditionally thought to be the setting for the earliest episodes in Boccaccio's *Decameron*. In 1888 it was purchased by Janet and Henry Ross. Nearby (right) is *SAN MARTINO A MENSOLA, a Benedictine church of the 9C, founded by St Andrew, thought to have been a Scotsman and archdeacon to the bishop of Fiesole, Donato, who was probably from Ireland. In the graceful 15C INTERIOR is a *triptych of the Madonna enthroned with two female saints by Taddeo Gaddi, and, on the high altar, a triptych with the donor Amerigo Zati by a follower of Orcagna (1391), known as the Master of San Martino a Mensola. In the N aisle is an *Annunciation by a follower of Fra Angelico, and a *Madonna and four saints by Neri di Bicci. A tiny MUSEUM contains a wooden *casket, decorated with paintings by the school of Agnolo Gaddi, which formerly contained the body of St Andrew and a reliquary bust of the saint (late 14C). Nearby is VILLA I TATTI (entrance on Via Vincigliata), the home of Bernard Berenson (1865–1959), the art historian and collector, and left by him to Harvard University as a Center of Italian Renaissance Studies. It contains his library (open to post-doctorate scholars) and *collection of Italian paintings (not open to the public, but shown to scholars with a letter of presentation by previous appointment). The Italianate garden was laid out by Cecil Pinsent in 1908–15. The pretty by-road continues up the hill through woods past the castles of Vincigliata and Poggio to (6km) Fiesole (see Rte 2A). In Via Vincigliata at the bottom of the hill are two plaques recording the writers and artists who lived and worked in the neighbourhood. The Villa Boccaccio (Via di Corbignano) was owned by the father of Giovanni Boccaccio who probably spent his youth here.

From Ponte a Mensola the road continues up to Settignano winding across the old road; both have fine views of the magnificent trees on the skyline of the surrounding hills. 7.5km **Settignano** (178m), a peaceful village, is known for its school of sculptors, most famous of whom were Desiderio and the brothers Rossellino. In the church is a Madonna and Child with two angels, attributed to the workshop of Andrea Della Robbia. In the lower Piazza Desiderio there is a superb view of Florence.

The numerous narrow lanes in and around Settignano, mostly with splendid views over unspoilt countryside are well worth exploring on foot. In Via Capponcina is *Villa Michelangelo* (No. 65; no adm.) where Michelangelo passed his youth. Via Rossellino diverges right from the narrow main road of Settignano to *Villa Gamberaia* (No. 72; 2km) which has a famous •garden (open weekdays 8–17; entrance fee; ring), remarkable for its topiary, azaleas, and ancient cypresses and pine trees.

C. Villamagna

Bus No. 23 from the station to Bagno a Ripoli, and from there Bus No. 48 to Villamagna.

From Piazza Ferrucci (Pl. 12) a road leads to Viale dei Mille for Bagno a Ripoli (see Rte 25), from which a road diverges left for the hamlet of Rimaggio. From here a pretty by-road leads up to *Vicchio di Rimaggio* with the church of San Lorenzo, just to the right of the road, in front of an old farmhouse and well, beside a group of cypresses and a palm tree. It is preceded by a portico and over the door is a good fresco of St Lawrence with two angels by the circle of Cosimo Rosselli. The interior (only open on Sunday) contains two 15C ciborium and a Madonna and Child attributed (from this work) to the Maestro di Vicchio di Rimaggio (c 1300). From Rimaggio a road (signposted Rosano and Pontassieve) continues through *Candeli* (5-star hotel *Villa La Massa*) with the church of Sant'Andrea, which contains a Madonna attributed to Bicci di Lorenzo. The narrow road continues uphill (with a fine view of the Arno). At a road fork is the entrance gate of *Villa La Tana*, impressively sited. This once belonged to Bianca Cappello but was rebuilt in 1740. The road now traverses woods before reaching (12km) **Villamagna** with the *Pieve di San Donnino* (if closed, ring at the priest's house at No. 1 in the lane above the church to the right). The church was founded by the 11C, and it preserves its Romanesque aspect. In the S aisle, stucco relief of the Madonna and Child surrounded by a 17C painting, and a triptych by Mariotto di Nardo, and the body of the Blessed Gherardo in a 16C urn. At the E end of the S aisle, frescoes attributed to the Maestro di Signa, and near the high altar, 16C Crucifix. At the E end of the N aisle •Madonna and Child with two saints by Francesco Granacci, who was born in Villamagna. On the N altar, fine 15C painting of the Madonna and saints in its original frame, and above the 16C font, a 14C painting of Saints John the Baptist and Anthony Abbot. On the opposite side of the main road a lane leads to Villa il Poggio, a Mannerist building. A road (signposted) leads up past the Oratory of the Blessed Gherardo with remains of 14C and 15C frescoes, to *Incontro* a splendid view point (557m).

The return to Florence may be made by continuing along the road from Villamagna through the Case di San Romolo and then descending (with wonderful views) through cypress woods to rejoin the main road along the S bank of the Arno. Rosano, 5km E is described in Rte 3.

D.   Poggio Imperiale and Pian de' Giullari

Bus No. 11 from Piazza San Marco and Via dei Strozzi for Poggio Imperiale.
Also Bus No. 38 (infrequent service) from Porta Romana for Poggio
Imperiale (Largo Fermi) and for Pian de' Giullari.

Outside Porta Romana (Pl. 13,14) Viale del Poggio Imperiale, a long straight
cypress avenue lined with handsome villas surrounded by gardens leads
up to the huge Villa of **Poggio Imperiale** (now a school; adm. readily
granted by previous appointment) with a neo-classical façade by Pasquale
Poccianti and Giuseppe Cacialli (1814–23). After 1565 this was the
residence of the grand-dukes of Florence. Some of its rooms are decorated
by Matteo Rosselli (1623), and others by Giuseppe Maria Terreni (1773). To
the left of the villa, in Largo Fermi, is the entrance to the *Observatory of
Arcetri*. Via San Leonardo (described in Rte 1K) leads back towards
Florence while Via Guglielmo Righini winds up past *Villa Capponi* (No. 3),
with a beautiful 16C *garden, to *Torre del Gallo*, reconstructed in medieval
style by Stefano Bardini in 1904–06. The road coninues to the pretty little
village of **Pian de' Giullari** (1st-class restaurant *Omero*, 11 Via Pian de'
Giullari) where *Villa di Gioiello* (No. 42) was the house where the aged
Galileo lived, practically as a prisoner, from 1631 until his death in 1642 (for
admission, ask at the observatory).

E.   Monteoliveto and Bellosguardo

Bus No. 13 (red) from the Station to Viale Raffaello Sanzio (for Monteoliveto)
and Piazza Torquato Tasso (for Bellosguardo). Bus No. 42 (infrequent
service) for Bellosguardo (going on to Marignolle) from Porta Romana.

On the S bank of the Arno, near Ponte della Vittoria (Pl. 5) is the thickly
wooded hill of MONTEOLIVETO with some beautiful private villas. It is
reached via Viale Raffaello Sanzio and (right) Via di Monteoliveto (Pl. 9).
A military hospital occupies the convent of the church of *San Bartolomeo*
(for adm. ring at No. 72A). It contains frescoes by Bernardino Poccetti and
Sodoma (Last Supper; very damaged), and an altarpiece by Santi di Tito.
The road ends in front of an entrance to the *Villa Strozzi* (open daily,
9–dusk), a beautiful wooded park, not kept as well as it might be.

The adjoining hill to the S is aptly called **Bellosguardo** (Pl. 9), with superb
views of Florence. It can be reached by foot from Monteoliveto by the pretty
Via di Monteoliveto, but the most direct approach from the centre of
Florence is from Piazza San Francesco di Paola (Pl. 9). In the piazza is an
ex-convent (No. 3; no adm.) bought by the sculptor Adolf Hildebrand in
1874, surrounded by a beautiful park, and the fantastic Villa Pagani built
by Coppedè in 1896. Via di Bellosguardo climbs uphill, with a view (right)
of *Villa dello Strozzino* a beautiful Renaissance villa. On the right, beside
a group of pine trees, is *Villa Brichieri-Colombi* (No. 20) owned in 1849–73
by Miss Isa Blagden who was often visited here by the Brownings. Henry
James wrote *The Aspern Papers* while staying at the villa in 1887.

A road on the left leads to the *Torre di Bellosguardo* with a delightful
garden. From the quiet Piazza di Bellosguardo is the entrance to the *Villa
dell'Ombrellino*, where Violet Trefusis lived until her death in 1973. It was

ostentatiously restored in 1988 as a trade centre. Via San Carlo leads out of the opposite side of the piazza to *Villa di Montauto* where Nathaniel Hawthorne stayed in 1859. Via Piana continues from Piazza di Bellosguardo to Via di Santa Maria a Marignolle which leads left (no entry to cars) to *Villa La Colombaia* (No. 2), now a convent school, where Florence Nightingale was born.

F.   The Certosa del Galluzzo

Bus 37 from the Station.

Outside Porta Romana Via Senese (Pl. 13) climbs uphill, and continues through (5km) the village of *Galluzzo* (First-class restaurant *Da Bibe*, 1 Via delle Bagnese, Ponte all'Asse), just beyond which, well seen on a picturesque hill on the right of the road, is the *Certosa del Galluzzo. Visitors are conducted by a monk (9–12, 15 or 14.30–17 or 18; closed Monday). The monastery was founded in 1342 by Niccolò Acciaioli. In the CHURCH is the *tomb-slab of Cardinal Agnolo II Acciaioli, now attributed to Francesco da Sangallo. The CHAPTER HOUSE has another expressive tomb-slab by Francesco da Sangallo, and a fresco of the Crucifixion by Mariotto Albertinelli. The secluded *GREAT CLOISTER with tondi by the Della Robbia, is surrounded by the monks' cells, one of which may be visited. On the upper floor of the PALAZZO DEGLI STUDI, a fine Gothic hall, is a picture gallery with five frescoed *lunettes of the Passion cycle by Pontormo, detached from the cloister, painted while he was staying in the monastery in 1522, and Florentine paintings of the 14C and 15C.

From (7.5km) *Le Rose* a long but pleasant walk follows a narrow road through beautiful countryside up to Impruneta (described in Rte 13A). Another road from Galluzzo via San Felice a Ema leads up to *Pozzolatico*, where the church of Santo Stefano has a painting of the Madonna delle Grazie by Jacopo del Casentino (c 1340), inserted into a larger painting by Giovanni Martinelli (1647) of saints Dominic, Catherine, and the Mysteries of the Rosary. This road continues via San Gersolé to Impruneta (see Rte 13A).

G.   Poggio a Caiano and Artimino

Information Office. APT of Prato, 48 Via Cairoli, Prato (Tel. 0574/24112).

Buses (COPIT or CAP) from 9 Largo Alinari every half hour (in c 30mins) to Poggio a Caiano. From Poggio a Caiano bus via Comeana to Artimino in 20 minutes, and via Seano to Carmignano (in 20mins).

From Porta al Prato (Pl. 1) Via delle Porte Nuove (signposted for Pistoia) leads out of Florence though an unattractive part of the city. 6km **Peretola** was the home of the Vespucci family before they moved to Florence. The church of Santa Maria contains a *tabernacle by Luca Della Robbia (1441). The small airport at Peretola (see Rte 1) is beside the motorway from Florence to the coast. At the Firenze-Nord exit, a few kilometres N, is the church of San Giovanni Battista, built in 1960–64 by Giovanni Michelucci.

The Certosa del Galluzzo

The uninteresting road for Poggio a Caiano continues through the suburb of (9km) *Brozzi*, where the church of Sant'Andrea has frescoes by Domenico Ghirlandaio and pupils. From (13km) *San Piero a Ponti* a road leads N to Campi Bisenzio (2km).

Campi Bisenzio, now a large industrial suburb (35,000 inhab.) of Florence, has ancient origins. It was granted privileges in 780 by Charlemagne. Situated in low-lying ground, it has often been subject to flooding from the river Bisenzio. In Piazza Matteotti are *Palazzo del Podestà*, with coats of arms on its façade, and the *Pieve di Santo Stefano*, founded in 936. It was restored in neo-classical style in 1835 and given its façade in 1938. It contains two fine stoups, a fresco of the Annunciation by Paolo Schiavo, a painting of St Anthony Abbot and the angel by Francesco Curradi (c 1650), and an altarpiece of the Madonna and Child with saints attributed to Sebastiano Mainardi. In the adjoining Teatro della Pieve is a fresco fragment of the Annunication and Holy Trinity attributed to Raffaellino del Garbo. The *Teatro Dante* was built by Falcini in 1871. Across the Bisenzio is the *Rocca Strozzi* rebuilt in 1377 and the church of *Santa Maria* which contains a chapel frescoed by Mariotto di Cristofano in 1420, and a 15C Crucifix.

18km **Poggio a Caiano**, a pleasant village at the foot of Monte Albano, is famous for its royal *VILLA (open 9–13.30), rebuilt in 1480 by Giuliano da Sangallo for Lorenzo il Magnifico. It became his favourite country villa, and was used by the Medici dynasty, including Francesco I and Bianca Cappello (who both died here on the same day in 1587), and subsequently by the Austrians and French grand-dukes, and the kings of Italy. It is surrounded by a fine park and garden (open 9–dusk). The fine rectangular building stands on a broad terrace surrounded by a colonnade. A classical Ionic portico on the first floor with the Medici arms in the tympanum bears a beautiful polychrome enamelled terracotta frieze attributed to Andrea del Sansovino (c 1490; a copy of the original which is now kept inside the villa). The semicircular steps were added by Pasquale Poccianti in 1802–07.

On the GROUND FLOOR are a little 17C theatre and a billiard room charmingly decorated in the 19C. On the FIRST FLOOR is the *SALONE, with a barrel vault, and two frescoes by Franciabigio and Andrea del Sarto illustrating incidents in Roman history paralleled in the history of Cosimo il Vecchio and Lorenzo. They were completed by Alessandro Allori. The remarkable *lunette of Vertumnus and Pomona is a very fine work by Pontormo. In another room are a series of delightful large still-lifes by Benedetto Bimbi.

From the main street of Poggio a Caiano a road (signposted) leads SW for (3km) *Comeana*, near which is the *TUMULUS OF MONTEFORTINI, now covered with oak trees, beside the road (entrance gate on the left; admission 9–12 except Monday). It contains an Etruscan chamber tomb and dromos (c 620 BC). Since 1980 excavations have been in progress of a second tomb (no adm.) built some 30 years earlier in the same tumulus, with a circular inner chamber supported by a central column 6m high. The main road winds up steeply through pretty woods to emerge beside (7km) the beautiful ***Villa di Artimino**, designed by Bernardo Buontalenti in 1594 for Ferdinando I. In a delightful position surrounded by superb Tuscan countryside, this is one of the finest Medici villas. This hill top site, between the Ombrone and Arno rivers was occupied by an Etruscan settlement from the 7C BC. Finds from excavations (still in progress) of the Etruscan-Roman settlement and its necropoli are exhibited in the MUSEO ARCHEOLOGICO COMUNALE in the basement of the villa (open 9–12.30 except Wednesday; Saturday 9–13, 15–19). These include a rare *incense burner in Bucchero ware (7C BC) with an elegant stand and an *amphora (late 6C BC or early 5C BC), both found at Prato di Rosello; and a well preserved service for use at banquets in bronze (4C BC).

On a little hill in front of the villa is the charming medieval borgo of **Artimino** (4-star hotel *Paggeria Medicea*, and first-class restaurant *La Delfina*), with a fine Romanesque church.

From Poggio a Caiano another pretty by-road (signposted) leads to (5km) *Carmignano* where the church of San Michele contains a remarkable altarpiece of the *Visitation by Pontormo (c 1530). This area has been famous since the 14C for its wine (produced with the addition of cabernet grapes), in particular at Bacchereto (restaurant *La Cantina di Toia*) and Capezzana (red wine, rosé, and 'vin santo'). At *Seano* a sculpture park was opened in 1988 with works by the native sculptor Quinto Martini. The road continues across Monte Albano past the Romanesque church of San Giusto to descend to (20km) *Vinci*, described in Rte 11.

H.   The Medici villas of Careggi, La Petraia, and Castello. Sesto Fiorentino

Bus No. 14C from the Station or Via de' Pucci to the Villa di Careggi (the penultimate request stop before the terminus). Bus No. 28 from the Station for La Petraia, Castello, and Sesto. A bus is recommended to traverse the uninteresting N suburbs of Florence, but pretty country walks may be taken in the hills behind Careggi and La Petraia.

From the Fortezza da Basso (Pl. 2) Via del Romito and its continuation Via Corridoni lead N to (3km) Piazza Dalmazia in the suburbs of Rifredi. The broad Viale Morgagni leads up to Careggi, which has given its name to the main hospital of Florence. At the top of the hill, beyond the buildings of the hospital, is the **Villa Medicea di Careggi**, in a well-wooded park, now used as offices by the hospital (adm. only with special permission). A 14C castellated farmhouse here was enlarged (and a loggia added) by Michelozzo for Cosimo il Vecchio in 1434. This was the literary and artistic centre of the Medicean court, and the meeting place of the famous Platonic Academy which saw the birth of the humanist movement of the Renaissance. In the villa, Cosimo il Vecchio, Piero di Cosimo, and Lorenzo il Magnifico all died. In 1848 it was restored by Francis Sloane. Walks may be taken in the hills behind Careggi at the foot of Monte Morello. A road follows the Terzolle stream past the little oratory of the Loggia dei Bianchi, with a miniature cupola, through the hamlet of *Serpiolle* (first-class restaurants *Strettoio*, 7 Via di Serpiolle and *Dulcamare Club*, 2 Via Dante da Castiglione), and continues through beautiful countryside up to *Cercina* (first-class restaurants *Trianon*, and *I Ricchi*) with a fine Romanesque church.

From Piazza Dalmazia Bus No. 28 continues along the busy Via Reginaldo Giuliano. Just beyond (5km) the locality of Il Sodo (request stop), a narrow road to the right leads up to **Villa della Petraia** (adm. 9–dusk). Once a castle of the Brunelleschi, the villa was rebuilt in 1575 for the Ferdinando I by Buontalenti. In 1864–70 it was a favourite residence of Victor Emmanuel II, and in 1919 it was presented to the State by Victor Emmanuel III. A pretty garden and moat precede the villa, which still preserves a tower of the old castle. On the upper terrace is the base of a fountain by Tribolo and Pierino da Vinci. A magnificent PARK, with ancient cypresses, extends behind the villa to the E. The Villa is shown on request. The courtyard has decorative *frescoes illustrating the history of the Medici family, by Volterrano and Cosimo Daddi. In a room here is displayed the bronze group of Antaeus and Hercules by Ammannati from the fountain in Villa di Castello. The rooms were furnished as state apartments in the 19C. On the first floor the private apartments, decorated in neo-classical style, contain the original bronze statue of *Venus by Giambologna, removed from the fountain in the garden. The gaming room is a remarkable 'period piece' hung with 17C paintings.

In Via della Petraia is Villa *Il Bel Riposo* where Carlo Lorenzini (Collodi) lived while writing *Pinocchio*, and the *Villa Corsini* rebuilt in 1698 by Antonio Ferri, with an interesting Baroque façade. A plaque records the death here in 1649 of Sir Robert Dudley. The villa and garden are sometimes open for exhibitions and concerts in May. In front of the villa Via di Castello leads shortly to **Villa di Castello** (adm. to the gardens only, as for La Petraia), now the seat of the Accademia della Crusca, founded in 1582, for the study of the Italian language. The villa was acquired by Giovanni and Lorenzo di Pierfrancesco de'Medici, Lorenzo il Magnifico's younger cousins, around 1477. Here they hung Botticelli's famous 'Birth of Venus'. The typical Tuscan *GARDEN, described by numerous travellers in the 16C and 17C, was laid out by Tribolo for Cosimo I in 1541. The *fountain by Tribolo was crowned by a bronze group by Ammannati (now kept in Villa della Petraia). The gardens also contain a grotto, a colossus by Ammannati, and an orangery. At the bottom of the avenue in front of the villa is the trattoria *Soldi*, the successor to the *Osteria Tricci* frequented by Carlo Lorenzini (see above).

Lovely country walks may be taken on the hillside above Via Giovanni da San Giovanni. A narrow rural road (Via di Castello; parallel to the main road lower down the hill) continues beyond Villa di Castello towards Sesto passing *Quinto* where *La Montagnola* (ring at No. 95 on Saturday or Sunday, 10–13) is a tumulus containing a remarkable domed tholos burial chamber of the Etruscan era.

The bus route ends at (9km) **Sesto Fiorentino**, a small town (41,000 inhab.; 4-star hotel *Villa Villoresi*, 2 Via Ciampi, Colonnata; 3-star *Park Hotel Alexander*, 200 Viale XX Settembre). At the entrance on the left is *Villa Corsi Salviati*, where exhibitions are held, with an 18C garden. Next to the Ginori porcelain factory, entered at No. 31 Via Pratese, is the MUSEO DELLE PORCELLANE DI DOCCIA (adm. Tuesday, Thursday, and Saturday 9.30–13, 15.30–18.30) in a fine building by Piero Berardi (1965). It contains a large well-displayed *collection of porcelain made in the famous Doccia factory founded by Carlo Ginori in 1735. The firm, known as Richard-Ginori since 1896, continues to flourish. Across the road, in an inconspicuous one-storey warehouse, Ginori seconds can be purchased.

At the foot of the hills is the *Villa Ginori* at Doccia, with a huge park and cypress avenue, created by Leopoldo Carlo Ginori in 1816. Here exceptionally interesting remains of the old Ginori factory survive. From Sesto a road leads inland via Colonnata to the *Strada Panoramica dei Colli Alti* which skirts the wooded slopes of *Monte Morello* (934m), with magnificent views, as far as Via Bolognese (see Rte 3).

3

The Mugello and the Val di Sieve

The **MUGELLO** is the area N of Florence which extends either side of the upper basin of the Sieve river. The beautiful landscape consists of wooded hills rising above the cultivated valley. The small towns of Borgo San Lorenzo, San Piero a Sieve, and Scarperia contain interesting buildings, and Vicchio is famous as the birthplace of Giotto. Numerous churches and villas are dotted around the hills. The **Alto Mugello** extends up to the Apennine passes and the border with Emilia-Romagna. The **Val di Sieve** is the area NE of Florence around the wine-growing centres of Pontassieve and Rufina. The whole area has been opened up to hiking along nature trails: information from the *Comunità Montana*, who publish a guide and a map, and from the Associazione Turismo Ambiente, both in Borgo San Lorenzo. Borgo San Lorenzo was severely damaged by earthquake in 1919, and the Mugello suffered further in the last World War from its proximity to the 'Gothic' Line across the Apennines.

Information Office and accommodation booking service at the *Consorzio Turistico Mugello*, 7 Via Garibaldi, Borgo San Lorenzo (Tel. 055/8458045). Comunità Montana Mugello, 45 Via Togliatti, Borgo San Lorenzo (Tel. 055/8495346). Associazione Turismo Ambiente, 29 Piazza Dante, Borgo San Lorenzo (Tel. 055/8458793).

Approaches by road from Florence. There are two direct roads from Florence to the Mugello, the Via Faentina (N302), the most attractive road, and the Via Bolognese (N65) which offers a slightly faster approach. The Faentina can also be joined at l'Olmo from a beautiful secondary road which leads along the hills beyond Fiesole (see Rte 2). The Val di Sieve can be reached directly from Florence E along the Arno on the Arezzo road (N69) as far as Pontassieve, and then by N67 which follows the Sieve N to Rufina and Dicomano.

The distances from Florence following a circular route in a clockwise direction from the Via Faentina as described in the route below, are as follows: 17km *Polcanto*—29km **Borgo San Lorenzo** (**San Piero a Sieve**, 5.5km W; **Scarperia**, 4km N). N551—36km **Vicchio**—44km *Dicomano*—54km *Rufina*—61km **Pontassieve**—66.5km *Le Sieci*—79km **Florence**.

Bus services. SITA and CAP provide a frequent service from Florence to San Piero a Sieve (in 50mins) and to Borgo San Lorenzo (in 1 hour). Other services connect Borgo San Lorenzo to San Piero a Sieve, Cafaggiolo, and Scarperia; and Vicchio, Dicomano, etc.

Florence city buses (ATAF) run along Via Bolognese as far as Pratolino (No. 25); and along Via Faentina as far as La Maddalena (No. 12) and Olmo (No. 70 from Fiesole).

Railway. A secondary line from Florence to Faenza runs via Pontassieve, Rufina, Dicomano, and Vicchio to Borgo San Lorenzo (in 60–70 minutes). There are long-term plans to reactivate the secondary line along the Faentina from Florence to Borgo San Lorenzo (out of action since the Second World War).

FROM FLORENCE TO SAN PIERO A SIEVE VIA THE VIA BOLOGNESE, 26km. The **Via Bolognese** which leaves Florence N of Piazza della Libertà (Pl. 3) at Ponte Rosso, is the old Roman road to Bologna. Beyond La Lastra the road climbs up to Trespiano, with the large cemetery of Florence. At Pian di San Bartolo Via della Docciola diverges left for the pretty Romanesque church of Cercina in lovely countryside N of Careggi (see Rte 2H). Just beyond Montorsoli a scenic road diverges left to skirt the foothills of Monte Morello as far as Calenzano (see Rte 2H). The main road now skirts the long ruined walls of the huge park of Villa Demidoff, the entrance of which is at (12.5km) **Pratolino** (4-star hotel *Villa Demidoff*, with swimming pool; first-class restaurant *Villa Vecchia*). Some 17–18 hectares of the splendid well-kept park of **Villa Demidoff** are open to the public in the summer (1 May–end of September), Thursday, Friday, Saturday, and fest. 10–20; car park on the left of the main road. A colossal statue of *Appennino (1579–80) here, by Giambologna, presents one of the most extraordinary sights in Italy. In the Medici villa (demolished in 1824) Galileo stayed in 1605–06 as tutor to Cosimo, eldest son of Ferdinando I.

On the right a pretty by-road diverges for L'Olmo on the Faentina (see below), and an alternative road for Montesenario. The main road now descends left with a fine view of the Carza valley to (18km) Vaglia. On the right a by-road leads to the little hill resort of *Bivigliano* (5km; 3-star hotel *Giotto*; 2-star camping site *Poggio degli Uccellini*) with the church of San Romolo (open at weekends) which contains a Della Robbian terracotta, and a 15C wood statue of St John the Baptist. A by-road (signposted) leads along a ridge up to the convent of **Montesenario** (7km), on a hill top (817m). On foot, there is a path up through the woods past the cemetery and some grottoes; for drivers, there is a car park at the top of the hill. Here seven Florentine merchants became hermits and established the Servite Order of mendicant friars in 1233. The *views are superb, and include (on a clear day) the whole Mugello valley. In the piazzale are two statues (1754) by Pompilio Ticciati. The church and convent were enlarged by Cosimo I in 1539, and then rebuilt in 1717. The clock tower dates from 1834. The CHURCH (open daily) has an 18C interior with elaborate stuccoes and a fresco by Antonio Domenico Gabbiani in the vault. In the sanctuary is a

Crucifix in polychrome stucco by Ferdinando Tacca, and two paintings by Tommaso Redi. In the choir, behind, are paintings by Giuseppe Bezzuoli (Assunta, 1849), Giuseppe Cassioli (St Joseph, 1937), and Pietro Annigoni (Seven founders of the Order, 1985). The Oratory of San Filippo contains a 15C polychrome terracotta Deposition group. Off the nave is the Chapel of the Seven Founders added in 1933 in a neo-Gothic style by Giuseppe Cassioli (who also made the urn over the altar). Above the door into the Sacristy, which contains two grisaille paintings, is a 14C painting of the Madonna and Saints. In the refectory of the CONVENT (admission on request) is a frescoed *Cenacolo by Matteo Rosselli.

The Via Bolognese continues and forks left from the road into (26km) **San Piero a Sieve**, described below.

The **Via Faentina** leaves Florence N of Piazza delle Cure (N of Pl. 4) and outside the city crosses the steep road which connects the hills of San Domenico di Fiesole (view of the Badia Fiesolana) and Careggi (view of Villa Salviati). It now follows the floor of the Mugnone valley which opens out at *Pian di Mugnone*, where a new road right leads up to Fiesole (see Rte 2). Just beyond the village of *Le Caldine* (where some unattractive new building has recently taken place) is the convent of **La Maddalena** on the right of the road. This was a hospice of the Dominican convent of San Marco, and it is now run by two friars. Here Fra Bartolomeo lived and painted several fresoes, including the Noli me Tangere in the little chapel in the orchard. Vistors ring at the convent (preferably 10–12, 16–18) and are conducted by a friar. The convent was built c 1470–85 probably on a design by Michelozzo. The church contains a *Madonna in Maestà attributed to the Master of the Horne triptych, and an Annunciation by Fra Bartolomeo above a presepio with terracotta figures attributed to Andrea Della Robbia. The portico, cloister, and refectory are also usually shown.

The road now becomes much prettier, traversing olive groves and vineyards and farms dotted with cypresses. At *La Querciola* the road begins to climb gently. Just beyond (13km) *L'Olmo* (3-star hotel and restaurant *Dino*; trattorie *Casa del Prosciutto*, and *Da Mario*, Torre di Buiano) is a crossroads (on the right is a beautiful road from Fiesole, and on the left is a road for Pratolino, see above). The main road continues straight on to reach the summit of Vetta Le Croci (first-class restaurant *Feriolo*, just over the hill, and pizzeria *Las Vegas*) before descending into the Mugello, with a landscape of fields and austere wooded hills. Beyond (17km) *Polcanto* the road continues to descend and then the view opens out. A by-road (left) from Polcanto leads steeply up through beautiful countryside with views of the Mugello valley to the *Badia di Buonsolazzo*, a Benedictine foundation with a worn 18C façade. The by-road continues to join a secondary road to Vaglia on the Via Bolognese (see above). The Via Faentina continues past (right) the church of Santa Felicità at (23km) *Faltona*. The church (usually locked), with a tall tower, contains a stained glass window (in the chapel of the Rosario, 1647) of St Felicity with her seven children, recently restored and attributed to the circle of Andrea del Castagno. The road continues right for Borgo San Lorenzo (leaving the road for San Piero a Sieve on the left) past the well-kept 18C *Villa Guiducci a Serravalle* (with a painted coat of arms on the bright yellow façade).

The view opens out and takes in the wide valley of the Sieve. Beyond the Sagginale crossroads (see below) a modern bridge leads into (29km) **BORGO SAN LORENZO** (14,800 inhab.), the main town of the Mugello, in the centre of the Sieve valley. Up until the 1950s it was a thriving market town, and since the 1960s numerous small industries have set up factories on the plain towards Scarperia.

Information Offices. *Consorzio Turistico Mugello* (information office and hotel booking service), 7 Via Garibaldi. *Comunità Montana Mugello* (which also provides information about hiking), 45 Via Togliatti (Tel. 8495346).

Buses. Frequent services (SITA and CAP) from Florence in 1 hr (and a wide network throughout the Mugello).

Car Parking, Piazza Dante.

Railway Station on the Florence–Faenza secondary line, from Florence via Pontassieve, Rufina, Dicomano, and Vicchio (infrequent services in 60–70 minutes).

Hotel. 3-star: *Villa Ebe* at Ferracciano, 3km outside.

Market on Tuesdays.

History. Of ancient foundation, Borgo San Lorenzo was once a possession of the Ubaldini, and from the 10C was owned by the Bishop of Florence. In a central position on a crossing of the Sieve it became a dominion of Florence after 1290. It suffered a severe earthquake in 1919. The famous Chini ceramic factories, founded by Galileo and Chino Chini, both natives of Borgo, were active here from 1906–44, producing notable ceramic decoration, stained glass, etc., much of it still to be found in the town.

In the pleasant old centre (now closed to traffic) of the town is the *Palazzo del Podestà* with numerous well-preserved coats of arms on its façade (including Della Robbian works). It is now the seat of the Biblioteca Comunale: on the ground floor are more coats of arms and frescoes including a 16C Florentine Madonna and Child with saints. Nearby is the large **Pieve di San Lorenzo**, first mentioned in 941 and rebuilt in the 12C. It was altered later and restored in 1937 after earthquake damage. The campanile is described below. The INTERIOR has pretty side altars erected in 1503. NORTH AISLE: first altar, 17C Florentine school, Saints Anthony Abbot and Anthony of Padua; second altar, Matteo Rosselli, Madonna and Saints Domenic and Francis; third altar, Bachiacca (attributed), *Saints Benedict, Sebastian, and Domenic (with angels in the lunette above); fourth altar, Jacopo Vignali, Madonna in glory with Saints (removed). Over the HIGH ALTAR, 14C painted Crucifix, and in the apse, mural painting by Galileo Chini (1906). At the end of the SOUTH AISLE, *Madonna, a ruined fragment attributed to Giotto. Fourth altar, Agnolo Gaddi (attributed), *Madonna enthroned with angels; third altar, Paolo Colli (died 1822), St Michael, and a 15C polychrome terracotta bust of St Lawrence. Beyond a 16C fresco of the Madonna (removed), the second altarpiece of the Lamentation over the Dead Christ is by Cesare Velli (1591).

Outside the church is a *Tabernacle of St Francis*, brightly decorated in 1926 with paintings and polychrome terracotta by the Chini workshop (restored in 1989). Corso Matteotti divides the old town roughly in half. Just before it passes beneath a gate with a clock tower (which still keeps the hours) a side street right leads to the foot of the unusual *Campanile of San Lorenzo*, built in 1263 above the apse. It is circular beneath and irregularly hexagonal above. Corso Matteotti continues towards a less attractive part of the town past the police station with a ceramic eagle by Chini, and some way further on ends beside the SANTUARIO DEL SANTISSIMO CROCIFISSO on the edge of the town. This centrally-planned building was built by Girolamo Ticciati in 1714–43 on the site of an oratory dedicated to a miraculous Crucifix venerated since c 1400. It was ruined in the earthquake of 1919 but has been reconstructed. INTERIOR. The fine high altarpiece of the guardian angel protecting Borgo from the earthquake of 1835 is by

Giuseppe Bezzuoli. Behind it is kept the miraculous Crucifix attributed to the school of Giovanni Pisano, exhibited only on the first Sunday of every month. The eight paintings of the Passion of Christ are by Luigi Sabatelli and the right altarpiece (the Baptism of Constantine) is by Ignazio Hugford. The Cappella della Compagnia, off the left side of the church, has stained glass by the Chini workshop (1922).

On the left of the sanctuary is the deconsecrated Gothic church of SAN FRANCESCO (privately owned; ring for adm. at the ex convent) with an interesting Cistercian interior with Giottesque frescoes recently restored. Nearby is the large *Villa Pecori-Giraldi*, with a 16C façade and a 19C tower. Owned by the Comune it is being restored (interesting Art Nouveau details in the interior). The park is open to the public.

On the other side of the town, on Piazza Dante, with a public garden, is the headquarters of the *Misericordia* (1908) with a neo-Gothic exterior and a majolica Pietà by Galileo Chini over the doorway. Inside the chapel are two side altars and two kneeling angels in enamelled terracotta by Galileo Chini, who also painted the apse.

FROM BORGO SAN LORENZO TO MARRADI AND PALAZZUOLO SUL SENIO. An annual race is held on this road from Faenza to Florence in spring known as the *100 kilometri del passatore*. The Faentina, followed by the railway, continues N of Borgo San Lorenzo past (2km) an avenue on the left of the road which leads to *San Giovanni Maggiore* (open on Sunday), surrounded by farm buildings. It has a portico and an 11C octagonal campanile. Founded in the 10C, the church was rebuilt by Francesco Minerbetti in 1520–30 and transformed in the 19C. It contains an elegant 12C *ambone. The stained glass is by the Chini factory, and the nave was frescoed in 1843 by Pietro Alessi Chini.

The main road continues through Panicaglia to (9km) *Ronta*, a quiet little summer resort, and the *Madonna dei Tre Fiumi* (3-star hotel *Tre Fiume*) in a fine position. The road climbs to (18km) the *Colle di Casaglia* (913m) at the watershed between the Sieve and Lamone valleys. Here is the junction for a road to Palazzuolo sul Senio (see below). The road descends the Lamone valley to (36km) **Marradi** (3-star hotel *Il Lamone*; first-class restaurant *Il Camino*), which lies in a narrow stretch of naturally defended valley at the foot of the Apennines which divide Tuscany from Emilia Romagna. It came under Florentine dominion from 1428 onwards. Its capture in 1944 made a breach in the German 'Gothic' line. The Piazza Le Scalelle is named after a mountain pass which was the scene of a victory of the citizens of Marradi in 1358 over Corrado Lando. On the outskirts of the town is the Teatro degli Animosi, built in 1792 by Giulio Mannaioni (recently restored and reopened). A huge old water-mill, now abandoned, survives from the early 20C. A by-road leads to *Badia del Borgo* (first documented in 1025), reconstructed in 1741–65. In the sacristy are preserved 15C paintings attributed to the Master of Marradi.

A winding mountain road (11.5km) connects Marradi with **Palazzuolo sul Senio** (3-star hotel *Senio* with restaurant; 2-star camping site *Visano*) in the Senio valley to the NW. It was ruled by the Ubaldini until 1362 when it came under Florentine dominion. In the picturesque 14C *Palazzo dei Capitani* is the *Museo della Vita e del lavoro delle genti di Montagna*, a fine local ethnographical museum (usually open in the afternoon). Next to it, above a garden, is the 17C church of Santi Carlo e Antonio with an interesting interior. The parish church of Santo Stefano contains Florentine 16–17C paintings, decorations by Dino Chini (1945), and a small museum. The medieval *Pieve di Misileo* (rebuilt in 1781), 8km from Palazzuolo, preserves a Romanesque crypt and a 15C painting of the Madonna and Saints (recently restored).

Another road leads N from Borgo San Lorenzo via *Luco di Mugello* (where the hospital in a former monastery has a beautiful Renaissance courtyard), to *Grezzano* (7km). Here in the *Casa d'Erci*, an old farmhouse, is a delightful private museum (open on holidays 14.30–18.30; summer 15.30–19.30) of agricultural implements and artisans' tools, all of them still in working order, illustrating life in the Mugello up until the last War. It is organised by a group of local volunteers.

A road (5.5km) leads W from Borgo San Lorenzo to **San Piero a Sieve** (2-star hotel _La Felicina_ with restaurant; 3-star camping site _Mugello Verde_, at La Fortezza), at a crossroads connecting the Mugello plain with the Apennine passes via Scarperia and Barberino del Mugello, and where the river Sieve meets the Carza. The _Pieve di San Pietro_, at the entrance to the village on the main road from Vaglia, was founded in the 11C and altered in the 18C. The baptismal font is a fine work by the Della Robbia. Above the high altar is a wood Crucifix attributed to Raffaello da Montelupo. The stained glass windows and painting of St Peter are interesting. Outside is a statue of St Peter by Girolamo Ticciati (1768) and a war memorial. Across the main road Via della Compagnia ascends past a little 13C oratory to _Palazzo Adami_ with terracotta decorations. A country track continues up to the large 16C _Fortezza di San Martino_, surrounded by pine woods, designed for the Medici by Bernardo Buontalenti to guard Florence from the N. It is one of the most interesting examples of Renaissance military architecture left in Tuscany. It is open only in summer on weekends. From Palazzo Adami, Via dei Medici descends through Piazza Gramsci past the large _Villa Schifanoia_ (formerly Medici) built in terraces on the hillside with a dovecot in the tower, and (right) an ancient house with arches, past the _Municipio_ with polychrome majolica decoration (1925), into the central Piazza Colonna.

Outside the village, just after a bridge over the Sieve, a by-road (3km; signposted) leads left to **Bosco ai Frati**, a charming little convent (four friars live here) in pretty wooded country (known locally for its mushrooms). Visitors are conducted (closed 12–15). The convent was founded before 1000 and the Franciscans came here in 1212. In 1273 St Bonaventura was staying in the convent when he became Cardinal. It was purchased by Cosimo il Vecchio in 1420 and he employed Michelozzo to restore the church and convent (he added the fine porch behind the church). Off the cloister a little Museum contains a *Crucifix attributed to Donatello (restored after earthquake damage). Another Crucifix attributed to Desiderio da Settignano was stolen in 1969.

A few kilometres W of San Piero a Sieve are the delightful Medici fortified villas of Trebbio and Cafaggiolo. They are reached by the main road (N65) to Barberino di Mugello which diverges from the Vaglia road 2km S of the village. Soon after the turn there is a view of Trebbio on its hill to the left of the road, and an unsurfaced road (signposted; 2km) ascends through pretty woods to the little hamlet around the **Castello del Trebbio** in a lovely elevated position. The castle (privately owned; for adm. telephone the Associazione Turistico Ambiente, 055 8458793), surrounded by cypresses, was built by Michelozzo for Cosimo il Vecchio in 1461 as a country residence. It remained the property of the Medici until 1644. A beautiful Italianate 15C garden with a long 17C pergola survives. The villa was the residence of Giovanni Dalle Bande Nere and Maria Salviati, and Amerigo Vespucci may have been a guest here in 1476.

The main road continues and soon skirts the garden railing of the **Villa di Cafaggiolo**, a huge castle well seen from the road (privately owned; adm. as for Trebbio). It is surrounded by a park with some fine trees, although one of the cedars of Lebanon in front of the villa has recently been damaged in a storm. This was the first country villa built by Michelozzo for Cosimo il Vecchio. It was erected in 1451 on the site of a castle. Leo X stayed here in 1515, and it was the favourite country house of Ferdinando I and of the Lorraine grand-dukes. The impressive exterior, which formerly had two towers and was surrounded by a moat, is more interesting than the interior, which has some 19C decorations restored in 1887 by the Chini brothers on

The Villa di Cafaggiolo, built in 1451 by Michelozzo for Cosimo il Vecchio

the ground floor. In 1500 Pierfrancesco de' Medici founded a ceramic manufactory in the buildings to the left of the villa. It was famous for its products especially up to c 1520.

FROM SAN PIERO A SIEVE TO BARBERINO DI MUGELLO AND THE FUTA PASS, N65, 25km. From the road fork 2km SW of San Piero, N65 diverges left from N503 and soon passes the by-road for Trebbio and then skirts the villa of Cafaggiolo (described above). The Barberino road is being realigned to avoid the huge artificial lake of *Bilancino* under construction since 1984. The dam here will control the waters of the Sieve (and their confluence with the Arno at Pontassieve in times of flood), and increase Florence's water supply, although legal proceedings are in process to discover how the funds have been used. At (7km) a by-road leads right for *Galliano* (4km), founded in 1048 by the Ubaldini at the foot of an Apennine pass (remains of its fortifications survive). The Pieve has a dome frescoed by Tito Chini (1920). It contains a Madonna and Child attributed to Margaritone di Arezzo and a Madonna and Child with saints attributed to the school of Ghirlandaio. In the adjoining oratory is an Annunciatory Virgin by Davide Ghirlandio. In the church of Santo Stefano a Rezzano is a Madonna and saints attributed to Filippino Lippi. The main road (realigned) continues left for (11km) **Barberino di Mugello** (2-star camping site *Il Sergente*, località Monte di F), well known because of its vicinity to the Florence–Bologna motorway. A borgo grew up here in the 11C around a castle of the Cattani. Of great strategic importance on an Apennine pass, it was sacked by many armies, including that of Sir John Hawkwood (in 1364). It was badly damaged in the last War. In Piazza Cavour is Palazzo Pretorio, and a portico attributed to Michelozzo. The Pieve contains a precious organ (16C–19C), and the Oratory next door has good woodwork. The church of *Cavallina* (2km S) contains a fine carved tabernacle attributed to Mino da Fiesole, and a 16C Madonna and Child with saints. Also just outside Barberino is the *Badia di Santa Maria a Vigesimo* with a fine façade and interior of 1740–47. Beneath the organ of 1744 is a rococo cantoria. The paintings include a 15C Virgin Annunciate and a Birth of the Virgin by Ignazio Hugford. The church of Sant'Andrea at *Camoggiano* (2km SW, across the motorway) has a pretty façade (1470) with a little portico, and a Della Robbian font. Next door is Palazzo Cattani with a good courtyard.

17km A by-road leads to the *Pieve of San Gavino Adimari* rebuilt in 1267, with an 18C interior and an interesting tomb slab carved with Christian symbols. The main road climbs past a turning for *Panna* (Trattoria *Ede Giuliani*), where mineral water is bottled, to (25km) the **Passo della Futa** (903m) on the main watershed of the Apennines. The strongest German defences in the 'Gothic' line were here, but the position was turned by the capture of the Giogo Pass and Firenzuola. Beyond the pass the road descends slightly to (27km) *Traversa*, and passes beneath the rocky Sasso di Castro. At (31km) *La Casetta* a steep road to Firenzuola and Imola descends to the right, while this road climbs to (36km) *Pietramala* (851m), a summer and winter holiday resort. Beyond (37km) the *Passo della Raticosa* (968m) begins the descent into Emilia (old custom-house on the boundary), see *Blue Guide Northern Italy*.

From San Piero a Sieve N503 leads N to Scarperia (4km). Just before entering Scarperia the 18C façade of the church of *Santa Maria a Fagna* is clearly seen to the right of the road. An inconspicuous by-road (yellow sign post) leads up to the church (ring for admission at the house on the right). Founded before 1018, the façade and interior were decorated in 1770. The contents include a handsome 12C *ambone and font, an Assumption of the Virgin, signed and dated 1587 by Santi di Tito, a 15C Florentine Madonna and Child attributed to Fra Diamante or *Pseudo Pier Francesco Fiorentino*, and a wax early-19C sculpture of the Dead Christ by Clemente Susini.

Scarperia (5700 inhab.) was founded in 1306 by the Florentines to protect her territories from invading armies from the N across the Apennines. It preserves its interesting rectangular plan laid out on either side of the main road which connected Florence to Bologna (now Via Roma) with the castle in the centre. In 1415 it became the seat of a Vicariato. The craft of making knives has been practised here probably since the 14C; it was a flourishing industry from the 15C up until the early 20C. In 1542 the village suffered from an earthquake, and after the Lorraine grand-dukes opened the new road across the Futa pass in 1752, Scarperia lost its importance. At the entrance to the town is the little *Oratorio della Madonna dei Terremoti* with a charming fresco of the Madonna and Child enthroned (c 1448) attributed to the circle of Francesco d'Antonio (or the school of Filippo Lippi). Beyond the little public garden (with a view) is the walled garden of the neo-Gothic Villa 'Il Torrino' (1930). The main road runs straight up to the centre of the town with the splendid *Palazzo dei Vicari* (adm. when the Biblioteca Comunale is open, usually in the afternoon), built in 1306 perhaps on a design by Arnolfo di Cambio. It has a very tall tower and numerous coats of arms all over its façade, some in enamelled terracotta by the Della Robbia and Benedetto Buglioni. The imposing atrium (restored in 1889 by Gaetano Bianchi), covered with more coats of arms and late-14C frescoes (including a Madonna and Child), leads into the long rectangular courtyard which stretches as far as the side of the hill (being shored up after landslips). The staircase leads up past a huge fresco of St Christopher (c 1412) to the first floor. Here is a fine fresco of the Madonna and Child with saints by the school of Ridolfo del Ghirlandaio (1554). The Sala del Consiglio has more frescoes (15–19C) with coats of arms, etc. The Sala del Sindaco may also be visited. There are long-term plans to open a museum in the castle after its restoration.

In the piazza, opposite Palazzo dei Vicari, is the parish church of *Santi Jacopo e Filippo* founded in the 14C but rebuilt, with a neo-Gothic campanile. In the interior, on the left side: first altar, Matteo Rosselli, Crucifixion and saints; second altar, Annunciation, a fine painting recently restored and attributed to Giovanni Balducci. In the chapel to the left of the main altar, small marble tabernacle, an early work by Domenico Rosselli and a small wood Crucifix attributed to Jacopo Sansovino. In the apse, late-15C wood Crucifix. In the chapel to the right of the main altar is a beautiful marble tondo of the Madonna and Child by Benedetto da Maiano (in its original wooden frame). The second altarpiece on the right side (Birth of the Virgin) is by Matteo Rosselli, and on the wall is a fragment of a 15C fresco. Also in the piazza, with a large window, is the *Oratorio della Madonna di Piazza* (door usually unlocked) with a Gothic tabernacle enclosing a fine painting of the Madonna and Child by Jacopo del Casentino (restored in 1986), within a 15C marble frame.

By the right flank of Palazzo dei Vicari, at No. 19 Via Solferino is the *Museo dei Ferri Taglienti*, an artisan's workshop (open and sometimes in use 15–19; Sat also 9.30–12.30; in winter by appointment at the Biblioteca Comunale) showing how knives were manufactured. From the public gardens (see above) a road runs down the edge of the hillside by the *Oratorio della Madonna del Vivaio* (closed since 1960), built on a design by Alessandro Galilei in 1724–41. It is a centrally-planned church surmounted by a tall drum and lantern, with an interesting neo-classical interior.

Sant'Agata, 3km W of Scarperia, has an interesting Pieve (open all day), documented since 984. The exterior is prettily decorated and the low tower has a clock. The interior is remarkable for its unusual columns on huge square bases which rise directly to the wooden roof beams. At the W end the baptismal font is enclosed by Romanesque marble intarsia panels (1175; formerly part of an ambone). On the wall is a Romanesque statuette. In the chapel to the right of the high altar, Mystical Marriage of St Catherine, a fine painting by Bicci di Lorenzo enclosed in a 16C wood tabernacle. On the triumphal arch are two tabernacles with the Madonna and Annunciatory Angel attributed to the bottega of Cristofano Allori. Over the W door, Romanesque statue of St Agata. The high altarpiece attributed to Giovanni del Biondo (c 1377) or Jacopo di Cione has been removed for restoration. Beside the 17C Palazzo Salviati, Chiasso Salviati leads out of the village into open country. Below the church is a Romanesque bridge and old water mill. A delightful little private museum, the *Teatrino degli Automi Meccanici di Faliero Lepri*, has mechanical tableaux of local peasant life (1920–50), open on holidays.

Another country road from Scarperia (signposted Luco di Mugello) skirts the racing circuit and passes the isolated little church of *San Michele a Figliano* which contains a font and altar by the Chini manufactory (who also designed the war memorial outside). The narrow road continues past *Villa Frescobaldi a Corte* with a fine park to the church of San Giovanni Maggiore, just off the road from Borgo San Lorenzo to Marradi (described above).

FROM SCARPERIA TO FIRENZUOLA, 20km. The road from Scarperia skirts the hedge of the garden of the neo-classical Villa il Pelagio (left), once a residence of the Borghese, then climbs steeply to (10km) the *Giogo di Scarperia* (882m) on the Apennine watershed. It then descends past *Rifredo* to (20km) **Firenzuola** (2-star camping site *Lo Stale*), a 14C Florentine colony, with a gateway at either end of its arcaded main street. It was laid out on symmetrical lines within rectangular bastions, designed by Antonio da Sangallo the Elder, but it was very badly damaged in the last War. The German 'Gothic' line was pierced by the taking of Firenzuola by the American fifth Army in September 1944 after heavy fighting. The road then follows the Santerno river through hills with interesting rock formations with numerous quarries of pietra serena. Just before (35km) *Moraduccio*, on the border with Emilia Romagna (see *Blue Guide Northern Italy*) is (right) a *British Military Cemetery*.

From Borgo San Lorenzo (see above) two roads, on either side of the river Sieve, continue to Vicchio. The prettier road which follows the S bank via

Sagginale, forks at *Santa Maria ad Olmi*, a conspicuous church with a bell tower, next to an elegant villa. The church dates from the 16C and contains a 15C tabernacle which encloses a 14C fresco, and paintings by Alessandro Allori and Carlo Portelli (if closed, ring at No. 4). Francesco I and Bianca Cappello stayed in the villa in 1585 when Alessandro Allori painted Bianca's portrait in fresco (detached in 1871 and now exhibited in the Tribuna of the Uffizi).

From Olmi a secondary road (the *Via delle Salaiole*) leads S to Polcanto (7km, see above). It passes the Villa de Le Viterete (1624), the buildings of which line the edge of the road next to a little chapel (the garden façade, difficult to see, has a loggia). Beyond, also on the left of the road, is the 15C Villa La Bartolina (recently restored) with a fine ground floor loggia of four arches. The road continues along the floor of the unspoilt valley to the little village of Poggiolo-Salaiole. The narrow road then climbs steeply up through woods to emerge on the Via Faentina just S of Polcanto.

On the left of the Sagginale road is *Lutiano Nuovo*, a little group of houses with a roadside tabernacle protecting a ceramic Madonna and Child by the Chini (1914). A road diverges right for the church of *San Cresci* (2km), in a lovely position above the valley. It has a splendid tall campanile with windows on four stories. Founded in the 9C, it was rebuilt in 1701–04 by Giovanni Battista Foggini (reconstructed after the earthquake in 1919). 33km *Sagginale* has a circular church built in 1969. A Madonna and Child with two angels by the Master of the Madonna Straus, and a silver reliquary bust of San Cresci by Giovanni Battista Foggini and Bernardo Holzmann also belong to the church. Beyond the village (3km) a turning right leads to *Campestri* (3-star *Villa Campestri* in a beautiful villa). Nearby is *Barbiana* where Don Lorenzo Milani (1923–67) founded a remarkable local school.

The road continues to Ponte a Vicchio where a picturesque bridge crosses the Sieve into (36km) **Vicchio** (2-star hotel *Montelleri*; 2-star camping sites *Vecchio Ponte* and *Valdisieve*), famous as the birthplace of Giotto and Fra Angelico. Benvenuto Cellini had a house here from 1559–71 (on Corso del Popolo; plaque). Part of the walls of 1324 survive. In Piazza della Vittoria is the polygonal Torre dei Cerchiai beside a neo-classical loggia. The centre of the little town is Piazza Giotto which has a bronze monument to the painter by Italo Vagnetti (1901). The Museo Civico *Beato Angelico* (closed) has an interesting collection of works of art from churches in the region. A few kilometres outside Vicchio, signposted off the main road to Borgo San Lorenzo, is *Vespignano* where the house in which Giotto (1266 or 1267–1337) is thought to have been born has been restored and opened to the public. It contains photographs of his major works (ring for admission: summer, Tuesday, Thursday, Saturday, and Sunday, 15–19; winter, Saturday and Sunday, 15–19). On the hillside above is the church of San Martino which contains a Madonna and Child by Paolo Schiavo and a tabernacle by Mino da Fiesole. A path leads across fields to the little *Cappellina della Bruna* protected by cypresses, which preserves a damaged fresco attributed to Paolo Schiavo (restored in 1985).

The main road continues from Vicchio to (44km) **Dicomano**, a flourishing small market town of ancient origins, with some arcaded streets. The town hall occupies a large neo-classical building (1888). A road leads up above the town to the 12C Romanesque *Pieve di Santa Maria* with a squat campanile (if closed ring at the priest's house, No. 25 on the left). The small INTERIOR has low stone arcades and a wood roof. On the S wall is a polychrome terracotta relief of the Marriage of St Joachim and Ann by the Della Robbian school. A painting of the Madonna of the Rosary by Santi di

Tito has been removed for restoration. At the end of the S aisle, Nativity attributed to the school of Bronzino in a splendid Mannerist frame. On the E wall, Assumption by Francesco Curradi in another fine frame. Behind the altar is a tiny Della Robbian polychrome tabernacle. N aisle, Giorgio Vasari (attributed), Madonna and saints; school of Ghirlandaio, Madonna enthroned with saints; and a beautiful 14C triptych of the Madonna with Saints. The little cloister has been restored.

On the N side of the town is the *Oratorio di Sant'Onofrio*, a splendid neo-classical building by Giuseppe Del Rosso (1796), preceded by a portico of four columns (the interior is being restored). The church of *Sant'Antonio* (rebuilt in 1938; usually locked) contains a Della Robbian relief (1504; heavily restored after damage in 1919) and a 14C Madonna and Child with saints. Important Etruscan excavations have taken place SE of Dicomano at *Frascole* (6C BC).

FROM DICOMANO TO SAN GODENZO AND THE PASSO DEL MURAGLIONE, 18km. The road (N67) ascends beside the Godenzo torrent to (10km) **San Godenzo** (2-star hotel *Silvano*), noted for its *ABBEY CHURCH, a massive Romanesque building founded in 1028 by Jacopo il Bavaro, Bishop of Fiesole. It stands above the main street of the town, in Piazza Dante Alighieri. The plain stone interior has the presbytery raised above the crypt. On the parapet is a pretty frieze of inlaid marble. The polyptych of the Madonna and saints attributed to Bernardo Daddi was repainted in 1533. The apse mosaic of the Coronation of the Virgin is by Giuseppe Cassioli (1929). In the left aisle is an Annunciation attributed to Franciabigio, and a wooden *statue of St Sebastian by Baccio da Montelupo (1506; restored in 1988). In 1308 a meeting took place in the abbey of members of the Guelf party in exile from Florence, including Dante. A by-road leads SW to *Castagno d'Andrea* (7km), thought to have been the birthplace of the painter Andrea del Castagno (1417 or 1419–57). In the parish church (rebuilt after the War) are frescoes of the Crucifixion by Pietro Annigoni (1958). Here is an entrance to the Parco Naturale del Monte Falterona, Campigna e delle Foreste Casentinesi (see p. 348). The main road continues (18km) to the **Passo del Muraglione** (907m), on the watershed. It is named after the massive wall erected here in 1836 by Leopoldo II to shelter travellers from snow and icy winds. From here the road descends to cross the border with Emilia Romagna just before *San Benedetto in Alpe* (see *Blue Guide Northern Italy*). On the border to the N, where the Troncalosso and Acquacheta rivers meet, is the charming *Acquacheta Waterfall* (130 m), sung by Dante (*Inferno*, XVI, 94-102).

The main road (N69) continues S from Dicomano. Beyond the road (N556) which leads left for *Londa* (where Etruscan remains have been found) and Stia in the Casentino (see Rte 24) is (51km) a by-road (signposted; left) for the Pieve di San Bartolomeo in Pomino (8km).

The beautiful road winds up through vineyards past some lovely old farmhouses. At *Castiglioni*, with a 12C church (altered in 1926) there is a view below of the tiny little fortified borgo of Castello di Castiglioni. Beyond *Petrognano*, with a church rebuilt in 1925 and the 18C Villa Budini Gattai, and Rimaggio, the tower of the pieve can be seen ahead. *San Bartolomeo in Pomino* was founded in the 12–13C (if closed, ring at no. 60). It has an attractive tall basilican interior with stone arches and a raised chancel. One of the capitals has interesting carved figures. On the left altar, Madonna and Saints Sebastian and Anthony Abbot, a fine work attributed to the Master of San Miniato, and on the wall a Della Robbian Madonna and Child with two saints. On the right wall is a detached fresco of St James with its sinopia. The stained glass and mosaic lunette of the Madonna with two angels outside the W door date from 1933.

54km **Rufina** (3-star hotel *La Speranza*) has been famous as a wine-growing centre since 1760 (*Chianti Rufina*). Above the town (but hidden by its park) is the 16C *Villa di Poggio Reale*, approached by a long cypress avenue. It is the seat of the *Museo della Vite e del Vino della Valdisieve* (closed for restoration), illustrating wine production in the area.

The tall 12C tower of *Montebonello* is conspicuous on the other side of the river where a road (signposted left) leads to *Santa Maria in Acone* (4km). The road crosses a stream and then narrows to climb uphill. An unsurfaced road leads past a farm and ends in front of the church (key at the house next door). The lunette over the main door, the apse and the high altar were decorated by the Chini at the beginning of this century. A painting of the Madonna and saints by the school of Ghirlandaio has been removed to the Misericordia at Pontassieve.

61km **Pontassieve** (16,500 inhab.), another important centre of the *Chianti Rufina* wine trade, stands at the confluence of the Sieve and the Arno. The old Medici bridge (1555; attributed to Bartolomeo Ammannati; restored) across the Sieve, can be seen upstream from the main road bridge. The town was severely damaged in the Second World War.

FROM PONTASSIEVE TO THE PASSO DELLA CONSUMA, 16km. The road (N70) for the Casentino branches left from the Arezzo road (N69) outside Pontassieve. It climbs beyond another fork (keep left) and passes a by-road (left) which leads up to *Nipozzano*. The picturesque hamlet is spread out along a ridge backed by cypresses, and includes the 17C Villa Albizi (Frescobaldi) behind a low wall, a church, and remains of an 11C castle. There are pretty farmhouses in the vicinity and views all the way to Vallombrosa. The farm produces a well-known wine (the cellars can sometimes be visited by appointment). The main road climbs through vineyards to (5km) *Diacceto* where the church of San Lorenzo (open only on weekends), rebuilt in 1872, contains a Della Robbian Madonna and Child with saints. From here a road leads S to **Pelago** (1.5km). A festival called 'On the Road' of buskers, street players, etc. is held here in July. Opposite a little Oratory preceded by a portico (and containing a small 15C wood Crucifix), a road leads into Piazza Ghiberti, named after the great sculptor Lorenzo, who was born here, probably in 1378. This delightful ancient market square preserves its old pump and a medley of houses. Via Roma leads out of the piazza past an old tower, and steps continue up past the handsome town hall and beneath two arches to the tiny Piazza Cavalcanti at the top of the village, with the flank of the church. In San Clemente a small museum was opened in 1994. The works from churches nearby include a triptych by Niccolò di Pietro Gerini. The main road continues to (9km) Borselli. A few hundred metres along the Pomino road (left) is the Romanesque church of *Tosina* which contains a beautiful triptych by Mariotto di Nardo (1389; restored in 1989). 16km *Consuma* (*Dal Consumi* for good snacks), a summer and ski resort a few metres below the pass (1023m) connecting the Pratomagno with the main Apennine chain. The road beyond, which descends into the Casentino, is described in Rte 24.

The Villa of *Altomena*, 5km SW of Pontassieve, is reached from the Arezzo road at Carbonile (by-road signposted for Paterno). The road climbs up to the drive (left; gate open) which leads up past interesting farmhouses to Altomena. A Guidi castle and a church have been incorporated into the villa which is surrounded by extensive vineyards and olive groves. The church contains a Madonna and Child with saints attributed to the circle of Domenico Ghirlandaio.

A by-road leads across the Arno from Pontassieve to **Rosano**, in a peaceful position by the river. By a pretty tabernacle a narrow road leads shortly to the well-kept Benedictine convent of *Santa Maria*, founded in 780, and now housing some seventy nuns. The church has a Romanesque façade and a fine 11–12C campanile (ring for admission on the right of the courtyard at the closed order). In the interior the presbytery is raised above the pretty crypt which has a 12C altar. In the right aisle, font (1423) and (right of the high altar), Annunciation by Giovanni dal Ponte (1434). On the E wall is a fine painted Crucifix (in very poor condition) by an unknown master of the late 12C or early 13C. In the chapel at the base of the campanile, Annunciation by Jacopo di Cione. A 16C wood ciborium has been removed to the convent. Mass is celebrated with Gregorian chant at 7am on weekdays and at 10am on holidays. The nuns have a laboratory for the restoration of books. A beautiful road climbs to Villamagna (described in Rte 2).

The main road continues from Pontassieve to (66.5km) *Le Sieci*. Here, on the left of the main road, is the *Pieve di San Giovanni Battista a Remole* with a fine tall campanile. The church is usually open 16–18.30; if closed ring at the priest's house in the garden beyond the portico. In the right aisle is the font made up from various coloured marbles in 1753, behind a 15C balustrade. On the wall is a statuette of St John the Baptist by the bottega of Giovanni Della Robbia. At the end of the aisle is a 15C ciborium in pietra serena. On the E wall, *Crucifixion, with the Madonna and St John, attributed to the school of Botticelli. In the chapel to the left, 14C fresco fragments and a *Madonna and Child, attributed to the Master of Remole, named after this work.

A by-road (signposted) leads N from Le Sieci to Santa Brigida (10km). The road follows the river to *Molino del Piano*. At a fork a road leads right signposted for Doccia. Above the road on the left can be seen the castle of *Torre a Decima*, approached by a pretty road lined on one side by cypresses. It was owned by the Pazzi family from the 13C, and was restored in 1950. The wine cellars can sometimes be visited by appointment. The road continues up to *Doccia* on the top of a hill in a beautiful position. Here the church of Sant'Andrea (entrance through the little courtyard behind) contains a tiny Della Robbian tabernacle and a Madonna and saints by the school of Ghirlandaio. The Crucifix and saints by Ignazio Hugford is in very poor condition. Outside is a misused medieval well. A narrow road below Doccia is signposted for Santa Brigida. It winds up and down through woods and lovely rolling hills, with a view left of the castle of Torre a Decima. Beyond Fornello is La Villa with a handsome villa, where another road comes in from Molino del Piano. 10km **Santa Brigida** (pizzeria). On the left of the road is the church with a square tower and an unusual plan. It contains a *Madonna and Child with two saints attributed to the Maestro di San Martino alla Palma, a 16C painted Crucifix, and a little carved tabernacle of 1483. On the intrados of the triumphal arch there are unusual carvings. At the W end are two 16C polychrome busts in niches. The apse has interesting frescoes. From the terrace there is a lovely view of the unspoilt countryside. The road continues down (keep left) to the *Castello del Trebbio* (not to be confused with the Castello di Trebbio outside San Piero a Sieve), right on the road. It was built by the Pazzi in the 13C but has been restored. Visitors are invited into the courtyard. The road continues steeply downhill lined with cypresses to the road which runs along the floor of the valley. To the right it leads past the pieve di Lubaco with a Romanesque apse to the crossroads of *La Vetta* on the roads from Florence and Fiesole to Polcanto (described at the beginning of this Rte); to the left it leads back to Molino del Piano.

The main road continues through (68km) *Le Falle*, where another pretty country by-road (right) leads up towards Fiesole via *Gricigliano* where the 15–16C Villa Martelli, with a fine garden, is now a monastery (the monks sell produce, etc. and Mass is held here in Gregorian chant on Sundays), and the hamlet of *Monteloro* (restaurant).

Beyond *Compiobbi* the main road passes (72km) the *Florence British Military Cemetery*, with 1551 graves, and **Rovezzano**, now on the outskirts of Florence. In Piazzetta Benedetto da Rovezzano is a tabernacle with a Crucifixion by Franciabigio. The Church of *San Michele* (rebuilt in 1840) contains a painted Crucifix dated 1400, and a Madonna enthroned by the Maestro della Maddalena. The church of *Sant'Andrea a Rovezzano* has a fine Romanesque campanile. In the neo-classical interior with frescoes by Luigi Ademollo, is a beautiful relief of the Madonna by the bottega of Luca Della Robbia, and an early-13C painting of the Madonna and Child. In the canonica is kept a marble statuette by a follower of Giovanni di Balduccio. The *Villa Favard*, surrounded by a park, was rebuilt in the 19C. 79km **Florence**.

4

Prato

PRATO (163,000 inhab.) is a rapidly expanding industrial town, known as the Manchester of Tuscany, and long famous for its wool factories; it is one of the most important centres of the textile industry in Europe. In 1992 it became the capital of a new Province. It is surrounded by extensive suburbs, but it has a peaceful old centre which preserves some beautiful monuments, all within its old walls.

Information Office. APT, 51 Via Luigi Muzzi (N of the Duomo), Tel. 0574/35141, with information office at No. 48 Via Cairoli (Tel. 0574/24112).

Railway Stations. *Centrale*, E of the town across the Bisenzio for all main line trains; services on the Florence–Lucca line stop also at *Porta al Serraglio*, 200 metres N of the cathedral.

Buses. Frequent services (via the motorway) from Florence (near the Railway Station) by CAP (terminal in Piazza Ciardi, with a stop in Via del Serraglio) and *Lazzi* (terminal in Piazza Stazione, with a stop in Piazza S. Francesco).

Parking. The centre is closed to traffic: parking in Piazza Mercatale or Piazza dei Macelli.

Hotels. 4-star: *President*, 20 Via Simintendi (Pl. 1). 3-star: *Flora*, 31 Via Cairoli (Pl. 2); *Giardino*, 4 Via Magnolfi (Pl. 3); *San Marco*, 48 Piazza San Marco (Pl. 4); *Milano*, 15 Via Tiziano (Pl. 5). 2- star: *Il Giglio*, 14 Piazza San Marco (Pl. 6). Rooms to let at the *Villa Rucellai*, Via di Canneto.

Restaurants in the historic centre. Luxury-class: *Baghino*, 9 Via dell'Accademia; *Osvaldo*, 13 Via Fra Bartolomeo. First-class restaurants: *La Candela*, 27 Via Cambioni; *San Domenico*, 62 Via Guasti; *La Cucina di Paola*, 16 Via Banchelli. Pizzerie and *tavole calde*: *Brogi*, 7 Piazza Duomo; *Chez le crouton*, 51 Via Carraia.

Theatres and annual festivals. *Teatro Comunale Metastasio*, with a renowned theatre season (October to April). *Teatro il Fabbricone*, Viale Galileo. The *Prato Fair* is held in September (with a historical pageant on 8 September). A big general market is held on Mondays at the Mercato Nuovo.

History. Although probably already settled in the Etruscan period, the first recorded mention of Prato is in the 9C. It became a free commune in the 12C and after 1351 came under the influence of Florence. The manufacture of wool in the city had reached European importance by the 13C, and it received further impetus in the following century through the commercial activity of the famous merchant Francesco di Marco Datini. Its textile factories continue to flourish, and it has become the centre of the 'rag-trade' in Europe. As an industrial centre, its population is expanding faster than almost any other city in central Italy.

Piazza del Duomo is a large square (closed to traffic) where many streets converge around the cathedral. The fountain dates from 1863 (by Emanuele Caroni and Ulisse Cambi). The *Duomo was founded in the 10C, but the present Romanesque building was begun in 1211 by Guidetto da Como. The unusual FAÇADE (1385–1457), partly striped in green and white marble, is crowned with a quadrilobe open sculptured frieze. Above the main portal is a *lunette with the Madonna and Saints Stephen and Laurence by Andrea Della Robbia (1489). The *PULPIT OF THE SACRED GIRDLE, designed by Donatello and Michelozzo (1434–38), is protected by a charming roof. The dancing putti by Donatello were replaced here by casts in 1972 (the originals are displayed in the Museo dell'Opera del

Duomo, see below). The Holy Girdle (see below) is displayed from the pulpit in a traditional ceremony on 1 May, Easter Day, 15 August, 8 September, and Christmas Day. The right *flank of the cathedral, the oldest part of the building, has beautiful blind arcading and Romanesque inlaid marble decoration, and two fine doorways. The handsome CAMPANILE also dates from the early 13C, except for the last storey which was added c 1356 by Niccolò di Cecco del Mercia.

INTERIOR (closed 12–16). The nave is supported by massive shiny green marble columns with good capitals, and the deep arcades are decorated with green and white striped marble. The whole building has been undergoing restoration since 1983; at present work is underway at the crossing. Immediately to the left is the *CHAPEL OF THE SACRED GIRDLE, built in 1385–90 to house the greatly revered relic which is traditionally considered to be the girdle (*Cintola*) which the Madonna gave to St Thomas at her Assumption. It was brought to Prato from the Holy Land in 1141. The splendid bronze *screen was begun in 1438 by Maso di Bartolomeo and continued by Antonio di Ser Cola and Pasquino di Matteo (1467). On the altar is a statuette of the *Madonna and Child, one of the best works of Giovanni Pisano (1317). The chapel is entirely frescoed by Agnolo Gaddi with stories from the life of the Virgin and of the Holy Girdle. On the altar opposite, in the S aisle, wood Crucifix by the bottega of Giovanni Pisano. Above the W door, Assumption of the Virgin by Ridolfo del Ghirlandaio. The *pulpit in the nave is by Mino da Fiesole and Antonio Rossellino.

The beautiful TRANSEPT AND EAST CHAPELS, thought to have been designed by Giovanni Pisano, were added in 1317–68. A balustrade (incorporating some sculpted marble panels of 1487 by Francesco di Simone Ferrucci), by Bernardino Radi and Gherardo Silvani (1637) precedes the high altar on which is a bronze Crucifix by Ferdinando Tacca (1653). The fine bronze candelabrum is by Maso di Bartolomeo. The CHOIR is decorated with celebrated *frescoes by Filippo Lippi (helped by Fra Diamante). This is one of the most beautiful fresco cycles of the early Renaissance (1452–66), and the monumental figures repay close study (coin-operated light). On the right wall: scenes from the Life of St John the Baptist; the Salome in the *Banquet of Herod is supposed to be a portrait of Lucrezia Buti, the nun who was first Lippi's model and then his wife. On the left wall: scenes from the life of St Stephen. Filippo Lippi also designed the beautiful stained glass window (except for the lower register which is modern). SOUTH TRANSEPT. The tabernacle of the Madonna dell'Ulivo (1480), designed by Giuliano da Maiano, contains a statue of the *Madonna and Child and a bas-relief of the Pietà by his brothers Benedetto and Giovanni. The painting of the Death of St Jerome by Filippo Lippi has been temporarily removed to the Museo dell'Opera del Duomo (see below). The second chapel right of the choir is frescoed by Alessandro Franchi (1873–76). The 13C wood figure of Christ was part of a Deposition group. In the first chapel right of the choir (Cappella dell'Assunta; coin operated light in the choir) are 15C frescoes of the life of the Virgin and of St Stephen. The lower scenes are by Andrea di Giusto, and the upper *scenes (the vault, two lunettes, and the Presentation in the Temple on the right side) are now attributed to the hand of Paolo Uccello as early works (c 1430). In the first chapel left of the choir (restored) are more early 15C frescoes; and in the second chapel is the *tomb of Filippo degli Inghirami (died 1480) and a fine stained glass window with the Visitation and Nativity. Above the door into the sacristy, monument to Carlo dei Medici by Vincenzo Danti. The chapel of the

Sacrament in the NORTH TRANSEPT has a carved entrance arch by Giovanni Camilliani (1544), and an altarpiece by Zanobi Poggini (1549).

To the left of the Cathedral, beside *Palazzo Vescovile* with a 15C loggia, is a little courtyard with a 16C fresco in a tabernacle. Here is the entrance to the **Museo dell'Opera del Duomo** (adm. 9.30–12.30, 15–18.30; fest. 9.30–12.30; closed Tuesday). It is arranged in rooms off the old cloister, part of which is a unique survival from the 12C, with tiny slender columns with exquisite capitals, and green and white marble decoration. Room I displays 14C paintings, including a Madonna and Child, and two Evangelists and two saints by Giovanni Toscani. R. II: Illuminated 15C anthem books, and two late-16C embroidered copes. Off the cloister: Sculpted *panels of dancing putti by Donatello from the Pulpit of the Sacred Girdle (outside the cathedral, see above), here displayed at eye level (but damaged by restoration in 1939; one panel has been removed for further restoration); Maestro della Natività di Castello, Madonna and Child enthroned with saints (from the church of Santi Giusto e Clemente at Faltugnano); Fra Diamante, Annunciation; Filippino Lippi, *St Lucy; Paolo Uccello (attributed) or the Master of Prato, *Jacopone da Todi (detached fresco); *reliquary for the sacred girdle, an exquisite work by Maso di Bartolomeo (1446). A treasury contains reliquaries, chalices, thuribles, reliquary busts, and a pax by Danese Cattaneo. The last room contains a painted Crucifix by the school of Botticelli; Michele Tosini, portrait of Lapo Spighi; Carlo Dolci, guardian Angel. Also temporarily displayed here, Filippo Lippi, death of St Jerome (from the cathedral). From the cloister there is also access to the medieval arches (*Le Volte*) beneath the transept of the Duomo, with early-15C frescoes, the 14C altar of the Holy Girdle, a small antiquarium, and some remains of the earlier church. A very unusual medieval pavement here is composed of some one hundred pieces of pottery kitchen ware.

Opposite the right flank of the Duomo Via Mazzoni (called the Corso), the main street of the town, leads to the handsome PIAZZA DEL COMUNE, with a statue (1896) of the Merchant of Prato (see below), and a pretty little fountain by Ferdinando Tacca (1659; the original statue of the young Bacchus and the basin are preserved inside Palazzo Comunale, see below). Here stand the arcaded late-18C Palazzo Comunale (by Giuseppe Valentini; a worn Medici stemma of 1550 survives on the corner, by Battista del Tasso) and the splendid **Palazzo Pretorio** (being restored). The main stone façade with its Gothic windows and outside staircase, was added to a medieval core in the early 14C, and the battlements completed in the 16C. The palace houses the *Galleria Comunale and the Museo Civico (adm. 9.30–12.30, 15–18.30; fest. 9.30–12.30; closed Tuesday), founded in 1852.

FIRST FLOOR. Frescoed *tabernacle by Filippino Lippi (1498), restored after severe damage in the last War. It was formerly on the corner of a house in Piazza del Mercatale (see below) purchased by Filippino for his widowed mother, who had been a nun at the nearby convent of Santa Margherita. Portrait of Baldo Magini, by Ridolfo del Ghirlandaio; Madonna and Child, by Lodovico Buti. A small adjacent room with cupboards and jars from the old pharmacy of the hospital, is used for lectures, etc. Beyond is the 14C Salone (being restored), with a fine roof.

SECOND FLOOR. On the stairs is the alabaster model by Lorenzo Bartolini for the Demidoff monument in Florence. The MAIN HALL contains the most important *works in the collection. Bernardo Daddi, story of the Sacred Girdle, Madonna and saints; Fra Bartolomeo, Madonna and Child (fresco fragment); Giovanni di Milano, polyptych; Pietro di Miniato, Coronation of the Madonna; Lorenzo Monaco (workshop), Madonna enthroned with saints; Luca Signorelli (attributed), tondo of the Madonna and Child with saints; Filippino Lippi, Madonna and Child with saints; Raffaellino del Garbo, tondo of the Madonna and Child with St John; Andrea di Giusto, Madonna and Child with saints, Filippo Lippi, Madonna del Ceppo (with Francesco di Marco Datini), Nativity; Francesco Botticini, Madonna and Child with saints; Zanobi Strozzi, predella; Piero di Lorenzo Pratese, predella; Andrea Della Robbia, St Anthony Abbot (lunette). The next two rooms contain later paintings, notably Battistello ('Noli me tangere'), and works by Gaspare Vanvitelli.

THIRD FLOOR (closed many years ago for repairs): later paintings including works by Gian Domenico Ferretti (Annunciation), Francesco Morandini (Tobias and the Angel), Giovanni Battista Naldini, Bilivert, etc. Here also is a fine collection of plaster-casts by Lorenzo Bartolini, who was born near Prato at Savignano (1777–1850).

At the foot of the stairs of the **Palazzo Comunale** (entrance at No. 2) is the original *fountain with the young Bacchus by Ferdinando Tacca, removed from the piazza outside. Upstairs the Sala del Consiglio (shown on request 8–14, except fest.) has a fine ceiling, two 15C frescoes, and a series of portraits in handsome frames (some by Alessandro Allori) of the grand-dukes of Tuscany, and of Cardinal Niccolò of Prato by Tommaso di Piero Trombetto.

Via Cairoli leads out of the piazza through a little square with the 19C façade of Palazzo Buonamici and its hanging garden. No. 19 is the Baroque Palazzo Gatti and beyond is the 16C Palazzo Novellucci. Beside a tall medieval tower is Piazza Santa Maria delle Carceri with the Palazzo della Canonica by Giuseppe Valentini adjoining the church of *Santa Maria delle Carceri** (closed 12–16.30), a masterpiece of the early Renaissance. It is one of the most important works by Giuliano da Sangallo, begun in 1485 (the exterior was left incomplete in 1506). The Greek-cross plan is derived from the architectural principles of Alberti and Brunelleschi. It was built where a miracle was performed in 1484 by the image of the Virgin painted on a prison wall (hence *Carceri*). The exterior, in green and white marble, recalls the Romanesque buildings of Florence (the last side was completed in the 19C). In the domed centrally-planned INTERIOR pietra serena is used to emphasise the structural elements. The beautiful enamelled terracotta frieze and tondi of the Evangelists are by Andrea Della Robbia. The stoup, with a bronze statuette of St John the Baptist, is by Francesco da Sangallo, son of the architect, and the stained glass windows date from the 15C.

On a mound next to the church is the *Castello dell'Imperatore** (restored). It was probably built in 1237–48 to protect Frederick II's route from Germany to southern Italy, and is typical of the Hohenstaufen castles of the south. The empty interior (adm. 9.30–12.30, 15–18.30; fest. 9.30–12.30; closed Tuesday) is of little interest, except for the walkway (closed for restoration) which provides a good view of the city and countryside. Concerts and plays are held here in summer.

From Piazza Santa Maria delle Carceri Via Cairoli leads to the **Teatro Comunale Metastasio** (admission on request at No. 59) with an elegant interior built in 1827–30 by Luigi Cambray Digny. It has a high theatrical reputation. Via Mazzini continues towards *Piazza San Marco* with a sculpture (1969–70) by Henry Moore, while Via Verdi skirts the theatre building to a crossroads with Via Garibaldi. On the right this road leads shortly to the huge PIAZZA MERCATALE, surrounded with a medley of pleasant buildings. Here the modern church of **San Bartolomeo** (the 14C church was destroyed

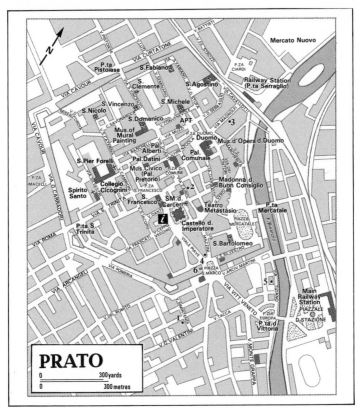

PRATO

| 0 | 300 yards |
| 0 | 300 metres |

in the Second World War) has a 15C marble tabernacle on the high altar with a painted Crucifix of the 14C Pistoian school above. The paintings include a tondo (above the W door) in a fine frame by the school of Botticelli, and works by Santi di Tito, Leonardo Mascagni, Livio Mehus (Rest on the Flight, at the end of the left wall), and Empoli. In the crypt is a fine wood Crucifix of the 14C. In the other direction, Via Garibaldi (see above) passes the oratory of the *Madonna del Buon Consiglio* (No. 53; if closed ask at Santa Maria delle Carceri), with a Della Robbian lunette (and other works by the Della Robbia in the interior).

Opposite the entrance to the castle is the E end of the Romanesque church of **San Francesco**, with a handsome striped marble façade. At the foot of the altar steps is the tomb of Francesco di Marco Datini (see below), by Nicolò Lamberti (1412). On the N wall is the tomb of Gimignano Inghirami (died 1460), attributed to Bernardo Rossellino. From the charming 15C cloister (planted with olive trees) or from the sacristy is the entrance to the CHAPTER HOUSE (or Cappella Migliorati) with good and well-preserved frescoes by Niccolò di Pietro Gerini (c 1395) of the Crucifixion, and stories from the life of St Anthony Abbot and St Matthew.

Via Santa Trínita leads out of the square. In Via Silvestri (right) is the church of the SPIRITO SANTO (open only for services; at other times ring at the Cappella Musicale at No. 21). The entrance is through a pretty little portico with Ionic columns. In the nave is a Presentation in the Temple by Fra Diamante, possibly to a design of Filippo Lippi, and a Madonna and Child with St Anne attributed to Sogliani. The high altarpiece of the Pentecost is by Santi di Tito. In the presbytery is a high relief of St John the Baptist (15C) and an *Annunciation and a predella by the school of Orcagna.

In front of the church of San Francesco (see above) is the *Biblioteca Roncioniana* in a building of 1751–66 (in the vestibule is a Tobias and the Archangel attributed to Andrea Della Robbia). Via Rinaldesca leads to the huge *Palazzo Datini** on the corner of Via Ser Lapo Mazzei, with unusually large projecting eaves. This was the residence of Francesco di Marco Datini, the famous Merchant of Prato (1330–1410), whose life is described in a book by Iris Origo. Part of the decoration and some of the sinopie survive of the exterior mural paintings, attributed to Niccolò di Pietro Gerini and others, which illustrated the story of the life of Datini. His papers and business documents (including over 140,000 letters), all of which were carefully preserved by him, provide a unique record of medieval life; they are housed in an archive in the palace. Part of the ground floor, including the courtyard, is open (9–12, 15–18 except Saturday afternoon and Sunday): at the foot of the stairs is a fresco of St Christopher and a room with a painted vault and a portrait of Datini, dressed in red. Another room with a frescoed lunette of the Redeemer above the door has delightful painted decoration with woods and animals, and a good vault. The frescoes are attributed to Niccolò Gerini and Arrigo di Niccolò di Prato. Beyond is **Palazzo degli Alberti**, the seat of the Cassa di Risparmio bank, which owns a particularly interesting collection of works of art (adm. on request, preferably by previous appointment; 8.30–12.30, 15–16, except Saturday and Sunday). The works, arranged in a gallery overlooking the banking hall, include: Giovanni Bellini, *Crucifix (with an interesting landscape); Filippo Lippi (attributed), Madonna and Child; Caravaggio, Christ crowned with Thorns. The fine 17C Tuscan paintings are by Matteo Rosselli, Leonardo Mascagni, Sigismondo Coccapani, Giovanni Battista Vanni, Lorenzo Lippi, Giovanni Bilivert, Carlo Dolci (Charity), Cesare and Pietro Dandini, Francesco Furini, Sustermans, and Bernardino Mei. The collection of marble sculptures by Lorenzo Bartolini include *Faith* and some portrait busts. On the stairs are two paintings by Galileo Chini.

In front of Palazzo Datini a road leads to Via Pellegrino on which is the pretty little church of *San Pier Forelli* (1838) with a barrel vault and semicircular apse lit from a semi-dome. Nearby is the huge 18C *Collegio Cicognini*, a well-known school attended by Gabriele D'Annunzio. Via Santa Caterina leads up to a little piazza in front of the church and convent of **San Nicolò** (for admission ring at the convent school), with an 18C interior. On the right wall are two 14C frescoes, and the high altarpiece of the Assumption is by Alessandro Gherardini. In the sacristy is a fine enamelled terracotta lavabo (1520) attributed to Santi Buglioni. The interesting convent has an 18C nuns' choir.

From Palazzo Alberti, Via Banchelli leads right and Via Guasti left to the church of **San Domenico**, which has an arcaded flank; founded in 1283 it was finished by Giovanni Pisano before 1322. It contains a 17C organ, on which Domenico Zipoli (born in Prato in 1688 and died in Argentina in 1726) probably played. Over the high altar is a Baroque baldacchino. SOUTH AISLE. Second altar, Crucifix by Niccolò Gerini; third altar, St Vincent Ferrer attributed to Pier Dandini; fifth altar, Madonna and saints and angels by Camillo Sagrestani. NORTH AISLE. Second altar, Madonna appearing to St Philip Neri, by Matteo Rosselli; fourth altar, Crucifix before St Thomas

Aquinas, by Francesco Morandini; fifth altar, Annunciation, signed by Matteo Rosselli. In the CHAPTER HOUSE (off the cloister) interesting early 15C frescoes of the life of St Dominic attributed to Pietro di Miniato were uncovered in 1984.

In the adjoining convent is a **Museum of Mural Painting** (entered from the church, or from No. 8 in the piazza; open 9–12 except Tuesday). It houses detached frescoes from buildings in the town and surrounding area. The well-displayed works include: Niccolò di Pietro Gerini, Tabernacolo del Ceppo (with its sinopia); Maestro delle Madonne (?), Madonna and Child; Antonio di Miniato, Madonna enthroned with saints (1411); Volterrano, Christ attended by angels; sinopie of the Cappella dell'Assunta in the Duomo, attributed to Paolo Uccello; graffiti *decoration from Palazzo Vaj of courtly scenes (15C). Also objects from the church treasury and a charming collection of ex-votos.

Opposite the façade of San Domenico is the church of *San Vincenzo e Santa Caterina de' Ricci* (open at 17), with a fine interior of 1733. In the convent are mementoes of St Catherine de' Ricci (1522–90) who lived here (canonised in 1746). In Via San Vincenzo, at No. 24 is the church of *San Clemente* in another convent (closed order; service at 18.00).

Via Convenevole leads from Piazza San Domenico past the little church of *San Michele* (the church of the Misericordia) with an altarpiece of the Assumption by Alessandro Allori (1603) and a Romanesque Crucifix. At the end of Via Convenevole Via della Stufa leads left to a piazza in front of the church of **Sant'Agostino**, erected in 1271, but since considerably altered. The INTERIOR contains 16–17C altarpieces, including, in the N aisle (2nd altar), a Madonna designed by Vasari (and executed by Giovanni Battista Naldini), and (3rd altar) St Thomas of Villanova, by Lorenzo Lippi. In the chapel at the end of the N aisle, Sacred Conversation, by Empoli (who also painted the Immaculate Conception and saints on the second S altar). A door in the N wall leads into the garden of the cloister; to the left is reached the CAPPELLA DI SAN MICHELE with a damaged frieze of saints (14C) and a relief of a Madonna and Child by the school of Ghiberti. The CHAPTER HOUSE, beyond, has a fine cross-vault and a 14C fresco of Christ in Pietà.

Nearby is the church of *San Fabiano* (entrance on request at No. 28 Via del Seminario; see the Plan). Interesting fragments of the pre-Romanesque monochrome mosaic pavement with figures of animals, sirens, and birds, are displayed in the cloister and on the W wall (the façade can be seen from Via Giovanni di Gherardo which skirts the walls).

In front of San Michele (see above), Largo Carducci leads back to Piazza del Duomo.

On the S outskirts of the town (in a Textile Institute at No. 9 Viale della Repubblica) is the MUSEO DEL TESSUTO (adm. usually on request, week-days 9–12). It contains a collection of textiles from the 5C AD to the present day (including examples of embroidery, tapestry, lace, velvet and damask), a display of looms, etc.

Between the motorway exit (Prato-est) and Viale della Repubblica is the **Centro per l'arte contemporanea Luigi Pecci**, designed by Italo Gamberini, and opened in 1988 (adm. 10–19 except Tuesday). The huge, well illuminated galleries are used for contemporary art exhibitions. There is also an open-air theatre, library, auditorium, snack bar, etc.

The road from PRATO TO BOLOGNA (100km; N325) follows the main railway line across the Apennines. It ascends the Bisenzio valley through (11km) the wide upland basin of *Vaiano*, with its 13C campanile. There is a small archaeological and liturgical collection (15C–19C) in the Badia. On a secondary road between Prato and Vaiano is *Figline di Prato* with the Romanesque Pieve of San Pietro (14–15C frescoes; and a small museum of 14–17C paintings and church silver). In the hills to the right of Vaiano is *Savignano*, the birthplace of the painter Fra Bartolomeo della Porta (1475–1517) and of the sculptor Lorenzo Bartolini (1777–1850). Passing (right) the ruined 12–13C castle of *Cerbaia*, the road reaches (21km) *San Quirico di Vernio* (278m), a substantial village with two residences (16C and 18C) of the Conti family. The watershed is crossed by an indefinite pass just before (31km) *Montepiano* (700m), a summer resort. Here the 11–12C Badia di Santa Maria contains 13–14C frescoes. Emilia is entered near (40km) *Castiglione dei Pepoli*, see *Blue Guide Northern Italy*.

The old road from Prato to Pistoia (19.5km) passes (7.5km) *Montemurlo*, where the medieval Guidi castle was the scene of the last attempt of the partisans of the Florentine Republic to overthrow the power of the Medici (1537).

5

Pistoia and its province

PISTOIA (93,200 inhab.) is a lively old Tuscan town with an unusual number of beautiful churches, whose character recalls its position between Florence and Pisa. Many of them have good sculptures. It is an important horticultural centre, particularly noted for the cultivation of ornamental plants. There are extensive nurseries on the surrounding plain.

Information Office of the *APT Abetone, Pistoia, Montagna Pistoiese* in Palazzo dei Vescovi, Piazza Duomo (Tel. 0573/21622).

Railway Station, Piazza Dante Alighieri, with services on the Florence–Viareggio line (from Florence, 34km in 35–45mins).

Buses from Piazza San Francesco (COPIT) to Abetone, Cutigliano, San Marcello Pistoiese, etc.; and to Florence (in 1 hour). From Piazza Dante Alighieri (*Lazzi*) to Florence (in 45mins); and to Prato, Montecatini Terme, Lucca, Viareggio, Pisa, Livorno, Forte dei Marmi, La Spezia, etc.

Parking. The centre is closed to traffic: parking at the ex-Officine Meccaniche Breda, off Via Pacinotti.

Hotels. 3-star: *Patria*, 8 Via Crispi (Pl. 1); *Milano*, 12 Via Pacinotti (Pl. 2). 2-star: *Firenze*, 42 Via Curtatone (Pl. 3). 4km E at Pontenuovo, *Il Convento* (3-star).

Restaurants. First-class: *San Jacopo*, 15 Via Crispi; *La Vela*, 12 Piazza dell'Ortaggio. Trattoria: *Tonino*, 159 Corso Gramsci. Snack bar *Frisco*, 58 Piazza San Francesco. 1st-class restaurants on the outskirts of the city: *La Cugna*, Località La Cugna, 238 Via Bolognese; *Rafanelli*, Località Sant'Agostino, 47 Via Sant'Agostino.

Annual Festival. The *Giostra dell'Orso*, a medieval jousting tournament, is held on 25 July in Piazza del Duomo.

History. *Pistoia* is first mentioned as the scene of Catiline's defeat in 62 BC. It was a republic in the 12C but was seized by the Florentines in 1306 and in 1315 by Castruccio Castracani (died 1328), a military and political adventurer. From 1329 it existed under the protection of Florence, whose fortunes it shared, as the Medici arms on the walls testify. As an ironworking town in medieval times, it gave its name to the pistol (originally a dagger, afterwards a small firearm), and indirectly to the Spanish pistole coin, so called as smaller than the French crown. The Breda works here are famous for the production of railway carriages and buses; a new factory was built in 1973 on the outskirts of the town between the railway and the motorway (the huge old *officine*, off Via Pacinotti, have been abandoned and are at present used as a car park). Guittone Sinibaldi, called Cino da Pistoia (1270–1337), the friend of Dante, was born here; also Clement IX (Giulio Rospigliosi), Pope in 1667–69.

The approaches from Florence (or from the station) enter the town on the site of the S gate; from here Via Vannucci and Via Cino lead to Piazza Gavinana. Corso Fedi, on the right before the piazza, leads to the church of **San Domenico** built c 1280, probably to the design of Fra Sisto and Fra Ristoro, with 14C alterations.

The INTERIOR is particularly interesting for its sculptured funerary monuments. The fine stained glass in the E window dates from 1930. SOUTH SIDE. Tomb of Filippo Lazzari, by Bernardo and Antonio Rossellino; third altar, St Sebastian by Giacinto Gimignani. In a niche with 14C fresco fragments, notable sculpted tomb effigy of Beato Lorenzo da Ripafratta (died 1457). Beyond the fourth altar, Gothic tomb of Andrea Franchi; fifth altar, Assumption by Matteo Rosselli. SOUTH TRANSEPT. Empoli, St Charles Borromeo with members of the Rospigliosi family, and 17C Rospigliosi funerary monuments (the busts are attributed to Bernini). In the chapel to the left of the presbytery, Cristofano Allori, St Domenic receiving the Rosary (with a portrait of the artist discussing his payment for the painting with the sacristan of the convent) and more 17C monuments. The organ, by Rovani da Lucca, dates from 1617.

A door in the S aisle leads into the CLOISTER in which is buried, in an unknown spot, the body of Benozzo Gozzoli, who died here in 1497 during the plague. In several rooms off the cloister are interesting frescoes (many detached from the church) shown by a monk (ring at No. 1 Piazza San Domenico). The CHAPTER HOUSE has a damaged fresco of the Crucifixion by an unknown master of the mid-13C, with its *sinopia, thought to be the oldest known. The REFECTORY has more good frescoes from the church. A small MUSEUM contains other frescoes including one with the portraits of Dante and Petrarch. Some of the frescoed lunettes of the life of Mary Magdalene, detached from a cloister, are by Giovanni da San Giovanni and Matteo Rosselli. Outside the entrance to the library: Journey of the Magi, attributed to the school of Benozzo Gozzoli; *St Jerome kneeling, thought to be an early work by Verrocchio (also attributed to Domenico Veneziano and Antonio del Pollaiolo); and *St Mary Magdalene (14C Sienese; removed).

On the other side of Corso Fedi is a little garden with palm trees, an equestrian statue of Garibaldi (1904) and amusing lamp-posts. The **Chapel of Sant'Antonio Abate (del Tau)** (open 9–13 except Sunday) was built in 1360 by the monks who cured the sick and disabled (who wore a 'T' or Greek *Tau* on their cloaks, probably symbolising a crutch). The fine Gothic vaulted interior is entirely frescoed with *scenes from the life of St Anthony Abbot and the story of the Sacred Girdle, and, in the vault, the Creation. These are by Niccolò di Tommaso (1372), probably with the help of Antonio Vite (formerly attributed to Bonaccorso di Cino and Masolino). A display of sculpture is to be arranged in the crypt.

In the adjoining *Palazzo del Tau* the **Centro Marino Marini** was opened in 1990 (adm. 9–13, 15–19 except Sunday afternoon and Monday). Here, well arranged in the numerous small rooms of the former convent are graphic works and plaster-casts by the sculptor who was born in Pistoia (1901–66). Farther on, on the left, is the church of

San Paolo, with a fine façade of 1291–1302. Over the later door are a St Paul between two angels by Jacopo di Mazzeo, and (high up on the pinnacle) a figure of St James, attributed to Orcagna. Inside is a 14C wood Crucifix (left wall).

Via Crispi leads N from Piazza Garibaldi to the church of **San Giovanni Fuorcivitas** of the 12–14C. The handsome striped N side, with a blind arcade surmounted by two blind galleries, serves as a façade. The fine portal bears a relief of the Last Supper by Gruamonte (1162). In the dark INTERIOR (light on right side), with stained glass of 1908, the *pulpit is by Fra Guglielmo da Pisa, a follower of Nicola Pisano (1270). The *stoup, with the theological and cardinal Virtues in the middle of the church is by Giovanni Pisano. On the W wall is a large Cross (13–14C). Over the altar on the right side, tondo of the Madonna and Child by the 15C Florentine school. The high altar is made up of 12C intarsia panels from the Duomo. On the right wall of the sanctuary, St John the Evangelist and stories from his life, by Giovanni di Bartolomeo Cristiani (1370); on the opposite wall, polyptych by Taddeo Gaddi (1353–55), and St Roch by Bernardino di Antonio del Signoraccio. On the altar on the N side of the nave, *Visitation in white glazed terracotta thought to be the work of Luca Della Robbia. Above the door, 15C wood statue of St Lucy. By the W end of the church, through the entrance to the Cinema Verdi, can sometimes be seen the charming cloisters.

Farther along Via Cavour, Via Roma leads left past (right) the *Palazzo della Cassa di Risparmio*, an interesting building of 1905 by Tito Azzolini (with interior decorations by Galileo Chini) which stands opposite the old *Palazzo del Capitano del Popolo* (1283), on the corner of Via di Stracceria. The low medieval buildings here (which now have interesting old shop fronts) were used by the workmen who constructed the Baptistery (see below). Beyond is *Piazza della Sala*, a delightful medieval market square, with a well (1453) surmounted by the Florentine *Marzocco* (1529). The large **Piazza del Duomo** has two handsome Gothic public buildings, as well as the Duomo, Baptistery, and Campanile. Above the far corner rises the tall medieval *Torre di Catilina*.

The ***Duomo** has an arcaded Romanesque Pisan façade. The porch was added in 1311, and the high arch in the barrel vault is beautifully decorated by Andrea Della Robbia, as is the *lunette above the central door. The separate *CAMPANILE was originally a watch tower, and is thought to have been adapted to its present use, with the addition of the three tiers of arches, in 1266 by Fra Guglielmo di Pisa, or in 1301 by Giovanni Pisano.

A cathedral in Pistoia is documented as early as the 5C. The present church, dedicated to the Lombard Saint Zeno, erected c 1220 was drastically altered at the end of the 16C, but work in 1951–66 restored it as far as possible to its Romanesque form. At this time the fine wood ceiling, decorated in 1388, was exposed. In 1145 Bishop Atho built the **Chapel of St James** in part of the S aisle (with a separate entrance), to conserve the precious relics of the apostle, St James the Greater, who became patron saint of the city. Pilgrims from Pistoia to his famous shrine at Santiago di Compostela bought back the relics in 1144. For this chapel the silver altar was commissioned in 1287 which since 1953 has been displayed in a chapel in the S aisle. Bishop Atho's chapel was demolished in 1787. Next to the chapel was the sacristy which was robbed by Vanni Fucci in 1293, recorded by Dante ('*Inferno*', XXIV) as the *Sagrestia dei belli arredi*. This is now incorporated in part of the Cathedral Museum (see below).

INTERIOR (closed 12–16). WEST WALL. Funerary monument of St Atho, famous Bishop of Pistoia, with reliefs showing the Bishop receiving the reliquary of St James, attributed to Cellino di Nese (1337). The *font is by Andrea Ferrucci da Fiesole, on a design by Benedetto da Maiano. In the

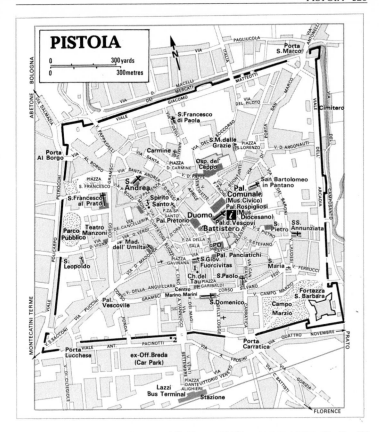

lunette above the door, fresco of St Zeno (12C?). SOUTH AISLE. On the W
wall is a Gothic window surrounded by beautiful fragments of 14C frescoes,
attributed to Bonaccorso di Cino, all that remains of the famous Chapel of
St James (demolished in 1787; see above). On the aisle wall, *tomb of Cino
da Pistoia, thought to be by Agostino di Giovanni on a design by Cellino di
Nese (1337). The painted *Crucifix is by Coppo di Marcovaldo (and his son
Salerno, 1275).

The CHAPEL OF ST JAMES (opened by the sacristan; fee), formerly the
Chapel of the Crucifix, was decorated in 1839, and since 1953 has housed
the famous *ALTAR OF ST JAMES, a masterpiece of medieval goldsmiths'
work. It is decorated with numerous silver and partially gilded bas-reliefs
and statuettes. It was commissioned in 1287, and remodelled and added to
during successive generations (up to 1456). It was restored in 1953. It is
made up of a dossal, the earliest part, attributed to Pace di Valentino, with
a statue of St James enthroned which was added by Maestro Giglio in 1353.
The altar frontal below with fifteen scenes from the New Testament was
completed in 1316 by Andrea di Jacopo di Ognabene. The two panels on
either side of the altar are the work of Francesco di Niccolò and Leonardo
di Ser Giovanni (1361–71). The panel on the left flank, with stories from the

life of St James, includes two half figures of prophets which were added in 1400 by Brunelleschi (who may also have executed the standing figure of St Augustine, and the seated figure of an Evangelist). Behind the altar is a charming 15C Flemish tapestry.

Beside the steps down to the crypt, in a Gothic niche, are fine 14C frescoes and a triptych with the Crucifixion (1429). In the chapel at the end of the aisle is a good altarpiece of the Coronation of the Virgin with Saints Baronto and Desiderio by Mattia Preti, and Moses receiving the tables of the law by Luigi Sabatelli and the Entombment by Giuseppe Bezzuoli (1845–6). The CHOIR was designed in the early 17C by Jacopo Lafri. The frescoes are by Passignano and the high altarpiece of the Resurrection is by Cristofano Allori. The colossal statues of Saints James and Zeno are by a certain Vincenzo (1603), a pupil of Giambologna. To the right, at the top of the sanctuary steps stands a bronze candelabrum by Tommaso di Bartolomeo (1442). On the N wall of the Choir is a fresco fragment of the Madonna attributed to Coppo di Marcovaldo. At the end of the NORTH AISLE is the CHAPEL OF THE SACRAMENT. Here (S wall) is the *Madonna di Piazza with Saints John the Baptist and Zeno (usually covered), the only documented work left by Verrocchio (1485), probably with the help of Lorenzo di Credi. Opposite is a *bust of Archbishop Donato de' Medici, variously attributed to Antonio Rossellino or Verrocchio. On the altar, ciborium of 1662. In the N aisle are a frescoed 14C Madonna and a seated statue of pope Leo XI. At the W end of the aisle is the *tomb of Cardinal Niccolò Forteguerri projected by Verrocchio (1476–83) with Christ in Glory surrounded by angels and statues of Faith and Hope. The figure of Charity (on the left) was added by Lorenzetto in 1515, and the bust and sarcophagus and the frame set up in 1753. Two sides of the Romanesque CRYPT survive, and fragments from the earlier church can be seen here including panels from the pulpit by Guido da Como (1199; dismantled in the 17C). On a lower level is the 17C crypt.

The *Baptistery is a beautiful octagonal building entirely decorated on the outside by bands of green and white marble. It was started in 1337 by Cellino di Nese, traditionally thought to be on a design by Andrea Pisano, and finished in 1359. The capitals and reliefs above the main entrance and the Madonna (attributed to Tommaso and Nino Pisano) in the tympanum are particularly fine. On the right is a tiny Gothic pulpit of 1399. The wood doors are the work of Pier Francesco di Ventura (1523). In the bare brick INTERIOR (closed 12.30–15.30 and on Monday; in winter on weekdays open only 9–12.30) is the font with fine intarsia panels by Lanfranco da Como (1226). The statue of St John the Baptist is by Andrea Vaccà (1724). **Palazzo dei Vescovi**, founded on this site at the end of the 11C and finished in the 12C (and enlarged in the 14C) was beautifully restored in 1982 by the bank which now owns it and uses part of it as offices. It contains an **archaeological section**, and the *Museo della Cattedrale di San Zeno (guided tour on Tuesday and Thursday at 8.30, 10, 11.30 and 15.30 and Friday at 8.30, 10, 11.30, 14.30, 15.30 and 16.45).

In the basement is displayed material found during excavations in the area of the palace, from the Roman period onwards, including two Etruscan cippi used in the foundations, and a hoard of medieval ceramics found in a well. The excavations themselves are shown and explained in detail. MUSEO DELLA CATTEDRALE DI SAN ZENO. The first room contains a Roman cinerary urn (2C AD) with a carriage drawn by four horses, found during excavations in the Duomo. The 15C illuminated choirbooks are displayed in rotation. One of the two *reliquaries, is by Rombolus Salvei (1379), and the other by Maestro Gualandi (1444). Also displayed here: octagonal ebony and ivory coffer by the bottega degli Embriachi (late 15C); chalice of 1384 signed by the local goldsmith Andrea di Pietro Braccini; and a polychrome wood statue of an angel with the head of the Baptist, an interesting work thought to be by a French sculptor (c 1361). Beyond are two 14C Sienese marble statuettes; the *reliquary of San Zeno, made by the local goldsmith Enrico Belandini while in Aix-en-Provence in 1369; the Cross of St Atto (c 1280), and the chalice of St Atto, attributed to Andrea and Tallino d'Ognabene (1286). The fresco of the Crucifixion is by Giovanni di Bartolomeo Cristiani (1387). In the 12C SACRISTY OF ST JAMES (which was attached to the Chapel of St James, formerly in the Duomo, see above) is the *reliquary of St James, by Lorenzo Ghiberti and his bottega (1407). A spiral staircase leads up to a room with 17C vestments, and 18C church silver. Another room has been reconstructed to contain *tempera murals by Giovanni Boldini (1868), with scenes of pastoral life and of the sea at Castiglioncello. They were detached from the Villa La Falconiera near Pistoia, where the Falconer family entertained Boldini and other Macchiaioli painters. Beyond a room with two 16C carved panels by the local sculptor Ventura Vitoni (1442–1522) which survived the fire in 1641 which destroyed the choir in the Duomo, is more 17C church silver. The 12C CAPPELLA DI SAN NICOLÒ, the Bishop's private chapel, contains 14C fresco fragments. Steps lead up to the top of the Romanesque façade of the cathedral (now closed in), above the present loggia. Another room has 17C reliquaries, including the reliquary of St Bartholomew (1663). The SALA SINODALE contains fragments of battle scenes, among the oldest medieval frescoes in Tuscany, and a triptych by Giovanni di Bartolomeo Cristiani.

On the W side of the piazza is **Palazzo Pretorio** (being restored), a Gothic building of 1367 and later, which has a good courtyard, with painted and sculptured armorial bearings of magistrates. On the opposite side of the piazza is **Palazzo del Comune**, another fine Gothic building of 1294, with later additions. On the façade is a curious black basalt head which has probably been here since 1305. The palace houses the **Museo Civico** (adm. 9–13, 15–19; fest. 9–12.30; closed Monday). Stairs lead up to the piano nobile. SALA DEI DONIZELLI. 13C *panel of St Francis, with stories from his life; 14C painting of Mourning over the dead Christ; Master of 1310 (attributed), polyptych of the Madonna and saints; 14C Tuscan statues; Mariotto di Nardo, Madonna enthroned with four angels; chalice by the local goldsmith Andrea di Piero Braccini; Francesco di Valdambrino, angel; Mariotto di Nardo and Rossello di Jacopo Franchi, Annunciation and saints; three paintings of the Madonna enthroned and saints by Lorenzo di Credi, Ridolfo del Ghirlandaio, and Gerino Gerini; 15C marble relief of the Madonna and Child. SALA DEI PRIORI. Bernardino di Antonio Detti, Madonna della Pergola; Agnolo di Polo, bust of the Redeemer; a 15C and a 16C statue of St Sebastian; Fra' Paolino, Annunciatory Angel and Virgin Annunciate. Stairs lead up past the *Centro Michelucci*, with drawings and models of works by the architect Giovanni Michelucci (1891–1991), born in Pistoia, and a section of 20C Pistoian paintings, to three rooms on the top floor. The SALONE contains late-16C and 17C paintings, including works by Gregorio Pagani, Matteo Rosselli, Il Cigoli, Empoli, Francesco Curradi, Carlo Saraceni (Madonna and Child, attributed), Giacinto Gimignani, Antonio Domenico Gabbiani, Lo Spagnoletto (portait of Lanfredino Cellesi of Pistoia), Giuseppe Gambarini, and a contemporary copy of Carlo Maratta's portrait of Clement IX. The decorative arts displayed here include Venetian glass, and Italian majolica. The PUCCINI COLLECTION includes:

Giovanni di Bartolomeo Cristiani, Madonna enthroned with angel musicians; Frankfurt Master, triptych; Maso di San Friano (bottega), angels and the Madonna; Giovanni Battista Naldini, Holy Family; Il Cigoli, marriage of St Catherine; Mattia Preti, Susannah and the Elders; Pietro Dandini, portrait of the doctor Tommaso Puccini. The last room contains 18C and 19C works by Luigi Sabatelli, Anton Raphael Mengs (portrait of cardinal Francesco Saverio de Zelada), and Gilbert Stuart Newton, and historical canvases by Enrico Pollastrini and Giuseppe Bezzuoli (and Puccini portraits).

A 17C covered passageway links Palazzo Comunale with the Duomo high up above the narrow Ripa del Sale which descends to **Palazzo Rospigliosi** (No. 3), opened to the public in 1990 (adm. Tuesday–Saturday, 10–13, Tuesday, Thursday, and Friday also 16–19). Here is housed the **Museo Diocesano**. The palace was left to the cathedral by the last member of this branch of the Rospigliosi family in 1981. In the apartment on the piano nobile Pope Clement IX (Giulio Rospigliosi) probably stayed in the sumptuous bedroom. It contains original furnishings and 17C and 18C frescoes. The interesting 17C paintings (with fine frames) include numerous works by Giacinto Gimignani (1606–81, a native of Pistoia) and his son Ludovico, as well as works by Jacopo Vignali, Lorenzo Lippi, and Felice Ficherelli. Three more rooms contain the MUSEO DIOCESANO (well labelled). The contents include an early 14C coffer, a small polychrome terracotta figure of the kneeling Virgin (c 1460), 12–16C silver Crosses, and 15–19C church silver.

Via Pacini and Via San Pietro lead to the disused 12C church of **San Pietro**, with a characteristic façade; over the main portal is a relief of Christ giving the keys to St Peter, the Madonna, and the Apostles.

Ripa del Sale descends to Via Pacini; straight across Via San Bartolomeo leads to the disorderly piazza in front of the church of *San Bartolomeo in Pantano* which was the church of a famous Benedictine monastery founded c 761. Here in 1001 died Count Ugo of Tuscany. The church was enlarged in 1159 and has a fine FAADE with a relief (1167) over the door of Christ and the Apostles, possibly by Gruamonte. The beautiful basilican INTERIOR with large capitals has a 13C Tuscan fresco of Christ in majesty in the apse. On the walls other fresco fragments have been exposed. The *pulpit by Guido da Como (1250), still Romanesque in spirit, has one column resting on a crouching figure thought to represent the sculptor. The altarpieces include (S aisle) works by Ignazio Hugford and Giovanni Maria Butteri, (S transept) Alessio Gemignani, and (N transept) Matteo Rosselli., and (N transept) Matteo Rosselli.

Via Pacini leads N to the **Ospedale del Ceppo**, founded in 1277, and still in use. The fine portico has recently been attributed to Michelozzo, with modifications by Giovanni Battista di Antonio di Gerino (c 1480). It is decorated with a colourful enamelled terracotta *frieze (1514–25), excellently carved and very well preserved (cleaned in 1984). It depicts the seven works of mercy by Giovanni Della Robbia, with the help of Santi Viviani Buglioni; the seventh was added by Filippo di Lorenzo Paladini in 1584–86. Between the scenes are the cardinal and theological Virtues, also by Giovanni Della Robbia. Beneath are medallions with the Annunciation, Visitation, and Assumption and the arms of the hospital, of the city, and the Medici, by Benedetto Buglioni and Giovanni Della Robbia. To the left of the hospital, above the door of the adjoining church, is a Coronation of the Virgin by Benedetto Buglioni (1512), the oldest work of the series.

To the E of the hospital in Piazza San Lorenzo, is the church of **Santa Maria delle Grazie** or *del Letto*. It was built in 1451 and was formerly attributed to Michelozzo, but the fine presbytery is now generally considered to be the work of the local architect Ventura Vitoni. The high altar has a fine silver tabernacle (1641) and the 14C bed, held to be miraculous, which gave its name to the church is preserved in a chapel on the left.

From the Ospedale del Ceppo, Via delle Pappe and Via del Carmine (left) lead to Via Sant'Andrea in which is the church of *Sant'Andrea, with another good 12C façade by Gruamonte and his brother Adeodato who signed the relief of the Journey and Adoration of the Magi (1166). In the long narrow interior (similar to San Bartolomeo in Pantano; coin-operated light) is a 14C font of the Pisan school, and a hexagonal *pulpit with dramatic reliefs by Giovanni Pisano (1298–1301), perhaps his masterpiece. He was probably helped by Tino da Camaino. In the apse is a statuette of St Andrew of the school of Giovanni Pisano (formerly on the façade), and in the S aisle, in a 15C tabernacle, a wood Crucifix by Giovanni Pisano. At the end of the N aisle, Madonna of Humility, by Niccolò di Mariano (15C Sienese).

At the end of Via Sant'Andrea is Piazza San Francesco, with the church of **San Francesco** (formerly known as *San Francesco al Prato*) begun in 1289, with a façade completed in 1717. The wide open-roofed nave with damaged remains of frescoes (and an altarpiece of the Raising of Lazarus by Alessandro Allori on the fourth left altar), ends in a wide vaulted transept with five E chapels. Behind the high altar (lights to right switched on by request) are 14C frescoes showing strong Giottesque influence, possibly the work of a pupil, Puccio Capanna. In the chapel to the left is a splendid fresco cycle of the *allegory of the triumph of St Augustine, by the Sienese school. 14C frescoes also decorate the second chapel to the right of the choir. In the S transept are interesting remains of a huge frescoed Crucifix, attributed to the Master of 1310. A door in this transept leads through the Sacristy to the CHAPTER HOUSE (not always open) both of which retain good late-14C frescoes, notably on the E wall of the latter, the Tree of Life with a Crucifixion, possibly by Pietro Lorenzetti. The 14C CLOISTER is beyond. In Corso Gramsci, S of the church, is the *Teatro Manzoni*, inaugurated in 1694, and altered in the mid-18C by Il Bibbiena.

From Piazza San Francesco Via Bozzi and Via Montanara e Curtatone lead back towards the centre of the town. To the left is the church of the **Spirito Santo**, founded by the Jesuits in 1647 with a good Baroque *INTERIOR by the Jesuit father Tommaso Ramignani, beautifully restored, with its contents, in 1988. Cardinal Giulio Rospigliosi, on becoming Pope Clement IX in 1667, commissioned Gian Lorenzo Bernini to design the high altar, and Pietro da Cortona to paint the high altarpiece of the Apparition of Christ to St Ignatius. The ciborium in pietre dure, ebony, and gilded bronze, also dates from this time. North side. First chapel, Ottaviano Dandini, Deposition (and the two small works on either side); second chapel, 17C wood robed statuette of the Madonna of Loreto, and early 18C paintings of the Nativity and Conception. The little organ on the left (and its decorative counterpart opposite) are by the Flemish organ-maker Willem Herman (1663). The contemporary carved confessionals are also noteworthy.

In Via della Madonna, which leads right off Via Montanara e Curtatone, is the 15C basilican sanctuary of the **Madonna dell'Umiltà**, built by Ventura Vitoni (1495), a pupil of Bramante. The DOME, a conspicuous feature of the city when viewed from the plain, was added by Vasari in 1562. The main portal dates from the 17C. The fine barrel vaulted VESTIBULE contains 18C frescoes illustrating the history of the basilica. The octagonal centrally planned INTERIOR is an interesting example of High Renaissance architecture. SOUTH SIDE. On the first altar, Lazzaro Baldi, Rest on the Flight into Egypt; second altar, Francesco Vanni, Adoration of the Magi; third altar, Il Poppi, Assumption. On the first altar left of the high altar, Lodovico Buti (on a design by Vasari), Annunciation; second chapel on the left, Passignano, Adoration of the Shepherds. The marble HIGH ALTAR by Pietro Tacca (with two angels by Leonardo Marcacci) encloses a miraculous 14C fresco of the Madonna of Humility, attributed to Bartolomeo Cristiani, around which the sanctuary was built.

Environs of Pistoia

At **La Verginina**, 4km NW of Pistoia, is a small *Zoo* (open daily 9–dusk), created in 1970 on a pleasant hillside (trattoria *Bischio*). A pretty road continues beyond the zoo through the Valle del Vincio via Momigno to (19km) Femminamorta (860m). A by-road from here leads (2km) to the pretty village of *Serra Pistoiese*, with an 11C Romanesque pieve. N633 leads S from Femminamorta via Marliana Montecatini, described below.

A few kilometres E of Pistoia, at the **Fattoria di Celle** on the Santomato road, is the interesting private collection of Giuliano Gori of modern and contemporary art with a sculpture park (admission by appointment; Tel. 0573/479907).

PISTOIA TO ABETONE, 49km, bus in 1hr 45mins. This route, constructed in 1776–78 by Leonardo Ximenes, traverses the *Montagna Pistoiese* or Pistoian Apennines. The Pistoia by-pass skirts the Breda works (1973) and continues past a turning (left) for the Zoo (see above). The Bologna road diverges to the right while N66 climbs steeply through woods and several villages to (10.5km) *Cireglio* with a few hotels and restaurants (restaurant *Da Ildo* at Piteccio). At (11.5km) *Piastre* is the junction with the by-road from Piteglio (described below); the main road bends right and now follows the river Reno. At (19.5km) *Pontepetri* is the junction with the road from Pracchia (see below). N66 continues left, parallel to a higher by-road linking the resorts of Maresca and Gavinana. The Imperial defeat of the Florentine army at Gavinana in 1530, in which both commanders, Francesco Ferrucci and Philibert, Prince of Orange were killed, sealed the fate of the Republic (a fine equestrian monument of 1920 by Emilio Gallori and the Museo Ferrucciano here commemorate the battle).

Beyond Bardalone the road becomes prettier with a view of the mountains; it climbs to 820m before descending to (29km) **San Marcello Pistoiese** (623m; APT Abetone-Pistoia-Montagna Pistoiese, 28 Via Marconi, Tel. 0573/630145; 3-star hotel *Il Cacciatore* with restaurant). It is the most important summer resort on the Pistoian Apennines, and there is a good view of the mountains ahead to the left. The road descends to cross the river Lima with several old dams, and (at 32km) joins N12 from Lucca. 37km *Cutigliano* (670m; numerous 3-star and 2-star hotels; first-class restaurant *Fagiolino*, 1 Via Carega), to the right of the road, is a tidy little resort. The 14C Palazzo Pretorio is covered with coats of arms, and in the nearby church of the Compagnia is an enamelled terracotta high altarpiece of the Madonna between Saints Anthony and Bernardine of Siena by the Della Robbia. On the edge of the village, beside two horse-chestnut trees is the parish church. In the light interior is a high altarpiece of a miracle of St Bartholomew by Sebastiano Vini, and on the left wall of the sanctuary is a Circumcision by Giovanni da San Giovanni. At the end of the left aisle is a fine wood altarpiece which encloses the Birth of the Virgin by Nicodemo

Ferrucci. The winter sports facilites include a funicular to *Doganaccia* (1540m), another ski resort, and to Croce Arcana (1730m).

Beyond (42km) *Pianosinatico* (948m) the road ascends through the splendid forest that still clothes the Tuscan slope of the mountains. *Rivoreta*, 3km N of Pianosinatico, has a local Ethnographical Museum. 50km The *Passo dell'Abetone* (1388m) takes its name from a huge fir-tree which has long disappeared. Round the road summit, still on the the Tuscan side of the boundary with Emilia, has developed **Abetone**, one of the best-known ski resorts in the Apennines, specially favoured by Florentines. Numerous ski-lifts and chair-lifts ascend to the snow fields. It is also much visited in summer (swimming pools, tennis courts, etc.). APT information office (Tel. 0573/60231). Two 4-star hotels, and numerous 3-star and 2-star hotels; first-class restaurant *La Capannina*, 254 Via Brennero. Bus services run to Bologna, Florence, Pisa and Ferrara. The road (described in *Blue Guide Northern Italy*) continues via Pievepelago at the foot of Monte Cimone, the highest peak in the Northern Apennines (2165m) in Emilia Romagna to Modena. The return to Pistoia from San Marcello Pistoiese can be made by the windy and narrow by-road (N633) via Migliorini and Piteglio (trattoria *La Chiocciolina* at La Lima) which passes through pretty countryside. It climbs to Prunetta where the road from Montecatini is joined to descend to *Piastre* (see above).

PISTOIA TO THE PASSO DELLA PORRETTA, 14km, N64. This is the Bologna road, followed by the *Porrettana* railway which until 1934 was the main line across the Apennines. The mountain stretch between Pistoia and Porretta Terme, opened in 1863 is particularly fine. On the outskirts of Pistoia, this route soon diverges to the Abetone road to ascend the Valle di Brana, with fine views downhill. 5km *La Cugna*. At (14km) *La Collina* the road reaches the summit of the *Passo della Porretta* (or *della Collina*; 932m) and enters Emilia, described in *Blue Guide Northern Italy*.

An alternative route from Pistoia (N362) to Bologna follows the Abetone road (see above) as far as (19km) *Pontepetri*, and then descends the Reno valley via (23km) *Pracchia* (616m; hotels), a summer resort fashionable between the Wars, at the mouth of a long railway tunnel (3km) on the border of Emilia.

PISTOIA TO VINCI, 24km. A fine road, in parts lined with pine trees, leads due S from Pistoia to (7km) Casalguidi, then traverses the Albano hills with spectacular views, via Baronto, to (24km) *Vinci*, described in Rte 11.

PISTOIA TO MONTECATINI, PESCIA, AND COLLODI, N435, 28km. The A11 motorway from Florence to the sea follows this road as far as Montecatini; it then bends S for Altopasicio (exit at Chiesina Uzzanese for Pescia and Collodi). Outside Pistoia, beyond the huge Breda factory, the motorway, road and railway traverse the low pass between the Apennines and Monte Pisano. The tall tower of the old fortress of *Serravalle Pistoiese* is conspicuous ahead. The road climbs over the pass beside Serravalle and emerges above the wide plain of Lucca stretching towards the sea. On a hill with chestnut woods, but disfigured by quarries, stands a tower of Monsummano Alto (described below).

The little spa of **Monsummano Terme** (4-star hotel *Grotta Giusti*, with swimming pool; 18-hole golf course in località Pievaccia), at the foot of the hill, with vapour baths, was once visited by the wounded Garibaldi. In the large piazza with a statue of Giuseppe Giusti (1809–50), the Tuscan poet, who was born here, is the parish church of *Santa Maria della Fontenuova* built in 1605 and surrounded by a portico with frescoed lunettes by Giovanni da San Giovanni (1630). In the pretty INTERIOR there is a fine ceiling and organ. In the S transept, Piero Dandini, Madonna with St Joachim and Anne. Over the high altar, venerated fresco of the Madonna and Child. In the N transept, Matteo Rosselli, Adoration of the Magi. A delightful MUSEUM (opened on request) contains works by Matteo Rosselli, Cristofano Allori, and a Cross in ivory attributed to Giambologna. At the end of the piazza is the *Osteria dei Pellegrini*, a fine building of 1609–16, with a portico in travertine. Just out of this end of the piazza, at the corner of Viale Martini, is *Casa Giusti*, which houses a museum relating to the poet. From the piazza various grotte are signposted; these are caverns in the hillside used as spas. A narrow road (also signposted) leads up round the hill to *Monsummano Alto*, a fortified medieval village at this strategic position defending the pass between the plain of Lucca and the valley of Pistoia. The road enters the ruined hamlet beside the tallest pentagonal tower. A path leads straight on to the 12C church with its campanile beside a picturesque group of houses, most of them abandoned. At the end of the ridge can be seen another gate on the hillside below. There is a fine view of the plain.

The main road descends to the plain and on a hill-top to the right Montecatini Alto comes into view. 15km **MONTECATINI TERME** (20,600 inhab.) is the best known of Italian spas, with an international reputation. It became famous at the beginning of the 20C, when the monumental thermal establishments were built. They are spaciously laid out and surrounded by attractive well-kept parks. The warm saline waters are taken, both internally and externally, for digestive troubles. The season runs from May to October.

Information Offices. *APT Montecatini–Valdinievole*, 66 Viale Verdi (Tel. 0572/772244). *Società delle Terme*, 41 Viale Verdi (where tickets for the mineral water, etc., can be purchased).

Railway Stations. *Centrale*, Piazza Italia, and *Succursale*, Piazza Gramsci (the most convenient to visitors, as the nearest to Viale Verdi). All trains on the Florence–Viareggio line stop at both stations; from Florence local trains in 50mins.

Bus services (Lazzi) from Via Toti to Pistoia, Prato, Florence, Lucca, Pisa, Pescia, Livorno, and Viareggio.

Funicular Railway from Viale Diaz to Montecatini Alto (usually open May–October 10–13, 15–20; in August 9–midnight; services c every half hour).

Hotels. There are two 5-star, twelve 4-star, sixty-two 3-star, and ninety-eight 2-star hotels, most of them open only from March or April to October or November. The most famous hotel (5-star, with a Luxury-class restaurant) is the *Grand Hotel e la Pace*, 1 Via della Torretta. Information and booking service at the *Associazione Provinciale Albergatori* (APAM), 66 Via delle Saline.

Restaurants of all categories all over the town. Luxury-class: *Enoteca da Giovanni*, 25 Via Garibaldi. First-class: *San Francisco*, 112 Corso Roma.

History. Ugolino Simoni (1348–1425), born in Montecatini, made a fundamental study of the mineral waters of Italy, including those of Montecatini. Although probably known in Roman times, and used by the Medici, they were first developed on a grand scale by the Austrian Grand-duke Pietro Leopoldo in 1773–82. By the beginning of this century Montecatini was one of the most famous spas in Europe. Giuseppe Verdi often stayed at the *Locanda Maggiore*, and wrote the last act of *Otello* here (1887). Most of the thermal buildings were built in 1928 on a project drawn up in 1915–18 by Ugo Giovannozzi for the Società delle Terme.

The centre of Montecatini is **Viale Verdi** on which are all the most important buildings; at the upper end is a view of Montecatini Alto. From the unattractive Piazza del Popolo (the church of Santa Maria Assunta was built in 1962) the avenue ascends past the *Gambrinus* café in a piazza with a colonnade and decorative lamp-posts. The monumental *Town Hall* (and post office) built in 1919, stands opposite the *Società delle Terme* which runs the spas. The spas, used for drinking water and bathing, are all situated in the fine park beyond. The elaborate *Terme Excelsior* (open all year) was built in 1909 by Bernardini in a florid mixture of styles. The handsome extension was added in 1968. The *Terme Leopoldine* (which probably cover the most ancient spring) was rebuilt in 1926 by Ugo Giovannozzi in a classical style (the temple bears a dedication to Asculapius). At the end of the Viale rise the splendid buildings of the **Terme Tettuccio**, the most famous thermal establishment in Montecatini, whose waters were mentioned as early as 1370. It was also rebuilt by Giovannozzi in 1925–28, although it preserves an inner façade by Gaspare Paoletti (1779–81). The café, reading room, and drinking gallery are all sumptuously decorated with ceramics, murals, statuary, and wrought-iron work by Galileo Chini, Ezio Giovannozzi (brother of Ugo), and many others.

Beyond the *Terme Regina*, on Viale Diaz, is the *Accademia d'Arte 'Dino Scalabrino'* (open May–Oct, Mon, Wed & Fri 15.30–19.30) with a gallery with works by Galileo Chini, Giovanni Fattori, Lorenzo Viani, Pietro Annigoni, and others, and a small historical museum. Also on Viale Diaz is the Funicular Station for Montecatini Alto (see below). In the extensive well-kept park beyond the Tettuccio are the *Terme Tamerici* and the *Terme Torretta* both built at the beginning of the century by Bernardini in a neo-Gothic style. On the hillside above is the *Parco della Panteraie* with fine woods (and a swimming pool). The central *Railway Station*, with handsome marble decoration, dates from 1937. The huge *Kursaal*, once the Casinò, was sold in 1989 and again in 1994, and may one day be restored.

Montecatini Alto (or *Montecatini Valdinievole* 4-star hotel *Park Hotel-Le Sorgenti*; at Pieve a Nievole; first-class restaurants *Le Pietre Cavate* and *Uno Più* at Pieve a Nievole; 3-star camping site *Belsito*, at Vico) is reached from Montecatini Terme by funicular (see above) or road (5km). It is an old hill town (290m) in a spectacular position. Here the men of Lucca were defeated in 1315 by Uguccione della Faggiola, leader of the Ghibellines of Pisa. Above the attractive piazza with several cafés and the Teatrino dei Risorti, an amusing building dating from the early 20C, on a hill planted with cypresses and ilexes, is the Prepositurale of San Pietro (open only for services). A small museum of vestments, reliquaries, and paintings here has been closed indefinitely. Walks may be taken in the pleasant surroundings, especially in the Val di Nievole, to the N.

The main road continues into (18km) **Borgo a Buggiano**, outside which (left of the road) is the huge *Villa di Bellavista*, built at the end of the 17C by Antonio Ferri, with frescoes by Pier Dandini. It is owned by the State and has been partly restored as an exhibition centre. The parish church (*Santissimo Crocifisso*) of Borgo a Buggiano was rebuilt in 1771. INTERIOR (all the works are labelled). On the nave pilasters are four paintings by Fra Felice da Sambuca (1777). On the first altar on the S side, Fra Paolino da Pistoia, Madonna enthroned with saints, and in the S transept, Bernardino del Signoraccio, Madonna of the Rosary with Saints Dominic and Francis (1500–10). Behind the high altar, wood *Crucifix thought to date from the early 14C and two terracotta statues of the Madonna and St John the Evangelist attributed to the workshop of the Buglioni. On the N side (second altar), Giacomo Tais, Madonna and saints, and (first altar), Alessandro Allori, martyrdom of St Agatha. A charming small MUSEUM (opened on request) contains church silver, vestments, a 14C painted reliquary, numerous Crosses, etc., some from Buggiano Castello. Two paintings (15C and 16C) from the pieve of Stignano may also be exhibited here.

Beyond the railway, a by-road (1km) leads up through olive groves past a large tabernacle on the right of the road with 15C frescoes of the Madonna and Child and two angels, etc. (restored in 1991) to **Buggiano Castello**, a charming old village, extremely well preserved. Many of the handsome houses, have attractive red plaster finish. It is best to leave the car on the road below, and walk up through the castellated gateway. Beyond the *ex-convent of Santa Scolastica* with a pretty loggia with tiny columns high up on its façade, is the delightful little piazza below the flank of the church, with the *Palazzo Pretorio* (recently well restored) with numerous coats of arms including some in Della Robbian enamelled terracotta. Through an arch there is a view of the plain and the church tower of Stignano. The PIEVE was founded in 1038. The wide interior has fine capitals. At the W end are a *font and lectern (c 1250). South side, second altar, Giovanni del Brina, Madonna and four saints (1571); third altar, Bicci di Lorenzo (or his school), Annunciation. Over the high altar is a small wood Crucifix (possibly dating from the 14C). In the chapel to the left of the sanctuary, the Madonna and saints in the style of Andrea del Castagno (1498) has been removed for restoration. North side, second altar, Giovanni del Brina, Madonna of the Rosary. A 16C terracotta Madonna and Child has been removed from the niche for restoration; first altar, 16C painting of the Baptism of Christ (in very poor condition). At the top of the hill are remains of the medieval *Rocca*.

At **Ponte Buggianese**, 4.5km S of Borgo a Buggiano, in the church of San Michele Arcangelo, are frescoes of the Passion cycle by Pietro Annigoni (1910–88), including a striking Last Supper in the apse.

Beyond Borgo a Buggiano a by-road diverges right for *Stignano* (1.5km), a hamlet in a fine position where Coluccio Salutati (1331–1406), Chancellor of the Florentine Republic, was born (plaque). The church of Sant'Andrea, with a Romanesque campanile, is usually locked. Two paintings have been removed and are in store in the church of Borgo a Buggiano.

23km **PESCIA** (18,200 inhab.) is a busy town which has expanded to the S. It has a very unusual plan, laid out longitudinally on both sides of the Pescia river: on the left bank is the cathedral and on the right bank the exceptionally long market square (Piazza Mazzini) with the town hall. Since the Second World War it has become an important horticultural centre particularly noted for asparagus, carnations, lilies, and gladioli. The striking flower market built in 1951 by Giuseppe Gori was superseded by an even larger one in 1980 (by Leonardo Savioli) on the S outskirts of the town.

Information Office. *APT Montecatini Terme-Valdinievole*, 66 Viale Verdi, Montecatini.

Railway Station, c 1km S of the town on the Florence–Viareggio line; local trains from Florence in c 1 hr.

Car Park behind the church of San Francesco.

Bus Services (COPIT) to Collodi (in 25mins), and Uzzano, Castelvecchio, and the other small villages in the vicinity.

Hotel. 3-star: *Villa delle Rose*, Via del Castellare (near the railway station).

Restaurants. First-class: *Cecco*, 84 Via Forti. Trattoria: *La Buca*, 4 Piazza Mazzini.

Biennale del Fiore (flower show) in early Sept (next in 1996).

History. The town grew up in the Middle Ages and was governed by a Vicario. As an ally of Florence, it suffered a severe defeat by Lucca and the Guelf party in 1281. The town expanded in the 16C and 17C.

The centre of the town is **•Piazza Mazzini**, a huge long narrow square which characterises the general layout of the town. At the upper end is the town hall in *Palazzo del Vicario* covered with coats of arms (restored in the 19C). In the loggia (seen behind an iron grille) is a war memorial by Libero Andreotti. A neo-Gothic outside staircase connects the palace to the *Can-*

celleria and the *Torre Civica*. Among the fine palaces in the piazza is Palazzo Della Barba (No. 79) on a design traditionally attributed to Raphael. The Renaissance church of the **Madonna di piè di Piazza** closes the S end of the square. It was built in the 15C by Buggiano and preserves its exterior, although the interior dates from 1605 (the wood ceiling is by Giovanni Zeti). Over the high altar is a venerated 15C fresco of the Madonna in the centre of a painting by Alessandro Tiarini which includes a view of Pescia. The last palace on the W side of the piazza was built c 1530 by Baccio d'Agnolo (but was reduced in size at the beginning of this century). *Ruga degli Orlandi* runs parallel to the Piazza on its W side. Among the handsome palaces here is the decorative *Palazzo Forti* (No. 42). Farther N is the church of the *Santissima Annunziata* (closed), built in 1713–20 by Antonio Ferri. It contains a painting of St Charles Borromeo by Volterrano. In Piazza Santo Stefano (left) there is a view of the Castello di Bareglia (now the convent of San Francesco di Paola) on the hillside. The church of **Santi Stefano e Niccolao** is approached by a pretty outside staircase (thought to be by Agostino Cornacchini). Founded in 1068 the church was reconstructed in the 18C. INTERIOR. South Aisle, first altar, two wood statues of the Annunciatory Angel and the Virgin Annunciate; the Virgin is attributed to Matteo Civitali. On either side of the second altar are two paintings of St Sebastian and St Michael by Agostino Ciampelli. In the sanctuary, Madonna and four saints by Ercole Bazzicaluva (17C), and, on the right wall, Madonna and Child with angel musicians (and the Epiphany below), a fine 15C painting.

In front of the church is the 18C Palazzo Galeotti, seat of the *Biblioteca Comunale* and the **Museo Civico** (open Wednesday, Friday, and Saturday, 10–13; Thursday 16–18; or by request at the Library). The works are unlabelled. LOWER FLOOR. Room 1: Neri di Bicci, *Annunciation and two saints; Lorenzo Monaco (attributed), triptych of the Madonna and two saints (1464); Master of Santa Cecilia (attributed), Madonna and Child. Room 2: lunette of the Madonna and Child with a bishop saint and St Dorothy, attributed to Benedetto Pagni da Brescia (a pupil of Giulio Romano). Room 3: Neri di Bicci, Coronation of the Virgin; Santi di Tito, Christ and St Mary Magdalene. Beyond is a room of the Galeotti palace with 18C decorations. UPPER FLOOR. Room 1: garland by the Della Robbia; Benedetto Pagni, Resurrection of Christ (restored in 1991); Giovanni da San Giovanni (attributed), St John the Baptist in the desert. Beyond a room with mementoes of the musician Giovanni Pacini who lived in Pescia from 1855 to 1867, there is a library with the papers of the historian Giovan Carlo de' Sismondi who lived in Pescia in the early 19C. The last room has a collection of local material belonging to the Comune, and a plan of the city dating from 1621.

On the right of Santo Stefano a short road leads up to another quiet little piazza in front of the *Palazzo del Podestà*, a handsome 13C building altered over the centuries. Here is a *Gipsoteca* with the works of the sculptor Libero Andreotti who was born in Pescia (1875–1933), open Wed & Fri 16–19; Sat 10–13; last Sun of month 16–19; winter: Fri 15–18, Sat 10–13, last Sun of month 15–18.

On the left, by the campanile of Santo Stefano (restored in 1388) Via San Policronio leads up beneath an archway to a bridge over a stream. From here a charming country lane continues uphill, past a tabernacle and skirting the walls, to the *Castello di Bareglia*, converted into the convent of San Francesco di Paola in 1674, with a pretty loggia. The church (1713) contains paintings by Giacomo Tais. On the other hill (left of the stream), called *Colle dei Fabbri*, in the church of an ex-convent (now a hospice) is a painting of St Philip Neri by Carlo Maratta.

Ponte San Francesco leads across the Pescia torrent to Piazza San Francesco with the *Teatro Pacini*, founded in 1717 (altered in the 19C and reopened in 1991), and the church of **San Francesco**, first built in the 13C, but later altered. In the INTERIOR a number of paintings have recently been restored. SOUTH WALL, frescoed lunette, detached from the exterior; second altar, painting of the eleven thousand Martyrs (1577; removed for restoration); third altar, *St Francis with six stories from his life signed and dated 1235 by Bonaventura Berlinghieri. Painted only nine years after the saint's death, it is considered to be one of the most faithful images of him. SOUTH TRANSEPT, St Charles Borromeo by Rodomonte Pieri and Francesco Nardi. In the SACRISTY is a large fresco of the Crucifixion attributed to Puccio Capanna. In the chapel to the right of the sanctuary, remains of frescoes attributed to Nicolò Gerini or Bicci di Lorenzo, and other frescoes dated 1431. In the SANCTUARY with fresco fragments, on the left wall is an interesting painting of a miracle of St Anthony by Giovanni Martinelli. In the chapel to the left of the sanctuary, triptych of St Anne by Angelo Puccinelli (1335), and on the left wall, Deposition by Passignano. The altarpiece in the NORTH TRANSEPT of the martyrdom of St Dorothy is a fine work by Jacopo Ligozzi. NORTH WALL, Lodovico Cigoli (attributed), St Louis of Toulouse, St Elizabeth of Hungary, and St Anthony before St Francis. In the large Chapel of the Immacolata (early 16C) there is a 15C wood statue of the Madonna and Child, and a Pietà attributed to Cristofano Allori. Also off this side is the *CAPPELLA CARDINI, a beautiful architectural work derived from Brunelleschi and attributed to Buggiano. It is in urgent need of structural repair and restoration; the 15C Crucifix has been temporarily removed to another part of the church. The frescoes are by Neri di Bicci.

Via Battisti leads out of the piazza past the hospital of *Santi Cosma e Damiano*, built in 1762, with a coat of arms on its façade, and modern hospital buildings. Set back from the road on the left is the little church of *Sant'Antonio Abate* (1361; closed), which contains fine early 15C frescoes attributed to Bicci di Lorenzo, and a wood *Deposition group dating from the 13C. At a crossroads by a bridge can be seen (left) *Palazzo Ricci* (1635) with a pretty little marble fountain at the foot of its façade. Via Cavour (beware of traffic) leads on to the **Duomo**, with a massive Gothic campanile (the top was added in 1771), once a tower in the walls. Founded in the 10C, it was rebuilt in 1726 and has a façade dating from 1895 in the Renaissance style. The INTERIOR was designed in 1693 by Antonio Ferri. Off the SOUTH SIDE opens the Cappella Turini built by Baccio d'Agnolo. The funerary monument of Baldassare Turini has two male figures by Raffaello da Montelupo and an awkward effigy by Pierino da Vinci. The painting of the Madonna del Baldacchino by Pietro Dandini is a fine copy of the original by Raphael, removed to the Pitti by Ferdinando dei Medici in 1697. Beside the high altar (by Vaccà) is a lectern made up from Romanesque sculptures from the ambone of the old church. NORTH SIDE, third chapel, altar by Andrea Pozzo and an altarpiece of the martyrdom of St Lawrence by Antonio Domenico Gabbiani; second altar, Madonna and saints by Antonio Franchi. Behind the cathedral is the little church of *San Michelino* (closed; deconsecrated), an interesting Romanesque building.

Beneath the campanile of the Duomo an arch leads into a courtyard. Here is the entrance (at the top of outside stairs) to the *Biblioteca Capitolare* (admission on request in the mornings). In the *Cappella del Vescovado* is a lovely small enamalled terracotta *triptych of the Madonna between Saints James and Blaise, a late work of Luca Della Robbia. Over the altar is a painting of the Madonna and saints by Domenico Soldini (1592). In front of the cathedral is the 18C church of *Santa Maria Maddalena* with a pretty dome. In the sacristy is kept a venerated carved Crucifix. Via Giusti continues out of the town, passing beneath the *Porta Fiorentina* erected in 1732 by Bernardo Sgrilli in honour of Gian Gastone dei Medici.

In Piazzale Leonardo de Vinci in the S part of town is a small *Museum of Archaeology and Natural History* (open Tues, Wed, Thurs & Fri 9–13; Tues also 15–17.30), with finds from the Valdinievole.

From behind San Francesco, a road (unsignposted) leads up through olive groves to **Uzzano**, a charming, quiet little village, extremely well preserved, with pretty gardens and orchards. The entrance is through a narrow archway. It is best to park in Piazza Umberto where the Palazzo del Capitano del Popolo has a loggia on the ground floor. From the terrace there is a view of the plain crowded with greenhouses. Via Barsanti leads up to the church with a decorative little façade and massive campanile. The interior has two vaulted chapels at the W end with worn 15C frescoes, a 13C stoup, a font with a rare 16C wood cover, and (in a niche) a lifesize Della Robbian statue in polychrome terracotta (in very poor condition) of St Anthony Abbot. From the lawn there is a view of Pescia with its two huge flower markets.

In the two pretty green valleys of the Pescia river are numerous paper mills (some now abandoned) and a number of picturesque villages well worth exploring from *Pietrabuona*, with remains of its castle. They include: *Medicina*, *Fibbialla*, above the Val di Torbola, *Aramo*, *San Quirico*, and (12km) **Castelvecchio**, with the fine Romanesque pieve of San Tommaso. Beyond *Stiappa* (16.5km) is *Pontito*, the highest village in the valley. It has an interesting fan-shaped plan. It was the birthplace of Lazzaro Papi (1763–1834) who translated Milton's *Paradise Lost*. Another road from Pietrabuona leads up to *Vellano* (11km), with the pieve di San Martino founded in 910.

The main road continues from Pescia. 27km Turning for **Collodi** (1km N), famous for the Baroque gardens of the huge Villa Garzoni, conspicuous on the hillside. The birthplace of the mother of Carlo Lorenzini (1826–90; born in Florence), it gave him the pen-name under which he wrote *Le Avventure di Pinocchio*, first published in 1881 and later translated into 63 languages. On the right of the road is the entrance to the spectacular *Gardens of Villa Garzoni* (admission daily 9.30–dusk), now situated in disappointing surroundings. Much visited by tourist groups, they are administered in a pretentious fashion. The terraced gardens were laid out on this steep hillside c 1650 and embellished in 1786. They are decorated with yew hedges, fountains, and statues. From the hemicycle, beyond a sloping parterre, a double staircase leads to an upper terrace at the foot of a scenographic cascade, bordered by two water staircases. At the left end of the terrace is the green theatre laid out with box hedges. At the top is a colossal statue of Fame, and, beyond, enclosed by cypresses, an 18C bath-house with separate enclosures for men and women, near a screened gallery for an orchestra.

Paths lead up through the ilex woods to the VILLA itself, or CASTELLO (closed indefinitely for restoration). The castle was bought by the Garzoni in the early 17C and in 1652 they transformed it into a villa. It contains frescoed architectural perspectives attributed to Angelo Michele Colonna and 18C furniture.

The peaceful old village of **Collodi** climbs up the hill behind the villa. It is best approached on foot by the stepped lane which leads up beside the wall of the villa; otherwise a very narrow road leads up from the square outside the gardens (very limited parking space at the top). The picturesque hamlet (no cars) has incredibly steep stepped lanes which lead up to the church. There are views of the valleys on either side of the ridge.

Across the river is the entrance to a CHILDRENS' PARK (open daily 8.30–dusk) built in 1956 to commemorate Pinocchio (much visited by school excursions). There is a bronze monument to the puppet hero by Emilio Greco and a piazza with mosaics illustrating the life of Pinocchio by Venturino Venturini. The *Osteria del Gambero Rosso* restaurant was designed by Giovanni Michelucci in 1963. A garden was laid out in 1971 with sculptured tableaux recalling episodes from the book, and an exhibition hall, also designed by Michelucci was opened in 1987.

The road continues up the valley beyond Collodi passing numerous paper mills (some of them now abandoned but interesting monuments of industrial architecture). A by-road left is signposted for **Villa Basilica**. The ancient *PIEVE has a delightful exterior and fine interior (12–13C). In the apse is an unusual painted *Cross by Berlinghiero Berlinghieri. The font now serves as a fountain in the piazza outside.

Also near Collodi is **San Gennaro** (3km). It is approached via a by-road which leaves the main Lucca road (N435) just after it crosses the river. The narrow road, which has open views, winds gently up past olives, pine trees, and cypresses. The domed campanile (1840) of the church can be seen ahead. It stands between a large villa and the interesting Romanesque façade of San Gennaro. The church (usually locked) contains an ambone of 1162 and two 15C terracotta statues of the Annunciation. In front is a little terrace with lime trees.

6

Lucca

LUCCA (86,600 inhab.) is one of the most beautiful small towns in Tuscany. It is surrounded by magnificent 16–17C ramparts which are its most remarkable feature. It conserves much of its Roman street plan, and is especially rich in Romanesque churches. There are also an unusual number of private walled gardens within the walls.

Information Offices. APT, 2 Piazza Guidiccioni; Information Office, Vecchia Porta di San Donato, Piazzale Verdi (open every day 9–19), Tel. 0583/419689.

Railway Station, Piazzale Ricasoli, a few hundred metres S of the Baluardo di San Colombano and the Duomo. Services on the Florence-Viareggio line, slow trains stopping at numerous stations (from Florence, 78km in 70–90 minutes).

Buses (CLAP and *Lazzi*) from Piazzale Verdi for Florence (via the motorway, frequent service in 1hr), Montecatini, Prato, Pistoia; for Bagni di Lucca, Barga, Castelnuovo di Garfagnana, etc; for Pisa, Livorno; for Viareggio, Carrara; and for Abetone.

Car Parking is not allowed inside the walls for longer than 90 minutes except with an hourly tariff. Visitors are therefore strongly advised to park outside the walls in one of the free car parks (the most convenient of which is *Le Tagliate*, outside Porta San Donato. Limited space is sometimes available off the Viali Carducci, Margherita, del Prete, and Giusti, or outside the station or Piazza Risorgimento. There is a special car park for caravans (with facilities) in Via Luporini outside Porta Sant'Anna.

Hotels within the walls. 3-star: *Universo*, 1 Piazza del Giglio (Pl. 1); *La Luna*, 12 Corte Compagni (Pl. 2); *Piccolo Hotel Puccini*, 9 Via di Poggio. 2-star: *Ilaria*, 20 Via del Fosso

(Pl. 3); *Diana*, 11 Via del Molinetto (Pl. 6). Outside the walls. 4-star: *Napoleon*, 1 Viale Europa. 3-star: *Rex*, 19 Piazza Ricasoli (Pl. 4); *Celide*, 27 Viale Giusti (Pl. 5). In the environs. 4-star: *Villa la Principessa* (with swimming pool) at Massa Pisana, 3.5km outside the town on the N12 for Pisa; *Villa San Michele* at San Michele in Escheto. 2-star: *Villa Casanova* (with swimming pool) at Balbano, 10km W of Lucca towards Massaciucolli.

Restaurants within the walls. Luxury-class: *Antico Caffé delle Mura*, 4 Piazzale Vittorio Emanuele; *Buca di Sant'Antonio*, 1 Via della Cervia; *Antica Locanda dell'Angelo*, 21 Via Pescheria. First-class: *Il Giglio*, 3 Piazza del Giglio; *All'Olivo*, 1 Piazza San Quirico. Simple trattorie and pizzerie: *Da Giulio*, 47 Via delle Conce; *Trattoria Gli Orti*, 17 Via Elisa; *Trattoria Leo*, 1 Via Tegrini. Restaurants outside Lucca. Luxury-class: *Solferino* at San Macario in Piano. First-class: *Casina Rossa* at Ponte San Pietro; *La Mora* at Sesto di Moriano. The ramparts (described below) provide a delightful place to **picnic**.

An **Antique Market** is held in Piazza San Martino on the third Sunday of every month (and on the preceding Saturday).

History. Stone implements discovered in the plain of Lucca show that it was inhabited some 50,000 years ago. The Roman colony of *Luca* was the scene in 56 BC of the the meeting of Caesar, Pompey, and Crassus to form the First Triumvirate. The town is reputed to have been the first place in Tuscany to have accepted Christianity and its first bishop was Paulinus, a disciple of St Peter. In 552 the Goths were besieged here by Narses. In the Middle Ages it was an important city under the Lombard marquesses of Tuscany, and later was constantly at war with Pisa and Florence. Under the rule of Castruccio Castracani, in 1316–28, Lucca achieved supremacy in Western Tuscany, but his death was followed by a period of subjection to Pisa (1343–69). Charles IV then gave the Lucchesi a charter of independence, and it maintained its autonomy, often under the suzerainty of noble families, until 1799. In 1805 Napoleon presented the city as a principality to his sister Elisa Baciocchi, and in 1815 it was given to Marie Louise de Bourbon as a duchy. Lucca produces large quantities of olive oil.

The Romanesque churches were greatly admired by John Ruskin who spent much time here (at the Hotel Universo) studying them. The sculptor Matteo Civitali (1435–1501) was born in Lucca, and nearly all his works remain in the town. Pompeo Batoni (1708–87), however, painted his fashionable portraits mainly in Rome. The city is the birthplace also of the musicians Luigi Boccherini (1743–1805) and Giacomo Puccini (1858–1924) whose forbears had for four generations been organists of San Martino, though he himself was only a chorister at San Michele.

The nearest entrance to the town from the Florence motorway and the Station is through Porta San Pietro at Piazza Risorgimento. A footpath also leads directly from the piazza in front of the station across the lawn at the foot of the walls through the bastion of San Colombano and up over the walls to the piazza beside the apse of the Cathedral. The gates, bastions, and walls are described in detail at the end of this route. From Porta San Pietro Via Carrara leads left to Via Vittorio Veneto which leads into the town across Via Garibaldi. PIAZZA NAPOLEONE was laid out in 1806 in front of the Napoleonic residence, and planted with plane trees. The statue of Marie Louise de Bourbon, Duchess of Lucca in 1815–24, is by Lorenzo Bartolini. Here is the huge **Palazzo Ducale**, in part designed by Bartolomeo Ammannati in 1578 and enlarged by Filippo Juvarra in 1728.

The palace stands on the site of a much bigger castle (which occupied almost a fifth of the town) built for Castruccio Castracani, probably by Giotto, in 1322. Most of this was demolished by the populace in 1369 in anger against the Pisans who had occupied it. The palace became the seat of the Lords of Lucca until 1799, and then the ducal residence. It is now used as Provincial government offices, and by the Prefecture. Behind the building (reached through Ammannati's Cortile degli Svizzeri) is the huge Dominican church of **San Romano** (closed, but being restored), which contains the tomb of St Romanus by Matteo Civitali (1490). Opposite the façade is a neo-Gothic stable block.

Adjoining Piazza Napoleone is Piazza del Giglio, with the neo-classical façade of the *Teatro del Giglio*, built in 1817 by the local architect Giovanni Lazzarini. It was one of the most important opera houses in Italy in the early 19C, and here in 1831 was given the first performance of Rossini's *William Tell* (with Niccolò Paganini playing in the orchestra). Beyond is Piazza San Giovanni with a pretty walled garden next to the church of *Santi Giovanni e Reparata, reopened in 1992. The fine portal of 1187 was preserved when the façade was erected in 1589. The interior (1160–87) has Roman columns with Romanesque capitals, a late-16C coffered ceiling, 19C funerary monuments, and frescoes attributed to Giuliano di Simone. At the E end can be seen the 9C crypt of San Pantaleone (which preserves his relics). Off the N side is the Baptistery with a remarkable roof of 1393. The excavations here show the 12C font above a square 9C font which partially covers the earliest palaeochristian font. The excavations (separate ticket) carried out in 1969–92 below the church revealed five building levels. Here can be seen a fragment of the mosaic pavement of a Roman Domus (1C BC), traces of Roman baths (2C AD), and the remains of the huge geometric mosaic pavement of the first church (4C–5C) on this site which was the cathedral of Lucca up to 715. Its nave is occupied by conspicuous round kilns used during the construction of the present church.

The attractive PIAZZA SAN MARTINO and the adjoining Piazza Antelminelli have a delightful miscellany of buildings from different periods: the Romanesque cathedral, the 14C building of the Opera del Duomo (now restored as the Museo della Cathedrale, see below) next to a 13C tower house and the 16C Oratory of San Giuseppe, the 16C Palazzi Sanminiati (on either side of a little garden with palm trees), and the fine Palazzo Micheletti (1556) with a charming walled garden, by Bartolomeo Ammannati (above which can be seen the roof of the Baptistery). The circular fountain dates from 1835.

The *Cathedral (*San Martino*) was consecrated in 1070 by Pope Alexander II, who had begun the rebuilding while bishop of Lucca. EXTERIOR. The asymmetrical *FAÇADE is decorated with delightful sculptures in the Pisan-Lucchese Romanesque style. The statue of St Martin is a copy of the original 13C work, now inside the cathedral. The upper part, with three tiers of arcades, is signed by Guidetto da Como (1204). The columns are beautifully designed. The lower part of the embattled *CAMPANILE dates from 1060, the upper from 1261. The three wide Romanesque arches (the one on the right smaller to accommodate the campanile) lead in to the PORTICO, again beautifully decorated with sculptures, begun in 1233, and partly the work of Guido Bigarelli da Como, recently restored. The exquisite decorative details are carried out in pink, green, and white marble. On either side of the central door, bas-reliefs depict the story of St Martin and the months of the year. Over the left doorway is a relief of the Deposition, and under it an Adoration of the Magi, perhaps early works by Nicola Pisano. Over the right doorway, in the architrave, is the meeting of St Martin with the Arians, and in the lunette, the Beheading of St Regolus. On the right pier of the portico is a symbolic labyrinth (12C). The sides of the building are also beautiful, as well as the exterior of the *APSE, with its arcades and carved capitals, surrounded by a green lawn.

The tall *INTERIOR (closed 12–15 or 15.30) was rebuilt in the 14–15C in a Gothic style, with a delicate clerestory, and a beautiful inlaid pavement designed by Matteo Civitali. On the entrance wall, the sculpture of *St Martin dividing his cloak was removed from the façade. It dates from the 13C or possibly the early 14C. The two stoups are by Matteo Civitali (1498).

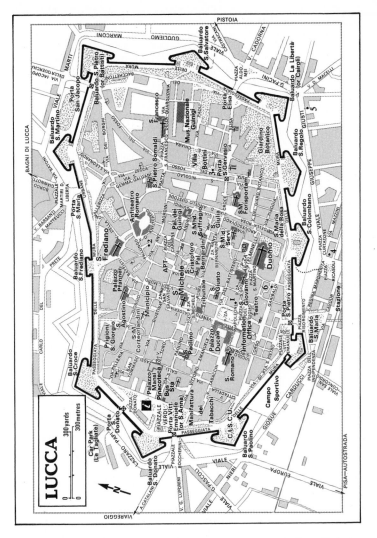

SOUTH AISLE. First altar, Passignano, Nativity; second altar, Federico Zuccari, Adoration of the Magi; third altar, Tintoretto (and his school), Last Supper (harshly restored); fourth altar, Passignano, Crucifixion; fifth altar, Michele Ridolfi, Resurrection (1825). The pulpit is by Matteo Civitali. A door leads into the SACRISTY. The altar was designed in 1835 and incorporates an early-15C bas-relief of St Agnello. The altarpiece of the Madonna and saints, with a good predella, is by Domenico Ghirlandaio, and the lunette of the Dead Christ attribued to a follower of Filippino Lippi. The 17C organ is the work of Domenico Zanobi.

SOUTH TRANSEPT. *tomb of Pietro da Noceto (1472), a beautiful Renaissance Humanist work, by Matteo Civitali, who also sculpted the tomb of Domenico Bertini (1479) here. The two angels flanking the tabernacle in the chapel of the Holy Sacrament, and the altar of St Regulus (1484), right of the sanctuary, are also the work of Civitali. The modern bronze high altar was installed in 1987, and part of the marble screen by the school of Civitali moved to the side chapels, despite local protest. The stained glass in the apse is the work of Pandolfo di Ugolino of Pisa (1485), and the choir stalls by Leonardo Marti (1452). On the high altar is a 14C Sienese triptych.

NORTH TRANSEPT. Altar with figures of the Risen Christ and Saints Peter and Paul, by Giambologna (the predella with a view of Lucca is of slightly later date). The celebrated *TOMB OF ILARIA DEL CARRETTO GUINIGI, with a serene effigy, is the masterpiece of Jacopo della Quercia (1405–06), and one of the most original works of the very early Renaissance. The sarcophagus may be the work of Francesco di Valdambrino. It was the subject of a controversial restoration in 1989. In the Cappella del Santuario, *Virgin and Child enthroned with saints by Fra Bartolomeo (1509). In the middle of the N aisle is the octagonal marble *TEMPIETTO, also by Civitali (1484), built to house the famous *VOLTO SANTO, a wooden likeness of Christ, supposed to have been begun by Nicodemus and miraculously completed. According to tradition, it was brought to Lucca in 782. It was greatly revered for centuries (and many copies made of it); the favourite oath of the English King William Rufus is said to have been *Per Vultum de Lucca*. The effigy is usually assigned stylistically to the 13C, probably a copy of an 11C work (in its turn perhaps modelled on a Syrian image of the 8C). On the outside of the Tempietto is a statue of St Sebastian by Civitali. NORTH AISLE. Fifth altar, Stefano Tofanelli, Assumption (1808); fourth altar, Jacopo Ligozzi, Visitation; third altar, Giovanni Battista Paggi, Annunciation (1597); second altar, Alessandro Allori, Presentation of Maria in the Temple (restored in 1989); first altar, Giovanni Battista Paggi, Birth of the Virgin.

The **Museo della Cathedrale** in Piazza Antelminelli (adm. daily 10–14; summer 10–18) was reopened in 1992 in modernized rooms on four floors. On the right of the ticket office is a room with elaborate goldsmiths' work made to decorate the Volto Santo, including a *frieze of 1382–84, a 17C crown, a huge jewel made in France in 1660, and a sceptre of 1852. The Evangelists by Domenico Fancelli (1663) were used to decorate the tempietto. R.I has illuminated codexes, including some by Martino di Bartolomeo. The Oratory of San Giuseppe has fine 17C gilded wood decorations. Upstairs R.II has a tiny wood pyx (1174), a Limoges *reliquary coffer showing the martyrdom of St Thomas Becket, and an ivory diptych from Constantinople (506). The famous *Croce dei Pisani is an elaborate Crucifix almost certainly commissioned by Paolo Guinigi in 1411 from Vincenzo di Michele da Piacenza. The 15C reliquary of St Sebastian is by Francesco Marti. R.III displays a 15C wood cupboard, part of the marble screen from the Duomo by Matteo Civitali, and paintings by Vincenzo Frediani. A crozier by Francesco Marti has been removed. R.IV has three paintings by Leonardo Grazia da Pistoia, Agostino Marti, and Zacchia il Vecchio. The two carved tondi of the head of the Baptist are by Masseo Civitali and Vincenzo Consani. R.V has goldsmiths' work of the 16C and 17C. On the top floor R.VI has late 17C–early 19C church silver. The sculptures in R.VII include the head of a bishop or a Pope (late 11C), 'Fra Fazio', a quaint 14C work, 14C–15C sculpted heads from the cathedral, the head of a man and a colossal statue of *St John the Evangelist by Jacopo della Quercia, two statuettes of prophets by Francesco di Valdambrino, and two classical female heads dating from c 1480. From here can be visited the Torre Belevedere and a walkway with a view of the piazza.

From Piazza San Giovanni a short road leads N across Via del Battistero (with numerous antique shops) to the 12C church of *San Giusto* (left), with a pretty façade and good portal. Farther on, across Via Santa Croce, in the picturesque Via Fillunga, is the 13C church of *San Cristoforo* with a fine interior (now used for exhibitions). It is the burial place of Matteo Civitali (died 1501) and also serves as a War memorial (the walls are covered with the names of the Dead). Beyond are two old towers, one, with a bell, dating from the 13C. Via Roma ends on the left in the delightful *PIAZZA SAN MICHELE, on the site of the Roman Forum and still the centre of the life of the city. The pavement and columns date from 1699–1705. The statue of Francesco Burlamacchi is by Ulisse Cambi (1863). On the left is *Palazzo Pretorio* (1492; enlarged 1588), in the portico of which is a statue by Arnaldo Fazzi (1893) of Matteo Civitali, traditionally thought to be the architect of the original building.

*San Michele in Foro** is typical of the Pisan Romanesque style as developed in Lucca. Mentioned as early as 795, the present church was largely constructed in the 11C and 12C, though work continued until the 14C. The imposingly tall *FAÇADE is richly decorated with coloured marbles, carved columns, and capitals. The upper part and lateral arcading date from the 14C when it was intended to raise the height of the nave (the project was abandoned because of lack of funds). On the tympanum is a huge statue of St Michael Archangel. On the SW corner is a copy of a Madonna by Civitali (see below). The façade was often sketched by Ruskin.

In the INTERIOR (closed 12.30–15) the vaulting, which covers a traditional beamed roof, was carried out in the early 16C. On the W wall, 14C frescoes, the *Madonna by Civitali from the façade, and an organ dating from 1804. In the apse hangs a Crucifix painted in the late 12C. SOUTH AISLE. First altar, white enamelled terracotta relief of the Madonna and Child, now attributed to Luca Della Robbia. Beyond a Martyrdom of St Andrew by Pietro Paolini, on the second altar is an unusual sculpted figure of St Michael (1658). SOUTH TRANSEPT. Monument to Bishop Sylvester Giles (see below) by Vincenzo Consani (1876); painting of St Filomena (1867); *Saints Helena, Jerome, Sebastian, and Roch, by Filippino Lippi. NORTH TRANSEPT, Marriage of the Virgin by Agostino Marti, and a Madonna and Child by Raffaello da Montelupo (1522), a high relief that formed part of the tomb (destroyed in the 19C) of Sylvester Giles, Bishop of Worcester, who died in Italy in 1521. In the N aisle, between the second and first altars, St Catherine, by Antonio Franchi.

Opposite the W door, Via di Poggio leads to Corte San Lorenzo where, at No. 9, is the entrance to the **Birthplace of Giacomo Puccini**. The house (open 10–13, 15–18; in winter 11–13, 15–17; closed Monday) contains interesting mementoes of the composer.

Via San Paolino continues Via Roma W to **San Paolino**, by Baccio da Montelupo and Bastiano Bertolani (1515–36), with a fine façade. The INTERIOR has small early-16C stained glass windows. SOUTH SIDE: first chapel, Il Riccio, Holy Trinity (1566); third chapel, 15C polychrome wood statue of St Ansano, by Francesco di Valdambrino; fourth chapel, Pietro Testa, St Theodore. The two small cantorie in the nave are by Nicolao and Vincenzo Civitali; Giacomo Puccini often played on the 19C organ. SOUTH TRANSEPT. In the right chapel is the Burial of St Paulinus and three other

Detail of the west façade of San Michele in Foro, Lucca

saints, a very unusual 14C painting attributed to Angelo Puccinelli. In the chapel opposite, Gerolamo Scaglia, Miracle of St Paulinus, and Madonna and Child with saints by Lorenzo Zacchia (1585). In niches on either side of the presbytery, 14C wood statues (removed). In the chapel to the left of the presbytery, Coronation of the Virgin, with a view of Lucca, an unusual 15C work. In the chapel opposite, Lorenzo Castellotti, St Joseph, and a 16C Madonna and Child. NORTH SIDE: fourth chapel, Paolo Guidotti, martyrdom of St Valerio, rare stone statuette of the Madonna and Child dating from the end of the 13C brought from Paris by merchants in the Middle Ages; second chapel, Francesco Vanni, Madonna and Child; first chapel, Giovanni Domenico Lombardi, Deposition. The stoup is by Nicolao Civitali.

Nearby, in Via Galli Tassi, is the **Museo Nazionale di Palazzo Mansi** (adm. 9–19; fest. 9–13; Monday closed). The piano nobile of the 17C palace has rooms decorated in the 17C–19C and the Pinacoteca is especially interesting for its 17C paintings (many with good frames), and Medici portraits.

A fine staircase leads up to the impressive loggia with Tuscan columns, and (left) the SALA DA PRANZO with mirrors, and 18C painted decorations by Francesco Antonio Cecchi. The SALONE DEL BALLO has late-17C frescoes by Giovanni Gioseffo Dal Sole. In the little chapel is a copy of a Madonna by Mabuse. The **Pinacoteca** is arranged in the four rooms beyond (the pictures are not all labelled but there is a hand-list in each room). **Room I** (the Salone): Leandro Bassano, Winter Landscape; Jacopo Ligozzi, Madonna appearing to St Giacinto; Paolo Veronese, St Peter the Hermit before the *Consiglio Veneto*; Luca Giordano, St Sebastian; Beccafumi, *Scipio; Domenichino, Samson; Carlo Dolci, St John the Baptist, St Anthony Abbot; Giovanni Battista Naldini or Giovanni Balducci, Prayer in the Garden; Orazio Marinari, David; Jacopo Vignali, *Tobias and the angel; Ventura Salimbeni, Portrait of a lady as St Catherine of Alexandria; Rosa da Tivoli, two landscapes; Salvator Rosa, two battle scenes; Federico Zuccari, self-portrait; Rutilio Manetti, *Triumph of David; Orazio Gentileschi, Mary Magdalene; Francesco Furini, Circe. **Room II** contains a fine collection of *portraits: Sustermans, portrait of a young woman, Cardinal Gian Carlo de Medici; Bronzino, Cosimo I in armour (one of several versions of this well-known portrait), Ferdinando de' Medici as a boy; Pontormo, *portrait of a boy (once thought to be Alessandro de' Medici); Bronzino, Don Garzia de' Medici as a child; Federico Barocci, Federico Ubaldo della Rovere at the age of two; Sustermans, Maria Maddalena d'Austria; Alessandro Allori, Bianca Cappello; Sustermans, Cardinal Leopoldo, Vittoria della Rovere. **Room III**: Andrea Schiavone, St Mary Magdalene; Vincenzo Catena, Holy Family; Sodoma, Christ carrying the Cross; good copy of a Madonna and Child with St Anne and the young St John by Andrea del Sarto; Jacopo Bassano, Adoration of the Shepherds; Tintoretto, two male portaits; Francesco Avanzi, Madonna and Child (the only known work by this 16C Milanese artist). **Room IV**: battle scenes by Salvatore Rosa, Bergognone, and Rosa da Tivoli; Paul Brill, landscapes; Michel Sweerts, portrait of a boy.

Off the Salone del Ballo (see above) are three small drawing rooms hung with 17C Flemish tapestries. The pretty bedroom, with an alcove, has 18C hangings made in Lucca. Beyond another room with a Holy Family with St Anne attributed to Van Dyck, is a room with a portrait of Antonio Santini as a boy by the 17C Flemish school. On the left are two 19C rooms with 18C still lifes and a painting of Danae by Denis Calvaert.

Via San Paolino ends in **Piazzale Verdi** with the old **Porta San Donato**, described with the ramparts at the end of this route.

Via Calderia leads N from Piazza San Michele to the church of *San Salvatore*, a 12C church with good sculpture by Biduino above its S portal. Via del Moro, behind, is lined with medieval mansions. Via Cesare Battisti winds between 17–18C palazzi towards the tall campanile of the church of *San Frediano* (1112–47). The façade is unusual for its large mosaic on a gold ground, possibly the work of Berlinghiero Berlinghieri (13C; restored in the 19C). It represents the Ascension (with the Apostles below). The church replaced an earlier basilica and has its apse at the W end.

In the splendid basilican *INTERIOR the columns of the nave have hand-some classical capitals. At the beginning of the S aisle is a magnificent *font (probably dating from the mid 12C), in the form of a fountain covered by a small tempietto, sculpted with reliefs of the story of Moses, the Good Shepherd, and the Apostles. Behind the font is a lunette of the Annunciation attributed to Andrea Della Robbia. Nearby are two interesting frescoes detached from behind the organ on the W wall. In the corner is the *Virgin Annunciate, a polychrome wood statue by Matteo Civitali (coin-operated light). Above the entrance is the organ, attributed to Domenico di Lorenzo. Beneath it, two framed detached frescoes: Amico Aspertini, Madonna and Child with saints, and a Visitation. Near the font is the 17C Chapel of Santa Zita (died 1278), with paintings of miracles of the saint by Francesco del

Tintore, and a 13C frescoed Crucifixion above the altar. Outside is a high relief of St Bartholomew by the Della Robbia, and an altar carved by Matteo Civitali. In the next chapel is an interesting painting of the Deposition by Pietro Paolini. In the last right chapel, wood relief of the Assumption by Masseo Civitali (in a marble frame). On the left wall of the presbytery is a huge marble monolith, probably from the Roman amphitheatre. In the Cappella Trenta (fourth chapel in the N aisle) is an elaborately carved *altarpiece by Jacopo della Quercia (1422: assisted by Giovanni da Imola) and two pavement tombs by the same artist: opposite is an Immaculate Conception and saints, by Francesco Francia. Outside the chapel is a statue of St Peter by Vincenzo di Bartolomeo Civitali. The second N chapel contains beautiful early *frescoes by Amico Aspertini (c 1508–09). They depict stories of San Frediano, St Augustine, and the bringing of the Volto Santo to Lucca, with interesting local details and classical ruins in the landscapes.

SW of the church is **Palazzo Pfanner** (formerly *Moriconi-Controni*), built in 1667, with a delightful galleried outside staircase. The 18C *garden, with fine statuary, can also be seen from the avenue along the walls (see below). On the first floor of the palace is a collection of 18–20C local costumes (not at present open to the public). Nearby is the 14C church of SANT'AGOSTINO, with a plain unfinished façade, and its small campanile resting on arches of the *Roman Theatre*. Inside, a little Baroque chapel was built in 1620 to house a venerated fresco of the Madonna del Sasso.

Across Via San Giorgio, Via del Loreto leads to **Santa Maria Corteorlandini**. The apse and S side of the church reconstructed in 1187 survive; the façade dates from the late 17C. The pretty interior with painted decoration dates from 1715–21. Over the W end is an elaborate and unusual organ gallery. The E end, with painted decoration by Angelo Maria Colonna is covered for restoration. Over the first altar in the S aisle, Madonna and saints attributed to Matteo Rosselli, and over the second altar in the N aisle, Birth of the Virgin by Francesco Vanni. A door in the N aisle leads to a chapel built in 1662 in imitation of the Santa Casa di Loreto. Outside is a fresco by Filippo Gherardi, and a polychrome wood *statue of St Nicholas of Tolentino by Francesco di Valdambrino (1407; still not returned here since its restoration). A precious collection of silk altar frontals (17–18C) made in Lucca belongs to the church.

Via San Giorgio leads back to Via Fillungo which leads left to the **Roman Amphitheatre**. The medieval houses which follow the ellipse of Via dell'Anfiteatro incorporate some of the brick arches of the amphitheatre. Its arena now forms a delightful *piazza, created in 1830–39 by the local architect Lorenzo Nottolini. From Via dell'Anfiteatro, Via Canuleia and Via Chiavi d'oro lead S to Via Sant'Andrea with the famous **Guinigi Tower**, 41m high, with trees growing on its summit (open daily, 9–19; winter 10–16). This stands beside the CASE DEI GUINIGI, two large brick Gothic palaces facing each other on Via Guinigi, Nos 29, and Nos 20–22, both built in the 14C and remodelled in the 16C.

During the rule of Castruccio Castracani, the Guinigi were one of the richest families in Lucca, particularly involved in the silk trade. The family continued to take an active part in the government of the city up to the 19C, and the last descendants of the family left the tower to the Comune of Lucca. The upper part of the tower is ascended by an iron staircase and on the top is a delightful little garden of six ilex trees. The view takes in the city and its tree-planted walls, and the hills beyond. To the S is the flank of the cathedral and the curious dome of the baptistery of San Giovanni; farther to the right is the campanile of San Michele, behind which can just be seen the rear of its tall façade (with an outside staircase). Nearer at hand is the high medieval bell-tower in Via Fillungo. To the N the tall campanile of San Frediano stands beside the conspicuous mosaic on its façade. Nearby the oval shape of the amphitheatre can be seen, and the campanile and white colonnaded façade of San Piero Somaldi; farther round is the white façade and rose window of San Francesco near the castellated roof of Villa Guinigi. To the E, the top of Santa Maria Forisportam with its campanile is visible.

Via Guinigi returns N to Via Mordini which leads right to Via Fratta. Just to the N is the church of **San Pietro Somaldi**, founded in 763. The church was rebuilt at the end of the 12C, and work continued up to the 14C. The grey and white banded façade dates from 1248, though the relief above the central door is by Guido da Como and assistants (1203). INTERIOR. SOUTH AISLE: first altar, Zacchia da Vezzano, Assumption (an unusual painting dated 1532); second altar, a good 17C painting of the Annunciaton; third altar, Giovanni Marracci, St Bona; at the end of the aisle, 14C frescoed lunette of the Madonna and Child. NORTH AISLE: On the altar at the E end, Nicolau Landucci, Holy Family (1840); third altar, Antonio Franchi, St Peter; second altar, highly venerated Madonna and Child by Sebastiano Conca; first altar, Saints Anthony Abbot, Bartholomew, Francis, Domenic, and Andrew, a good painting attributed to Raffaellino del Garbo.

Via Fratta leads to a crossroads by the pretty canal (formerly the moat outside the medieval walls) which runs along Via del Fosso. Here stands the *Madonna dello Stellario*, a statue set up in 1687 on an ancient column. Carved on its base there is an interesting view of Lucca from outside the walls at the Porta San Donato. Nearby is a neo-classical fountain by Lorenzo Nottolini. Beyond the canal and column rises the marble façade of **San Francesco**, a church rebuilt in the 14C (the upper part of the façade was finished in 1930). INTERIOR. SOUTH SIDE: second altar, Sebastiano Conca, Madonna and saints; between the second and third altars, unusual monument to Giovanni Guidiccioni (1500–41), with a fine statue of the Madonna and Child attributed to Vincenzo Civitali; in the chapel to the right of the high altar, *lunette of the Presentation of the Virgin in the Temple and the Marriage of the Virgin, a detached fresco of remarkably high quality (but very damaged) by the 15C Florentine school. NORTH SIDE: fifth altar, Passignano, Noli me tangere; fourth altar, Federico Zuccari, Nativity; between the fourth and third altars, funerary monuments to the musicians Luigi Boccherini (1743–1805) and Francesco Geminiani (1687–1762). In the cloister is the tomb of Bonagiunta Tignosini (1274) with a ruined fresco by Deodato Orlandi.

Nearby is the unusual brick VILLA GUINIGI, a castellated suburban villa built in 1418. The austere building has been restored to house the **Museo Nazionale Guinigi** (open 9–14 except Monday) which contains a fine collection of sculpture and paintings from Lucca and its province. In the garden is a Roman mosaic (1–2C AD), and a group of carved Romanesque lions from the medieval walls. Room I (left of the portico) displays Bronze Age and Villanovan finds from near Lucca, and material from the Etruscan settlement of Serchio. R.II: Four Ligurian tombs (reconstructed); Etruscan tomb with gold jewellery and an Attic krater (3C BC). Beyond are Roman finds from the city including an altar of 40–30 BC found in Piazza San Michele, mosaics, marble heads, etc. SOUTH PORTICO: Medieval architectural fragments and a tomb-slab of a member of the Antelminelli family attributed to Jacopo della Quercia. R.III: Fine examples of Lucchese sculpture (8–14C) including a transenna with a relief of Samson and the lion; fragment of a statue of St Martin (12–13C) from the Duomo; bas-reliefs from the church of San Jacopo in Altopascio; statuette of the Madonna and

Child attributed to Biduino (late 13C); gold jewellery etc. found in a Lombard tomb (600–650 AD). R.IV: Virgin annunciate, attributed to Nino Pisano; marble statues by various masters from a polyptych attributed to Priamo della Quercia (see below, RXII). R.V–VII are closed for rearrangement. They contain fine *works by Matteo Civitali; weights and measures of Lucca (18–19C), and neo-classical reliefs from Palazzo Ducale by Vincenzo Consani.

Stairs lead up to the Pinacoteca. R.X (being rearranged). Francesco Traini, St Michael Archangel; 'Ugolino Lorenzetti', St John the Evangelist, *Madonna and Child; Berlinghiero Berlinghieri, painted Cross; Maestro del Bambino Vispo, Saints; Deodato Orlandi, Madonna and Child. R.XI. Zanobi Machiavelli, Madonna and Child and saints; Madonna and Child after Filippo Lippi; two reliefs by the bottega of Donatello. R.XII. Neroccio Landi, Assumption; intarsia panels from the sacristy of the Duomo by Masseo Civitali and Cristoforo Canozzi da Lendinara. R.XIII. Works by Bernardino del Castelletto, the Master of the Tondo Lathrop, Amico Aspertini, Matteo and Masseo Civitali. R.XIV: Fra Bartolomeo, *Madonna della Misericordia (1515), *God the Father with Saints Mary Magdalene and Catherine. R.XV: Intarsia views of Lucca by Ambrogio and Nicolao Pucci (1529) from the Cappella degli Anziani in the Duomo. Works by Riccio, Daniele da Volterra (Deposition), and Vasari (Immaculate Conception). R.XVI. Works by Aurelio Lomi, Jacopo Ligozzi, Domenico Passignano, Ludovico Cigoli, and Federico Zuccari. R.XVII. Works by Pietro da Cortona, Guido Reni, Giovanni Lanfranco, and Rutilio Manetti. R.XVIII–XX contain 17C–18C works. On the ground floor are two rooms of medals and coins minted in Lucca up to 1843.

From Piazza San Francesco, Via del Fosso on the line of the medieval walls leads S between a canal (formerly the moat) and the garden wall of **Villa Bottini** (*Buonvisi*; entrance on Via Elisa), a fine building of 1566 with two façades, surrounded by a pretty walled garden (open 9–14), with beautiful magnolia trees, and a nymphaeum (in very poor repair) attributed to Buontalenti. The interior, with many rooms frescoed by Ventura Salimbeni, has been restored by the Comune and it is now used for conferences and it contains a newspaper library. In July and August concerts are usually held in the garden. Opposite the entrance in Via Elisa is the church of the *Santissima Trinità* (1589; key from the adjoining convent) which contains a sentimental Madonna della Tosse, by Matteo Civitali. *Porta San Gervasio* (1255) is the best of the gates remaining from the second enceinte.

Inside the gate Via Santa Croce continues to the piazza in front of *Santa Maria Forisportam, another fine church with a marble façade in the 13C Pisan style, named from having been outside the city gates until 1260. Above the left door is a fine architrave with a lion and a griffon, and in the lunette above the right door is a 13C statuette of a bishop saint. Above the central door is a 17C relief of the Coronation of the Virgin. The pleasant grey INTERIOR was altered in 1516 when the nave and transepts were raised. On the W wall a paleo-Christian sarcophagus has been adapted as a font. SOUTH AISLE: first altar, Gerolamo Scaglia, Coronation of the Virgin (with a 15C fresco fragment below); fourth altar, Guercino, *St Lucy. The ciborium in pietre dure and bronze in the S transept dates from c 1680. The handsome HIGH ALTAR was designed by Vincenzo Civitali (and finished in the 18C). In the N transept is a neo-classical monument to Antonio Mazzarosa by Vincenzo Consani (1870) and an altarpiece of the *Assumption, a much darkened painting by Guercino. In the SACRISTY, off the S transept, is a Dormition and Assumption of the Virgin by Angelo Puccinelli

(1386) and a Madonna and Child by Pompeo Batoni. A small museum is to be arranged in some adjoining rooms with sculpture (including a 12C Madonna enthroned from the façade), church silver, altar frontals, a missionary museum, fossils, Roman material, etc.

Via della Rosa leads S to the charming little oratory of **Santa Maria della Rosa** (locked), built in 1309–33 in the Pisan Gothic style. Inside are some traces of the original Roman wall.

Via Santa Croce leads back towards Piazza San Michele across Piazza Bernardini (dominated by its 16C palazzo). To the right, in Piazza del Suffragio, is the *Oratorio di Santa Giulia* (13–14C; closed). Via Roma continues into Piazza San Michele (see above).

The Ramparts

A walk around the top of the 16–17C *ramparts (4195m) which enclose the town completes a visit to Lucca. The road has been completely closed to traffic and some of the bastions have been restored, while others are being restored. They have been planted with trees since the 16C (although some of these are now diseased and are being replanted) and provide delightful views of the town and of the Apuan Alps. The avenues and parks are beautifully maintained. The earliest circle of walls of which traces have survived date from the Roman period; new walls were built in 1198. The present fortifications, extremely well preserved, were carried out in 1544–1650. The walls are 12m high and 30m wide at the base, and have eleven bastions, on many of which guardhouses survive. The interiors of some of the bastions have been restored, with their complicated defence works, armouries, ammunition stores, passages, etc. Outside the walls are grassy fields on the site of the moat (the recent construction of a car park at the foot of the Baluardo di San Martino has been justly criticised). There were originally only three gates. The walls were never put to use but must have served as an effective deterrent to Lucca's enemies. They were built on a system afterwards developed by Vauban, and recall the ramparts of Berwick-on-Tweed in Scotland and Verona. The guardhouse on the Baluardo di San Paolino is aptly occupied by an international centre for the study of urban enceintes (CISCU, see below).

The **Baluardo di San Paolino** (see the Plan) dates from 1594–1642. In the delightful park is a monument to the musician Alfredo Catalani by Francesco Petroni. The guardhouse at No. 21 is the seat of CISCU (*Centro Internazionale per lo Studio delle Cerchia Urbane*), founded in 1967, with a photo archive and library relating to the history of urban enceintes. Admission is courteously granted by appointment and the bastion shown. It was restored in 1967 and has an interesting interior which incorporates a remarkable vaulted central hall of the 15C defensive tower on this site, as well as various corridors, an armoury, and a well and drinking trough for the horses.

A splendid double avenue of plane trees planted by Marie Louise de Bourbon in the early 19C leads along the ramparts to the **Baluardo di Santa Maria** designed by Francesco Paciotti and constructed by Matteo Civitali in 1562. Here is a 19C piazzale with a statue of Victor Emmanuel II by Angelo Passaglia, and two 13C lions from the medieval walls. The *Antico Caffè delle Mura* (now a restaurant) was built in 1840 by Cesare Lazzarini. The avenue passes beneath a loggia above the florid **Porta San Pietro**, the most important entrance to the town (1566; by Alessandro Resta), which preserves its original doors and portcullis (the side gates were added in 1846). From here there is a view of the campanile of San Giovanni and the roof of the Baptistery. Beyond is the flank and apse of the Duomo beneath a bank planted with magnolia trees. On the **Baluardo di San Colombano** (being restored) are two more 13C lions, and the ruins of a medieval tower. The interior was restored in 1967. From the **Baluardo di San Regolo** there is a view down Via del Fosso with its canal which runs along the line of the walls built in 1198. On the bastion there is a children's playground and an ilex grove around a bust of Mazzini on a column. The **Botanical Gardens**, laid out in 1820 by Bernardino Orsetti (admission weekdays 8–13) can be approached from here. An extremely interesting garden for specialists, it includes medicinal plants, a cedar of Lebanon (1820), a sequoia, a camphor tree, and a three-stemmed ginkgo tree. The ramparts (here planted with ilexes) now skirt the wall of the Botanical Gardens. The **Baluardo La Libertà** (or *Cairoli*) is asymmetrically placed at the SE corner of the fortifications.

There is a view of the Torre Guinigi from the avenue as it crosses above the neo-classical **Porta Elisa**, opened in 1809. At the end of Via Elisa can be seen Porta San Gervasio in the medieval walls. The **Baluardo di San Salvatore** is walled off for restoration. Here can be seen remains of a medieval fortification (a rectangular enclosure with four wells on the left of the path). From the **Baluardo di San Pietro** (or *Cesare Battisti*) there is a splendid view of the Apuan Alps. The ramparts pass above **Porta San Jacopo** (opened in 1930) to reach the **Baluardo di San Martino**, the foot of which has recently been disfigured by a car park. The interior was restored in 1967, and ruins of a medieval tower can be seen here. The avenue passes beneath the loggia above **Porta Santa Maria** (1593), one of the three original gates. The **Baluardo di San Frediano** is a small rectangular bastion protected by grassed earthworks (1554). Many trees have had to be felled here because of disease. From the walls there is a splendid view across fields (traversed by paths) and trees to the mountains beyond. Inside the walls stand the campanile and apse of San Frediano, and the pretty garden decorated with statues of Palazzo Pfenner. The viale skirts a prison wall as far as the **Baluardo di Santa Croce** with remains of a medieval tower. The guardhouse here has two columns and is vaulted below. The walk now passes beneath the loggia of the handsome **Porta San Donato** (1639) with two statues of San Paolino and San Donato by Giovanni Lazzoni. This replaced the **old Porta San Donato**, built in the medieval walls in 1591, which is conspicuous nearby in Piazzale Verdi. This area of the town, formerly called Prato del Marchese was used from the 18C onwards for football games, horse races, etc. The gateway, on a design by Ginese Bresciani, was beautifully restored in 1976 and is now the APT information office. The line of the old walls can also clearly be seen here, and the foundations of the drawbridge outside the gate. A handsome stable block of 1876, at the foot of the ramparts, may one day be restored as a conference centre. The **Baluardo di San Donato** is beautifully planted with trees. The bastions pass above **Porta Sant'Anna** (or *Vittorio Emanuele*), opened in 1910 to return to the Baluardo di San Paolino.

Environs of Lucca

The environs of Lucca are noted for their fine villas and gardens built between the 16C and 19C, although only three of them are at present open to the public (many others are being studied and may be restored and opened to the public). In the foohills, NE of the town, is the late 17C VILLA REALE (at *Marlia*, 8km), once the home of Elisa Baciocchi. Here Niccolò

Paganini, Metternich and John Singer Sargent stayed. It was bought in 1923 by Anna Laetitia (Mimì) Pecci-Blunt (1885–1971). She opened the *Galleria La Cometa* in Rome in the 1930s, and became a well-known collector of Italian art. The house is not open to the public, but the 17C Orsetti *garden, with notable statuary and a 'theatre', is shown 1 March–30 November at 10, 11, 15, 16, 17, 18 except on Monday.

At *Segromigno* (10km) is the 17C VILLA MANSI (adm. 10–12.30, 14.30–16.30; summer 9.30–13, 14.30–19; Monday closed). Part of the garden altered by Juvarra in 1742 survives near the house, with a pescheria, the *Bagno di Diana*, and fine statues. The 'English' park was created in the 19C. The villa has late-18C decorations, including frescoes of the Myth of Apollo in the Salone by Stefano Tofanelli. At *Camigliano*, nearby, is the VILLA TORRIGIANI (adm. April–October, 9.30–11.30, 15–19.30; winter: Saturday and Sunday only 9.30–11.30, 14.30–17) with a rococo façade, and fine park. It contains 17C and 18C paintings and a collection of porcelain.

A few km S of Lucca, off the N12 on a by-road to Pozzuolo in the VILLA BERNARDINI (località Vicopelago) built in 1600–15 by Bernardo Bernardini with a (modern) garden which includes an 18C 'theatre' (adm. 9.30–12, 14.30 or 15–17 or 19.30).

FROM LUCCA TO MONTECATINI, 27km. The road (N435) passes (5km) *Lunata*, with its tall Romanesque campanile, which lies 2km S of *Lammari*, where the parish church contains a tabernacle, Matteo Civitali's last work. 11km Turning for *Montecarlo* (6km SE), well known in Tuscany for its production of good wine (red and white; *Michi, Buonamico*, etc.). 5km farther S, just beyond the motorway, is *Altopascio*, where Castruccio beat the Florentines in 1325. The Order of the Knights of Altopascio (*del Tau*) ran a hospice for pilgrims here in 1084, and it has since been famous for its hoteliers. It is also well known for its bread. The main road continues past a turning (at 15km) for San Gennaro and Collodi (described in Rte 5), and through (19km) Pescia, in the province of Pistoia to (27km) Montecatini.

At *Badia di Cantignana*, 6km S of Lucca, was born Carlo Piaggia (1827–82), the African explorer who (with Romolo Gessi) first circumnavigated Lake Albert.

On the plain to the S of Lucca (well seen from the motorway) is a monumental *Aqueduct* built by Lorenzo Nottolini, c 1823, to bring water to the town from Monte Pisano.

7

The Garfagnana

The beautiful upper valley of the Serchio N of Lucca is known as the **GARFAGNANA**. It is well-wooded and richly cultivated. Lying between the Apennines and the Apuan Alps the scenery is spectacular in the side valleys and on the higher ground. In the centre of the valley is Castelnuovo di Garfagnana situated between the Parco delle Alpi Apuane and the Parco dell'Orecchiella in the Apennines. In the lower valley is the interesting village of Barga.

Information Offices. *Castelnuovo di Garfagnana: Comunità Montana della Garfagnana*, and *Centro Accoglienza e Visite del Parco Alpi Apuane*; Piazza delle Erbe (Tel. 0583/65169); Pro Loco, Loggiato Porta. *Consorzio Operatori Turistici*, Via Roma (hotel booking service, Tel. 0583/644473). *Bagni di Lucca*: APT, 139 Via Umberto I. *Borgo a Mozzano: Comunità Montana della Media Valle del Serchio*, 100 Via Umberto. *Barga*: Pro Loco, Piazza Angelio.

A magnificent **railway line**, with fine scenery, follows the valley from Lucca to Aulla (91km in c 2hrs 15mins). It is served by local trains stopping at all stations including Bagni di Lucca, Barga, and Castelnuovo di Garfagnana (in c 1hr).

Bus services from Piazzale Verdi in Lucca (CLAP) to Bagni di Lucca, Barga, Castelnuovo di Garfagnana, Vagli, etc. Services run by *Lazzi* also to Bagni di Lucca.

Hotels. *Castelnuovo di Garfagnana*. 2-star: *Da Carlino*. Near the *Parco dell'Orecchiella*. 3-star: 'California', Corfino (Villa Collemandina); *Il Grotto*, Villetta (San Romano Garfagnano). 2-star: *Panoramico*, Corfino; *La Baita*, Corfino; and *Il Casone*, Passo Radici (Casone di Profecchia). Near the *Parco delle Alpe Apuane*. 4-star: *Lo Scoiattolo*, Passo Carpinelli (Minucciano). 3- star: *Mini Hotel*, Gramolazzo (Minucciano). 2-star: *Belvedere*, Carpinelli (Minucciano); *Le Alpi*, Vagli Sotto. Near *Barga*. 3-star: *Villa Libano*, 6 Via del Sasso; *La Pergola*, Via Sant'Antonio. At *Bagni di Lucca*. 3-star: *Bridge*, Piazza Ponte a Serraglio; *Corona*, 78 Via Serraglio, *Bernabò*, Bagni Caldi. 2-star: *Svizzero*, 30 Via Casalini. 1-star: *Roma*, 110 Via Umberto I.

Camping sites: Castelnuovo di Garfagnana: *Parco La Piella* (2-star); Giuncugnano: *Argegna* (summer only) (2-star).

Restaurants: numerous trattorie, especially good in the mountain areas around the Parco dell'Orecchiella, including *Il Casone* at Casone di Profecchia, and *Da Carlino* at Castelnuovo di Garfagnana. At Bagni di Lucca: first-class restaurants: *Vinicio, Del Sonno, Circolo Forestieri* and *Boccale Due*.

Hiking and **horseback riding** are organised along some 350km of nature trails in the Apuan Alps and the Apennines (with overnight stays in mountain refuges). Information from the Comunità Montana in Castelnuovo di Garfagnana.

Road from Lucca (N12).—24km Turning for **Bagni di Lucca**. N445—42km **Barga**—56km **Castelnuovo di Garfagnana**—67km *Camporgiano*—(92km *Casola in Lunigiana*—115km *Aulla*).

From Lucca N12 leads N to (9km) *Ponte a Moriano* (first-class restaurant *La Mora*). At *Vinchiana*, 2km farther on, a road winds up through beautiful scenery to (5km farther) *San Giorgio di Brancoli* where the Romanesque church has an *ambone and a font, both 12C, a St George of the Della Robbian school, and a 14C painted Crucifixion. A bridge leads across the Serchio from Ponte a Moriano and the more interesting road now follows the W bank of the Serchio past (18km) *Diecimo* (at the tenth Roman mile from Lucca), with its 13C Romanesque church. From here a by-road (for Pescaglia) leads shortly to *Celle dei Puccini*, the home of Puccini's ancestors (their house can be visited; Saturday and Sunday, 15–19; or by appointment). At (22km) *Borgo a Mozzano* the church contains expressive 16C sculptures and a wooden figure of St Bernardine by Matteo Civitali. The conspicuous *Ponte della Maddalena* is a remarkable ancient footbridge over the Serchio. There are many Romanesque churches in the vicinity.

A road recrosses the river for (29km) **Bagni di Lucca** (150m; for hotels and restaurants, see above), a little spa with warm sulphur and saline waters, somewhat off the main valley on N12. It is divided into several districts including Bagni Caldi and Bagno alla Villa. Noted for its waters since the 12C, it was particularly fashionable as a residence of the nobility of Lucca and foreigners from the 17C up until the end of the 19C. Its famous visitors have included Shelley, Byron, Browning (who advised Tennyson, Poet Laureate, to stay here in 1851), and Walter Savage Landor. Here the novelist Francis Marion Crawford (1854–1909) was born, and in the little Protestant cemetery Ouida lies buried.

Bagni di Lucca is entered by *Ponte a Serraglio*, from which the lower road leads left along the river overhung with pretty trees to the *Casinò* (being restored) built by Giuseppe Pardini and founded in 1837 as the first licensed gaming house in Europe. A plaque on the house beside it records Alphonse de Lamartine's stay here in 1825. The upper road leads through woods to the pretty spa of BAGNI CALDI, with the *Stabilimento Jean Verraud* (early 20C). In the other direction a road leads from the bridge to LA VILLA, a typical little spa (APT information office). The *Palazzo del Circolo dei Forestieri* here was built in 1923–24, and the *Teatro Accademico* in 1790 (restored 1986). The old English Chemist still has the royal coat of arms. Here, in the public gardens, is the neo-Gothic *English Church* built in 1839 by Giuseppe Pardini and on the hillside above the royal stables built in 1811.

A road leads up to the tiny hamlet of BAGNO ALLA VILLA, once an elegant residential district and now possessing an air of decadence. *Villa Buonvisi* was built in Piazza di Sopra in 1570, and Montaigne stayed here in 1581. The village was restored in 1669 for the visit of the grand-duchess Vittoria della Rovere, and more houses, including the Casa Mansi built at that time. In 1722 James Stuart, the Old Pretender came here with his wife Clementina Sobieska and stayed at the Villa Buonvisi. In 1811 Elisa Baciocchi, having received the principality of Lucca from her brother Napoleon, transformed Palazzo Orsetti into her summer residence, and this period of splendour for Bagno alla Villa continued during the Bourbon duchy. In 1818 Shelley and Mary Wollstonecraft lived in the Casa del Chiappa, and in 1822 Byron stayed with his friend John Webb who owned the Villa Buonvisi. The baths here were rebuilt in the 17C.

The main road through the Garfagnana, keeping to the E bank of the Serchio, enters the country of the Castracani family, whose tombs and castle adorn the village of *Ghivizzano* (right). The village of *Coreglia Antelminelli*, also to the right of the main road, contains an interesting church and a museum of 18–20C figurines (open weekdays 8–13; fest. in summer, 8–13, 16–19) for which the locality is famous.

42km **BARGA** (11,000 inhab.) is the most important place in the lower Serchio valley (for hotels, see above). It has expanded at the foot of its hill (410m) leaving the little old village remarkably peaceful. By the bastion, with a war memorial, a monument to Antonio Mordini (1819–1902), and a huge cedar of Lebanon, cars can be parked. Beyond the old *Porta Reale* (or *Mancianella*) the narrow *Via di Mezzo* winds up and down through the centre of the village. It passes the church of the *Santissima Annunziata* built in 1595 with decorative stuccoes, beside Palazzo Mordini. Beyond Palazzo Cordati which follows the curve of the street is a little piazza in front of the *Teatro dell'Accademia dei Differenti*. A theatre was first built here in 1689 and the present building dates from 1795 (being restored). Above is a view of the Duomo and its campanile (described below). *Piazza Angelio* is named after Pietro Angeli (1517–96), the Humanist, whose bust is on the corner of his house. Here is the local tourist office, and concerts are often held in this attractive piazza. Via di Mezzo continus to *Piazza del Comune* (or Salvi) with a picturesque loggia (once a market place), with the Florentine Marzocco. Palazzo Pancrazi houses the town hall. In the adjacent Piazza Garibaldi is the handsome 16C *Palazzo Balduini*, perhaps on a design by Bartolomeo Ammannati.

From Piazza Comune a steep flight of steps lead up to the church of *Santissimo Crocifisso* with a pleasant façade. It contains wooden stalls and a decorative gilded wood high altar. Via della Speranza leads out of the village through Porta Machiaia and over the interesting old Ponte dell' Acquedotto. Steps continue up from the Santissimo Crocifisso to the grassy terrace in front of the Duomo. From here there is a splendid view which takes in the snow-capped Apuan Alps and the Apennines. The Roman-esque *•Duomo* (restored in 1920 after earthquake damage) has a fine exterior built in the local white stone (*alberese*), and an embattled campanile. It dates from the 9C–14C with later alterations. The flank of the earliest church serves as the façade which has an interesting main door. The N doorway has a carved architrave.

In the dark INTERIOR is a handsome stoup beneath a fresco of St Lucy. The painting of St Christopher dates from the 18C (probably by Stefano Tofanelli). The sculpted 13C •pulpit is attributed to Guido Bigarelli of Como (or his pupil). In the main apse is a huge imposing figure of •St Christopher in polychrome wood (early 12C). The stained glass tondo above is on a cartoon attributed to Lorenzo di Credi. In the chapel to the right of the high altar is a terracotta altarpiece of the Madonna with Saints Sebastian and Roch (restored), and Della Robbian works. In the chapel to the left of the high altar is a large painted Crucifix (15C) and a 16C painting of St Joseph with a view of Barga (in an elaborate frame), with a Byzantine Madonna and Child. The contents of the rich TREASURY, which include a chalice by Francesco Vanni, are at present kept in the Canonica.

Across the grass is the *Palazzo Pretorio* with a loggia and a small archeological museum. Steps lead down past a pretty garden to the *Conservatorio di Sant'Elisabetta* (ring for admission). In the church is a fine high altarpiece in enamelled terracotta attributed to Benedetto Buglioni. A large 15C Crucifix has been removed for restoration. Via del Pretorio returns to the Porta Reale. Outside the gate, below Via Marconi by the hospital, is the church of *San Francesco*, with fine polychrome enamelled terracottas attributed to the bottega of Andrea Della Robbia.

The by-road which leads from Barga to Fornaci di Barga passes a farm and cemetery next to the pieve of *Loppia*, founded in the 9C, with a worn Romanesque façade.

A pretty road continues beyond Barga to *Tiglio Alto* where the church contains 14C statues of the Annunciation, reminiscent of those in the cathedral of Carrara.

From the main road a bridge leads across the Serchio to *Gallicano*. A by-road leads up to the hermitage of *Calomini* (9km), excavated in the rock in the 12C (the double loggia dates from the 18C). It is opened by Capuchin monks from Lucca in May–September. A road continues along the Turrite from Gallicano to the *Grotta del Vento* (14km), above Fornovolasco, a huge cave extending for hundreds of metres below the Apuan Alps (guided tours every hour, 10–12, 15–18; in winter only on fest.).

The main road continues N to (45km) *Castelvecchio Pascoli*. Nearby on the hill of Caprona is the house (open 10–13, 14.30 or 15–17 or 18.30; closed Monday) where Giovanni Pascoli (1855–1912) lived from 1895 until his death. The house has remained as it was with its original furnishings and it contains mementoes and MSS. of the poet. He is buried in a chapel here (the tomb was designed by Leonardo Bistolfi). 56km **Castelnuovo di Garfagnana** (6,500 inhab.), the centre of the Garfagnana, situated where the Turrite river meets the Serchio, and the headquarters of the *Comunità Montana della Garfagnana* (see the beginning of this route). In Piazza Umberto I are remains of the 13C *Rocca* or governor's palace, the residence in 1522–25 and in 1640–42 of the poets Ludovico Ariosto and Fulvio Testi when they were governors of the district. Via Fulvio Testi leads up past a little piazza with a recently restored façade of the Rocca (now used as the town hall) past the local tourist office to the *Duomo*, rebuilt in 1504. In the interior (left wall), *St Joseph and angels, a beautiful enamelled terracotta altarpiece (attributed to Verrocchio, or the Della Robbia); Madonna and two saints attributed to Michele di Ridolfo Ghirlandaio and an Assumption by Santi di Tito. In the chapel to the right of the sanctuary, 14C Crucifix.

Via Castracani leads down to the old *Porta Miccia* with a bridge (1324) over the Serchio. On the other side of the river, in Via Marconi, is the *Teatro Alfieri*, dating from 1860, by Giovanni Carli), now used as a cinema. There is a market in Castelnuovo on Thursdays. Near the village is the *Fortezza di Monte Alfonso* (1579).

From Castelnuovo a spectacular mountain road leads over the Apuan Alps to Massa (41km, see Rte 8). At 17km it diverges right from the road which tunnels through the Galleria del Cipollaio to descend to Seravezza (Rte 8). Beyond Arni the road passes through an unpaved tunnel under Monte Altissimo (1589m) before descending to Massa.

Castelnuovo is the starting point for excursions (including hiking and horseback riding; map and information from the Park Office in Castelnuovo di Garfagnana) in the **Parco Naturale delle Alpi Apuane**, a protected area since 1985 and interesting for its spectacular mountain scenery between Versilia and the Serchio valley. On both sides of the mountain chain are marble quarries. The fauna include wild boar, deer, mountain goats, etc. The highest peak is *Monte Pisanino* (1946m). At *Vagli* is a large lake formed by the dam of a hydroelectrical plant (1946). Every 10 years or so when the lake is drained (last time in 1994) the borgo of Fabbriche di Careggine, founded in the 13C, re-emerges. Near *Campocatino* (LIPU wildlife office) are interesting shepherds' huts built with dry-stone walls and slate roofs. Some of them date from the 17C and are being restored. The hermitage of *San Viviano* is perched on an isolated rock nearby. Most of the hotels are in the comune of Minucciano in the N part of the park.

On the other side of the valley is the **Parco dell'Orecchiella** in the Apennines with meadows in the green upland plains and extensive woods. For hiking and horseback riding, information and map from the 'Comunità Montana' in Castelnuovo di Garfagnana. A road from Castelnuovo follows the left bank of the Serchio past *Sambuca*. Beyond *San Romano in Garfagnano* is *Verrucole* with the ruins of a castle which belonged to the Gherardenghi. From Vibbiana the road continues up to Orecchiella with a Visitors' Centre. From here a path (2km) leads to a little Botanical Garden with Alpine plants on the *Pania di Corfino* (1300m), founded in 1984 (open July–Sept 9–12.30, 14.30–18). There are some hotels near *Corfino* (see the beginning of this Route).

From Castelnuovo a road (N324) leads across the Apennines towards Modena and Pievepelago (see *Blue Guide Northern Italy*). It passes *Pieve Fosciana* with an interesting church and *Castiglione di Garfagnana* (7km) with 14C walls. The church preserves a Madonna (1389), the only signed work by Giuliano di Simone of Lucca. *Villa Collemandina* has a Romanesque church with two altars by Matteo Civitali. A secondary road diverges from N324 just S of Castiglione for *San Pellegrino in Alpe*

(16km from Castelnuovo di Garfagnana) with an interesting local ethnographical museum. It occupies 14 rooms of the 12C hospice which served travellers crossing the Apennines, and illustrates peasant life in the area (open 9.30–13, 14.30–19; October–May, 9–12, 14–17; closed Monday). The church has more fine works by Matteo Civitali. A few kilometres above San Pellegrino is the pass of *Foce delle Radici* (1529m), with winter sports facilities.

67km *Camporgiano.* The 15C castle contains a museum with an archaeological section and a collection of medieval and Renaissance ceramics (open 9–12; summer also 15–18). The picturesque road now climbs past *Giuncugnano* beside the pretty upland plain of *Argegna* to (82km) the *Foce di Carpinelli* (842m). It enters the valley of the Aulella at (92km) *Casola in Lunigiana* which, with (115km) *Aulla*, is in the province of Massa-Carrara, described in Rte 8.

8

Versilia and the province of Massa-Carrara

VERSILIA is famous for its beaches which stretch N from the famous resort of Viareggio all the way to Forte dei Marmi in the narrow coastal plain at the foot of the splendid Apuan Alps. In summer the coast is crowded with holiday-makers, many of them from Florence. The little inland town of Pietrasanta, as well as Camaiore and Seravezza are attractive and have buildings of interest. The marble quarries above Carrara are world famous. The inhabitants of the small towns of **MASSA** and **CARRARA**, although they live only a few kilometres apart, are proudly independent of each other. Their province takes in the whole of the NE corner of Tuscany, and includes the *Lunigiana* in the Magra river valley and the interesting town of Pontremoli, although this area has perhaps more in common with Liguria than with Tuscany.

Information Offices. *APT Versilia*, 10 Viale Carducci, Viareggio (Tel. 0584/48881), with information offices at Forte dei Marmi, Lido di Camaiore, and Marina di Pietrasanta. The *Comunità Montana Alta Versilia* has its headquarters at Seravezza, where a 'Pro Loco' office is also open in summer. *APT Massa-Carrara*, 24 Lungomare Vespucci, Marina di Massa (Tel. 0585/240046), with an information office at Marina di Carrara, 5 Piazza Menconi (Tel. 0585/632218).

Road distances from Viareggio to Pontremoli.—11km *Camaiore*—20km **Pietrasanta**—25km *Seravezza.* N1 (Aurelia)—37km **Massa**. N446dir—44km **Carrara**—59km *Fosdinovo*. N446, N63—80km *Aulla*. N62—90km *Villafranca in Lunigiana*—102km **Pontremoli**.

A **Motorway** (A12) follows the coast from Viareggio to Carrara, with exits at Versilia (for Pietrasanta and Seravezza), Massa and Carrara. It continues to a junction with the motorway to La Spezia where the A15 motorway diverges right up the Magra valley for Parma (exits at Aulla and Pontremoli).

Railway on the main Pisa–Genoa line from Viareggio via Pietrasanta and Massa to Carrara (and Sarzana). From Sarzana a secondary line diverges up the Magra valley via Aulla and Pontremoli.

Buses. A comprehensive network (run by *Lazzi*) serves all the towns in the area.

Numerous **hotels** of all categories in the coastal resorts of Versilia. Camping sites near Torre del Lago Puccini. Information from APT offices and *Associazione Alberghieri*, 1 Via Leonardo da Vinci, Viareggio.

VIAREGGIO (55,700 inhab.) is the main town of Versilia, and the most popular seaside resort on the W coast of Italy. It first became fashionable in the early 19C and it retains an old-fashioned air with an esplanade planted with palm trees, Art Nouveau houses, and huge old grand hotels and cafés.

Information Office, APT, 10 Viale Carducci.

Railway Station, Piazza Dante (with a tourist information office open in summer).

Buses from the station (circular service) along the sea-front (Viale Carducci) to Lido di Camaiore and Forte dei Marmi; also inland to Camaiore; from Piazza Mazzini to Pisa; to Lucca and Florence; to La Spezia; and to Torre del Lago Puccini. *Lazzi* service in summer to Pisa airport.

Hotels. Viareggio has seven 4-star, sixteen 3-star, and some forty 2-star, and eighty 1-star hotels (some of them seasonal).

Restaurants of all categories abound (including trattoria *La Darsena*).

The **Carnival** held in February is one of the most famous in Italy. The parade of allegorical floats (many of them topical) takes place on Shrove Tuesday and the first and second Sunday of February at 14.30, and on the third Sunday of February at 17.30.

Shelley and his friend, Lieutenant Williams, drowned on 8 July, 1822, when their little schooner *Ariel* sank off Viareggio on a voyage from Livorno to La Spezia. Their bodies, washed ashore on the beach of Il Gombo, N of the mouth of the Arno, were there cremated in the presence of Trelawny, Byron, and Leigh Hunt. Shelley's ashes were collected and buried in the Protestant cemetery at Rome.

In this century regular visitors to Viareggio have included D'Annunzio, Isadora Duncan, Eleonora Duse, Carlo Carrà, Felice Carena, Giovanni Papini, Luigi Pirandello, and Roberto Longhi. Since 1929 the 'Premio Viareggio' has been awarded annually here for a work of literature.

The town retains its regular plan from the early 19C when it was laid out by Lorenzo Nottolini on a chessboard pattern with long avenues parallel to the seafront and numerous parks. After Paolina Bonaparte built her villa on the edge of the sea in 1820 it became one of the first seaside resorts in Europe. Numerous decorative buildings (in Viale Carducci, Via Michelangelo Buonarroti, Via Ugo Foscolo, Via Antonio Fratti, etc.) survive from the Art Nouveau and Art Deco periods, many with frescoes and graffiti as well as external ceramic decoration (much of it by Galileo Chini). Among the architects who worked here were Giovanni Lazzarini, Alfredo Belluomini, and Roberto Narducci. A splendid double promenade, with a roadway and a footway, leads along the shore from the Giardini d'Azeglio to Piazza Puccini. Some old bagni (bathing establishments) survive here. At the inner corner of the Giardini d'Azeglio is Piazza Shelley, with a bust of the poet by Urbano Lucchesi (1894). At 2 Via Machiavelli is the *Museo Preistorico e Archeologico A. C. Blanc* (9–13; fest. 16–19; closed Mon). In Piazza Mazzini the first *Ospizio Marino* survives, built in 1854–61 by Giuseppe Barellai as a model hospital. Beautiful pine-woods extend along the shore in either direction from the town, and there is a distant view of the Apuan Alps. The outer harbour is busy with boat-yards and a 16C tower guards the inner basins where there is a port.

The fine road along the coast to Forte dei Marmi passes (5km) the **Lido di Camaiore**, another extended bathing resort. It is the first of a series of more or less exclusive resorts which stretch all the way along the coast to (30km) Marina di Carrara. They are extremely crowded (mostly with Florentines) in summer. Called **Forte dei Marmi, I Ronchi, Marina di Massa** and **Marina di Carrara** they are laid out on regular plans with long straight roads parallel to the shore and consist of elegant villas and hotels surrounded by gardens. The sea and wide beaches, separated from the road by colourful beach huts, are not as clean as they once were. All the resorts have spectacular views inland to the Apuan Alps (often snow-capped) and white marble quarries. The most elegant bathing resorts along this stretch of coast are Forte di Marmi and I Ronchi, with numerous villas and samll hotels set in thick vegetation. 3-star hotel *Astoria Garden*, 10 Via Leonardo da Vinci; restaurants *Lorenzo* and *Tre Stelle*. The pine-woods were severely damaged in a tornado in 1977. The beaches are mostly private and have splendid views of the mountains. In Forte dei Marmi Aldous Huxley wrote *Crome Yellow* in 1921, and two years later, *Antic Hay*. The Molo, a low pier, is the scene of the evening 'passeggiata'. The only high building on the shore is the round Torre Fiat, a skyscraper built as an industrial holiday colony. Marina di Carrara is interesting as a marble port.

Torre del Lago Puccini, recently developed as a holdiay resort with numer-ous camping sites, is reached from Viareggio (road signposted) along the Viale dei Tigli, a fine avenue of lime trees which borders the *Macchia Lucchese*, a protected area of woods. It can also be reached from Piazza d'Azeglio by bus, or, in summer by boat from Largo Risorgimento. Viale dei Tigli ends at Viale John Kennedy which leads right to the sea; to the left Viale Marconi and Viale Puccini lead under the motorway to the **Lago di Massaciuccoli**. Torre del Lago Puccini adopted the name of Giacomo Puccini (1858–1924) who made his bohemian home on the lake where he enjoyed shooting waterfowl. The little lakeside resort is somewhat dis-turbed by the close vicinity of the motorway. On the waterfront, surrounded by a garden, is the VILLA which Puccini built (guided tours every half hour, 9.30–12.30, 16–18.30; winter 10–12, 15–17.30; closed Monday). All his operas except the last, *Turandot*, were to a great extent written here. The house preserves mementoes of Puccini and his tomb is in the chapel. An opera festival is held on the lakeside in summer in an open-air theatre. Outside is a bronze statue of Puccini by Paul Troubetzkoy (1925). It is possible to take boat trips (30 minutes; enquire locally) on the lake to visit the marshes. Sine 1979 the lake has been part of the *Parco Naturale Migliarino-San Rossore-Massaciuccoli* which protects the coast from Viareggio to Livorno (information from the *Consorzio del Parco*, 4 Via Aurelia Nord, Pisa; see also the end of Rte 9).

The other side of the lake, which is prettier, is reached by the road from Viareggio for Lucca via Massarosa (8.5km). At Quiesa (10.5km) a by-road leads right for the village of **Massaciuccoli**. By the right side of the road, marked by two cedars of Lebanon (yellow signpost) are the unenclosed remains of a *Roman villa* discovered in 1935. It belonged to the Venulei, a Pisan family, in the 2C AD. Above the excavations is a small Antiquarium. A mosaic pavement with fantastic animals made of stone tesserae was lifted and restored in 1987 (open summer daily exc Mon 17–20; fest. 9–13, 17–20; in winter on request). On the other side of the road a path (signposted) leads up through olive groves in five minutes to remains of small *Roman baths* (unenclosed) on the hillside below the church (which can also be reached by car from the Lucca road). There is a fine view of the lake from here. At the entrance to the village (a few hundred metres from the Roman villa) a road (unsignposted) leads down to a canal from the lake beside two picturesque old houses. Beyond two bridges a walkway raised on stilts (beware of broken planks!) continues across the marshes to the lakeside where there are hides and fishing huts.

From Massaciuccoli a road is signposted to Lucca across a hill with some disused quarries, and then down through woods. It passes the conspicuous 14C castle of *Nozzano* (see Rte 10). Nearby is *Arliano*, with a very ancient pieve.

From Viareggio a road (signposted) leads along a canal to (11km) **Camaiore**, a pleasant little town in a fine position surrounded by the foothills of the Apuan Alps. It is built on a regular plan with long straight streets. First-class restaurants in the environs include: *Emilio e Bona* at Lombrici; *La Dogana* and *Cavallino Bianco* at Capezzano Pianore, and *Il Vignaccio* at Santa Lucia. The *Collegiata* (1278) has been much altered. In the presbytery is an Assumption with Saints Peter and Paul by Benedetto Brandimarti (late 16C). At the end of the left aisle, Communion of the Apostles by Piero Dandini, and on the third left altar, 14C wood Crucifix. In the baptistery the font dates from 1387. Next to the tiny little Romanesque church of *San Michele* (being restored) are the 17C premises of the Confraternità del Santissimo Sacramento which now houses a *Museo di Arte Sacra* (open in winter on Saturday 10–12; in summer, Tuesday and Saturday 16–18; if closed ring at No. 71). It contains a Flemish *tapestry with the Last Supper and scenes of the Passion, dated 1516, on a cartoon by Pieter Pannemaker; fine vestments, church silver, and a wood statue of the Virgin Annunciate (restored) attributed to the 15C Lucchese school (Matteo Civitali?). Off the Corso is the *Badia di San Pietro*, founded by the Benedictines in the 8C, and rebuilt in the 11C. Outside a 14C portal survives from the convent walls. The church contains a Baroque altar and remains of a 14C fresco. The approach road from the sea passes the prominent church of the *Francescani*, with an 18C choir and a marble statue over the high altar dating from 1689.

In the environs of Camaiore is the Romanesque *Pieve of San Giovanni Battista e Santo Stefano* which contains a Roman sarcophagus (2C AD), used as a font, and a triptych by 'Maestro Gerio' (1443). The village of *Nocchi* (4km) also has an interesting church. Other churches worth a visit in the environs towards Viareggio include *Mommio*, *Corsanico* (with a precious organ built by the Venetian Vincenzo Colonna in 1602–06), *Conca di Sotto*, and *Stiava*. Nearer Massarosa is *Pieve a Elici* where the restored 11C church in a beautiful position has a sculpted high altar, a stoup and ciborium attributed to Lorenzo Stagi and an old fresco of the Madonna and Child.

From Camaiore the Viareggio road soon meets the busy Aurelia which continues N to (20km) **PIETRASANTA**, the main inland town of Versilia (23,000 inhab.), which has long been famous for its highly skilled marble workers, and for its bronze foundries. Numerous artists come here to study the techniques of sculpture. A pleasant small town it has retained its interesting plan with four long straight parallel streets which run at right angles through Piazza Duomo. On the outskirts of the town are some interesting old marble works (some dating from the Art Nouveau period).

Railway Station on the main Pisa–Genoa line (slow trains only).

Car parking in Piazza Statuto.

Hotels. 3-star: *Palagi*, 23 Piazza Carducci; and numerous hotels of all categories at the coastal resort of Marina di Pietrasanta.

First-class **restaurants**: *Il Gatto Nero*, *Da Sci* and *Il Fico*.

18-hole **golf course** *Versilia*.

History. The town was founded by Guiscardo da Pietrasanta, the Podestà of Lucca in 1255, and thrived under the lordship of Castruccio Castracani in 1316–28. In the following centuries its possession was disputed between Genoa, Lucca, and Florence. From the 16C up until c 1820 it declined because of the presence of malaria in the surrounding marshes. Famous natives include the sculptors Lorenzo and Stagio Stagi (1455–1506 and 1496–1563) and Eugenio Barsanti (1821–64), inventor (with Felice Matteucci) of the internal combustion engine.

*Piazza Duomo has a fine group of buildings and a splendid view of the castle and walls climbing a wooded hillside. Behind the monument to the Grand-duke Leopoldo II (by Vincenzo Santini, 1843) is a column bearing the Florentine *Marzocco* by Donato Benti, and a wall fountain. The **Duomo** (or *Collegiata di San Martino*), first built in 1256 and enlarged in 1330, has a white marble façade with a beautiful rose *window by the Riccomanni, a local family of sculptors. Above the three portals are unusual sculpted lunettes. The 16C bas-relief of St John the Baptist is by Stagio Stagi, and the coat of arms (1513) is that of the Medici pope, Leo X. The unfinished brick campanile is attributed to Donato Benti.

The INTERIOR has fine marble altars and confessionals. The frescoes in grisaille are by Luigi Ademollo (1825). The two stoups are by Stagio Stagi, and the *pulpit is by Lorenzo Stagi (1504), with a staircase by Andrea Baratta. The interesting 17C altarpieces in the aisle are in poor condition. At the end of the S aisle, 15C statue of the Virgin Annunciate. In the S transept, Nativity by Piero Dandini. In the handsome chapel to the right of the sanctuary is preserved a late Gothic painting of the Madonna and Child with Saints John the Evangelist and John the Baptist (exhibited only on certain religious festivals). On either side of the sanctuary are two candelabra by Sergio Stagi and two bronze angels by Ferdinando Tacca. Over the high altar is a Crucifix, also by Tacca. The carved marble *stalls are also by Stagi. In the N transept, Madonna of the Rosary, by Matteo Rosselli. At the end of the N aisle is an unfinished statuette of St John the Baptist by Stagio Stagi, who also carved the two capitals on the pilasters of the crossing. The sacristy and baptistery (opened by the sacristan) are also interesting: the font is by Donato Benti.

Beyond the campanile is the 16C Palazzo Moroni with a pretty staircase. It houses the MUSEO ARCHEOLOGICO VERSILIESE (usually open Tuesday–Thursday, 9–12, Saturday 15–18, Sunday 10–12) with local finds from the Neolithic to Roman periods. Another section has medieval and Renaissance ceramics found during the restoration of the convent of Sant'Agostino after 1970. The 14C church of **Sant'Agostino**, with a handsome façade, has been closed for many years. It has been deconsecrated and is being restored as a hall for concerts and lectures. The ex-convent and cloisters (entrance to the right) have been restored as a cultural centre and the seat of the Biblioteca Comunale. Here is the *Museo dei Bozzetti* (open 9–12, 14.30–19; Saturday and Friday, 14.30–19; closed Monday and Sunday), with plaster models by various sculptors notably Leone Tommasi (1903–65). Via della Rocca leads up past a few palm trees and the domed bell tower of Sant'Agostino to the **Rocca di Sala**, on the hillside planted with olive trees. The fortress was originally built by the Longobards, and reconstructed in 1324 by Castruccio Castracani. It contains a 15C palace built by Paolo Guinigi. On the other side of the square is the *theatre* (18C; recently restored), and at the far end of the square can be seen the *Rocca Arrighina* inside the Porta Pisana near the Torre delle Ore. A house here has a plaque recording Michelangelo's stay in 1518.

In Via Mazzini (where a plaque marks the house of Stagio Stagi) is the Misericordia next to the church of *San Biagio*. It contains an altarpiece of the Madonna enthroned by the local painter Lorenzo Cellini. A statue of San Biagio by Francesco da Valdambrino has been removed for restoration.

On the outskirts of Pietrasanta, near the hospital, is the church of *San Salvatore*, founded in 1523. In the cloister are lunettes of the life of St Francis by Luigi Ademollo. The long straight Viale Apua leads directly to the sea at Marina di Pietrasanta. It passes the park (right) of *La Versiliana* in Fiumetto, where D'Annunzio stayed at the beginning of the century. Built in 1886, it is now used for plays, concerts, exhibitions, etc.

On the S outskirts of the town (signposted off the Lucca road by the cemetery) is the by-road for **Valdicastello Carducci**. It passes the *Pieve di Santi Giovanni e Felicità* amid olive trees, a very ancient church. It has a fine rose window, and contains an early sarcophagus and 14C frescoes. In the courtyard is a well by Giuseppe Stagi (1559). Valdicastello was the birthplace of the poet Giosuè Carducci (1835–1907). The house can be visited on Saturday (9–12) and Sunday (15–18), in summer: Tues–Sun 17–20. The church contains a marble tabernacle by Stagio Stagi.

A road continues away from the coast towards Seravezza. It passes (23km) *Vallecchia* with the pieve of Santo Stefano, another ancient church with interesting sculptures including a pulpit by Andrea Baratta (1681), a bas-relief attributed to Donato Benti, and a Madonna and Child of the 14C. 25km. **Seravezza** attractively situated in a narrow ravine surrounded by high mountains, with numerous quarries and marble works. Michelangelo stayed here while looking for marble in 1517. The tree-lined streets are built along the Versilia river (its waters white from marble) between two bridges. A tourist office is open by the river in summer. The *Duomo* (1503; finished in the 17C), on the right bank of the river beside a group of handsome houses, has a castellated campanile and a dome. The wide interior has fine marble altars and confessionals. The high altar has a picture of St Laurence on the grille in marble inlay. Behind and above it is a marble reliquary and a Cross. In the chapel to the left of the high altar is a font by Stagio Stagi (recently restored).

On the left bank of the river, some way upstream, is *Palazzo Mediceo* built for Cosimo I in 1555 by Ammannati (recently restored). It is now the seat of the Biblioteca Comunale. The courtyard has a well with a charming fish above it. Opposite the palace is an old marble works.

A road leads along the floor of the Vezza valley past numerous small quarries and some waterfalls. At Ponte Stazzemese (7km) a road leads right and climbs through Mulina for **Stazzema** (12.5km), a climbing centre, in a splendid position at the foot of oddly-shaped mountains. Just before reaching the village, the road passes the church of SANTA MARIA ASSUNTA (if closed ring at the canonica) on the edge of the hill, preceded by a charming paved forecourt with a porch overlooking the valley. The first church on this site dates from the 9C; it was enlarged in the 13C and 14C. The façade has a fine 15C rose window and interesting carvings.

The columns in the interior have fine capitals, Gothic on the left, and Renaissance on the right. The wood ceiling dates from after 1630. The organ at the W end is attributed to Filippo Tronci (1775). On the W wall is a 16C bas-relief of the Baptism of Christ. At the end of the right aisle, marble statue of St Anthony Abbot, attributed to Nicolao Civitali or Leonardo Riccomanni. The high altar dates from 1649 and bears an altarpiece of the Assumption attributed to Matteo Rosselli. The tabernacle on the right wall of the sanctuary and fine portal of the sacristy are both attributed to Lorenzo Stagi. On the left wall of the sanctuary is a very unusual painting of the Assumption, with angels, saints, and apostles, attributed to a Catalan painter of the 14–15C.

From outside the church a cobbled path (300m) leads down through woods to the *Santuario del Piastraio* (open only for occasional services, but visible though an open window), with an 18C interior and a painting attributed to a certain Guglielmo Tommasi (1772). The road ends at the quiet little village on a ridge of the hill with a clock tower of 1739.

A by-road leads N from Seravezza via Fabbiano for *Azzano*, passing the 13C pieve of *La Cappella* in a fine position with a view of the marble quarries and Monte Altissimo. Michelangelo is known to have used marble from quarries in this area. On the façade is a fine rose window, and inside an hexagonal ciborium.

A by-road off the Stazzema road leads to *Retignano*, with another ancient church which contains a font attributed to Donato Benti and carved altars by Lorenzo Stagi

(1486) and Benti (1532). The road continues to *Levigliani*, an ancient village and a centre for climbing in the Apuan Alps.

The Aurelia (N1), 4km S of Seravezza continues parallel to the coast and passes into the province of Massa Carrara. At 34km is a turning for *Montignoso* (right of the road; 2-star hotel *Pasquilio*, with restaurant) with fine views. Higher up is *Sant'Eustachio* where the church contains a fine small seated statue of the Madonna and Child (in wood) attributed to Tino da Camaino, and a beautiful painting of the Florentine school (dated 1424) at the E end with the Madonna and four saints and the story of the patron saint in the predella. A marble statue of St Eustachio dates from 1906. The marble mosaic high altar and confessionals were made by the inhabitants in the 1950s.

37km **MASSA** is a provincial capital situated at the foot of the narrow Frigido valley, below the Apuan foothills. It has greatly expanded since the Second World War and now has a largely modern aspect (68,000 inhab.). Founded in the Middle Ages, it was the capital of the Malaspina duchy of Massa-Carrara from 1442 to 1790. Numerous orange and lemon trees were planted here in the early 19C, notably in the central *Piazza degli Aranci.* Here also is a grandiose marble monument with lions and an obelisk dating from 1861, and the huge *Palazzo Cybo Malaspina* with a delightful red façade by Alessandro Bergamini of 1701. The courtyard is by Gian Francesco Bergamini (1665). The **Duomo**, reached by Via Dante Alighieri has an imposing marble façade of 1936.

The 18C INTERIOR was decorated at the end of the 19C. RIGHT AISLE. The baptistery has an early-15C font by Riccomanni. First altar, Matteo Rosselli (attributed), Coronation of the Virgin; third altar, Luigi Garzi (school of Maratta), Saints John the Evangelist, John the Baptist, Peter, and James. Stairs lead down from the right aisle to the funerary chapel of the Cybo Malaspina with tomb-slabs of the ducal family and two funerary monuments. The tomb of *Eleonora Malaspina (died 1515) by Pietro Aprili (influenced by the monument of Ilaria del Carretto by Jacopo della Quercia in the Duomo of Lucca) was beautifully restored by local craftsmen. The monument to Lorenzo Cybo is by the school of Stagio Stagi. RIGHT TRANSEPT. Marble altarpiece in high relief by Andrea and Tommaso Lazzoni (1672). The CHAPEL OF THE HOLY SACRAMENT (by Giovanni Francesco Bergamini) dates from 1675–94. The fine *altar (1694) was designed by Bergamini to preserve the fresco fragment of the Madonna and Child by Pinturicchio (from the Cybo chapel in Santa Maria del Popolo in Rome). Also here is a triptych attributed to Filippo Lippi and a Nativity in enamelled terracotta by Benedetto Buglioni. On the HIGH ALTER, bronze Crucifix and six candlesticks by Ferdinando Tacca. In the LEFT TRANSEPT is a highly venerated wood *Crucifix of the early-13C. LEFT AISLE, third altar, Carlo Maratta, Immaculate Conception. There is also an interesting MUSEUM (only open by appointment, Tel. 0585/42643).

The *Rocca* or **Castello Malaspina**, on a high hill, is reached by a narrow (signposted) road. It was first built in the 11–12C, and the Renaissance palace of the Malaspina was enlarged in the 16–17C. A building of the highest interest, it has been closed for many years for restoration. At its foot is the oldest district of Massa called *Rocca* with very narrow streets (but few old houses) and the church of *San Rocco* which has an interesting 16C Crucifix, attributed to the local sculptor Felice Palma. In the modern part of the town towards the sea is the church of *Santa Maria degli Uliveti*; a wood sculpture of St Leonard by Jacopo della Quercia has been removed to the Canonica. There is an Ethnological Museum illustrating peasant life in the Apuan Alps at No. 85 Via Uliveti. The church of *San Giacomo Maggiore* in Via Piastronata contains an interesting 15C painting of the Madonna del Carmine by the Lombard School. The church of *San Sebastiano* (1957) contains a 17C Pietà by Felice Palma.

From Masssa a spectacular mountain road leads over the Apuan Alps via Antona and Arni to Castelnuovo di Garfagnana (see Rte 7). This was constructed in 1880 to provide access to the quarries on Monte Altissimo.

A pretty back road (the *Strada del Foce*) connects Massa to Carrara across the hills. It traverses woods and quarries and has good views of the mountains. 44km **CARRARA** (67,700 inhab.) is a flourishing town, world famous for its white marble.

Railway Station, 3km from the centre of the town, on the Genoa–Pisa line.

Bus Services (CAT) from Via del Cavatore to Marina di Carrara and the railway station (every 10mins); to the Fantiscritti quarries and Colonnata; and to Massa, Fosdinovo, and Pontremoli.

Car parking off Via Cavatore, or (with an hourly tariff) in the main squares.

Hotels. 3-star: *Michelangelo*, 3 Corso Fratelli Rosselli. 2-star: *Da Roberto*, 5 Via Apuana; and many more at Marina di Carrara.

Restaurants. Trattoria: *Roma di Prioreschi*, 1 Piazza Cesare Battisti. At Colonnata: (First-class) *Locandapuana* and *Venanzio*.

History. The earliest record of Carrara's existence dates from 963 when it was given to the bishops of Luni. It then passed into the hands of Lucca and Genoa before becoming part of the duchy of the Malaspina with Massa in 1442. It has been known for its marble since Roman times, and is now one of the main centres in the world for marble production. Carrara has also been well known in Italy since the 19C as a centre of the Anarchist movement.

The most interesting part of the town is around the good Romanesque *Duomo, altered in the 13C when the attractive Gothic storey was added to its façade (being restored). In the handsome S flank is a 13C portal, the usual entrance. The charming apse and campanile can be seen in the courtyard of the Canonica from which there is a view of the marble quarries in the Apuan Alps. The well proportioned INTERIOR has rough marble walls and huge capitals. There are interesting fresco fragments all over the church. SOUTH AISLE. Beyond the first altar is the Arca di San Ceccardo, supported by two 17C putti. Farther on are two charming 14C *statues of the Annunciation showing French influence. At the end of the aisle is the altar of the Holy Sacrament, with a Madonna and Child by Clemente da Reggio (16C) and in niches on either side, two statues (in very high relief) of Saints John and Thomas. The vault is frescoed by Acquilio Bernardino (1518). On either side of the PRESBYTERY are fine carved screens. Over the high altar is a painted 14C *Cross by Angelo Puccinelli. The pulpit, decorated with coloured marbles, dates from 1541. At the end of the NORTH AISLE the altar of the Assumption has a statue of the Madonna attributed to Moschino (17C) and two statues of Saints Catherine and Jerome. On the N wall, recomposed marble ancona with seated statues of the Madonna and Child with four saints, and an interesting 15C bas-relief beneath. Beyond is a small bas-relief which may represent Countess Matilda of Canossa crowned by Pope Gregory VII. A door leads into the BAPTISTERY (if closed, admission on request through the sacristy) which contains a large 16C hexagonal font for total immersion with an unusual little cupola in polychrome marble on top. The other font is another good work of the 16C.

At the W end of the N aisle is a fine carved arch over the altar (perhaps by Giroldo da Como) and a Crucifix made as a model by Pietro Tacca flanked by two Baroque statues of the Annunciation. At the W end of the S aisle is an altar carved in 1869 by Pietro Lazzerini di Tommaso.

The fountain in the piazza with a statue of Andrea Doria was left unfinished by Baccio Bandinelli. In the square is a red house (plaque) believed to have sheltered Michelangelo on his visits to buy marble. The pretty narrow Via Santa Maria leads away from the Duomo. It passes some interesting old doorways and, at No. 14, the unusual *Casa Repetti* with animal reliefs and little slender columns. It ends in front of the 17C church of the Carmine by a monument to Mazzini (1892) and the pink 17C façade of a palace now the seat of the *Accademia di Belle Arti*, entered from the other side, where it incorporates the old Malaspina castle (restored). On the lawn outside is a small statue of Pietro Tacca by Carlo Fontana (1900). A carved Roman marble relief (now very worn) found in the quarries of Fantiscritti with the signatures of Giambologna (1598) and Canova (1800) is at present in the courtyard (admission sometimes on request). The pleasant Piazza Gramsci has trees (including palms) and views of the hills and quarries. Via Giorgi leads down to the handsome Piazza Alberica with some fine red 17C palaces, and a white marble pavement. An interesting old road runs along the Carrione stream, just out of the square. In the nearby Piazza Garibaldi is the neo-classical *Teatro degli Animosi* by Giuseppe Pardini (1840).

From Piazza Gramsci Via Roma leads straight down to the 19C *Piazza Matteotti* with evergreen trees, and the monumental *Politeama Verdi* (1892; being restored). In Via Verdi, on the corner of Via Pelliccia, is an amusing mushroom coloured Art Nouveau building (No. 16). A number of interesting old-fashioned shop fronts are preserved in Carrara.

A long straight avenue (Viale XX Settembre) leads down to Marina di Carrara on the seafront. It passes a modern building which houses a permanent exhibition of marble quarrying and craftsmanship (open in summer; enquire at the Municipio). Outside the cemetery of Turigliano, in a pleasant little garden, a colossal white marble monolith by Sergio Signori (left unfinished at the sculptor's death in 1990) bears the dedication 'to Gaetano Bresci from the Anarchists'. Bresci assassinated King Umberto I in 1900 and died a year later in prison. The local government voted in favour of erecting a monument to him in 1986.

The famous **Marble Quarries** in the Apuan Alps which have been worked for over 2000 years are well worth a visit. They produce about one million tons of white marble a year, and over 170 quarries are now in use. They are situated in three valleys: *Colonnata, Fantiscritti* and *Ravaccione*. They can all be reached by road (signposted from Carrara). There is a bus to Colonnata six times a day (three on fest.), and to Fantiscritti (Ponte di Vara) on weekdays (four times a day). The quarries of Fantiscritti are perhaps the most interesting, since they are approached past the Ponte di Vara, the old railway bridge, and there is a museum (see below).

Up until the end of the last century marble was extracted from the mountainside by hand. Wooden wedges were inserted along the natural fissures in the marble. By keeping these wet they would swell and eventually the block of marble would fracture. A hand saw was also used, together with water and sand, by two workers, who were able to cut into the marble at a rate of about 5cm a day. A radical change in quarrying methods occurred at the end of the last century when steel wire, several hundred metres long, was introduced. This, still with the help of sand and water, can cut into the marble at a rate of c 10–20cm an hour. Diamond wire and diamond point saws are now also widely used. Once the blocks were extracted they used to be sent down the mountainside on a slide using ropes and wooden rollers, and then transported by wagons drawn by up to ten bullocks in pairs. A railway was constructed between 1876 and 1891 from the quarries to Marina di Carrara. This is no longer used, but the track which traverses tunnels and the high Ponte di Vara has been converted into a road which is now used by the lorries which climb up into the quarries on rough roads to pick up the marble. It is then transported either to Marina di Carrara for shipping, or to one of the numerous saw mills in and around the town which cut up the marble into slabs and polish it before exportation.

There is a delightful private outdoor *Museum* (open daily) by the Fantis-critti quarries which illustrates the history of marble quarrying by means of instruments and tools and remarkable life-size sculptures in marble. From here rough roads lead up through the quarry, and another road follows the old railway tunnel to the Ravaccione quarries.

From Carrara the Lunigiana can be reached staying within Tuscany, by a beautiful minor road (N446dir) which climbs up through Gragnana. 53km. Turning for *Campo Cecina* (1300m; 10km), in the Apuan Alps with a fine panorama of the marble quarries. The road now runs through woods along the edge of the hills with views towards the Apuan Alps, and then towards the sea. 59km **Fosdinovo**, a medieval fortified borgo on the border between Tuscany and Liguria. It is in a beautiful position on a hill top with views of the Apuan Alps, the valley of the Magra, and the gulf of La Spezia. It became a feudal stronghold of the Malaspina in 1340 and they remained here until 1820. Since 1867 the CASTLE has been owned by the Malaspina-Torrigiani family. It probably dates from before the 13C, and has been well restored. It is usually open (tel. 0187/68891), and is shown on a guided tour (c half an hour). In 1981 much of the furniture was stolen. The most interesting rooms are the tiny *Camera di Dante* where the poet is supposed to have stayed as a guest in 1306, which has a frescoed niche of Christ in Pietà with the kneeling figure of a Malatesta crusader, and the Great Hall with frescoes illustrating Dante's visit by Gaetano Bianchi (1882). From the enclosed loggia there is a fine view of the village and the plain extending towards the sea. The battlements can also be visited. Exhibited in various rooms of the castle are: 16–19C arms and armour, a peacock from a 17C merry-go-round, Montelupo ceramics, and coins minted in Fosdinovo in 1661–69.

From the castle a narrow paved street runs through the borgo to the parish church of *San Remigio*, which has a pleasant grey-and-white interior with colourful Baroque marble altars. On the right side, Madonna (second altar) and a bas-relief of the Liberation of Souls from Purgatory (last altar), both by Giovanni Baratta. The choir has carved wood stalls, and on the E wall, high up in a niche, is a seated *statue of St Remigio (c 1300). At the end of the left side, funerary monument of Galeotto Malaspina (died 1367) with his effigy (fully armed) beneath a Gothic canopy. On the W wall are two interesting small bas-reliefs, and near the door the 16C font. A few steps lead down from the E end to the *Oratorio del Santissimo Sacramento*, with more elaborate, well-carved marble altars and a 17C wood Crucifix. Just beyond San Remigio, preceded by a marble balustrade and pavement, is the unusual white marble façade (1666) of the *Oratorio dei Bianchi* (closed for restoration). The 14C polychrome wood statue of the Virgin Annunciate which belongs to the church is at present shown in San Remigio only on 25 March and 8 September.

The road which winds down past olive groves from Fosdinovo towards the sea passes through an ancient archway at *Caniparola* (*trattoria dell'Arca*) where the handsome Villa Malaspina, with a pretty garden, dates in its present form from 1724. This road meets the Aurelia on the border with Liguria. Places of great interest nearby which form part of Lunigiana, include Castelnuovo Magra, Luni, and Santo Stefano di Magra, all described, together with Sarzana, the gulf of La Spezia and the rest of Liguria, in *Blue Guide Northern Italy*.

A pretty road (N446) winds down from Fosdinovo to join the road (N445) to Aulla and the Magra valley near (71km) *Soliera*, in the valley of the Aulella.

N445 leads E past the ancient *Pieve di Codiponte* (10km) to *Casola in Lunigiana* (12km) with a local ethnographical museum (temporarily closed). About 7km S is the little spa of *Equi*. The road continues to *Giuncugnano* (26km), beyond which is the valley of the Garfagnana, described in Rte 7.

From Soliera, *Fivizzano* (8km NE; 2-star hotel *Il Giardinetto*, with restaurant) can be reached by N63 which leads to Reggio Emilia (see *Blue Guide Northern Italy*) via the Passo del Cerreto (1261m). It is a small town enclosed in ramparts by Cosimo I dei Medici. Nearby is the 14C castle of Verrucola.

N63 continues left to (80km) **Aulla** beneath the picturesque 16C fort of Brunella; there is a natural history museum and botanical garden here related to the Lunigiana (9–12, 14–18 except Monday). N62, accompanied by the A15 motorway to Parma, continues up the Magra valley through the district known as the **Lunigiana**, named after the Roman city of Luni, in Liguria. 90km *Villafranca in Lunigiana*, with a local ethnographical museum in an old mill (9–12, 15 or 16–18 or 19 except Monday). 102km **PONTREMOLI** (trattoria *Da Bussè*) lies in a strategic position among the chestnut-clad foothills of the Apennines. There was a castle here in 990, and a medieval borgo grew up between the Magra and Verde rivers. Now Pontremoli is a pleasant little town (10,700 inhab.) with some 17C and 18C palaces. Via Cavour and Via Mazzini traverse the town from the Porta Parma to the Porta Fiorentina on the line of the ancient Via Francigena. The central Piazza della Repubblica is separated from Piazza Duomo by a clock tower. Here is the Municipio with a portico (and the tourist information office in the courtyard), and the fine Palazzo Pavesi (No. 1; 1734–43) attributed to Giambattista Natali. Opposite the town hall is the 18C Pretura.

The **Duomo** was built by Alessandro Capra in 1636–87. The FAÇADE by Vincenzo Micheli dates from 1881, with a lunette mosaic by Annibale Gatti and two statues by Antonio Bucci of Seravezza. The bronze doors are by Riccardo Rossi of Carrara (1965). The elaborate INTERIOR, hung with chandeliers, has gilding and stuccowork, and marble altars and confessionals. The 1st N chapel has a 17C altarpiece and a 16C painting of the Madonna enthroned. In the sanctuary are four 18C paintings by Giuseppe Bottani, Giuseppe Peroni, Giovanni Domenico Ferretti, and Vincenzo Meucci. In the S transept is an elaborate carved altar by Lorenzo Franzoni (1808) and in the N transept, an altar dating from 1654 and a painting by Pierre Subleyras (in very poor condition). On the left wall is a 19C Deposition by Giuseppe Collignon. In the spandrels of the dome are 19C frescoes of the Evangelists by Giovanni Gaibazzi. The chapel of the Holy Sacrament, on the right of the presbytery, is a fine work of 1828.

Opposite the Duomo is the neo-classical *Palazzo del Vescovo*, with an outside staircase.

The winding Via Garibaldi leads gently up to Porta Parma past a series of handsome doorways and several Baroque palaces. On the left, Vicolo del Piagnaro, a lovely old lane, continues up past some old houses to the **Castello del Piagnaro** with the **Museo delle Statue-Stele** (admission 9–12, 14–17; summer 9–12, 16–19; Monday closed). The castle, founded in the 10C was enlarged in the 14C and several times destroyed. In the Middle Ages it was of fundamental importance to the defence of the Via Francigena (or *Strada della Cisa*), the road across the Apennines from Emilia into Tuscany. It contains a collection of remarkable statue-stele of the Lunigiana cult found over the last two centuries in the Magra valley. Fifty-nine of these statue-menhirs, which date from prehistoric times up to the Roman era (but mostly from the Bronze Age), have so far been found in Lunigiana, and the museum provides a complete documentation of them all. The original ones are displayed in Room III, while R. V and VI contain casts of the others.

Just out of Piazza Duomo (see above), off Via Garibaldi, Via della Cresa leads beneath a few arches to the narrow old Ponte della Cresa across the Verde river. Via Ricci Armani continues from Piazza della Repubblica past (left) Palazzo Dosi dating from the early 18C by Giovanni Battista Natali, with a courtyard, to Via Cavour with a Baroque palace at No. 15. At the end are some fortifications by the Ponte del Casotto. The bridge leads across the Verde river to a lane which continues to the church of *San Francesco* (marked by its Romanesque campanile). The unusual and attractive entrance portico is by Giovanni Battista Natali (1740). The church contains a fine painting of the Ecstasy of St Francis by Gianbettino Cignaroli (18C) on the E wall, and a lovely relief on the second left altar attributed to Agostino di Duccio. The unusual composition shows a half-figure of the Madonna with the Child lying in front of her, and a frame of cherubs' heads.

From the end of Via Cavour, opposite a palace with a pretty double loggia in the courtyard and a palm tree, Ponte Battisti (rebuilt after the War) leads across the Magra beneath an arch which connects the bright orange church of *Nostra Donna* to the old stone *Castelnuovo* (12–14C). The fine rococo church built by Giovanni Battista Natali (1738) is closed for restoration. It contains frescoes by Sebastiano Galeotti, and altarpieces by Alessandro Gherardini and Giuseppe Galeotti. In the piazzetta is the Teatro della Rosa. Via Mazzini runs parallel to the Magra past a pink palazzo with statuary on the balconies. At No. 30 is the office of the *Comunità Montana della Lunigiana*. Beyond Piazza Dodi begins Via Pietro Cocchi where at No. 7 is Palazzo Damiani (18C; in very poor repair) and at No. 24 is a neo-classical palace (1807).

On the S outskirts of the little town is the church of the *Annunziata* (for adm. ring at priest's house nearby), with an unusual tall façade (1937). It contains an octagonal tabernacle attributed to Jacopo Sansovino (1527), and paintings by Luca Cambiaso. The chapel of San Niccolò is decorated by Giovanni Battista Natali, and the sacristy has a vault painted by Francesco Natali and carved benches and cupboards by Francesco Battaglia (1676).

9

Pisa

PISA (104,300 inhab.), standing on the Arno a few miles from its mouth, is famous for its beautiful Piazza del Duomo, with the Cathedral, Leaning Tower, and Baptistery. The building of these splendid monuments was begun in the 11C and 12C when Pisa was a great maritime Republic. In the 13C and early 14C Nicola Pisano and his son Giovanni decorated both the inside and outside of the Duomo and Baptistery with their remarkable sculptures. Pisa has a flourishing university (founded in the 14C) as well as the renowned Scuola Normale university college, but it is now a somewhat austere town and many of its churches and palaces are in very poor repair. The Lungarni along the two banks of the river, lined with some fine palaces, are still a special feature of the town (and the seagulls on the Arno are a reminder of its proximity to the sea).

Information Offices. APT (Pl. 15), 26 Via Benedetto Croce, Tel. 050/40096 (Information Offices in Piazza del Duomo (Pl. 2), and at the main railway station).

Airport. *Galileo Galilei* (San Giusto), 3km S for international services to London, Paris, and Frankfurt, and internal flights to Rome, Milan, Turin, Cagliari, Catania, etc. Airport Railway Station (*Pisa Aeroporto*) with express train services every hour in one hour via Pisa Central to Florence. Bus no. 7 from the airport via Pisa central railway station and Lungarno Pacinotti to Piazza Garibaldi and Borgo Stretto.

Railway Stations. *Centrale* (just beyond Pl. 15, 2), Viale Gramsci for all services, one of the main railway junctions in central Italy, with services to Florence, Genoa, Turin, and Milan, and to Grosseto and Rome. For buses to the centre of the city, see below. *Aeroporto* with services via Pisa central to Florence. *San Rossore* (Pl. 1) served by all trains on the Lucca line and a few slow trains on the La Spezia line.

Town Buses. No. 1 from the central railway station via Ponte Solferino, Lungarno Simonelli, Via Bonanno Pisano and Piazza Manin to Piazza del Duomo. From the Duomo it returns to the Station via Via Santa Maria, Lungarno Pacinotti, Ponte di Mezzo, and Via Mazzini. **No. 7** from the central railway station to Borgo Stretto (see above). **Country Buses** run by the *Azienda Pisana Trasporti* and *Lazzi* from Piazza Sant'Antonio (Pl. 14) for Lucca, Florence, Livorno, Versilia, Marina di Pisa, etc.

Hotels. 4-star: *Grand Hotel Duomo*, 94 Via Santa Maria (Pl.2;1); *Cavalieri*, 2 Piazza della Stazione (south of Pl. 15); *D'Azeglio*, 18 Piazza Vittorio Emanuele (Pl.14;3). 3-star: *Villa Kinzica*, 4 Piazza Arcivescovado (Pl. 2; 4); *Royal-Victoria*, 12 Lungarno Pacinotti (Pl.11;2). 2-star: *Amalfitana*, 44 Via Roma (Pl. 6;6).; *Villa Primavera*, 43 Via Bonanno Pisano (Pl. 5;7); *Leon Bianco*, 6 Piazza del Pozzetto (Pl. 11;5).

Restaurants. Luxury-class: *Il Ristoro della Faggiola*, 1 Via della Faggiola; *Sergio*, 1 Lungarno Pacinotti. First-class restaurants: *Taverna Kostas*, 39 Via del Borghetto; *Osteria dei Cavalieri*, 16 Via S. Frediano; *Alle Bandierine*, 4 Via Mercanti; *La Mescita*, 2 Via Cavalca; *Turiddo*, 12 Piazza S. Frediano. Trattorie and cheap eating places (including self-service restaurants and pizzerie): *Mago di Oz*, Via del Borghetto; *Ambarabà*, Via Cavalca; *Il Montino*, 1 Vicolo del Monte; *Castelletto*, 12 Via del Castelletto; *La Grotta*, 103 Via S. Francesco; *Caffè Federico Salza*, 46 Borgo Stretto.

Annual Festival. In June the *Festa di San Ranieri*, commemorating the patron saint of the city St Ranieri (1117–60), is celebrated with candle-light festivities on the Arno and the *Gioco del Ponte*, a sham fight between the people living on either side of the Arno. The combatants wear 16–17C costumes, and the day ends with a procession of both parties.

History. The origins of the city are uncertain, but the site near the sea seems to have been settled by at least 1000 BC. An Etruscan town, it expanded in the 4C BC and became a Roman colony from the 2C BC, when, situated on a lagoon, it was a naval and commercial port. It continued to flourish under the Lombards in the 7C and 8C. By the 11C Pisa had become a maritime republic, rivalling Genoa, Amalfi, and Venice. Constantly at war with the Saracens, Pisa captured from them Corsica, Sardinia, and the Balearic Isles (1050–1100), and at the same time combined war and trade in the East. The wealth of the Pisans was proverbial. In 1135, assisting Innocent II against Roger of Sicily, Pisa destroyed Amalfi; but subsequently joined the Ghibelline party, and remained proudly faithful to it, even though surrounded by Guelf republics. The 12C was the period of her greatest splendour when she was one of the most important cities in Europe. But in 1284 Pisa was defeated by the Genoese in the naval battle of Meloria and lost her maritime supremacy; from then onwards the city had to submit to a succession of lordships, including those of the Gherardesca family (1316–41) and of Gian Galeazzo Visconti (1396–1405). The Florentines gained possession of Pisa in 1406, and after one or two unsuccessful efforts at rebellion it became a quiet refuge of scholars and artists, a university having been established in the city in 1343 by pope Clement VI. When Charles VIII entered Italy in 1494 he was expected to restore Pisa's liberty, but he broke his promise, and Florence took final possession of the city in 1509. In 1944 the town was bombarded by both German and Allied artillery; the Camposanto and the area near the station suffered worst, and further damage was caused when all the bridges were blown up. Disappointing and disorderly reconstruction work resulted in an unusually high number of unattractive buildings in various parts of the town.

The most illustrious native of Pisa is Galileo Galilei (1564–1642), physicist and astronomer. The mathematician Leonardo Fibonacci (1165–1235) was also born here. Pisa was visited by Landor in 1819–21, by Shelley in 1820–22, and by Byron in 1821, and here Browning brought his bride in 1846, before they settled in Florence. Titta Ruffo (1877–1953), the famous baritone, was born in Pisa.

Art. The Romanesque architecture of Pisa, a remarkable development of the North Italian Romanesque style, had a far-reaching effect on the neighbouring cities, spreading as far afield as Prato and Arezzo, and also into Sardinia, and leaving its imprint on the Gothic buildings that appeared later in the city. Pisan sculpture at the same time was an important influence in the advance from hieratic formalism, its greatest exponent being Nicola Pisano (c 1200–80), probably a native of Apulia who came to live in Pisa. His son Giovanni also produced some splendid sculptural works. In the 14C Nino Pisano, and his son Andrea were the best sculptors at work in the city. In painting Pisa produced no great master, but Giunta Pisano (fl. 1202–55) is believed to be the earliest painter whose name is inscribed on any extant work.

A. Piazza del Duomo

From the railway station, the most pleasant route on foot to Piazza del Duomo (a walk of 30–40mins) is via Viale Gramsci, Corso Italia, Ponte di Mezzo, Borgo Stretto, Via Ulisse Dini, Piazza Cavalieri, Via dei Mille, and Via Santa Maria. Bus No. 1 from the station to Piazza del Duomo; or Bus No. 7 to Piazza Garibaldi, and from there on foot.

··Piazza del Duomo, or *Campo dei Miracoli* (Pl. 2), with its bright marble monuments, is one of the most remarkable sights in Italy. The splendid Romanesque buildings of the Cathedral, Baptistery, and Campanile (Leaning Tower) are spaciously laid out in a rational arrangement and superbly set off by the green lawns between them. They are enclosed to the N by the Camposanto and the crenellated city walls in an almost rural setting. The piazza lies well NW of the centre of the city and, unlike most other Italian cathedral towns, it does not provide the focus of city life.

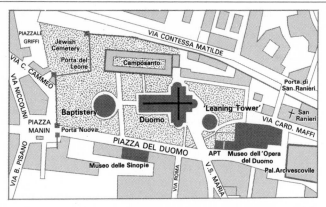

Admission. The **Baptistery**, **Camposanto** and **Museo dell'Opera del Duomo** remain open throughout the da , 9–dusk (8–19.40 in summer). The **Museo delle Sinopie** is open from 9–12.30, 15–dusk. The **Duomo** is open 7.45–12.45, 15–dusk. The **Campanile** is not at present open to the public. There are inclusive tickets for 4 or 2 of the above monuments or museums. A ticket for the Duomo has to be bought at one of the museums or at the offices of the Opera del Duomo, just N of the Duomo. In the vicinit of the piazza are a tourist information office, WCs, and numerous souvenir stalls.

The **•Duomo** (Pl. 2), begun by Buscheto in 1063, and continued by Rainaldo, is one of the most celebrated Romanesque buildings in Italy, and the prototype of the Pisan style of architecture in which a strong classicism survives. It was restored in 1602–16 after a serious fire in 1595.

The building stands on a white marble pavement and is covered inside and out with black-and-white marble, toned on the exterior to a delicate grey and russet. The •FAÇADE shows four tiers of columns with open galleries, with a row of seven tall arches below. In the left-hand arch is the tomb of Buscheto. The bronze doors were remodelled after the fire by various sculptors of the school of Giambologna. The W door is open in summer; otherwise the usual entrance is from the S transept, opposite the PORTALE DI SAN RANIERI, with bronze •doors by Bonanno da Pisa (1180; restored in 1989). Above is a lunette with a 15C Madonna and Child and two angels by Andrea di Francesco Guardi. Outside the transept is a copy made in 1930 of a beautiful Greek vase (original in the Camposanto).

The cruciform INTERIOR (admission, see above) is over 94.5m long and 32m wide (72m across the exceptionally deep transepts). The 68 pillars have 11C capitals in imitation of classical ones. The rich ceiling of the nave was remodelled after 1596. Some of the small stained glass windows (restored in 1947–48) are attributed to Alesso Baldovinetti. The two stoups (1) bear statues by Felice Palma (1621), perhaps on a design by Giambologna. WEST WALL. The tomb of Matteo Rinuccini (2) incorporates a Crucifix by Pietro Tacca. The 14C fresco of the Crucifixion (3) is attributed to Bernardo Falconi. The Frosini funerary monument (4) has a bas-relief of the Deposition by Giovanni Battista Vaccà (1702). On the walls of the SOUTH AISLE, between the altars, are hung a series of large 18C canvases, all of them labelled. First altar (5), Cristofano Allori, Madonna and saints (1610; perhaps completed by Zanobi Rosi in 1626); second altar (6) Francesco Vanni, Disputation of the Holy Sacrament (with a figure on the left attributed to Annibale Carracci); third altar (7) Andrea del Sarto and

Giovanni Antonio Sogliani, Madonna delle Grazie. Beyond a historical painting (8) by Sebastiano Conca, the fourth altar (9) has a carved lunette of God the Father by Bartolomeo Ammannati. SOUTH TRANSEPT. On the first altar (10), carved by Stagio Stagi, Madonna and Child with saints by Giovanni Antonio Sogliani and Perin del Vaga. The two early-18C paintings (11, 12) are by Domenico Muratori and Benedetto Luti. The CHAPEL OF SAN RANIERI (13) has 17C sculptures by Francesco Mosca, and a marble and bronze coffer by Giovanni Battista Foggini which contains the remains of Pisa's patron saint (1117–60). The *tomb of the Emperor Henry VII (14) was sculpted by Tino da Camaino (1315) with a fine effigy (it has been partly reassembled here; other statues are in the Museo dell'Opera del Duomo). The Renaissance altar (15) was carved by Pandolfo Fancelli. On the altar right of the choir (16), Christ on the Cross by Giovanni Bilivert.

Beneath the oval dome frescoed by Orazio Riminaldi (1627) are remains of a Cosmatesque pavement; another fragment, discovered near the high altar in 1977, may date from the end of the 11C. In the centre of the outside face of the triumphal arch is a large 14C fresco of the Madonna and Child attributed to the Master of San Torpè. The balustrade at the entrance to the CHOIR bears two bronze angels by Giambologna and assistants (1602). The wooden throne and benches have good marquetry work. The stalls (15C) were reconstructed in 1616 from what survived of the fire. On the entrance piers, in rich frames, are a delightful *St Agnes (17) by Andrea del Sarto and a Madonna by Giovanni Antonio Sogliani. The marble lectern and candelabra are by Matteo Civitali. On the walls beneath the cantoria are paintings by Andrea Del Sarto: *Saints John, Peter, Margaret and Catherine. The Crucifix on the high altar is by Giambologna; the angel on the column to the left is by Stoldo Lorenzi (1483). Round the APSE (admission only with special permission): Sodoma, Descent from the Cross (1540) and Sacrifice of Abraham (1542); works by Sogliani, and Beccafumi. On the intrados of the apse arch are frescoed angels by Domenico Ghirlandaio (restored). In the apse is a fine mosaic, the *Redeemer enthroned between the Madonna and St John the Evangelist, a 13C work completed by Cimabue in 1302.

The *PULPIT in the nave (18; light) by Giovanni Pisano (1302–11; perhaps with the assistance of Tino da Camaino), removed in 1599 after the fire, was reconstructed in 1926. It is a masterpiece of Gothic sculpture. The columns, on plain bases, resting on lions, or carved into figure sculpture, have statues of sibyls above the capitals, and florid architraves. Above, deeply carved relief panels representing scenes from the New Testament are separated by figures of prophets. The bronze lamp hanging over the nave, supposed to have suggested to Galileo the principle of the pendulum, was in fact cast by Battista Lorenzi in 1587, six years after the discovery.

On the altar to the left of the presbytery (19) is a much venerated 13C painting of the Madonna to which the Pisans are traditionally supposed to have turned in times of trouble since 1225. The painting of the Birth of the Virgin (20) is by Corrado Giaquinto. NORTH TRANSEPT. Funerary monument of Archbishop d'Elci by Vaccà (1742). In the Cappella del Sacramento (21), bronze and silver ciborium by Giovanni Battista Foggini (1685), and sculptures by Chiarissimo Fancelli (1625) and Francesco Mosca (c 1563). In the arch high above (difficult to see) is a mosaic of the Annunciation attributed to Gaddo Gaddi. On the altar (22), carved by Stagio Stagi is a Miracle of Christ by Aurelio Lomi. The NORTH AISLE is hung with more large 18C paintings (all labelled). Fourth altar (23), 16C bas-relief in the lunette of the Madonna appearing to St Ranieri; third altar (24), Ventura

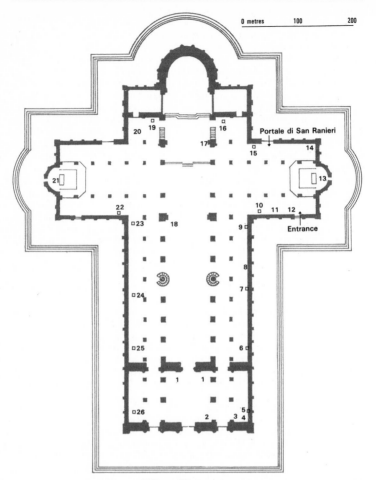

Pisa Duomo

Salimbeni, God the Father and saints; second altar (25) Passignano, Holy Spirit and martyrs; first altar (26), Giovanni Battista Paggi, Christ on the Cross and saints.

Superbly sited at the E end of the cathedral rises the *Campanile, the famous **Leaning Tower** (Pl. 2). It is a beautiful work, circular in plan and having eight storeys of round arches, six open galleries, and a bell-chamber of smaller diameter. The tower, 54.5m high, leans 4.5m out of the perpendicular. It is one of the most original bell-towers in Italy, apart from its marked inclination which has accounted for its world-wide fame. It has been closed to the public since 1990 for safety and conservation reasons.

Begun in 1173, the tower was only 10.5m high when a subsidence of the soil threw it out of the perpendicular. During the 13C the architect in charge appears to have been Giovanni di Simone, who endeavoured to rectify the inclination as the building proceeded. By 1301 the building had risen as far as the bellchamber, and Tommaso di Andrea da Pontedera completed the tower in the late 14C as it now stands. A spiral staircase (294 steps) leads to the top (splendid *view). Galileo made use of it in his famous experiments on the velocity of falling bodies. The lean has been increasing by c 1mm a year, and a long and complicated operation being carried out on the subsoil in an attempt to stabilise the structure. In 1992 steel cables were inserted around the base of the tower, and between the first and second galleries.

The *Baptistery (Pl. 2), W of the Duomo, is a noble circular building begun in 1152 by Diotisalvi. The Gothic decoration was added to the Romanesque building by Nicola Pisano (1270–84) and his son Giovanni (1297). The Gothic dome and cusped arches were added in the 14C by Cellino di Nese. There are four portals, of which the most elaborate, facing the Duomo, is embellished with foliated columns and a Madonna by Giovanni Pisano (copy; original in the Museo dell'Opera). The handsome INTERIOR (admission, see above) has a two-storeyed ambulatory, and is decorated with bands of black-and-white marble. A staircase leads up to the gallery. The beautiful octagonal *font of white marble, carved and inlaid in mosaic, is by Guido da Como (1246). The statue of St John the Baptist is by a local artist, Italo Griselli (1880–1958). The 13C altar stands on a raised mosaic pavement. The *pulpit, by Nicola Pisano, is signed and dated 1260. Resting on slender pillars bearing figures of the Virtues, it bears panels sculptured in bold relief (Nativity, Adoration of the Magi, Presentation, Crucifixion, and Last Judgement).

The *Camposanto (Pl. 2), or cemetery, was begun in 1278 by Giovanni di Simone, and completed in the 15C. The bright marble exterior wall has handsome blind arcading and a Gothic tabernacle over one door with statues attributed to the bottega of Giovanni Pisano. The interior (admission, see above) is in the form of an oblong cloister, lit by graceful traceried windows (never filled with glass), around a lawn. It is traditionally said that Archbishop Lanfranchi (1108–78) brought shiploads of earth from the Holy Land to form a burial-ground here. It was decorated with extremely important frescoes in the 14C and 15C by Taddeo Gaddi (1300), Andrea Bonaiuti, Antonio Veneziano, Spinello Aretino, Piero di Puccio (1377–90), and Benozzo Gozzoli (1468–84). From the 14C onwards Roman sculptures were collected here, including a huge collection of sarcophaghi. All these works were severely damaged in the Second World War, when the roof fell in. The frescoes (also ruined by exposure to the elements) have now all been detached for reasons of conservation, and some are displayed in a gallery here; the sinopie are preserved in the Museo delle Sinopie (see below). In the walks, bitterly cold in winter, are numerous pavement tombs.

The ROMAN SCULPTURE AND SARCOPHAGHI in the Camposanto made up one of the most important classical collections in Europe in the early Renaissance. Many of these have been destroyed or removed, but a remarkable series of 84 sarcophaghi, most of them dating from the 3C AD, remain (although many of them are very damaged). Some of them were re-used by Pisan citizens in the Middle Ages. Over the centuries funerary monuments were also erected here, some of which were later removed. The monuments are being cleaned and re-arranged.

SOUTH WALK. Left of the entrance (outer wall): sarcophaghi of the 2C and 3C, and (inside wall) two neo-classical monuments and two Roman statues. The large wall tomb (cleaned in 1991), at the end of this walk, is that of Francesco Algarotti (died 1764), the physicist.

The Baptistery, Pisa

WEST WALK (rearranged in 1991, when the monuments were cleaned). The oval sarcophagus with two male figures in togas, dating from the mid-3C AD, was re-used in the 14C by the Falconi family. On the wall, funerary monument of Francesco Vegio by Francesco Ferrucci (Il Tadda) with remains of 16C frescoes by Agostino Ghirlanda around it. Behind a Roman sarcophagus with figures of Genii (3C) is the wall tomb of Counts Bonifazio and Gherardo della Gherardesca attributed to a Pisan sculptor and dated 1330–40. The sarcophagus is decorated with arcaded niches with the Pietà and saints, and the figure of the defunct is flanked by the Annunciatory angel and the Virgin Annunciate. Beyond the small funerary monument of Selvaggia Borghini with her profile by Enrico Van Lint (1829), in the centre of this walk is the large wall momument of Bartolomeo Medici (1573), with a bust and an obelisk attributed to Niccolò Tribolo. The harbour chains of the ancient port of Pisa, displayed here, were carried off by the Genoese in 1342 (and returned by them in 1860). On two plinths, busts of Carlo Metteucci by Giovanni Duprè (1869) and of Giorgio Regnoli by Reginaldo Bilancini (1860). On the wall is a bust of Amedeo of Savoy by Cesare Zocchi (1897). The sarcophagus (one of the earliest in the Camposanto) with festoons was the tomb of Bellicus Natalis, consul in 87 AD. On the wall is the funerary monument of the painter Giovanni Battista Tempesti, with a seated female figure by Tommaso Masi (1804), and at the end of the N Walk is the large monument to Francesco Sanseverino Murci by Francesco Mosca decorated with coloured marbles. At the end of the wall, funerary monument of Lorenzo Pignotti (died 1817), the physicist, with a good relief by Stefano Ricci. A granite column serves as a base for a marble crater of the 1C BC. The frescoes (late-16C–early-17C) are by Aurelio Lomi (Esther and Assuero) and Paolo Guidotti (story of Judith and Holofernes).

NORTH WALK. Outer wall: two 3C sarcophaghi, and that of Larcius Sabinus (mid 2C AD); inner wall: tomb of Rafidia, a freedwoman (1C AD). A door in the outer wall leads into the CAPPELLA LIGO DEGLI AMMANNATI, with the tomb of the Pisan doctor who died in 1359. On the left is a huge room built in 1952 to house some of the frescoes detached from the S walk of the Camposanto, including *Triumph of Death, Last Judgement, stories of the Anchorites, etc. These have been variously attributed to Orcagna, Francesco Traini, Vitale da Bologna, Buffalmacco, etc. but are generally held to be by an unknown 14C master named from these frescoes the Master of the Triumph of Death (1360–80). Liszt was inspired by these scenes to create his '*Totentanz*'. Also here, Crucifixion by the Maestro della Crocifissione di Camposanto (c 1380), and Taddeo Gaddi, Patience of Job. The gallery on the other side of the Cappella degli Ammannati contains photographs of other frescoes formerly in the Camposanto (and some of them totally destroyed in the War) by Buffalmacco, Francesco Traini, Benozzo Gozzoli, etc. In the centre, Greek *vase (2C–1C BC), with dancing nymphs and satyrs and Dionysiac scenes carved in low relief, a superb work which was studied by sculptors of the Renaissance. It was formerly outside the Cappella di San Ranieri of the Duomo (and replaced there by a copy in 1930).

NORTH WALK (right of the door into the Cappella Ammannati). Outer wall, 2C and 3C sarcophaghi re-used in the Middle Ages, including a large one illustrating the myth of Phaedra and Hippolytus, re-used in 1076 for Beatrice, mother of Countess Matilda of Canossa. Beyond a fragment of a monochrome mosaic with birds, is a door into the CAPPELLA AULLA with a polychrome terracotta Assumption attributed to Giovanni Della Robbia (damaged). To the right of the door, beyond three 3C sarcophaghi is one decorated with Satyrs and Meanads and Dionysiac scenes on the cover, and one showing the myth of Meleager hunting the Caledonian boar. On the inner wall: several small sarcophaghi for children. Beyond two steps, two fine large sarcophaghi, one with a battle scene between Romans and barbarians (very damaged), and one with niches with the figures of the Muses (and on the cover a marriage bed with a husband and wife).

EAST WALK (being re-arranged). Tomb with an effigy of Filippo Decio (died 1535) by Stagio Stagi; seated female statue (1842) by Lorenzo Bartolini for the tomb of Count Mastiani; tomb of the scientist Mossotti (died 1863), with a reclining female figure by Giovanni Duprè. The CAPPELLA DEL POZZO (closed) with a dome, was built at this end of the Camposanto in 1594. On the wall here can be seen the nails and part of the preparation used for the intonaco for the frescoes.

SOUTH WALK. Outer wall: inscribed decrees ordaining honours for Gaius and Lucius Caesar, nephews of Augustus; Roman milestones (2C). On the inner wall, the second sarcophagus right of the door has winged Victories holding a medallion (on which was later carved a medieval coat of arms). Outer wall (beyond the door): sarcophagus with winged Victories inscribed with the name of Aelius Lucifer, a freedman; two oval sarcophagi with lions attacking their prey; sarcophagus with an open door symbolising the entrance to the after life; sarcophagus with hunting scenes illustrating the myth of Meleager and the Seasons, with a marriage bed and husband and wife on the cover.

On the S side of the lawn is the former OSPEDALE NUOVO DI MISERICORDIA (13–14C), where the *Museo delle Sinopie del Camposanto Monumentale (Pl. 2; admission, see above) was opened in 1979. A sinopia is the name given to the sketch for a fresco made on the rough wall (prepared with *arriccio*) in a red earth pigment (called *sinopia* because it originally came from Sinope on the Black Sea). The sinopia was then gradually covered with *grassello*, another type of wet plaster, as work proceeded day by day on the fresco itself. By detaching a fresco from the wall it has been possible in many instances to recover the sinopia from the inner surface. The 14–15C frescoes of the Camposanto (see above) were severely damaged in the last War and had to be detached: the sinopie were then restored and are now displayed together here.

A platform provides a view of three huge *panels with stories of the Anchorites, the Last Judgement and Hell, and the Triumph of Death, all generally attributed to the Master of the Triumph of Death (but thought by some scholars to be by Buffalmacco). On the far (end) wall, Crucifixion by Francesco Traini and Ascension, attributed to Buffalmacco. On the N wall, Theological Cosmograph by Piero di Puccio. On the last wall are smaller sinopie (very damaged) by Spinello Aretino, Antonio Veneziano, Andrea Bonaiuti, and Taddeo Gaddi. On the upper level are frescoes and sinopia fragments by Buffalmacco (Incredulity of St Thomas, Resurrection, etc.) On the ground floor the sinopie are by Piero di Puccio and Benozzo di Lese.

The *Museo dell'Opera del Duomo (for admission, see above) was opened in 1986, using the latest methods of security and display, in the former chapter house of the Cathedral behind the Leaning Tower. The collection includes works of art from the Duomo, Baptistery, and Camposanto. The fine building, with a double loggia, overlooking a little garden, has good views of the Leaning Tower. Handlists are supplied.

GROUND FLOOR. **R. 1** displays 19C models in wood and alabaster of the monuments in Campo dei Miracoli. **R. 2** contains casts of the first pulpit made for the Duomo by Guglielmo in 1162. **R. 3**: 12C sculpture from the Duomo, showing Islamic and French influences. The intricately carved transenna (probably an altar frontal) is attributed to Rainaldo. On the left wall are capitals and inlaid marble panels from the façade of the Duomo (their original postitions are shown on a diagram). In front is a long transenna from the presbytery by the school of Guglielmo, carved on the back of a Roman panel with a frieze of dolphins. The striking polychrome wood Crucifix is attributed to a Burgundian artist. The splendid bronze *griffin (11C) and the basin and capital (10C) are Islamic works brought from the East as war booty. The statue of St Michael is attributed to Biduino, and the seated statue of David playing the cithern shows the influence of Provence sculptors. The small **R. 4** displays a late-12C *capital from the Campanile. **R. 5** contains 13C heads from the exterior of the Baptistery (their original positions are shown on a diagram) and fragments from the transenna. **R. 6**, a pretty barrel vaulted room with wall paintings, displays the Gothic statues (very worn) from the summits of the triangular tympanums on the exterior of the Baptistery. They are by Nicola and Giovanni Pisano, and assistants. Facing them are busts of *Christ blessing, by Nicola Pisano, between the Madonna and St John the Evangelist, originally above the main entrance of the Baptistery facing the Duomo.

In the corridor and R. 7 are parts of the late-13C frieze with carved rectangles which ran round the base of the exterior of the Duomo. **R. 7** displays sculptures by Giovanni Pisano, including a (headless) Madonna and kneeling figure representing Pisa, formerly part of an allegorical group with the Emperor Henry VII. The Madonna and Child and Saints John the Evangelist and John the Baptist were removed from the main door of the Baptistery. The half-length Madonna del Colloquio is a beautiful composition. **R. 8** contains works by Tino da Camaino: fragments of the font from the Duomo; statues of the Annunciation and two deacons from the tomb of the Emperor Henry VII in the S transept of the Duomo; the tomb of St Ranieri (his first work, 1301–06); and the seated Henry VII between dignitories of the state. **R. 9.** Funerary monuments of two archbishops by Nino Pisano. **R. 10.** Funerary monument of Archbishop Pietro Ricci by the Florentine sculptor Andrea di Francesco Guardi; architectural fragments by Matteo Civitali, and the workshop of Lorenzo and Stagio Stagi.

The Cathedral treasury is displayed in **RR. 11 and 12**: 12C Cross, known as the Croce dei Pisani in bronze and silver; two 12C Limoges enamelled caskets; Tuscan embroidered altar-frontal (1325); and a cope, also dating from the 14C. The *girdle with five reliefs decorated with enamels and precious stones dates from the end of the 13C or beginning of the 14C. Also displayed here: 15C reliquary of St Clement, and an 11C ivory casket. The ivory statuette of the *Madonna and Child, is a superb work by Giovanni Pisano (1299–1300), originally over the main altar in the Duomo. The Crucifix is also by Giovanni Pisano. In the 17C chapel (R. 12) are displayed 17C reliquaries and the service of gilded church silver (French, 1616–17) given by Maria de' Medici to Archbishop Bonciani.

Stairs lead up to the FIRST FLOOR. **R. 13**: paintings by a follower of Benozzo Gozzoli (Madonna and Child, four saints, and patrons), and by Battista Franco and Aurelio Lomi. Marble angels by Tribolo and Silvio Cosini. **R. 14**: 18C paintings by Giuseppe and Francesco Melani and Giovanni Domenico Ferretti. **R. 15** displays wood intarsia: allegories of Faith, Hope, and Charity, by Baccio and Piero Pontelli (1475) are displayed opposite two works by Cristoforo da Lendinara. Also here are panels from choir-stalls by Guido da Seravallino. **R. 16**: two liturgical parchment scrolls, known as *Exultets* (12C and 13C), with illuminations, 14C illuminated choirbooks, and a 16C wooden lectern. **RR. 17–19**. Church vestments (16–19C). **R. 21**: engravings and watercolours by Carlo Lasinio (1759–1838) responsible for the restoration of the Camposanto. The delightful copies in watercolour of the frescoes of the Camposanto provide a precious record of them before their almost total destruction in the War. **RR. 22–24** contains an archaeological collection displayed by Lasinio in the Camposanto in 1807: cinerary urns, sarcophaghi, busts, including one of Julius Caesar, Etruscan urns, and Egyptian antiquities. The exit from the museum is along the PORTICO on the ground floor where the colossal *half-figures of Evangelists, prophets, and the Madonna and Child, by Nicola and Giovanni Pisano from the exterior of the Baptistery (1269–79) are displayed.

The handsome Renaissance *Palazzo Arcivescovile*, also in Piazza Arcivescovado, has a bright yellow façade and an attractive 16C courtyard (with a statue of Moses by Andrea Vaccà, 1709). A flying bridge connects the palace with its walled garden across Via Capponi. At the end of Via Corta is the church of *San Ranieri* (often closed) which contains a fine painting of the Madonna and Saints by Aurelio Lomi.

The 12C castellated **walls** which enclose the N and W side of Piazza del Duomo were pierced by the *Porta del Leone* (opposite the W end of the Camposanto) in the 13C. The gate was named after the Romanesque lion which survives here. Through the closed wooden gates can be seen part of the *Jewish Cemetery* which was moved here in the 16C, and surrounded in 1801 by a high wall. The *Porta Nuova*, the present exit from the piazza, replaced the Porta del Leone in 1562.

B. Piazza dei Cavalieri, Borgo Stretto, and the churches of Santa Caterina and San Francesco

From Piazza del Duomo, Via Santa Maria runs S. Opposite the end of Via dei Mille the short Via Luca Ghini leads to the entrance to the **Botanical Gardens** (Pl. 6; adm. 8–13, 14–17.30; Saturday 8–13; fest. closed; ring at the door on the left). Founded in 1543 by Luca Ghini, and on this site since 1591, this is the oldest university botanic garden in Europe. The large building which houses the Botanic Institute was built in 1890, and in the same year the two fine palm trees from Chile were planted here. The old garden is laid out in rectangular beds (well labelled) in front of the Institute. At the end on the left is the original building which housed the Botanic Insitute, its façade decorated in imitation of a grotto with shells and pebbles. The gardens (damaged in a hurricane in 1994) contain notable examples of palm trees, ginkgos, magnolias, and camphor trees.

Via dei Mille continues left and soon passes the Romanesque church of *San Sisto*, with a fine interior, beautifully restored. It is decorated with banners and on the W wall are 14–15C ships' masts, and a 14C Arab inscription. The high altar dates from 1786. ***Piazza dei Cavalieri** (Pl. 7), once the centre of the city, was named from the Knights of St Stephen, an order founded by Cosimo I in 1561 to combat the Turkish infidel, in imitation of the Knights of Malta. **Santo Stefano dei Cavalieri** (Pl. 7; open 9–12.30; also in the afternoon on Saturday and Sunday), their church, has a hand-some façade by Giovanni de' Medici (1594–1606), son of Cosimo I, and an unusual campanile by Vasari (1572).

The fine INTERIOR by Vasari (1565–69) is usually decorated with the banners captured from the infidel (these have been temporarily removed for restoration). The ceiling (1604–13) has good paintings by Cigoli, Jacopo Ligozzi, Cristofano Allori, and Empoli. 17C carved wood ornaments (attributed to Santucci) and lanterns from the galleys of the knights are displayed in various parts of the church. The two fine organs date from 1734 and 1569. The high altar, with a statue of the patron saint, is by Giovanni Battista Foggini. The five tempera paintings in grisaille (on the N, S, and W walls) are attributed to Empoli, Alessandro Allori, Vasari, and Ligozzi (or Stradano). Above the pretty pulpit by Chiarissimo Fancelli (1627; restored in 1930), with pietre dure inlay, is a painting of the Madonna and Child by Aurelio Lomi. The two stoups were designed by Vasari and carved by Fancelli. In the monumental side aisles are white marble confessionals. On the S side: first altar, Vasari, stoning of St Stephen; second altar, Crucifix attributed to Tacca. On the N side: second altar, Bronzino, Nativity; first altar, Lodovico Buti, Miracle of the Loaves and Fishes.

To the left of the church is PALAZZO DEI CAVALIERI, formerly *della Carovana*, modernised in 1562 by Vasari, with spectacular graffiti decoration, designed by him (much restored). It is now the seat of the SCUOLA NORMALE SUPERIORE, a university college of extremely high standing, founded by Napoleon in 1810, and modelled on the Ecole Normale

Supérieure in Paris. It incorporates a large medieval hall of the old Palazzo del Popolo, now used as a lecture hall. Concerts are given here from December to May. Outside is a statue of Cosimo I by Francavilla (1596).

The **Palazzo dell'Orologio**, closing the N side of the square, occupies the site of the old *Torre dei Gualandi* or *della Muda* (later the Torre della Fame), the 'mews' of the eagles that figure in the Pisan coat of arms. Here in 1288 Count Ugolino della Gherardesca, suspected of treachery at the battle of Meloria, and his sons and grandsons were starved to death (Dante, *Inferno*, XXXII). The building is now used as a library by the Scuola Normale, and the tower can be seen from the entrance, incorporated in the structure.

Via Ulisse Dini leads down to **Borgo Stretto** (Pl. 7), a pretty arcaded shopping street in the centre of the town (closed to private traffic), with wide pavements. Some of the porticoes date from the 14–15C. Off the narrow old Via Notari (parallel to the right) a daily market is held in *Piazza delle Vettovaglie*, with porticoes dating from 1544 (but damaged in the War). In Borgo Stretto is the church of **San Michele in Borgo**, built in the 11C, with a 14C façade by Fra Guglielmo Agnelli, typical of Pisan Gothic. In the interior (damaged in the last War) are good capitals. Over a door on the W wall (at the end of the N aisle) is a detached 13C fresco of St Michael. On the altar in the N aisle, Crucifix (a 14C Pisan work), and over the high altar, Madonna and saints by Baccio Lomi. Borgo Stretto ends at the central Piazza Garibaldi on the Arno (described in Rte 9C).

From Borgo Stretto, opposite Via Ulisse Dini (see above), the narrow Via San Francesco leads to the church of SANTA CECILIA (1103) with a façade and campanile decorated with majolica plaques (replaced by copies). Inside, a handsome Romanesque column at the W end supports a corner of the campanile. Over the high altar, Martyrdom of St Cecilia by Ventura Salimbeni. To the N, across the huge Piazza Martiri (planted with plane trees), stands the large church of **Santa Caterina** (Pl. 4, 8), built for the Dominicans in the 13C, with a façade in the Pisan Gothic style of 1330. The huge INTERIOR has a colourful E window of 1925. On the S wall, tomb of Gherardo di Compagno (1419), and St Catherine of Alexandria by Aurelio Lomi. A chapel off the S side which serves as a war memorial contains a Pietà by Santi di Tito. In the chapel to the right of the high altar, relief of the Madonna and saints by the school of Donatello. On either side of the presbytery, *statues of the Annunciation by Nino Pisano. In the N transept, Fra Bartolomeo, Madonna and saints. N Wall. Francesco Traini, *Apotheosis of St Thomas Aquinas; second altar, Cesare Dandini, St Vincent Ferrer; tomb of Archbishop Simone Saltarelli (died 1342) by Nino Pisano; first altar, Raffaello Vanni, St Catherine of Siena receiving the stigmata.

To the NE (see the Plan) are vestiges of *Roman baths*, uncovered in 1942. From Via Cardinale Maffi there is a dramatic view of the Leaning Tower. In the other direction, Via San Zeno leads NE to (c 400m) the little Romanesque chapel of **San Zeno** (Pl. 4; usually closed) of ancient foundation, showing various architectural styles from the 10C and incorporating Roman fragments in its façade. It has been deconsecrated and is now used for exhibitions, concerts, and conferences. Outside Porta San Zeno Via Vittorio Veneto skirts a fine stretch of the city walls.

Via San Francesco (see above) continues E to the Gothic church of **San Francesco** (Pl. 8), with a good campanile. The handsome plain façade was finished in 1603. INTERIOR. SOUTH SIDE: first altar, Empoli, Baptism of Christ; second altar, Giovanni Battista Paggi, Resurrection; third altar, Passignano, St Peter receiving the keys from Christ; fourth altar, Santi di Tito, St Francis receiving the stigmata. In the Gothic chapel of St Filomena

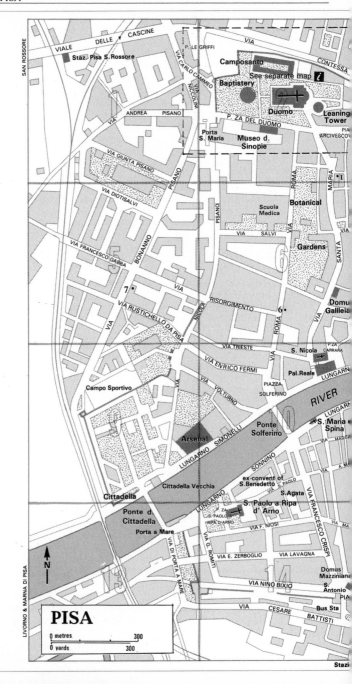

SAN ROSSORE

VIALE DELLE CASCINE

Staz. Pisa S.Rossore

VIA CARLO CAMMEO

VIA NICCOLINI

P. LE GRIFFI

VIA

CONTESSA

Camposanto

See separate map *i*

Baptistery

Duomo

Leaning Tower

ANDREA PISANO

VIA

P. ZA DEL DUOMO

PIA
ARCIVESCOV

Porta
S. Maria

Museo d.
Sinopie

VIA GIUNTA PISANO

VIA DIOTISALVI

PISANO

ROMA

MARIA

•I

Scuola
Medica

Botanical

VIA FRANCESCO GABBA

BONANNO

VIA

PISANO

VIA SALVI

Gardens

SANTA

VIA

7•

VIA RUSTICHELLO DA PISA

VIA NICOLA

RISORGIMENTO

6•

ROMA

Domu
Galilei

VIA TRIESTE

VIA

S. Nicola

P. ZA
CARRARA

VIA ENRICO FERMI

Pal. Reale

LUNGARN

Campo Sportivo

VIA

VIA VOLTURNO

PIAZZA
SOLFERINO

RIVER

LUNGARN

Arsenal

LUNGARNO SIMONELLI

Ponte
Solferino

S. Maria
Spina

VIA MADO

Cittadella Vecchia

LUNGARNO

SONNINO

ex-convent of
S. Benedetto

S. PAOLO

S. Agata

S. Paolo a Ripa
d'Arno

VIA A. M

Cittadella

Ponte d.
Cittadella

P. ZA
S. PAOLO
RIPA D'ARNO

VIA FRANCESCO CRISPI

Porta a Mare

VIA DI PORTA A MARE

VIA G. ROMITI

VIA F. NIOSI

VIA E. ZERBOGLIO

VIA LAVAGNA

VIA MA

LIVORNO & MARNA DI PISA

N

VIA NINO BIXIO

Domus
Mazziniana

S.
Antonio

PIA

VIA

CESARE

BATTISTI

Bus Sta

PISA

0 metres   300
0 yards   300

Stazi

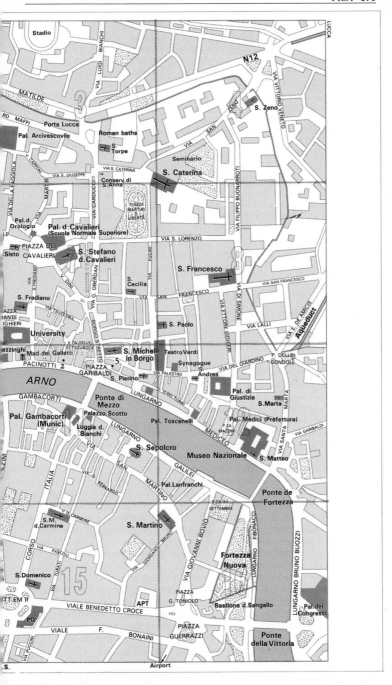

Stadio

MATILDE

RD MAFFI Porta Lucca

Pal. Arcivescovile

Roman baths

S. Torpe

Seminario

S. Caterina

VIA S. CATERINA

Conserv.di
S.Anna

PIAZZA
MARTIRI
D.
LIBERTA

N12

S. Zeno

VIA VITTORIO VENETO

LUCCA

VIA DELLA FAGGIOLA

Pal.d.
Orologio

Pal. d.Cavalieri
(Scuola Normale Superiore)

VIA S.GIUSEPPE

VIA S. LORENZO

PIAZZA DEI
CAVALIERI

Sisto

S. Stefano
d.Cavalieri

S. Frediano

S.
Cecilia

S. Francesco

VIA SAN FRANCESCO

VIA DI SIMONE

VIA LALLI

VIA E. DE AMICIS
Aqueduct

PIAZZA
DANTE
ALIGHIERI

University

Mad. dei Galletti

PACINOTTI 2

ARNO

GAMBACORTI

Pal. Gambacorti
(Munic)

S.
FRANCESCO

S. Paolo

VIA ETTORE SIGHIERI

S. Michele
in Borgo

Teatro Verdi

Synagogue

S.
Andrea

PIAZZA
GARIBALDI

S. Pierino

Ponte di
Mezzo

Palazzo Scotto

Loggia d.
Bianchi

LUNGARNO

Pal. Toscanelli

VIA DEL GIARDINO

P. DELLE
GONDOLE

Pal. di
Giustizia

S.Marta

Pal. Medici (Prefettura)

MEDICEO

P.ZA
MAZZINI

VIA SANTA

VIA GARIBALDI

MARTA

S. Sepolcro

Museo Nazionale

S. Matteo

GALILEI

Pal.Lanfranchi

Ponte de
Fortezza

VIA ITALIA

S.M.
d.Carmine

S. Martino

P.ZA XX
SETTEMBRE

Fortezza
Nuova

LUNGARNO FIBONACCI

VIA GIOVANNI BOVIO

LUNGARNO BRUNO BUOZZI

S.Domenico

VITT EM II

PO

VIALE BENEDETTO CROCE

APT

PIAZZA
G. TONIOLO

Bastione d.Sangallo

Pal. dei
Congressi

VIALE

F.

BONAINI

PIAZZA
GUERRAZZI

Ponte
della Vittoria

Airport

is a tomb of 1414. On the high altar is a large marble reredos by Tommaso Pisano. In the vault, frescoes by Taddeo Gaddi (1342). The E window has good stained glass dating in part from the 14C. In the second chapel to the right of the high altar, Crucifixion and saints by Spinello Aretino. In the third chapel left of the high altar are remains of 14C frescoes. The vaulting in the N transept bears the campanile. In the SACRISTY a chapel is frescoed by Taddeo di Bartolo, and on the walls are sinopie by Niccolò di Pietro Gerini of the frescoes by him in the chapter house. NORTH SIDE: fifth altar, Francesco Vanni, St Francis; third altar, Ventura Salimbeni, Assumption.

On the S side of Via San Francesco is Piazza San Paolo, where the abandoned church of *San Paolo all'Orto* retains the lower part of a handsome 12C façade (propped up for restoration). Farther S is *San Pierino* (1072–1119; closed), which has a large cr pt (seen from the outside). Via Palestro, with the *Teatro Verdi* (1867; small museum), and *Synagogue* (1648; restored in 1865 b Marco Treves), leads E to *Sant'Andrea*, another good 12C church (closed; used b a cultural societ). Be ond the huge *Palazzo di Giustizia* (1938–58) Via Giusti and Via del Giardino lead to Piazza delle Gondole, on a canal, with a 16C fountain. Here is the end of the *Aqueduct* built b the Medici in 1601–13 to bring water to the cit from Asciano (c 6km awa). The low brick arches are ver well preserved. In Via Santa Marta is the church of *Santa Marta*, with an interesting 18C interior.

Several streets lead S from San Francesco to the Lungarno Mediceo, on which is the Museo Nazionale di San Matteo (described below).

C. The Museo Nazionale di San Matteo and the Lungarni north of the river

The ex-convent of San Matteo (used as a prison in the 19C) has been occupied since 1947 by the **Museo Nazionale di San Matteo** (Pl. 12; adm. 9–19; fest. 9–13; closed Monday). The museum has been partially closed for many years, and by no means all of the collection is yet on display. The rooms are un-numbered, and most of the works are poorly labelled. In the entrance hall, sarcophagus with the Good Shepherd (4C AD). Off the attractive brick CLOISTER, with sculptural fragments, are four rooms which display 16C pottery and the Tongiorgi *collection of majolica tondi from Pisan church façades and ceramics (10C–18C), including numerous Islamic pieces. Another room contains high reliefs from San Michele. FIRST FLOOR. **Room 1** (left). Early Tuscan painted Crucifixes (12–13C), including one signed by Giunta Pisano, and one (recently restored) signed by Berlinghiero; and early Pisan panel paintings including St Catherine with stories from her life (13C). **R. 2**: panels by Deodato Orlandi and the Maestro di San Torpè (early 14C); Francesco Traini, *polyptych of St Dominic with stories from his life (signed), Madonna and Child with saints; Lippo Memmi, polyptych. At the end of the room: Simone Martini, *polyptych (signed 1319–21); works by Giovanni di Nicola, and a wood statue of the Virgin Annunciate by Agostino di Giovanni. **R. 3** (right): 14C and 15C Pisan wood sculptures; works by Francesco di Valdambrino; *Madonna del Latte, a half-length polychrome marble gilded statue from Santa Maria della Spina by Andrea and Nino Pisano; Nino Pisano, Christ in pietà, wooden high relief of the Madonna and Child, and marble statuette of the Madonna and Child (the last two from Santa Maria della Spina); Andrea and Nino Pisano, *Annunciatory angel, a wooden statue from San Matteo.

Virgin Annunciate, attributed to Francesco di Valdambrino, Museo Nazionale di San Matteo, Pisa

In the long gallery (**R. 4**) overlooking the cloister are sculptural fragments, which were arranged in the 19C in the Camposanto. They include French and Pisan statuettes (including two by Tino da Camaino and Nicola Pisano) and capitals carved by Giovanni di Balduccio. **R. 5**. Displayed on stands to the left: Barnaba da Modena, Madonna enthroned, Madonna and Child; Antonio Veneziano, Assunta, and processional standard with the Crucifixion and St Ranieri. Also in R. 5: works by Jacopo di Michele; polyptychs by Martino di Bartolomeo; Taddeo di Bartolo, Processional standard with the Crucifixion and St Donnino; Cross in rock crystal decorated with miniatures

(Venetian, early 14C; removed); Maestro di Barga, processional standard (Crucifixion and St Ursula). On the stands opposite: Taddeo di Bartolo, Madonna and saints and two angels; Spinello Aretino, Coronation of the Virgin, fragment of a polyptych, six frescoed heads; Agnolo Gaddi, two fragments of a polyptych; works by Luca di Tommè, Cecco di Pietro, and Francesco Neri da Volterra.

In the short gallery (**R. 6**), are four polychrome wood statues by Francesco di Valdambrino. **R. 7**. Works by Turino di Vanni. **R. 8** Masaccio, *St Paul; Michelozzo, stucco relief of the Madonna and Child; Fra Angelico, Madonna of Humility; Donatello, reliquary *bust of St Rossore (or St Luxorious), a splendid work in gilded bronze (1424–27) from S. Stefano dei Cavalieri; Master of the Castello Nativity, Madonna and Child with angel musicians; Neri di Bicci, Coronation of the Virgin; Zanobi Machiavelli, Madonna and saints. **R. 9** contains three paintings by Benozzo Gozzoli, a painted terracotta bust of the Redeemer by the circle of Verrocchio, and a bronze bust of a saint attributed to Michelozzo.

In the last long gallery (**10**): *Madonna of Humility by Gentile da Fabriano, two altarpieces of the Madonna and saints by Domenico Ghirlandaio, an enamelled terracotta tondo by Benedetto Buglioni, and a Madonna in Adoration by Andrea della Robbia. The last room (**11**) has 15C and 16C works in poor condition. A tempera *painting on canvas of Christ blessing attributed to Fra Angelico has been removed. Later works are now kept in Palazzo Reale (see below).

In the little piazza outside the museum is the church of **San Matteo**, founded in 1027. The pretty blind arcading and the E end of the Romanesque church can be seen along the Lungarno. The church (and façade) was reconstructed after a fire in 1607. The handsome Baroque INTERIOR with paintings in marble frames, marble stoups and confessionals, was damaged in the War but beautifully restored in 1990. It contains fine 17C and 18C paintings. The 18C vault fresco of the Glory of St Matthew is by the local painters Giuseppe and Francesco Melani. SOUTH SIDE: stories from the life of St Matthew by Jacopo Zoboli and Marco Benefial on either side of the S altar, which has a painting of Christ in Judgement with the Madonna and saints by Clemente Bocciardi. The high altarpiece of the calling of St Matthew by Francesco Romanelli is flanked by two oval paintings by Giuseppe Melani. NORTH SIDE: stories from the life of St Matthew by Sebastiano Conca and Francesco Trevisani on either side of the N altar which has a 13C Pisan painted Crucifix (the head is ruined) and the Madonna and St John the Evangelist and angels painted by Stefano Marucelli. Beneath the nuns' choir, Madonna and Child with angels and saints, by the 16C Florentine school.

Palazzo Medici (now the Prefecture), on the left of the piazzetta, was built in the 13–14C and owned by the Medici from 1446. Lorenzo il Magnifico often stayed here with his friend Politian. It was restored to its medieval aspect in 1879 by Ranieri Simonelli. In Piazza Mazzini is a statue of Mazzini by Giuseppe Andreoni (1883). The attractive **Lungarno Mediceo** continues along the river. Next to *Palazzo Roncioni* (No. 16) with a handsome façade by Giovanni Stefano Marucelli (1630), where Madame de Stael stayed in 1815–16, is *Palazzo Toscanelli* (formerly Lanfranchi), with a fine 16C façade. It was occupied by Byron in 1821–22, and is now the seat of the State Archives. Via delle Belle Torri runs parallel to the Lungarno here; fragments of some of the 12–13C tower houses survive incorporated into unattractive new buildings. In Piazzetta Cairoli is a column surmounted by a pretty statue of Abundance by Pierino da Vinci (1550).

The small but busy **Piazza Garibaldi** (Pl. 11), at the end of Ponte di Mezzo, is at the centre of the city. The bronze statue of Garibaldi is by Ettore Ferrari (1892). The 18C Palazzo del Casino dei Nobili has three high arches. The arcaded Borgo Stretto (described in Rte 9B) leads N from the piazza. **Ponte di Mezzo** (Pl. 11), rebuilt in 1950, is on the site of the Roman bridge over the Arno. It has been the scene of the annual Gioco del Ponte (in June) since the 15C. **Lungarno Pacinotti** continues along the river past Hotel Victoria opened in 1842 (where Charles Dickens stayed in 1845). *Palazzo Agostini* (or *dell'Ussero*; No. 26) has early-15C terracotta decoration on its façade. Here is the *Caffè dell'Ussero* opened in 1794, and famous as the meeting place of writers during the Risorgimento (it preserves mementoes of its famous patrons, including Giuseppe Giusti, and Renato Fucini). Via Curtatone e Monatanara leads away from the river to the **University**, on this site since 1473. The present façade dates from 1907–11. The splendid courtyard survives from 1550. A Studio existed in Pisa as early as the 12C, and the university was founded in 1343. It has a high reputation. Beyond the university, in Via Cavalca (right) can be seen the high *Torre del Campano* (13C). On the opposite side of Via San Frediano is the church of **San Frediano** (Pl. 7; 11C), with a good façade. It preserves columns and capitals in its altered INTERIOR which has delightful 17C confessionals. In the S aisle, first chapel, 13C painted *Crucifix, and on the right wall, Aurelio Lomi, Adoration of the Magi. In the chapel to the right of the high altar is an amusing Baroque altar. In the chapel to the left of the high altar are three paintings by Alessandro Tiarini. On the N wall, Ranieri Borghetti, Saints Paul and Bartholomew; third and first chapels, paintings by Ventura Salimbeni.

On Lungarno Pacinotti the tiny church of the *Madonna dei Galletti* has an attractive 17–18C interior with a good ceiling, and a fresco of the Madonna and Child by Taddeo di Bartolo over the high altar flanked by two wooden 18C angels. At No. 43 is *Palazzo Lanfreducci* (or *Upezzinghi*), also known as the *Palazzo alla Giornata*, with a fine white marble façade by Cosimo Pugliani (1594). *Palazzo Mazzarosa* (No. 45) dates from the 19C. In Piazza Francesco Carrara is a good statue of the Grand-duke Ferdinando I by Pietro Francavilla (1594). The huge **Palazzo Reale** (Pl. 10; No. 46), built on to an old tower house, has a plain façade begun in 1584 by Bernardo Buontalenti for Francesco I de' Medici. It is now the seat of the Soprintendenza ai Monumenti and is used for exhibitions. The collection of the surgeon Antonio Ceci (1852–1920) is displayed in four rooms (adm. weekdays 9–13). It contains paintings by Michele di Matteo, Francesco Francia, Andrea Boscoli, Bernardo Strozzi, Valerio Castello, Magnasco, Pieter Brueghel, Frans Francken, and Jan Brueghel (an exquisite little Holy Family). The collection also includes 18–19C ivory miniatures, drawings by Elisa Toscanelli, furniture, small bronzes and medals, and porcelain (French and far Eastern). More material from the Museo Nazionale di San Matteo is to be exhibited here including paintings by Francesco Francia, Rosso Fiorentino (Rebecca and Eliezer at the well) and Guido Reni (*Sacred and Profane Love; a drawing and a painting), Giuseppe Maria Crespi and Bernardo Strozzi. A small painting of the Crucifixion is attributed to Herri met de Bles.

Behind the palace, in Via Santa Maria, is the church of **San Nicola** (Pl. 10), founded c 1000, but much altered over subsequent centuries. In the 13C *campanile is a remarkable spiral staircase on which Bramante (according to Vasari) modelled his Belvedere staircase in the Vatican.

INTERIOR. SOUTH SIDE. First altar, Francesco Traini, *Madonna and Child; second chapel (on the wall) St Charles Borromeo by Giovanni Bilivert; fourth chapel, St Nicholas of Tolentino protecting Pisa (clearly depicted) from the plague, c 1400. The 17C chapel to the right of the high altar was decorated by Matteo Nigetti, who also designed the high altar (flanked by two statues by Felice Palma). In the chapel to the left of the high altar, Crucifix attributed to Giovanni Pisano. From this chapel is the entrance to the sacristy which contains a polychrome wood Madonna attributed to the school of Jacopo della Quercia. NORTH SIDE: fourth chapel, *Madonna and Child, statue attributed to Nino Pisano; 2nd chapel, altarpiece of the Annunciation by Giovanni Bilivert (in very poor condition).

At No. 26 Via Santa Maria is the *Domus Galileiano*, opened in 1942 to commemorate the famous scientist Galileo, born in Pisa. It has a fine librar (admission granted to scholars). Next door is the birthplace of the scientist Antonio Pacinotti (1841–1912). Farther on, the modern Palazzo Da Scorno incorporates a large Romanesque capital into its unattractive façade.

Lungarno Pacinotti ends at *Ponte Solferino*, rebuilt in 1974 after its collapse in the flood of 1966. **Lungarno Simonelli** continues to the *Arsenal*, a boatyard built by the Medici grand-dukes in 1548–88. On the façade (in very poor repair) are marble masques and five inscriptions. The buildings are now used as stables for horses by the Ministry of Agriculture. Beyond rises the tall medieval **Cittadella** or *Fortezza Vecchia* (Pl. 9), with the Torre Guelfa, enlarged in the 15C. *Ponte della Cittadella* (1957; first built in the 13C) leads to the S bank of the Arno (see below).

D. The south bank of the Arno

At the S end of Ponte della Cittadella is the 13C *Porta a Mare* (Pl. 13), and abandoned ruins of a bastion in the walls. On the river can be seen the old gate of the Navicelli canal (now covered over) which was begun by Cosimo I in 1541 to connect Pisa with Livorno. Inside the Porta a Mare is a large Art Nouveau villa with a tower (No. 12), with good wrought-iron work and palm trees in its garden. In this remote part of the city a spacious piazza with trees (and a splendid view of the tall Cittadella across the river) opens out in front of the church of *San Paolo a Ripa d'Arno* (Pl. 14), founded in 805. The splendid façade (restored in 1944) probably dates from the 13C and the N flank has fine blind arcading. The solemn bare interior (closed) has a handsome Roman sarcophagus, and a fine Romanesque capital (second on left). Behind the E end, surrounded by a lawn with a few trees, is the unusual Romanesque chapel of *Sant'Agata*, a tiny octagonal brick building (after 1063). On the other side of Via San Paolo is the wall of the *ex-Convent of San Benedetto* (1393), the courtyard of which has been restored by a bank in an incongruous style. The façade on the Lungarno, beyond the little church (closed) has terracotta decoration carried out in 1850 by Domenico Santini.

Lungarno Sonnino leads along the river to Ponte Solferino, just beyond which is the charming little church of *Santa Maria della Spina* (Pl. 10), a gem of Pisan Gothic architecture (1230, finished in 1323), named after a thorn of the Saviour's crown, the gift of a Pisan merchant. It was restored after War damage. The interior is usually open Mon, Wed & Fri 10–12, Tues, Thurs & Sat 17–19.

From the bridge Via Crispi leads S towards Piazza Vittorio Emanuele II and the Station. It ends in front of the church of *Sant'Antonio* (1341; reconstructed after the War). Nearb , at No. 71 Via Mazzini is the **Domus Mazziniana** (open 8–13 except Sunda), built in 1952 on the site of a house destro ed in the War where Giuseppe Mazzini died in 1872, while visiting his friends the Rosselli under the false name of John Brown. It contains mementoes of Mazzini and a librar specialising in the Risorgimento. In Piazza Sant'Antonio is a mock-Gothic tram station (now used as a bus station) near a stretch of the cit walls. Across Piazza Vittorio Emanuele II, with a bronze statue of the king b Cesare Zocchi (1892) is the church of *San Domenico* (closed) in Corso Italia. Corso Italia returns N to Ponte di Mezzo past the church of **Santa Maria del Carmine** (Pl. 15) founded in 1325 and enlarged in 1612 (restored). Inside, on the right of the entrance is a painting of St Teresa b Cosimo Gamberelli. On the S side, Andrea Boscoli, Annunciation, and be ond a prett pulpit of 1705, Madonna and saints b Baccio Lomi. The altarpieces on the N side are b Alessandro Allori (Ascension), and the school of Aurelio Lomi (saints).

Lungarno Gambacorti continues to the handsome *Palazzo Gambacorti* (No. 1), built by Pietro Gambacorti in 1370–80, and now the town hall. In Piazza XX Settembre, at the S end of Ponte di Mezzo, is the *Loggia dei Banchi* built by Cosimo Pugliani (1603–05), on a design by Bernardo Buontalenti, as a market place. From here Corso Italia (Pl 11, 15; closed to traffic; described above), the main street on the S bank of the Arno, leads due S to Piazza Vittorio Emanuele II and the Station. Lungarno Galileo continues along the river to **San Sepolcro** (Pl. 11), an octagonal church with a very unusual pyramidal roof built in the 12C by Diotisalvi, probably for the Templars, and restored in 1975. It is now below the level of the road. The striking interior lit by small windows, has tall pilasters forming a high Gothic arcade around the brick pyramidal roof. The font has stone reliefs by Mario Bertini (1956). Lungarno Galileo continues to *Palazzo Lanfranchi* (now owned by the Comune) dating from the Middle Ages but rebuilt in the 16C (and recently restored). Via Lanfranchi leads S to Via San Martino, a handsome street, and one of the best preserved in the city. Here is the church of **San Martino** (Pl. 16), begun in 1332 and consecrated in 1477 (restored in 1969–75). On the façade is a copy of a relief of St Martin (the original is now inside the church). The INTERIOR has an open timber roof. At the W end are detached frescoes of the life of Mary by Giovanni di Nicola. SOUTH SIDE. The 13C painted Crucifix with stories of the Passion is by Enrico di Tedice. First altar, Aurelio Lomi, St Andrew. Above the entrance into the side chapel, 14C relief of St Martin and the beggar by Andrea da Pontedera. The chapel, with a pretty barrel vault, has two detached frescoes and sinopie attributed to Antonio Veneziano. Second altar, Palma Giovane, St Benedict; third altar, Passignano, Madonna and Child (removed). NORTH SIDE. Second altar, Jacopo Ligozzi, Mary Magdalene in front of the Crucifix; first altar, Giovanni Sordo (Mone), Annunciation.

At No. 19 Via San Martino is a Roman relief of a female figure, a fragment of a 3C sarcophagus (restored in 1988). Known as *Kinzica*, it is named after a legendary Pisan heroine who saved Pisa from the Saracens in 1004.

At the end of Ponte della Fortezza (1959; first built in 1286) is the ruined *Palazzo Scotto* to the right of which is the 17C Palazzo Chiesa. Here Shelley lived in 1820–22 (plaque), the period of *Epipsychidion*, inspired by the Contessina Emilia Viviani, and of *Adonais*. Lungarno Fibonacci follows the wall of the ruined *Fortezza Nuova* built in 1512 by Giuliano da Sangallo. It now encloses a public garden known as the *Giardino Scotto*.

Environs of Pisa

FROM PISA TO MARINA DI PISA, 12km. A road (signposted for Marina di Pisa; buses from Piazza Sant'Antonio) leaves Pisa on the S bank of the Arno and crosses the Aurelia. Lined by a long straight avenue of plane trees, it skirts the Arno, with boat building yards and fishing huts, etc. The road passes close to (6km: left) the church of ***San Piero a Grado** (in need of restoration), built on the site where St Peter is said to have landed on his journey from Antioch to Rome. Excavations have confirmed the existence of a building here in the 1C AD. In Roman times this was the site of the last ferry across the Arno. The present Romanesque basilica dates from the 10–12C. The pretty EXTERIOR has blind arcading and incorporates Roman and medieval architectural fragments and friezes. The 11C ceramic basins (some of them from Tunisia, Marocco, and Spain) have been replaced by copies (the originals are displayed in the Museo Nazionale di San Matteo in Pisa). The 13C campanile was destroyed in 1944. The entrance is through a central lateral door. The INTERIOR is unusual in having apses at both the E and the W ends. The re-used columns have a great variety of Roman capitals. At the W end a ciborium covers an area of excavations of earlier churches on this site including two apses, one dating from the 3–4C and one from the 8–9C. Here a granite half-column (which formerly supported the ancient altar) marks the spot where St Peter is supposed to have preached. The 16C loggia was built in the apse at the W end to support a cantoria. Against the walls of the church are numerous ancient architectural fragments found in the excavations, and four inscriptions in pietra serena (formerly part of the 17C high altar) which recount the story of St Peter. Also here is an interesting carved wood 16C confessional. The *fresco cycle in the nave is attributed to Deodato Orlandi (1300–12). Above portraits of popes from St Peter to John XVII (1003) are scenes from the life of St Peter and St Paul.

12km **Marina di Pisa** (hotels and a camping site; first-class restaurant *Da Gino*, 2 Via delle Curzolari), is a pleasant old-fashioned bathing resort (with several Art Nouveau houses) at the mouth of the Arno, first developed in 1869. It is backed by dense pinewoods, whose seeds are used in making confectionery.

Between the Arno and the Serchio lies the **Tenuta di San Rossore**, a summer estate of the President of the Republic, with bird and animal sanctuaries (wild boar, deer, etc) donated to the State in 1988. This area, and the *Tenuta di Tombolo* to the S, and (beyond the Serchio) Migliarino and Massaciuccoli (see Rte 8) have been protected since 1979 as the PARCO NATURALE MIGLIARINO–SAN ROSSORE–MASSACIUCCOLI, although the trees are threatened with disease, the rivers polluted, and the coastline is being eroded. Part of the Tenuta di San Rossore (entrance on Viale delle Cascine) is open on fest. 8.30–17.30 or 19.30; bus No. 11 from Piazza Vittorio Emanuele (three times a day on fest.). From Migliarino a private road leads beneath the railway line to the mouth of the Serchio at *Marina di Vecchiano*, one of the most beautiful parts of the coastline with interesting bird life. Other areas are nature reserves (information from the *Consorzio del Parco*, Via Aurelia Nord 4, Tel. 050/525500). On the beach of *Il Gombo*, N of the mouth of the Arno, Shelley's body was washed ashore in 1822 (see Rte 8). Allan Ramsay, the painter, was more fortunate and escaped with his life from a shipwreck here in 1736 on his first jouney to Rome. To the S of Marina di Pisa the modern resort of *Tirrenia* (with numerous hotels of all categories, and camping sites) extends towards Livorno (see Rte 10).

FROM PISA TO SAN GIULIANO TERME, 7km. A road (N12) leaves Pisa outside the N stretch of walls and runs along a canal constructed by Cosimo I lined with ancient plane trees. 7km **San Giuliano Terme** (3-star hotel at Rigoli *Villa di Corliano*), is a small spa at the foot of Monte Pisano, whose spring waters have been known since ancient times. New thermal buildings were constructed here in 1744 by Francesco Pecci for the Grand-duke Francesco I. A bust and plaque mark the Casa Prinni where Shelley stayed in the summer of 1820. The road continues up Monte San Giuliano past olive groves (with a view back of Pisa), through a tunnel, and then descends towards Lucca (see Rte 6). The old road to Lucca, slightly longer, passes between the 14C castle of *Nozzano* (being restored), a Luccan outpost and the Pisan castle of *Ripafratta*.

Calci, with the important Certosa di Pisa, 13km E of Pisa is described in Rte 11.

10

Livorno

LIVORNO is a busy and lively town with a maritime air, which, since the 1970s has become the biggest container port in Italy (169,000 inhab.). It was laid out on a polygonal plan in 1576 by Bernardo Buontalenti for the Medici who constructed the fortifications and surrounded it by a deep moat (the *Fosso Reale*). In the 19C the city expanded on open symmetrical lines. Although it suffered systematic destruction from bombing in 1943, part of the Medici defence works survive, as well as numerous monumental 19C buildings, and the town was well reconstructed. The spacious seaboard is particularly attractive. It has a well-known street market where American goods are sold (Camp Darby, a US army base is nearby). The town was called by the English *Leghorn*.

Information Offices. APT, 6 Piazza Cavour (Tel. 0586/898111; information offices open in summer at the Molo Mediceo, and at the passenger terminal (Calata Carrara), near the Stazione Marittima.

Railway Station, Piazza Dante, c 1km from Piazza Grande (Bus No. 1). Frequent train service to Pisa in 10–20mins, and local trains to Florence via Pisa and Empoli in 1hr 20mins. Express services to Rome and Genoa on the main line along the coast.

Town Buses. No. 1 from the railway station to Piazza Grande; No. 2 from Piazza Cavour to the Museo Civico in Via della Libertà (and on to Antignano or Montenero).

Country Buses. *Lazzi* services from Piazza Manin to Empoli, Florence, Pisa, Viareggio, Lucca, etc.; ATL services from Piazza Grande to Castiglioncello, Cecina, Piombino, etc.

Car parking. Much of the centre of the city has restricted access for motorists (except residents) from 7.30–19.30. Car parking off Viale Carducci, Viale Italia, or at the Railway Station. Car park (with hourly fee and reduction for long-term parking), 5 Scali Bettarini.

Maritime Services. Boats from Porto Mediceo run by Toremar to *Capraia*, daily in 3 hrs (once a week via Gorgona in 3½hrs). Car Ferries from Calata Carrara run by Corsica Ferries and *Navarma* to *Corsica*; Sardinia Ferries (from Calata Carrara) and *Compagnia Sarda Navigazione Marittima* (from Calata Tripoli) to *Olbia*; Sicil Ferry from Calata Tripoli to *Palermo*; 'Alimar' from Calata Carrara to *Barcellona*.

Hotels. 4-star: _Palazzo_, 196 Viale Italia (Pl. 1). 3-star: _Gran Duca_, 16 Piazza Micheli (Pl. 2); _Gennarino_, 301 Viale Italia (Pl. 3); _Atleti_, 50 Via dei Pensieri (near the Hippodrome, off Viale Italia, towards Antignano). At _Antignano_ on the sea (6km S): _La Capinera_, 32 Via del Castello (2-star).

CAMPING SITE (2-star) _Miramare_, 220 Via del Littorale (open in summer). Youth Hostel, Villa Morazzana.

Restaurants. Livorno is famed for its fish restaurants (fish is always more expensive than meat). First-class restaurants: _La Barcarola_, 63 Viale Carducci; _Il Sottomarino_, 48 Via Terrazzini. At Antignano: _La Capinera_, 32 Via del Castello. Simple trattorie: _Carlo_, 43 Via Caprera; _Da Galileo_, Via della Campana (off Via Garibaldi); _Cantina Senese_, 95 Borgo Cappuccini; _Enoteca Doc_, 42 Via Goldoni. A characteristic cheap dish served in pizzerie to be eaten standing up (or taken away) is the _torta_, made from chick-peas.

Sea-bathing S of the town beyond Antignano at Il Romito (rocks) or at Quercianella (private beaches; fee).

History. Though a fortress here was the subject of dispute between Pisan, Genoese, and Florentine overlords from the early Middle Ages, Livorno dates its rise from 1571, when the new port was begun by decree of Cosimo de' Medici. Ferdinando I (1587–1609) continued the work and employed Sir Robert Dudley, son of the Earl of Leicester, Elizabeth I's favourite, to construct the great mole (1607–21). Sir Robert, a marine engineer, built warships and administered the port for the grand-duke. Ferdinand, by his proclamation of religious liberty, made the town a refuge for persecuted Jews, Greeks who had fled from the Turks, converted Moors expelled from Spain and Portugal under Philip III, and Roman Catholics driven from England under the penal laws. They were joined by many Italians fleeing from the oppression of their own states, and by exiles from Marseilles and Provence. The policy of Ferdinand was pursued by his successors, and Livorno became a great port, now the third largest in Italy. As a neutral port it was able to supply numerous ships for the naval battles against Napoleon, and Lord Nelson came here in 1793. In 1749 Sir Joshua Reynolds landed here on his only visit to Italy, and Tobias Smollett, Byron, and Shelley all lived at Montenero on the outskirts of the town (see below). In the mid-19C Livorno became a well-known bathing resort. Robert Stephenson built the railway line from Livorno to Pisa which was opened in 1844; it terminated at the neo-classical Stazione Ferroviaria Leopoldo (San Marco; see the Plan), now closed. Giovanni Fattori (1825–1908), the Macchiaioli painter and Pietro Mascagni (1863–1945), composer of 'Cavalleria Rusticana' were both born here. Another native was Amedeo Modigliani (1884–1920), the artist. In 1984 two sculptures were dredged up from the Fosso Reale and acclaimed by numerous art critics to be lost masterpieces by Modigliani. They were soon proved to be fakes made by a group of young students, and the incident was recognised as one of the most successful hoaxes of recent years.

Nearly 5km off Livorno rises the reef of _Meloria_, where the maritime power of Pisa was crushed by the Genoese in 1284; hereabouts also in 1653 an English trading fleet was routed by the Dutch.

The _railway station_ is a fine Art Nouveau building (1910) by Pietro Via. Beside it, in Piazza Dante, are the remains of a spa hotel built in 1905 by Angelo Badaloni. The long, wide _Viale Carducci_, with an avenue of trees and pretty lamp posts, leads due W towards the centre of the city. Beyond an old factory building of 1906 are the _public gardens_ laid out in 1854, and the monumental **Cisternone**, a water cistern built in 1829–32 by Pasquale Poccianti, with a classical portico and exedra. Via de Larderel continues past the large neo-classical _Palazzo Larderel_ (1832–50) into the huge **Piazza della Repubblica**, known as the _Voltone_ since it rests on a wide vault over the Fosso Reale (which still flows beneath it; see below). It was laid out in 1834 by Luigi Bettarini: on the great expanse of pavement rise fine lampposts and two statues, one of Ferdinando III by Francesco Pozzi (1837), and one of Leopoldo II by Emilio Santarelli (1885). To the N is a good view of the moated Fortezza Nuova (described below). Via Grande continues past the handsome _Cisternino_, another fine neo-classical building designed by

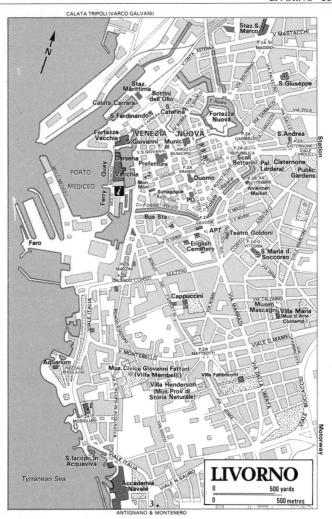

CALATA TRIPOLI (VARCO GALVANI)

ANTIGNANO & MONTENERO

Poccianti in 1827. In Via Madonna (right) three Baroque façades survive among the unattractive modern buildings: the former churches of the Annunziata (1605), and of the Concezione (1599), both by Alessandro Pieroni, and the 18C façade of San Giorgio degli Armeni.

Piazza Grande, in the centre of the city, was a huge square laid out in the 16–17C and formerly surrounded by porticoes by Alessandro Pieroni (only a fragment survives at the SW corner). It was greatly reduced in size when a much criticised modern bulding was built in the centre, so that it is now divided from Largo Municipio to the N. The **Duomo** was begun in 1587, modified in 1606 by Alessandro Pieroni, and completed in 1609 by Antonio Cantagallina. It had to be virtually rebuilt in 1954–59, after severe damage in 1944. The Doric portico which precedes the façade (and which was an integral part of the design of Piazza Grande) is attributed to Inigo Jones. During the restoration of the INTERIOR three paintings were installed in the ceiling: Passignano, Assumption; Empoli, Madonna and Child with St Francis of Assisi; and Jacopo Ligozzi, Triumph of St Giulia. Among the funerary monuments on the S wall, the most notable is that of Alessandro Del Borro by Giovanni Battista Foggini. On either side of the high altar are two small heads of angels by François Duquesnoy, killed in Livorno by his brother in 1643. On the right wall, Translation of the body of St Giulia by the local painter Tommaso Gazzarrini (1834) opposite a Miracle of St Francis by Giuseppe Bezzuoli. The transepts were added in the 18C (reconstructed after the War).

In Large Municipio, N of Piazza Grande, is *Palazzo Municipio* by Giovanni Del Fantasia (1720), with a bell tower and a double staircase added by Bernardino Ciurini. On the left is the 17C *Palazzo di Camera di Commercio*, designed with three large arches by Annibale Cecchi. On the corner of Via della Posta is *Palazzo Granducale* (now Palazzo della Provincia) designed in the 17C by Antonio Cantagallina (and reconstructed after the War). Via San Giovanni (once the main street of the old town, but now without character) leads out of the W side of the piazza past the 17C church of *San Giovanni* (restructured) which contains a high altar by Ferdinando Tacca. To the right a road leads across a bridge to *Via Borra*, one of the most important streets in the city in the 18C (among the palaces here, some of which are being restored, is Palazzo delle Colonne at No. 29, designed by Giovanni Battista Foggini). Beyond the next pretty bridge is the 18C octagonal church of *Santa Caterina* (being restored; it contains a Coronation of the Virgin behind the high altar by Vasari). This area, laid out in 1629–44, is known as **Nuova Venezia**, because of its numerous canals. From the bridge there is a good view right of the wall of the **Fortezza Nuova** built in 1590 on a design by Giovanni de' Medici, Vincenzo Bonanni, and Bernardo Buontalenti. It is surrounded by a moat, and the interior has been laid out as a pleasant public park (open daily 8–dusk; the entrance is near a palm tree). It is sometimes used for exhibitions.

From Santa Caterina (see above) Via San Marco traverses the interesting Via dei Floridi with houses built above the old bastions, to the façade of the former *Teatro di San Marco* where a worn plaque records the founding of the Italian Communist Party here in 1921. A modern school building has recently been built behind the façade. The Scali del Rifugio skirts the canal past the ex-convent of Santa Caterina where Sandro Pertini (1896–1990; elected President of the Republic in 1978) was held as a political prisoner during the Fascist regime (plaque set up in 1977). To the right a roadway descends above an archway giving access to the canal. The *Bottini dell'Olio* (1705–31) here were the last important building constructed in Livorno by the Medici, on a project by Giovanni Battista Foggini. The warehouse could store some 24,000 barrels of oil; the fine vaulted hall has been restored and is now used for exhibitions. Amidst evident signs of bombing from the last War is the church of **San Ferdinando**, recently restored, with a good 18C interior (also by Foggini) and excellent marble sculptures by Giovanni Baratta.

Beside the main harbour for the fishing fleet in the *Darsena Vecchia* (1591), in Piazza Micheli, is the famous ***Monumento dei Quattro Mori**, a monument to Ferdinando I with a statue of him by Giovanni Bandini (1595), and four Moorish slaves in bronze (1623–26), the masterpieces of Pietro Tacca. On the wall of the Medici fortifications here (restored as part of a hotel) is a plaque set up in 1896 by John Temple Leader to Sir Robert Dudley (see above). Nearby, facing a scenographic piazza with a colossal equestrian statue of Victor Emmanuel II by Augusto Rivalta (1882) is the huge *Palazzo del Governo* (now the Prefecture), a Fascist building of 1942 with monumental white marble bas-reliefs (1954). In the harbour is the wall of the crumbling **Fortezza Vecchia**, the most important of the Medici defence works in the city. It was built to the design of Antonio da Sangallo in 1521–34, and embodies part of a Roman castrum, the so-called Matilda Tower (11C), and remains of a Pisan fort of 1377. From Piazza Micheli a bridge leads to the ferry quay in the *Porto Mediceo*, and on the other side of the Fortezza Vecchia is another ferry quay near the Stazione Marittima. Some way farther N, at the entrance to the port, is the tall *Torre del Marzocco*, attributed to Lorenzo Ghiberti (1439).

From Piazza Micheli the ugly Via Grande, with monotonous square arcades, leads past two copies of the fountains made by Tacca for the monument to Ferdinando I (see above) but instead installed in Piazza Santissima Annunziata in Florence, back to Piazza Grande (described above). Behind the Duomo Via Cairoli (closed to traffic) leads S towards Piazza Cavour. At the beginning on the left is the church of *Santa Giulia* (1603) with attractive benches and confessionals in the interior. Over the high altar is a painting of the patron saint with stories from her life, attributed to the 'Maestro di Varlungo'. Beyond an 18C courtyard is the Cappella di San Ranieri (1696–1701), with interesting pavement tombs. Off Via Cairoli, behind the Post Office, in Via del Tempio is the *Synagogue*, built in 1962 on a design by Angelo Di Castro, after the destruction of the old synagogue in the War. Via Cairoli ends in **Piazza Cavour** (statue by Vincenzo Cerri, 1871) across two branches of the attractive **Fosso Reale**, built as a defensive moat around the town by the Medici c 1559. In the centre of the Scali Aurelio Saffi which skirts the left-hand canal, is the huge russet-coloured building of the *Central Market* set up in 1894 by Angelo Badaloni. It has eight caryatids by Lorenzo Gori in its impressive interior. On the opposite side of the canal is the huge Benci school building in a similar colour, also by Badaloni, and the neo-Gothic façade of the *Dutch Church* (1864). Off this side of the canal (see the Plan) is Piazza XX Settembre, laid out in 1819 by Poccianti around the neo-classical portico of the church of *San Benedetto* built in 1819 on a design by Angelo Pampaloni. Since 1944 the piazza has been the site of the famous *Mercatino* where American goods are sold (open every morning).

Via Verdi leads to the right out of Piazza Cavour, past the neo-Gothic *Waldensian Church*, built in 1845 by Rumball as the Presbyterian Church of Scotland, to the entrance (No. 59) to the **Old British Cemetery** (for the key to the gate apply at the offices of the Misericordia, 9–12, 15–18.30; fest. 9–12). Probably opened in the 16C, this was for many years the only Protestant cemetery in Italy. Many of the monumental tombs date from the 1660s. Tobias Smollett (see below) was buried here in 1773 (the tomb, with an obelisk and Latin inscription, is to the right of the centre). The cemetery was visited by Shelley, Longfellow, and Fenimore Cooper and was closed in 1840 when the new cemetery was opened in the N suburbs. The Anglican church outside, with a classical temple façade, was built by Angiolo Della Valle in 1840. It is now used by the Misericordia as a chapel.

Off Via Rossi, the other side of Piazza Cavour, Via Goldini leads to the *Teatro Goldoni* (1843–47) where in 1921, at a Congress of the Socialist Party, a schism resulted in the founding of the Italian Communist Party (see above). A short way further E, across Corso Amedeo, is the church of *Santa Maria del Soccorso* (1835) by Gaetano Gherardi, with a painting of St Lawrence by Enrico Pollastrini (1862) in the first S chapel. In Via Calzabigi (see the Plan) is the entrance (No. 54) to the **Museo Mascagnano** (adm. as for Museo Civico), opened in 1985 in a 19C Castelletto to commemorate Pietro Mascagni (1863–1945), the Livornese musician. Among numerous mementoes are Mascagni's musical scores, his piano, photographs, manuscripts, etc. In the park of Villa Maria (entered from No. 22 Via Redi) is a *Modern Art Gallery* (10–13 except Monday).

The 19C Villa Fabbricotti, over 1km S of Piazza Cavour, approached along the unattractive, straight Via Marradi and Via della Libertà (best reached by Bus No. 2 from Piazza Cavour) is surrounded by a public park open daily 8–dusk. The **Museo Civico** was formerly exhibited here. Works by Giovanni Fattori and the Macchiaioli have been moved to Villa Mimbelli (see below). The earlier works are to be exhibited elsewhere. They include: Maestro della Natività di Castello, Adoration of the Child; Borgognone, Battle scene; circle of Botticelli, Madonna and Child; Neri di Bicci, Crucifixion; Carlo Cignani, Deposition; Beato Angelico, *Head of the Redeemer crowned with thorns (a very unusual and striking work); and Greek and Russian icons with interesting examples of the Cretan School (16–17C).

There is an exit from the park on Via Roma, where, at No. 234 is the *Villa Henderson*. A new building in the park houses the *Museo Provinciale di Storia Naturale* (open 9–12.30, 16–19 except Sat afternoon & fest.).

Towards the sea, in Via San Iacopo in Acquaviva, the 19C *Villa Mimbelli* houses the **Museo Civico Giovanni Fattori** (open 10–13, 16–19 exc. Mon), opened in 1994. It contains 135 *paintings by the Macchiaioli painter Giovanni Fattori born in Livorno. These include battle scenes at Montebello and the Madonna delle Scoperta, country scenes in the Maremma and Roman Campagna, and portraits (including a peasant woman and Signora Martelli at Castiglioncello). Other Macchiaioli painters represented include Silvestro Lega (Peasant Girl), Vincenzo Cabianca, Telemaco Signorini, Serafino da Tivoli, Giovanni Boldini (including a portrait of Cabianca), Cristiano Banti, and Angiolo Tommasi. There are also good works by Enrico Pollastrini (1871–76) and Plinio Nomellini. A fine public park surrounds the villa.

The pleasant **Viale Italia** (see the Plan) skirts the shore with a wide promenade passing gardens and elegant seaside houses, and 19C hotels and bathing establishments. On the Piazzale Mascagni, a pretty terrace built out into the sea, is the *Aquarium* (10–12, 16–19 or 14–17 in winter; closed Monday) and, farther on, the huge *Naval Academy*, founded in 1879, next to the 17C church of *San Jacopo in Acquaviva*, sited where St James the Greater is supposed to have landed on his way to Spain; St Augustine also is said to have stayed here after his baptism. The Viale continues past Art Nouveau houses and the attractive suburbs of *Ardenza* (with a neo-classical crescent, built in 1840, overlooking the sea), and *Antignano*, built as bathing resorts.

Above Antignano is **Montenero** (193m). It is 9km from the centre of Livorno; reached from Ardenza by the Strada di Montenero, followed by bus No. 2 from Piazza Cavour. A funicular railway opened in 1909 (or a winding road) mounts the hill. Here Tobias Smollett (born in 1721) lived for the last two years of his life and finished *Humphrey Clinker*. Byron, who spent a holiday at the Casa Dupuy, may have sailed from here in his boat, the 'Bolivar', to visit Shelley at the Casa Magni at Lerici. While staying at the Villa Valsovona near here in 1818, Shelley wrote his tragedy *The Cenci*. On a voyage by boat from Livorno to La Spezia on the 8 July 1822 Shelley and his friend Lieutenant Williams drowned (their bodies were recovered near Viareggio, see Rte 8).

The pilgrimage church of MONTENERO (1676) contains a miraculous painting of the Madonna, supposed to have sailed by itself in 1345 from the island of Negropont (Euboea) to the shore of Ardenza. The painting has been attributed to Margaritone di Arezzo, or the Pisan school (Il Gera). The basilica owns a remarkable collection of 19C and 20C ex-votos.

11

Florence to Pisa via Empoli and San Miniato

Information Offices. For Empoli and Vinci, APT Florence (Tel. 055/290832); from San Miniato to Pisa, APT Pisa (Tel. 050/40096).

Road, N67. This is not a very attractive road as it has been ribbon-developed and is lined with small factories. The N bank of the Arno, although it has some interesting villages, is generally less attractive and more built-up than the countryside S of the Arno. The route described below includes a long detour to the S of the Arno and the distances are as follows: 13km *Lastra a Signa*—25km *Montelupo Fiorentino*—32km **Empoli** (**Vinci**, 11km)—44km **San Miniato**—55km *Montopoli in Val d'Arno*—66km *Palaia*—89km *Casciana Terme*—105km *Pontedera*—112km *Cascina*—117km *Vicopisano*— 129km *Certosa di Pisa* and *Calci*—143km **Pisa**.

A Superstrada, a fast four-lane highway was completed in 1991 from Florence to Pisa and Livorno on the S bank of the Arno, and it follows N67 closely. It begins in the S suburbs of Florence near Scandicci (well signposted). It is generally preferable to the old main road (N67) and has exits at all the main places of interest: 23km *Montelupo Fiorentino*—29km **Empoli**—39km **San Miniato**—45km *Montopoli*—54km *Pontedera*— 81km **Pisa**.

Railway, the main line from Florence to Pisa. Frequent service to Pisa in 55mins, via Empoli (in 20mins). Slow trains on this line also stop at Montelupo, San Miniato Basso, etc. One of the earliest lines in Italy, it was built on a project by Robert Stephenson for the Tuscan grand-dukes (1838–40; completed in 1844–48).

Buses (*Lazzi*) from Florence for Lastra a Signa, Montelupo, Empoli, etc. From Empoli (*Lazzi* and COPIT) frequent services for Vinci (in 20mins).

The old road out of Florence (N67) traverses the huge suburb of *Scandicci* where much new building has taken place since the War. To the S, about 2km beyond Vingone, is San Paolo a Mosciano, where in the Villa Mirenda (next to the little cemetery and church) D.H. Lawrence stayed in 1926–27 while completing *Lady Chatterley's Lover* (first published in Florence in 1928). The main road continues through unattractive suburbs and under the Autostrada del Sole, and just beyond a power station at (8km) Casellina a by-road (signposted) leads to the church of *San Martino alla Palma* (c 4km SW; open only for services; at other times ring at the green door under the portico) in a magnificent position in low rolling hills (well seen from the main road). It was founded in the 10C, and contains a charming Madonna by a follower of Bernardo Daddi known, from this painting, as the Master of San Martino alla Palma (1325–30). About 1km beyond (9km) *Piscetto*, and 5mins to the right of the road, is the church of *Santi Giuliano e Settimo*, an 8C building, altered in subsequent centuries. About 2km NW of (11km) *Fornaci* is the BADIA DI SAN SALVATORE A SETTIMO, a 10C abbey, rebuilt for Cistercians in 1236–37, walled and fortified in 1371, and restored since 1944. The church has a rebuilt campanile and a Romanesque façade with a round 15C window. It is open only for services; at other times ring the (inconspicuous) bell by the gate to the left of the façade. INTERIOR. Over the second altar on the S side, Lodovico Buti, martyrdom of St Lawrence (1574). Behind the high altar in pietre dure is the choir with a Della Robbian enamelled terracotta frieze of cherubim and the Agnus Dei, and two frescoed tondi of the Annunciation by the school of Ghirlandaio. On the left of the high altar is a little marble *tabernacle, beautifully carved and attributed to Giuliano da Sangallo. The chapel on the left of the high altar has good *frescoes (in poor condition) by Giovanni di San Giovanni (1629). The wall-tomb on the N side dates from 1096. In the sacristy are kept two paintings formerly displayed in the church, one of the Adoration of the Magi and one an unusual scene of Christ at the sepulchre, both attributed to Ghirlandaio or his school. The interesting remains (carefully restored) of the MONASTERY (now privately owned, but sometimes courteously shown; ring at the cloister) include much of the old fortifications, and the chapter-house and remarkable vaulted lay brothers' hall.

13km **Lastra a Signa** (first-class restaurant *Antica Trattoria Sanesi*), a large village near the confluence of the Vingone and the Arno, once famous for the production of straw hats. The old centre (right of the main road) is remarkable for its walls built in 1380, with three gates. Here is the *Loggia di Sant'Antonio* (it has been undergoing restoration for many years, now almost completed), formerly a hospital erected at the expense of the Arte della Seta in 1411. The portico of six arches (the seventh is walled up) has traditionally been attributed as an early work to Brunelleschi. Nearby is the *ex-Palazzo Pretorio*, a little building (in need of restoration), with the escutcheons of many podestà. Just out of the main square is the church of *Santa Maria* (for admission ask at the Misericordia) with a Madonna and Child by the school of Cimabue (removed for restoration).

Just beyond the town, off the main road (signposted), is the church of SAN MARTINO A GANGALANDI, at the end of an attractive row of houses. Founded in the 12C or earlier, it has a restored campanile and a 15C loggia at the side. The baptistery at the W end is decorated on the exterior and in the vault with frescoes by Bicci di Lorenzo and his school (1432; restored in 1982). The font was sculpted by a follower of Ghiberti. Here is hung a painting of St John the Baptist attributed to Bernardo Daddi (1346; in very poor conditon). Over the first S altar is an unusual painting of five female saints, attributed to Piero Salvestrini da Castello, a pupil of Poccetti; over the third S altar, Immaculate Conception by Matteo Rosselli (1615). The fine semicircular apse was decorated in pietra serena by Leon Battista Alberti, who was rector here from 1432–72. The high altar bears the date 1366. On the N wall is a large detached fresco of St Christopher, and fragments of 14C frescoes over the second altar. Above a little room with fine capitals, now used as the sacristy, off the left side of the church, a small MUSEUM has recently been arranged (admission on request, preferably by appointment). It contains 18C church silver and paintings including a Madonna of Humility by Lorenzo Monaco (from San Romolo a Settimo), a triptych with the Assumption and four Saints by Bicci di Lorenzo and a Madonna and Child attributed to Jacopo del Sellaio.

In the hills to the SW is the castle of *Malmantile* (1424), an outpost of Castracani against the Florentines, celebrated in a poem by Lorenzo Lippi.

25km **Montelupo Fiorentino** (3-star hotel *Baccio da Montelupo*), is an attractive village at the meeting of the Pesa with the Arno. Its 14C fortifications still determine the layout of the old centre. It was fortified by the Florentines in opposition to the now demolished stronghold of Capraia, beyond the river; thus the wolf (*lupo*) was to devour the goat (*capra*). In the 15C and 16C Montelupo was one of the most important centres of ceramic production in the Mediterranean. Baccio da Montelupo (1469–1535) and his son Raffaello (c 1505–66), both sculptors and architects, were born here.

The approach road passes the fine *Villa dell'Ambrogiana* (used as a prison), a Medici hunting lodge on a square plan with four angle towers. It was reconstructed after 1587, possibly on a design by Buontalenti. It had a garden on the Arno with fountains and grottoes. Across the Pesa river is the main street of Montelupo, off which roads lead up towards the castle hill past the *Palazzo Pretorio* (restored, with a neo-Gothic loggia), now the seat of the MUSEO ARCHEOLOGICO E DELLA CERAMICA (open 9–12, 14.30–19 excluding Mon; Sun 14.30–19), arranged in 1983–89. The modern display is accompanied by detailed explanations. On the GROUND FLOOR is the archaeological collection. Room I contains Paleolithic finds, and R. 2 Bronze Age weapons. Imported vases from Greece and Southern Italy, and Etruscan and Roman material are displayed in R. 3. Room 4, with remains of 15C frescoes, displays the medieval collection. UPPER FLOOR. RR. 5 and 6 contain a didactic display of ceramic manufacture. R. 7: The Paolo Azzati collection of ceramics. R. 8–10: majolica produced in Montelupo from the 14C to the 18C, arranged chronologically.

In Via Bartolomeo Sinibaldi, just below the museum, is the church of *San Giovanni Evangelista* with a *Madonna enthroned with Saints Sebastian, Lorenzo, John the Baptist, and Roch by Botticelli and his workshop. At the top of the castle hill is the church of *San Lorenzo* (the custodian lives nearby) with fresco fragments signed and dated 1284 by Corso di Buono. The tall, square campanile was probably once a tower of the castle.

Along the road for San Casciano in Val di Pesa, 2km S of Montelupo, is the *Pieve di Sant'Ippolito* of the 11C, with a marble ciborium by a 15C Florentine sculptor.

Across the Arno is *Capraia* (see above). Excavations in progress at *Montereggi alla Castellina* have revealed Etruscan and Roman remains. *Limite*, 3km W, is well known for its boat builders. To the E of Montereggi, on the hill of *Bibbiani* is a villa with gardens laid out in the mid-19C by Cosimo Ridolfi (often visited by Giacomo Puccini). They are open April–July, and mid September–October on Friday and Sunday at 9 and 11 (information from the Comune di Capraia e Limite).

32km **EMPOLI** is a pleasant small town (44,100 inhab.) spaciously laid out (after damage in the last War) around two long parallel shopping streets either side of the small piazza in front of the Collegiata. It has long been famous for its glass factories, and is now an important commercial centre of the clothing industry.

Information Office (Pro Loco), Piazza Farinata degli Uberti.

Railway Station (10 minutes' walk from the Collegiata) on the main Florence–Pisa line with frequent services (express trains from Florence in 20mins; local trains in 30mins). Empoli is also a junction for the Florence–Siena secondary line.

Buses (*Lazzi*) from Piazza della Stazione for Florence (in c 70mins), Lastra a Signa, Montelupo, etc.

Hotels. 3-star: *Tazza d'oro*, 16 Via Giuseppe del Papa; *Commercio*, 16 Piazzetta Ristori; *Il Sole*, 18 Piazza Don Minzoni.

Restaurants. First-class restaurants: *Bianconi*, 70 Via Tosco-Romagnola (2km outside the town on the Florence road); *Il Galeone*, 67 Via Curtatone e Montanara. Simple trattorie: *Il Petrarca*, 122 Viale Petrarca; *Sciabolino*, 14 Via Ormicello; *Da Cioffi*, 333A Via Valdorme.

Glassworks. *Consorzio Centrovetro*, Piazza Guido Guerra and *Consorzio Toscanavetro*, Piazza Gramsci.

History. In 1984 excavations revealed Roman remains in the centre of Empoli. The town grew up around the church of Sant'Andrea after 1119. Here in 1260 the Ghibelline party held their famous 'parliament' after their victory at Montaperti; the proposal to raze Florence to the ground was defeated by Farinata degli Uberti, who is honoured for his protest by Dante (*Inferno*, X). The glassworks of Empoli have long been known for their production of green glass, including the characteristic wine fiasco (protected by straw) which was first produced here in large quantities at the beginning of this century. Jacopo Chimenti, the painter, known as Empoli (1551–1640) was a native of the town.

From the station the wide straight Via Roma leads to *Piazza della Vittoria* and the oratory of the *Madonna del Pozzo*, with an interesting plan by Andrea Bonistalli (1621). A long nave surrounded on the exterior by a portico precedes a pretty octagonal domed sanctuary. At No. 16 in the piazza is the *House of Ferruccio Busoni* (1866–1924), the musician, which has a small museum. From the right flank of the oratory Via Giuseppe del Papa leads to the Canto del Pretorio where on the right is *Piazza Farinata degli Uberti*, the pleasant arcaded central square which has a large fountain with four amusing lions by Luigi Pampaloni (1827). A local museum of Paleonthology (open Thurs, Sat & Sun 17–20) with a well illustrated collection of fossils from the Pliocene period including numerous shells, found in central Tuscany.

The **Collegiata di Sant'Andrea**, documented as early as 780, was begun in its present form in 1093. The handsome black-and-white marble FAÇADE recalls that of San Miniato al Monte in Florence. It was probably begun in the mid-12C, and the upper part is a successful imitation carried out when the church was enlarged in the 18C by Ferdinando Ruggeri. The marble portal dates from 1546.

The INTERIOR by Ruggeri has a ceiling painting by Vincenzo Meucci and Giuseppe del Moro which was reconstructed after severe damage in the last War. On the W wall, fresco of Christ with instruments of the Passion attributed to Raffaello Botticini. SOUTH SIDE. First chapel, venerated 14C Crucifix, and a painting of 1808 symbolising the recovery from the plague. Second chapel, interesting detached 14C Florentine fresco of the Martyrdom of St Lucy (with white oxen). On the high altar by Zanobi del Rosso (1785), triptych by Lorenzo di Bicci. On the E wall, fresco of the Martyrdom of St Andrew by Ferdinando Folchi (1862). To the left of the presbytery is the entrance to two oratories, the second of which is used as a sacristy. Here are the remains of a Della Robbian tiled pavement around the altar. Outside the chapel at the end of the left transept is a very ruined fresco of St Joseph attributed to Empoli (right). The statuette of the Madonna on the altar (repainted) is attributed to the bottega of Buglioni. NORTH SIDE: (fourth chapel) 17C painting of the Madonna and saints, and (first chapel) reliquary cupboard of c 1724.

In the courtyard to the right of the façade is the entrance to the ***Museo della Collegiata di Sant'Andrea**, one of the first local museums in Tuscany, founded in 1859, which contains fine works of art from the Collegiata and other churches in the area, as well as private donations. The museum was reopened in 1990 and the sculptures, frescoes, and paintings (many of them recently restored) are beautifully displayed and well labelled (admission 9–12; Thursday, Friday, and Saturday also 16–19; closed Monday; the ticket includes admission to the church of Santo Stefano degli Agostiniani, see below).

GROUND FLOOR. **Room 1** was formerly part of the church of San Giovanni Evangelista, transformed into a baptistery in the 15C and connected by a passageway to the Collegiata. Here is a *font dated 1447, an exquisite and unusual work recently attributed to Bernardo Rossellino. The *fresco of Christ in Pietà (detached from the window wall in 1946, and restored in 1987) is a superb work by Masolino (1424–25). Also here are frescoes and sinopie of Saints by Lo Starnina (1409). **R. 2**: stoup of 1557; lectern of English workmanship donated to the Collegiata in 1520; bas-relief of the Madonna and Child attributed to Mino da Fiesole; small tondo of the Madonna and Child, an early work by Tino da Camaino; terracotta dossal of the Madonna enthroned with Saints attributed to Santi di Buglioni.

FIRST FLOOR. **R. 3** contains 14C and 15C paintings. Master of 1336 (Pistoian school), Madonna and Child with saints; works by Niccolò di Pietro Gerini; Lorenzo di Bicci, Crucifixion and Virgin of the Holy Girdle; early 15C painting for an altar step of the Miracle of the Almond Tree and the brotherhood of the Compagnia del Crocifisso, which took place in Empoli in 1399; Ambrogio di Baldese (attributed), Madonna del latte; Agnolo Gaddi (attributed), triptych; Cenni di Francesco, saints; Mariotto di Nardo, Madonna and Child. The polychrome wood statue of *St Stephen is signed and dated 1403 by Francesco da Valdambrino. **R. 4**: Rossello di Jacopo Franchi, triptych; Master of Signa, saints; Lorenzo Monaco, Madonna enthroned with saints; Filippo Lippi, Madonna enthroned between angels and saints (a very small work); Lorenzo Monaco, *Madonna of Humility with four saints (1404); Bicci di Lorenzo, Madonna and saints. The polychrome wood statue of the penitent *Magdalene is dated 1455 and is attributed to Don Romualdo da Candeli and Neri di Bicci. **R. 5** displays works by Francesco Botticini and his son Raffaello. The *tabernacle of St Sebastian (c 1475) contains exquisite paintings of two angels by Francesco Botticini and a beautiful statue of St Sebastian by Antonio Rossellino. Also by Francesco Botticini, Annunciation, and angel musicians. Works by Raffaello Botticini include Saints Sebastian and Jerome, and a predella. **R. 6**: Jacopo da Empoli, Incredulity of St Thomas; 17C Florentine painter, Assumption of the Virgin; tabernacle of the Holy Sacrament, an elaborate work by Francesco and Raffaello Botticini; Jacopo del Sellaio, Madonna and Child, Madonna and saints; Giovanni Antonio Sogliani, St Blaise (in a splendid frame); Pier Francesco Fiorentino, Madonna enthroned with saints. The upper walk of the CLOISTER (closed in winter) displays Della Robbian works in enamelled terracotta, including a tondo of the Holy Father by Andrea and dossals by Benedetto Buglioni and his bottega. A precious collection of ten illuminated missals (13–16C) will be displayed in the museum in the future.

Near the museum, in Via dei Neri, is the 14C church of **Santo Stefano degli Agostiniani** (open 10–12 except Sunday & Monday). The church, with no façade, is important for its remains of frescoes by Masolino. INTERIOR. The organ at the W end, with an elaborate gallery of 1756, dates from 1558. SOUTH SIDE. The first chapel was frescoed with the Legend of the True Cross in 1424 by Masolino; the scenes were destroyed in 1792 except for the intrados of the entrance arch, the window frame, and a niche with trompe l'oeil shelves. However the *sinopie have survived here. Beyond the second chapel with a 17C wood dossal, the fourth chapel has remains of frescoes and sinopie (restored in 1989) attributed to the bottega of Bicci di Lorenzo. Here has been placed a damaged tomb slab of an Augustinian monk dated 1432. Beyond is the entrance to an ORATORY (1510) with carved benches by Nofri d'Ascanio and a copy of a Deposition by Cigoli (removed by Ferdinando II and now in the Galleria Palatina in Florence), carried out in 1690 by Antonio Domenico Gabbiani. In the SOUTH TRANSEPT are more fresco fragments by Masolino: a group thought to represent the pupils of St Ivo, and a lunette of the *Madonna and Child with two angels. To the right of the high altar is the entrance of the Oratory of the Santissima Annunziata, with two beautiful *statues of the Annunciation by Bernardo Rossellino (c 1447). In the chapel on the left of the high altar, Passignano, Adoration of the Shepherds (1621). NORTH SIDE. Fourth chapel, altarpiece of the Assumption by Mario Balassi (1659); the third chapel was decorated in 1759–63 with frescoes by Vincenzo Meucci and Giuseppe Del Moro. Second chapel, Rutilio Manetti, Martyrdom of St Catherine (1627) and frescoes by Ottavio Vannini. In the first chapel, the Madonna of the Rosary by Francesco Furini encloses a painting of St Nicholas of Tolentino protecting Empoli from the plague by Bicci di Lorenzo (1445).

At the far end of Via Giuseppe del Papa is Via della Noce, in which are remains of the *Porta Pisana* (1487; damaged in the last War), the only part to survive of the once-famous walls of Empoli.

Churches of interest in the environs of Empoli include *Santa Maria a Ripa* (works by the Della Robbia, Santi Buglioni, Giovanni Antonio Sogliani), *Pianezzoli* (15C pulpit and a Madonna and Child with saints signed and dated 1593 by Ludovico Cigoli) and *Monterappoli* (fresco attributed to Raffaello Botticini).

On the E outskirts of Empoli is the unattractive suburb of PONTORME, birthplace of the painter Jacopo Carucci, called Pontormo (1494–1556; plaque set up in 1956 by Emilio Cecchi on No. 97 on the main road). The small church of *San Michele* (identified by its tall domed campanile; inconspicuous sign off the main road) contains *St John the Evangelist and *St Michael (c 1519) by Pontormo. In a niche with very faded frescoes of the Baptism of Christ, also attributed to Pontormo, is a handsome round 15C marble font. On the fine gilded wood high altar is a ciborium and two paintings by Girolamo Macchietti of St Michael Archangel and St John the Baptist. In the chapel to the left of the high altar, *Immaculate Conception by Lodovico Cigoli (c 1590). A short distance from the church, on the outskirts of the village, is the church of *San Martino*, with a brick façade which incorporates a bellcote. The attractive simple interior (if closed, ring at the house on the right) contains (behind the left altar), a good 15C fresco fragment of two saints (restored in 1985). On the left of the apse arch is a statuette of the Madonna and Child by Michele da Firenze. Above, on either side of the apse arch are two paintings of five saints attributed to Giovanni Toscani.

On the SW slope of Monte Albano, 11km N of Empoli, in beautiful countryside, is the little village of **Vinci** (3-star hotels), famous as the birthplace of Leonardo da Vinci (1452–1519). The restored 13C *Castle* of the Guidi houses a particularly interesting *MUSEUM (open daily 9.30–18 or 19), beautifully rearranged in 1986. It contains numerous *models of the machines invented by Leonardo, exhibited beside facsimiles of his drawings (well labelled, also in English). Next door is the *Biblioteca Leonardiana*, a library relating to Leonardo (open Tuesday–Friday, 15–19). The nearby church of *Santa Croce* preserves the font in which Leonardo is supposed to have been baptised. The road continues up to the hamlet of *Anchiano*, higher up on the hill (also approached by an old path, c 2km long), amidst magnificent olive groves. Here is the house which is traditionally thought to be the actual birthplace of Leonardo. It was restored in 1952 as a humble memorial to him (open 9.30–13, 14.30–17 except Wed). In the lower town, preceded by a porch, is the church of the *Santissima Annunziata*, with an Annunciation (over the high altar), attributed to Fra Paolino da Pistoia.

The road continues from Vinci across Monte Albano with splendid views to Pistoia (see Rte 5).

2km SE of Vinci is the Pieve di Sant'Ansano in Greti founded before 998, which preserves interesting sculptures and a painting by Rutilio Manetti.

Cerreto Guidi, 8km NW of Empoli, is a centre of wine production (*Chianti Putto*). 2-star hotel *Il Tegolo*, with restaurant. The Villa Medici here has been restored and opened to the public (9–19; fest. 9–14). It is approached by a splendid double ramp built in brick to a design of Buontalenti. The villa, incorporated in a castle, was begun in 1565. The early Medici grand-dukes used the palace which now contains portraits of the family, and decorations carried out in the early 20C. The small Baroque garden was designed in the 18C by Ferdinando Ruggeri. In the church next door (open only on Sunday) is a *font by Giovanni or Andrea Della Robbia.

Beyond the road (N429) which diverges S for Castelfiorentino and Certaldo (see Rte 15) is (44km) **SAN MINIATO** (22,800 inhabitants), a pretty little town in a fine position, formerly known as *San Miniato al Tedesco*.

Information Office, Piazza del Popolo.

Railway Station. *San Miniato-Fucecchio* in San Miniato Basso, on the Florence–Pisa line (slow trains only in 35mins from Florence).

Hotel. 3-star: *Miravalle*, 3 Prato del Duomo (with first-class restaurant). **Restaurants** (both first-class): *Canapone*, Piazza Bonaparte; *Collebrunacchi*, 12 Via Collebrunacchi (in the environs).

History. On the site of an 8C church dedicated to the Florentine martyr San Minias, the Lombard town became the seat of the Imperial Vicariate in Tuscany. Here Countess Matilda was born in 1046. The Rocca was built by Frederick II in 1240. From the tower, Pier della Vigna (Dante *Inferno*, XIII, 31–78), his minister, is supposed to have killed himself. From 1369 San Miniato came under Florentine dominion.

At the highest point of the town was the *Rocca* built by Frederick II. Only two towers remain of the castle; the highest one, conspicuous for miles around, was rebuilt after its destruction in the last War. Paths lead up to the gardens around it. The second massive square tower now serves as the belfry of the Duomo, in the *Prato del Duomo* with pretty trees. The **Duomo** was built c 1195, but later altered and restored in 1860. The Romanesque brick façade was decorated with blue and brown ceramic bowls probably manufactured in North Africa. Some of these were removed in 1979 to be exhibited in the Museo Diocesano. In the INTERIOR the pulpit and funerary monuments in the aisles are by Amalia Duprè. On the first altar in the S aisle is a Nativity (in very poor conditon) by Aurelio Lomi. Over the high altar is a 17C wood Crucifix. In the N transept, Francesco di Angelo Lanfranchi (*Lo Spillo*), Deposition (1528), restored in 1988. Over the first altar in the N aisle, Cosimo Gamberucci, Raising of Lazarus.

Next to the Duomo is the **Museo Diocesano** (open 9–12, 14.30–17.30, except Monday; in winter open only on Saturday and Sunday) into which works of art have been collected from churches in the region. The works are all labelled. Room 1: sculptural fragments; detached fresco fragment of a Maestà by the Maestro degli Ordini. R. 2: Neri di Bicci, Madonna and Child with saints; Rossello di Iacopo Franchi, St Catherine of Alexandria, and a scene of her martyrdom; Cenni di Francesco di Ser Cenni, St Jerome translating the Bible (which was signed and dated 1411) and a predella scene with the saint being fed by the angel); school of Orcagna, St Michael Archangel (and a scene of his fight with the devils). Giovanni da San Giovanni (attributed), detached fresco of the Annunciation and prophets, and two frescoed heads. Cases display liturgical objects and church silver. R. 3: two drawings by Lodovico Cigoli; Master of Santi Quirico e Giulitta (attributed; formerly thought to be by Filippo Lippi), small Crucifixion (c 1430); Andrea del Verrocchio (attributed), *Redeemer, a bust in terracotta (with traces of polychrome); Francesco Granacci, Madonna enthroned with saints; Jacopo di Michele (*Il Gera*), processional standard, painted on both sides, with the Flagellation and Crucifixion; Antonio Maria Ferri, wood model of the church of the Crocifisso (see below); circle of Andrea del Castagno (or an early work by Andrea), Madonna of the Holy Girdle; Fra Bartolomeo (with assistants), Circumcision. The two rooms upstairs display paintings by Matteo Rosselli, Il Poppi, and Lodovico Cigoli (including the sacrifice of Isaac). The two large paintings of the Deposition and the Way to Calvary are unusual 17C works by the Tuscan-Flemish school.

Opposite the Duomo is the 12C *Palazzo dei Vicari dell'Imperatore*, and the handsome 17C *Palazzo Vescovile* with a curved façade. Three flights of steps lead down beneath the palace to Piazza della Repubblica where the big 17C *Seminario* has a fine façade (the painted decoration and the medieval shop-fronts beneath have been restored). Via Vittime del Duomo leads out of the piazza beneath an arch down to the old PALAZZO COMU-NALE, the town hall. The Council Chamber on the first floor (admission on request) has a fresco of the Madonna and Child between saints by Cenni di Francesco di Ser Cenni. On the ground floor (entered from the street; unlocked on request at the town hall) is the 15C ORATORY OF THE MADONNA DI LORETO with delightful frescoes probably dating from 1413 and attributed to Arrigo di Niccolò and others, and a fine wood ancona with 16C Florentine paintings. A scenographic staircase leads up the *Sanctuary of the Crocifisso*, an unusual builing on a Greek-cross plan by Antonio Maria Ferri (1705–18; restored in 1990, open Sat & Sun). It contains 18C frescoes by Antonio Domenico Bamberini. The statues outside include (in a niche) the Risen Christ by Francesco Baratta.

Farther on a road climbs left to the huge church of *San Francesco* built in 1276 on the hillside below the Rocca (and completed in 1480). In the interior on the left wall is a fresco fragment of St Christopher by the school of Masolino.

From Piazza della Repubblica (see above) Via Conti descends to *Piazza del Popolo*, the centre of San Miniato, with the church of **San Domenico** (reopened after restoration in 1994). Of ancient foundation, the interior has 18C frescoes on the upper walls attributed to Antonio Domenico Bamberini. In a chapel at the end of the right side (left of the door into the sacristy) is the tomb of Giovanni Chellini, a Florentine doctor who died in 1461, with a fine effigy now attributed to Pagno di Lapo Portigiani (on a model by Donatello, who was Chellini's patient). It was recomposed here in the 19C. The altarpiece of the Madonna and Child is by Domenico di Michelino and the Master of the Johnson Nativity. In the adjacent chapel (right of the sanctuary) are restored 14C frescoes of the life of the Virgin and (on the pilaster) St Lawrence, a fragment attributed to the bottega of Masolino. A Madonna and Child by the Master of San Miniato has been removed. The Sanctuary was frescoed in 1900 by Galileo Chini. In the chapel opposite the one with the Chellini monument is a Deposition and two saints in a fine ancona by Il Poppi (recently restored). In other parts of the church are interesting frescoes by the 15C Florentine school and altarpieces by Francesco Curradi, Giovanni Battista Vanni, and Antoniazzo Romano.

Via IV Novembre continues past a number of handsome palaces. In a little piazza the 16C *Palazzo Grifoni* (with a loggia), attributed to Giuliano di Baccio d'Agnolo, is being restored after it was half destroyed in the War. Via Carducci continues past the church of the *Santissima Annunziata* (1522), centrally planned, with an octagonal cupola (over the altar is a worn 14C fresco of the Annunciation), and farther on (left; No. 15 Via Roma) is the Conservatorio and church of *Santa Chiara* (closed) which contains a Crucifix by Deodato Orlandi and a Noli me tangere by Lodovico Cigoli.

A road leads from San Miniato Basso N across the Arno to Fucecchio, Castelfranco di Sotto and Santa Maria a Monte. **Fucecchio** (5km; 19,000 inhab.), with light industries, was founded before the 11C. It was beseiged in 1323 by Castruccio Castracani and after 1330 came under Florentine rule. In the central Piazza Vittorio Veneto a long flight of steps leads up to the large church of *San Giovanni Battista*, founded in the 10C and rebuilt in the 18C. It contains on the N side (first altar) a Madonna and saints (in very poor condition) by the 16C Florentine school beneath a fragment of a Baptism of Christ, and (on the last altar) a 16C marble relief of the Madonna and Child. On the left side of the church is a terrace with a panoramic view. Here is the church of *San Salvatore* (Misericordia) preceded by a pretty loggia. In the interior (closed order of nuns), on the third S altar, is an Allegory of the Conception by Giorgio Vasari (one of several versions of this painting by the artist).

In the piazza, opposite Palazzo del Podestà, another flight of steps leads up to an old palace which now houses the Biblioteca Comunale. It is being restored and will house the *Museo di Fucecchio*, with some archaeological material, and paintings by Zanobi Machiavelli (*Madonna in Adoration), the Maestro dei Paesaggi Kress (Trinity and Evangelists), and Berlinghiero Berlinghieri (saints).

A secondary road follows the N bank of the Arno via *Santa Croce sull'Arno* (8km) with some 430 tanneries which produce 35% of Italian leather, to *Castelfranco di Sotto* (11km), on low ground beside the Arno, severely damaged in the last War, and by the Arno flood of 1966. It preserves its rectangular plan. Beyond an old gate, a road leads to the main piazza with the 15C Palazzo Comunale with a portico facing the flank of the church of San Pietro, which contains a painting by Alessandro Allori, a fine 13C statue of St Peter, and a 14C Annunciation group.

The road continues to SANTA MARIA A MONTE (15km). It has an interesting circular plan and all its streets are curving. Its castle had strategic importance in the Middle Ages and was contested by Florence, Lucca, and Pisa. From Piazza della Vittoria, where a large yellow palace houses the town hall, Via Carducci leads down and continues right round the village. It passes a terrace with a view of the built-up plain of the Arno beside a fine palace and the church of *San Giovanni Evangelista*. In the interior the baptismal font has fine sculptures by Domenico di Giovanni Rosselli (1468). On the right of the high altar (behind glass; difficult to see) is a *statue of the Madonna and Child enthroned in polychrome wood of 1255. At the E end is a 14C Crucifix. Over the side door is an unusual dark stone ambone supported by two lions, with carvings and (unfinished) inlaid marble decoration. Above the attractive E end are worn frescoes by Luigi Ademollo. The *Canonica* next door has a large (but damaged) Della Robbian tondo over the door. Via Carducci continues back to Piazza della Vittoria past another pretty curving street with a nice row of little houses. Various winding streets lead up around the top of the hill and the site of the castle which was never repaired after severe War damage.

On the S bank of the Arno the superstrada and the old road below San Miniato continue to *San Romano*, scene of the indecisive battle of 1432 between the Florentines and the Sienese. There is a good collection of old pharmacy jars in the Farmacia Mannelli. A by-road leads S to (55km) MONTOPOLI IN VAL D'ARNO in pleasant farming countryside. There was a fortress here by the 8C. On the approach road (preceded by a portico and a palm tree) is the church of *Santa Marta* (usually closed) which contains a Raising of Lazarus by Lodovico Cigoli and a Madonna with souls in Purgatory by Santi di Tito. The road leads up past the flank and campanile (formerly a tower of the castle) of the large church of *Santo Stefano* (if closed; ring at No. 5). In the pleasant interior (S side) the baptistery has a large 16C oval font, and a chapel containing a 14C Crucifix. Beyond the second altar, with a Madonna of the Rosary by Francesco Curradi, is a Resurrection by Orazio Fidani. North side. Ludovico Cigoli (attributed), Prayer in the Garden; 2nd altar, Jacopo Vignali, Madonna with Adam and Eve, a striking painting, signed and dated 1664. On the wall is an interesting small painting of the Annunciation (1513), and, above, a lunette with God the Father. On the first altar, fresco of the Holy Family of 1519. The road continues to Piazza Michele da Montopoli from which a short road leads to a remarkably high and wide arch at the foot of a hill on which the castle was built. The road continues up, and beyond the town hall facing a little piazza with a view and an old tower, it narrows into a track.

The old road and superstrada continue direct via Pontedera to Pisa, but it is well worth making the long detour described below S from Montopoli to Palaia and Casciana Terme, and other attractive villages in the beautiful hilly countryside S of the Arno.

From Montopoli a pretty country road leads S up through woods to (66km) **Palaia**, first mentioned in 980. There are views of the distant hills to the S towards Volterra and N towards the Apennines. The approach road leads left around the little hill, with a view of the large 13C *Pieve di San Martino* outside the village. It is approached by a signposted road but is usually closed (it was over restored in the 19C). Porta Fiorentina leads into the long Piazza della Repubblica (closed at the far end by another gate). Above Porta Fiorentina is the campanile of the little 12C church of *Santa Maria* with a plain façade (closed). Via del Popolo leads out of the piazza under a gate with a clock and up past (left) the inconspicuous church of *Sant'Andrea* with a brick façade and small tower. In the interior are two fine statues of the Madonna and Child on the right and left of the high altar: the one on the right in painted wood is signed and dated 1403 by Francesco da Valdambrino, and the one on the left in terracotta is attributed as an early work to Giovanni Della Robbia. On the left wall are parts of a terracotta altar frontal with figures of saints, by the school of Andrea Della Robbia. On the E wall, Crucifix attributed to the school of Giovanni Pisano. At the top of the village there is a fine view from the Rocca.

From Palaia a road continues to (76km) *Capannoli* on the floor of the Era valley and on a road (N439) to Volterra.

Peccioli is a pleasant little village 6km S of Capannoli. A road leads up from the market square in front of the church of the *Carmine* (closed) to the central piazza. Here is the unusual E end of *San Verano*, next to an amusing bell-tower crowned with circular battlements. The church is entered by the side door. It was founded in the 12C, but later altered and restored after the War. The Romanesque Pisan façade looks out over the plain. In the interior on the right side is a 13C Madonna and Child attributed to Enrico di Tedice. The Oratory (1580) off the left side has a fine carved wood ceiling (the paintings from it by Jacopo Vignali have been removed for restoration). Here is hung a Madonna and four saints by Neri di Bicci. A 14C Crucifix and a 13C painting of St Nicholas of Bari also belong to the church. In the piazza, opposite the E end of the church, is the restored *Palazzo Pretorio* (No. 5) with coats of arms high up on the façade, some in enamelled terracotta.

Outside the village (well signposted) is a small park with life-size models of dinosaurs and a childrens' playground (open daily).

From Capannoli a by-road continues W for 6km to meet the road S for (89km) **Casciana Terme**, an attractive little spa surrounded by low hills planted with olives and vineyards. It has tree-lined streets and small hotels (3-star and 2-star) and some Art Nouveau houses. It was known for its waters in Roman times and in the Middle Ages (when they were taken by Countess Matilda). In 1311 Pisa built baths here and it became well known again in the 18C. It has warm anti-rheumatic waters used for both bathing and drinking. The season runs from April to November. In the central Piazza Garibaldi is the handsome neo-classical façade of the *Terme* by Giuseppe Poggi (1870). Behind are the new spa buildings (being enlarged) and a park. Just off the piazza is the tourist information office (called the *Ritrovo del Forestiero*). There are numerous small furniture factories in the area.

A pretty by-road leads up to **Casciana Alta** (3km), a hamlet with a spacious piazza with plane trees, and a terrace overlooking lovely countryside. Here the church of San Niccolò with a cupola, has a heavily decorated neo-classical interior with orange Corinthian columns. The painting of the Hospitality of St Julian is by Orazio Fidani. A polyptych by Lippo Memmi belongs to the church (removed). A road continues to **Crespina** (11km). The Macchiaioli artist Silvestro Lega often stayed and painted in this area. Above the village is the church of San Michele with a statue of the saint on the façade. A painting of St Michael Archangel by Bernardo Daddi belongs to the church. From the church, Via Montegrappa (signposted *La Guardia*), Via San Rocco, and Via Belvedere lead in c 2km (keep left) to the beautiful 18C *Villa di Belvedere*, with a monumental flight of steps on the façade, approached by an ancient cypress avenue and preceded by a handsome garden. The elegant little 18C domed chapel was built by Mattia Tarocchi in 1775–84 and decorated by Giovanni Battista Tempesti. It contains a painted Cross by the Master of San Torpè. The countryside here is particularly lovely.

A narrow road which traverses pretty country and passes a neo-classical oratory preceded by a portico leads E to **Lari** (16km), a little village built in a circle around the foot of a huge Medici fortress with splendid brick bastions. A gate leads through the outer walls and then steps (signposted) lead up round the bastion to the entrance to the castle (open 8.30–20; fest. 10–20; in urgent need of restoration). Inside is a little paved courtyard with a well and numerous coats of arms on three walls including many in enamelled polychrome terracotta. It is possible to walk around the ramparts. For adm. to the interior, Tel. 0587/685274. The church at its foot was restored in 1910. On either side of the choir, the two marble statues of the Annunciation are attributed to Andrea Guardi. On the left wall is a beautiful tabernacle with a Madonna and Child in enamelled terracotta surrounded by a garland, by Giovanni Della Robbia (1524). In a niche off the right side is a painting of the Madonna by Francesco Melani, highly decorated. *Cevoli*, 3km E, has a conspicuous church beside a cemetery with a large semicircular apse which contairs the only known painting signed by Andrea de Pisis (who helped Benozzo Gozzoli with the frescoes in the Camposanto in Pisa), dated 1490. From here it is a short distance down to the road from Casciana Terme to Ponsacco, see below.

From Casciana Terme a straight road follows the river valley N to Ponsacco and crosses the superstrada into (105km) **Pontedera**, a busy market town (26,500 inhab.) making motor-scooters. The old road (N67) for Pisa continues W into (112km) **Cascina**, a centre of the furniture trade, beneath Monte Verruca (563m), a prominent peak of Monte Pisano. It was the scene of a Florentine victory over the Pisans in 1364. It now has unattractive surroundings with numerous small factories, but the main Corso Matteotti is lined with porticoes for the whole of its length. At the beginning on the left, behind a railing, is the little 14C *Oratory of San Giovanni* (if closed, ring at the convent school next door at No. 9). The Gothic vaulted interior contains a cycle of frescoes by Martino di Bartolomeo (1398) in extremely poor condition, including saints in Gothic niches and scenes from the Old Testament above. The altarpiece of the Annunciation by Luca di Tommè was removed to Florence many years ago. Farther along the main street, between the town hall and a palace with an attractive balcony, Via Palestra leads to Piazza della Chiesa with three churches and a 15C tower. Only the 12C *Pieve di Santa Maria* is open regularly. It has a fine basilican interior with handsome columns and a seated terracotta statue of the Madonna and Child (early 16C; in the chapel to the right of the apse). The church of *San Benedetto*, 3km W of Cascina on the main road, has a splendid English alabaster (14C).

A road leads across the Arno to (117km) **Vicopisano**, a village situated on a little hill which still has a number of towers and part of its fortifications, restored by Brunelleschi after it was taken by the Florentines in 1407. It is bordered on the S by a canal built by the Medici grand-dukes to deviate the course of the Arno which now flows 2km S. At the foot of the hill is the Torre del Brunelleschi (c 1406) in the walls which mount the hillside. Near it is the *Torre delle Quattre Porte* resting on a vault, once open on four sides. On the other side of the hill, a narrow road can be followed up on foot past the Municipio, with a tower, to the 14C *Palazzo Pretorio*, with numerous coats of arms. It is in very poor condition and part of it is privately owned, but it is being restored. Above, on top of the hill, is the tower of the castle (now enclosed in a private garden) and below can be seen a number of other towers. Outside the village (near Piazza Cavalca) on flat ground by the main road is the fine 12C Romanesque *Pieve*. It contains a sculptured wood group of the Deposition (12–13C) and (in a niche on the left side) a large statue of St John the Baptist, a fine work dating from before 1390 and recently attributed to Nino Pisano. It was restored in 1990 and the arms and head probably date from the 17C. The little baptismal font dates from the 15C.

A rather unattractive road continues past the little spa of *Uliveto Terme* (well known for its mineral water) and the conspicuous Torre degli Uperrighi at Caprona on the very edge of a quarry, towards Calci. Soon the huge (129km) ***Certosa di Pisa** comes into view on low ground, now in a disappointing setting. This is one of the largest monumental monasteries in the country. The Charterhouse was founded in 1366 and reconstructed in the 18C. It was built to house 60 Carthusian monks, but the monastery was closed in 1973. Guided tours are given every half hour: winter 9–16; summer 9–18; fest. 9–12; closed Monday.

In the FIRST COURTYARD is the monumental façade (1718) of the church and the two wings of the monastery. To the right, an elaborate gateway (1768), decorated in the form of a grotto with shells and pebbles, leads into the garden. The CHURCH has colourful frescoes by Giuseppe and Pietro Rolli and a marble lectern in the form of an angel by the school of Bernini. The E end (with a high altarpiece by Volterrano) is being restored. The side chapels contain altarpieces including a Crucifix by Bernardino Poccetti, and St Bruno by Jacopo Vignali. The CAPPELLA DEL ROSARIO and CAPPELLA DELLA SACRA FAMIGLIA have decorations by Giuseppe Maria Terreni. The CHIOSTRO GRANDE has an elaborate fountain and white marble porticoes by Giovanni Battista Cartoni (1636–51). It is surrounded by the spacious monks' cells, one of which is shown. The smaller CHIOSTRINO CAPITOLARE survives from the 15C (the well dates from 1614). Beyond the CAPPELLA DEL CAPITOLO is the REFECTORY with a Last Supper by Bernardino Poccetti and 18C frescoes by Pietro Giarrè. The elaborate GRAND-DUCAL APART-MENT where distinguished guests stayed, has period furniture and stuccoes by Angelo Maria Somazzi and more frescoes by Pietro Giarrè. The 17C CHIOSTRO DEL PRIORE has an unusual double well. A TERRACE looks out over the monastery garden and fish tanks (and to the right, in the distance, can be seen the Leaning Tower and Baptistery of Pisa). A grand staircase (by Michele Fossi) leads down to the courtyard and vestibule.

In a wing of the monastery (and in a covered loggia, once used by the monks to take their exercise) the University of Pisa has recently arranged the MUSEO DI STORIA NATURALE, founded at the University in 1591 by Ferdinando I (open Wed, Fri & Sun 10–12.30, 16–18.30; Tues, Thurs & Sat 18–23; closed Mon). The collection is extremely interesting and some of it still displayed in showcases of 1752.

Near the Certosa is the straggling unattractive village of (130km) *Calci*. From the piazza with four palm trees a road leads shortly to the PIEVE, founded in 1088–98, marked by its massive square unfinished campanile. The attractive façade in the Pisan style has decorations in two shades of grey. The basilican INTERIOR has fine columns and capitals. The large monolithic rectangular *font has an interesting sculpted front (mid-12C) by an artist influenced by Biduino. Beside the unusual robed figure of Christ in the centre is a gnome, symbolising the river Jordan. On the right is St John the Baptist; the other figures represent the Madonna and two angels. The pretty marble confessionals date from 1757. On a pilaster of the church is a 13C head of Christ which has been adapted as a copy of the Volto Santo of Lucca. On the altar right of the high altar, Madonna and Child with saints signed by Aurelio Lomi (who may also have painted the Adoration of the Shepherds in a chapel off the right side of the church). In the sacristy is kept a beautiful late-14C painting of the *Madonna and Child.

A secondary road via Mezzana continues into (143km) **Pisa**, see Rte 9.

12

Pisa to Monte Argentario: the Tuscan Maremma

The **MAREMMA** is the name given to the marshy coastal plain which stretches from Cecina, some 50km S of Pisa, to the Argentario and the border with Lazio. The name may be derived from the Spanish *marisma* meaning marsh. It has also come to refer to the *Colline Metallifere* further inland and to the promontories of the Uccellina and Monte Argentario. The typical vegetation which includes dunes covered with the low *macchia* *mediterranea* (with myrtle and juniper thickets) backed by woods of pines, elms, oaks, and ash, and, further inland, thick forests of ilexes and cork trees, survives in part. The wildlife has been protected in places, notably in the Parco Naturale della Maremma, and the World Wildlife Fund sanctuaries at Bolgheri, the lagoon of Orbetello, and the marsh of Burano, remarkable for their birdlife. The swamplands were for centuries abandoned. Later malaria caused poverty and the gradual decline of the population, and the Maremma Grossetana became notorious for its brigands. Attempts to reclaim the marshes by building canals and draining the land, made from the 16C onwards, were hampered by economical and technical difficulties. On the succession of Leopoldo II as Grand Duke of Tuscany in 1824 a 20-year plan was drawn up to reclaim arable land, build roads, and repopulate the villages by encouraging various industries. It is only since 1928, with the introduction of mechanisation and the elimination of malaria, that the Maremma has been able to flourish economically and benefit from the growing tourist industry.

Road, Via Aurelia (N1). A busy road, recently realigned and made into dual carriageway.—19.5km **Livorno** (described in Rte 10)—41km *Castiglioncello*—55km *Cecina*—80km *San Vincenzo* (for **Populonia**, 17km, and **Piombino**, 22km)—90km *Venturina* (for *Campiglia Marittima*, 4km)—106km *Follonica* (for **Castiglione della Pescaia**, 22km)—130km *Grilli* (for **Vetulonia**, 5km)—153km **Grosseto** (described in Rte 19)—159km *Rispescia* (for *Alberese*, 9km and the **Parco Naturale della Maremma**)—176km *Fonteblanda* (for *Talamone*, 4km)—193km *Orbetello Scalo* (for **Orbetello**, 4km and **Monte Argentario**, 6km).

The **Via Aurelia** was built c 241 BC to link Rome with the Etruscan towns on the Tyrrhenian coast. It left Rome at Porta Aurelia (now Porta San Pancrazio) and reached the shore at Alsium (Palo Laziale), a port of the Etruscan city of Caere (Cerveteri) then followed the coastline to Cosa. In c 109 BC it was extended to Populonia, Pisa and Genoa. It ended in Gaul at Forum Julia (Fréjus, on the French Riviera). The modern road follows roughly the same line, although in places it now runs further inland.

Railway. This route is followed by the main line from Pisa to Rome. Only slow trains stop at the coastal towns: Castiglioncello, Rosignano, Vada, Cecina, Bolgheri, Castagneto Carducci, San Vincenzo, Campiglia Marittima, Follonica, Talamone, Orbetello Scalo (from Pisa to Orbetello Scalo in over 2hrs). Some of the fast trains from Pisa stop at Grosseto (in 1hr 30mins).

Buses run by ATL from Livorno along the coast to Castiglioncello, Cecina, Piombino, etc. Services run by RAMA from Grosseto to Castiglione della Pescaia, Vetulonia, Alberese, Talamone, the Argentario, and Capalbio.

Accommodation at the coastal resorts. The coast from Livorno to the Argentario has numerous seaside resorts, which are extremely crowded in summer. Detailed up-to-date information about hotels, apartments, and camping sites is available from the APT of Livorno (Tel. 0586/898111) for the stretch of coast as far as Piombino, and from the APT of Grosseto (Tel. 0564/454510) for the area from Follonica to the Argentario and the border with Lazio.

The Via Aurelia (N1) leads out of Pisa S of the Arno and runs beneath the A12 motorway to (11km) *Stagno* in the midst of the former marshes of the Arno, drained (c 1620) by Sir Robert Dudley, and now occupied by a huge oil refinery. Here N67bis diverges inland; it is now part of a superstrada recently completed from Livorno to Florence (see Rte 11). Across the canal the Livorno by-pass begins: Livorno is described in Rte 10. Beyond Livorno the Aurelia has been improved and made into dual-carriageway as far as the Cecina by-pass. Instead the old road hugs the shore, and beyond the seaside suburbs of Ardenza and Antignano, passes (32km) *Quercianella*, a little seaside resort with beaches backed by pine woods (3-star hotel *Villa Margherita*, and 1-star hotel *Villa Verde*).

41km **Castiglioncello** is a large resort on a promontory (information office open in summer at 967 Via Aurelia). It has numerous hotels of all categories (most of them closed in winter), including (4-star) *Villa Godilonda*; (3-star) *Atlantico*, *Martini*, and *San Domenico*. Trattoria *La Baracchina*, Punta Righini. At (43km) *Rosignano Solvay* are the factories processing the soda from the Saline di Volterra. The old town of *Rosignano Marittimo* is 4km inland (trattoria *San Marco* in località San Marco). The Museo Civico (with Etruscan and Roman material) in Palazzo Bombardieri is open 9–13, 16–19 excluding Mon. This area is known for its wine (*Montescudaio*). At (48km) *Vada* the railway from Pisa via Colle Salvetti joins the main line. There are numerous campsites here near the beaches, which are less crowded than those of Castiglioncello.

55km **Cecina** (Information Office in Largo Cairoli open in summer; 3-star hotel on the Aurelia *Il Palazzaccio*; first-class restaurant *Scacciapensieri*, 33 Via Don Minzoni; trattoria *Antica Cecina*, 17 Via Cavour) is the junction for Volterra (described in Rte 16), which lies 42km inland along N68. At San Pietro in Palazzi, 2km outside the town, is the early-19C *Villa La Cinquantina* (open Mon, Wed, Fri & Sat 7.15–13.15; Tues & Thurs 14–20) with an Etruscan and Roman collection. A local ethnographical museum is also displayed here. The pretty little medieval village of *Casale Marittimo* lies 11km inland (restaurant *Le Volte*). *Marina di Cecina* has numerous 3-star hotels (including 'Gabbiano') and 2-star hotels (including *Azzurra*) and 3-star camping sites.

64km. A by-road leads to the coast where *Marina di Bibbona* and *Forte di Bibbona* also have numerous 3-star and 2-star hotels, and 3-star camping sites. 67km *San Guido*. A splendid ˙avenue of cypresses, nearly 5km long, planted in 1801 by Camillo Della Gherardesca, leads from the main road up to the delightful little village of *Bolgheri* where the poet Carducci spent his childhood (1838–49). The cypress avenue is the subject of a famous poem by him. The white and rosé wines of Bolgheri are particularly good, and *Sassicaia* is considered the best Cabernet wine of Italy. On the coast here is the RIFUGIO FAUNISTICO DI BOLGHERI (2100 hectares) a remarkable wildlife oasis created in 1960, and jealously protected from new building by the local authorities. The landscape, typical of the Maremma, includes umbrella pines, ilexes, cork trees, and dunes covered with the vegetation known as the *macchia*. This was once a hunting reserve of the Della Gherardesca, and the wild animals here include deer and wild boar, and there are a great variety of migratory birds. It is open 15 October to 15 April on Fridays and the first and third weekend of each month, 9–12, 14–16.30. Only 12 people at a time are allowed to visit the reserve; it is necessary to book at the *Vigili Urbani* at Castagneto Carducci. 72km. Another road leads inland to the pretty little village of *Castagneto Carducci*. Near the Aurelia is the 3-star *Nuovo Hotel Bambolo* with restaurant, and the 3-star *La Torre di Donoratico*. First-class restaurants *Bagnoli*, at Bagnoli, and *Il Cacciatore* at Castagneto. On the coast is the resort of *Castagneto-Donoratico* with more hotels and camping sites.

80km **San Vincenzo** is a well known large seaside resort extended to the S by the Riva degli Etruschi, a vast bungalow colony. Information Office, Via Alliata. Numerous hotels of all categories include the 4-star *Park Hotel I Lecci* and the camping sites include the 3-star *Park Albatros*. Famous luxury-class restaurant *Gambero Rosso*; first-class restaurant *Il Bucaniere*.

At San Vincenzo N1 runs inland (see below), while another road, on the line of the Roman Aurelia, continues due S along the coast for Populonia (17km) and Piombino (22km).

12km S a by-road diverges right for **Baratti** (5km), a little port on a pretty bay with good beaches. It was one of the most important ports of ancient Etruria. Iron from Elba and perfumes, amulets and objects from Syria, Egypt, and Greece were traded here as early as the 8C BC for tin and copper from the mines of the nearby hills known as the *Colline Metallifere* (metalliferous hills). Here in the sea in 1968 was found a silver amphora decorated with 132 concave medallions in bas-relief thought to be from Antioch and to date from the 4C, possibly the work of a Syrian silversmith. It is now exhibited in the Archaeolgical Museum of Florence. A Roman ship 20m long containing objects from the Middle-East was discovered at a depth of 18m in 1974. A damaged marble female figure was discovered in a sunken boat in 1990 and may be exhibited in the local museum after restoration.

The road passes the **Necropolis of Populonia** (San Cerbone) on the sea. It was first excavated in 1919 and is important for the study of the development of Etruscan funerary architecture (open daily 9–dusk). Several interesting large tumulus tombs dating from the 7–5C BC are shown as well as one in the form of an edicola. Remains found here of two iron chariots, bronze figurines etc., are now in Florence. Another necropolis known as *Porcareccia* in woods nearby and a 'factory' area where iron was worked in the Etruscan era, are shown only by special request. The tombs here, covered by enormous slag heaps, were excavated in the first half of this century and some of the contents are in the Museum of Populonia. The road continues uphill past an opening in the woods leading to some underground tombs (hypogeum) known as the *Bucche delle Fate*. A footpath leads on to the Cala di San Quirico on the S side of the promontory.

The road ends at the little castellated village which preserves the name of **Populonia**, encircled by walls, the Etruscan section of which is formed of huge blocks of stone. With the Roman conquest and the siege of Sulla the town began to decline. In 546 it was sacked by Totila and given by Charlemagne to Pope Hadrian I c 780. St Cerbone, the last bishop of Populonia was obliged to transfer the bishopric to Massa Marittima in 842. The *Castle* may be visited (9.30–12.30, 14.30–dusk, except Mondays) from which there is a magnificent view stretching from Punt'Ala to the Apuan hills and the islands of Elba, Corsica, and Capraia. The *Museo Etrusco Gasparri* (opened on request, tel. 0565/29512) is a private museum which was opened in 1956. It illustrates the development of local civilisation from the Iron Age to the Roman period. There are objects in bronze and terracotta from the surrounding necropoli and a number of Attic, Apulian and Etruscan vases. Photographs record the most interesting finds, which are kept in Florence.

The main road continues S to **Piombino** (22km), with 39,000 inhabitants, situated at the S end of the Massoncello promontory, once an island. Information office open in summer in Piazzale Premuda; 4-star hotel *Centrale* and 3-star hotel *Collodi* and camping sites. It is an old seaport which has thrived in recent years and is now entirely dominated by large and ugly metal works. It is the port for Elba (see Rte 30). Cesare Borgia built the *Fortress* in 1501 and the fortifications were rebuilt by Grand-duke Cosimo I in 1543. Earlier projects sketched by Leonardo da Vinci remained on paper. The *Cathedral* (Sant'Antimo) has a marble lunette over the baptismal font of the Madonna and Child with two angels in adoration by Andrea Guardi (1460–70). Buses run from the station to Porto Vecchio (for the Elba boats, see Rte 30) in 10mins; to Volterra (2hrs); and to Livorno (2hrs). A branch railway runs to Campiglia in 20mins.

90km *Venturina* is at an important crossroads. **Campiglia Marittima**, 4.5km N, is a prosperous little town with wide views. The medieval district round the *Rocca* preserves parts of its walls including the Porta Pisana and Porta Fiorentina, the 13C *Palazzo Pretorio* studded with coats of arms, and many old houses. The Teatro dei Concordi was restored in 1991. Outside the town on a hill next to the cemetery is the *Pieve di San Giovanni*, a fine example of Romanesque Pisan architecture of the 11–12C. It has a polychrome marble façade and a side portal with a carved architrave attributed to the workshop of Biduino (mid-12C). The nearby marble quarries, already exploited by the Romans, provided marble for the Cathedral of Florence. Slag heaps and remains of furnaces survive in the Val di Fucinaia. ROCCA SAN SILVESTRO, c 5km N of Campiglia, is a little 10C mining town abandoned in the 15C and exceptionally well preserved: it is one of the most important medieval mining sites in Europe. Extensive excavations are in progress (for adm. ask at the Municipio of Campiglia, Tel. 0565/839111).

Another road (N398) leads inland from Venturina. **Suvereto** (9km) preserves parts of its old walls, and next to the medieval gate is the Romanesque church of *San Giusto* which has a porch decorated in the Byzantine style. The main street leads past the 17C *Chiesa della Madonna* to the fine *Palazzo Comunale* (early 13C). The former convent of *San Francesco* in Piazza della Cisterna has a good cloister. Remains survive of the 14C Aldobrandeschi *Rocca*. A fine wine (red and white) is produced here, known as *Val di Cornia*. A short distance N is the charming hill-top village of *Belvedere* which has extensive views. **Frassine** (21km) is an ancient village with ruins dating from the Lombard period. The Sanctuary of the Madonna (restored) has a carved wood Madonna and Child by the 14C Pisan school, and an interesting collection of ex-votos (16–19C) in the transept. This road continues to climb towards Monterotondo Marittimo (33km; see Rte 18).

Beyond Venturina the Aurelia reaches the sea again just before (106km) **Follonica**, an unattractive industrial town (16,700 inhab.; first-class restaurants: *Leonardo Cappelli* and *Paolino*, Piazza XXV Aprile) situated on the gulf of the same name, with views of Elba and the promontory of Piombino. APT information office, Viale Italia. It has a popular sandy beach with numerous 3-star and 2-star hotels (including *Miramare*), and a 1-star camping site *Pineta del Golfo*. Iron furnaces, supplied from the iron mines of Elba, have existed here since ancient times. Under the Medici the furnaces became a state monopoly for the production of arms and ammunition (cannon balls). The iron foundry created by Leopoldo II in 1834 was bombed in 1947 and abandoned in 1962: only the impressive iron entrance gate by Carlo Reishammer survives. The same architect also built the parish church of *San Leopoldo*, in an interesting combination of cast iron, stone, plaster, and wood. A footpath through beautiful Mediterranean vegetation runs along the cliffs down to the little *Cala Martina* from which Garibaldi escaped by boat in 1849 (commemorated by a column). A little further on is *Cala Violina*, a small bay famous for its clear water and sandy beach. The beautiful town of Massa Marittima, 19km inland, is described in Rte 18.

FROM FOLLONICA TO GROSSETO VIA CASTIGLIONE DELLA PESCAIA, N22, 44km. This route follows the line of the Roman road and provides an alternative approach to Grosseto to the busier Aurelia. Beyond the Alma river at (11km) *Pian d'Alma* a road diverges right to **Punta Ala**, situated at the S end of the Gulf of Follonica, in thick pine woods. Formerly a natural beauty spot, with only a watch tower, it became the property of Italo Balbo in 1929 and, since the Second World War, has been transformed into a luxury holiday resort equipped with a golf course (18 holes) and other sports facilities (4-star hotels *Piccolo Hotel Alleluja* and *Gallia Palace* with restaurant; and 3-star *Punta Ala*). From Pian d'Alma another road runs inland to the peaceful village of **Tirli** (9km; 410m). 1-star hotel *Edera*, and first-class restaurant *Tana del Cinghiale*. Here the inhabitants of Castiglione sought refuge against the attacks of pirates in the 16C. It grew up near the site of a hermitage of the legendary St Guglielmo who, together with St George, is traditionally venerated in the Maremma. The parish church (17C) has altars and stuccoes by Andrea Ferrari of Lugano (1674). A footpath leads into chestnut woods with extensive views where pleasant walks may be taken (the small modern chapel of Sant'Anna marks the site of the hermitage). N322 touches the coast just N of Castiglione. There are numerous exclusive holiday villas at *Roccamare* among pine trees with private beaches beyond low sand dunes, and large 3-star camping sites at

Le Rocchette. The road passes Riva del Sole, a Swedish holiday resort created in the 1960s, with hotels and camping sites by the wide sandy beach.

22km **Castiglione della Pescaia** (7700 inhab.) is the most famous and attractive resort on the Maremma coast, very crowded in summer, but extremely pleasant in other seasons. APT information office, Piazza Garibaldi. It has numerous hotels of all categories (including the 3-star *Miramare* with restaurant, and 2-star *Corallo* with restaurant), camping sites, and trattorie. Its small harbour, which was strategically important in Etruscan and Roman times, is now crowded with yachts and boats. It belonged to Pisa in the 12C and was later conquered by Alfonso of Aragon, Siena, and Florence. The Medici Grand-duke Ferdinando I rebuilt its walls in 1608 around the Aragonese fort on the hill overlooking the harbour. The old town, restored in recent years, is entered through an arched gateway and a street leads up to the *Castle* from which there are extensive views along the coast and inland across the plain to the hills. A pretty street winds round inside the walls. The *Parish Church*, which was largely rebuilt after the War, has a bell-tower which dominates the sky-line. In the cemetery is buried the writer Italo Calvino (1923–85) who lived nearby from 1972 until his death.

N322 continues S through a beautiful wood of umbrella pines near fine beaches towards Marina di Grosseto. Off this road, just beyond Castiglione, a footpath to the left leads to the Ponte a Cateratte next to the *Casa Rossa*. This interesting building in brick and travertine, with three arched sluices, was designed in 1767 by Leonardo Ximenes, a Spanish Jesuit and an expert in hydraulics. It stands above converging canals built to control the waters between the Ombrone and the sea, and was part of one of the earliest projects to reclaim the Grosseto plain. A local ethnographical museum may be opened here, and there are plans to protect the fauna and flora of the surrounding marshland. The swamp which gradually developed as a result of the silting up of the canal at Castiglione and periodical floods of the Ombrone and other rivers, was the primary cause of malaria and the consequent poverty and decline of the population in the district. Farther along the coast are *Marina di Grosseto* (10km) with hotels (including 3-star *Lola Piccolo*) and camping sites, and *Principina a Mare* (12km), another resort (3-star hotel *Grifone*) in woods, which has been greatly developed in the last twenty years.

From Castiglione (see above) the most interesting route to Grosseto now runs inland alongside the Bruna river, which marks the N boundary of the former Lago Prile, the salt lake of Etruscan and Roman times which gave access to the harbours of Vetulonia and Roselle. At (28km) *Ponti di Badia* (trattoria) an unsurfaced road to the right crosses the Bruna and leads to a hillock with remains of the *Badia al Fango*, a Benedictine monastery on the site of the Roman Villa Clodia, where Catullus' beloved Lesbia is said to have resided. Formerly a small island or peninsula, it served as the port of the Lake of Castiglione during the Medici period. It commands an extensive view over the plain of Grosseto (standing out across the marshes to the W is the Casa Rossa, described above). 31km On the left, at the entrance to an avenue of cypress and pine trees which leads to the estate of *La Badiola*, is a simple stone with a Cross erected in 1989 to commemorate Leopoldo II who used to stay here, and whose love and concern for the Maremma were fundamental in bringing back to life this area which had suffered from centuries of neglect. 34km *Macchiascandona* (trattoria) where the road diverges right across the plain to (44km) Grosseto (see Rte 19).

Beyond Follonica the modern Via Aurelia (N1, being improved) turns inland and offers the fastest approach to Grosseto. From (112km) *Scarlino Scalo* a by-road (right) leads up to the little hill town of *Scarlino* (6.5km). It preserves its medieval streets and houses, besides remains of its castle. The Romanesque church of San Donato has been remodelled. A monument to Garibaldi has a touching inscription recalling the help the villagers gave to the hero at the time of his escape. Beyond the station of Scarlino is an important pyrite mine. 116km. By-road right for Caldana.

This road leads past *Gavorrano* (6km), a small town on a wooded hill (8400 inhab.), in the vicinity of which are stone and marble quarries. The parish church (1927) has a fine sculpture of the Madonna del Carmine by Giovanni di Agostino. The road continues to *Ravi* (10km), another little mining town beautifully situated on a slope of

Monte Calvo. The hill (469m) can be explored on foot, and offers spectacular views stretching from Massa Marittima to Monte Amiata and the Argentario. *Caldana* (13km) is a village in a beautiful natural setting which preserves its old walls. The church of San Biagio has a fine 16C façade in travertine in the style of Antonio da Sangallo il Vecchio. The simple and elegant interior has arched bays, windows, and cornices picked out in grey stone against the white plaster. In the vicinity is a quarry of Porta Santa marble.

The Aurelia continues to (120km) the station of Gavorrano, where a by-road (left; signposted Roccastrada) passes near *Castel di Pietra* (172m, footpath) where Pia de' Tolomei was allegedly murdered by her husband (Dante, *Purgatorio*, V, 130–136). The new Aurelia now follows the railway while the more interesting road bears S to (130km) *Grilli*. Here a by-road on the right leads in 5km to the hill-top village of **Vetulonia** (344m), on the site of the city of Vetulonia or Vetluna, one of the richest and most flourishing Etruscan cities.

The discovery of several necropoli has confirmed the documented description of Vetulonia as an important member of the Etruscan Confederation. Its identification was officially established in 1887 when the name was changed from Poggio Colonna. The earliest tombs date from the late 9C BC. The period of greatest prosperity was in the 8–7C BC and the numerous tombs excavated at the end of the last century, some of them outstanding in size, were particularly rich in terracotta vases and objects in bronze, silver, and gold. These are now to be found in various museums, principally in Florence and Grosseto. The Romans defeated the Gauls here in 224 BC, and are said to have borrowed from Vetulonia the insignia of their magistrates—the fasces, curule chair, and toga praetexta—and the use of the brazen trumpet in war.

From the Etruscan and Roman town there survive remains of the citadel wall (covering a circuit of 5km), as well as traces of a street of houses, with drains and cisterns. At the top of the town (fine views) are several medieval houses and the parish church, originally Romanesque, with an impressive bell-tower. The local Antiquarium, renovated and enlarged, is due to re-open soon. From Via dei Sepolcri may be reached the domed Tumulo della Pietrera and the Tumulo del Diavolino, the most remarkable tombs in the 8–7C necropolis: they have been allowed to fall into a state of neglect and can no longer be visited inside.

At the foot of the hill of Vetulonia, the road to the S passes another necropolis, and then branches right to the village of *Buriano* (10km; 239m), which is dominated by the massive ruins of its 10C Rocca. The church, built in 1302, has a fine tower. Inside is a 15C stained glass window representing the Birth and Assumption of the Virgin, a fresco fragment of an Epiphany dated 1524, and a wooden statue of St Guglielmo. The by-road continues S to the crossroads at Macchiascandona, on the road from Castiglione della Pescaia to Grosseto (described above).

At 138km this road meets N73 from Roccastrada, described in Rte 19A. 139km *Braccagni* is the modern suburb of MONTEPESCALI perched high up above the plain of Grosseto. It is a small medieval town on a hill of olive trees, 3km off the Aurelia. The old walls survive in part and there is a terrace with panoramic views towards the sea and N towards Monte Leoni. The small 14C church of *San Lorenzo*, at the entrance to the town, has a fresco of the Assumption by the school of Bartolo di Fredi on the left wall. Picturesque streets lead up to the castle tower, with a large clock, and the pretty stone façade of the Romanesque church of *San Niccolò*. Inside are numerous fragmentary frescoes and four charming scenes of the life of the Virgin dated 1389, by a close follower of Bartolo di Fredi. The *altarpiece by Matteo di Giovanni of the Madonna and Child enthroned with saints and angels is from San Lorenzo. Over the high altar is a fine 14C painted Crucifix of the Sienese school.

A new stretch of the Aurelia by-passes (153km) **Grosseto** (see Rte 19) to the E, crosses the Ombrone (the Classical Umbro, one of the chief rivers of Etruria), and continues to (159km) *Rispescia*. Here a by-road leads towards the coast for *Alberese* (9km), a small pleasant village built on a spacious plan in 1951 at the N entrance to the *PARCO NATURALE DELLA MAREMMA, an area of some 70 sq. km designated a national park in 1975 which stretches S across the beautiful wooded and roadless *Monti dell'Uccellina* (417m) to Talamone. The 15 kilometres of coastline here survive as perhaps the best preserved in Italy.

At the crossroads before Alberese a road to the right leads through pine woods to *Marina di Alberese*. This unspoilt beach, backed by thick pinewoods planted in the mid-19C, begins at the estuary of the Ombrone river. On the right bank of the river is the remarkably well preserved (private) *Palude della Trappola*. The beach extends S as far as Cala di Forno at the foot of the Monti dell'Uccellina where there are natural grottoes. Farther on, the rocky slopes of the Uccellina plunge straight into the sea: the beautiful coastline and distinctive vegetation, which includes dwarf palm trees, can be seen from a boat. Tickets to the park must be purchased at the *Park Information Office* (Tel. 0564/ 407098) at Alberese. Here a bus leaves on the hour every hour (9–dusk) on Wednesday, Saturday, and fest. (but from 15 June until 30 September the service is only open at 7 and 16 on Wednesday, Saturday, and fest.) for the centre of the park (10mins) from which various itineraries are indicated along marked footpaths (most of them require a minimum of three hours; children are welcome). The vegetation in the park varies from woods of pine trees, ilexes, elms, and oaks to marshlands, and the typical Mediterranean *macchia* of myrtle and juniper bushes. Animals which run wild here include the famous white long-horned cattle, deer, foxes, goats, wild cats, horses, and wild boar. The cattle and horses are herded by cowboys known as *butteri* (rodeo at Alberese in August). Migratory birds and numerous aquatic species abound. Behind the church of Alberese is the entrance (pedestrians only; open daily) to the *Itinerario Faunistico*, a beautiful walk of less than an hour through a protected area, where deer and other wild animals can usually be seen. The *Museo della Cultura Popolare Grossetana* at Alberese is at present closed. Within the park the *Torre della Bella Marsilia* is the lonely remnant of the castle of Collecchio, home of the Marsili of Siena. In 1543 the castle was destroyed by the corsair Barbarossa and the entire household murdered except for the lovely Margherita, who was carried off to the harem of the Sultan Suleiman the Magnificent, soon to become his legitimate sultana and the mother of Selim II. Farther N are the romantic ruins of the 12C abbey of *San Rabano*, with a well preserved bell-tower. Several other ruined towers along the coast are also visible from the Aurelia. Another entrance to the park near Talamone is described below.

The Aurelia skirts the park as far as (176km) *Fonteblanda* (trattoria 'Ristoro Buratta'), where a road leads right towards Talamone (4km) on the bay which forms the S boundary of the park. The road passes olive groves and the cemetery, on the right, with an interesting funerary chapel in an Oriental Art Nouveau style. A short way beyond an unsurfaced road to the right (500m; signposted 'Parco Naturale della Maremma') leads past the site of a Roman villa and baths, to the S area of the Uccellina hills. Cars may be parked outside an enclosure with a stile. No ticket is required but visitors must leave the park before dusk. There are two footpaths (the longer walk takes approximately 2–2½hrs). They lead through the *macchia* and woods, and emerge on the coast overlooking the sea. These pretty and varied walks are especially beautiful towards sunset.

The approach to **Talamone**, a summer resort, is particularly striking with the castle silhouetted against the sky.

Hotels. 4-star: *Talamonio*, 3-star: *Capo d'Uomo*; 2-star camping site *Talamone*.

Restaurants (first-class): *La Buca*, and *Da Flavia*.

History. This was once an Etruscan city, said to have been founded by the Argonaut Telamon c 1300 BC. The medieval town developed on the rocky promontory and in the 14C and 15C Talamone became the port for Siena. Here also Garibaldi and the Thousand put in on their way to Sicily in 1860 to collect arms and ammunition and to land a party for a feigned attack on the Papal States.

The picturesque harbour with yachts and fishing boats at their moorings, lies at the foot of the steep village. Although damaged in the War, Talamone retains its charm and the walk up along the walls to the Rocca offers splendid views of the Argentario and island of Giglio. The 15C *Rocca*, an impressive block-like construction flanked by a tower, was rebuilt by the Sienese on the site of an Aldobrandeschi castle. There are plans to house a museum here relating to the Parco Naturale della Maremma. Lower down is Piazza Garibaldi (with a bronze bust of the hero) with the parish church (1953) which contains modern paintings and stained glass windows. Overlooking the harbour is a terrace which dominates the entrance to the village, with the War Memorial at the centre of a parapet. The ancient town of Talamone extended S of the bay beyond Fonteblanda. On the nearby hill of Talamonaccio, N of the Osa estuary, a temple was built to celebrate the victory of the Romans over the Gauls at the battle of Campo Reggio in 225 BC. Finds made during excavations here include the fragments of a splendid pediment of the temple which have recently been restored and are exhibited in Orbetello (see below).

The Aurelia continues S and crosses the river Osa, beyond which are hotels and camping sites in thick pine woods. The estuary of the Albegna is crossed just before (185km) *Albinia*, at a crossroads. Here a road leads right along the sandy spit of land known as the *Tombolo di Giannella* to the Argentario (described below). To the left N74 leads towards Manciano and Pitigliano (see Rte 23). The Aurelia skirts the extensive LAGOON OF ORBETELLO between the *Tombolo di Giannella* and the *Tombolo di Feniglia*, two tongues of sand which extend to the Argentario promontory, in the centre of which is Orbetello. The lagoon which is a refuge for some 200 bird species is protected by the World Wildlife Fund (Tel. 0564/862439). From (193km) *Orbetello Scalo* a road leads along a sandy isthmus to **Orbetello** (4km; 13,500 inhab.), an old-fashioned resort (considerably damaged in the War) beautifully situated in the middle of the lagoon with palm trees on the waterfront.

Information Office, Piazza del Duomo.

Car Park inside the walls (signposted), facing the lagoon.

Hotels. 3-star: *I Presidi, Sole*; 1-star: *Piccolo Parigi*.

Restaurants. First-class: *Il Nocchino*, 64 Via dei Mille; pizzeria *Gennaro*; trattoria *Al Tramonto*.

History. The position of Orbetello favoured settlements in ancient times. It was an Etruscan colony (remains of the town walls are still visible) and a place of importance in the Middle Ages. It became the capital of the *Stato dei Presidi*, which included Ansedonia, Porto Ercole, Porto Santo Stefano, and Talamone, the part of Sienese territory retained by Spain, after she had allied herself to Cosimo I to bring about the fall of Siena in 1557. In 1646 the town held out against a two-month siege by the French. All these coastal towns were incorporated into the Grand Duchy of Tuscany in 1808. On the approach to the town the road passes the former airfield from which Italo Balbo led a formation flight of seaplanes across the Atlantic to celebrate the tenth anniversary of Fascism at the World Fair of Chicago in 1933.

The road leads through one of the elegant gateways built by the Spaniards when they fortified the town; another reminder of this Spanish stronghold is the unusual *Polveriera Guzman* (powder-works), on the SE side, which has been recently restored. The *Cathedral* (Santa Maria Assunta) has a •façade of travertine stone with an upper triangular section containing a rose-window, above which is a niche with a statue of St Biagio. The arch and sides of the portal, dated 1376, are finely carved. The church was almost entirely rebuilt in the 17C and the decoration and floor tiles are Spanish in taste. The pretty chapel of St Biagio has an early Romanesque marble •altar-frontal carved with Biblical symbols, peacocks, and vine branches. To the right in Piazza Garibaldi is the *Palace of the Spanish Governor* with a porticoed façade and clock-tower, at the foot of which is a bust of Garibaldi. On the left of the palace the Corso leads to Piazza del Plebiscito with the *Municipio* decorated with coats of arms and a War Memorial at the centre. The pediment from the temple of Talamone (see above) is exhibited in *Palazzo Comunale* (Piazza della Repubblica), open Sat & Sun 10–12, 16–19.30.

A dyke, 1.5km long, built by Leopoldo II in 1842, joins Orbetello to **MONTE ARGENTARIO** (635m), usually known simply as *L'Argentario*, an almost circular peninsula once covered with thick woods of ilexes and oaks but which has suffered greatly from deforestation and forest fires. It is covered with wild flowers in spring. The beauty of the promontory can best be appreciated from the sea. Porto Santo Stefano and the smaller Porto Ercole are now famous as exclusive holdiay resorts with harbours for yachts and lively fish markets.

From Orbetello a road leads S along the coast of the Argentario past the TOMBOLO DI FENIGLIA a beautiful sandy isthmus 6km long and 1km wide which joins the peninsula to the mainland at the S end of the lagoon of Orbetello. Woods were felled here at the beginning of the 19C, replaced by a forest of pine trees planted at the beginning of this century. It is now one of the finest forests on the coast and is a protected area with a lovely sandy beach (and a 1-star camping site, and a trattoria). It is traversed by a footpath (also open to cyclists) some 7km long. A port for private boats recently constructed at Cala Galera nearby has eroded the coastline.

Porto Ercole (7km from Orbetello), now an important resort (4-star hotel *Il Pellicano*), has a particularly sheltered port with fortifications of the Spanish period. Etruscan in origin, it thrived until the 15C when, through poor administration and the threats of pirates, it fell into decline. Porto Ercole was an important military and naval base of the Spanish *Stato dei Presidi*. At the entrance to the old town is an elegant gate, surmounted by a bell, with a plaque commemorating the painter Caravaggio who is said to have died offshore here in 1610. Steep steps lead up to the parish church and to the ruined Rocca, from which there is an extensive view. Near the seafront is the 16C *Palazzo Consani*, the residence of the Governor, with a view across the harbour towards the modern district of Le Grotte. Towering above Porto Ercole are three impressive fortresses. *Forte Santa Barbara*, to the W, is the largest (26,000 square metres). It was built by the military architect Giovanni Camerini with three circles of walls, a moat and draw-bridge. Opposite are *Forte San Filippo*, a rectangular structure with four triangular bastions and a moat, begun in 1558 by the same architect, and the *Forte Stella*, named after its star-shaped inner fortress.

The road along the N coast of the Argentario from Orbetello leads past the TOMBOLO DI GIANNELLA at the N end of the lagoon of Orbetello (3-star and 2-star camping sites). At *Santa Liberata* there are excavations of a large

Roman villa and fish farm. The road winds along the coast down to the harbour of **Porto Santo Stefano**, 10km W of Orbetello. The port was first developed in the 15C and the Spanish fort dates from 1560. It is now a popular summer resort (APT information office, 55 Corso Umberto; 3-star and 2-star hotels, including 3-star *Villa Domizia* at Santa Liberata; first-class restaurant *Trattoria del Ponte*), but its charm has been greatly impaired by War damage and excessive rebuilding. This is the port for the Isola del Giglio, see below.

A *Strada Panoramica* (39km) encircles the promontory through a varied landscape with interesting vegetation. It provides splendid views. From Porto Santo Stefano it passes along the coast high above cliffs planted with vineyards, olive groves, and orange and lemon trees. The *Cala Grande* is one of the most beautiful bays along the coast. A parapet faces the island of Giglio and provides an ideal point from which to enjoy the sunset. As the road winds round the S side of the promontory the scenery becomes increasingly varied with steep cliffs, rocky bays and grottoes, rocks emerging from the sea and two small islands. The road deteriorates (no guard rails) and is interrupted by an unsurfaced stretch of c 4km which is steep and arduous but worth exploring. There are wild uncultivated areas with occasional watch-towers and houses before the road reaches the bays with the sandy beaches of the grand summer hotels and villas on the approach to Porto Ercole.

A road (13km) diverges from the main road near Orbetello to climb inland up to the *Punto Telegrafo* at the summit. It passes the motherhouse of the Passionist Order, founded by St Paul of the Cross (Paolo Danei, 1694–1775). Eight monks now live here; the small church (1735) has altarpieces by Sebastiano Conca and Pietro Aldi. The road continues through Mediterranean vegetation and ilex woods which shelter numerous wild flowers, with splendid views, to end at a mast and military installations.

From Porto Santo Stefano (see above) car ferries and hydrofoils run frequently (in c 1hr) to the pretty **Isola del Giglio**, 17.5km W. Information from *Toremar* (Tel. 0564/814615) and *Maregiglio* (Tel. 0564/812920). 3-star and 2-star hotels at Campese and Giglio Porto (including 2-star *Pardini's Hermitage*, Cala degli Alberi). 1-star camping site at Sparvieri *Baia del Sole*. Rooms to let at Campese, Castello and Giglio Porto. The island has an area of 21 sq. km and a little grey granite fortess-village (bus from the port), and vineyards. Pathways lead down to the sandy beach from the village. The island is crowded at weekends in summer, and new buildings are spoiling its natural beauty. In 1961 in the bay of Campese a boat was discovered offshore some 50m below the surface, shipwrecked c 600 BC. Its cargo of Greek and Etruscan ceramics, including numerous aryballos and Corinthian ware, wooden flutes, and a rare bronze Corinthian helmet, has mostly been recovered, and in 1985 part of its keel, 3m long, was salvaged. Oxford University has been in charge of the project.

The island of **Giannutri**, to the SE, which has been threatened with tourist development, has ruins of a Roman villa of the family of Domizi Enobardi. Boats from Giglio in summer.

From Orbetello Scalo (see above) the Aurelia continues along the coast. At (198km) a by-road leads right to the resort of **Ansedonia** (3km), on a promontory with elegant villas in thick vegetation. The road ends at the little *port* by the Torre Puccini, where Puccini composed part of 'Tosca'. This is the site of the PORT OF COSA, formerly connected to a lagoon (part of the Lago di Burano), now silted up. The lagoon was connected to the sea by the *Bagno* or *Spacco della Regina* a natural cleft in the rock 260m long; this was later replaced by the so-called *'Tagliata Etrusca'* a shorter channel cut through the rock (still clearly visible), designed also to prevent the silting up of the harbour. A project to construct a port for private boats threatens to damage these interesting remains.

The flat-topped hill (113m) above is the site of the Roman city of **Cosa** (adm. daily 9–14), founded in 273 BC and later called Ansedonia, in a beautiful position with fine views. The usual entrance is by the Porta Fiorentina in the polygonal walls which had 18 towers. Uphill on the left is the Forum, Temple of Concordia, amphitheatre, and curia. Higher up are the Porta a Mare, the Capitolium with two temples, one dedicated to Jupiter and the other (larger with a triple cella) to Mater Matuta, and the third gate. A path returns downhill past the Domus Dominus, the governor's residence and the excellent little museum.

On the other side of the Aurelia a by-road (signposted Villa Romana) leads inland past the ruins of a Roman villa (*delle Colonne*) whose interesting perimeter wall has unusual cylindrical towers. The road continues for c 1km; the second road on the left (unsurfaced) mounts a small hill (not signposted; keep left) to a house in pine trees, beside which a sign for the *scavi archeologici* indicates the overgrown ruins of the Roman villa of *Settefinestre* in a romantic setting (on the hillside below, beside a fence). Excavations (some of them since covered over) in 1976–81 by student volunteers from Tuscany and London revealed remains of a large villa of the 1C BC (probably abandoned by the mid 2C AD), with farm buildings attached. Numerous rooms with geometric mosaic floors were identified, and part of its front wall (3.5–4.5m high), as well as wall-paintings of the second and fourth Pompeian style. The farm (with wine and olive presses, and buildings thought to have been used as pigsties) appears to have been run by slaves whose modest quarters have also been found. The visible remains, now abandoned, include the high wall with buttresses and arches.

The Aurelia continues towards Rome, and, at 207km, is the turning for **Capalbio** (3-star hotel *Bargello*; first-class restaurants *Da Maria* and *Da Carla*; trattoria *Toscana*), well seen from the main road, a charming little medieval village, 6km NE, which has recently become fashionable as an exclusive summer resort. It is in a beautiful position on a low hill above thick ilex, cork, and oak woods once typical of the Maremma, in the centre of a game reserve. The area is famous for its wild boar (fair in September). The walkway along the walls can be followed on two levels. The grave of Domenico Tiburzi, the most famous brigand of the Maremma, lies half in and half out of the cemetery. A legendary figure, the terror of upper Lazio and the Maremma, he was finally caught and shot in 1896 aged 60, after being on the run for 24 years. At *Pescia Fiorentina*, 9km E, an old iron foundry survives, of great interest to industrial archaeologists (there are long-term plans to restore it). It also has a modern sculpture garden known as the *Giardino dei Tarocchi*. On the other side of the Aurelia is Capalbio station, and across the railway line, by an old red farmhouse, is the LAGO DI BURANO, a marshy lagoon 4km long at the S limit of the Tuscan Maremma. It has an area of some 300 hectares and is now a bird sanctuary administered by the World Wildlife Fund, where a remarkable variety of birds can be seen from September to April (on Sundays at 10 & 14.30; Tel. 0564/898829). The Torre di Buranaccio here dates from the 15C. There is a fine beach at *Chiarone* to the E. The Aurelia now leaves Tuscany to enter Lazio. It crosses the Fiora just before (226km) Montalto di Castro and the turning for the interesting Etruscan remains of Vulci, described in *Blue Guide Rome and environs*.

13

Florence to Siena: the Chianti

The fastest route between Florence and Siena is the superstrada (56km) which starts S of Florence beside the 'Certosa' exit of the A1 motorway, and reaches Siena on its N outskirts. It runs roughly parallel to the Cassia (N2; described in Rte 13B) and has exits at all the main places of interest. It is a poorly engineered road, with no emergency lane, and is usually very busy. It has no service stations. If time permits, by far the pleasantest approach to Siena from Florence is by one or other of the routes described below.

A. The Via Chiantigiana

The Via Chiantigiana road derives its name from the hilly region between Florence and Siena known as the **Chianti** district. Here the world-famous red wine called Chianti Classico is produced from a careful blend of white and black grapes perfected over many centuries including Sangiovese, Canaiolo, Malvasia del Chianti, and Trebbiano Toscano. This ruby-coloured wine is generally considered the best of the Tuscan Chianti wines. Only Chianti grown in a limited geographical area (including San Casciano Val di Pesa, Greve, Castellina, Radda, and Gaiole) can be called Classico, and bear the black cock (*gallo nero*) trademark. Among the less famous but most genuine wines of this area are *Castello di Ama* and *Nozzole*.

The road traverses beautiful countryside past vineyards and olive groves surrounding the typical, elegant farmhouses known as *case coloniche*. Many of these were built in the 18C during the agricultural reforms carried out by the Grand-duke Pietro Leopoldo, and they are often splendidly sited with characteristic towers (formerly dovecots). Some of them have been carefully restored in the last few decades, often by foreigners, and Chianti has become a fashionable place to live. Also in this area are many old Romanesque churches (*pieve*) and feudal castles. For those with time and their own transport, it is well worth deviating from the route described below to explore the magnificent countryside, which is perhaps at its most beautiful in October and November when the range of autumn colours offered by the great variety of deciduous trees contrasts with the pines and cypresses, and the golden vines alternate with silver olive trees, often planted in reddish soil. At this time the sky can be either bright blue or animated by striking clouds and, at sunset, an unforgettable sight.

Information Offices. APT of Florence (Tel. 055/290832) for Impruneta, Greve, and Panzano; and APT of Siena (Tel. 0577/280551) for Radda, Gaiole, Castellina in Chianti, and Castelnuovo Berardenga.

Road, N222, 70km.—10km *Grassina*—17km turning for **Impruneta** (4km)—18km *Strada*—29km **Greve in Chianti**—37km *Panzano*—39km turning for **Radda in Chianti** (10km), *Badia di Coltibuono* (19km), and **Gaiole in Chianti** (24km)—49km **Castellina in Chianti**—60km *Quercegrossa*—70km **Siena**.

Buses. To Impruneta services run by CAP c every hour from Florence (Largo Alinari, off Piazza della Stazione) in 40mins. Frequent services run by SITA from Florence (SITA bus station, on Piazza Stazione) to Greve in 1hr. Some services leave Florence by Porta Romana, and run via Galluzzo and the Cassia as far as Terme di Firenze, and others leave Florence by Piazza Beccaria, and run via Ponte a Ema, Grassina, Ugolino, and Strada in Chianti.

From Greve the bus continues to Panzano (and, infrequently, to Lamole, Radda and Castellina). Another SITA service (once or twice a day) via Grassina, Greve, and Panzano to Radda and Gaiole (in 2hrs).

Accommodation. There are a number of fine hotels in beautiful quiet positions in the country, mostly 3-star and 4-star, and nearly all of them with swimming pools. There is a scarcity of cheaper hotels and camping sites, although numerous localities offer *Agriturism* accommodation. Restaurants also tend to be expensive in the Chianti region. In many of the larger estates the wine cellars may be visited, and wine purchased.

Florence is left by Piazza Ferrucci at the S end of Ponte San Niccolò (Pl. 12). The road signposted to Grassina traverses a piazza in front of the BADIA A RIPOLI, a pretty 16C porticoed church flanked by its tall campanile. A Benedictine convent, founded in 790, it became a Vallombrosan monastery in the 12C. Since its suppression in 1808 it has been a parish church. The interior, enlarged in 1598, has a Latin-cross plan with a crypt. It was restored to its original state in 1930 when the later painted decoration and stucco-work was destroyed. The altarpieces include: Agostino Veracini, St John Gualberto (c 1744); Nicodemo Ferrucci, Crucifixion and saints; Jacopo Vignali, Madonna and Child (1630); Giovanni Camillo Sagrestani, Scene from the life of Countess Matilda (1706), and Francesco Curradi, Madonna and Child in glory. In the sacristy are fine inlaid cupboards and a frescoed frieze attributed to Bernardino Poccetti (1585).

From the S end of the piazza the Chiantigiana leads to (5km) *Ponte a Ema*. At the crossroads (Croce del Carota) a by-road leads left in 1km to the ORATORIO DI SANTA CATERINA DELL'ANTELLA (key with the veterinary clinic next door). The stone façade was originally frescoed (the lunette over the doorway representing the Madonna and Child by Spinello Aretino is in the Depositi delle Gallerie Fiorentine). The nave is divided into two bays with cross-vaults containing figures of the Evangelists. On the walls is a *cycle of frescoes of the life of St Catherine by Spinello Aretino (c 1390). Flanking the apse are figures of Saints Anthony and Catherine attributed to Pietro Nelli (c 1360). Another cycle of frescoes of c 1360, also devoted to St Catherine and attributed to the Master of Barberino decorates the apse. The original altarpiece by Agnolo Gaddi has been removed.

The Chiantigiana (N222) continues S passing beneath the motorway at San Piero a Ema. 10km **Grassina**, a large village which is noted for its Good Friday Passion play. The golf-course at (14km) *Ugolino* (18 holes) was created in 1933 to satisfy the British colony in Florence (the first golf course was made in the grounds of one of the Demidoff properties in 1889). The Club House was built by Gherardo Bosio and the greens beautifully landscaped between olive trees, cypresses, and pines. Impruneta appears in the distance on the range of hills to the right and is reached via a by-road (4km) which diverges from this road just before (18km) Strada.

Impruneta (correctly, L'Impruneta; 275m), is a large village (13,600 inhab.) on a plateau, where the great cattle fair of St Luke is still celebrated (mid-October), although it has now become a general fair. 2-star camping site open in summer at Bottai *Camping Internazionale*; restaurant *I Tre Pini* at Pozzolatico. The clay in the soil has been used for centuries to produce terracotta for which the locality is famous. The kilns here still sell beautiful pottery (flower pots, floor tiles, etc). In the large central piazza (where the fair is held) is the COLLEGIATA (*Santa Maria dell'Impruneta*), with a high 13C tower, and an elegant portico by Gherardo Silvani (1634).

The INTERIOR was restored, after severe bomb damage in 1944, to its Renaissance aspect which it acquired in the mid-15C under the Pievano Antonio degli Agli. SOUTH SIDE. First altar, Cristofano Allori, martyrdom of St Lawrence; second altar, Passignano, Birth of the Virgin. In the nave chapel, bronze Crucifix attributed to Giambologna. At the entrance to the presbytery are two CHAPELS (c 1452) by Michelozzo, with beautiful *deco-ration in enamelled terracotta by Luca Della Robbia. They were recon-structed and restored after bomb damage. The chapel on the right was built to protect a relic of the True Cross given to the church by Pippo Spano in 1426. It contains an enamelled terracotta ceiling and an exquisite relief of the Crucifixion with the Virgin and St John in a tabernacle, flanked by the figures of St John the Baptist and a bishop saint. Beneath is a charming predella of adoring angels. The chapel on the left protects a miraculous painting of the Virgin traditionally attributed to St Luke which was ploughed up by a team of oxen in a field near Impruneta. For centuries it was taken to Florence to help the city in times of trouble. It had to be 'restored' in the 18C by the English painter Ignazio Hugford. The beautiful ceiling is similar to the one in the other chapel. The frieze of fruit on the exterior incorporates two reliefs of the Madonna and Child. The figures of Saints Luke and Paul flank a tabernacle which contains the image of the Madonna and Child (usually covered; exposed only on religious festivals). The silver altar frontal designed by Giovanni Battista Foggini replaces a 15C relief now exhibited in the treasury (see below). The large high altarpiece (1375) was partially recomposed after it was shattered in the War. It is the work of Tommaso del Mazza and Pietro Nelli. On the N side of the nave are 16C inlaid stalls and a 15C cantoria. In the baptistery is a late-16C font with a 14C relief of the Baptism of Christ. A door beneath the portico on the right leads into two CLOISTERS; off the second (left) is the little CRYPT (11C), with sculptural fragments.

The TREASURY (entrance on the left of the church door; adm. Friday, 10–13, Saturday 15–18.30; Sunday 10–13, 15–18.30; in summer: Thursday and Friday 10–13, Saturday and Sunday 10–13, 16–19.30). Above the portico of the church are displayed a gilded silver *Cross attributed to Lorenzo Ghiberti (c 1420–25); two paxes attributed to Antonio di Salvi; a Cross of the 13C and 14C; fifteen silver votive vases of 1633; and 17C and 18C church silver. The marble schiacciato relief attributed to a follower of Donatello shows the discovery of the miraculous painting of the Madonna of Impruneta (see above). In two other rooms are displayed eleven illumi-nated *choirbooks including one attributed to Lippo di Benivieni (c 1310–20), five attributed to the bottega of Pacino di Bonaguida (mid 14C), and three by Antonio di Girolamo da Ugolino (1537–39). The patchwork cushion and linen and silk veil were found in the tomb of Bishop Antonio degli Agli (died 1477) in 1944. Vestments are to be exhibited in another room.

The Chiantigiana (see above) continues to (18km) *Strada*, where the Romanesque church of San Cristofano has a Crucifix by the school of Donatello. The road leads across the *Passo dei Pecorai* (344m; 2-star hotel *Da Omero* and trattoria *Casprini da Omero*). At the crossroads (21km) of *Le Bolle* a by-road leads uphill to *Vicchiomaggio* (1km), a medieval castle, where the wine cellars may be visited. 29km **Greve in Chianti**, a pretty market town (10,000 inhab.), is one of the centres of the wine trade (an annual fair is held in the third week of September). 3-star hotel *Del Chianti*, 86 Piazza Matteotti (with swimming pool), and *Agriturist* farmhouses in the vicinity. Restaurant *Bottega del Moro* and trattoria *Borgo Antico* at Lucolena, 7km E. Greve has a particularly attractive triangular piazza with ample terraces above porticoes and a monument to Giovanni da Verrazzano (died 1528), the explorer of the North American coast. In Piazza Matteotti is a little puppet theatre which gives regular performances for children in summer. A by-road leads W to the charming little village of *Montefioralle* (1.5km), the birthplace of the Vespucci family. It is perched on a hill, and partly surrounded by its old walls, and has remains of a medieval castle (trattoria *Taverna del Guerrino*). In the church of Santo Stefano are a large 13C icon of the Madonna and Child by a Florentine painter, and the Trinity with four saints and an Annunciation with Saints John the Baptist and Stephen, both 15C Florentine works. An unsurfaced road branches off beyond the village to *San Cresci*, an unusual Romanesque church in a beautiful position, and continues, through woods, to Badia di Passignano (5km; see Rte 13B).

37km **Panzano** (478m), originally a medieval castle, has partly preserved its old walls and towers. 3-star hotels *Villa Sangiovese*, 5 Piazza Bucciarelli (with swimming pool) and *Villa Le Barone* (with swimming pool), 19 Via San Leolino. The church of Santa Maria (completely renovated a century ago) has a late Gothic Madonna and Child framed by a painting of saints and angels attributed to Bernardo di Stefano Rosselli. In the nearby oratory is an Annunciation attributed to Michele di Ridolfo del Ghirlandaio. Just beyond Panzano is its pieve, *San Leolino*, beautifully situated on a hill. The simple Romanesque church has a 16C porch and three naves with three apses. It contains an *altarpiece of the Madonna between Saints Peter and Paul, and stories from their lives, attributed to Meliore di Jacopo (mid-13C), a triptych by the Maestro di Panzano (15C), a Madonna enthroned with two angels by the 15C Florentine school, a polyptych (over the high altar) by Mariotto di Nardo (dated 1421), and two glazed terracotta tabernacles attributed to Giovanni Della Robbia. On the left wall is a reliquary bust of St Euphrosynus (a local saint who was venerated in a nearby oratory). The church gives on to a 15C cloister.

39km. An alternative (but much longer) route (N429, N408, N484; 68km) to Siena diverges left from the Chiantigiana via Radda and Gaiole (described below). It traverses beautiful countryside in the heart of the Chianti region.

6km. By-road left for the **Castello di Volpaia** (3km; 617m) in a splendid panoramic position. Trattoria *Podere Terreno alla Via della Volpaia*, 21 Via di Volpaia. Volpaia was once a hostel for pilgrims, and wine has been produced here since the 11C. In the tiny fortified hamlet there is a small Renaissance church called *La Commenda*. Modern art exhibitions are held here in September. 10km **Radda in Chianti**, another major wine centre. The surrounding district can be explored in all directions to enjoy the wonderfully varied and beautiful countryside. 4-star hotel *Relais Vignale* (with swimming pool), and *Agriturist* farmhouses. Trattoria *Le Vigne*, Podere le Vigne. Radda preserves parts of its walls and fortifications which encircle the medieval town. The Palazzo Comunale has numerous coats of arms on its façade and a 15C Florentine fresco of the Madonna and Child. Opposite are steps leading to the church of San Niccolò with a 15C Crucifix. Outside the town is the 15C convent of San Francesco with a later portico.

Three kilometres E of Radda the main road for Siena turns S, but the more interesting route continues E for (19km) **Badia di Coltibuono**, a Vallombrosan abbey, built on the site of an 8C hermitage, surrounded by beautiful oak and pine woods. The monastery has been transformed into a villa (with a restaurant and wine cellars). The main structure in grey stone dates from the 11–12C and it has an impressive crenellated tower; the church may be visited. At a crossroads near the Badia, N408 leads S to (24km) **Gaiole in Chianti**, another traditional centre of the wine industry. 4-star hotels with swimming pools: *Castello di Spaltenna*, and *Residence San Sano* at Lecchi, 6km S, and numerous *Agriturist* farmhouses. Just beyond, on a hill to the right, is the medieval castle of *Vertine*. Opposite, on the left, an unsurfaced road climbs up to the village of *Barbischio*, picturesquely perched on a hill in a setting of rocks and wild vegetation. 27km. By-road on the left for the impressive castle of *Meleto* (1km), one of the best preserved in the Chianti district. It has two massive circular towers dominating extensive vineyards. 30km. The direct road for Siena (53km) continues S while N484 diverges left for (35km) the crossroads of the Madonna di Brolio where a cypress avenue leads to the *Castle of Brolio*, the home of the Ricasoli family since the 12C, and well-known for its wine. Strategically placed at the S end of the Chianti hills, it was for centuries disputed between Florence and Siena. Its impressive fortifications, dating in part from the 15–16C, were heavily restored in the 19C and the house rebuilt in 1860 in Sienese Gothic style (open daily 9–12, 15–18). The 14C chapel has a modern mosaic on the façade and contains a polyptych by Ugolino di Nerio (14C); in the crypt are the family tombs. Bettino Ricasoli, the eminent statesman and philanthropist, died here in 1880. The magnificent view to the S stretches from Monte Amiata to Siena and the hills beyond.

N484 continues S past (42km) a by-road for *San Gusmé* (1km), on a hill, one of the most picturesque villages in the area. An excellent white wine ('Val d'Arbia') is produced in this area. The main road passes the splendid 18C Villa Chigi (the gardens are open fest. 10–dusk) on the outskirts of (47km) **Castelnuovo Berardenga**, where the church of Santi Giusto e Clemente has a *Madonna and Child signed and dated 1426 by Giovanni di Paolo. 4-star hotel *Borgo San Felice*, with swimming pool; and trattoria *Bottega del Trenta*. Trattoria *Nonna Luisa* at Corsignano. 51km Junction with the main road (N326) from Arezzo to Siena. 58km By-road for *Montaperti* (signposted right for Colle di Montaperti), the hill (3km) where the Florentine Guelf army was defeated by Siena on 4 September 1260. A pyramid commemorates the battle. Nearby is the *Pieve di Sant'Ansano* (founded in the 7C). A footpath leads to an octagonal chapel over the spot where the saint was martyred. 68km **Siena**, see Rte 14.

The Chiantigiana winds downhill and crosses the river Pesa before climbing again with spectacular views of woods, vineyards, olive groves, and scattered *case coloniche*. 49km **Castellina in Chianti** (578m), a small medieval town, with a 15C castle and town gate, which dominates the Arbia, Elsa, and Pesa valleys. In the vicinity are a number of hotels with swimming pools: *Villa Casalecchi*, *Tenuta di Ricavo* (both 4-star); *Belvedere di San Leonino*, *Salivolpi* (both 3-star), and numerous *Agriturist* farmhouses. 2-star camping site *Luxor Quies* open in summer. Trattoria *La Torre* in Piazza del Comune. Castellina has a modern suburb which meets the demands of the expanding wine trade. In the parish church (rebuilt after the last War) is a detached fresco of the Madonna and Child by Lorenzo di Bicci, and the shrine of St Fausto, invoked in times of torrential rain or drought.

A by-road leads to Radda (see above; 10km) passing the impressive Etruscan tomb of *Montecalvario* (7C BC) surrounded by pine trees on the left just outside Castellina.

FROM CASTELLINA TO POGGIBONSI (20km). This is a particularly beautiful road. 15km. On the left is the little 12C Romanesque church of *San Pietro a Cedda*, with a carved architrave over the front and side doors, a square bell-tower, and an apse decorated with blind arcades. The simple *interior (open only for Mass on Saturday at 17.30, and Sunday at 10.30) is entirely built of stone, with a timber roof. A large transversal arch resting on the elaborately carved capitals of two half columns divides the nave. The apse has a lancet window and delicately carved decoration. There are two frescoes of saints (15C) and a reproduction of a triptych of the Madonna and Child with saints of the 15C Florentine school (the original has been removed to the Museo Civico of Colle Val d'Elsa). A little beyond is a fine view of the castle of Strozzavolpe on a hill to the left (described in Rte 13B).

The main road now runs along a ridge from which can be enjoyed a variety of extensive views before descending to (60km) *Quercegrossa*. The village has a restored Romanesque church with a moving Pietà group in painted terracotta by Francesco di Giorgio Martini and an assistant (probably Giacomo Cozzarelli). At 64km a by-road (6km) leads through beautiful country to the *Certosa di Pontignano*, a monastery founded in 1343 with three High Renaissance cloisters. It is now attached to Siena University and used for conferences. The church (at present closed for restoration) contains frescoes by Bernardino Poccetti. From the road is a splendid view of Siena beyond undulating fields and vineyards. The Chiantigiana continues into (70km) **Siena**, see Rte 14.

B. The Via Cassia

Information Offices. APT of Florence (Tel. 055/290832) for San Casciano Val di Pesa and Tavarnelle; and APT of Siena (Tel. 0577/280551) for Poggibonsi and Monteriggioni.

This route follows the last stretch of the **Via Cassia**, the Roman road, paved c 154 BC, built from Rome to Florence (for the Cassia S of Siena, see Rte 20). Although longer than the superstrada which follows it closely, it offers the advantage of passing through beautiful and varied countryside and many places of interest.

Road, N2, 70km.—18km **San Casciano in Val di Pesa**—27km turning for *San Donato in Poggio* (8km) and *Badia a Passignano* (5.5km)—32km **Tavarnelle in Val di Pesa**—34.5km *Barberino Val d'Elsa*—44km **Poggibonsi**—50.5km *Staggia*—55.5km **Monteriggioni**—70km **Siena**.

Buses. Frequent services run by SITA. From Florence via Porta Romana, Galluzzo, San Casciano, San Donato in Poggio, to Tavarnelle in 1hr 20mins; also via Sant'Andrea in Percussina to San Casciano and Mercatale. From Florence via Porta Romana, Galluzzo, Poggibonsi, Colle Val d'Elsa and Monteriggioni to Siena in 1hr 40mins. From Florence (non-stop) via the superstrada to Siena many times a day in 1hr 15mins.

Florence is left by Porta Romana (Pl. 13, 14). Via Senese continues past the Certosa del Galluzzo (see Rte 2), and at the superstrada and motorway roundabout N2 begins. It traverses (7km) *Tavarnuzze*, and, just beyond, a road diverges right for Sant'Andrea in Percussina.

This road leads through a wood to the hamlet of **Sant'Andrea in Percussina** (3km; first-class restaurant *Scopeti*) with the *Albergaccio* where Niccolò Machiavelli lived in exile from 1513 and wrote *Il Principe*; the hostelry here succeeds the one frequented by the politician and writer. The Romanesque church of Sant'Andrea has an elegant Renaissance interior with a small dome, a Presentation in the Temple by Pietro Confortini (1606) and some fragmentary frescoes (14–15C). The road continues past Spedaletto to a path left leading to *Santa Maria a Casavecchia*, a Romanesque church beautifully situated with a view of Brunelleschi's dome in the distance. Inside is a relief of the Assumption in glazed terracotta by Benedetto Buglioni (c 1515). This road rejoins the Cassia just N of San Casciano (see below).

N2 follows the river Greve and passes the *US Military Cemetery* where are buried 4403 American soldiers who died in service N of Rome in 1944–45. It continues past the public swimming pool at the *Terme di Firenze* and then begins to wind uphill. A by-road to the left (signposted) leads to the Romanesque church of *Santa Cecilia a Decimo* (5km). A church existed here in the time of Charlemagne, but the present structure, including an impressive bell-tower, dates from the 12C. The portico was added in the 16C. The interior, elegantly decorated with stucco-work (1728) has three naves divided by arches resting on pilasters. Over the altar is a Madonna and Child with Saints Lawrence and Cecilia by Michele di Ridolfo del Ghirlandaio. The panel of the Madonna and Child in the nave is by Cenni di Francesco. Behind the church are picturesque old farm buildings.

18km **San Casciano in Val di Pesa** is a small town (14,500 inhab.) situated on a hill (310m) which dominates the beautiful hilly landscape of the Chianti district with extensive views all around. Pro-Loco tourist office, Tel. 055/210895; 3-star hotel *L'Antica Posta*; trattorie: *Cantinetta del Nonno*, 18 Via IV Novembre; *Nello*, 64 Via IV Novembre; and *Matteuzzi*, 8 Via Certaldese. The road continues to a car park with steps to the town centre. Inside the walls it is a short walk to Piazza Pierozzi with a clock-tower under which is an arch leading to the *Collegiata*, rebuilt in 1793 on the site of a Romanesque church. Over the baptismal font is a fresco of the Madonna and Child with Saints John the Baptist and Stephen by an early 15C Florentine master. Above the high altar is a painted wood Crucifix by the workshop of Baccio da Montelupo, and, in the choir, Glory of St Cassiano by Luigi Pistocchi. On the altar to the left, Madonna and Child, a detached fresco (c 1500), and on the left wall of the nave, Annunciation by Fra Paolino. In Via Roma is the church of *Santa Maria del Gesù* (known as 'Il Suffraggio') where a *MUSEO D'ARTE SACRA was opened in 1989 (adm. Saturday 16.30–19; fest. 10–12.30, 16–19). It contains works from San Casciano and from many of the nearby country churches. Inside, on the high altar, Madonna and Child by Lippo di Benivieni, and other 15C and 16C paintings including a Coronation of the Virgin by Neri di Bicci (1481). Behind the altar, a 14C Sienese wood Crucifix and four gilded bronze processional Crosses (14–15C). In a little room on the right, polychrome marble statue of the Madonna and Child inscribed Gino Micheli (1341). In the nuns' choir are important works including a Madonna and Child by Ambrogio Lorenzetti and the San Michele altarpiece, a rare 13C Florentine work, attributed to Coppo di Marcovaldo, both from the church of Sant' Angelo l'Abate at Vico l'Abate, Master of the Horne Triptych, Madonna and Child; Master of San Lucchese, painted Crucifix; end wall, Simone Pignoni, Martyrdom of St Lucy; Master of San Iacopo a Mucciana, triptych of the Madonna and Child with saints (1398); Cenni di Francesco, Madonna and Child. In the centre is a marble pedestal, possibly of a baptismal font, composed of carvings representing the Annunciation, Nativity, and Annunciation to the Shepherds, attributed to the Master of Cabestany (French or Spanish, second decade of the 12C). Seven cases contain church silver, vestments, etc.

From Piazza Pierozzi Via Morrocchesi leads past some interesting buildings to the church of the *Misericordia* (Santa Maria del Prato), a 14C Gothic church rebuilt in the late 16C (if closed, entrance through the Confraternity). It contains a fine collection of *works (well labelled) including a painted Crucifix with the mourning Virgin and St John by Simone Martini (c 1325); Madonna and Child (behind the high altar) by Ugolino di Nerio, who also painted the St Peter and St Francis; Ecstasy of St Francis by Francesco Furini; Madonna of the Rosary and Circumcision by Jacopo Vignali; marble pulpit with the Annunciation by Giovanni di Balduccio (1339). Outside the old walls, next to a terrace with a fine view, is *San Francesco* with a bell tower (1492). The church was rebuilt and the portico added in the 18C. In the interior, on the left, is an altarpiece of the Madonna and Child between Saints Francis and Mary Magdalen by Biagio d'Antonio, and, right, a Sienese Crucifix (c 1360).

FROM SAN CASCIANO TO CERBAIA, 6.5km. The road passes several Romanesque churches in picturesque settings with attractive views. They are generally open only for services on Sunday morning, but at other times ring at the priest's house. Most of their contents have been removed for safe keeping to the Museum in San Casciano (see above). Just outside San Casciano a narrow by-road diverges steeply left (signposted *Vivai Orlandi*) to *Santa Maria ad Argiano*, a Romanesque church largely rebuilt in the 18C. 2.5km Road (right) for *San Martino ad Argiano*. The Romanesque church façade has terracotta decorations and an 18C portico. Next to it is the Oratory of the Santissima Annunziata, which has fine 17C furniture, an Annunciation by Cesare Dandini and a painting of Saints Augustine, Ambrose, and Carlo Borromeo by Fabrizio Boschi. 3.5km. A cypress avenue leads to the villa and church of *San Pietro a Montepaldi*, with a simple Romanesque façade and Baroque interior. Beyond (4.5km) *Talente*, a by-road leads left to *San Giovanni in Sugana*, one of the oldest and most important Romanesque churches in the diocesis of Florence. It was considerably restored and provided with a cupola in the 16C. It contains some glazed terracotta works by the Della Robbia and Buglioni, and a Crucifixion by Pier Dandini. It preserves parts of its original structure and has an elegant 16C cloister with an upper loggia, carved doorways and a two-light Romanesque window. At (6.5km) **Cerbaia** this road meets the Via Volterrana described in Rte 15.

FROM SAN CASCIANO TO CERTALDO, 22km. The pretty road, which diverges right from the Cassia just S of San Casciano, winds upwards to the tiny village (7km) of **San Pancrazio**. In a little piazza at the top of the hill is the Romanesque *Pieve* (10C) beside a fortified tower (the key may be obtained from the priest's house next door). It has a 17C portico, and three naves divided by pilasters (restored). The paintings include a Madonna and Child attributed to Taddeo Gaddi, and a Crucifixion by Santi di Tito, 1590. The road continues to (12km) **Lucardo**, in a beautiful position on a hill. The charming church of San Martino (key from the adjacent canonica) was renewed inside in the Baroque period and decorated with stuccowork. Behind the main altar is a Madonna and Child with Saints Peter, John the Baptist, Martin, and Justus attributed to Ridolfo del Ghirlandaio and a Madonna and Child with saints by an anonymous 17C Florentine artist. The nearby castle, commanding a fine view, with a tower and parts of the walls still extant, is recorded from the 8C. 16km Beyond a fine *casa colonica* with a tower is an unsurfaced road to the left which leads to the **Pieve di San Lazzaro a Lucardo**, dating from the late 11C and one of the finest examples of early Romanesque architecture in the Florentine area. It is surrounded by medieval buildings and has a massive tower (the upper part is restored) next to the remains of the former cloister. The church is built entirely of sandstone and has a basilican plan with three naves divided into seven bays by thick pilasters, and a raised chancel terminating in three apses. The crypt was discovered during restoration work. There are frescoes on the left wall and on two pilasters by Cenni di Francesco. The portico over the entrance dates from the 19C. The road continues through rolling countryside with a view of San Gimignano as it approaches (22km) **Certaldo**, see Rte 15.

A pretty road leads from San Casciano to Mercatale (5km) passing the 16C Villa Le Corti, attributed to Santi di Tito, and, beyond *Calcinaia*, a chapel, formerly belonging to the Strozzi family, with a fresco of the Pietà attributed to Bronzino. Just before Mercatale an unsurfaced road diverges left to *Luiano* (2.5km), a group of houses including a villa near the small Romanesque church of Sant'Andrea (11C) at the top of a footpath. A fresco of the Presentation of the rule of St Clare to St Francis (mid-14C Florentine school) is due to be detached and removed to the San Casciano museum. 2km beyond *Mercatale* (Restaurant *Il Salotto del Chianti*), at the crossroads known as Le Quattro Strade, the road to the right leads past an old fortified farmhouse to *Santo Stefano a Campoli*, a 10C church, with a 17C portico. Inside (key in the afternoons from the house next door) are a Madonna and Child with saints, attributed to Giuliano Bugiardini and a Madonna and Child with the infant St John by the 15C Florentine school. From Le Quattro Strade a road leads E to join the road from Impruneta to Greve (see Rte 13A).

The Cassia continues S past *Bargino* (first-class fish restaurant *del Pesce*). At 27km a road branches left for San Donato in Poggio and Badia a Passignano.

The by-road leads S and then another pretty by-road (signposted) leads left uphill to **Badia a Passignano** (5km; 341m; restaurant and pizzeria *La Scuderia*; and 1st-class restaurant *La Cantinetta* at Rignana, 3km S), in a delightful setting, enclosed by cypress trees and surrounded by vineyards and olive groves. A chamber music festival is held here at Pentecost (early June); information from the *Amici della Musica*, Tavarnelle Val di Pesa (Tel. 055/8076426). The monastery was founded in 1049 by St Giovanni Gualberto, a Benedictine monk who fought against simony in the Church and created the Vallombrosan Order. He died at Badia a Passignano in 1073. The tall medieval tower survives, but the rest of the building was reconstructed in the late 19C, when the crenellations were added to the walls. A cypress avenue leads to the main entrance, while a flight of stone steps approaches the little village church of SAN BIAGIO (14C), with remains of 15C frescoes inside. The abbey church (see below) has a simple stone façade dating from the mid-13C.

An arched doorway leads to the MONASTERY (open on Saturdays and Sundays; or on request) through a terrace with an Italianate garden on the right. The façade and towers date from the end of the last century when, after the monastic suppressions, the monastery was privately owned. The return of the small Vallombrosan community here dates from 1986. The CLOISTER, access to which is through a fine 15C stone doorway with a carved and inlaid door, was begun by the architect Jacopo Rosselli in 1470. The upper storey loggia, which was closed in and provided with windows in the 18C, has frescoes of the life of St Benedict by Filippo d'Antonio Filippelli (1483). From the cloister there is a view of the bell-tower, completed in 1297, and the red brick dome added in 1602. The large 15C REFECTORY has a *cenacolo, a life-size fresco representing the Last Supper, painted by Domenico and Davide Ghirlandaio in 1476. The two lunettes above of Adam and Eve driven out of Paradise and Cain slaying Abel are by Bernardo Rosselli. There are also remains of other frescoes and a monumental fireplace.

A small CHAPEL, with a fresco of the Annunciation by Filippelli, has stairs to the CHURCH. The interior, originally Romanesque, was remodelled in the late 16C. The choir-stalls were carved by a Vallombrosan monk, Michele Confetto, in 1549; the two paintings decorating them of the Nativity and the three Archangels are by Michele di Ridolfo del Ghirlandaio. The SACRISTY, off the S transept, dates from the 15C. It contains a stone tabernacle with painted wood shutters made for St Giovanni Gualberto's *reliquary bust. This superb work is composed of a silver and silver gilt head made in Siena in the 14C to which was added, slightly later, the supporting base decorated with scenes from the saint's life in coloured enamel within gilt pinnacled frames. In 1598–1602 Domenico Cresti, a native of the village, and known as *Il Passignano* remodelled the E end of the church creating three chapels, a transept and a dome (frescoed by Giuseppe Nicola Nasini in 1706). Passignano decorated the *central chapel with the fresco of God the Father in Glory in the vault, the four Cardinal Virtues in the spandrels, and the Evangelists in painted niches. He also painted the three large altarpieces representing the Apparition of St Michael on Mount Gargano (S wall), the Apparition of the Madonna (centre), and St Michael defeating Lucifer (N wall). The statues of Saints Peter and Paul are by Andrea Ferruzzi. The chapel on the right is dedicated to St Sebastian and St Atto, a Vallombrosan abbot. All the paintings, including the frescoes in the S transept illustrating the life of Atto are by Benedetto Veli (1600). The *North Chapel is dedicated to St Giovanni Gualberto and contains his tomb beneath the reclining marble figure by Giovanni Caccini (1580). The design of the chapel and the Glory of the saint frescoed in the vault are by Alessandro Allori (1580), who also painted, with assistants, the scenes of the saint's life in the N transept, and the large fresco of the transportation of the relics, depicting numerous portraits among the clergy and congregation. The altarpiece of the chapel which shows Pope Celestino III proclaiming the saint's canonisation in 1193 is by Giuseppe Nicola Nasini (1709). The two other altarpieces, the Ordeal by Fire of St Peter Igneus (right) and Giovanni Gualberto forgiving his brother's murderer and praying before the Crucifix of San Miniato (left) are by Giovanni Butteri (1600). Steps lead down to the small 10C crypt.

The main road continues past *Sambuca* (2-star hotel *Torricelle Zucchi*) and then climbs uphill through a wood. Just before reaching San Donato a turning to the right leads to *Morrocco* (2km). A short road leads up (left) to the Carmelite convent of *Santa Maria del Carmine*, founded in 1481. The church is flanked by a loggia with remains of 15C frescoes. Inside is a glazed terracotta lunette of the Annunciation by Andrea Della Robbia and a portrait of Niccolò di Giovanni Sernigi, founder of the convent, attributed to Luca Della Robbia. The most important paintings, including several panels by Neri di Bicci, have been removed to the Museum of Tavarnelle (see below). A venerated 13C icon formerly on the high altar was stolen in 1980.

San Donato in Poggio (first-class restaurant *La Toppa*) is 8km from the Cassia. Just outside the village is the PIEVE, a beautiful Romanesque church of the late 12C, with three apses, built out of large blocks of cream-coloured *alberese* stone. The upper part of the square crenellated tower is of darker pietraforte stone. Simple piers divide the interior into three naves, the central nave being considerably higher than the side aisles. A little chapel on the right contains a *baptismal font by Giovanni Della Robbia (1513) with reliefs of the life of St John the Baptist, and a small collection of paintings among which is a Coronation of the Virgin by Giovanni del Biondo. Over the high altar is a painted 15C Crucifix. A steep incline leads to the main street which traverses the fortified medieval village of San Donato. The central piazzetta has an elegant Renaissance palace and, behind the well, in the right-hand corner, a Romanesque oratory known as the Compagnia, built of brick with an oculus on the façade. Farther on are remains of the old walls and a gateway with picturesque views.

About 1km beyond the Pieve, on the Castellina road, is the sanctuary of the *Madonna di Pietracupa* (open daily at 11), a late-Renaissance church (1595) surrounded by a portico. The simple Latin-cross interior has the main altar and transept carved in pietra serena, and three altarpieces by Passignano; the one on the high altar surrounds a venerated image of the Madonna. The beautiful road continues to Castellina in Chianti (10km; see Rte 13A) along a ridge with magnificent views across the Elsa valley towards San Gimignano and the hills beyond.

32km. On the outskirts of **Tavarnelle**, on the left, some 500m along a narrow road, is the Romanesque church of *San Pietro in Bossolo* in a lovely position with wide views. In the canonry, beyond a little cloister, a MUSEO DI ARTE SACRA was opened in 1989 with works of art and liturgical objects from other churches in the district. The paintings include a Madonna and Child with two angels attributed to Meliore (c 1280); Jacopo Franchi, Madonna and Child; Neri di Bicci, Pietà, Madonna and Child enthroned with saints, Mourning Virgin and St John, and a portrait of Niccolò Sernigi who commissioned all these works for the convent of Morrocco in 1473–75; Master of Tavarnelle, Madonna and Child with saints; Lorenzo di Bicci, Madonna and Child; Jacopo da Empoli, Madonna and Child with the infant St John; Ugolino di Nerio (attributed), Madonna and Child between Saints Peter and John the Evangelist; and Master of Marradi, Madonna and Child enthroned with two angels. There is also a fine collection of church silver, vestments, ex-votos, and reliquaries (13–19C).

The main road runs through the lengthy village of Tavarnelle (youth hostel *Ostello del Chianti*, 137 Via Roma, and *Agriturist* farmhouses; first-class restaurant *La Fattoria* at La Romita, 3km N; and trattoria *Il Frantoio*, at Marcialla, 4km W), at the end of which is the church of *Santa Lucia a Borghetto*, on the right. This Franciscan church (13C) is one of the few examples of Gothic architecture in the district. Typically sober in form, and built from simple bricks and pebbles, it contains fresco fragments and a 14C Florentine painted Crucifix. Something survives of the former cloister on the right.

The Cassia continues to (34.5km) the little village of **Barberino Val d'Elsa** (373m; 2-star camping site *Semifonte*). It preserves its defence walls and a gateway at either end of the main street, which is named after the poet

Francesco da Barberino (1264–1348). The 14C *Ospedale dei Pellegrini,* just inside the walls, is now the Public Library. There are several elegant palaces (restored), including the *Palazzo Pretorio* with coats of arms on the façade. The church of *San Bartolomeo* was rebuilt by Giuseppe Castellucci at the beginning of this century. A Madonna and Child by Bicci di Lorenzo and a bronze bust of Beato Davanzato by Pietro Tacca are preserved in the Canonica.

FROM BARBERINO VAL D'ELSA TO CERTALDO, 15km. This by-road leads through beautiful countryside. 2km Road left for the **Pieve di Sant'Appiano**, a 10C Romanesque CHURCH largely rebuilt in brick in the 12C after its tower fell down destroying much of the original building. The interior is finely proportioned with brick columns separating the nave from the aisles, and carved capitals. To the right of the entrance from the Romanesque cloister is a marble tomb slab carved with the effigy of Raffaello Gherarduccio dei Gherardini (1331). The chapel left of the choir has remains of frescoes and a Madonna and Child with saints by a 16C Florentine artist. Against the wall on the left is the shrine of St Appiano, which was originally under the main altar. According to tradition, St Appiano was the first evangeliser of the Val d'Elsa. In the nave are three frescoes of saints by the school of Ghirlandaio. The CLOISTER, which still preserves a fine door and three windows of the original sacristy, leads to the nearby CANONICA. It has a 15C hall with fresco decoration and the arms of the Catellini family, protectors of the pieve, and a small collection of paintings awaiting restoration. In front of the simple façade of the church are four columns which formed part of the former BAPTISTERY (pulled down in the early 19C) which had an unusual octagonal plan with a dome and crypt. Next to the cloister an ANTIQUARIUM has recently been opened. It contains Etruscan and Roman objects from the surrounding district (open Saturday and Sunday, 15–19). This by-road continues past the picturesque medieval village of *Linari* and rejoins the Cassia 2km before Poggibonsi (see below).

The Certaldo road passes the Villa of Petrognano before reaching (5km) a crossroads where there is a circular chapel surrounded by cypresses. It is known as *La Cupola* since it reproduces in miniature Brunelleschi's cupola of Florence Cathedral. It was built in 1597 by Santi di Tito to commemorate the former town of *Semifonte,* originally enclosed in star-shaped walls, in a strategic position close to the Francigena and Volterrana roads. Under the Conti Alberti it became so powerful that it was a threat to Florence, and was raised to the ground by Henry VI after a siege lasting from 1198 to 1202. The *Cupola* which forms a charming landmark, is now being restored by the local authorities. The road passes (6km) the church of *Santa Maria a Bagnano.* Its precious paintings have unfortunately had to be removed for safekeeping and are now housed temporarily in the canonica of Certaldo. Works from other churches in the neighbourhood have also been removed to Certaldo. The by-road continues to (15km) **Certaldo**, see Rte 15.

44km **Poggibonsi** (3-star hotel *Europa* at Calcinaia, 2km S; trattoria *Italia,* 34 Via Trento and *La Galleria*), is an unattractive commercial town of 25,000 inhabitants and an important road centre which has developed since the last War. Little remains of the old town except for the restored church of *San Lorenzo* in Piazza Savonarola which has a 14C Crucifix attributed to Giovanni d'Agostino. The Gothic *Palazzo Pretorio,* on the corner of Via Repubblica beside a crenellated medieval tower, has coats of arms on the façade. The *Collegiata,* opposite, rebuilt in 1860, has a marble baptismal font of 1341 and, in the apse, a painting of the Resurrection, attributed to Vincenzo Tamagni. Dominating the town on a hill is the castle of *Poggio Imperiale* begun for Lorenzo il Magnifico by Giuliano da Sangallo and continued by Antonio da Sangallo the Elder in the first half of the 16C.

The Cassia continues S. 45km. By-road left (unsurfaced) to *Luco* and the 14C *Castle of Strozzavolpe* (open on the third Sunday in October for the festival of San Luco). Romantically situated above a deep gorge, it is enclosed by battlements with a drawbridge at the entrance beneath a tall square tower. The view embraces Siena, San Gimignano, and Castellina in Chianti. Another by-road left off the Cassia (signposted *Il Magione*) leads back towards Poggibonsi, and then right downhill (400m) to a charming group of medieval buildings beside the small church of *San Giovanni al Ponte* (11–12C). This is one of the best preserved of the many hospices for pilgrims which formally lined the VIA FRANCIGENA, recorded from the 10–13C as the pilgrim route from France to Rome. It was described in detail by Sigeric, Archbishop of Canterbury, on his return journey from Rome in 990–994. The Cassia continues to the left while N541 diverges towards Colle Val d'Elsa (see Rte 17).

Just off the Colle road, a by-road leads uphill to the right past the Gothic arches of the so-called *Fonte delle Fate* (13C), surrounded by trees. The road winds up left to the Romanesque church of **San Lucchese** (1.5km), rebuilt and enlarged in the 14C (and damaged in the last War). The simple nave has a copy of a Noli me Tangere by Raffaellino del Garbo (destroyed in the War), and, in a niche on the right, a fresco of the Madonna and Child with saints attributed to Bartolo di Fredi. A door opens on to the cloister with 16C frescoes depicting the story of St Lucchese, a holy layman (died 1260) who devoted himself and his wealth to helping the poor. In the sacristy is a 14C cupboard decorated with painted figures of apostles and saints attributed to Niccolò di Segna or Memmo di Filippuccio. The apse window is by Rodolfo Margheri (1945). To the left of the transept above the arch of the Chapel of St Lucchese are late-14C frescoes illustrating the life of St Stephen by the Master of San Lucchese who has recently been identified with Cennino Cennini. On the left wall of the transept, Miracle of St Lucchese by an anonymous 14C painter. The vault and walls of the chapel were frescoed in the 19C. Along the N wall of the nave is another frescoed lunette with St Nicholas of Bari by Bartolo di Fredi and a large Della Robbia polyptych dated 1514. There is a fine view of the surrounding countryside.

50.5km *Staggia*, a small village enclosed in its medieval walls with an impressive castle and fortifications (14–15C). Next to the church of Santa Maria Assunta (heavily restored but with a round stained-glass window at either end of the transept) is a small Museum (ring at the priest's house for the key, or at the pharmacy opposite). It houses an important altarpiece by Antonio del Pollaiolo representing the *Communion of St Mary Magdalen; a 14C Sienese Madonna and Child; a Deposition by Angelo Salimbeni; and some fresco fragments and liturgical objects.

55.5km **Monteriggioni**, a beautifully preserved medieval fortified village, standing on a hillock. (First-class restaurant *Il Pozzo*; at Strove: 4-star *Residence San Luigi* and 3-star hotel *Casalta*, both with restaurant; first-class restaurant *Piccolo Castello* at Castello). Its 13C *WALLS, complete with fourteen towers (mentioned by Dante: *Inferno*, xxxi, 41–44), provide a romantic view from below. Inside the walls in the main square is a small Romanesque church with a pretty façade. The main street leads on to the other entrance gate from which there is a fine view. Off the other parallel street is a public garden.

Abbadia Isola, c 3km W, is a former Cistercian abbey in a small village. The Romanesque church of the 11–12C was largely rebuilt after the octagonal cupola collapsed in the 18C. The basilican interior, beautifully proportioned, has alternating piers and columns and three apses, with a simple crypt beneath the elevated choir. Two detached fresco lunettes on the right of the nave are by Taddeo di Bartolo and Vincenzo Tamagni. On the left wall is a large fresco of the Assumption by Tamagni and a baptismal font with a carved relief representing the Baptism of Christ (1419). The splendid *Maestà by the so-called Master of Badia a Isola, a follower of Duccio, is now in the Pinacoteca of Siena, and the *polyptych by Sano di Pietro is in the church of San Francesco at Colle Val d'Elsa.

61km. By-road right for the little church of *San Lorenzo al Colle* (4km; at present closed), on Monte Maggio, where frescoes were discovered in 1986. 67km The Cassia joins the Via Chiantigiana to enter (70km) **Siena**, described in Rte 14.

14

Siena

SIENA, with 59,000 inhabitants, capital of the Tuscan province of the same name, is the second most interesting town in Tuscany after Florence. It preserves its medieval character to a remarkable degree, and has been largely unspoilt by new buildings. Its beautiful Gothic buildings include the Cathedral and Palazzo Pubblico, as well as numerous churches. The delightful Sienese school of painting produced, in the first half of the 14C, masterpieces by Duccio di Buoninsegna, Simone Martini, and Pietro and Ambrogio Lorenzetti, all of whose work is well represented in the Pinacoteca, Palazzo Pubblico, and Museo dell'Opera del Duomo. The Campo is one of the most remarkable squares in Italy. The seventeen *Contrade* or wards into which the town is divided still manage to play an active part in the life of the city, culminating in the famous Palio horserace which has survived as perhaps the most spectacular annual festival in Italy, in which the whole city participates. The town is built on a Y-shaped ridge (320m) and spreads into the adjacent valleys; the streets are consequently often steep, and to pass from one part of the city to another it is often necessary to cross a deep valley. For this reason, and also because its treasures are unusually scattered, several days are needed for an adequate visit.

Information Offices. APT, 43 Via di Città (Pl. II; 6); Information Office at No. 56 Piazza del Campo (Pl. II; 6; Tel. 0577/280551).

Railway Station (N of Pl. II; 1), in an unattractive part of the town at the bottom of the hill c 1.5km N of it; buses from the piazza (opposite the Station) to Piazza Gramsci (Pl. I; 6) in 7mins.

Buses (SITA) from Piazza San Domenico (Pl. II; 1) to Florence (Piazza Stazione) c every hour in 1hr 15mins (via the superstrada). Also to Grosseto, Lucca, and Arezzo. TRA-IN town buses (and for the environs) from Piazza Gramsci (Pl. I; 6).

Parking. The centre has been entirely closed to traffic. Parking areas are clearly indicated at the entrances to the town; best near San Domenico (Pl. I; 5, 6); also near the Stadium, the Fortezza, and La Lizza, except on market day (Wednesday) and on Sunday (when football matches are held). Other car parks at Fontebranda (Pl. I; 9) and at the Railway Station (N of Pl. I; 2). Free car parking (with minibus service every 15mins) on the outskirts of the town at: *Due Ponti* (beyond Porta Pispini; Pl. I; 12; bus to Logge del Papa, Pl. II; 7), and at *Coroncina* (beyond Porta Romana, Pl. I; 16; bus to Piazza del Mercato Pl. II; 11). Other car parks are under construction (below Forte di Santa Barbara, etc.). Permission to enter the centre of the city (for access to hotels and garages) can be obtained from the *Vigili Urbani* (town police) at San Domenico or No. 7 Viale Tozzi.

Hotels. 4-star: *Park Hotel*, 16 Via Marciano (beyond Pl. I; 1; towards the Florence superstrada), with swimming pool; *Jolly Hotel Excelsior*, 1 Piazza La Lizza (Pl. I; 6; 2). 3-star: *Athena*, 55 Via Mascagni (Pl. I; 13; 1); *Palazzo Ravizza*, 34 Pian dei Mantellini (Pl. II; 13; 3); *Minerva*, 72 Via Garibaldi (Pl. I; 6; 4); *Duomo*, 38 Via Stalloreggi (Pl. II;

13; 5); *Chiusarelli*, 9 Via Curtatone (Pl. II; 1; 6). 2-star: *Lea*, 10 Viale XXIV Maggio (Pl. I; 9; 7). **In the environs**. 4-star (all with swimming pools): *La Certosa di Maggiano*, 82 Via di Certosa (beyond Pl. I; 16); *Villa Patrizia*, 58 Via Fiorentina (beyond Pl. I; 1); *Villa Scacciapensieri*, 10 Via di Scacciapensieri (near the Osservanza; beyond Pl. I; 4). 3-star: *Castagneto*, 39 Via dei Cappuccini (beyond Pl. I; 9). **Youth Hostel**, *Guidoriccio*, 89 Via Fiorentina, località Stellino (on the N outskirts towards the Florence superstrada; bus No. 15 from Piazza Gramsci).

Camping Site (3-star): *Siena Colleverde*, 47 Via di Scacciapensieri (open mid-March–mid-October; bus No. 8 from Piazza Gramsci).

Restaurants. Luxury-class: *Alla Speranza*, 33 Piazza del Campo. First-class: *Da Mugolone*, 8 Via dei Pellegrini; *Grotta del Gallo Nero*, 67 Via del Porrione; *Grotta Santa Caterina*, 26 Via Galluzza; *L'Angolo*, 13 Via Garibaldi; *Renzo*, 14 Via delle Terme; *Spadaforte*, 13 Piazza del Campo; *Il Ghiottone*, 68 Via Massetana. Simple trattorie and pizzerie: *La Vecchia Osteria*, 8 Via San Marco; *Osteria dell'Artista*, 11 Via Stalloreggi; *Da Vasco*, 6 Via del Capitano; *Hosteria il Carroccio*, 32 Via Casato di Sotto; *La Speranza*, 35 Piazza del Campo (attached to a luxury-class restaurant; see above); *Pizzeria il Riccio*, 44 Via Malta; *Pizzeria O'Pazzariello*, 22 Viale Curtatone; *Pizzeria Roberto*, 26 Via Calzoleria; *Quattro Venti*, 68 Via San Pietro. In the environs. Luxury-class: *Antica Trattoria Botteganova*, 29 Via Chiantigiana. Simple trattoria: *La Colombaia*, 61 Strada Chiantigiana, località Malafrasca. **Pasticceria** *Nannini*, 24 Via Banchi di Sopra for *panforte* and other traditional Sienese sweets.

Picnic places near Fontebranda (Pl. I; 9), outside Porta Laterina and Porta San Marco (Pl. I; 13), and in front of the Basilica of the Servi di Maria (Pl. I; 12, 16).

Theatres. *Dei Rinnovati*, Palazzo Pubblico. Concerts in the Accademia Musicale Chigiana, 89 Via di Città (Pl. II; 10; music week in August).

English Church, St Peter's, Via Garibaldi (Pl. I; 6), open for occasional services.

History. Siena appears in history as *Saena Julia*, a Roman colony founded by Augustus. Under Charlemagne the town had its own counts, and about 1125 it became a free republic, which soon entered into rivalry with Florence. The town took the part of the Sienese pope Alexander III, chief of the Lombard League, against Barbarossa, who besieged Siena without success in 1186. But afterwards, as head of the Tuscan Ghibellines, Siena helped the exiles from Florence and defeated that city at the famous battle of Montaperti in 1260. When the Ghibellines were defeated by Charles of Anjou in 1270, Siena established a Guelf oligarchy of the middle class (popolo grasso) ruled by a Council of Nine. In 1348 the town was devastated by the Black Death when over three-quarters of the population died. In 1355–69 it was attacked by Charles IV, and in 1399 it came under the power of Gian Galeazzo Visconti, who was scheming to hem in Florence. After his death the city regained its liberty for a while, but Pandolfo Petrucci (*Il Magnifico*) made himself autocrat in 1487. Another spell of liberty was marked by victory over the Florentines and Clement VII (1526), but the Spaniards captured Siena in 1530, and Cosimo I de' Medici entrusted the final suppression of the Sienese to the bloodthirsty Marquis of Marignano, who took the city in 1555 after a disastrous siege of 18 months. Some 700 families, refusing to live beneath the Medici yoke, migrated to Montalcino, where they maintained a republic until 1559 when that too was handed over to Florence by the treaty of Cateau Cambresis. From then on Siena shared the history of Florence and Tuscany. On 3 July 1944 French Expeditionary Forces entered Siena unopposed.

Illustrious natives of Siena (other than painters and sculptors, see below) include Pope Alexander III (died 1181), St Catherine of Siena (Caterina Benincasa; 1347–80), made a Doctor of the Church in 1970, Lelio Sozzini (1525–62) and his nephew Fausto (1539–64), the forerunners of positivism, and Senesino (Francesco Bernardi; 1680–1750), the castrato mezzo-soprano, star of Handel opera in London.

Since the 13C the city has been divided into three **Terzi**: *di Città*, *di San Martino*, and *di Camollia*, and each Terzo subdivided into wards, or **Contrade** by the Comune for administrative purposes. In the 14C there were 42 Contrade, reduced in the 16C to 23. Since 1675 there have been 17 Contrade, each with a headquarters, with a small museum, beside its oratory, run by an assembly elected by all those born in the Contrada over 18 years of age. Children are baptised at an open-air font in the Contrada. The names and headquarters of each Contrada are as follows: *Aquila* (eagle), Casato di Sotto; *Bruco* (caterpillar), 48 Via del Comune; *Chiocciola* (snail), 37 Via San Marco; *Civetta* (owl), Via Cecco Angiolieri; *Drago* (dragon), 19 Piazza Matteotti; *Giraffa* (giraffe), 18 Via delle Vergini; *Istrice* (porcupine), 87 Via Camollia; *Leocorno* (unicorn), 15 Via di Follonica; *Lupa* (she-wolf), 71 Via di Vallerozzi; *Nicchio* (scallop shell), 68 Via dei Pispini; *Oca* (goose), 13 Vicolo del Tiratoio; *Onda* (wave), 111 Via Giovanni Duprè; *Pantera* (panther), Via San Quirico; *Selva* (wood), Piazzetta della Selva; *Tartuca* (tortoise), 21 Via Tommaso Pendola; *Torre* (tower), 76 Via di Salicotto; and *Valdimontone* ('montone', mountain goat), 6 Via Valdimontone. The oratories and museums of each Contrada are only open on certain days of the year (enquire at the APT office) or by appointment in advance.

Every year 10 Contrade are selected to compete in the famous **CORSA DEL PALIO**, a horserace which takes place twice a year in the Campo: on 2 July (Visitation) and 16 August (the day after the Assumption). The later and more important contest was first run in 1310; the earlier race was established in 1659. Rivalry between the Contrade is strongly felt and provides an extraordinary atmosphere of excitement in the city throughout the summer. The prize is the *Palio* (also known as the *drappellone* or *cencio*), a banner designed anew each year which goes to the winning Contrada, not an individual, and celebrations continue for many weeks after the victory, in which the horse is the main protagonist.

Three days before the *Palio* the horses are drawn by lot by each Contrada. The jockeys instead are chosen in advance (and paid for) by each Contrada. There are six dress rehearsals, the last one on the morning of the race called the *provaccia*. At 14.30 or 15 the horse and jockey are blessed in the church of each Contrada, a remarkable ceremony in which everyone is invited to keep silent (and no flash photography is allowed) in order not to disturb the horse; it is only when it is well outside the church that cheering and singing explodes. At 16.30 or 17 in Piazza Duomo (well seen from Via del Capitano) a parade forms, led by the dignatories of Siena and members of each Contrada in Renaissance costume, drummers, knights, and horses. It then processes round the Campo to the accompaniment of the tolling of the bell in the Torre del Mangia, and with two flag throwers performing the *sbandierata* for each Contrada. At the end a triumphal chariot drawn by four white oxen bearing the *Palio*, with eight buglers and three Sienese dignatories enters the Campo from Casato di Sotto, ringing a bell. The crowd wave flags as it passes. The *Palio* is hung up at the corner of the Campo near Via dei Pellegrini (beside the starting posts). The horses and jockeys (riding bare back) enter from the courtyard of Palazzo Pubblico.

The horses have to line up behind a rope, and another horse (drawn by lot) canters up from behind outside the rope: when he is at the level of the rope the *mossiere* should let the rope fall so that they all start together (*la mossa*). The timing is extremely difficult and for this reason there are usually a number of false starts (which are signalled by a loud bombarda or cannonshot which recalls the jockeys to the starting point). It can take some 40 minutes to start the race (after three false starts the order of horses is changed). The *mossiere* is rushed out of the Campo as soon as the race starts as his decision is often contested. The race consists of three laps of the Campo, and it is the horse that wins (even if it is riderless). Celebrations by the winning Contrada last all night (and the horse eats at the head of the table at the banquet held in its honour). The following morning (from 8.30 or 9 onwards) the Captain, flag throwers, drummers, and horse of the winning Contrada process around the city with the Palio visiting the headquarters of each Contrada (except that of their traditional enemies). Each Contrada honours the winners by joining them in flag throwing. The banner of the winning Contrada is flown from Palazzo Pubblico.

Siena is closed to traffic for several days before the Palio. You can buy tickets (not cheap) in advance for the stands or terraces or for the area inside the railings of the fountain; but the most exciting way to see the race is from the centre of the Campo (free standing room only) which is crowded with spectators. All entrances to the Campo are closed some time before the ceremony begins; the last one to close is at Via Duprè. The Campo can hold about 30,000 people.

Art. Sienese architecture, representing a blend of the Gothic style with the Italian spirit, produced the fine Palazzo Comunale, the Cathedral, and numerous palaces. The Renaissance was late in influencing Siena (chiefly through Bernardo Rossellino and Giuliano da Maiano). The architects Lorenzo Maitani (1275–1330), Francesco di Giorgio Martini (1439–1502), and Baldassarre Peruzzi (1481–1537) were natives of the town. Sculpture was represented by Nicola and Giovanni Pisano, Tino da Camaino, Agostino di Giovanni, Goro di Gregorio, and others of their school in the 13C and early 14C; later Jacopo della Quercia (1371–1438) gathered round him numerous pupils, and the school renewed its splendour (c 1450–1550) in Neroccio di Bartolomeo, Il Vecchietta, Giovanni di Stefano, Francesco di Giorgio Martini (see above), Giacomo Cozzarelli, Lorenzo di Mariano (Il Marrina), and Bartolomeo Neroni (Il Riccio). From the 13C to 15C many sculptors produced splendid painted wood statues, for which Siena is particularly famous, including Francesco di Valdambrino, Mariano d'Agnolo Romanelli, and Domenico di Niccolò dei Cori.

The justly famous Sienese school of painting, which flourished from the second half of the 13C to the first half of the 14C, *arte lieta fra lieto popolo*, began with Guido da Siena. The most important painter was Duccio di Buoninsegna (c 1260–1319), contemporary with Cimabue, who painted his celebrated 'Maestà' in 1311 (now in the Museo dell'Opera del Duomo), which was for a long period the inspiration of the school. His art was carried on by Simone Martini (1284–1344), the friend of Petrarch, and by Lippo Memmi (fl. 1317–47), and it reached maturity in Pietro and Ambrogio Lorenzetti (fl. 1306–50). Later came Taddeo di Bartolo, Domenico di Bartolo, Sano di Pietro, Matteo di Giovanni (the boldest painter of the school), Benvenuto di Giovanni, Lorenzo di Pietro (see above), Stefano di Giovanni (Sassetta), Francesco di Giorgio Martini (see above), Giovanni di Paolo, Bernardino Fungai, Pietro di Francesco Orioli, and Girolamo del Pacchia. At the beginning of the 16C Sodoma, influenced by the art of Leonardo da Vinci, introduced a new spirit among the artists already mentioned and their immediate successors (Fungai, Domenico Beccafumi, Brescianino). In the later 16C and early 17C artists active in the city included Francesco Vanni, Ventura Salimbeni, Rutilio Manetti, and Bernardino Mei. In the 19C the town produced the painter Cesare Maccari (1840–1919), and sculptor Giovanni Duprè (1817–82).

The WALLS OF SIENA survive almost entire (well seen from Via Girolamo Gigli, Via Peruzzi, etc, Pl. I; 16, 12, 8, and 7) but, of the original 38 gates, only eight are extant. These are (from the W clockwise): *Porta Camollia, Porta Ovile, Porta Pispini, Porta Roma, Porta Tufi, Porta San Marco, Porta Laterina*, and *Porta Fontebranda*.

The three main streets of Siena, the Banchi di Sopra, the Banchi di Sotto, and Via di Città, meet at the so-called *Croce del Travaglio* opposite the *Loggia della Mercanzia* (Pl. II; 6), begun in 1417 from the plans of Sano di Matteo; the upper story was added in the 18C. The five statues of saints (1456–63) are by Antonio Federighi and Vecchietta, the former of whom carved the marble bench (right) beneath the portico. The Mercanzia held a commercial tribunal here, famous for its impartiality, to which even foreign States resorted.

A.   The Campo and Palazzo Pubblico

Steep alleys lead down from Via di Città and Via Banchi di Sotto to the ****Campo** (Pl. II; 6), the piazza of Siena and centre of civic life, laid out in the 12C. First paved in red brick and marble in 1327–49, it has the remarkable form of a fan or scallop-shell and slopes down to the Palazzo Pubblico on the flat SE side. Occupying the site of the Roman forum, it is the scene in summer of the famous Palio. It is enclosed by a picturesque medley of palaces (with restaurants, cafés, and shops); the only survivor of the original 14C buildings, besides the splendid Palazzo Pubblico, is *Palazzo Sansedoni* which follows the curve of the piazza at the NE end of the semicircle. Although it was reconstructed in 1767, it dates from 1340, with three stories of Gothic windows and a tower asymmetrically placed.

The *Fonte Gaia* is a tame reproduction (1858; by Tito Sarrocchi) of the original fountain by Jacopo della Quercia (see below).

The ***Palazzo Pubblico** (Pl. II; 6) was built in an austere but graceful Gothic style in 1297–1310, with characteristic Sienese arches at street level. The lower part is built of stone, the upper part of brick; the top storey of the wings was added in 1681. The central section has four storeys, and the whole façade is crowned with battlements. The slim, tall tower (102m high), known as the *Torre del Mangia, was built by Muccio and Francesco di Rinaldo in 1338–48 in ruddy brown brick. The beautiful stone cresting, probably designed by Lippo Memmi, is thought to have been constructed by Agostino di Giovanni. The tower may be climbed (see below). At its base is the *Cappella di Piazza* (1352–76), an open loggia built to commemorate the deliverance of the city from the plague in 1348. Most of the statues are by Mariano d'Agnolo Romanelli (1376–80). The chapel was heightened above the four pilasters with arches and a beautiful carved architrave by Antonio Federighi in 1463–68.

The ground floor is used as municipal offices, but the upper floor, with its superb frescoes of the Sienese school from Simone Martini and Ambrogio Lorenzetti to Sodoma, and the **Museo Civico** is open (daily 9.30–13.30; April–October 9–18.30; Sunday & fest. 9–13).

The door beside the loggia leads into the *Cortile del Podestà* (14C). On the left is the entrance to the tower (see below), and on the right is the ticket office and an iron staircase (1979) which leads to the UPPER FLOOR. On the landing is a case of Sienese ceramics, mostly 17–18C. The first four rooms of the museum were opened in 1985 to display paintings which form part of the MUSEO CIVICO (diagrams are provided in each room). Room 1: 16–18C non-Sienese and foreign schools, including works by Felice Brusasorci, Johann Heinrich Schonfeld, and Il Bamboccio. R. 2: (right) and R. 3 contain 16–17C Sienese paintings including works by Alessandro Casolani, Il Pomarancio, Ventura Salimbeni, and frescoes and sinopie by Sodoma detached from the Cappella di Piazza. R. 4: 17–18C Sienese paintings (Domenico and Rutilio Manetti) and a case of church silver.

The SALA DEL RISORGIMENTO was designed in 1878–90 and decorated under the direction of Luigi Mussini to illustrate the life of Victor Emmanuel II by Sienese painters including Amos Cassioli and Cesare Maccari. Here are 19C busts of famous Sienese, and sculptures by Tito Sarrocchi (Flora) and Giovanni Duprè (reclining figure of a child). A flight of stairs leads up to the spacious LOGGIA with a view of the covered market building and orchards beyond. It has a restored timber ceiling. Here are preserved remains (partly restored) of the very damaged Fonte Gaia which was one of the masterpieces of Jacopo della Quercia (1409–19). It was removed from the Campo (see above) in 1844, and dismantled in 1858. The SALA DELLA SIGNORIA is the seat of the Consiglio Comunale. The 16C lunettes are decorated with frescoes illustrating events in Sienese history.

The SALA DI BALIA is entirely frescoed with *scenes from the life of Pope Alexander III by Spinello Aretino and his son Parri (1407–08), including a splendid naval battle. The damaged entrance wall is being restored. Also here is an inlaid seat by Barna di Turino. The ANTICAMERA DEL CONCIS-TORO contains some detached frescoes (one attributed to Ambrogio Loren-zetti), a 14C painted Crucifix, Madonna and Child attributed to Matteo di Giovanni, and wood statues attributed to Jacopo della Quercia and his workshop. The SALA DEL CONCISTORO has a marble doorway by Bernardo Rossellino (1448). The *vault is frescoed by Beccafumi (1529–35), illustrating heroic deeds of ancient Greece and Rome. Three large Gobelins

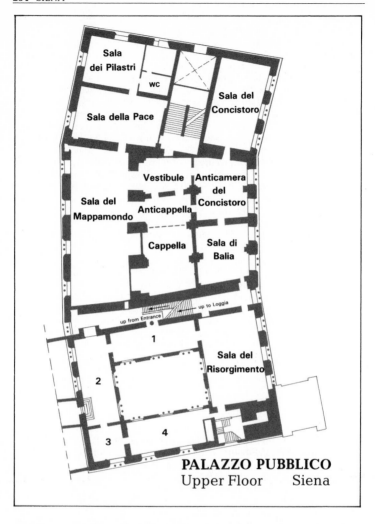

Sala dei Pilastri

WC

Sala del Concistoro

Sala della Pace

Vestibule

Anticamera del Concistoro

Sala del Mappamondo

Anticappella

Cappella

Sala di Balia

up to Loggia

up from Entrance

1

Sala del Risorgimento

2

3

4

PALAZZO PUBBLICO
Upper Floor   Siena

tapestries (removed) represent the elements Earth, Air and Fire; five other tapestries also usually exhibited here are 16C Florentine works. Above the door, Judgement of Solomon attributed to Luca Giordano.

In the VESTIBULE is a ruined fresco of the Madonna from the loggia by Ambrogio Lorenzetti, and the gilded bronze she-wolf (part of the arms of Siena, evincing pride in her Roman origin), by Giovanni di Turino (c 1429), removed from the exterior of the palace. The ANTICAPPELLA is decorated with frescoes by Taddeo di Bartolo illustrating the Virtues and famous Roman and Greek heroes and divinities, and a colossal St Christopher. Two 15C intarsia panels and a case of goldsmiths' work (12–17C) are also displayed here. The CAPPELLA, with a fine wrought-iron screen (1435–45) on a design attributed to Jacopo della Quercia, is also frescoed by Taddeo di Bartolo, with scenes from the life of the Virgin (1407–08). The altarpiece is by Sodoma. The 15C chandelier in wrought iron and gilded polychrome wood is by Domenico di Niccolò dei Cori (1420–30) who also carved the *stalls (1415–28).

The SALA DEL MAPPAMONDO was named after a circular map of the Sienese state painted for this room by Ambrogio Lorenzetti (see below). The Council met here before 1342. Here is the famous *Maestà, the earliest work of Simone Martini (1315; partly repainted by him in 1321), a beautiful Madonna seated beneath a baldacchino borne by apostles and surrounded by angels and saints. It was restored in 1990–93. On the opposite wall is the famous fresco of *Guidoriccio da Fogliano, Captain of the Sienese army, setting out for the victorious siege of Montemassi, a delightful work (partly repainted, but cleaned in 1981), traditionally attributed to Simone Martini (1330). Since 1977 it has been the subject of a heated debate among art historians, some of whom suggest it may be a later 14C work, and therefore no longer attributable to Simone Martini. The fresco beneath, discovered in 1980, and thought to date from 1315–20, which represents the deliverance of a borgo (with a castle) to a representative of the Sienese Republic has been variously attributed to Duccio di Buoninsegna, Pietro Lorenzetti, or Memmo di Filippuccio. The traces of a circular composition here are thought to mark the position of the lost fresco of the Sienese state which gave its name to the room (see above). On either side are *Saints Victor and Ansanus, by Sodoma. On the long wall: Victory of the Sienese at Poggio Imperiale by Giovanni di Cristoforo Ghini and Francesco d'Andrea (1480), and Victory at Val di Chiana, by Lippo Vanni, both predominantly in burnt sienna. On the pilasters below (left to right): (in the angle) Blessed Bernardo Tolomei by Sodoma (1533); St Bernardine by Sano di Pietro (1450), and St Catherine of Siena by Vecchietta (1461).

The *SALA DELLA PACE was the room of the Nine who ruled Siena after 1270. The remarkable allegorical *frescoes by Ambrogio Lorenzetti (1338) are considered the most important cycle of secular paintings left from the Middle Ages. On the wall opposite the window is an Allegory of Wise Government: on the entrance wall are illustrated the effects of Good Government in the town and countryside. The city represents Siena. Opposite is an Allegory of Evil Government (very damaged) with its effect on the town and countryside (very damaged). The SALA DEI PILASTRI contains 13–15C paintings including a *Maestà, a splendid huge painting by Guido da Siena (second half of the 13C, but dated 1221), a 13C Crucifix, part of a polyptych by Martino di Bartolommeo, a stained glass window with St Michael Archangel by Ambrogio Lorenzetti; an Annunciation by Niccolò di Ser Sozzo; and some carved wooden painted and inlaid coffers. The *massacre of the Innocents by Matteo di Giovanni (1482) belongs to the church of Sant'Agostino.

The entrance to the tower, the **Torre del Mangia** is on the left-hand side of the Courtyard. Stairs lead up to the ticket office (adm. see above), and then out onto a little roof terrace at the foot of the tower. A stone staircase continues up past the mechanism of the clock. Higher up there is a view of the church of Santa Maria dei Servi, before the two bells are reached. Narrow wooden stairs continue right up to the top of the lantern with another bell. There is a splendid view: to the NW are the Campo and San Domenico with the tree-covered Fortezza; to the NE in the foreground the domed church of Santa Maria Provenzano and San Francesco, and a stretch of walls enclosing fields beyond. On the hill behind is the Osservanza. To the SE can be seen the church of Santa Maria dei Servi with its tall brick campanile, and orchards, and to the SW the church of Sant'Agostino and the Duomo, with the tall nave of the *Duomo Nuovo*.

B. The Cathedral and Museo dell'Opera del Duomo

In Piazza del Duomo is the *Cathedral (Pl. II; 9; open all day 7.30–17 or 19.30) dedicated to the *Assumption*. It is the earliest of the great Tuscan Gothic churches, despite certain Romanesque elements. It is known that Nicola Pisano was involved as architect in the 13C.

The first church on this site probably dates from the 9C, and a second building is traditionally thought to have been consecrated in 1179. The present cathedral was under construction from c 1215 and the cupola was completed in 1263. In 1316 it was enlarged under the direction of Camaino di Crescentino. After 1285 the façade was begun on the plans of Giovanni Pisano, and in 1339 a scheme was adopted by which an immense nave was to be constructed S of the original church, which was to become a transept. Lando di Pietro and Giovanni di Agostino began this herculean task, but the plague of 1348 and the political misfortunes of the city compelled its abandonment. The original plan was resumed, leaving the huge unfinished nave to record the ambition of the Sienese. The building measures 89m by 24m (52.5m across the transepts). The apse was completed in 1382. The upper part of the façade, in the style of the Cathedral of Orvieto, was added by Giovanni di Cecco after 1376.

EXTERIOR. Marble steps, flanked by columns bearing the she-wolf of Siena (the originals attributed to the workshops of Giovanni Pisano and of Urbano da Cortona are now in the Museo dell'Opera del Duomo, see below), ascend to a plinth of white marble inlaid with black, on which the cathedral stands. The *FAÇADE in polychrome marble is remarkable for its magnificent statuary, now mostly replaced by copies (originals in the Museo dell'Opera). The lower part, with three richly decorated portals of equal height and size, with triangular pediments, was designed by Giovanni Pisano in 1284–85 and 1296–97 who, together with his pupils, was responsible for the sculptures of prophets, philosophers, and patriarchs. The architrave (covered for restoration) of the main portal bears stories from the life of the Virgin, an early work by Tino da Camaino. The upper part of the façade, with a great rose window, was added in the second half of the 14C in a less harmonious design; in the three gables are bright 19C Venetian mosaics. On the E side the *CAMPANILE (1313) rises from the transept (on the base of an earlier tower); its six storeys, banded in black and white, are pierced by windows whose openings increase in progression from single to sixfold. The door into the S transept (*Porta del Perdono*) bears the cast of a tondo of the Madonna and Child, almost certainly by Donatello (original in the Museum). On the roof of the nave and S transept are copies of 14C statues of the Apostles (originals in the *Cripta delle Statue*) placed here in 1681 when they were removed from the interior and replaced there by statues by Giuseppe Mazzuoli (in turn removed in the 19C to the Brompton Oratory, London). On the left flank of the Cathedral is the lapidary stone of Giovanni Pisano who was buried here.

The dichromatic style of the exterior, familiar from many Tuscan Romanesque churches, is repeated with greater emphasis in the *INTERIOR. Here the elaborate use of bands of black and white marble on the walls and

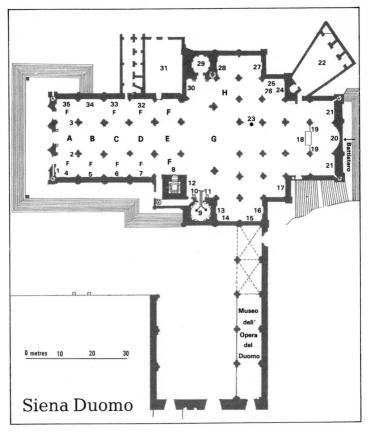

Siena Duomo

columns provides a magnificent effect. The round arches of the nave support a pointed vaulting. The interior contains numerous important sculptural works.

*PAVEMENT. The floor of the whole church is ornamented with a remarkable series of 56 marble designs, of which the oldest (1373) are in simple graffiti (black outlines on the white marble), while the others are inlaid with black, white, or (after 1547) colours. Some have been replaced by copies (the originals are in the Museo dell'Opera). Those in the nave and aisles are usually uncovered, but the earliest parts beneath the cupola, and in the apse and transepts, are covered by protective flooring and are shown only from 7–22 August. More than 40 artists, most of them Sienese, worked at this pavement: the most original and productive of whom was Beccafumi who executed 35 scenes from 1517 to 1547. The scenes in the nave (the letters below refer to the plan of the Duomo) are as follows: Ermete Trismegisto (A; Giovanni di Stefano); Sienese wolf with symbols of her allies (B; 14C); Wheel with the Imperial eagle (C; 14C); Hill of Virtue (D; Pinturicchio); Wheel of Fortune and Power (E; attributed to Domenico di Niccolò dei Cori). In the side aisles (F) are figures of ten sibyls (1481–83), designed by Guidoccio Cozzarelli, Neroccio di Bartolomeo, Benvenuto di Giovanni, Matteo di Giovanni, Antonio Federighi (Erythaean Sibyl in the S aisle), and Urbano da Cortona.

The thirteen scenes beneath the cupola (G) are by Domenico Beccafumi (1521–24) and Giovanni Battista Sozzini. In the transepts are scenes by Beccafumi, Benvenuto di Giovanni, Matteo di Giovanni, Francesco di Giorgio, Antonio Federighi, Neroccio di Bartolomeo, Domenico di Bartolo and Pietro del Minella (Death of Absalom, 1447; S transept). In the N transept the splendid scene of the Massacre of the Innocents by Matteo di Giovanni (H; 1482; restored in 1790) is left uncovered. At the E end are scenes by Domenico di Niccolò dei Cori (story of David, 1423).

NAVE. The carved columns of the main W door are attributed to Giovanni di Stefano (1483). The reliefs of the pedestals are by Urbano da Cortona. The glass in the rose window represents the Last Supper (1549; by Pastorino de' Pastorini, a pupil of Guglielmo de Marcillat). The monument (1) to Paul V (Camillo Borghese) in a fine niche by Flaminio del Turco has a statue by Domenico Cafaggi (1592). The two stoups (2, 3) are beautifully carved by Antonio Federighi. Above the nave arches are a monotonous series of busts of popes produced from 1495 onwards by means of terracotta moulds. SOUTH AISLE. First altar (4) Domenico Maria Canuti, St Gaetano (1681); second altar (5) Annibale Mazzuoli, ecstasy of St Jerome (1725); third altar (6) Raffaello Vanni, St Francis of Sales (1654); fourth altar (7) Pier Dandini, mystical marriage of St Catherine (1671). Above the doorway to the campanile (8) is the tomb of Bishop Tommaso Piccolomini, a fine work (1484–5) by Neroccio di Bartolomeo Landi. Beneath it are six bas-reliefs by Urbano da Cortona. The hexagon of the dome was decorated at the end of the 15C with gilded statues of saints attributed to Giovanni di Stefano, and figures of patriarchs and prophets in chiaroscuro, by Guidoccio Cozzarelli and Benvenuto di Giovanni. During restoration work in 1982 on the dome, sculptures were discovered on the capitals and brackets of one of the windows and attributed to Nicola Pisano. SOUTH TRANSEPT. The circular Baroque CAPPELLA CHIGI (9) was built for Alexander VII in 1659–62, almost certainly on a design by Bernini to house the Madonna del Voto. The statues are by Antonio Raggi (St Bernardine), Ercole Ferrata (St Catherine), and Bernini: St Jerome (10) and St Mary Magdalene (11). Above the statues are marble bas-reliefs of 1748. Maratta painted the Visitation (in very poor condition) and the Flight into Egypt is a mosaic after a painting by the same artist. The Madonna del Voto, a fragment of a larger painting, is by a follower of Guido da Siena.

This venerated painting has been the traditional focus of entreaty of the Sienese in time of crisis. On six occasions in their history the inhabitants have placed the keys of their threatened city before it and prayed for deliverance. The first occasion was before the battle of Montaperti; the latest on 18 June 1944, a fortnight before the liberation of Siena. It is surrounded by gilded bronze angels by Ercole Ferrata. The bronze statue in the chapel is by Arturo Viligiardi (1918).

The organ (12) was designed by Bernini. The Roman Baroque monument to Alexander III (13) was completed by Ercole Ferrata. On the altars: (14) Luigi Mussini, St Crescenzio (1867) and (15) Mattia Preti, St Bernardine (1670). On the wall, monument to Alexander VII (16) by Antonio Raggi, on a model by Bernini. The marble pavement tomb of Bishop Carlo Bartoli (died 1444) was designed by Pietro del Minella and carved by Federighi. The CHAPEL OF THE SACRAMENT (17) has a fine altar by Flaminio del Turco (1585) and an altarpiece of the Adoration of the Shepherds by Alessandro Casolani.

The Duomo, Siena

CHOIR. The marble high altar (18) is by Baldassarre Peruzzi (1532); the huge bronze *ciborium is by Vecchietta (1467–72). At the sides the uppermost angels carrying candles are by Giovanni di Stefano (1489), the lower two are by Francesco di Giorgio Martini (1490). The Cross and candelabra are to a design of Riccio (1570). The eight candelabra in the form of angels (19) on brackets against the pillars of the presbytery are fine works by Domenico Beccafumi (1548–51). In the apse (20), fresco of the Ascension by Beccafumi (altered in 1812), and, on either side (21) frescoes by Ventura Salimbeni. The round window in the apse contains *stained glass (1288) from cartoons by Duccio, probably the oldest existing stained glass of Italian manufacture. The intarsia *choir-stalls are of varying dates: 1362–97, by several artists under Francesco del Tonghio; 1503, by Giovanni da Verona; and those by Riccio and his school, 1567–70. To the left of the altar is the entrance to the SACRISTY and CHAPTER HOUSE (22; sometimes shown on request), the former with frescoes (1412) now attributed to Benedetto di Bindo. Beyond a vestibule with a fine bust of Alexander VII by Melchiorre Caffà, a follower of Bernini, is the chapter house, with a Madonna and Saints by Pietro di Francesco Orioli.

NORTH TRANSEPT. The octagonal *pulpit (23) is a remarkable Gothic work by Nicola Pisano (1265–68), completed six years after his famous pulpit in the Baptistery of Pisa. He was assisted by his son Giovanni, and by Arnolfo di Cambio.

Around the base of the central column are the figures of Philosophy and the seven Liberal Arts, and at the top of the columns, the Christian Virtues, Evangelists, and Prophets. The seven panels beautifully carved in high relief symbolise the Redemption, with scenes from the life of Christ and two scenes of the Last Judgement. They are divided by another series of carved figures, including a beautiful Madonna and Child. The elegant staircase was added in 1543 to a design of Riccio.

The transept altar (24) has an altarpiece by Francesco Vanni. The *tomb of Cardinal Riccardo Petroni (25; died 1313) is by Tino da Camaino, the design of which was frequently copied throughout the 14C. In front (26) is the bronze pavement *tomb of Bishop Giovanni Pecci, signed by Donatello (1426). The monument to Pius II (27) is by Giuseppe Mazzuoli (1694); that of Pius III (28) is by Pietro Balestra (1703).

The *CAPPELLA DI SAN GIOVANNI BATTISTA (light; 29) is a graceful Renaissance structure probably by Giovanni di Stefano (1492). The elegant portal is by Marrina (and the classical bases to the columns by Antonio Federighi); the wrought-iron gate is the work of Sallustio Barili. In the interior are (restored) frescoes by Pinturicchio including three scenes from the life of St John the Baptist (removed), and portraits of two kneeling figures (the one shown in the robes of the Order of St John is Alberto Aringhieri, the founder). The statue of St Ansanus is by Giovanni di Stefano; that of St Catherine is by Neroccio. The bronze statue of *St John the Baptist (removed) is one of Donatello's later works (1457) which recalls his St Mary Magdalene in Florence. The font was beautifully carved c 1460 by Antonio Federighi. Outside the chapel (30) is the monument to Marcantonio Zondadari by Giuseppe and Bartolomeo Mazzuoli.

In the NORTH AISLE is the entrance to the *LIBRERIA PICCOLOMINI (31) (open every day 10–13, 14.30–17; summer 9–19), one of the most delightful creations of the Renaissance. It was founded in 1495 by Cardinal Francesco Piccolomini (afterwards Pius III) to receive the library of his uncle Aeneas Silvius Piccolomini (Pius II). Its marble façade is by Marrina (1497); above the altar (right) was placed a relief of St John the Evangelist attributed to Giovanni di Stefano. The large fresco above by Pinturicchio shows the coronation of Pius III. The bright interior consists of a hall decorated with colourful and highly decorative *frescoes by Pinturicchio and his pupils (1502–9) in an excellent state of preservation. Raphael is thought to have contributed to the design of some of the scenes. They represent ten episodes from the life of Pius II (beginning to the right of the window): 1. Aeneas Silvius goes to the Council of Basle; 2. He presents himself as envoy to James II of Scotland; 3. He is crowned as poet by Frederick III (1442); 4. He is sent by the Emperor to Eugenius IV (1445); 5. As Bishop of Siena, he is present at the meeting in 1451 of the Emperor Frederick and his betrothed Eleonora of Portugal outside the Porta Camollia; 6. He is made Cardinal by Calixtus III (1456); 7. He becomes Pope (1458); 8. He proclaims a crusade at Mantua (1459); 9. He canonises St Catherine of Siena (1461); 10. He arives, dying, at Ancona (1464). The beautiful vault decoration is also by Pinturicchio and his pupils. In the centre is the celebrated group of the *Three Graces, a Roman copy of an original by Praxiteles, acquired in Rome by Cardinal Francesco Piccolomini. It served as model to Pinturicchio, Raphael, and Canova. Here are exhibited the *choir books of the cathedral and the Scala hospital, illuminated by Liberale da Verona, Girolamo da Cremona, Sano di Pietro, and others. The ceramic floor has a beautiful design.

The great *PICCOLOMINI ALTAR (32) is by Andrea Bregno (c 1480). The statuettes in the four lower niches of *St Peter, St Pius, St Gregory, and *St Paul are documented early works by Michelangelo (1501–4), who may also have worked on the figure of St Francis above, which was begun by Pietro Torrigiani. The *Madonna and Child at the top, traditionally attributed to Giovanni di Cecco, is thought by some scholars to be Jacopo della Quercia's earliest work (c 1397–1400). The painted Madonna and Child over the altar (framed by marble reliefs) is attributed to Paolo di Giovanni Fei (c 1385). Third altar (33) Pietro Sorri, Epiphany (1588); second altar (34) Francesco Trevisani, Christ between Saints James and Philip; first altar (35) Francesco Trevisani, Martyrdom of the Four Soldier Saints.

Beside the façade of the Duomo is the long Gothic façade of *Palazzo Arcivescovile*, with marble black-and-white decoration on the ground floor and brickwork above (probably reconstructed in 1665).

Opposite the cathedral are the buildings of the **Ospedale di Santa Maria della Scala** (Pl. II; 9), founded in the 9C (the oldest document to have survived which mentions the hospital dates from 1090). There are long-term plans to transform this huge group of buildings into a cultural centre. The irregular Gothic façade has been modified over the centuries. The 14C PILGRIMS' HALL (*Sala del Pellegrinaio*) may be seen on request in the mornings. Until recently used as a hospital ward, it has delightful frescoes illustrating the history of the hospital and life within it, carried out in 1440–44. The first two bays are ruined. Over the two doors: Vecchietta, Story of the Blessed Sorore, mythical founder of the hospital, and, opposite, Domenico di Bartolo, Feeding the poor in the hospital. In the third two bays: Domenico di Bartolo, Birth and education of orphans in the hospital and the marriage of an orphan, and (opposite) Building work to enlarge the hospital. Fourth two bays: Priamo della Quercia, Investiture of the Rector of the hospital by the Blessed Agostino Novello, and (opposite) Domenico di Bartolo, Distribution of Alms. In the last two bays: Domenico di Bartolo, Healing of the sick, and (opposite) Celestine III granting rights to laymen for running the hospital. In the last two bays on either side of the windows, 16C nursing scenes in the hospital by Giovanni Navesi and Pietro Crogi.

Other parts of the hospital of great interest but not at present open to the public include the GREAT SACRISTY, with the Madonna del Manto by Domenico di Bartolo, and a fresco cycle by Vecchietta and his school (1446–49).

In another part of the hospital (entered from the S end of the piazza) the **Museo Archeologico Nazionale** (open 9–13.30; fest. 9–12.30) was arranged in 1993. Founded in 1933 and formerly exhibited in Palazzo della Sapienza, it contains Etruscan and Roman material. The first section, the Antiquarium, is devoted to private collections. The Bonci Casuccini collection has material from Chiusi including a terracotta canopic vase and throne (6C BC). The large Bargagli Petrucci collection has finds from Sarteano (including numerous cinerary urns). The Chigi Zondadori collection includes a carved Roman sarcophagus front (2C AD). At the end of the hall is the Mieli collection with bucchero ware and bronzes from Chiusi. The material from the Accademia dei Fisiocritici includes coins, small bronzes, and lamps. The topographical collection opens with material from Siena, including finds from the Roman villa at Pieve al Bozzone. Upstairs is displayed material

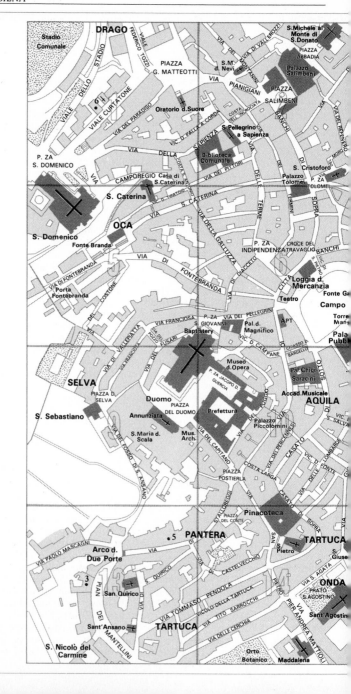

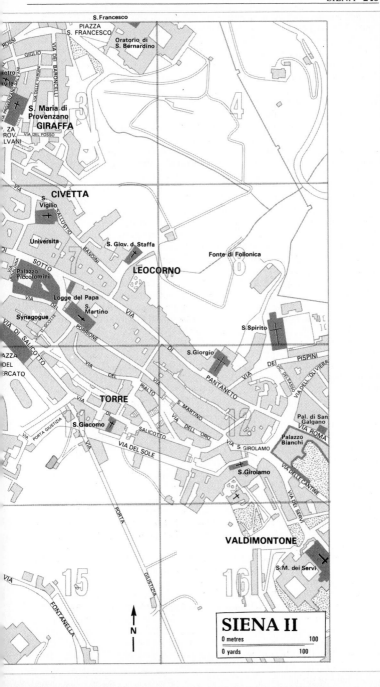

S.Francesco

PIAZZA
S. FRANCESCO

Oratorio di
S. Bernardino

ROSSI

GIGLIO

VIA DEI BARONCELLI

ietro
vile

S. Maria di
Provenzano
GIRAFFA

ZA
ROV.
LVANI

VIA DEL FOSSO

CIVETTA

S.
Vigilio

VIA SALLUSTIO

4

Università

BANDINI

S. Giov. d. Staffa

Fonte di Follonica

SOTTO

LEOCORNO

8

Palazzo
Piccolomini

Logge del Papa
S.
Martino

S.Spirito

Synagogue

VIA DI SALICOTTO

PORRIONE

VIA

DI

S.Giorgio

PISPINI

AZZA
DEL
RCATO

VIA DELL'OLIVIERA

VIA DEI TASSO

VIA

DEL

RIALTO

PANTANETO

VIA

TORRE

DI

S. MARTINO

Pal. di San
Galgano

VIA ROMA

S.Giacomo

PORTA GIUSTIZIA

SALICOTTO

VIA DELL'ORO

12

Palazzo
Bianchi

VIA

VIA DEL SOLE

S. GIROLAMO

VIA DELLE CANTINE

S.Girolamo

VIA DEI SERVI

PORTA

DI

GIUSTIZIA

15

VALDIMONTONE

16

S-M. dei Servi

VIA

FONTANELLA

↑
N
|

SIENA II

| 0 metres | 100 |
| 0 yards | 100 |

from Sienese territory, and in the last section of the hall finds from Murlo (including a terracotta frieze of horses in bas relief), Valle d'Elsa, Chianti, Monteriggioni, Colle and Casole d'Elsa.

The church of the hospital, dedicated to the **Annunziata** (Pl. II; 9; entered by the Gothic doorway at the left end of the façade) was rebuilt in 1466. The fine hall INTERIOR has been attributed to Guidoccio d'Andrea, Vecchietta, or even Francesco di Giorgio Martini. The carved and painted wood ceiling is by Benvenuto di Giovanni, Pellegrino di Mariano, Agostino d'Andrea and Domenico di Cristofano. On the S wall, on the first altar, is an Assumption by Pietro Locatelli, and on the second altar is a painted Crucifix of c 1330. The organ was built by Piffaro of Siena (1514–19); the organ case is traditionally attributed to Peruzzi and is decorated with two polychrome reliefs in roundels attributed to Ventura Turapilli. Raised high above a flight of steps is the main altar, with a relief on the altar frontal of the Dead Christ by Giuseppe Mazzuoli, on top of which is a bronze statue of the *Risen Christ by Vecchietta (1476). Two candle-bearing angels are by Accursio Baldi (1585). In the huge apse is a fresco by Sebastiano Conca (1732). On the N wall (second altar) is a Vision of St Teresa by Ciro Ferri, and (first altar) an Annunciation attributed to Giovanni Maria Morandi. By the door is a stoup by Urbano and Bartolomeo da Cortona (1453).

Opposite the S flank of the Duomo is Palazzo del Governatore dei Medici (Palazzo Reale), now the Prefecture, rebuilt in 1593. Beyond, Piazza Jacopo della Quercia occupies the site of the unfinished nave of the *Duomo Nuovo* (see above): the marble arcades survive as well as the façade and side portal which give some idea of the size and beauty of the projected building. Its S aisle has been converted into the *Museo dell'Opera del Duomo (Pl. II; 10; admission daily 9–13.30; mid-March–September, 9–19.30). GROUND FLOOR. SALA DELLE STATUE. Original *statues and sculptural fragments from the façade of the cathedral, by Giovanni Pisano and his school, constituting one of the most important groups of Italian Gothic sculpture. In the centre, bas-relief of the Madonna and Child with St Anthony Abbot and Cardinal Antonio Casini, by Jacopo della Quercia, and a tondo of the Madonna and Child almost certainly by Donatello (from the Porta del Perdono of the Duomo). Works by Urbano da Cortona (St Peter, St Bernardine in Glory); (left wall) fragments of four symbolic animals sculpted by Giovanni Pisano; (near the grille) two wolves nursing twins, from the columns outside the Duomo, one attributed to the workshop of Giovanni Pisano and one to the workshop of Urbano da Cortona. In the floor, fragments of the original pavement of the Duomo. At the end, altarpiece of the Baptism of Christ, by Andrea del Brescianino (1524).

FIRST FLOOR. SALA DI DUCCIO. **Maestà, by Duccio di Buoninsegna (1308–11), a huge celebrated work painted on both sides, divided in 1771 to show both faces: Madonna and Child enthroned and the Story of the Passion. Until 1505 it hung over the high altar in the Cathedral, and it was of fundamental importance to the Sienese school of painting. Also *Birth of the Virgin, by Pietro Lorenzetti, and *Madonna and Child, an early work by Duccio (from the church of Santa Cecilia in Crevole). A room to the left contains illuminated MSS., drawing projects related to the cathedral and Piazza del Campo, and a drawing of the pavement of the cathedral by Giovanni Paciarelli (1884). A room to the right displays gilded wood statuettes of the Madonna and Child and four saints (from the church of San Martino), generally attributed to Jacopo della Quercia and Giovanni da Imola, but possibly by Antonio Federighi. The statue of St John the Baptist from the church of San Giovanni is attributed to Jacopo della

Quercia or his bottega. In the small room beyond are polychrome wood statues: a late-14C carved Crucifix is flanked by the Madonna and St John the Evangelist by Domenico di Niccolò dei Cori (1415). The St John the Baptist is by Francesco di Giorgio Martini (1464) and St Savino by Guido di Giovanni (1393–95), painted by Paolo di Giovanni Fei.

SECOND FLOOR. The SALA DEL TESORO contains croziers, reliquaries (including the reliquary of St Galgano from the end of the 13C), and paxes. The Crucifixes include *Christ on the Cross in wood by Giovanni Pisano, an early masterpiece (c 1280; restored in 1987). Sculptural works include three busts (from statues) of saints, by Francesco di Valdambrino in polychrome wood (1409), and 12 statues of saints attributed to Giuseppe Mazzuoli (models for the marble statues now in the Brompton Oratory, London). In a small room off the treasury is displayed the *treasury of the Chigi chapel in the Duomo which has beautiful Roman and French works of the early 17C. SALA DELLA MADONNA DAGLI OCCHI GROSSI. In the centre, the *Madonna dagli Occhi Grossi, by a Sienese painter known as the Maestro di Tressa (1220–30). It adorned the high altar of the cathedral before Duccio's Maestà. Ambrogio Lorenzetti, four saints; Giovanni di Paolo, St Jerome; and four small paintings by Sodoma. The painting of *St Bernardino of Siena by Sano di Pietro is flanked by two paintings showing the saint preaching in the Campo and in Piazza San Francesco; Gregorio di Cecco, polyptych; Sano di Pietro, Madonna and Child with saints. SALA DEI CONVERSARI. Works by Matteo di Giovanni; Beccafumi, *St Paul; Il Pomerancio, Madonna and Child with saints; altar frontals. The SALA DEI PARATI contains vestments and a marble statue of a child by Giovanni Duprè. From here is reached the SCALA DEL FALCIATORE, a stair which winds up to the façade of the 'new' cathedral (extensive views of the city and countryside).

The side door of the *Duomo Nuovo*, between the incomplete nave and the cathedral, is a beautiful Gothic *portal (the sculptures by Giovanni d'Agostino have been removed to the Cripta delle Statue and replaced by casts). From here a steep flight of steps constructed in 1451 descends to the Baptistery. Half-way down is the entrance to the so-called CRIPTA DELLE STATUE (closed since 1992). Here may be seen part of the exterior wall of the Duomo before it was enlarged and remains of the crypt. Rooms I and II contain statues of apostles from the exterior of the Duomo by followers of Giovanni Pisano, including three now attributed to Tino da Camaino (1317–18). The angel from the cusp of the façade is by Tommaso Redi. In the third room are remains of the crypt with primitive fresco fragments with scenes from the Passion by the school of Guido da Siena (c 1270–80; the earliest known frescoes of the Sienese school). Also here are the two splendid carved columns and lions by Giovanni Pisano from the main door of the Duomo, and the seated statue of the Redeemer and two angels from the lunette of the side door of the *Duomo Nuovo* by Giovanni d'Agostino (c 1345; see above).

At the bottom of the steps is the *Baptistery (Pl. II; 6; beneath part of the cathedral) with a noble but unfinished Gothic façade by Domenico di Agostino (1355). The INTERIOR (March–Oct 9.30–18 or 19; winter 9–13, 14.30–17), finished c 1325 probably by Camaino di Crescentino has a beautiful hexagonal *FONT, one of the most interesting sculptural works of the early Renaissance (1417–30). The gilded bronze panels in relief illustrate the life of St John the Baptist: the Angel announcing the birth of the Baptist to Zacharias, by Jacopo della Quercia; Birth of the Baptist, and his

Detail of the Incredulity of St Thomas, from Duccio's Maestà in the Museo dell'Opera del Duomo, Siena (engraving by Timothy Cole, 1888)

preaching, by Turino di Sano and Giovanni di Turino; Baptism of Christ and St John in prison, both by Lorenzo Ghiberti; *Herod's Feast by Donatello. The six statues at the angles are by Donatello (Faith and Hope), Giovanni di Turino (Justice, Charity, and Prudence), and Goro di Ser Neroccio (Fortitude). The marble tabernacle above was designed by Jacopo della Quercia who carved the five statues of prophets in niches and the crowning statue of the Baptist. The four bronze angels are by Donatello and Giovanni di Turino. The 15C *frescoes were restored in 1993. On the two lateral vaults nearest the entrance are figures of the Apostles and Saints attributed to Agostino di Marsiglio. The four Apostles in the central bay are by Vecchietta, who also frescoed the three vaults nearest the altar with the Articles of the Creed, the apsidal arch with the Assumption of the Virgin and a glory of angels, and the three lowest scenes in the apse of the Annunciation, Flagellation, and Way to Calvary. The three Passion scenes above in the apse are by Michele di Matteo Lambertini (c 1451–55). In the large lunette left of the apse are scenes of the Miracles of St Anthony of Padua by Benvenuto di Giovanni (c 1460) and in the large lunette right of the apse, Washing of the Feet by Pietro di Francesco Orioli (1489).

Immediately E of the Baptistery is the *Palazzo del Magnifico*, built for Pandolfo Petrucci from the plans of Cozzarelli, who designed also the bronze ornaments of the façade (1504–08).

C. The Pinacoteca Nazionale

The **Pinacoteca Nazionale** (Pl. II; 14) is the most important gallery for the study of the great Sienese masters, including Duccio di Buoninsegna, Ambrogio and Pietro Lorenzetti, and Sassetta, all of whom are well represented. The collection also includes fine works by Sodoma. The Pinacoteca has been housed since 1932 in the handsome 14C *Palazzo Buonsignori*, restored in 1848. It is open daily Tues–Sat 9–19; Monday 9.30–13.30; fest. 8–13; winter daily 8.30–13. The display is strictly chronological. Many of the paintings have been restored; others are in the course of restoration. There are long-term plans to move the collection to the ex-Ospedale di Santa Maria della Scala, see Rte 14B, and a number of rooms have a provisional arrangment. The first floor is often used for exhibitions so that the permanent collection has to be temporarily re-hung or closed.

SECOND FLOOR. The first two rooms illustrate the origins of the Sienese school of painting. **Room 1**: Maestro di Tressa (attributed), *altar frontal, partly in relief representing Christ blessing between symbols of the Evangelists, and scenes from the Legend of the True Cross, the first securely dated work (1215) of the Sienese school; 2. Margarito d'Arezzo (attributed; c 1270/80), St Francis; 597. Crucifix, with Passion scenes (first years of the 13C); 8. **Guido da Siena**, three scenes from the Life of Christ, one of the first paintings known on canvas. **R. 2**: Guido da Siena (attributed), *16. Madonna and Child, dated 1262, 7. Reredos with Madonna and saints; 15. Guido da Siena, or a follower of the late 13C (known as the Maestro del Dossale di San Pietro), St Peter enthroned with stories from his life; works attributed to Guido da Siena or his followers, including (9–13) scenes from the Life of Christ; 313. Maestro del Dossale di San Pietro, St Francis and stories from his life (from the church of San Francesco in Colle Val d'Elsa).

RR. 3 and 4 contain works by **Duccio** and his followers. **R. 3**: *28. Duccio di Buoninsegna and assistants, polyptych of the Madonna and saints; 39. Ugolino di Nerio (attributed), dossal; Niccolò di Segna, 38. Four saints, 46. Crucifix (1345); 47. Duccio di Buoninsegna and assistants, polyptych, Madonna and saints, a late work; 21. Circle of Segna di Bonaventura,

Crucifix (from the church of San Giusto in Siena). **R. 4**: *20. Duccio, the Madonna dei Francescani, a tiny work of jewel-like luminosity, considered to be one of his masterpieces (c 1285; much ruined); 18. School of Duccio (attributed to the Maestro di Città di Castello), Madonna and Child (from the church of San Pellegrino, Siena); 40. Segna di Bonaventura, four saints; works attributed to the 'Maestro di Città di Castello'; Ugolino di Nerio (attributed), 36. Crucifix, 34. Crucifixion and St Francis.

In **RR. 5–8** are paintings by **Simone Martini** and **Ambrogio** and **Pietro Lorenzetti**. **R. 5**: minor painters of the 14C, including Bartolo di Fredi (104. Adoration of the Magi), and Luca di Tommé. **R. 6**: Simone Martini, *Madonna and Child (from the Pieve of San Giovanni Battista in Lucignano d'Arbia), *Pala di Beato Agostino Novello (from the church of Sant'Agostino, formerly in the Museo dell'Opera del Duomo); Lippo Memmi, 595. Madonna, 19. Madonna and Child with saints (fresco fragment). **R. 7**. In the main part of the room: 76. Maestro di Ovile, Madonna and Child; 598. Ambrogio Lorenzetti, Crucifix (very damaged); Paolo di Giovanni Fei, 116. Birth of the Virgin and saints, 300. Madonna and Child with saints; Maestro di Ovile, 61. Assumption, St Peter enthroned between saints (from the church of San Bartolomeo a Sestano); 317. Maestro di San Lucchese (attributed to Cennino Cennini), Birth of the Virgin. In a side room (**7A**): Ambrogio Lorenzetti, 77. Madonna and Child between Saints Mary Magdalene and Dorothy, 77A. Lamentation, 90, 314. (by a follower of Ambrogio) Saints Peter and Paul (from the church of San Michele a Sant'Angelo in Colle, Montalcino); Pietro Lorenzetti, Madonna and Child (from the Pieve di Santi Leonardo e Cristoforo at Monticchiello, near Pienza); Ambrogio Lorenzetti, 605. Madonna and Child, 92. Allegory of the Redemption; 147. Pietro Lorenzetti, Crucifixion. In the other side room (**7B**): Ambrogio Lorenzetti, 70–1. Two small landscapes (a city by the sea, and a castle on the edge of a lake), perhaps part of a larger decoration, 88. Annunciaton, the last dated work by this artist (commissioned in 1344), 65. Madonna between saints and doctors of the church; Pietro Lorenzetti, *Madonna enthroned (from the church of Sant'Ansano a Dofano, near Monteaperti), 578–9. Saints Agnes and Catherine of Alexandria, two panels from a polyptych. **R. 8**: Pietro Lorenzetti, 50. Madonna and Child with saints.

The first side of the loggia (**R. 9**) displays works of the 14C Sienese and Florentine schools, including: 607. Niccolò di Pietro Gerini Crucifixion with St Francis; 67. Angelo Puccinelli, St Michael enthroned with saints; 119–125. Spinello Aretino, Coronation and Dormition of the Virgin, parts of a polyptych. Beyond the Chapel (**R. 10**) is **R. 11** which displays the late-14C Sienese school. Taddeo di Bartolo, 55. Crucifix, *128. Triptych, *131. Annunciation, Dormition, and Saints Cosmas and Damian (signed and dated 1409). The second side of the loggia (**R. 9**): 60. Bernardo Daddi, triptych, dated 1336; 157. Lorenzo Monaco, Madonna and saints; *164. Domenico di Bartolo, Seated Madonna with angel musicians (dated 1433); 171. Michelino da Besozzo, marriage of St Catherine (the only signed work by this artist).

RR. 12–19 display Sienese painting of the 15C. **R. 12** is devoted to **Giovanni di Paolo**: 173. St Nicholas of Bari and other saints (signed and dated 1453), *200. Crucifixion (signed and dated 1440), inside the polyptych of San Galgano. A Madonna and Child from the church of San Simeone at Rocca d'Orcia is also temporarily displayed here. **R. 13**: Giovanni di Paolo, 206. Madonna dell'Umiltà, 172. Last Judgement; Sassetta, 9. Presentation in the Temple, 95,87. Prophets, 168–9. Saints, 167. Last Supper, 166. Temptation of St Anthony (all from an altarpiece painted in 1423–26).

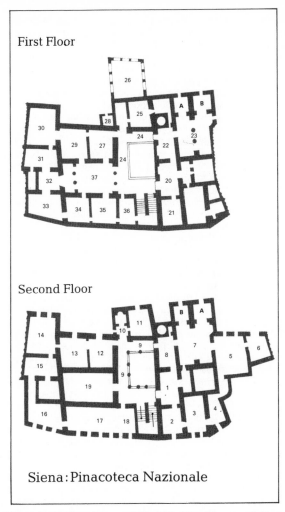

First Floor

Second Floor

Siena : Pinacoteca Nazionale

R. 14: Neroccio di Bartolomeo, 295, 285, 281. Three paintings of the Madonna and Child with saints; Matteo di Giovanni, *286. Madonna and Child with angels (signed and dated 1470); Francesco di Giorgio Martini, 288. Madonna and Child with an angel, 277. Annunciation; 400. Matteo di Giovanni, Madonna and Child with saints and angels; 437. Francesco di Giorgio Martini, Nativity and saints; 280. Matteo di Giovanni, Madonna and Child; 282. Neroccio di Bartolomeo, Madonna and Child (signed and dated 1476); 432. Matteo di Giovanni, Maestà. 278. Neroccio, Madonna and Child. 274–6. Francesco di Giorgio Martini, story of Joseph (very damaged). **R. 15**: late 15C works including three paintings of the Adoration of the Shepherds: 414b. by Matteo di Giovanni, 390, and 279. by Pietro di Domenico. In the corridor: Maestro dell'Osservanza, 218. Martyrdom of St

Bartholomew and Christ in Pietà (very damaged), 216. Predella of the altarpiece in the Basilica of the Osservanza. **R. 16**: **Sano di Pietro**, 265. St Jerome in the desert; 246. Polyptych, signed and dated 1444; 227. Assumption; 240, 272. Saints. **RR. 17–18**: Sano di Pietro, 233, 255. Predelle, 241. Madonna appearing to Pope Calixtus III (with a view of Siena). **R. 19**: Vecchietta, 210. Madonna and Child with saints, (in the centre), *204. Painted cupboard for reliquaries (from Santa Maria della Scala) with scenes from the Passion and lives of the saints; Francesco di Giorgio Martini, 440. Coronation of the Virgin, and a detached fresco of the Madonna enthroned with angels from the Villa Piccolomini di Vignano; kneeling figure in terracotta of Mary Magdalene by Cozzarelli.

On the stairs down to the FIRST FLOOR are fresco fragments by Domenico di Bartolo from the Ospedale di Santa Maria della Scala. **R. 20**: 309. Girolamo da Cremona, Annunciation; 581. Benvenuto di Giovanni (attributed), Noli me Tangere. **R. 22** has two paintings by the Maestro di Volterra. **R. 23**: Umbrian and Umbrian-Sienese schools. In one part of the room (23A): 379, 381, 393. Girolamo del Pacchia (attributed), Charity, Fortitude, and Justice; 495. Pinturicchio, Holy Family with the young St John; 503. Girolamo Genga, Madonna and Child; 407. Umbrian-Sienese painter of the early 16C, Nativity. In the other part of the room (**23 B**): 333, 334. Girolamo Genga, Ransom of prisoners, and Flight of Aeneas and Anchises from Troy (frescoes detached from Palazzo del Magnifico).

R. 27. Works by Brescianino (650–2. Charity, Hope, and Fortitude) and **Beccafumi** (420. St Catherine receiving the Stigmata). **R. 29**. Works by Marco Pino and Beccafumi (Birth of the Virgin, and Coronation of the Virgin from S. Spirito). **R. 30** contains the splendid large *cartoons by Beccafumi for the pavement of the Duomo (restored). **R. 31**. Girolamo della Pacchia, Annunciation and Visitation (from S. Spirito); *352. **Sodoma**, Scourging of Christ, a superb work (1511–14). Beyond **R. 32** with more works by Sodoma is **R. 37** with two masterpieces by Beccafumi (*427. Descent into Hell and *423. St Michael and the rebel angels). Sodoma, 443. Christ in limbo and 413. Deposition. Also here are four statues by Marrina (Annunciation, Madonna in Adoration, and the Risen Christ). Other works not at present on view include paintings by Francesco Maffei, Giuseppe Bazzani, Rutilio Manetti, Simondio Salimbeni, and Francesco Vanni.

In a room on the THIRD FLOOR the small paintings of the COLLEZIONE SPANNOCCHI, formed in the 17C, are arranged. Dürer, St Jerome (a signed work); Lorenzo Lotto, *Nativity; Francesco Furini, Mary Magdalene; Flemish works; Giovanni Battista Moroni, two portraits of gentlemen; Bernardo Strozzi, St Francis; Paris Bordone, *Annunciation, Holy Family; Bartolomeo Montagna, Madonna and the Redeemer (two fragments of a larger work); Palma Giovane, the bronze serpent (signed and dated 1598); Padovanino, Rape of Europa; 16C Flemish school, portrait of a jeweller; Girolamo Mazzola Bedoli, portrait of a young man.

D.   The Terzo di Città

From the W side of the Campo *VIA DI CITTÀ (Pl. II; 10, 6), bordered by handsome mansions, winds upwards to the S. To the left (No. 89) is the 14C **Palazzo Chigi-Saracini** (Pl. II; 10), a characteristic Sienese Gothic fortified palace with splendid three-light windows. It houses the renowned ACCADEMIA MUSICALE CHIGIANA, founded in 1932 by Count Guido Chigi

Saracini. The academy holds international courses in July and August and concerts are given in the theatre built in 1923 in 18C style. Exhibitions are held in the palace periodically of parts of the famous *CHIGI-SARACINI COLLECTION of works of art. The huge collection was formed at the end of the 18C by Galgano Saracini, and is particularly important for its Sienese works, ranging from the 13–17C. Most of it is now owned by the Monte dei Paschi bank (the Accademia Chigiana owns the remaining part of it). Admission to scholars is sometimes granted by previous appointment at the head office of the Monte dei Paschi bank in Piazza Salimbeni (see Rte 14F). The paintings include: Maestro di Tressa (early 13C), Madonna and Child; Margarito d'Arezzo, painted Cross; Pisan follower of Francesco Traini, St Paul; works by Mariotto di Nardo, Sano di Pietro, and Matteo di Giovanni; a tabernacle by the Maestro dell'Osservanza, a tondo by Botticelli and his bottega; and fine works by Sassetta, including the *Adoration of the Magi. Later masters represented include Bernardino Mei. There is also a collection of small sculptures, drawings, archaeological material, etc.

To the right (No. 128) is the splendid Renaissance *Palazzo Piccolomini delle Papesse*, built by Caterina Piccolomini, sister of Pius II, from the plans of Bernardo Rossellino (1460–95); it is now occupied by a bank. Then comes *Palazzo Marsili* built in brick in 1444–50 (restored). Next to it is the 15C *Palazzo Marsilli-Libelli* (seat of the Soprintendenza per i Beni Ambientali e Architettonici) which bears the Piccolomini coat of arms attributed to Urbano da Cortona or Vecchietta.

Parallel to Via di Città **Casato di Sotto** (Pl. II; 10) leads gently uphill from the Campo past a number of fine palaces. On the left is *Palazzo Chigi* (No. 15), constructed in the early 16C, and the birthplace of Alexander VII (plaque). Palazzo dei Conti della Ciaia (No. 23) has a façade designed by Francesco Brandini (1715). From Vicolo del Salvatore (left) there is a fine view of the Basilica dei Servi di Maria (see Rte 14E). Beyond is the beige-coloured *Palazzo Ugurgeri* (No. 39) with graffiti decoration. On the right Vicolo di Tone leads up to Via dei Percennesi, a very narrow street with flying arches and tall medieval houses in the heart of the CONTRADA DELL'AQUILA (Pl.II; 10). Off the left side of Casato di Sotto two flights of steps in Vicolo della Fonte lead down to a handsome public fountain beneath the road, protected by a high arch (1359). Near the end of Casato di Sotto is the *Oratorio dei Tredicini*, the oratory of the Contrada dell'Aquila, built in 1630. The high altarpiece is by Bernardino Mei. Costa Larga leads back up to Piazza Postierla (see below).

Via di Città ends in *Piazza Postierla* (or *I Quattro Cantoni*; Pl. II; 10) where a column (1487) with a fine iron standard-holder is surmounted by a she-wolf (recently replaced by a copy). In Via del Capitano (right), which leads to Piazza Duomo (described in Rte 14B) are the 16C Palazzo Piccolomini Adami (on the left, at the corner) and the late-13C Palazzo del Capitano (No. 15). In the piazza is a chemist's shop with furniture dating from c 1830.

Via di Stalloreggi begins in Piazza Postierla and leads up through the CONTRADA DELLA PANTERA (Pl. II; 13, 14), the oldest part of the city with numerous medieval houses. In Piazza del Conte is the fountain used for baptisms in the contrada. The ex-*Palazzo dei Bisdomini* (No. 43) is one of the best Gothic palaces to survive in the city. It stands on the corner of Via di Castelvecchio, at the beginning of which is a pretty tabernacle protecting a fresco of the Pietà (called the Madonna del Corvo) by Sodoma. Via di Castelvecchio diverges left through an interesting old part of the town. Some way along on the left, two arches admit to a little fortified 'piazza' on a hill. Via di San Quirico is wider and ends at the little church of San Quirico. Via di Stalloreggi continues down to the Arco delle Due Porte (see below).

From Piazza Postierla, Via di San Pietro leads past Palazzo Bonsignori, seat of the Pinacoteca Nazionale (described in Rte 14C), next to which is the church of *San Pietro alle Scale* (Pl. II; 14), rebuilt in the 18C with a pleasant interior. On the N wall are a fragment of a fresco of St Catherine in very poor condition, attributed to Liberale da Verona, and five panels by Ambrogio Lorenzetti. On the high altar, Flight into Egypt, by Rutilio Manetti.

Via di San Pietro continues down past (left) the Casato di Sopra (a winding old street which meets the Casato di Sotto; see above), to the Arco di Sant'Agostino, beyond which is the church of **Sant'Agostino** (Pl. II; 14), dating from 1258. From the terrace there is a good view of the town and countryside. The church has been closed since 1982, but is sometimes used for exhibitions. The attractive bright INTERIOR was remodelled in 1749 by Vanvitelli. It has particularly interesting early-17C altarpieces. SOUTH SIDE. First altar, Astolfo Petrazzi, Communion of St Jerome; second altar, Perugino, *Crucifixion. The *PICCOLOMINI CHAPEL has three beautiful Sienese works: an *Epiphany by Sodoma, a *Massacre of the Innocents, by Matteo di Giovanni (1482; removed to the Palazzo Pubblico since its restoration), and a lunette fresco of the *Madonna seated among saints by Ambrogio Lorenzetti. The pala of the Blessed Agostino Novello by Simone Martini, also painted for the chapel, is at present in the Pinacoteca Nazionale. Fourth altar, Ventura Salimbeni, Calvary. In the SOUTH TRANSEPT the Cappella Bichi has two splendid frescoes in grisaille of the Birth of the Virgin and the Nativity, attributed to Francesco di Giorgio Martini (discovered in 1978). Above are two monochrome lunettes by Signorelli. The majolica pavement dates from 1488. In the adjacent chapel, 15C wood statue of the Madonna and Child (removed for restoration). The HIGH ALTAR is by Flaminio del Turco. Beneath it is a reliquary of the Beato Agostino Novello. NORTH TRANSEPT. In the first chapel, a fresco with a view of Jerusalem has recently been discovered; second chapel, fresco fragment by Bartolomeo Neroni (Il Riccio) of a sepulchral monument; and Rutilio Manetti, Temptations of St Anthony. The wooden statues in the transepts have been removed; one is attributed to Jacopo della Quercia, and the other (the seated Madonna wearing a crown and holding the standing Child) is by Giovanni di Turino (1420; restored in 1986). The funerary monument to Agostino Chigi (died 1639) has statues by Tommaso Redi. NORTH AISLE. Third altar, Francesco Vanni, Baptism of Constantine; (beyond the door), Carlo Maratta, Conception; Giovanni Francesco Romanelli, Adoration of the Shepherds.

In the Prato di Sant'Agostino is the entrance (No. 4) to the *Accademia dei Fisiocritici*, founded in 1691 by Pirro Maria Gabrielli. It has geological, mineralogical, and zoological collections (open weekdays 9–13, 15–18, except Thursday afternoon). From Sant'Agostino Via Sant'Agata leads to the church of *San Giuseppe*, the oratory of the CONTRADA DEL CAPITANO DELL'ONDA. The brick façade dates from 1653 and the marble bust of St Joseph is by Tommaso Redi. The octagonal cupola was probably designed by a follower of Baldassarre Peruzzi, and it has a centrally planned 16C interior. The walled Via di Fontanella circles the cultivated hillside beside a font beneath the apse of Sant'Agostino. It joins Via Mattioli (see below). Beyond the Arco di San Giuseppe the picturesque Via Giovanni Duprè descends through the Contrada dell'Onda to Piazza del Mercato (Pl. II; 11) from which Palazzo Pubblico with its loggia and tower is seen from the rear. In the other direction are fields and orchards, and below the piazza is a public fountain.

To the SE of Sant'Agostino Via Pier Andrea Mattioli leads past the entrance (No. 4) to the **Botanical Gardens** (Pl. I: 14), on a steep slope, transferred here in 1856 (open 8–17; Saturday 8–12; closed fest.). Beyond is the neo-classical façade (1839) of the church of the *Maddalena* which contains paintings by Antonio Bonfigli and Raffaello

Vanni. Via Mattioli ends at **Porta Tufi** (Pl. I; 15), a fine gateway erected c 1326. Outside the gate is the *Misericordia Cemetery* (1843–74), with tombs decorated by Tito Sarrocchi, Cesare Maccari, Amos Cassioli, Giovanni Duprè and others.

From the Prato di Sant'Agostino, Via della Cerchia leads SW towards Pian dei Mantellini. It ends beside the church of *Santi Niccolò e Lucia*, with 17C frescoes and wood carvings in the interior. On the S altar is a venerated Madonna in an 18C frame. The high altarpiece of the Martyrdom of St Lucy is by Francesco Vanni (1606); above is a fresco by Ventura Salimbeni. On either side of the presbytery, two 15C polychrome statues: St Lucy attributed to a Sienese sculptor close to Francesco di Giorgio Martini and St Nicola (with an unusual head, attributed to a follower of Giovanni di Stefano).

Beyond, in the wide Pian dei Mantellini is the Carmelite convent and church of **San Niccolò al Carmine** (Pl. II; 13; also called *Santa Maria del Carmine*), with a huge campanile. INTERIOR. SOUTH SIDE. Bartolomeo Neroni and Arcangelo Salimbeni, Adoration of the Shepherds; in the niche, Assumption with angels playing musical instruments, and saints, a damaged fresco attributed to Benedetto di Bindo. Over the altar, Domenico Beccafumi, *St Michael. In the chapel of the Sacrament, off the S side, in a fine 16C frame, Birth of the Virgin and the Redeemer by Sodoma. At the end of the S side a painting of Saints, signed and dated 1593 by Francesco Vanni, surrounds the Madonna dei Mantellini (replaced by a photograph while it is being restored). The 17C high altar attributed to Tommaso Redi bears an earlier ciborium. Behind the altar a small Byzantine painting of the Madonna and Child has been removed. On the NORTH SIDE, Alessandro Casolani, martyrdom of St Bartholomew, and, over the altar, Girolamo del Pacchia, *Ascension (in poor condition). At the W end of the wall, Giuseppe Collignon, Holy Family appearing to saints (1825). On the W wall, Stefano Volpi, Crucifixion. In the SACRISTY (admission on request), formerly a private chapel, with interesting architectural details, is a statue of St Sigismondo by Giacomo Cozzarelli (in polychrome terracotta) and a painting of the Annunciation by Raffaello Vanni (recently restored). Part of the CONVENT is now used by the university; the 16C cloister with frescoes by Giuseppe Nicola Nasini (1710) can be seen at No. 44.

Pian dei Mantellini has several handsome buildings which follow its curved shape. To the right of the church, at No. 40, is *Palazzo Incontri*, a handsome neo-classical palace by Serafino Belli (1799–1804) with pilasters and busts in roundels. Beyond, at No. 28 is the façade of the former church of the *Conservatorio delle Derelitte* (by Riccio, c 1554). Opposite the flank of the Carmine is *Palazzo del Vescovo* (Celsi Pollini Neri) attributed to Baldassarre Peruzzi. It has a second façade in the narrow lane which leads up to a fine medieval tower next to the little church of *Sant'Ansano* (usually closed), built in 1441 by Pietro del Minella, Antonio Federighi, and others. It contains a precious stained glass tondo of St Ansano atributed to Cozzarelli, a high altarpiece by Rustichino, signed and dated 1617, and two 15C frescoes of the Adoration of the Magi and St Ansano. To the right of the church is the *Istituto di Santa Teresa* (1877–81). In front of Sant'Ansano, Via Tommaso Pendola leads through the CONTRADA DELLA TARTUCA (Pl. II; 13), with its oratory, built by members of the contrada in 1682–85. The stucco relief on the high altar is by Giovanni Antonio Mazzuoli. The panel in the pavement, in imitation of that of the Duomo, was designed by Arturo Viligiardi (1891). The two paintings of Miracles of St Anthony are by Giuseppe Nicola Nasini. Parallel to the S is Vicolo della Tartuca, a medieval blind alley with a flying bridge, and Via Tito Sarrocchi, with the house (No. 35) where Beccafumi lived from 1516.

Off the other side of Pian dei Mantellini Via San Marco leads down through the CONTRADA DELLA CHIOCCIOLA (Pl. I; 14). At the beginning on the left is the façade of the former church of San Marco next to a relief of the Lion of St Mark (1954). Farther on, at No. 37, in a courtyard behind an iron gateway is the church dedicated to Santi Pietro e Paolo which serves as the oratory of the contrada della Chiocciola. Built in 1645 on a design by Flaminio del Turco, it has a high altarpiece by Andrea del Brescianino. Farther down, at the fork with Via della Diana is the delightful 18C chapel of the *Madonna del Rosario*. In front is a Renaissance well. On the right side of Via San Marco is the huge convent of *Santa Marta* with a long façade probably by Il Tozzo, follower of Peruzzi (1535). On the opposite side, at No. 149, is a tabernacle with Christ on the Cross by Ventura Salimbeni. Outside Porta San Marco (c 1326) there is a fine view of the countryside.

Pian dei Mantellini ends at the *Arco delle Due Porte* (Pl. II; 13). High up on the wall of a house (No. 7) is a tabernacle with an early 14C fresco, thought to be the oldest tabernacle in the town. Just inside the gate is a house (on the right; plaque) where Duccio di Buoninsegna lived. The 16C tabernacle has a fresco attributed to Baldassarre Peruzzi (or Bartolomeo di Davide).

Via di Stalloreggi, which leads up to Piazza Postierla is described above. From the gate Via Paolo Mascagni leads downhill to *Porta Laterina* which preserves its wooden doors. Near it is a huge bastion in the walls designed by Baldassarre Peruzzi. Outside the gate is a delightful view of the walls as far as Porta San Marco with olive groves and orchards outside them and unspoilt countryside beyond.

From the Arco delle Due Porte, Via del Fosso di Sant'Ansano, a narrow pretty road, curves N beneath the huge building of Santa Maria della Scala (see Rte 14B) which covers the hill on the right. Beyond the low wall on the left are fields planted with olives and vines. The road ends at Piazza della Selva in the CONTRADA DELLA SELVA (Pl. II; 9). Here is *San Sebastiano* (*in Valle Piatta*), the oratory of the contrada. This small church is attributed to Domenico Ponsi (1507) or Baldassarre Peruzzi. It contains a Madonna and Child with saints by Benvenuto di Giovanni, and two paintings of c 1630 by Astolfo Petrazzi (Epiphany) and Rutilio Manetti (Crucifixion). The stepped Vicolo di San Girolamo leads up to Piazza del Duomo (see Rte 14B).

Via di Valle Piatta and (left) Via del Costone descend to the *Fonte Branda (Pl. I; 10), the oldest and most abundant spring in Siena. It was mentioned as early as 1081 and covered over in 1248 with brick vaults by Giovanni di Stefano. The water is channelled from a large reservoir. The font marks the entrance to the Terzo di Camollia (see Rte 14F). On the hill above, San Domenico is conspicuous, and a pretty lane leads uphill (right) from the spring to Vicolo dei Tiratori which passes under the house of St Catherine (entrance in Costa Sant'Antonio, described in Rte 14F).

E.   The Terzo di San Martino

From the NE angle of the Campo, Via Rinaldini leads to *Palazzo Piccolo-mini (Pl. II; 7), which faces Via Banchi di Sotto, a handsome building of the Florentine Renaissance, probably designed by Bernardo Rossellino and begun by Porrina in 1469. In the courtyard are good suspended capitals by Marrina (1509). The palace contains the ARCHIVIO DI STATO, one of the finest extant collections of archives. The exhibits (open weekdays 9–13) include charters and other manuscripts, autographs, Boccaccio's will, and a unique series of book bindings, among them the *Tavolette di Biccherna*, the painted covers of the municipal account-books, some by the most famous artists of the 13–17C. The study room is open to students in the morning (except 15–30 August).

Opposite are the administrative offices of the *University*, founded c 1240, at the side of which Via San Vigilio leads to the church of **San Vigilio** (Pl. II; 7). The fine ceiling has paintings by Raffaello Vanni. The third chapel on the S side has a marble altar by Tommaso Redi and Dionisio Mazzuoli and reliefs attributed to Mazzuoli. The high altar dates from 1688; the two paintings on either side are by Francesco Vanni. The third altar on the N side has a bronze Crucifix attributed to Pietro Tacca and two sculpted half-figures attributed to Giuseppe Mazzuoli. This area is part of the CONTRADA DELLA CIVETTA whose oratory is in Via Cecco Angiolieri, and whose headquarters is in the restored Castellare degli Ugurgieri.

Via San Vigilio ends at Via Sallustio Bandini opposite the Renaissance *Palazzo Bandini Piccolomini* (built c 1465 by Antonio Federighi, now used by the University). This characteristic street descends past two more interesting Bandini palaces on the bend of the road, opposite a high wall with two stone 13C lions (perhaps formerly bearing columns on a church façade), and ends in Piazzetta Grassi. Here is the church of *San Giovannino della Staffa*, now the oratory of the CONTRADA DEL LEOCORNO (Pl. II; 7). It contains works by Raffaello Vanni and Rutilio Manetti, and a 14C Madonna and Child by Francesco di Vannuccio.

Via Banchi di Sotto ends at the elegant **Logge del Papa** (Pl. II; 7; being restored). It was built for Pius II by Antonio Federighi (1462). The decorations are attributed to Francesco di Giorgio Martini. Next to it is the church of **San Martino** (Pl. II; 7; mentioned in a document of the 8C), with a façade by Giovanni Fontana (1613). The pleasant INTERIOR by Giovanni Battista Pelori dates from after 1537. SOUTH SIDE, second altar, Guido Reni, Circumcision; third altar, Guercino, Martyrdom of St Bartholomew; fourth altar, marble statue of St Thomas of Villanova attributed to Giovanni Antonio Mazzuoli. The Baroque high altar, with a ciborium, is attributed to Giuseppe Mazzuoli. On the wall of the choir are two sepulchral monuments attributed to Bartolomeo Mazzuoli. NORTH SIDE. Fourth altar, Giuseppe Mazzuoli, Madonna and Child; third altar, Domenico Beccafumi, *Nativity. On the W Wall is a painting of the Madonna protecting Siena (1528). and two pretty organs. NORTH SIDE. Fourth altar, Giuseppe Mazzuoli, Madonna and Child; third altar, Domenico Beccafumi, *Nativity. On the W wall is a painting of the Madonna protecting Siena (1528).

On the left of the Logge del Papa Via di Pantaneto descends to the church of **San Giorgio** (Pl. II; 12) with a good marble façade (1738) and a campanile of 1260. The INTERIOR has white stucco decoration. On the W wall is the tomb of Francesco Vanni (1656), with his bust in bronze by his sons Raffaello and Michele, the last of whom carried out the exquisite and very unusual marble panel. SOUTH SIDE, first altar, Placido Costanzi, Calling of St Peter; second altar, Niccolò Franchini, Death of the Virgin. In the S transept, Pietà with St Carlo by Vincenzo Meucci; Pietà with St Catherine, by Francesco Vanni, and a funerary monument by Giovanni Janssens (1748). The high altarpiece is attributed to Sebastiano Conca. In the N transept is a Vision of St Filippo Neri by Raffaello Vanni and a monument by Janssens.

Beyond the church, Via dei Pispini leads left to a piazza with a pretty fountain in which is the 16C church of **Santo Spirito** (Pl. II; 8, 12; closed for restoration). The cupola is attributed to Giacomo Cozzarelli (1508) and the portal to Baldassarre Peruzzi (1519). INTERIOR. SOUTH SIDE, first chapel, frescoes and paintings by Sodoma. The terracotta Nativity group is by

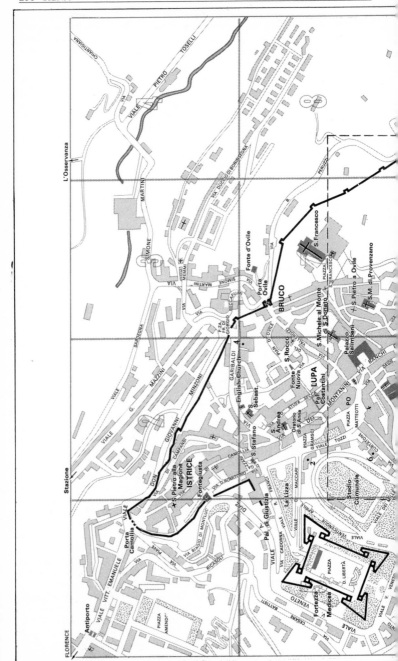

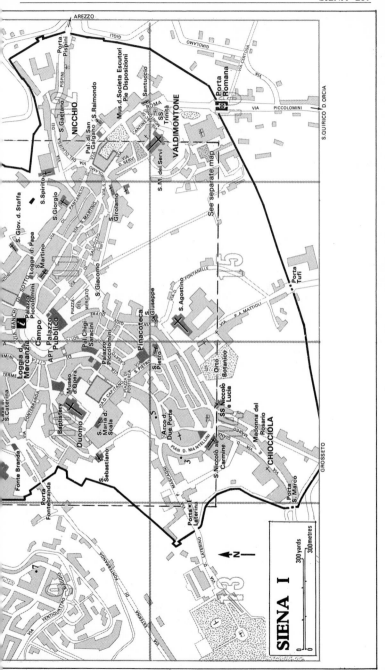

SIENA I

300 yards
300 metres

AREZZO

Porta Pispini

NICCHIO

S. Gaetano
S. Raimondo

Mus.d.Società Escutori Pie Disposizioni

Santuccio

Pal. di San Galgano

SS. Trinità

VALDIMONTONE

Porta Romana

VIA PICCOLOMINI

S.QUIRICO D'ORCIA

S. Spirito

S. Giorgio

S. Giov. d. Staffa

S. Girolamo

S. Giacomo

See separate map

Porta Tufi

S. Martino
Logge d' Papa

Palazzo Piccolomini

Campo

Loggia d. Mercanzia

APT

Palazzo Pubblico

Pal.Chigi Saracini

Palazzo Piccolomini

Pinacoteca

S. Giuseppe

S. Agostino

VIA P. A. MATTIOLI

TERME

S. Caterina

Museo d'Opera

Baptistery

Duomo

S. Maria d. Scala

S. Pietro

Arco d. Due Porte

SS. Niccolò e Lucia

Orto Botanico

GROSSETO

Fonte Branda

S. Sebastiano

S. Niccolò al Carmine

Madonna del Rosario

CHIOCCIOLA

Porta S. Marco

Porta Fontebranda

Porta Laterina

SIENA III

VENTIQUATTRO MAGGIO

VIA TERME

Ambrogio Della Robbia (1504). Second chapel, wood statue of St Vincent Ferrer by Giacomo Cozzarelli. Third chapel, Domenico Beccafumi, Coronation of the Virgin. Beside the high altar, four saints by Rutilio Manetti. NORTH SIDE, third chapel, Girolamo del Pacchia, Coronation of the Virgin, and a large painted Crucifix attributed to Luca di Tommé. Two wooden kneeling figures of St Jerome and Mary Magdalen are by Francesco di Giorgio Martini.

Via dei Pispini descends to a fork with Via dell'Oliviera at which is the church of *San Gaetano* (1683), with a pretty façade, the oratory of the CONTRADA DEL NICCHIO. Via dei Pispini continues down to the splendid *Porta Pispini* (or Porta San Viene; Pl. I; 12), dating from c 1326–28. The fresco painted by Sodoma above the gate has been detached and removed to the church of San Francesco. To the left of the gate, at an angle of the city walls, is the only surviving bastion of the seven designed by Peruzzi in the 16C to strengthen the earlier defences. On the right of the gate steps lead down to a public fountain. The church of *Sant' Eugenia*, 700m outside the gate (marked by its campanile) contains a Madonna, one of the finest works of Matteo di Giovanni.

Vicolo del Sasso, opposite Santo Spirito, leads shortly to Via Roma. On the right is *Palazzo Bianchi* (1804) with a large garden, on the wall of which is a pretty carved tabernacle dated 1477 by Giovanni di Stefano. Opposite is the Renaissance *Palazzo di San Galgano*, built in the style of Giuliano da Maiano (1474). The church of *San Raimondo al Rifugio* (closed many years ago) has a marble façade of 1660. It contains interesting 17C paintings, including works by Francesco Vanni and Rutilio Manetti. A Virgin Annunciate in wood by Jacopo della Quercia (1410–20), which belongs to the church, has been restored. At No. 71 Via Roma are the premises of the *Società Esecutori di Pie Disposizioni* (Pl. I: 12), with their MUSEUM (admission 9–13, except fest., ring on the first floor). This society of executors of benevolent legacies is the successor to the medieval lay brotherhood of the Compagnia della Madonna, suppressed in 1785. The paintings include: a lunette showing St Catherine of Siena leading Pope Gregory XI back to Rome, by Girolamo di Benvenuto; a Crucifix by the Duccio school; Madonna and Child by Sano di Pietro; Madonna and Child, Saints Peter and Paul, by Niccolò di Ser Sozzo, and Holy Family by Sodoma. The custodian conducts visitors across the road to another museum opened in 1981, donated by the Bologna-Buonsignori families, which contains an eclectic collection of prehistoric material, Etruscan and Roman ceramics and glass, jewellery, Deruta majolica, Chinese porcelain, the Portait of a Lady by Gino Severini, arms, etc. Via Roma ends at **Porta Romana** (Pl. I; 16), the largest double fortified gate of Siena (1328).

From Via Roma (opposite No. 71) Via Val di Montone (partly stepped) leads up past the ex-church of San Leonardo, now the headquarters of the CONTRADA DI VALDIMONTONE (Pl. I; 12), and the Oratorio della Santissima Trinità, the church of the Contrada. It has a splendid Mannerist interior. The vault is frescoed by Ventura Salimbeni and the stuccoes are by Brescianino and Lorenzo and Cristoforo Rustici. In the Sacristy is a Madonna and Child by Neroccio di Bartolomeo who also painted the beautiful frame.

Via Val di Montone ends at the church of **Santa Maria dei Servi** (Pl. I; 16), a large church with a massive brick campanile. From the top of the steps there is an unusual view of the Duomo Nuovo, the campanile and the Duomo, and Palazzo Pubblico. The spacious INTERIOR has lovely capitals. SOUTH AISLE. Above the first chapel, remains of 14C frescoes; second chapel, *Madonna del Bordone by Coppo di Marcovaldo, signed and dated 1261, partly repainted by a pupil of Duccio. On either side, two 16C paintings. Third chapel, Rutilio Manetti, Birth of the Virgin; fourth chapel,

Siena

Alessandro Franchi, Madonna and saints; fifth chapel, Matteo di Giovanni, *Massacre of the Innocents (1491; in very poor condition). SOUTH TRANS-EPT. On the right wall, Francesco Vanni, Annunciatory Angel. In the chapel, painted Cross attributed to Niccolò di Segna; above the sacristy door, Segna di Bonaventura, Madonna and Child. CHAPELS AT THE EAST END: second chapel⸍right of the sanctuary, especially interesting remains of frescoes (including the Massacre of the Innocents) attributed to Francesco di Segna, with the help of Niccolò di Segna and Pietro Lorenzetti. On the high altar, Bernardino Fungai, Coronation of the Virgin. In the first chapel left of the sanctuary, frescoed in the 19C, on either side of the altar are small frescoed tondi attributed to Giuseppe Nasini. The second chapel left of the sanctuary contains more good frescoes (scenes from the life of St John the Baptist) attributed to Francesco and Niccolò di Segna and Pietro Lorenzetti. The altarpiece of the Nativity is by Taddeo di Bartolo (1404). NORTH TRANSEPT. In the chapel, Giovanni di Paolo, Madonna of the Misericordia (signed and dated 1431). On the wall, Rutilio Manetti, Miracle of the Blessed Gioacchino Piccolomini (1633). Opposite is a painting of the Madonna and the plague in Siena by Astolfo Petrazzi painted to frame a painting of the Madonna del Popolo by Lippo Memmi (c 1325), removed several years ago to the Pinacoteca Nazionale. Also in this transept, Madonna Annunciate by Francesco Vanni. NORTH AISLE. Fifth chapel, Adoration of the Shepherds by Dionisio Montorselli and a 16C Dead Christ in polychrome terracotta. Fourth chapel, Francesco Curradi, Madonna and saints, and (left wall), Adoration of the Shepherds by Alessandro Casolani; second chapel, Madonna di Belvedere attributed to Jacopo di Mino del Pelliccaio and Taddeo di Bartolo and (on either side) 16C Sienese paintings. First chapel, Francesco Vanni, Annunciation. On the W wall, 18C marble statue of the Immacolata.

The return to the Campo may be made along Via dei Servi, Via San Girolamo (left) and Via di Salicotto (left again). Via di Salicotto runs through the CONTRADA DELLA TORRE (Pl. II; 11) whose Oratory of San Giacomo is on the left of the road beside No. 76 (ring for the custodian, 10–12, except Thursday). It contains a Crucifixion by Rutilio Manetti. In the last lane on the right, off Via di Salicotto, before the Campo, called Vicolo delle Scotte, is the *Synagogue*, a neo-classical building of 1756. The ghetto was in this area from 1571 to 1796.

F.   The Terzo di Camollia

From the Campo, Vicolo di San Pietro leads up to the Croce del Travaglio where *Via Banchi di Sopra* (Pl. II; 2, 6) begins. It leads N to Piazza Tolomei, where from the 11C the Sienese parliament used to assemble. *Palazzo Tolomei* (Pl. II; 6) is one of the oldest Gothic palaces in Siena (now owned by a bank), begun c 1208 and restored some 50 years later. Opposite is the church of **San Cristoforo** (Pl. II; 2) where the magistrates of the Republic officiated. It is one of the oldest churches in Siena. The neo-classical façade dates from 1800. INTERIOR. On the first altar on the N side, Girolamo del Pacchia, Madonna enthroned and saints (c 1508). In the N Transept is an unusual 15C fresco of the Pietà and Allegory of the Passion (in very poor condition), and a polychrome terracotta Madonna and Child. On the high altar, statuary group of the Translation of St Benedict, attributed to Giovanni Antonio Mazzuoli (1693). In the S Transept is a statuette of St Galgano in terracotta and white glazed enamel by the school of the Della Robbia. A painting of St George and the dragon attributed to the Maestro dell'Osservanza or Sano di Pietro has been removed from the S wall.

Via del Moro, flanking San Cristoforo, descends past an archway into the 13C cloister (restored in 1921) to the quiet piazza (from which a stretch of the city walls can be seen) in front of **Santa Maria di Provenzano** (Pl II; 3; 1594) with a pretty exterior. The Mannerist FAÇADE is by Flaminio del Turco (1604) with four statues (1816) and the dome was designed by Don Giovanni de' Medici. The INTERIOR has neo-classical furniture. On the W wall, monochrome painting by Bernardino Mei. SOUTH WALL. Giovanni Bruni, Birth of the Virgin (19C). The first elaborate marble altar by Flaminio del Turco encloses an altarpiece of the Mass of San Cerbone by Rutilio Manetti (signed and dated 1630). In the spandrels of the dome are 18C frescoes and the marble pavement beneath it dates from 1685. SOUTH TRANSEPT. Altarpiece by Francesco Rustici (1612) and, in the centre, Madonna by a pupil of Raffaello Vanni. On the high altar, designed by Flaminio del Turco, is a highly venerated 15C terracotta bust of the Madonna in honour of which the Palio of 2 July is run. The prize banner is preserved in the church before the race. On either side are two silver statues by Francesco and Giovanni Antonio Mazzuoli. The ciborium dates from 1734. The two organs are by Sebastiano Montese (1728). NORTH TRANSEPT. 17C Crucifix and two statues by Antonio Manetti (1837–39) and a 17C ciborium. NORTH WALL. Giovanni Bruni, Circumcision; on the altar, Dionisio Montorselli, Vision of St Catherine and Martyrdom of St Lawrence; Giovanni Bruni, Coronation of the Virgin. On the W wall, Bernardino Mei, Mass of St Gregory the Great.

To the right of the church, in Via delle Vergini, is the Oratory and headquarters of the CONTRADA IMPERIALE DELLA GIRAFFA (Pl. II; 3). Via

Provenzano Salvani leads along the left flank of Santa Maria to Via del Giglio in which (left) is the church of **San Pietro a Ovile** (Pl. II; 3). In the INTERIOR, on the E wall, fragment of an Annunciation attributed to Bartolo di Fredi and a painted Crucifix by Giovanni di Paolo. On the altar to the left of the high altar, 14C Crucifix, attributed to the Maestro del Crocifisso dei Disciplinati (the two wood figures of the Madonna and St John by Domenico di Niccolò dei Cori have been removed to the Pinacoteca Nazionale). On the N altar, Madonna enthroned and four angels by the Master of the Madonna di San Pietro a Ovile, now identified as Bartolomeo Bulgarini (replaced by a photo and removed to the Villa di Montarioso, see Rte 14G). On the wall is a fragment of a fresco of the Annunciation, a very early Sienese work. On the W wall, Sebastiano Folli, Holy Family and young St John (1614).

Via Provenzano continues to Via dei Rossi, and (right) to Piazza San Francesco (good view of the Osservanza), with the large Gothic church of **San Francesco** (Pl. I; 7), built in 1326–1475, all but destroyed in the fire of 1655, and afterwards used as a barracks for a long period. In 1885–92 it was heavily restored; the façade is by Vittorio Mariani and Gaetano Ceccarelli (1894–1913), but the pretty campanile survives from 1763. The cold INTERIOR has late-19C stained glass (restored after the War). High up on the W wall have been placed detached frescoes from the Porta Romana by Sassetta and Sano di Pietro, and from Porta Pispini by Sodoma. SOUTH WALL. Two frescoed tabernacles with the Visitation and saints by the 14–15C Sienese school. In a 14C carved tabernacle has been placed an ancient wood Crucifix. SOUTH TRANSEPT. In the chapel, fresco of a polyptych with the Madonna enthroned and saints by Lippo Vanni. The marble statue of St Francis (against the wall of the transept) has recently been attributed to a 15C sculptor influenced by Francesco di Valdambrino. CHOIR CHAPELS. Outside the fourth chapel to the right of the sanctuary, pavement tomb of 1541 with graffiti decoration (on a cartoon attributed to Beccafumi). In the third chapel, small relief of Mary Magdalene between two angels; second chapel, funerary monument of Cristoforo Felici, with a very unusual carved effigy by Urbano da Cortona (1462–87); first chapel right of the choir, 14C Sienese Madonna and Child (attributed to Andrea Vanni). On the left wall of the sanctuary, two busts of Silvio Piccolomini and Vittoria Forteguerri (father and mother of Pius II), made for their tomb and probably dating from the 15C. First chapel left of the choir, detached fresco of the Crucifixion by Pietro Lorenzetti; third chapel, two fine *frescoes by Ambrogio Lorenzetti, one with the Martyrdom of Franciscan monks and one with a scene of St Louis of Toulouse before Pope Boniface VIII. Fourth chapel left of the choir, Madonna and Child enthroned (restored), attributed to Jacopo di Mino. In the NORTH TRANSEPT is a chapel with a fine marble pavement by Il Marrina. NORTH WALL. Detached fresco of the Crucifix and St Jerome, sculptural fragments from the ancient church, and the huge monumental doorway by Francesco di Giorgio Martini removed from the façade of the church. The Renaissance CLOISTERS house the Faculty of Political Science of the University.

To the right of the church stands the **Oratorio di San Bernardino** (Pl. I; 7; 15C), on the spot where the saint preached (open April–Nov, 10.30–13.30, 15–17.30). The LOWER CHAPEL has lunettes frescoed with scenes representing the saint's life by 17C Sienese artists including Francesco Vanni, Domenico Manetti, Ventura Salimbeni, and Rutilio Manetti. The painting in the ceiling with a view of Siena (1580) is by Francesco Vanni. The paintings include a *Madonna and Child by Sano di Pietro, and works by

Astolfo Petrazzi and Bernardino Mei. In the vestibule on the first floor is a standard by Francesco Vanni and a bas-relief signed by Giovanni di Agostino (1341). The *UPPER CHAPEL, beautifully decorated by Ventura Turapilli (after 1496), contains good frescoes of 1518 by Sodoma (Present-ation, Visitation, Assumption and Coronation of the Virgin), Beccafumi (Marriage of the Virgin, Transition of the Virgin), and Girolamo del Pacchia.

Via dei Rossi, arched at either end, returns to Via Banchi di Sopra which ends (right) at **Piazza Salimbeni** (Pl. II; 2), laid out at the end of the last century when the three palaces were enlarged or restored. In the centre is *Palazzo Salimbeni*, enlarged in neo-Gothic style in 1866 by Giuseppe Partini. On the left is *Palazzo Tantucci* by Bartolomeo Neroni (1548), restored by Partini and, opposite, *Palazzo Spannocchi* which has a fine façade by Giuliano da Maiano in Via Banchi di Sopra, and a façade in the piazza by Partini in imitation of the Renaissance style. These three palaces form the seat of the MONTE DEI PASCHI DI SIENA, a banking establishment founded in 1624, which owns an interesting collection of works of art (admission only with special permission). It includes paintings by Sano di Pietro, Sassetta, Giovanni di Paolo, the Maestro dell'Osservanza, Benvenuto di Giovanni, Domenico Beccafumi, Rutilio Manetti, and Bernardino Mei. The bank also owns most of the Chigi Saracini Collection.

Costa dell'Incrociata descends from the piazza to Via della Sapienza. Here is the church of **San Pellegrino a Sapienza** (Pl. II; 2). The vault was frescoed in the 18C by Giuliano Traballesi. On the S side (behind glass) is a tiny ivory portable altar known as the *Madonna delle Grazie*, a precious work probably by a French craftsman, a rare survival from the 14C. On the wall beside it is a small incised marble Crucifix, a very unusual work (removed for restoration), recently attributed to Guccio di Mannaia (c 1310). On the S altar, Lorenzo Feliciati, Madonna of the Misericordia (1772). On the N and S walls are two fragments of a painting with St Paul and a bishop saint by a follower of Ambrogio Lorenzetti. On the high altar, Giuseppe Nasini, Birth of the Virgin. The N altarpiece of the Preaching of St Paul is by Alessandro Calvi. The six stucco statues in niches are by Giuseppe Mazzuoli the Younger. The beautiful painting, now attributed to the bottega of Simone Martini, of the Blessed Andrea Gallerani (founder of the Misericordia) has been restored but not yet returned to the church. Parallel to Via della Sapienza is the interesting medieval Vicolo della Pallacorda.

The **Biblioteca Comunale** (Pl. II; 2; open weekdays 9–20; Saturday 9–14) contains over 100,000 volumes and 5000 MSS., as well as illuminated missals, breviaries, and books of hours, St Catherine's letters, a 7C papyrus from Ravenna, drawings by Peruzzi and Beccafumi, a work by Dante with illuminations by Botticelli, and fine examples of bookbinding (including an 11C Byzantine work). Beyond, Costa Sant'Antonio descends from Via della Sapienza to the entrance to the **Casa di Santa Caterina** (Pl. II; 5; open 9–12.30, 15.30–18), the house where St Catherine of Siena was born, converted into a sanctuary after its purchase by the Comune in 1466.

Caterina Benincasa (1347–80), or Catherine of Siena, was the daughter of a dyer and took the veil at the age of eight. Her visions of the Redeemer, from whom she received the stigmata and, like her Alexandrian namesake, a marriage ring, have been the subject of countless paintings. Her eloquence persuaded Gregory XI to return from Avignon to Rome, and her letters (preserved in the Biblioteca Comunale; see above) are models of style as well as of devotion. She died in Rome, was canonised in 1461, and in 1939 was proclaimed a patron saint of Italy. She was made a doctor of the Church in 1970, the first female saint, with St Teresa of Avila, to be given this distinction.

The present entrance is through a PORTICO erected in 1941. Beyond, the charming little LOGGIA was built perhaps by Peruzzi or by his follower Giovanni Battista Pelori (1533). Here is (left) the ORATORIO DELLA CUCINA, the family kitchen converted into an oratory, which has the most interesting decorations. On the wall to the left of the entrance: paintings by Alessandro Casolani, Pietro Sorri (St Catherine liberating a woman possessed of the devil), Pomarancio, Lattanzio Bonastri and Gaetano Marinelli (1872). The altarpiece is by Bernardino Fungai, and on either side are two paintings by Riccio. On the wall right of the altar: paintings by Pietro Aldi (1872), Riccio and Arcangelo Salimbeni (1578), Pomarancio, and Alessandro Casolani. On the wall opposite the altar, is a curved painting in a niche by Francesco Vanni, and on either side, works by Pietro Sorri, Rutilio Manetti, and Francesco Vanni. The wood stalls date from 1518 and 1555, and the majolica pavement from the 16C. Opposite is the CHURCH OF THE CROCI-FISSO built in 1623 on the site of the Saint's orchard to house the Crucifixion (by the late-12C Pisan school) before which St Catherine received the stigmata at Pisa in 1375, now over the high altar. It is preserved in a cupboard decorated by Riccio. The marble high altar is by Tommaso Redi (1649). In the S transept is an altarpiece by Sebastiano Conca and in the N transept an altarpiece by Rutilio and Domenico Manetti. Stairs lead down to the CAMERA DELLA SANTA, St Catherine's cell, frescoed by Alessandro Franchi in 1896. It preserves a small painting of St Catherine receiving the stigmata by Girolamo di Benvenuto. Below is the ORATORIO DELLA TINTORIA or SANTA CATERINA IN FONTEBRANDA, now the oratory of the CONTRADA DELL'OCA and only open on special occasions. It was built in 1465 on the site of the dyer's workshop. It contains frescoes of five angels by Sodoma, and St Catherine receiving the stigmata and other scenes from her life, by Girolamo del Pacchia and Ventura Salimbeni. The splendid polychrome wood *statue of St Catherine is by Neroccio di Bartolomeo, sculpted for this oratory in 1475.

Vicolo del Tiratoio passes under the house of St Catherine and a pretty little lane leads downhill to the Fonte Branda, described in Rte 14D.

Costa Sant'Antonio is continued beyond Via Santa Caterina by Via della Galluzza which climbs steeply beneath numerous flying arches to Via di Diacceto. This street then leads (right) over Via di Fontebranda (view over a low wall of San Domenico) and emerges beneath an arch in Piazza San Giovanni outside the Baptistery (see Rte 14B).

San Domenico can be reached either by Via della Sapienza (see above) or from Costa Sant'Antonio, by taking Vicolo del Campaccio through the first archway on the left, a lane which climbs up above St Catherine's house to Via Camporegio. At the top of the hill of Camporegio stands the austere Gothic church of **San Domenico** (Pl. II; 5), begun in 1226, enlarged, damaged, and altered in successive centuries. The campanile dates from 1340 (altered in 1798). From the edge of the hill there is a view of the Duomo and Palazzo Pubblico above old houses on a hillside. The INTERIOR is built in the usual Dominican form, with a wide aisleless nave, transepts, and a shallow choir with side chapels. The CAPPELLA DELLE VOLTE, a chapel at the W end, contains the only authentic portrait of St Catherine, by her contemporary and friend, Andrea Vanni; in this chapel she assumed the Dominican habit and several of her miracles occurred. The paintings here are by Mattia Preti and Crescenzio Gambarelli. S Side: first altar, Alessandro Casolani, Birth of the Virgin (1584); beyond opens the CAPPELLA DI SANTA CATERINA (being restored). On the entrance arch, Saints Luke and Jerome, by Sodoma. The tabernacle on the altar, by Giovanni di Stefano

(1466) encloses a reliquary containing St Catherine's head. On the right and left of the altar are celebrated *frescoes by Sodoma (1526), representing the saint in ecstasy and swooning. The pilasters have good grotesques. On the left wall, the saint interceding for the life of a young man brought to repentance, also by Sodoma; on the right wall, Francesco Vanni, the saint liberating a man possessed. The beautiful pavement is attributed to Giovanni di Stefano. Above the steps down to the huge crypt (begun in the 14C, but usually closed) is a detached fresco of the Madonna and Child and a Knight attributed to Pietro Lorenzetti. The *Nativity is by Francesco di Giorgio Martini and an assistant. The Pietà in the lunette above is by Matteo di Giovanni and the predella by Bernardino Fungai.

Over the high altar is a fine *tabernacle with two angels, by Benedetto da Maiano (c 1475; difficult to appreciate because of the incongruous stained glass in the E windows). In the first chapel right of the altar have been hung fragmentary remains of frescoes by Andrea Vanni and Lippo Memmi, detached from the cloister, and a triptych of the Madonna and Child with Saints Jerome and John the Baptist by Matteo di Giovanni. In the first chapel left of the sanctuary, polychrome wood statue of St Anthony Abbot attributed to Giovanni di Turino. In the second chapel left of the altar, incongruous 18C frescoes by Giuseppe Nasini surround *St Barbara enthroned between angels and Saints Mary Magdalene and Catherine by Matteo di Giovanni, opposite a Madonna and Child with four saints by Benvenuto di Giovanni. On the third altar on the N side, Sodoma, four saints and God the Father and the Mysteries of the Rosary (surrounding a 14C Madonna and Child, removed for restoration). On the second N altar, Rutilio Manetti, Miracle of St Anthony Abbot.

From Piazza San Domenico Viale dei Mille leads above the STADIUM (Pl. I; 5, 6) on the floor of the valley, to the huge **Fortezza Medicea** (Pl. I; 5), or *Forte di Santa Barbara*, built for Cosimo I de' Medici by Baldassarre Lanci in 1560. On the bastions are avenues with delightful views. In the vaults is the *Enoteca Italica*, an exhibition of Italian wines (open 12–midnight).

From San Domenico the unattractive Viale Curtatone leads past the neo-classical *Evangelical Church* (1882) to the undistinguished *Piazza Matteotti* (Pl. II; 1) with the huge Post Office built in 1910 (by Vittorio Mariani). Here is the little *Oratorio delle Suore* (or *del Paradiso*) of the CONTRADA DEL DRAGO (Pl. II; 1), approached by a double staircase. The interior, decorated in 1693, has paintings by Francesco Rustici, Domenico Manetti, and Raffaello Vanni. The bust of St Catherine in polychrome terracotta is by Marrina.

From San Domenico Via della Sapienza and Costa dell'Incrociata return to Piazza Salimbeni (see above). Via Montanini continues N passing the little *Oratorio di Santa Maria delle Nevi* (Pl. II; 1; usually locked), an elegant Renaissance building (1471) attributed to Francesco di Giorgio Martini. The *altarpiece (Madonna delle Nevi) is by Matteo di Giovanni (1477).

Via di Vallerozzi descends steeply towards Porta Ovile. On the right Via dell'Abbadia leads up to Piazza Abbadia with the *Rocca di Palazzo Salimbeni* (14C; restored in the Gothic style in the 19C). High up in the courtyard can be seen the Medici coat of arms by Domenico Cafaggi (1570). In the piazza is the church of **San Michele al Monte di San Donato** (Pl. II; 2), transformed in 1691 and heavily restored. In the INTERIOR the inner door dates from 1918. SOUTH WALL. Antonio Buonfigli (attributed), Madonna of the Rosary, and (above) fresco fragments; first altar, Annibale Mazzuoli, Madonna and St Apollonia. Beyond the second altar, in a stucco frame, Crucifix and saints attributed to Antonio Buonfigli or Francesco Nasini. The SOUTH TRANSEPT has 18C paintings by Giovanni Battista Sorbi. Here is displayed a small polychrome wood group of the *Pietà, a very unusual work (restored in 1986) now attributed to Vecchietta. On the high altar are two marble angels in the manner of Giuseppe Mazzuoli. The CHOIR, with frescoes by Ademollo, is hung with paintings by Andrea Vanni, Benedetto di Bindo and Sodoma. The N transept has paintings by Antonio Nasini (1693). On the N side is a heavily restored wood statue of St Anthony.

Via di Vallerozzi continues down to the church of *San Rocco*, the oratory of the CONTRADA DELLA LUPA (Pl. I; 6), with a classical column outside bearing a bronze copy of the she-wolf of Rome. The interior has fine 17C Sienese paintings by Raffaello Vanni, Rutilio Manetti, and Ventura Salimbeni. From here it is a short way left, off Via Pian d'Ovile, to the brick *Fonte Nuova di Ovile* (Pl. I; 7; 1303) with two fine Gothic arches, reached by steps below the road. Via Vallerozzi ends at **Porta Ovile** (Pl. I; 7); on the left is a tabernacle with a fresco of the Madonna and Child with saints by Sano di Pietro. The fine gate dates from the 14C; outside there is a view back of a stretch of walls with orchards and old houses and the flank of the church of San Francesco. Steps go down to the picturesque *Fonte d'Ovile* (1262). Just inside the gate, in Via del Comune is the headquarters of the CONTRADA DEL BRUCO (Pl. I; 7), one of the most characteristic in the town. In the oratory is a Madonna and Child by Luca di Tommè. One of the poorest parts of the town in the Middle Ages, there was a revolt here in 1371 of the workers belonging to the Contrada.

Via Montanini continues N past (No. 92) *Palazzo Ottieri (Costantini)*, with a 15C façade attributed to Francesco di Giorgio Martini, with fine ironwork. Farther on, on the right, is the church of **Sant'Andrea** (Pl. I; 6), approached by steps added in 1755. It was founded in the 12C, transformed in the 18C, and restored in this century. In the INTERIOR on the S side are (first altar), fine 15C frescoes of the Madonna and Child with St Anne, and (second altar) a pretty stucco frame enclosing a fresco by Apollonio Nasini. Over the high altar, Coronation of the Virgin, signed and dated by Giovanni di Paolo (1445). On the N side (second altar), another fresco by Nasini enclosed in a stucco frame, and (first altar) fragments of 15C frescoes. On the W wall is a stucco bas-relief of the Madonna and Child by the 15C Sienese school. On Via Montanini is the *Oratorio di Sant'Anna in Sant' Onofrio* which preserves a half-length figure in terracotta of St Bernardine (right of the high altar) dating from the end of the 15C (in the manner of Cozzarelli). The stucco statues in the niches date from 1769.

Via Montanini ends at a fork with Via di Camollia and the unattractive Via Garibaldi on the curve of which (and considerably below the level of the road) is the church of *San Sebastiano* (locked), which contains early-17C frescoes. Via Camollia continues N and Via dei Gazzani diverges left for the church of *Santo Stefano* (closed for restoration), rebuilt in 1671–75. On the high altar is a polyptych by Andrea Vanni (1400) with a predella by Giovanni di Paolo. It also contains paintings by Rutilio Manetti and Antonio Bonfigli. The church is on the corner of *La Lizza* (Pl. I; 5, 6), a small attractive public park laid out in 1778 by Antonio Matteucci and Leopoldo Prucher with two diverging avenues of horse-chestnuts and cedars of Lebanon beside the Fortezza Medicea (see above). The good statue of Garibaldi is by Raffaello Romanelli. A market is held in this area on Wednesdays. The Palazzo di Giustizia was built here in 1986.

Via del Romitorio leads down from the church of Santo Stefano under a tunnel and past a little garden to the church of **Santa Maria in Portico a Fontegiusta** (Pl. I; 1, 2), an elegant little Renaissance church. On the brick façade is a fine marble portal (1489) with a frieze attributed to Giovanni di Stefano. The INTERIOR is in the form of a vaulted hall. The tiny round window on the W wall has restored 15C stained glass. The fresco on the right of the Visitation (1522) is attributed to Scalabrino. On the S altar, Bernardino Fungai, Coronation of the Virgin with saints. On the E wall (right of the high altar), Francesco Vanni, Intercession of the Blessed Ambrogio Sansedoni for the protection of Siena (portrayed below). The *HIGH ALTAR is a splendid work in marble in the form of a classical edicola by Marrina (c 1517) with a lunette of Christ in Pietà (by Michele Cioli da Settignano) and two winged Victories. It surrounds the highly venerated Madonna di Fontegiusto, a late 14C fresco. On either side of the altar are faded frescoes by Ventura Salimbeni and the large lunette above has a fine fresco of the Virgin in Glory by Girolamo di Benvenuto (1515). By the door on the N side is a tiny stoup in bronze, signed and dated 1480 by Giovanni delle Bombarde. On the N wall is a fresco (partly repainted) of the Sibyl announcing to Augustus the Birth of Christ, attributed to Baldassarre Peruzzi or Daniele da Volterra. A small MUSEUM has been arranged in an old tower. Among the contents are an interesting bronze ciborium, tradi- tionally attributed to Vecchietta, a polychrome wood statue of St Sebastian, attributed to Giovanni di Stefano, and a terracotta bust of St Bernardine attributed to Vecchietta.

From the front of the church of Fontegiusto the short Via Fontegiusto leads up beneath a pretty arch to Via di Camollia. On the right is the headquarters and oratory of the CONTRADA DELL'ISTRICE (Pl. I; 2). Via di Camollia continues left to the church of *San Pietro alla Magione* (Pl. I; 1) with a rebuilt façade and a Gothic portal. In the interior are numerous remains of detached 14C frescoes, and (in a niche on the right wall) a 15C sinopia of the Madonna and Child. The little marble tabernacle on the right of the sanctuary is derived from the façade of the Duomo. The adjoining 16C chapel contains a fresco of the Madonna and Child by Riccio. Surrounding the church are the restored buildings of the *Magione*, a medieval pilgrims' hospice founded by the Knights Templar.

Via di Camollia ends at the *Porta Camollia* (Pl. I; 1), rebuilt in 1604 and inscribed *Cor magis tibi sena pandit* to commemorate a visit of the Grand- duke Ferdinando I. A few steps beyond is a column recalling the meeting on this spot of Frederick III and Eleanora of Portugal in March 1451 (depicted in the frescoes in the Libreria Piccolomini, see Rte 14B). Beyond the column is the *Antiporto* or barbican (1675), in imitation of the Porta Romana. In Via Cavour, c 500m from the antiporta, is the brick *Palazzo dei Diavoli* or *dei Turchi* attributed to Antonio Federighi (1460). From either end of Via Camollia roads descend to Piazzale Francesco di Giorgio and the Viale Mazzini leading to the railway station.

G.   Environs of Siena

The convent and church of **L'Osservanza** is the most important Sienese church outside the walls. About 2.5km from Porta Ovile (see Rte 14F; Pl. I; 7), it is reached by Via Simone Martini and the 16C *Madonnina Rossa* (beyond the railway crossing). The basilica (admission 9–13, 16–19) was founded in 1423 by St Bernardine with the object of restoring the obser- vance of the original Franciscan rule, relaxed by papal dispensations. The convent was enlarged in 1476–90 probably by Francesco di Giorgio Martini and Giacomo Cozzarelli. It was confiscated by the city in 1874, and well rebuilt in 1949 after severe War damage. In the INTERIOR the stucco and terracotta roundels in the vaults and in the sanctuary are attributed to Giacomo Cozzarelli. On the W wall the two roundels with saints surrounded by garlands of fruit are attributed to Andrea Della Robbia. On either side of the entrance to the sanctuary, white glazed figures of the Annunciatory Angel and the Virgin in tabernacles, by Andrea Della Robbia. LEFT SIDE: first altar, Sano di Pietro, Madonna and Child, with four angels; second altar, Andrea Della Robbia, blue and white enamelled terracotta altarpiece of the Coronation of the Virgin; fourth altar, four saints by Andrea di Bartolo (1413). In the sanctuary is a fresco with its sinopia by Pietro di Francesco Orioli. RIGHT SIDE: detached fresco of the Crucifixion by Bartolomeo Neroni; third altar, Sano di Pietro, Madonna and Child with saints. On the right wall, St Elizabeth of Hungary by Girolamo di Benvenuto, and, on the left wall, St Bernardine by Pietro di Giovanni d'Ambrogio; fourth altar, triptych attributed to the Maestro dell'Osservanza, named from this painting. In the sacristy is a group of seven polychrome terracotta *figures mourning over the dead Christ, by Giacomo Cozzarelli (beautifully restored in 1984). A small MUSEUM contains a Head of Christ by Lando di Pietro (1338), all that remains of a wood Crucifix destroyed in 1944, and a *reliquary of St Bernardine by Francesco d'Antonio (1454). The *Certosa di Pontignano*, about 8km from Porta Ovile, is described in Rte 13A.

Near Porta Pispini (see Rte 14E; Pl. I; 12) the Strada di Busseto leads out of the town, and beyond the railway is the pretty little hamlet of *Sant'Agnese a Vignano*, visited by Stendhal. Here the villa of Cesare Brandi (1906–88), with a fine library and art collection, is used by the University of Siena as a Fine Arts Institute.

Outside Porta Camollia (see Rte 14F; Pl. I; 1), Via Caduti di Vicobello and the Strada di Vico Alto lead towards the *Villa di Vicobello* built on a hill for the Chigi by Baldassarre Peruzzi. It is surrounded by a large garden, the best preserved private 16C garden near Siena (admission by appointment).

The approach road for the Siena–Florence superstrada passes close to the *Villa di Montarioso*, now a seminary, with a collection of works of art from churches in the region not at present open to the public.

Outside Porta Romana (see Rte 14E; Pl. I; 16) is the *Certosa di Maggiano*, probably the first charterhouse to be founded in Tuscany. It was built in 1315 and suppressed in 1782; it is now restored as a hotel. The church has an interesting 18C interior (frescoes by the Nasini) and sculptures by the Mazzuoli.

FROM SIENA TO LECCETO, CASTELLO DI CELSA, AND CETINALE, 25km. From Porta San Marco (Rte 14D; Pl. I; 13) N73 (signposted for Roccastrada and Grosseto) passes near (3km; left) the battlemented *Villa di Monastero*, formerly the abbey of Sant'Eugenio (suppressed in 1810). About 500m farther on, a by-road on the right leads to (5km) the 12C CASTELLO DI BELCARO, in a lovely position (admission weekdays 14–16 on application), enlarged in the 16C by Peruzzi. The main road continues to (9km) a turning (right) for (11km) **Leceto** (326m) in thick ilex woods. This magnificent fortified monastery, founded on the site of an ancient hermitage, is now inhabited by Augustinian nuns and is therefore only partly visible (Mass on fest. at 17.00). The CHURCH has a simple Romanesque façade, partly covered by a portico with remains of frescoes. The interior was transformed in the late Baroque period and a marble screen placed behind the altar to separate the nave from the choir. In the nave are the two fine pavement tombs of Niccolò Saracini (1350) and Jacopo Magistri Martini (1499). On the nave wall are some interesting fresco fragments. The 'Madonna of Lecceto' by Ambrogio Lorenzetti is now kept in Villa di Montarioso (see above). A rare series of twenty choirbooks, with miniatures by Giovanni di Paolo and others, which belong to the monastery, are now preserved in the Biblioteca degli Intronati in Siena. Next to the church is the entrance to the *Cloister* (bell beside the door), built in brick on two storeys, with stone columns supporting the lower loggia. From here there is a good view of the impressive square battlemented tower.

This by-road continues to (15km) the little Romanesque-Gothic church of SAN LEONARDO AL LAGO (reached by a narrow track on the left; the signpost has been knocked down). Situated on a small hill (292m) it dominates a valley which was once a lake. It has a rose window over the doorway. In the interior, the apse is entirely frescoed with scenes of the Life of the Virgin (with angels in the vault), by Lippo Vanni (1360–70). To the right of the church (ring the bell) are remains of the former monastery, including the refectory with a Crucifixion frescoed by Giovanni di Paolo. The by-road leads uphill to (22km) the CASTELLO DI CELSA (504m), approached by an avenue of umbrella pines. Originally a medieval castle, it was transformed in the early 16C into a villa with a garden facing Siena, designed by Baldassarre Peruzzi. He may also have built the elegant circular chapel which is visible from the road. Although extensively restored, partly in neo-Gothic style, it presents a romantic sight in this isolated position. An unsurfaced road winds down through ilex and cypress woods S to (25km) CETINALE (337m), a grandiose villa in a superb position. It was built by Carlo Fontana for Cardinal Fabio Chigi in 1680. Its vast park, known as 'La Tebaide' was one of the celebrated curiosities of the Baroque era. Numerous statues of hermits and little chapels along the paths winding through the woods were intended to evoke an atmosphere of prayer and contemplation for the visitor. A steep flight of steps leads to the Romitorio (hermitage), a little building which dominates the surrounding landscape. There is also an English garden created since 1977. The most direct return from here to Siena is along the by-road which continues S via Ancaiano and Sovicille (described in Rte 19A) to rejoin N73.

15

Florence to Volterra

The fastest road to Volterra from Florence is via the Florence–Siena super-strada as far as (48km) the exit *Colle Val d'Elsa Nord*. Here N68 continues W past (51km) Colle Val d'Elsa (described in Rte 17). The beautiful road runs along a pretty ridge of hills with wide views including the towers of San Gimignano, 12km N (also described in Rte 17). The road then climbs through magnificent countryside to reach the distinctive open landscape around (78km) Volterra (described in Rte 16).

An alternative, but much slower route, described below, follows the **Via Volterrana**, considered one of the most beautiful roads in Tuscany. 18km *Cerbaia*—27km *Montespertoli*—39km **Castelfiorentino** (for **Certaldo**, 9km)—47km *Gambassi Terme*—50km turning for *Montaione and San Vivaldo*—55km *Il Castagno*—76km **Volterra**.

Information Offices. APT of Florence (Tel. 055/290832) for Castelfiorentino and Certaldo.

Railway. Services from Florence to Empoli in 20mins. From Empoli (with some through trains from Florence) to Castelfiorentino (in 15mins) and Certaldo (in 30 minutes).

Bus Services run by SITA (infrequent daily service) from Florence (via Porta Romana and Galluzzo) to Cerbaia, Montespertoli, Castelfiorentino, and Certaldo in 1hr 40mins. To Volterra along the Via Volterrana once a day in 2hrs 40mins.

Florence is left by Porta Romana (Pl. 18) and the Via Senese continues to Galluzzo. Here the Via Volterrana diverges right and winds upwards above the Certosa del Galluzzo (see Rte 2) with a fine view back over Florence and the surrounding hills. On the right is the Romanesque church of *Sant'Alessandro a Giogoli* (12C), in a pretty position, from which there is a view of *I Collazzi*, one of the grandest Florentine villas of the 16C. It is surrounded by olive trees and a park with cypresses and pines. The formal garden, which includes a splendid terrace of lemon trees from which there is a magnificent view, can sometimes be visited by appointment. The road continues through a wooded valley with pine groves, and beyond (18km) *Cerbaia* (Luxury-class restaurant *Tenda Rossa*) crosses the river Pesa and traverses Montagnana. 20km The *Villa of Montegufoni* is conspicuous on the right of the road. Originally a medieval castle of the Acciaiuoli family, its tower, built in 1386, was modelled on that of Palazzo Vecchio in Florence. The villa was rebuilt in the 17C; in 1909 it was purchased by Sir George Sitwell, and was the home of his three children, Edith, Osbert and Sacheverell, until Sir Osbert's death in 1969 (it is now a hotel-residence). The little church of San Lorenzo (rebuilt in the 17C) has a Crucifix by Taddeo Gaddi, a Madonna by Lippo di Benivieni, and a fresco of St Lawrence by Gian Domenico Ferretti (1764). Many paintings from the Uffizi were stored in the villa during the last War. The road proceeds through beautiful countryside and, at 24km, just past Baccaiano, a by-road diverges left to *Poppiano* (298m), a castle of the Guicciardini family famous for its wine (*Chianti Colli Fiorentini*), next to a little village with an old church.

27km **Montespertoli** (first-class restaurants *La Terrazza*, Viale Matteotti, and *Il Focolare* at Montagnana; and trattoria *Baccaiano* at Baccaiano), is a small town at the heart of another important wine-growing area (which produces *Chianti Putto*, *Chianti Colli Fiorentini*, *Montalbano* and *Galestro*). The main piazza, forming a triangle with a well at the centre, has an interesting 17C building enclosing the *Oratory of the Misericordia* with two gabled clock-towers surmounted by small bells. Also facing the piazza is the church of *Sant'Andrea* (16C, but rebuilt after the War) which has an early-12C baptismal *font, decorated with marble inlay. Over the high altar is a 14C Crucifix and there is also a damaged triptych by Niccolò Gerini.

Outside Montespertoli (2km along the Tresanti road) is the pieve of *San Pietro in Mercato* (open on Sunday at 11). Probably founded in the 10C, the present building was consecrated in 1057. It has a basilican plan with three apses and three naves separated by simple arched piers devoid of decoration. Left of the entrance, beneath a lunette with a fresco of the Baptism of Christ by the school of Ghirlandaio, is a 12C baptismal *font, with simple geometrical motifs inlaid in coloured marble. A MUSEUM in the conventual buildings is due to open in 1995 for works removed for protection from churches in the neighbourhood (including Sant'Andrea a Botinaccio, San

Biagio a Poppiano, Santa Maria a Torri, San Bartolomeo a Tresanti, and San Giusto a Montalbino.

The road continues along a ridge, with wide views on either side, to (39km) **CASTELFIORENTINO** (17,500 inhab.; 2-star hotel *Lami*), situated on the river Elsa, with the old walled town above on a rocky spur (108m). At the entrance to the LOWER TOWN (left) is the church of **Santa Verdiana** rebuilt in the 18C on the site of the former Romanesque church of Sant'Antonio. The elegant FAADE, with a portico, is by Bernardo Fallani and Giuseppe Manetti. The *INTERIOR, entirely decorated with frescoes by a group of 18C Florentine artists to an overall architectural design by Foggini, forms a unique and charming complex of exceptional freshness and luminosity. The nave vault, the twelve hemispherical domes of the side chapels and the paintings of the apse and altars depict the legend, miracles and apotheosis of Santa Verdiana. This local saint, after making a pilgrimage to Compostela and another to Rome, chose to live the rest of her life as an anchoress in a walled-up cell (in the church crypt). Renowned for her holiness, Verdiana died c 1242 after living 34 years in the company of two snakes which were sent, in answer to her prayers, to try her patience. The Glory of St Verdiana in the nave vault is by Alessandro Gherardini (1708), with painted architecture by Lorenzo il Moro. The cupola above the transept representing the saint received into heaven is by Matteo Bonechi (1716). The small domes were frescoed by Giovanni Camillo Sagrestani, Agostino Veracini, Ranieri del Pace, Antonio Puglieschi, and Niccolò Lapi. The altarpieces include: Jacopo da Empoli, Assumption of the Virgin (enlarged by Gherardini a century later with the addition of putti); Orazio Fidani, ecstasy of St Francis (1644); Simone Pignoni, charity of St Thomas of Villanova (1664); Giovanni Martinelli, Three saints; and Giovanni Domenico Ferretti, two scenes from the life of St Verdiana. Three large paintings dating from the 1630s (Reclusion of St Verdiana by Giovanni Battista Ghidoni, her death by Bartolomeo Salvestrini, and her funeral by Filippo Tarchiani), removed from the apse in the 19C, have been restored and will be returned here to their original frames, thus completing the recent restoration of the entire church.

In the *Canonica* of Santa Verdiana a small *Museum* is being installed with earlier works from the church, including paintings by Taddeo Gaddi, Taddeo di Bartolo, and Francesco Granacci. It will also house paintings and sculptures from the churches of Voltigiano, Cambiano, Ortimino, and Petrazzi, as well as illuminated manuscripts and liturgical objects. Across the garden in front of Santa Verdiana is the apse of *San Francesco*, a 13C Franciscan church built in brick, which was badly flooded in 1966 and is now being restored. It has 14C frescoes by Giovanni del Biondo.

Signposts (*Affreschi del Gozzoli*) indicate the way to the UPPER TOWN. Here at No. 41 Via Tilli (named after Michelangelo Tilli, the 17C physician, botanist, and philosopher) the **Biblioteca Comunale** (open Tuesday, Thursday, and Saturday 16–19; fest. 10–12, 16–19) houses detached frescoes by Benozzo Gozzoli from two chapels. The *TABERNACLE OF THE 'MADONNA DELLA TOSSE' comes from Castelnuovo d'Elsa, a few kilometres N of Castelfiorentino. A neo-Gothic chapel was built round it in the mid-19C to protect the frescoes, which have now been detached. The vault of the tabernacle has a figure of Christ and the four Evangelists. The trompe-l'oeil altarpiece represents the Madonna and Child enthroned with Saints Peter, Catherine, Margaret and Paul surrounded by angels holding up a red curtain. The Dormition of the Virgin and her Assumption are depicted on the two side walls. The frescoes were painted by Benozzo Gozzoli and his workshop in 1484. The larger •TABERNACLE OF THE VISITATION is dated 1490; badly damaged by damp and flooding, it was detached in 1965 from a chapel in Castelfiorentino when the fine sinopie were found. Although in fragmentary condition, the surviving scenes illustrating the life of the Virgin are a typical example of Gozzoli's charming narrative style. The episodes, painted in a rich range of colours, are transformed into scenes of everyday life, full of picturesque details, with architectural and landscape backgrounds.

Via Tilli leads into *Piazza del Popolo* with the *Municipio* on the left, surmounted by its clock tower and bell which chimes every hour when the little seated soldier called 'Membrino' strikes it with a hammer. Steps lead up from the piazza to the Romanesque church of *San Leonardo*, which was rebuilt inside in the 16C. It has a pretty cupola which is visible from the street along the left side of the church. This street climbs towards the 12C •**Pieve di Sant'Ippolito** (originally San Biagio, the parish church of the medieval Castello). It stands at the top of a flight of steps in a beautiful panoramic position dominating the countryside and the towers and roofs of the old town. The simple brick FAÇADE has a two-light window above which are decorative ceramic bowls. A marble inscription records the creation of the Tuscan League in 1197, the first Treaty between Volterra, Lucca, Siena, San Miniato, and Florence. The simple INTERIOR (extensively restored; if closed, the key is available from the old people's home next door) has fine proportions. Over the baptismal font is a frescoed lunette with a half-length figure of the Dead Christ and two angels (14C). Behind the high altar is a Crucifix of the same period. On the left side of the church is a bell-cote with three bells, one of which is dated 1253. The elegant apse is visible from the garden (access from the church sacristy) which is partly enclosed by the old walls with remains of two towers.

5km N of Castelfiorentino, on the road to Castelnuovo d'Elsa, is the chapel of the *Madonna della Tosse*, where Benozzo Gozzoli's frescoes (see above) will eventually be reinstalled. The road continues to Castelnuovo and (left; 3km) the *Pieve di Coiano*, situated on a hill (182m). This ancient church, founded in the 11C, has a Pisan-type façade with a two-light window above the doorway and remains of 14C frescoes inside.

CERTALDO (15,600 inhab.) is 9km S of Castelfiorentino on the main road (N429) from Empoli to Poggibonsi along the Elsa valley. In Certaldo Alto: 2-star hotel *Il Castello* with restaurant, and *Osteria del Vicario* (with rooms to let). 2-star camping site 10km W at Marcialla. The old town of Certaldo is on a hill surrounded by a modern industrial suburb. In the LOWER TOWN is the main square, *Piazza Boccaccio* (car park), with a marble statue by Augusto Passaglia (1879) which was commissioned to celebrate the fifth centenary of the death of Giovanni Boccaccio (1313–75), the celebrated author of the *Decameron*, who died at Certaldo, and may also have been born here. The pseudo-Romanesque church of *San Tommaso*, patron saint of Certaldo, was founded in 1843. The adjacent *Canonica* at present houses some of the works destined for the Diocesan Museum which is to be opened in the upper town. They include: a monumental 13C •Crucifix in polychrome wood, and a polyptych by Puccio di Simone from San Donnino; •Madonna and Child by the Master of Bagnano (Meliore?); triptych by a close follower of Duccio; Madonna of the Rosary by Bernardo Monaldi and other paintings from Santa Maria a Bagnano; detached fresco of the Madonna (standing in a niche) by Cenni di Francesco from San Martino a Maiano. The four predella •scenes of the life of Beata Giulia of Certaldo, are attributed to Paolo Uccello (from the church of Santi Michele e Jacopo, see below). They depict her saving a child by miraculously passing through a fire unscathed, and thanking the children of Certaldo with flowers for having brought her bread.

Certaldo Alto (signposted) is reached on foot in c 10min. Built almost entirely of brick, the upper town has considerable charm and maintains its medieval character, despite some War damage. Its walls and gateways, dating from the 13–15C, are well preserved. All the principal buildings, as well as some attractive houses, face onto Via Boccaccio. Half-way up on the left is the CASA DEL BOCCACCIO (rebuilt in 1947), with a tower and loggia, which was bought and restored in the early 19C by Marchesa Carlotta dei Medici Lenzoni. Boccaccio is known to have spent part of his later years here (or in the contiguous house), enjoying a peaceful and simple life. He was buried in the nearby church. The house (open daily 9–12, 15–18) is now occupied by a Museum and the *Centro Nazionale di Studi sul Boccaccio*, with a small library containing all the editions and translations of his writings. On the first floor is a fresco representing Boccaccio in his study which was commissioned from Pietro Benvenuti by the Marchesa Carlotta in 1826. On the left of the little piazza is the *Compagnia dei Bianchi* to which the Diocesan Museum is to be moved (see above).

Opposite is the church of SANTI MICHELE E JACOPO, whose simple brick façade dates from the 13C. The interior was restored to its original Roman-esque appearance at the beginning of this century. Temporarily placed on the right of the entrance is the *'Tabernacolo dei Giustiziati' a small frescoed chapel representing Christ being taken down from the Cross, saints and other scenes, painted by Benozzo Gozzoli and Giusto d'Andrea in 1466. South Side. In a niche is an urn containing the body of Beata Giulia, who lived thirty years walled up in a cell next to the sacristy in order to devote herself to prayer and meditation. Her death in 1367 was announced by the mysterious tolling of all the bells in Certaldo. The predella, formerly on the altar of her chapel, is now in the Diocesan Museum, see above. Nearby is a glazed terracotta relief of the Madonna of Mercy with two kneeling saints and two small Della Robbian tabernacles (c 1500) on either side of the altar. On the N wall a door leads to the pretty 16C cloister. Beyond, in a round niche, is a *bust of Giovanni Boccaccio by Giovan Francesco Rustici of 1503 with an epitaph; his modern tombstone is now in the centre of the nave. To the left of the entrance is a niche with a fresco of the Madonna and Child with saints of the 14C Sienese school.

Beyond the church is PALAZZO PRETORIO, originally the castle of the Conti Alberti, with its façade decorated with picturesque coats of arms in stone and glazed terracotta which record the Governors (*Vicari*) sent from Florence. The INTERIOR is open in summer 9.30–12.30, 16.30–19.30, and in winter 10–12, 15–18. Around the COURTYARD are the rooms where justice was administered, dungeons, and a chapel with a fresco of Doubting Thomas attributed to Benozzo Gozzoli. Several rooms have fine doorways and fireplaces and still preserve remains of their fresco decoration. There is also a small collection of Roman and medieval finds from local excava-tions. A staircase leads up to the rooms of the former governors where temporary exhibitions are held. A terraced garden and a walkway over-looking the defence walls provides a splendid view stretching from the hills of the Val d'Elsa to San Gimignano. Across the garden on the ground floor is the side entrance to the 13C church of *Santi Tommaso e Prospero* which contains a few damaged 15C frescoes and some sinopie by Gozzoli.

From Castelfiorentino (see above) the Volterrana proceeds S towards Gambassi Termi, shortly before which, on a slight rise to the left, is the

• PIEVE DI SANTA MARIA A CHIANNI, a Pisan-Romanesque church of the late 13C, with three orders of blind arches on the façade. The exterior is built of honey-coloured sandstone. Fine lancet windows and two tall halfcolumns with interesting capitals decorate the exterior of the N transept. The Latin-cross INTERIOR has a basilican plan and raised chancel with a wide transept and five apses (the central apse was altered in the 16C) separated by half-columns. The columns dividing the nave from the aisles differ in type and size and have capitals decorated with floral, geometrical, and anthropomorphic motifs. There is a copy by Santi di Tito of Andrea del Sarto's Gambassi altarpiece (now in the Pitti Gallery in Florence). 47km GAMBASSI TERME, a small spa (1-star hotels), which is known for its springs of *Acqua Pillo*, has an attractive public garden outside the *Palazzo Civico* which houses a small collection of Etruscan and Roman finds excavated in the area. The town was already known in medieval times for the production of glass. It was the birthplace of Domenico Livi who made some of the stained-glass windows of Florence Cathedral in the 1430s. 50km. By-road (right) for Montaione (3km) and San Vivaldo (7km).

Montaione (3km) on a hill (342m; 3-star hotel *Vecchio Molino*) now has an unattractive modern suburb. Etruscan and Roman in origin, the medieval Castello, which had survived with its walls, towers and gates almost intact, suffered considerable damage in the Second World War. The old town has a simple plan of three parallel streets with a central piazza. The 13C church of *San Regolo*, was rebuilt in 1635 by Scipione Ammirato il Giovane, to a design perhaps by Bartolomeo Ammannati. The imposing bell-tower dates from 1795. It contains a 13C Madonna and Child by a follower of Cimabue. The *Palazzo Pretorio* dates from the 14C and its façade is decorated with numerous coats of arms. It now houses a local *Museum* (opened on request at the Comune), which contains an interesting collection of fossils, minerals, and prehistoric stone implements.

From Montaione a road leads through woods to **San Vivaldo** (7km), situated in the Bosco di Camporena (404m). This was originally a hermits' retreat and is associated with Beato Vivaldo Stricchi of San Gimignano, a Franciscan tertiary, who was found dead in a hollow tree in 1320. A chapel was built on the spot under the custody of Franciscan friars. In 1500–15 a friar named Tommaso created here a mystical itinerary or ideal pilgrimage to the Sacro Monte, or Holy Mountain, of Jerusalem, with 30 chapels containing tableaux representing the Life and Passion of Christ. Not all of these survive but 18 have been restored. The sequence comprised: the Annunciation, Flight into Egypt, Supper in the house of Simon the Pharisee, Last Supper, Christ praying in the Garden of Gethsemane, House of Pilate, Flagellation and Mocking of Christ, Jesus Condemned, Way to Calvary, Meeting with Mary His Mother, Meeting with the Holy Women, Veronica, Crucifixion, Deposition, Noli me Tangere, Doubting Thomas, Ascension, Pentecost, and Ascension. The terracotta figures are mostly Florentine, from the Della Robbia and Buglioni workshops, although a few are attributed to the Sienese sculptors Rustici and Cozzarelli. The chapels lead to the 15C church of *Santa Maria in Camporena* with a portico. It houses a Romanesque Crucifix and an altarpiece of the Madonna and Child with Saints Jerome, Francis, and Vivaldo by Raffaellino del Garbo.

5km W of San Vivaldo, across a more open landscape with clay downs and some interesting rock formations, is the little hill-top village of *Castelfalfi* in a pretty position, overlooking an 18-hole golf course.

The Via Volterrano (Strada Provinciale N. 4) leads S to (55km) *Il Castagno*. San Gimignano (described in Rte 17) is 11km E. There is a fine view of Volterra in front of a range of hills. The road continues W through wild and sparsely inhabited countryside and, after crossing the river Era, proceeds uphill past woods and olive groves. Volterra is approached from the NW with the church of Santi Giusto e Clemente forming a prominent landmark.

On either side are dramatic views of the precipices and eroded slopes of Le Balze. 76km **Volterra** is described in Rte 16.

16

Volterra

VOLTERRA lies in a magnificent position on a precipitous hill (555m) with open views in every direction across a splendid yellow and grey landscape of rolling clay hills. It is an austere medieval walled town (13,000 inhab.), the successor to an Etruscan city of much greater extent. Almost all the buildings are constructed out of panchina, a kind of limestone which is the matrix of alabaster, and which is found here in abundance. The town has for long been famous for the traditional skill of its craftsmen in working alabaster, and some two hundred workshops here still produce objets d'art.

Information Office. IAT, 2 Via Turazza (Tel. 0588/86150).

Railway Station at Saline di Volterra, 11km SW in the valley, on a branch line (some trains are substituted by buses) to Cecina (in 40min). Bus connection with trains from Piazza XX Settembre. Cecina is on the main line from Pisa to Rome (slow trains only).

Buses. Services run by SITA from Florence via Castelfiorentino in 2hrs 40min. Other services from Florence and Siena via Colle Val d'Elsa, where a change is necessary. Buses from Volterra to Pisa, Massa Marittima, and San Gimignano.

Large underground **car park** at the entrance to the town just before Piazza Martiri della Libertà. Other car parks outside the walls.

Hotels. 4-star: *San Lino*, 26 Via San Lino; 3-star: *Etruria*, 32 Via Matteotti; *Albergo Villa Nencini*, 55 Borgo Santo Stefano (outside Porta San Francesco); *Hotel Sole*, 10 Via dei Cappuccini.

Camping site (2-star) *Camping Comunale Le Balze*, Via Mandringa (open April–October). **Youth Hostel** *Ostello della Gioventù*, Via Don Minzoni.

Restaurants. First-class: *Etruria*, Piazza dei Priori. Trattorie and pizzerie: *Il Pozzo degli Etruschi*, 28 Via delle Prigioni; *La Pace*, 29 Via Don Minzoni; *Pizzeria il Rifugio*, Piazza XX Settembre; *Da Badò*, 9 Borgo San Lazzaro; *Lo Sgherro*, Borgo San Giusto (beyond Porta San Francesco). Lovely places to **picnic** include the Parco Archeologico and the outskirts of the town, near San Giusto or overlooking the Balze.

Annual Festivals. *Astiludio* on 1 September with flag-throwing and processions. Theatre Festival in July. A large **market** is held in the town on Saturday mornings (near the Roman Theatre in summer).

History. *Velathri* was the northernmost of the 12 cities of the Confederation of Etruria Propria and one of the most prominent. In the 3C BC it became the Roman *Volaterrae*. It supported the cause of Marius against Sulla and underwent a siege of two years before falling to the troops of the latter. It gained some importance under the Lombards and was for a time the residence of the Lombard kings. After bitter struggles, it was subdued by Florence in 1361, and again in 1472 in the the War of Volterra waged by Lorenzo il Magnifico for control of its alum deposits, which ended in the sack of the city by the Florentines under the command of Federico da Montefeltro. Another rebellion was crushed by Francesco Ferrucci in 1530 and Volterra remained under Florentine dominion, and later under the Grand-duchy of Tuscany, until the unification of Italy in 1860. Its natives included the satirist Persius Flaccus (AD 34–62), St Linus, the reputed successor of St Peter in the papal chair, Pope Leo the Great (440–461), and the painter Daniele Ricciarelli da Volterra (1509–66).

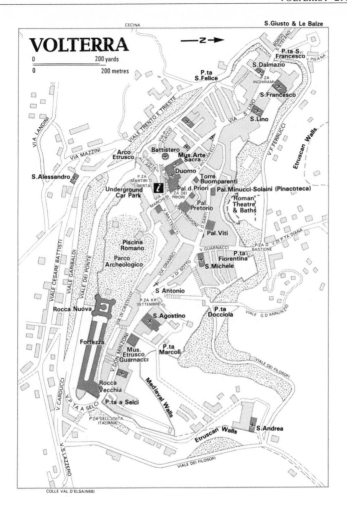

Piazza Martiri della Libertà forms the S entrance of the town; at the N end of the piazza Via Marchesi leads left to *PIAZZA DEI PRIORI, bordered by buildings medieval, or in the medieval style. Immediately to the left is the austere ***Palazzo dei Priori** (open weekdays, 9–13), with its battlemented tower, now the town hall, the oldest building of its kind in Tuscany. It was begun in 1208 and completed in 1257 by Riccardo da Como; the windows on the first floor were altered later and the upper part of the tower was rebuilt and modified in 1846. The vestibule is decorated with coats of arms, and steps lead up to the first floor with the Sala del Consiglio Comunale (admission when not in use), the council chamber of the town since 1257. The original timber ceiling was replaced by the present double cross-vault in 1516. On the end wall is a fresco of the Annunciation by Jacopo di Cione

(1383), and to the right, the Marriage Feast at Cana by Donato Mascagni; the remaining decoration is modern. In the next room, the Saletta della Giunta, are several paintings: Job and his wife by Donato Mascagni, the Birth of the Virgin by Ignazio Hugford, and the Adoration of the Magi by Giovanni Domenico Ferretti. Steps lead up to the bell-tower (at present closed) from which there is a magnificent view stretching as far as the sea.

To the right of Palazzo dei Priori is *Palazzo Vescovile*, originally the town granary, which was begun in the 14C. In between, set back from the piazza, is the N transept of the cathedral, decorated with horizontal bands of black-and-white marble. Across the piazza is a remarkable sequence of 13C architecture, beginning on the right with *Palazzo Pretorio*, surmounted by the Torre del Porcellino which derives its name from the sculpted boar on a bracket to the right of the top window. The vertical emphasis of the building is underlined by the narrow windows flanking the tower. The adjacent *Palazzo del Podestà* has three large rounded arches on the ground floor and two-light windows on the three upper storeys. The crenellated tower to the left, formerly a prison, adds to the variety of forms, openings, and use of stone. At the end of the piazza is the former *Palazzo Incontri*, now used as a bank, which has been considerably modified through the centuries. Facing it, at the opposite end of the piazza, is the modern *Palazzo Demaniale*, designed to harmonise with the older buildings.

Via Turazza leads out of the piazza to the left of Palazzo dei Priori. It passes the remains of the Romanesque transept and nave of the cathedral, and the late-18C *Oratorio della Misericordia*. This chapel contains a Crucifixion by Donato Mascagni (1602) over the altar, and paintings by Giovanna Forzoni (Agony in the Garden, 19C), Giuseppe Nicola Nasini (Birth of the Virgin), and Giuseppe Arrighi (St Anthony of Padua). In the beautiful *PIAZZA SAN GIOVANNI is the Baptistery, the Cathedral façade, and, at the far end, the Hospital of Santa Maria Maddalena. The **Cathedral** (or Basilica of Santa Maria Assunta; open all day) dates from the 12C, and the FAÇADE is a fine example of 13C Pisan architecture, with blind arches beneath the roof and three small round windows. The lower part was modified in the 16C with the addition of the three larger windows and the doorway, decorated in the lunette with green and white marble. The INTERIOR, which was rebuilt in the later 16C, has a Latin-cross plan with five apse chapels and an additional chapel at the end of each transept. The nave and aisles are divided by columns of painted stucco and capitals by Leonardo Ricciarelli. The long nave has a magnificent coffered ceiling designed by Francesco Capriani, and executed by Jacopo Pavolini (1580). SOUTH AISLE. First altar, Pieter de Witte (also known as Pietro Candido; 1578), the city of Volterra presented to the Madonna by her patron saints Giusto and Ottaviano; second altar, Francesco Curradi, Birth of the Virgin; third altar, Giovan Battista Naldini, Presentation of the Virgin (1590). SOUTH TRANSEPT. Outside the CHAPEL OF SAN CARLO BORROMEO, which preserves the wall of its Romanesque structure, is a Crucifixion by Francesco Curradi (1611). Inside are paintings by Matteo Rosselli (St Carlo), and the school of Guido Reni (St Mary Magdalen). The CHAPEL (1592) at the end of the transept has a fine ceiling with stucco decoration by Lionello Ricciarelli and frescoes by Giovanni Balducci. The pietra serena altar is attributed to Vasari, and the altarpiece of the Raising of Lazarus is by Santi di Tito (1592). In the painted niches are 18C frescoes of saints by Agostino Veracini. The two paintings of scenes from the Life of Christ are by Giovanni Balducci. The CHAPEL OF THE DEPOSITION has a *Deposition, a monumental and moving work of 1228 by a Pisan sculptor, with life-size figures in gilded and painted wood (restored in 1989). Behind is a small chapel (light switch on right) of the original Romanesque church, with fresco fragments representing Christ's Passion attributed to Taddeo di Bartolo.

To the right of the choir is the CHAPEL OF ST OTTAVIANO, whose body is preserved in a marble urn by Raffaello Cioli of Settignano (1522–25). St Ottaviano, a 6C hermit and one of Volterra's venerated patron saints, saved the city from a terrible plague in 1522. The choir stalls behind the high altar are by Andreuccio di Bartolomeo and Antonio del Tinghio (1404). Over the early-19C altar is a magnificent *tabernacle carved by Mino da Fiesole (1471): the Infant Christ stands above the chalice and pairs of adoring angels kneel beside the tabernacle door. Below, on the pedestal, are the Theological Virtues and four saints. The two kneeling angels holding candlesticks are by Andrea Ferrucci of Fiesole. Flanking the high altar are two *angels, also by Mino da Fiesole, kneeling on two elegant Gothic columns.

In the first chapel off the NORTH TRANSEPT is the marble tomb of St Ugo (1644), bishop of Volterra. In the next chapel is the *Madonna dei Chierici, a fine painted wood statue by Francesco di Valdambrino. The *CHAPEL OF ST PAUL, designed by Alessandro Pieroni in 1607, was built by Jacopo Inghirami, the admiral who won a victory over the Turks. The stucco decoration is by Giovanni Caccini and the *frescoes in the vault, depicting the life of St Paul, are by Giovanni da San Giovanni. The altarpiece of the conversion of St Paul is by Domenichino (Domenico Zampieri). There are also paintings of the decapitation of the saint by Francesco Curradi, and his mission to Damascus by Matteo Rosselli. Outside the sacristy is a holy water stoup by Andrea Sansovino and, over the door, the Immaculate Conception by Giovan Paolo Rossetti. The SACRISTY has 15C cupboards and some later furniture. A Baroque cupboard contains fine reliquary busts of the patron saints of Volterra.

NORTH AISLE. Third altar, Niccolò Circignani, Immaculate Conception (1586). The 13C Pisan *pulpit supported on columns borne by lions was put together in 1584 using various sculptural fragments. The reliefs represent the Sacrifice of Isaac, the Annunciation and Visitation, and the Last Supper. Second altar, *Annunciation, a painting of great harmony and beauty, full of light and space, with a landscape extending far into the distance. Formerly attributed to Mariotto Albertinelli, it is now generally accepted as the work of Fra Bartolommeo (1497). First altar, Francesco Cungi, Martyrdom of St Sebastian (1588). In the LADY CHAPEL are two niches with painted terracotta figures by an anonymous 15C sculptor representing the *Adoration of the Magi and the *Nativity, the latter with a charming frescoed background by Benozzo Gozzoli. On the W wall is the tomb of Monsignor Mario Maffei by Montorsoli (1537).

Facing the cathedral is the elegant, octagonal ***Baptistery**, a fine building in the local stone called panchina, with a façade decorated with horizontal bands of black-and-white marble. The doorway is framed with clusters of slender columns supporting a rounded arch above the architrave, which is carved with heads of Christ and the Madonna and the twelve apostles, and inscribed with the date 1283. The cupola was added in the 16C when the walls had to be heightened to counteract the thrust. The INTERIOR (at present closed for restoration) is of great simplicity, and unadorned except for six large niches. Inside the entrance is a holy water stoup formed of an Etruscan funerary stone. The large octagonal font in the centre is by Giuseppe Covoni (1759), and the statue of St John the Baptist by Giovanni Cybo (1769). The altar and 18C arched marble frame enclose an Ascension by Niccolò Circignani (1591). To the right of the altar is the original baptismal *font by Andrea Sansovino (1502), with marble bas-reliefs of the Baptism of Christ and four seated figures of Faith, Hope, Charity, and Justice.

To the left of the cathedral façade is the exterior of the Lady Chapel with a modern stone lunette representing Saints Giusto, Lino, and Ottaviano by Raffaello Consortini. Beside it is the tall, square CAMPANILE, dated 1493, which towers over the piazza. Closing the piazza on the left is the ex-hospital of *Santa Maria Maddalena* (restored as a study centre in 1990), with an elegant Renaissance portico. The *Oratorio* in Via Franceschini has 17C frescoes.

In Via Roma is the entrance to the **Museo d'Arte Sacra** (open 9.30–13) in *Palazzo Vescovile*. In the vestibule are bells (11C–15C) and bas reliefs probably by Agostino di Giovanni. In the first room: sculptures by Tino da Camaino, a bust of St Lino by Andrea della Robbia, and a silver reliquary bust of St Ottaviano by Antonio del Pollaiolo. The wooden tabernacle was painted by Bartolomeo della Gatta. The painted Madonnas are by Segna di Bonaventura, Neri di Bicci, and Taddeo di Bartolo, and the Crucifix dates from the 12C. In R. 2 is a gilded bronze Crucifix by Giambologna and church silver. R. 3 contains illuminated choir books and vestments. The *Madonna of Villamagna is by Rosso Fiorentino (1521), and the *Madonna of Ulignano is by Daniele da Volterra (1545).

Via Roma, which leads back towards Piazza dei Priori, crosses Via Ricciarelli and passes under the lofty archway of the 13C Buomparenti and Buonaguidi tower houses. The medieval Via Buomparenti leads into Via Sarti. On the corner (No. 1) is *Palazzo Minucci Solaini*, restored in 1982 to house the **Pinacoteca e Museo Civico** (open daily 9.30–18.30; November–March 9.30–13). The small, elegant palace with a loggia surrounding the courtyard is attributed to Antonio da Sangallo il Vecchio. The collection, mostly paintings by Tuscan artists formerly exhibited in Palazzo dei Priori, is small but choice. The works are arranged chronologically.

FIRST FLOOR. **R. 1**: 13C Tuscan Crucifix; Romanesque capitals and a sculptured lunette. **R. 2**: *Madonna and Child, and Crucifixion by an early-14C Sienese painter; *Saints Giusto and Ugo also by an anonymous early-14C artist; and a case of ivories (some of them casts). A chapel (**R. 3**) has a small altarpiece attributed to Francesco Conti. **R. 4**: *polyptych of the Madonna and saints, complete with its predella, signed and dated 1411 by Taddeo di Bartolo (from Palazzo dei Priori). **R. 5**: polyptych by Cenni di Francesco (1408). **R. 6**: *polyptych by the Portuguese painter Alvaro Pirez (c 1430); and two *statues of the Virgin and angel Gabriel by Francesco di Valdambrino (c 1410), originally in the cathedral. **R. 7** is now used as a restoration laboratory which is open to the public. **R. 8**: Stefano di Antonio Vanni, *Madonna and Child (1457); Priamo di Piero della Quercia (attributed), Madonnas, St Bernardine; and a small collection of ceramics including 17C black pottery inspired by Etruscan models. **R. 9**: mid-15C Florentine school, Nativity (a damaged but interesting work); Benvenuto di Giovanni, *Nativity and charming *predella scenes of the Life of the Virgin; Neri di Bicci, Saints Sebastian, Bartholomew and Nicholas of Bari (1477). **R. 10** has a painted terracotta Pietà by Zaccaria Zacchi. **R. 11**: Domenico Ghirlandaio, *Apotheosis of Christ with Saints Benedict, Romualdo, Attinia, and Greciniana (1492), with a beautiful landscape; Master of Santo Spirito, Madonna enthroned with saints; Leonardo Malatesta, Madonna and Child with saints (1516; inspired by Raphael's Madonna del Baldacchino). **R. 12**: Luca Signorelli, *Annunciation, one of the artist's masterpieces, and *Madonna and Child enthroned with Saints

John the Baptist, Francis, Anthony of Padua, Bonaventura, and Jerome (1491). The *Deposition signed and dated 1521 by Rosso Fiorentino, executed at the age of 26, is one of the major creations of Florentine Mannerist painting. Of overwhelming dramatic force, it is remarkable for its colour and technique.

SECOND FLOOR. **R. 1**. Daniele da Volterra, *fresco of Justice with the Medici arms (1532), detached from the vestibule of Palazzo dei Priori; Pieter de Witte, Deposition and Nativity; Niccolò Circignani, Annunciation and Coronation of the Virgin; Domenico Mascagni, Nativity of the Virgin (1599). **R. 2**: Fragments including a Head of the Madonna by Giuliano Bugiardini, and some small 15–16C Florentine and Flemish paintings. **R. 3**: Baldassare Franceschini (called 'Il Volterrano'), *Madonna and Child in glory with Saints Francis, Clare, John the Evangelist, Stephen, Mary Magdalen, and Paul (1639). More rooms are to be opened to display 17C and 18C silver, and the collection of coins and medals from the Museo Guarnacci.

In the spacious Via Sarti are several fine palaces including Palazzo Tortora Salvetti (on the left) and Palazzo Ruggieri Buzzaglia with two balconies (on the right). Farther down is the fine 16C façade of *Palazzo Viti* (originally Incontri), attributed to Bartolomeo Ammannati. In the early 19C the ground floor and courtyard, which had remained unfinished, were bought by the Accademia dei Riuniti and rebuilt as a THEATRE (at present closed), named after Persius Flaccus. The palace was acquired in 1850 by Benedetto Giuseppe Viti, an alabaster merchant, who had the interior redecorated for a visit of Vittorio Emanuele II in 1860. The entrance staircase (at No. 41) by Giovanni Caccini has a bust of the King and a plaque commemorating his visit. The piano nobile (which may be visited on request) has elegant period furniture and a unique collection of works in alabaster, as well as Indian and Chinese objects acquired by Viti during his trading expeditions in the East.

In the small Piazza San Michele is a 13C medieval tower and the church of *San Michele Arcangelo* which has a fine Pisan-Romanesque façade decorated with blind arches on two levels, divided by striped black-and-white marble decoration. In the lunette over the doorway is a 15C statue of the Madonna and Child. The interior was altered in 1827. To the left of the altar is a glazed terracotta *Madonna and Child attributed to Giovanni Della Robbia in a marble tabernacle.

Via Guarnacci leads N of the piazza to *Porta Fiorentina*, which preserves its old wooden doors. Just outside the gate is the entrance to the **Roman Theatre** (open 11–16), built at the end of the 1C BC and one of the best preserved in Italy. Excavations begun in 1952 by Enrico Fiumi revealed part of the cavea and scena, with Corinthian columns over 5m high. Numerous coins (3C BC–4C AD) found here are now in the Museo Guarnacci. Inside the portico, which was added a century later, are remains of baths.

From Piazza San Michele, Via di Sotto passes the Romanesque flank of the church and Via Docciola, a picturesque street with steps leading down between cypress trees to the *Fonti di Docciola*, a fountain protected by a brick vault supported on two large Gothic arches, dating from 1245. Nearby is the 13C *Porta di Docciola*. Via di Sotto broadens as it reaches Piazza XX Settembre. To the right is the 15C *Oratory of Sant'Antonio Abate*, inside which is a painting of the titular saint by Priamo della Quercia (1442). On the left is a war memorial and the church of **Sant'Agostino**, founded in the late-13C, but rebuilt in 1728. It has a basilican plan with three naves divided by Corinthian columns. Inside on the right is the tomb of Alessandro

Part of the scena of the Roman Theatre, Volterra

Riccobaldi (died 1523), decorated with skulls and cross-bones. In the S aisle is a 13C painted Crucifix (damaged) and a 14C fresco of the Madonna and Child in a marble tabernacle. A chapel to the right has monochrome frescoes, all copies after famous paintings, dating from 1912, and under the altar is a painted terracotta Pietà with a 14C fresco of the Madonna above. In the chapel to the left of the high altar is a Madonna with Saints Thomas of Villanova and Clare of Montefalco by Volterrano (1669), and, in the N aisle, the Madonna del Soccorso by Ulisse Giocchi (1614). On the entrance wall are fresco fragments of a large Crucifixion, detached from the Badia, attributed to a follower of Giotto.

At No. 15 Via Don Minzoni is the ***Museo Etrusco Guarnacci** (open daily, 9.30–18.30; Nov–March 9.30–13), one of the most interesting Etruscan collections in Italy, and extremely well displayed (also labelled in English). The nucleus of the collection was donated by Canon Pietro Franceschini in 1732, and it was subsequently enriched by the important bequest of the archaeological collection and library of Monsignor Mario Guarnacci (1701–85). The delightful building, with a garden has appropriate decorations and some of the original show-cases survive. The arrangement begins on the GROUND FLOOR with a prehistoric section demonstrating the existence of primitive communities in this territory, with finds from excavations, and maps. The Roman section includes portrait heads, reliefs, fragments of murals, and several mosaic floors from the theatre and baths. The Etruscan civilization, from the 10C BC onwards, is magnificently documented. Entire finds from tombs dating from the 8–7C BC are exhibited, with arms, household objects, fibulae and bronzes. From the 6C BC there are stele and fragments with inscriptions. The collection is particularly famous for its Etruscan cinerary urns, in alabaster or terracotta, mostly dating from the 3C BC, found locally and numbering over 600. The terracotta urns are probably the oldest. Many are sculpted with fine reliefs and the lids generally bear the recumbent figures of the dead, with the cup of life reversed.

On the walls of the staircase are Roman inscriptions and Romanesque fragments. FIRST FLOOR. RR. XIII-XIX contain cinerary urns arranged according to the subjects of the reliefs: Theban and Trojan cycles; Amazons, Ulysses, etc. R. XX: terracotta *tomb cover with strikingly realistic portraits of a husband and wife (early 1C BC). R. XXII contains lamps and works in bronze, including the famous bronze votive *figure of the early 3C BC, known as the 'Shadow of the Evening'. R. XXIII displays coins. R. XXIV: bronze figurines, bone and ivory objects, and jewellery. SECOND FLOOR. R. XXVII: fragments of a pediment. R. XXIX contains examples of tools used for sculpting marble and alabaster. R. XXX (with a fine view of the countryside around the town) has chosen examples of alabaster urns dating from the 3–2C BC. R. XXXI has examples of urns illustrating various themes. R. XXXII: portraits and large-scale reclining figures. R. XXXIII: mirrors. R. XXXIV: bronze objects. R. XXXV: marble statues, stele, and inscriptions. R. XXXVI: contains Etruscan pottery.

Opposite the museum, Vicolo Marchi leads to Via di Castello which has a magnificent view of the ***Fortezza**. This massive structure is composed of the Rocca Vecchia to the left, built by the Duke of Athens in 1343, joined by a double rampart to the Rocca Nuova on the right, which was added by Lorenzo il Magnifico in 1472–75. The Rocca Nuova forms a square, with circular towers at each corner, surrounding the battlemented tower known as *Il Maschio*. The Rocca Vecchia has a semicircular tower called 'La Femmina', and another tower next to the Porta a Selci beside the entrance. The Fortezza has always been a prison, and is still used as such. Via di Castello leads back to the town centre via the ***Parco Archeologico Fiumi**, a beautiful public garden (ideal for picnics) on the site of the Etruscan and Roman acropolis. There are fine views from the park which overlooks excavations of a Roman piscina or reservoir.

From Piazza San Giovanni (see above) Via Persio Flacco beside the Baptistery leads to Via Lungo Le Mura which continues downhill overlooking the valley to the S. It ends at the famous ***Porta all'Arco**, the main gateway to the Etruscan town, dating from the 4–3C BC, partly rebuilt by the Romans in the 1C BC. The splendid, impressive round arch is decorated with three monumental heads, supposed to be of Etruscan divinities. It has miraculously survived past sieges and modern warfare. A plaque to the right records how the citizens of Volterra saved it from destruction in 1944 by undertaking to fill it with paving stones overnight: *Ospite, quest'opera grande dei nostri maggiori minacciata dal furore di una barbara guerra fu serbata alla tua ammirazione soltanto da noi Volterrani.* From beneath the arch the pretty Via Porta all'Arco winds back uphill to Piazza dei Priori.

The centre of the old town has a maze of winding streets which run up and downhill, with narrow alleys, many of which are arched. From Piazza dei Priori Via Ricciarelli leads W past the Buomparenti and Buonaguidi tower-houses (see above), and other interesting houses including a fine rusticated palace, to the little *Oratory of San Cristofano*, inside which is a fresco of the Madonna attributed to Mariotto d'Andrea da Volterra. Via San Lino continues downhill. On the right is the church of *San Lino*, with a façade of 1513. The interior has a series of lunettes with scenes from the life of Christ by Cosimo Daddi (1618). On the S altar, Cesare Dandini, Birth of the Virgin; on the high altar, Francesco Curradi, Madonna in Glory with St Lino and other saints. On the N altar is a Visitation by Cosimo Daddi. The tomb of Beato Raffaele Maffei, the founder of the church, is by Silvio Cosini (1522) and the statues of Beato Gherardo and the archangel Raphael in the side niches are by Stagio Stagi.

The street ends at Piazza Inghirami, inside Porta San Francesco. To the left is the small church of *San Dalmazio*, which is still owned by the Inghirami family, with a Renaissance doorway (1516). It contains an altarpiece of the Deposition signed and dated 1551 by Giovan Paolo Rossetti, a native of Volterra. Opposite, above a slope, is the 13C church of **San Francesco**, which has been extensively rebuilt. On the S side of the nave: Giovan Battista Naldini, Immaculate Conception (1585); Niccolò Circignani, fresco of the Pietà; Alessandro Gherardini, hermits (1748). A door leads into the ·CAPPELLA DELLA CROCE DI GIORNO, built in 1315 next to the church, with its own entrance facing the piazza. The chapel was entirely painted with frescoes by Cenni di Francesco in 1410, representing the Legend of the True Cross and the Infancy of Christ. This is not only a rare and fascinating example of a narrative cycle, but it is also a description, in countless details, of the architecture and costumes of the period. On the main entrance wall, in a lunette, Seth receives the branch of the Tree of Sin and plants it on Adam's grave; and below, the Queen of Sheba predicts the future of the miraculous wood; left wall, the wood is used to make the Cross; next bay, St Helena identifies the True Cross; below, St Helena carries away the Cross; to the left, on the pilaster, St Francis receiving the stigmata; Chosroes, King of Persia, steals the Cross; vision of the Emperor Constantine, and the battle of Maxentius at the Milvian bridge; left of the door, the idolatry of Chosroes; right wall, Chosroes beheaded, and Heraclius, barefoot, brings the Cross back to Jerusalem; on the right pilaster, St John the Baptist. The second bay of the right wall represents the Nativity and Adoration of the Shepherds in the lunette, and a large, dramatic scene of the Massacre of the Innocents below. In the apse, from left to right, the Holy Sepulchre, above the Flight into Egypt; Death of the Virgin (damaged); Annunciation, above the Circumcision. The spandrels of the vault are frescoed by Jacopo da Firenze with figures of the Evangelists and saints standing on clouds against a blue sky. On the altar a Crucifixion attributed to Bartolomeo Neroni replaces Rosso Fiorentino's Deposition, now in the Pinacoteca. Over the entrance to the chapel is a tomb (1719) of a member of the Guidi family, who were patrons of the chapel.

The marble Baroque high altar contains a 15C image of the Madonna. In the crossing (left) is the tomb of Bishop Jacopo Guidi who died in 1588. On the left side of the nave is a Madonna and Child with saints by Vincenzo Meucci. At the entrance to the SACRISTY there is a holy water stoup in the form of a marble prow-like female figure of the vestal virgin Tuccia holding a sieve, dated 1522, and inscribed 'Innocens nihil timet' and 'Io Bap Bava'. In the sacristy is a group of terracotta figures by Zaccaria Zacchi, depicting the Pietà. Farther down the nave are a Crucifixion by Cosimo Daddi, the tomb of Mario Guarnacci (after whom the museum is named) in yellow-

and-white marble with reclining figures of Justice and Contemplation beside his portrait bust, and a Nativity by Giovanni Balducci.

Outside the 14C *Porta San Francesco*, one of the grandest and best preserved gateways of the town, Via del Borgo di Santo Stefano leads down past the ruined church of that name to the church and convent of *Santa Chiara*, which has a portico attributed to Ammannati. Nearby is an impressive tract of Etruscan walls. Borgo San Giusto continues downhill to (c 15 minutes) the church of **Santi Giusto e Clemente**, its eccentric tall façade rising above a grassy slope flanked by cypresses. It was founded in 1627 to replace an earlier church which disappeared into the Balze (see below), but only completed in 1775. In front of the façade are terracotta figures of the patrons and protectors of Volterra, Saints Giusto and Clemente (right), the titular saints (brother missionaries who came from Africa in the 6C), and (left) Saints Ottaviano and Lino. They stand on monolithic stone columns with Romanesque capitals. The grandiose INTERIOR has a Latin-cross plan with a single nave. SOUTH SIDE. Cosimo Daddi, Visitation; Giovanni Domenico Ferretti, St Francis Xavier preaching; Martyrdom of Saints Attinia and Greciniana (1642). In the S transept there is a photographic reproduction of a Madonna and Child by Neri di Bicci. On the main altar, flanking a marble urn, are the statues of Saints Giusto and Clemente. In the Cappella della Compagnia, ceiling fresco of Elisha and the angel by Volterrano (1631). NORTH SIDE. Pietro Dandini, Martyrdom of St Ursula, and saints surrounding the Madonna.

The road continues past a small gate (view) to end beside the restored Etruscan walls, overlooking the formidable precipice of LE BALZE, formed by the natural erosian of the Pleistocene clay here. Erosian and several earthquakes have not only engulfed the greater part of the earliest necropolis of Volterra and buildings of subsequent periods, but continues to be a threat. Off Via Pisana, on a hill, are the ruins of the BADIA which was abandoned after the earthquake of 1846 and subsequent landslides.

Below the Fortezza (see above) Viale dei Ponti, a beautiful panoramic road built by the Grand-duke Leopoldo II, runs beneath the medieval walls overlooking the Cecina valley. It runs parallel to the road to Florence (N68), off which, after c 1km, a by-road diverges to the left for the 15C church and monastery of **San Girolamo**, possibly designed by Michelozzo. Beneath the portico are two chapels with *reliefs, representing St Francis giving the Tertiary Rule to St Louis of France and the Last Judgement, both by Giovanni Della Robbia, and dated 1501. In a chapel to the right of the entrance is the Immaculate Conception by Santi di Tito. Flanking the high altar are a *Madonna enthroned with saints by Domenico di Michelino and the *Annunciation with Saints Michael and Catherine of Alexandria signed and dated 1466 by Benvenuto di Giovanni, a work of great charm and refinement. The two statues representing St Francis and St Jerome are by a follower of Cieco di Gambassi. In the four niches on the sides are stucco figures of saints by Mazzuoli. Not far from the church are remains of the few surviving Etruscan ipogee tombs (their contents are in the Museo Guarnacci).

17

San Gimignano and Colle di Val d'Elsa

Approaches by Road. The quickest route from Florence to San Gimignano is via the Superstrada del Palio for Siena as far as (40.5km) the exit for *Poggibonsi* (see Rte 13B). A pretty road leads W from Poggibonsi. 44.5. An unsurfaced road to the right winds steeply up to the *Villa of Pietrafitta* at the top of a cypress avenue (233m). The villa, which once belonged to Cardinal Mazzarin, has been extensively altered over the centuries. There is a small octagonal chapel next to the house dated 1584. The view extends over vineyards and olive groves to the surrounding hills. The main road continues to (51km) *San Gimignano*. A slower, but more attractive route from Florence is via the Via Cassia, see Rte 13B.

Colle Val d'Elsa is 14km SE of San Gimignano. It can also be reached direct from Florence by the Superstrada del Palio to (45km) the exit *Colle Val d'Elsa Nord* which is 3km from the town centre.

Frequent **buses** to San Gimignano from Florence; to Poggibonsi in 50mins (run by SITA), and from there services run by TRA-IN. To *Colle Val d'Elsa* services from Florence via Poggibonsi in 1hr (run by SITA).

Train services to Poggibonsi (on the line from Empoli to Siena, with some through trains from Florence). Frequent bus services from Poggibonsi station to San Gimignano and Colle Val d'Elsa.

SAN GIMIGNANO is a charming hill town (324m) of 7700 inhabitants, which has preserved its medieval appearance more completely than any other town in Tuscany. It can, however, be uncomfortably crowded with tourists (mostly on day tours from Florence or Siena) in spring and summer. The town is famous for its numerous towers which make it conspicuous from a great distance and provide one of the most remarkable views in Italy. It is surrounded by rich agricultural land, famous for its wine (notably the white *Vernaccia*) which was already renowned in the 14C. The countryside nearby is remarkably upspoilt and exploring the by-roads at random can be particularly rewarding.

Information Office. APT, 1 Piazza Duomo (Tel. 0577/940008).

Transport, see above.

Car Parks outside the walls.

Hotels. In the centre: 3-star: *Bel Soggiorno*, 91 Via San Giovanni; *La Cisterna*, 24 Piazza della Cisterna; *Leon Bianco*, 8 Piazza della Cisterna. In the environs: 3-star: *Le Renaie* at Pancole, 6km N, and *Pescille* at Pescille, 4km. **Camping site** (1-star) *Il Boschetto di Piemma*, 3km E at Santa Lucia (closed in winter). **Youth Hostel** *Ostello della Gioventù*, 1 Via delle Fonti. Numerous rooms to let and accommodation in farmhouses, etc. (information from Hotels Promotion, Via San Giovanni, Tel. 0577/940809).

Restaurants. First-class: *Dorandò*, 2 Vicolo dell'Oro; *La Stella*, 75 Via San Matteo. Numerous trattorie and pizzerie on or near Via San Giovanni. Beautiful places to **picnic** can be found in the surrounding countryside or near the Rocca.

History. The town derives its name from St Gimignano, a 4C bishop of Modena, traditionally venerated here. It was long known as *San Gimignano delle belle Torri* from the noble towers of its palaces, most of which were constructed in the 12–13C. Thirteen still survive out of the 76 traditionally thought to have existed. The town has

Etruscan origins and was later inhabited by the Romans. In medieval times it owed its prosperity to its situation on the Via Francigena, an important road for commerce and the main pilgrim route to Rome from northern and central Europe. Dante was sent here in 1299 as an ambassador of Florence to attach the smaller town to the Guelf League. After the devastation caused by the Black Death of 1348 San Gimignano came under the protection of Florence and there was an artistic revival in the 15C. However, the town declined commercially as a result of the deviation of the pilgrim route to the Elsa valley. The town suffered some damage in the Second World War.

The entrance to the town is through *Porta San Giovanni* (1262), finest of the town gates. Via San Giovanni, with a good view of the tall tower of Palazzo del Popolo at the end, continues past the little Pisan-Romanesque façade of the deconsecrated church of *San Francesco*. Beyond *Palazzo Pratellesi* (14C), now the Biblioteca Comunale, is the *Arco dei Becci*, another ancient gate beside several tall towers, forming part of the first circle of walls (12C). Beyond it opens the charming *PIAZZA DELLA CISTERNA, named from its well of 1237, with 13–14C buildings, notably *Palazzo Tortoli* with its two-light windows. A few paces to the N is *PIAZZA DEL DUOMO, another handsome medieval square with a number of towers. The crenellated Palazzo del Popolo, with its tower and loggia, stands to the left of the Collegiata, at the top of a flight of steps. Opposite the church is *Palazzo del Podestà* (1239, enlarged 1337), with an unusual vaulted loggia surmounted by the *Torre della Rognosa* (51m) which was once appointed the maximum standard of height in order to diminish rivalry in tower building.

The Romanesque *Collegiata (closed 12.30–14.30; summer 12.30–15.30), dating from the 11C, was solemnly consecrated by Pope Eugenius III in 1148 and enlarged in 1466–68 by Giuliano da Maiano. In the INTERIOR the aisle walls are entirely covered with two cycles of *frescoes (coin operated light in the nave), scarred by war damage and missing in a few parts, but mainly well restored. The beautiful New Testament scenes in the SOUTH AISLE, composed of 22 episodes on three levels representing the Life and Passion of Christ with a large Crucifixion scene in the fifth bay, are one of the great works of Italian Gothic painting. For long attributed to Barna da Siena (c 1381) and Giovanni d'Asciano, they are now thought to have been executed in 1333–41 by a master working in the bottega of Simone Martini, possibly Lippo Memmi assisted by Federico Memmi and Donato Martini. The Old Testament scenes in the NORTH AISLE, also on three levels, comprising 26 episodes relating to Genesis, Noah, Abraham, Joseph, Moses and Job are signed and dated 1367 by Bartolo di Fredi. On the WEST WALL, Last Judgement, Paradise, and Hell, by Taddeo di Bartolo (c 1410), full of details that have re-emerged since they were cleaned in 1990. On pedestals flanking the W door are two fine *statues of the Virgin Annunciate and the Angel Gabriel by Jacopo della Quercia (1421). They were painted in 1426 by Martino di Bartolomeo.

The sacristan shows the *CAPPELLA DI SANTA FINA, off the S aisle (the ticket includes the Museo d'Arte Sacra, Museo Civico, and Museo Ornitologico), a beautifully preserved Renaissance chapel built by Giuliano da Maiano (1468) to honour this patron saint of the town. The *altar and marble shrine with exquisite bas-reliefs are by Benedetto da Maiano (1472–77). The frescoes decorating the vault and walls of the chapel are by Domenico Ghirlandaio (c 1475): (right lunette) St Gregory announcing to Santa Fina her imminent death, and the miraculous flowering of violets on her wooden bed; (left lunette) Funeral of Santa Fina accompanied by three miracles (the healing of her nurse's paralysed hand, the blind choir boy's sight regained,

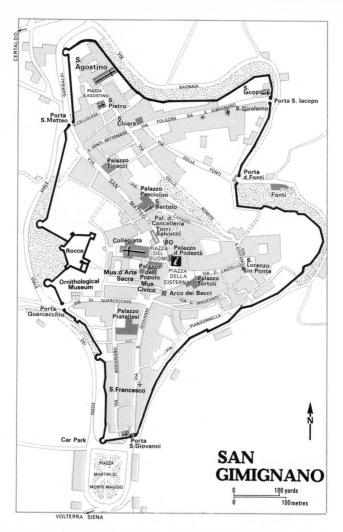

SAN GIMIGNANO

0 _____ 100 yards

0 _____ 100 metres

and the ringing of the church bells by angels). The saints and prophets are also by Ghirlandaio, possibly assisted by Sebastiano Mainardi. A very rare reliquary bust of gilded and painted leather decorated with coloured glass inlay, attributed to the Sienese sculptor Manno di Bandino (14C), is preserved in the shrine. HIGH ALTAR. Above is a *ciborium by Benedetto da Maiano. The choir stalls, pulpit and lectern are by Antonio da Colle.

An archway, surmounted by a statue of San Gimignano (1342), left of the church façade, leads into a courtyard where the *Baptistery* loggia has an Annunciation by Sebastiano Mainardi (1482) and a font of 1378. Here is the entrance to the small **Museo d'Arte Sacra**, with paintings, sculptures, and liturgical objects mostly from the Collegiata, and an Etruscan collection (open every day April–September, 9.30–19.30; winter 9.30–12.30, 14.30–17.30, except Monday). In the little CHAPEL on the ground floor are tomb-slabs, etc. In the adjoining room are paintings by Fra Paolino, Tamagni, Matteo Rosselli, a few sinopie by Benozzo Gozzoli and some very fine illuminated *choir books of the 14C.

On the FIRST FLOOR, the room to the left contains a wood figure of *Christ, of the type of the Volto Santo of Lucca, probably a Sienese work of the early 13C; 14C polychrome wood statues of the *Virgin and the angel Gabriel, formerly in the Collegiata; Benedetto da Maiano, marble *bust of Onofrio di Pietro, a work commissioned by the Comune of San Gimignano in 1493 to honour this distinguished citizen and scholar; a bust of the Redeemer by Pietro Torrigiani, and a Madonna and Child with St Sebastian and the Beato Bartolo by Vincenzo Tamagni. In the next room, *Madonna and Child signed by Bartolo di Fredi; red velvet *antependium, with doves and the monogram of Christ embroidered in gold, made in Florence in 1449, and a Crucifix attributed to Benedetto da Maiano. There is also a collection of 15–18C church silver, and a statue of St Anthony Abbot by Francesco di Valdambrino. Beyond a room with a marble angel by Goro di Gregorio and a sinopia by Tamagni is the LOGGIA with a small collection of Etruscan material found locally.

Behind the cathedral is the ruined **Rocca**, begun in 1353, now surrounded by a public garden partly enclosed by old walls. The surviving tower commands a remarkable *view of the town and surrounding countryside. Steps lead down to Via Quercecchio (with a fine view of Colle Val d'Elsa, Casole d'Elsa, and Radicondoli, with Monte Maggio in the distance) where a small deconsecrated church now houses an *Ornithological Museum* (same ticket and admission times as the other museums, see above).

Palazzo del Popolo (1288–1323), which still serves as town hall, was restored after war damage. The splendid tower, known as the Torre Grossa (54m) was begun in 1300. The fresco under the loggia, of the Madonna and saints, is by a 14C master. A passageway leads into a pretty courtyard with fresco fragments (two by Sodoma) and a stairway mounts to the **Museo Civico** (open 9.30–18 or 19.30; winter 9.30–13.30, 14.30–16.30; closed Mon). The SALA DEL CONSIGLIO, where Dante is supposed to have delivered his appeal, contains a large *fresco of the Maestà by Lippo Memmi (signed and dated 1317). This superb work, showing the Madonna enthroned beneath a canopy surrounded by angels and saints, with the podestà Mino de' Tolomei kneeling in adoration, recalls the famous work by Simone Martini in the Palazzo Pubblico in Siena. The fresco was subsequently enlarged and Benozzo Gozzoli is known to have added the two saints on the far left and right in 1466. The other walls are decorated with Sienese frescoes of hunting and tournament scenes (late 13C) and, on the end wall, the people of San Gimignano swearing allegiance to Charles of Anjou (ante 1292). The small adjoining room contains a fine polychrome marble *bust of Santa Fina (c 1498) and a terracotta bust of St Gregory, both by Pietro Torrigiani. The CHAPEL has a fresco of the Holy Trinity by Pier Franceso Fiorentino, a Pietà with symbols of the Passion by a follower of Neri di Bicci, and a Madonna and Child with five saints by Leonardo Malatesta da Pistoia (early 16C).

Stairs lead up to the PINACOTECA, with fine views over the town. In the CAMERA DEL PODESTÀ, a small room off the stair landing (left), are charming *frescoes of domestic scenes warning against the wiles of women, including Aristotle ridden by Campaspe, by Memmo di Filippuccio (early 14C). The fine *reliquary bust of St Ursula in polychrome and gilded wood is by the Sienese sculptor Mariano d'Agnolo Romanelli (late 14C), and the painted terracotta bust of Beato Bartolo is attributed to Torrigiani. In the MAIN HALL: Coppo di Marcovaldo, *Crucifix with Passion scenes, one of the masterpieces of 13C painting in Tuscany; another *Crucifix attributed to the Maestro delle Clarisse (c 1280–85); Guido da Siena, Madonna and Child enthroned (damaged; c 1280); Sebastiano Mainardi, Madonna and saints; Benozzo Gozzoli, *Madonna of Humility worshipped by two saints with a charming predella (1466); Filippino Lippi, two large tondoes of the *Annunciation, early works (1482), with a sensitive rendering of light; Pinturicchio, Madonna in glory with Saints Gregory and Benedict in a landscape (1512), one of the artist's last works; Domenico di Michelino, *Madonna and Child with four saints; Benozzo Gozzoli, *Madonna and Child with four saints, signed and dated 1466. In the two side rooms: Sienese school, Crucifix (c 1290); Memmo di Filippuccio, polyptych of the Madonna and Child with eight saints (c 1310); Bartolo di Fredi, female heads; Lorenzo di Niccolò di Martino, *reliquary tabernacle of Santa Fina, painted on both sides with stories of her life and miracles (c 1402); Sebastiano Mainardi, tondo with the Madonna and Child and two angels; Taddeo di Bartolo, polyptych (1394); Neri di Bicci, Madonna and Child, saints and angels; Taddeo di Bartolo, *St Gimignano and stories from his life (from the high altar of the Collegiata); Niccolò di Ser Sozzo, polyptych with the Assumption and saints (c 1345); Master of 1419, polyptych of San Giuliano; Lorenzo di Niccolò di Martino, triptych with St Bartholomew (1401). In the passage are various sculptural fragments and reliefs. The TOWER may be climbed to see the splendid *view.

Beyond the twin *Torri dei Salvucci*, *VIA SAN MATTEO, the most attractive street in the town, lined with medieval buildings, runs towards *Porta San Matteo* (1262). It passes *Palazzo della Cancelleria*, the Romanesque façade of the church of *San Bartolo*, and the 13C Pesciolini tower house, all grouped outside a double arch from an earlier circuit of walls: farther on is *Palazzo Tinacci*. Just inside the gate, Via Cellolese leads right for **Sant'Agostino**, an aisleless church consecrated in 1298 with three apsidal chapels. The entrance is by a side door. INTERIOR. To the right of the main door, in the CAPPELLA DI SAN BARTOLO (another patron saint of San Gimignano, 1228–1300) is a splendid *tomb by Benedetto da Maiano (1495). Set behind a draped marble curtain, this elaborate monument is composed of a predella with three scenes of the saint's life beneath the shrine with reliefs of two flying angels, above which are the three Theological Virtues seated in niches forming part of a reredos. Above, in a lunette, the Madonna and Child are flanked by two adoring angels. To the left, frescoes of Saints Gimignano, Lucy, and Nicholas of Bari by Sebastiano Mainardi, who also painted the four doctors of the Church in the vault. SOUTH WALL: Madonna and Child with eight saints, predella scenes and saints on the pilasters by Pier Francesco Fiorentino (1494); above, fresco of the Pietà by Vincenzo Tamagni. Beyond the side entrance, Christ and symbols of the Passion, by Bartolo di Fredi, who also painted the frescoes (c 1374) in the SOUTH APSE, representing scenes from the Life of the Virgin (Nativity, Presentation in the Temple, Marriage of the Virgin, and Dormition). Over the altar, Nativity of the Virgin with the donatrix and St Anthony Abbot on the right by Vincenzo Tamagni (1523). On the HIGH ALTAR, *Coronation of the Virgin above kneeling figures of Saints Fina, Augustine, Bartolo, Gimignano, Jerome, and Nicholas of Tolentino, signed and dated

San Gimignano

1483 by Piero del Pollaiolo. The CHOIR is entirely covered with *frescoes by Benozzo Gozzoli and assistants (1464–5) illustrating the life of St Augustine from his childhood to his death, in 17 scenes, full of charming details. The vault and pilasters are decorated with evangelists and saints, by Gozzoli's workshop. On the NORTH WALL, mystic marriage of St Catherine by Giovanni Balducci, and Madonna and Child with saints by Fra Paolino of Pistoia (1530). Beyond a door which leads into the SACRISTY and a pretty Renaissance CLOISTER, Sebastiano Mainardi, *fresco of St Gimignano blessing three dignitaries of the city (1487), above an effigy of Fra Domenico Strambi, the patron who commissioned the paintings for the high altar and choir. *Marble relief, with four half-length bishops in roundels, recently identified as part of the orignal shrine of San Bartolo and attributed to Tino di Camaino (c 1318). Beyond is a fragmentary fresco of the Madonna delle Grazie by Lippo Memmi, a marble pulpit of 1524, a large fresco of *St Sebastian interceding for the citizens of San Gimignano, painted by Benozzo Gozzoli in 1464 after the plague of that year, and a Deposition and saints attributed to Vincenzo Tamagni.

In Piazza Sant'Agostino is the Romanesque church of *San Pietro* which contains frescoes by Memmo di Filippuccio.

From Piazza della Cisterna (see above) Via del Castello leads E to the church of *San Lorenzo* (at present closed), built entirely of brick (1240). Inside are frescoes by Cenni di Francesco.

The *Circonvallazione* around the 13C walls (in need of restoration) provides fine views and access to picturesque parts of the town. All the minor churches are of interest for their architecture or paintings (or both), but nearly all of them are kept locked. Especially noteworthy are *San Girolamo*, with an altarpiece by Vincenzo Tamagni (1522), and *San Jacopo*, a charming little Pisan-Romanesque building, with a painting of St James by Pier Francesco Fiorentino. Outside Porta alle Fonte, just to the S, is an arcaded medieval public fountain, known as *Le Fonti*.

The **Pieve of Cellole**, one of the finest Romanesque churches of the Val d'Elsa, is 4km from Porta San Matteo. It is reached off the Certaldo road (left; signposted for Gambassi) and then by the second turning right. This charming church, which gave Puccini the setting for his *Suor Angelica*, is situated on a hill (395m) among cypress trees. It was completed in 1238 and the façade of beautifully cut travertine blocks has a simple doorway decorated with two stylised capitals of different shape. Above the lunette is an elegant two-light window. Inside, wide stone columns with capitals carved with stylised flowers, support the arches separating the nave from the aisles. The apse is decorated with blind arches and a narrow window. The hexagonal baptismal font is carved out of a single block of travertine. In the sacristy are two altarpieces (c 1500) and an impressive life-size Crucifix of polychrome wood. An Etruscan necropolis has been excavated in the area.

The road continues W to *Il Castagno* (8km) where it joins the Via Volterrana (see Rte 15). Certaldo (also described in Rte 15) is 13km N. of San Gimignano.

COLLE DI VAL D'ELSA (223m; 14,800 inhab.) is situated on a rocky spur on the left bank of the Elsa river. Although not often visited, it is a delightful little town with many interesting art treasures. The medieval upper town is particularly well preserved and its position offers magnificent views on all sides.

Information Office (open in summer) 18 Via Campana.

Transport, see the beginning of this Rte.

Car park beneath the walls with a flight of steps to the upper town.

Hotels. 3-star: *Villa Belvedere*, with restaurant, 2km outside the town at Belvedere; *La Vecchia Cartiera*, 5 Via Oberdan.

Restaurants. First-class: *L'Antica Trattoria*, 23 Piazza Arnolfo di Cambio; *Arnolfo*, 2 Piazza Santa Caterina.

History. In the Middle Ages the exploitation of the river through a system of canals gave rise to flourishing wool and paper industries. In the 12C Colle was an independent commune. It was repeatedly disputed between Siena and Florence: at the Battle of Colle, which was fought on the plain below the town in 1269, the Florentines routed the Sienese, thereby avenging the terrible Battle of Montaperti of 1260. Provenzano Salvani, the valiant veteran of Montaperti, but hated nephew of Sapa (Dante, *Purgatorio*, xiii, 100–138), met his end here. The town eventually came under Florentine dominion in 1333. Colle received the title of city in 1592. It is also associated with the manufacture of glass which is still produced here, giving employment to over 800 people. Arnolfo di Cambio (1232–1302), the famous sculptor and architect who built Palazzo Vecchio in Florence was born here.

The road from San Gimignano passes beneath the walls beside a car park, from which a short flight of steps leads to the UPPER TOWN. A street runs along a parapet at the back of the houses following the horse-shoe shape of the hill, with a fine view of the valley and countryside beyond. To the right, across the slopes of the public gardens, is an old stone bridge with irregular arches which leads to the monastery of **San Francesco**. The church has a Romanesque façade in sandstone with brick mouldings decorating the two-light window above the doorway. To the left is the entrance to the monastery (now a Seminary; ring the bell for access), with a fine Renaissance cloister off which is the entrance to the church. The interior, rebuilt in the 17–18C, has a single nave elegantly decorated with stuccowork and full of light. Over the high altar is a *polyptych, signed and dated 1479 by Sano di Pietro. It shows the Madonna and Child enthroned with Saints Benedict, Cyrinus, Donatus, and Justina; and the Annunciation above. The rich frame also includes saints on the pilasters and predella scenes. There are various fresco fragments, including a 14C Madonna and Child with an apostle, on the first altar to the right of the main entrance. On the next altar is a copy of the altarpiece of St Francis in Santa Croce in Florence. The Baroque tomb of the organist Antonio Giacobbi is dated 1740.

The view back towards the town is very picturesque. The road meets a squat, circular brick tower, once a fresh water cistern, to the right of which is the **Porta Nuova**, an impressive gateway attributed to Giuliano da Sangallo. It has two round battlemented towers on the outside. From here the main street, Via Gracco del Secco, leads back through the full length of BORGO SANTA CATERINA in the upper town, passing numerous interesting medieval and Renaissance houses with charming views. Opposite the hospital of San Lorenzo is the 17C church of *San Pietro* which has an Assumption by Pier Dandini. A short way along on the left is an oratory next to the church of *Santa Caterina*, which has an impressive group of lifesize figures in painted terracotta representing the *Lamentation and attributed to Zaccaria Zacchi (early 16C). The street continues past (left) *Palazzo del Municipio*, displaying the Medici arms, to a bridge (originally a draw-bridge), with a fine panorama on either side. It joins Borgo Santa Caterina to the old town (known as CASTELLO).

At the far end of the bridge the road passes beneath an archway incorporated in the fine *Palazzo Campana* (1539) by Giuliano di Baccio d'Agnolo, a stately building with handsome windows. Beyond several picturesque medieval houses is Piazza del Duomo with *Palazzo Pretorio* (1335) on the left, decorated with coats of arms. It has recently been restored to house the ARCHAEOLOGICAL MUSEUM (open Tues–Fri 15.30 or 16–17.30 or 18; Saturday and Sunday, 10–12; 15.30–18.30; closed Monday). It contains some 15–16C frescoes, including an Annunciation, discovered under whitewash; a small collection of Etruscan pottery and bronze objects excavated in the Elsa valley; the Terrosi Collection acquired in 1971; and recent finds from the necropoli of Le Ville and Pierini.

The *Duomo was originally Romanesque, as can be seen from the series of blind arcades along its N flank. It was rebuilt in 1603–19 and the façade was completed in 1815. It has been restored in honour of the city of Colle's 400 anniversary. The fine campanile (unfinished) dates from the early 17C. The INTERIOR has a Latin-cross plan. It contains numerous art treasures. The marble pulpit resting on earlier capitals and supporting columns has bas-reliefs dated 1465 attributed to Giuliano da Maiano. The first S Chapel of San Marziale has a miracle of the saint by Giovanni Paolo Melchiorri (1694). In the second Epiphany Chapel: Vincenzo Dandini, Adoration of the Magi (1673), Deifebo Burbarini, Baptism of Christ and Marriage at Cana; third chapel: Giovanni Antonio Galli, called Lo Spadarino, St Silvester baptising the Emperor Constantine; fourth chapel: Rutilio Manetti, *Nativity (1635), between Astolfo Petrazzi, Conversion of St Paul, and Martyrdom of St Peter. In the S transept is the CHAPEL OF THE SANTO CHIODO which was commissioned by Pius II for the relic of one of the nails supposed to have been used at the Crucifixion. It contains a *tabernacle attributed to Mino da Fiesole, a 16C wrought-iron screen by Drea di Lavaccio, and a bronze *lectern with a palm branch and eagle by Pietro Tacca. Hanging on the transept wall to the left of the chapel is a Nativity by Francesco Poppi (1567). Over the HIGH ALTAR is a bronze *Crucifix, a gift of the Grand-duchess Maria Maddalena of Austria given to the cathedral in 1629. It was designed by Giambologna but was presumably cast after his death by Pietro Tacca. To the left of the transept is the CHAPEL OF THE HOLY SACRAMENT which has an impressive altarpiece of the *Last Supper by Ottavio Vannini, signed and dated 1636. In the adjacent Baptistery is an Annunciation by Cosimo Gamberucci (1618). The fourth N *RESURREC-TION CHAPEL (1635–42) with paintings of the Resurrection, the Immaculate Conception, and Madonna and Child with saints by Filippo Tarchiani; in the third chapel, Niccolò Tornioli, St Gregory interceding for the plague-stricken in Rome (1643); two paintings of saints by Giovanni Rosi. In the second chapel, Ascension, Noli me tangere, and Doubting Thomas by Giuseppe Chiari. In the first chapel: Giovanni Odazzi, Dream of St Joseph, Marriage of the Virgin; Paolo de' Matteis, Flight into Egypt.

At the end of the pretty piazza is *Palazzo Vescovile*, which houses a Pietà by Ludovico Cigoli. Via di Castello continues alongside the palace past a large tabernacle on the corner next to the former Palazzo dei Priori, the façade of which is decorated with graffiti. The outside stairway leads up to the **Museo Civico** (open at the same time as the Archaeological Museum, see above) which is confined to three rooms. In the main room (used by the town council) are several altarpieces, some removed from the Duomo, all well labelled. A door leads into a chapel with a portico decorated with paintings by Simone Ferri (1581). Other works in the collection include: Girolamo Genga, *Madonna and Child; paintings and pastels by the local 19C artist Antonio Salvetti; Raffaellino del Garbo (attributed), Adoration of the Magi (a fresco detached from a tabernacle); Pier Francesco Fiorentino, Madonna and Child with saints; Felice Palma, marble bust of Lorenzo Usimbardi; sculptural fragments and capitals, and some interesting models of the old town of Colle. The last room has a well-head with bas-reliefs, and engravings by Valerio Spada, a native of Colle. The collection also houses a late-14C or early 15C triptych of the Madonna and Child with saints by Pseudo Ambrogio di Baldese from San Pietro a Cedda and a Madonna and Child with saints by Lorenzo di Bicci from San Giusto a Villore. Other works from churches in the neighbourhood are due to be installed here.

Opposite the museum is the arched loggia of the *Teatro dei Varii*, an ancient theatre which was enlarged in the 13C, and provided with an upper floor with Gothic windows in 1760. The street broadens into a charming small square on the right of which is the Romanesque church of **Santa Maria in Canonica** with a simple bell-tower. The stone façade has a rose-window and decoration in brick, with small blind arches under the roof. The interior, altered in the 17C, has a large *tabernacle of the Madonna and Child with saints by Pier Francesco Fiorentino. At the end of the street are more interesting houses and the *Tower-house of Arnolfo* dating from the early 13C. A covered alley (Via delle Volte) returns from here towards Palazzo Campana through the oldest part of the town. From a small street to the right a steep footpath (La Costa) paved with bricks descends to the LOWER TOWN. It meets Via Garibaldi at the Quattro Cantoni onto which face the four fine palaces of the Beltramini–Palazzuoli, Tommasi, and Sabolini. In a niche on Palazzo Beltramini is a marble relief of the Madonna and Child attributed to Tommaso Fiamberti. An archway leads to the church of **Sant'Agostino**. The façade (unfinished) dates from the 13C and the bell-tower is modern. The *INTERIOR has beautiful proportions, with columns separating the nave from the aisles. It was rebuilt by Antonio da Sangallo il Vecchio (1521). SOUTH AISLE. Francesco Curradi, Immaculate Conception; Taddeo di Bartolo, *Madonna and Child; Ridolfo del Ghirlandaio, *Deposition with saints, and a predella (1518); Giovanni Battista Pozzo, Martyrdom of St Catherine (1589). In the CAPPELLA BERTINI (1598), to the right of the choir, is a *Pietà with saints by Lodovico Cardi, called Il Cigoli, a Nativity by Giuliano Biagi (1591), and marble busts of Cosimo I by Francesco Bordoni, and Francesco Bertini by Giovan Battista Caccini. In the N aisle, Giovan Battista Paggi, St Andrew and saints, and the Annunciation (1586), marble *tabernacle, known as the Madonna di Piano, attributed to Baccio da Montelupo containing a fresco of the Pietà with Saints Anthony and Francis, in a 17C silver frame.

Beyond the church is the chimney of a former glass factory and a 15C paper factory (now a hotel). On the left opens the central PIAZZA ARNOLFO, with a War Memorial of 1925, porticoes on two sides and the obsolete railway station. To the NE is the *Banca del Lavoro*, a modern building in orange-painted steel and glass by Giovanni Michelucci. Beyond the former railway station, in Via di Spugna, is the *Cappella del Renaio*, with a Giottesque fresco of the Pietà over the altar, and, opposite, the 10C church of *Santa Maria a Spugna*, which has a Romanesque façade. Behind the church is the river Elsa, with remains of the Ponte di Arnolfo and a view towards the former Abbey of San Salvatore, now transformed into a farmhouse.

FROM COLLE VAL D'ELSA TO CASOLE D'ELSA, MENSANO, AND RADICONDOLI, 32km. The road for Volterra (N68) passes the impressive Porta Nuova (described above) on the left, and after 1km reaches the pretty little Renaissance church of *Le Grazie*. It has several early 16C frescoes and a venerated 14C image of the Madonna and Child. Part of a brick cloister may be visited on the right. Just past the church is the turning (left) for Casole d'Elsa. 7km A narrow road leads right for *BADIA A CONEO (open for Mass on Sundays at 9.15, or on request), in a beautiful position with wide views. This fine 12C Romanesque church, once part of a Vallombrosan abbey suppressed in the 16C, gives an impression of grandeur and simplicity. Entirely built in light grey stone, it has a simple façade with four blind arches and half-columns and two capitals decorated with foliate and animal motifs. The exterior of the apse has blind arcading with small stylised human heads. A wide arch to the right opens on to a courtyard with picturesque farm buildings on the site of the former cloister. The church has a Latin-cross plan with a single nave and three apses, of which only the central apse is visible from the outside. The beautiful INTERIOR is entirely faced with stone. Over the crossing is a dome, and the transept and apse are vaulted, while the nave has a timber roof. The nave has a transversal arch dividing it from the transept and another arch with carved capitals. Small blind arches and carved capitals decorate the apse.

The pretty road continues and climbs steeply up to the old town of (14km) **Casole d'Elsa**. The Romanesque COLLEGIATA was transformed in the Gothic style in the 15C (painstakingly restored after war damage). On the arch over the choir, which is divided into five chapels framed by Gothic arches, are remains of 14C frescoes of the Last Judgement attributed to Giacomo di Mino del Pellicciaio. To the left of the side entrance is the baptismal font over which is a small statue of the Baptist (1485). Along the S wall of the nave are a terracotta relief of the Nativity by Benedetto and Santi Buglioni, the *tomb of Bishop Tommaso Andrei (died 1303) by Gano da Siena, and several altarpieces (well labelled). In the S transept is a *Madonna and Child with four standing saints by Girolamo del Pacchia. The last chapel to the left of the choir has 15C Florentine frescoes on the vault. In the N transept is a detached fresco lunette of the *Madonna and Child enthroned with angels by a close follower of Duccio. A door leads to a large chapel known as the Chiesa di Santa Croce, which has a number of paintings including (flanking the altar) the *Virgin annunciate and angel Gabriel by Rutilio Manetti. In the nave on the N wall is the fine *cenotaph of Ranieri del Porrina (died 1315), by Marco Romano, with a full length effigy in a marble niche and two beautiful figures of *Virtues. Steps lead down to the crypt with remains of the earlier church. The last altarpieces in the nave include *Immaculate Conception and two saints by Amos Cassioli, and *St Augustine washing Christ's feet by Rutilio Manetti.

On the right of the church is the CANONICA, an interesting structure in stone and brick, with remains of a cloister, dating from c 1500. It is at present being restored and the MUSEO DELLA COLLEGIATA will be housed here. The collection includes: Segna di Bonaventura (attributed), *Madonna and Child; Andrea di Niccolò, *Madonna and Child enthroned with saints and angels, *Massacre of the Innocents; a ciborium by Alessandro Casolani; and illuminated manuscripts and liturgical objects.

Via Casolani passes the 14C *Palazzo Pretorio* (right), alleged to have been redesigned by Francesco di Giorgio Martini in 1487. It now houses the ANTIQUARIUM COMUNALE (open Saturday and Sunday 11–13, or by appointment) which contains finds, mostly Etruscan, from excavations in the neighbouring district. The 14C *Rocca* dominates the far end of the little town, overlooking an extensive landscape, with hills in the distance. On the outskirts of Casole, on a hillock, is the little Romanesque church of *San Niccolò* next to the cemetery. The frescoes inside are by Alessandro Casolani and Francesco Rustici.

The road continues towards Siena past (21km) the little village of **Mensano** (499m) with its walls and castle still in part extant. The 12C Romanesque church of *San Giovanni Battista* has a simple oblique façade with an oculus and a fine portal. The noble interior (restored in the 1950s) has a basilican plan with impressive monolithic stone columns dividing the nave from the aisles, and three apses. The *capitals, unusually large in size, and carved with an intricate assemblage of acanthus and other leaves, heads and fantastic animals, are by Bonamico, whose name is carved on a marble slab on the left side of the altar.

The road continues S, and beyond (30km) Casone, in a beautiful position (509m), it diverges right for (32km) **Radicondoli**. This little town preserves parts of its medieval fortifications, as well as picturesque streets and a few Renaissance palaces. The 16C Collegiata has an *altarpiece of the Assumption and Nativity by Pietro di Domenico and a Madonna attributed to Niccolò Tegliacci in a side chapel. The cemetery has a late-12C funerary chapel (the Pieve Vecchia) dedicated to San Simone. It has a Latin-cross plan with a single apse and a projecting transept. In the interior brick and stone are used to obtain a decorative effect. It contains some interesting pre-Romanesque carving. There is an annual summer festival at Radicondoli, during which concerts and theatre performances are held in the cloister of the Convento dell'Osservanza.

18

Volterra to Massa Marittima

Road, N68, N439, N441, 66km.—9km *Saline di Volterra*. N439—23km
Pomarance—33km **Larderello**—39km *Castelnuovo di Val di Cecina*—
50km turning for *Monterotondo Marittima* (3km)—61km Junction with
N441—66km **Massa Marittima**.
There is a **bus service** from Volterra which follows this route.

Information Offices. APT of Pisa (Tel. 050/541800) as far as Castelnuovo di
Val di Cecina; APT of Grosseto (Tel. 0564/454510) for Monterotondo Marittima and Massa Marittima.

From Volterra N68 winds down through rolling hills and *crete* to (9km)
Saline di Volterra, an industrial suburb of Volterra, named after its underground salt deposits which have been systematically mined since the 9C.
Here N439, a beautiful winding road, diverges left, with a fine view of
Volterra in the distance. It follows a ridge overlooking the Cecina valley,
characterized by white chalk hillocks or *Crete*, and then climbs towards
(23km) **Pomarance** (370m; 3-star hotel *Pomarancio*), a medieval town
which owed its prosperity to the wealth of minerals mined locally, and later
to the exploitation of natural vapour jets. In 1472 it came under the
dominion of Florence and exercised control over a vast area comprising the
upper Cecina valley and most of the surrounding Metalliferous Hills. It was
the birthplace of two painters called Pomarancio: Cristoforo Roncalli (1552–
1626) and Niccolò Circignani (c 1517–96). Parts of the old walls survive and
the *Porta Volterrana* was built at the N end of the town in 1326. *Palazzo
Pretorio*, first built in the 12C, has a Florentine Marzocco lion on the corner
and numerous coats of arms. Beyond an arch is the parish church of *San
Giovanni Battista* which was rebuilt in the 18C but preserves its Romanesque façade with blind arches. Inside are frescoes covering the nave and
apse, including a large Last Supper by Luigi Ademollo behind the altar. On
the altars in the nave are an Annunciation by Roncalli, and the Madonna
of the Rosary by Circignani. In the S transept chapel is a *Madonna and
saints by Vincenzo Tamagni (1525). The baptistery chapel has a charming
*Nativity group of painted terracotta figures attributed to Zaccaria Zacchi
with a background fresco of the Magi by Tamagni. A *Madonna and Child
enthroned with scenes of the infancy of Christ by a 13C artist, and a
Madonna of the Goldfinch dated 1329 by a Sienese painter have been
removed to the nearby Canonica. The contents of an Etruscan tomb
excavated near the church are in the Museum of Volterra. There are several
palaces of the Larderel and other local families and some medieval houses
and towers in the older part of the town facing S on a natural terrace of
rock. From here there is a distant view of the picturesque ruin of the *Rocca
di Sillano* (530m), a 12C castle with three circles of walls (which may be
reached from a by-road which diverges E, 4km S of Pomarance).

The road continues uphill passing chimneys and pipelines, with a distinct
smell of sulphurous springs, to (32km) *Montecerboli* (386m), which
preserves its medieval nucleus and a Romanesque Pieve built in brick. In
the new parish church is a triptych of the Madonna and Child with the two
St Johns by a 13C Pisan artist, and a 14C Sienese Crucifix.

33km **Larderello** (390m; 3-star hotel *La Perla*), noted for the production of boric acid. It was from the nearby natural vapour jets (known as *lagoni* or *soffioni*) that François De Larderel began to extract boric acid in 1818, the presence of which had been discovered by a German scientist, Franz Hoefer, in 1777. The small town built for the workers near the original industrial plant was named Larderello in 1846 by Grand-duke Leopoldo II. At the centre is the De Larderel palace which houses an interesting MUSEUM (open daily on request, 8–17), created by the National Electrical Company (ENEL) in 1955. It documents the scientific exploitation of the steam jets which was continued by Larderel's son and grandson, initially for the production of boric acid and later for electricity. Today there are 14 power stations fed by over 60 kilometres of pipelines. The residential area, rebuilt after damage from bombing in 1945, has a church by Giovanni Michelucci. There is also a late-Renaissance church dedicated to the Madonna of Montenero with a Gothic bronze pulpit. To the right of the church is a column with a bust of Leopoldo and another column commemorates a prize received at the Paris Exhibition of 1867. The bare landscape, with its pipelines, furnaces, and power stations covering some 170 sq km, with clouds of steam bursting from the ground, was understandably called the 'Valley of Hell'.

After a steep climb, the road descends to *La Perla* where there are baths recommended for rheumatism. The road then ascends to (39km) *Castelnuovo di Val di Cecina* (612m; 3-star hotel *Il Castagno*). This is a small industrial and agricultural town, also popular as a summer resort on account of its situation in ancient chestnut woods. It has a medieval and late-Renaissance district. A pretty by-road diverges left towards Radicondoli (see Rte 17). The main road winds up amid oak and chestnut trees on a ridge above the Pavone valley through very wild scenery. 50km. Turning (right) for *Monterotondo Marittimo* (3km), situated on a hill on a natural ravine, which preserves part of its 13C castle and a crenellated tower (restored) of the Palazzo Comunale. In the parish church of San Lorenzo is a Madonna and Child by the so-called Master of Monterotondo, an artist close to Duccio. This was the birthplace of the writer Renato Fucini (1843–1921). 2km W are the *Terme di Bagnolo* (550m) a spa (3-star and 2-star hotels), with hot springs (43° C). This road (N398) continues towards the coast via Frassine and Suvereto (described in Rte 12).

N439 leads along a high ridge with extensive views. At (61km) *Scuola* is the junction with N441 from San Galgano (see Rte 19A). On the right can be seen Follonica and the sea in the distance.

66km **MASSA MARITTIMA**, an ancient mining town (10,500 inhab.) in beautiful countryside. Mining in the surrounding Metalliferous Hills (rich in iron, copper, and lead ores) has taken place since Etruscan times, and was a flourishing industry in the Middle Ages (when the earliest known Mining Code was drawn up here), and again in the last century. The town's period of greatest glory was from 1225 to 1335 when it was an independent Republic: its splendid Duomo, with its remarkable sculptural works, dates from this time. Massa Marittima remains one of the most fascinating and enchanting towns in southern Tuscany.

Information Office in Palazzo del Podestà (Tel. 0566/902756).

The nearest **Railway Station** is at Follonica, 17km SW, on the main line from Pisa to Grosseto.

Buses from Follonica, Grosseto, and Volterra.

Car Parking outside the old town.

Hotels. 3-star: *Il Sole*, 43 Via della Libertà; 2-star: *Duca del Mare*, with restaurant, Piazza Dante Alighieri.

Restaurants. First-class: *Taverna Vecchio Borgo*, 12 Via Parenti. Trattoria: *Da Tronco*, 5 Vicolo Porte. Bar *Le Logge*, Piazza Garibaldi (specialising in Panforte).

Annual Festival. *Il Girifalco*, a cross-bow contest between the districts (or *Terzieri*) of the town, in traditional costume, takes place twice a year on the Feast of St Bernardine (20 May or the following Sunday), and on the second Sunday in August.

History. Massa Marittima was the birthplace of St Bernardine of Siena (1380–1444), who preached his last Lenten Sermons here. It flourished as an independent republic from 1225–1335, before falling under Sienese rule. From 1317 it minted its own silver coin, the *grosso*, which bore the figure of St Cerbone. The famous Mining Code drawn up at this time is one of the most important legislative documents to have survived from the Middle Ages in Italy.

The town is divided into two distinct parts, the Città Vecchia around the cathedral, and the Città Nuova on a hill above. Both districts were enclosed in the 13C circuit of walls, the extent of which reflects the prosperity of the medieval town prior to Sienese dominion in 1335. The Città Nuova and the Città Vecchia were then divided by the Sienese with an immense fortified wall which incorporated Porta alle Silici.

Access to the CITTÀ VECCHIA is either through the 13C Porta Salnitro, from which a road leads steeply up along the side of the Duomo, or from Porta dell'Abbondanza (or *delle Formiche*), behind the Duomo. In the delightful triangular *PIAZZA GARIBALDI (usually called Piazza del Duomo) the elegant architecture blends into the charming network of streets forming a unity that is both harmonious and varied. The *Duomo is magnificently positioned at an angle above an irregular flight of steps, with the campanile closing the vista. Dedicated to St Cerbone, the cathedral was begun in the early 13C. It has a splendid Romanesque EXTERIOR in travertine with blind arcading. The upper part of the FAÇADE, with exquisitely carved arches and capitals, symbols of the Evangelists, and a kneeling telamon, was added in the Pisan Gothic style in 1287–1314. The story of its patron saint, whose relics were transferred to Massa from Populonia in the 9C, is sculpted above the main doorway in a single marble block, probably by a 12C Pisan sculptor. The *bas-reliefs illustrate stories from the life of St Cerbone (see below): the saint is miraculously saved from shipwreck; he is thrown into the bears' den; he performs a miracle with two deer; he presents the Pope with a flock of geese; and he celebrates Mass in the presence of the Pope.

The INTERIOR, which has a basilican ground plan, has 14C stained glass in the rose window representing St Cerbone before Pope Virgilius. The apse was prolonged and provided with slender Gothic windows in the late 13C and the octagonal cupola was added in the 15C. The three naves are divided by travertine columns with magnificent capitals. The nave vault dates from 1626. To the right of the entrance is a series of *reliefs, thought to be pre-Romanesque, representing Christ with angels, the Apostles, and the Massacre of the Innocents. The splendid rectangular *FONT, carved in a single square block of travertine resting on three lions and a lioness, with reliefs of the life of the Baptist and Christ Blessing, is by Giroldo da Como (1267). The 15C tabernacle rising from its centre, with carved figures of prophets in niches and crowned by a marble statue of the Baptist, is by Pagno di Lapo Portigiani. In the SOUTH AISLE is a painting of the Birth of the Virgin by Rutilio Manetti, and, in a side chapel, a 14C Sienese fresco of Saints Lucy, Margaret, and Agatha, and some illuminated choirbooks in a case. In the CHAPEL OF THE CRUCIFIX is a painted *Crucifix, attributed

Massa Marittima

to Segna di Bonaventura, and an Immaculate Conception by Rutilio
Manetti. The HIGH ALTAR, resembling a triumphal arch, is by Flaminio di
Girolamo del Turco (1623). The polychrome wood *Crucifix, recently
restored, is now universally regarded as an autograph work by Giovanni
Pisano. Behind the high altar is the *ARCA DI SAN CERBONE, a marble urn
signed and dated 1324 by Goro di Gregorio, a masterpiece of Sienese
Gothic sculpture. The sculptor reveals great gifts as a story-teller and his
reliefs are full of charming details, spontaneity and poetry.

The story of St Cerbone, who was probably born in Africa in 493, is illustrated in the
following scenes: he escapes from vandals to the Maremma, where he leads a hermit's
life; he is condemned by Totila to be devoured by bears for giving shelter to enemy
soldiers, but instead the bears only lick his feet; after becoming Bishop of Populonia,
his parishioners object to his saying Mass before dawn and, since he will not change
his ways, denounce him to Pope Virgilius; the Pope sends a delegation summoning
the bishop to Rome; the envoys refuse Communion from Cerbone and are overcome
by thirst; in answer to the saint's prayers two female deer allow themselves to be
milked; three sick men he meets on the way to Rome are miraculously cured; at the
gates of Rome, Cerbone summons a flock of geese to accompany him, as a gift for the
Pope; he is received by Virgilius whom he invites to assist at Mass before dawn; at the
service the Gloria is sung by angels which is the reason why he said Mass so early, a
fact that his humility prevented him from divulging.

In the chapel to the left of the high altar is the *Madonna delle Grazie, with a Crucifixion and Passion scenes on the back, attributed to a follower of Duccio, possibly the young Simone Martini. On the wall are fragments of a Presentation in the Temple by Sano di Pietro, sawn into pieces and stolen in 1922. Steps lead down to the undercroft in which are displayed eleven Sienese statuettes of prophets and saints (c 1340), a silver-gilt reliquary Cross decorated with enamels by Andrea Pisano, a reliquary of two thorns of Christ's crown in crystal, silver and enamels by Goro di Ser Neroccio, and two angels in wood attributed to Vecchietta. The fresco of the Cruci-fixion in a lunette is by a 15C Sienese artist. NORTH AISLE. Annunciation by Raffaello Vanni (1643); fragmentary 15C fresco of the Adoration of the Magi; and 14C frescoes. To the right of the entrance is a 14C frescoed triptych above a 3C Roman sarcophagus relief.

The tall bell-tower is probably contemporary with the church, but the upper part is restored. Beside it is Palazzo Vescovile. On the other side of the piazza is the 13C **Palazzo del Podestà**, with steps leading up to the entrance, which houses the **Archaeological Museum** (open 10–12.30, 15.30–19 or 15–17; closed Monday), and the three most important works from the **Pinacoteca**: the *Maestà by Ambrogio Lorenzetti (c 1330) showing the Madonna and Child enthroned surrounded by saints, angels, and the theological virtues, a small Madonna by Sano di Pietro, and the angel Gabriel by Sassetta. The interesting archaeological material on the ground floor dates from the Paleolithic to Roman eras (well labelled), most of it found near the Lago dell'Accesa (see below). The unusual funerary stele carved in a stylised human form is reminiscent of the statue-stelae of Luni. The collection is due to be enlarged as a result of recent excavations. The Pinacoteca on the first floor is closed.

To the right of Palazzo del Podestà is the small 13C palace of the Conti di Biserno (the first-floor windows were added in the 16C), beside *Palazzo Comunale* with two robust crenellated towers (extensively restored). From the corner of Palazzo Vescovile, Via Ximenes leads to *Palazzo dell'Abbon-danza*, a 13C fountain with three large pointed arches, over which a granary was built in the 15C. From Piazzale Mazzini, nearby, there is a fine view of the cathedral apse and tower. In Via Corridoni, a short distance away, is the **Museo della Miniera** (guided visits daily, every half hour: winter 10–12, 15–16; summer 10–12.30, 15.30–19; closed in February). Situated in an abandoned mine, it demonstrates mining techniques and exhibits equip-ment, machinery, and specimens of minerals.

From Porta dell'Abbondanza two streets lead uphill to *Piazza Matteotti* in the CITTÀ NUOVA, with parallel intersecting streets, quite different in plan to the lower town. Here *Porta alle Silici*, part of the vast and impressive fortifications erected by the Sienese after their conquest of Massa in 1335, is connected to the older *Torre del Candeliere* by an immense flying arch. The clock tower, which was reduced to two-thirds of its original height by the Sienese, may be climbed (11–12.30, 17–19; closed Monday; winter on request). The Sienese fortress (on the site of the former Bishop's Palace) was partly destroyed in the 18–19C to make room for the hospital of Sant'Andrea. From the adjoining parapet there is a splendid view over the roofs of Massa to the surrounding countryside.

From Piazza Matteotti there is a view down to *Porta San Francesco*, beyond which is the 13C Franciscan church, reduced in length after a landslide. On the N side of the Piazza is *Palazzo delle Armi*, with an arched portico, where ammunition was stored. It now contains the **Museo di Storia e Arte delle Miniere** (open October–March on request; 1 April–15 July and in September, 10–11, 15–17). It documents excavations in the district, with reliefs, diagrams and photographs illustrating the development of mining from Etruscan to modern times. It preserves the Mining Code of 1310. On the upper floor are a selection of minerals, instruments, and tools, and a cast of an ape skeleton (*Oreopithecus Bambolii*), discovered in a lignite mine.

Corso Diaz leads to the church of •**Sant'Agostino**, founded in 1299. The simple façade has an oculus above an elegant doorway. The polygonal apse, pierced by arched Gothic windows (with modern glass), was designed by Domenico di Agostino (1348), who completed the Cathedral of Siena. The INTERIOR has a single NAVE, divided into bays by grandiose pointed arches. It is hung with a number of paintings: St Guglielmo attributed to Antonio Nasini; Flight into Egypt by Lorenzo Lippi; Madonna and Saints by Rutilio Manetti; and Annunciation by Jacopo da Empoli; tomb of the Augustinian theologian Michele Bellucci (died 1479) by Urbano da Cortona. In the ST LUCY CHAPEL, right of the choir, is a reclining effigy of St Lucy (the 15C original is in the Musée des Arts Decoratifs in Paris) and frescoes, one of them representing the presentation of the Mining Code of Massa attributed to Vincenzo Tamagni. In the CHOIR is a Nativity by Bartolomeo Ponti (1627) and frescoed angels on the left wall flanking a 15C marble tabernacle and, behind the high altar, •Adoration of Shepherds with Saints Bernardine and Anthony of Padua by Pietro di Francesco Orioli (c 1480). In the chapel on the left is a painted terracotta Madonna and Child of the Sienese school (c 1500). In the nave is a painting of the Visitation by Rutilio Manetti (1639). A door opens from the church on to the elegant CLOISTER and conventual buildings. Behind rises the tall slender bell-tower, which was built on to one of the towers of the city walls in 1627.

Next to Sant'Agostino is the façade of the former church of *San Pietro all'Orto*, now the premises of the Terziere della Città Nuova, which houses the paraphernalia for the annual Girifalco contest (see above). The rooms also contain a small collection of pottery and coins found locally, and some 14C frescoes recently discovered under whitewash. The beautiful old stepped Via Moncini returns downhill from Porta alle Silici to the cathedral.

Just outside Massa Marittima, on the road to Follonica, a by-road to the left leads to the LAGO DELL'ACCESA (8km). This small lake, 580m long and 400m wide, is set in a beautiful, tranquil landscape. It is next to the source of the river Bruna. Nothing remains of the Medici and Lorena iron foundry (another one was in the nearby village of Valpiana), but there is evidence that the fusion of metals here dates back to Etruscan times. Settlements and necropoli, excavated on the SW side of the lake, date from the 7C BC (the excavations are described in detail, and the finds exhibited, in the Archaeological Museum of Massa Marittima).

From Massa Marittima N441 leads to Follonica (17km) on the coast, described in Rte 12.

19

Siena to Grosseto

A. via San Galgano

Road, N73, 92km—10km turning for *Sovicille* (2km)—14km *Rosia*—19km
Junction with N541—30km *Bivio del Madonnino* (for **San Galgano**,
2.5km)—34km *Monticiano*—59km **Roccastrada**—77km Junction with NI—
92km **Grosseto**.

Information Offices. APT of Siena (Tel. 0577/280551) as far as Monticiano;
APT of Grosseto (Tel. 0564/454510) for Roccastrada.

Buses (several times a day) run by TRA-IN from Siena (Piazza San
Domenico) to Massa Marittima via Palazzetto stop at San Galgano. Services
run by RAMA from Grosseto (railway station) to Roccastrada. For services
from Siena to Grosseto, see Rte 19B.

N73 leaves the Siena by-pass at the 'Porta San Marco' exit. 10km. By-road
(right) for **Sovicille** (2km; 4-star hotel *Torre Pretale*). Just before entering
the village, the road passes (left) the *Pieve di San Giovanni Battista di
Ponte allo Spino*. This small 12–13C Romanesque church is built of evenly-
cut stone that has acquired a beautiful patina over the centuries. Its simple
façade is dominated by a bell-tower built on to a massive earlier tower. The
E end, with its three apses and raised crossing decorated with blind arches
may be seen from the footpath along the side of the church. The interior
has a basilican plan, with six pilasters dividing the three naves, which are
of equal height, and a timber roof. The transept and crossing are vaulted.
The capitals are richly carved with realistic and symbolic figures, as well
as geometrical and plant motifs, showing Lombard and possibly also French
influences. An archway to the right of the façade leads into the courtyard
which preserves part of the cloister and remains of the canon's house with
two fine Gothic windows. The village of Sovicille preserves parts of its
medieval walls and some picturesque houses. Facing the main square is
the much restored church of *San Lorenzo*, with an old campanile. Inside,
on the right of the nave, is a fresco of the Madonna and Child with saints
attributed to Alessandro Casolani. A pretty road leads N from Sovicille to
Ancaiano and the villas of Cetinale and Celsa, described in Rte 14G.

14km *Rosia* is an old village built on a slope at the foot of which is the
Pieve di San Giovanni Battista (13C). The church has an unusually broad
façade with three narrow windows and an arched doorway. On the right is
a fine Romanesque campanile with windows on four levels, decreasing
from four to one-light. In the interior are three naves supporting an open
timber roof. To the right of the entrance is a triptych of the Madonna and
Child with Saints Sebastian and Anthony Abbot by Guidoccio Cozzarelli,
and a rectangular marble baptismal font, carved with a bas-relief of Christ
and six angels (15C).

A by-road (left) leads along the Torrente Rosia and then climbs uphill
along a cypress avenue to *Torri* (1km; trattoria *Le Torri di Stigliano* at
Stigliano, 2km S), a tiny medieval village surrounded by its old walls.

Beyond an archway in the walls is a picturesque piazzetta, leading to an enclosure onto which faces the S flank of the Romanesque-Gothic church of *Santissima Trinità e Santa Mustiola*. Built in beautifully hewn stone, it has a fine carved doorway and three arched windows decorated with human and animal heads. The interior, which was heavily restored in the 19C, has a Madonna and Child by Luca di Tommé. To the left, under the arms of Pope Pius II with the date 1462, is the entrance to the *cloister of the former Vallombrosan monastery, now a private villa (open Monday and Friday, 9–12). This small cloister, built in brick, has loggias on three levels: the lowest arches are decorated with black-and-white marble and supported by a variety of columns with fine capitals. The middle loggia has octagonal brick columns, and the top loggia has slender wood columns. There are extensive woods above Torri, with fine views of Siena in the distance.

N73 continues from Rosia skirting a stream with wooded slopes on either side, and passing Ponte della Pia, an old bridge on the left, and a ruined castle on the right. 19km Junction with N541, a beautiful road from Colle Val d'Elsa (see Rte 17) which runs along the river Elsa in a wide valley. From the crossroads, with the column of Montarrenti erected by Leopoldo II (named after the castle on the hill), the road winds steeply up over a pass, with splendid views of plains, rocks, wooded slopes and distant hills, to (34km) *Frosini*, a medieval castle transformed into a villa, situated at the heart of a tiny village with a pretty Romanesque church. From the public garden on the S slope there is a fine view. The road passes beneath the castle before descending in a double bend to the valley. 35km By-road (right) through beautiful countryside with interesting old farmhouses to CHIUSDINO (7km), the birthplace of St Galgano. It is a typical hill-top village (564m), with a cluster of grey stone houses on narrow streets that wind up and down, often with steps and arches. The simple Romanesque *Church* has been extensively modernised. Nearby, in a pretty little piazza, is the *Chapel of the Compagnia*, with a relief of St Galgano over the portal, by Urbano da Cortona dated 1466. Almost next door is the *House of St Galgano*, with horizontal bands of brick decorating its façade, and another relief showing the saint in a wood by Giovanni d'Agostino. In the valley below the village is the Molino della Pile, a 12C mill.

30km *Bivio del Madonnino*. Here N441 diverges right towards Massa Marittima (see Rte 18) past (left; 2.5km) the ruined *Abbey of San Galgano (open daily 8–12, 14–sunset) in an isolated position on a plain in beautiful farming country. The abbey, once the chief Cistercian house in Tuscany, was built beneath the little hill-top mausoleum of St Galgano Guidotti (1148–81), canonised in 1185, on Monte Siepi. The church is a remarkable French Cistercian Gothic building (1218–88). In the 14C and 15C the abbey was corruptly administrated, and in the 16C the abbot sold off the leading of the roof which by 1786 had collapsed, and the buildings were subsequently abandoned. A small community of Olivetan nuns settled in what remains of the monastery in 1973. The FAÇADE, with three arched doorways separated by columns, is unfinished. The entrance to the church is on the right, past the CHAPTER HOUSE and a fragment of the cloister. The roofless CHURCH, with a grass-grown nave, and a magnificent E end, is one of the most romantic sites in Tuscany. The proportions are most impressive and the effect of the windows framing the sky unforgettable. The nave is divided by pillars with Gothic arches resting on beautifully carved capitals. The transept, forming a Latin-cross, is also divided by columns. The little rectangular detached CEMETERY CHAPEL also dates from the 13C.

On MONTE SIEPI, the little hill above, is the circular *CHAPEL OF SAN GALGANO (open, as above). This was erected in 1182 over the tomb of St Galgano and on the site where he lived as a hermit. The exterior, built in stone to a height of 4m and then in alternate bands of stone and brick, was completed in the 14C. The interior, one of the few centrally planned churches in Tuscany, has a conical-shaped cupola, built of concentric rings of red brick and white travertine. The sword in the stone at the centre commemorates St Galgano's renunciation of knightly pursuits in favour of a life of prayer before the Cross. A little 14C chapel has *frescoes and sinopie by Ambrogio Lorenzetti and his workshop (c 1344). In the central lunette is the Virgin in Majesty adored by saints and angels holding baskets of flowers, with the figure of Eve reclining in the foreground. Below, divided by the window, are the Virgin and angel Gabriel; it is interesting to note the differences in composition revealed by the detached sinopie on the adjacent wall. On the left wall are scenes from the life of St Galgano: the saint conducted to Heaven and his vision of St Michael in Rome. In the vault are medallions with figures of prophets. There is a splendid view of the abbey from the hill.

The main road continues from the Bivio del Madonnino, and after a short climb enters (34km) the village of **Monticiano** (382m; 2-star hotel *Da Vestro*), which came under Sienese dominion in the 13C. In the piazza, above a flight of steps, is the Romanesque church of *Sant'Agostino*, with a façade in travertine, and a fine portal and oculus. Here is preserved the funerary urn of Blessed Antonio Patrizi (died c 1311), an important figure in the Augustinian monastic movement in medieval Tuscany. The single-naved interior, redecorated in the Baroque period, has a frescoed polyptych of the Madonna and Child with saints, and a damaged Crucifixion (both dating from the 14C). On the left side of the nave is a painting of the Death of the Blessed Antonio Patrizi by Rutilio Manetti (c 1629). Off the pretty cloister is the *chapter house which has interesting 15C frescoes by three different hands. The Madonna and Child enthroned between St Augustine and the Blessed Antonio Patrizi, surmounted by the Annunciation, is attributed to a follower of Taddeo di Bartolo. The monochrome frescoes depicting Christ's Passion, silhouetted against a red background, and the scene of the Last Supper are by unknown painters. Farther uphill is the *Pieve di Santi Giusto e Clemente* with a Romanesque façade.

The road winds through woods of oaks and chestnuts passing beneath the fortified village of *Torniella*, from which there are fine views. 55km By-road (right) for Sassofortino (6km) and Roccatederighi (8.5km).

From Sassofortino (560m) *Monte Sassoforte* (787m) can be climbed, following paths through chestnut woods. From the summit there is a fine view over the Maremma plain. *Roccatederighi* (520m), picturesquely situated on a rocky spur of the Sassoforte, has another fine panorama. *Montemassi* (9km S) is an impressive ruined castle surrounded by a medieval village, overlooking slopes of olive groves. The castle fell to Guidoriccio da Fogliano in 1328, a victory celebrated by Simone Martini in his famous fresco in the Palazzo Pubblico in Siena. There is a particularly fine view from the ruins of the castle high above the village dominating the plain. In the church of Montemassi is a rather damaged Madonna by Matteo di Giovanni.

59km **Roccastrada** (475m; 3-star hotel *Caolino d'Italia*, at Piloni c 3km N), a medieval village which has expanded considerably in recent years thanks to various industries. There are some picturesque streets near the remains of the former fortress with fine views. The road winds downhill to (71km) Sticciano Scalo, preceded by an avenue of pine trees. On the top of a hill to the left is *Sticciano* (4km), an unspoilt village with a fine 13C Romanesque church. There are beautiful views, including one towards the wooded slopes of Monte Leoni (614m) which may be explored on foot. 77km N73 meets the Via Aurelia (N1), passing Montepescali (described in Rte 12).

92km **GROSSETO** (62,500 inhab.) is capital of the province of the same name. It is the chief town of the Tuscan Maremma, a district ravaged by malaria throughout the Middle Ages. Reclamation work was begun by the Lorraine grand-dukes of Tuscany, and the marshes were gradually drained. A *bonifica* on a large scale was undertaken after 1930 and Grosseto is now the centre of a rich agricultural zone. It suffered considerable damage in the Second World War.

Information Office. APT, 206 Via Monterosa (Tel. 0564/454510).

Railway Station on the Pisa–Rome main line (services from Pisa in 1hr 30min). **Buses** run by RAMA to all places in the province. **Parking** outside the ramparts.

Hotels include: *Bastiani Grand Hotel*, 64 Piazza Gioberti (4-star); *Leon d'Oro*, 46 Via San Martino, and *San Lorenzo*, 22 Via Piave, both 3-star. Luxury-class **restaurant** *Buca di San Lorenzo*, 1 Via Manetti.

History. Grosseto probably had Etruscan origins. In the 10C it became the seat of the Bishop of Roselle following a Saracen raid. After a century of conflicts, Grosseto was subjected to Siena in the 14C, and eventually came under the dominion of the Medici in 1559. Situated on the Ombrone river, the town derived its wealth from its port and nearby salt deposits.

The old town, which has a few medieval remains, is entirely enclosed in hexagonal brick ramparts, incorporating the 14C Sienese Cassero. These fortifications were built by the Medici in 1564–93, also as a defence against pirate attacks from the sea. The Sienese keep, originally a tower and courtyard with a gateway, was later roofed over and transformed into the governor's headquarters. It is now used for exhibitions. Five of the bastions were laid out as public gardens by Leopoldo II in 1835.

The main road (N1) which enters Grosseto from the W passes the railway station on the right, and terminates at the circular Piazza Fratelli Rosselli. Here are the Prefettura, with a classical colonnade, and Palazzo delle Poste (1930), a fine example of Fascist architecture. Corso Carducci leads through the Porta Nuova past the 12C façade of San Pietro on the left to Piazza Duomo on to which face Palazzo Comunale (1870) and the **Cathedral**. It was begun, on the site of an earlier church, by the Sienese architect Sozzo di Rustichino at the end of the 13C, but was largely rebuilt in the mid-19C. The neo-Gothic FAÇADE in pink-and-white marble, which was added in 1855, incorporates parts of the earlier decoration, including the symbols of the Evangelists, and a curious circular palindrome to the right of the main entrance recording its foundation in 1294. The S side has two Gothic windows and a doorway with fine carvings, also attributed to Sozzo. The remaining decoration was added by Casare Maccari in 1897. The brick bell-tower dates from the early 15C, but was completed later. The INTERIOR, forming a Latin-cross with three naves, was also decorated in the 19C with bands of contrasting marble. The temple-shaped baptismal font is by the Sienese sculptor, Antonio Ghini (1470). The rich marble high altar dates from 1649. In the N transept, in an elaborate frame, also by Antonio Ghini, is an Assumption by Matteo di Giovanni (c 1480).

To the right of the cathedral is Piazza Dante with a monument to Leopoldo II by Luigi Magi (1846). There is a portico on two sides and Palazzo della Provincia, in a neo-Gothic Sienese style, dates from the beginning of this century. Off Via Ricasoli is Piazza del Mercato, and leading off it is Via

Mazzini. Here at No. 61 is the *Museo di Storia Naturale* (open daily except Monday, 9–13, 15–19; fest. 9–13). It contains an interesting collection of mammals, birds and insects native to the region, as well as prehistoric remains and Neolithic finds, and a vast range of shell-fish.

The town centre is small and easy to explore. Off Piazza Indipendenza is the 13C church of *San Francesco*, with a simple façade pierced by a rose-window over the doorway. The interior, with a single nave and timber roof, has remains of frescoes including St Anthony Abbot and a large St Christopher. The painted *Crucifix over the high altar is attributed to Duccio (c 1285). To the right of the choir is the chapel of St Anthony with a fresco cycle illustrating the saint's life and virtues, by Francesco and Antonio Nasini (1683). The sacristy has an Annunciation by Francesco Curradi. To the left of the church is the cloister (much restored) with 14C fresco fragments. The fine well in travertine has a dedication to Ferdinando I dei Medici and the date 1590. In the contiguous Piazza Baccarini is the **Museo Archeologico e d'Arte della Maremma** (No. 3; installed here in 1975 but closed since 1992 for rearrangement). The fine archaeological collection, founded in 1865, has objects ranging from prehistoric to the Etruscan and Roman eras. Finds from excavations in the district are arranged systematically according to sites and well labelled. Of particular interest are the Roman statues discovered at Roselle. There is also an important medieval section, with Lombard objects, coins, gems, and pottery. On the upper floor is a collection of paintings formerly exhibited in the Museo Diocesano. It includes: Guido da Siena, *Last Judgement; 14-15C Sienese and Florentine works; Sassetta, *Madonna of the Cherries; Pietro di Domenico, Dead Christ. Among the later paintings is an altarpiece of the Madonna in Glory above a view of Grosseto by Alessandro Casolani of 1631. There are also some liturgical objects, sculptures, illuminated manuscripts and Renaissance coins, as well as an interesting photographic section which documents life in the Maremma in the 19C and early 20C.

B. via Paganico

Road, N223, 70km—20km *San Lorenzo a Merse*—24km **Bagni di Petriolo**—39km *Civitella Marittima*—46.5km **Paganico**—52.5km turning for *Campagnatico* (4km)—66km turning for **Roselle** (5km)—70km **Grosseto**.

Buses run by TRA-IN from Siena (Piazza San Domenico) follow this route.

Information Offices. APT of Siena (Tel. 0577/280551) as far as Bagni di Petriolo; APT of Grosseto (Tel. 0564/454510) S to Grosseto.

This is the fastest, but busiest, route to Grosseto. Although called a superstrada the road is not dual-carriageway. It is a beautiful road which passes through varied scenery, perhaps at its most lovely in spring when the yellow broom is in flower. From the Siena by-pass N223 runs S; it is worth looking back to see the magnificent view of the city spread over its hill. The road proceeds past scattered farmhouses with extensive views towards the hills on the right, and with Monte Amiata visible at times in the distance to the left. It continues along the Merse valley where rice is cultivated. At a bridge (20km) across the river (4-star hotel *Locanda del Ponte*) a road diverges right to *San Lorenzo a Merse* (2km), a pretty village perched on a hill. The main street leads up to the Romanesque church which has a stone façade decorated with green marble in the Sienese style. It has a timber roof and an apse pierced by a single lancet window. To the left of the church is a chapel, and beyond is the old castle in a panoramic position. This by-road leads on to Monticiano, described in Rte 19A.

The main road continues, and, at 24km a by-road to the left leads steeply down to **Bagni di Petriolo**, a little spa enclosed in its 15C walls, with an old chapel. Pope Pius II came here to benefit from the sulphurous water springs. The baths are open in summer on weekdays 6.30–13.30, 15.30–20 (1-star hotel *Bagni di Petriolo*, and 3-star hotel *Imposto* at Imposto). It is possible to bathe in the sulphur springs below the bridge on the banks of the Farma. The by-road continues uphill to the village of *Pari* in a beautiful position.

N223 crosses a spectacular viaduct dominating the Farma valley (4-star hotel *Terme di Petriolo*, with sulphur pools) and then passes through two long tunnels, before reaching (39km) the turning for *Civitella Marittima* (329m), well seen on the right. The old nucleus of houses is built over the remains of its walls. From this turning a road leads across the main road and then an unsurfaced road on the left winds down to a cypress avenue (c 1km) leading to the Romanesque church of *San Lorenzo al Lanzo*, in a particularly beautiful position in a deep valley. The very well preserved façade has half-columns flanking the doorway with interesting capitals, similar to those of Sant'Antimo. The interior is heavily restored and the former monastic buildings are now private.

46.5km **Paganico** (2-star hotel *La Pace*), a village situated on a loop of the river Ombrone in a strategic position for the defence of Siena from the south. It preserves its walls and gates almost intact: they were rebuilt in the mid-14C by Lando di Pietro, the architect of Siena cathedral. The church of *San Michele*, in the piazza, dates from the same period. Its single nave has a giant frescoed figure (damaged) of St Christopher. On the left of the nave is an altarpiece of the Madonna and Child with saints by Andrea di Niccolò (c 1480). Over the high altar is a Madonna and Child enthroned worshipped by saints by Guidoccio Cozzarelli. On the wall nearby is a very dramatic painted Crucifix of the late 15C. The *frescoes in the choir are a masterpiece of 14C Sienese painting. During recent restoration work the name of the artist Biagio di Goro Ghezzi and the date 1368 were discovered. On the soffit of the arch are half-length figures of saints and in the vault, the Evangelists. On the E wall (on either side of the window) is the Annunciation. The artist has made use of the window jambs to make the perspective of his composition more convincing (note the presence of the Infant Jesus and the Dove on the left). On the N wall is the Nativity, with angel choirs, and other charming details. Below are three scenes from the legend of St Michael. On the opposite wall is the Epiphany above a scene with St Michael dividing the Blessed from the Damned.

52.5km. By-road (left) for *Campagnatico* (4km; 275m), a pretty village on a ridge with remains of its old castle. At the entrance to the village on the left is the church of Santa Maria (closed for restoration). From the small piazza, with the Romanesque façade of the former hospital of Sant'Antonio, the main street leads up to the church of San Giovanni Battista. It has an elegant Gothic façade with a perforated rose window. The crenellated bell-tower probably formed part of the old fortifications. The interior, with a single nave and three apses, contains detached frescoes of the Life of the Virgin (from Santa Maria), signed and dated 1393 by Meo di Piero and Cristofano di Bindoccio. In the 19C horse breeding was encouraged here and several elegant houses have stables decorated with horses' heads.

55km. A by-road to the right leads to the hill-top village of *Montorsaio* (384m; 4km), on the edge of thick woods. The parish church has a Madonna and Child by Sano di Pietro and a late-Renaissance sacristy cupboard. In the nearby confraternity chapel of Santa Croce is a fine Crucifix (1629). From Montorsaio a footpath leads (in 1 hr, or 1hr 30min.) to the summit of *Monte Leoni* (614m), passing remains of the convent of San Bernardino (suppressed in 1751), with panoramic views.

63km. Signpost to *Nomadelfia*, a Christian community, founded in 1931 by Don Zeno Saltini (died 1981) to create a family, especially for young people in need: there are now over 300 members. 66km. Turning for the excavations of **Roselle**, reached by a well-signposted by-road (5km). One of the most important Etruscan cities in northern Etruria, it came under Roman dominion in the 3C BC. A bishopric was founded here in the Middle Ages. In 935 it was pillaged by the Saracens, and abandoned after 1138 when it became a quarry for the nearby villages. The pretty drive up Poggio Moscona through a wood passes several tombs (car park at the top). From a footpath on the left it is possible to get a view of a stretch of the cyclopean walls (6C BC), which enclosed the Etruscan town. They are approximately 3km long. The site is open to the public daily (1 May–31 August, 7.30–20.30; 1 September–31 October, and 1 March–30 April, 8.30–19.30; 1 November– 29 February 9–17.30). The footpath leading uphill overlooks the Roman road (formed of large flagstones) and the area comprising the Roman forum and basilica. Nearby are remains of a house with mosaic floors, a paved street, and drains. Towards the hill on the right, large statues of the Emperor Claudius and the Imperial family were discovered in a rectangular chamber; they are now in the museum of Grosseto. Beyond further excavations (still in progress) is the amphitheatre, 37m x 27m, with four entrances, in opus reticulatum of the 1C AD. On the adjacent hill traces of the earlier Etruscan settlement have been brought to light, together with remains of household objects, pottery, tiles, and unbaked bricks. There is evidence here that the Etruscans used a system of collecting rain water similar to the Roman *impluvium*. The view over the plain (formerly Lago Prile) is particularly beautiful. Near the modern village of Roselle, the waters of a spa known since antiquity, were deviated by the flood in 1966.

N223 crosses the new section of the Aurelia to enter (70km) **Grosseto** (described in Rte 19A).

20

The Via Cassia south of Siena

Road, N2, 63km—14.5km *Monteroni d'Arbia* (for **Asciano**, 16km)—16km *Lucignano d'Arbia* (for *Murlo*)—27km **Buonconvento** (for the **Abbey of Monte Oliveto Maggiore**, 9km)—30km By-road for **Montalcino** (14km), and **Sant'Antimo** (24km)—43km **San Quirico d'Orcia**—63km turning for *Radicofani* (10km).

Buses run by TRA-IN from Siena (Piazza San Domenico) to Asciano, Buonconvento (with services to Monteoliveto Maggiore), Montalcino, Sant'Antimo, and San Quirico d'Orcia.

Information Office. APT of Siena (Tel. 0577/280551).

The **Via Cassia**, the old Roman road between Rome and the N (see Rte 13B) leaves Siena by the Porta Romana (the Siena Sud exit on the by-pass). It runs through a remarkable landscape of bare clay hills known as LE CRETE. Beneath their deeply eroded slopes are scattered clusters of trees. Here and there are pretty farm houses, and the crests of the hills are often marked with pines and cypresses. The Cassia follows the river Arbia, lined with poplar trees, through *Isola d'Arbia* (with a pretty Romanesque church, on the left) and *More di Cuna* (with medieval brick buildings, on the right). 12km *Cuna*, just off the road on a hill to the right, is a rare example of a fortified medieval granary. It belonged to the hospital of Siena, Santa Maria della Scala, and is entirely built of brick with fortified walls, towers, and an arched gateway. Inside is a small chapel, with a 16C fresco of the Madonna and Child with saints, various houses, beautifully preserved, and a central 13C fortress. An immense ramp leads up to the first floor where grain was stored. There is a fine view of Siena. The road continues along the Arbia valley, known for its excellent white wine, to (14.5km) *Monteroni d'Arbia*, a medieval village surrounded by an industrial suburb. Here a road diverges left for Asciano.

FROM MONTERONI D'ARBIA TO ASCIANO, 16km. This pretty road traverses increasingly wild countryside reminiscent of the landscapes in the backgrounds of paintings by the Sienese masters (particularly those by Giovanni di Paolo). 9km. A by-road for Pievina leads in 500m to the ruined abbey of *Rofeno*, isolated on a hill with fine views all round. The road then descends to the valley, crosses the Ombrone and enters (16km) **Asciano** (5900 inhab.) through a gateway in the walls built by the Sienese in 1351. (Information Office, open in summer, on Corso Matteotti; 3-star hotel *Il Bersagliere*; first-class restaurant *Osteria della Pievina*, 5km NW; trattoria *Da Ottorino* at Sante Marie, 7km N.) Corso Matteotti, the main street, leads up to the Gothic church (left) of *Sant'Agostino* which has a simple brick façade. The interior has transversal arches and altars of grey stone; the first two enclose damaged 16C frescoes. Behind the high altar (the Madonna and Child by Matteo di Giovanni is a reproduction) is the marble tombstone of Giacomo Scotti by Urbano da Cortona (1487). To the left of the church is the 14C *Casa Corboli*, which preserves some 14C frescoes by the school of Lorenzetti. The house, which is at present being restored, will eventually become the Museo d'Arte Sacra (see below). Farther up on the left a covered passageway gives on to a picturesque courtyard with a well. The street continues uphill to the crenellated bell-tower of the *Torre Civica* (restored), opposite which is the *Antica Farmacia Francini Naldi*, with its elegant 19C cupboards displaying old pharmacy jars. A Roman mosaic floor discovered on the premises of the pharmacy may be visited on request. Via Cassioli, to the right, leads down past old houses to *Piazza del Grano* which has a fine fountain by Antonio Ghini (1450). Beyond is the 14C *Palazzo del Podestà* studded with 15C coats of arms.

The picturesque Via Bartolenga winds uphill ending opposite the *Collegiata di Sant'Agata*, approached by steps. This beautiful Romanesque-Gothic church, dating from the late 13C, has a travertine FAÇADE with three slender blind arches and an oculus, to the right of which is a fine campanile. The unusual INTERIOR has a broad nave and three apses with a dome resting on a circular drum, decorated with blind arches, and terminating in a lantern. There is a 15C Sienese Crucifix over the altar, a fresco of the Madonna and Child with two archangels by the school of Sodoma on the S wall, and a Pietà by Bartolomeo Neroni on the N wall. The most important paintings and sculptures belonging to the church are exhibited in the adjoining **Museo d'Arte Sacra** (open on request by appointment, Tel. 0577/718207 until it reopens in 1995). The works on view include: Master of the Osservanza, *triptych of the Birth of the Virgin with the Madonna of Humility and angels in the pinnacle; Barna da Siena, (attributed), Madonna and Child; Segna di Bonaventura, *Madonna; and an altarpiece by Francesco Vanni. The sculpture includes: *Virgin Annunciate and angel by Francesco di Valdambrino (c 1420); a 14C Crucifix; and 17C choir-stalls. Part of the collection is undergoing restoration and will eventually be exhibited in Casa Corboli (see above). These works include: Ambrogio Lorenzetti, *altarpiece with St Michael (from Badia a Rofeno); Matteo di Giovanni, *polyptych; Giovanni di Paolo, Assumption; Pietro di Giovanni d'Ambrogio, *triptych; Sano di Pietro, Madonna; and Taddeo di Bartolo, Annunciation.

To the right of the Collegiata, beyond the war memorial, a road leads up to the Romanesque-Gothic church of *San Francesco*, at present closed for restoration, in a fine position with a good view of the town and its circuit of walls. To the left of the Collegiata, at No. 36 Via Mameli, is a *Museum* of paintings (mostly portraits) and drawings by the local painter Amos Cassioli (1832–91), which was opened in 1991 (admission daily except Monday, 10–12.30 and in summer also 16.30–18.30). At the top of Corso Matteotti, which also converges on the main piazza, is the church of *San Bernardino*, now transformed into the *Museo Etrusco* (open as above). It has an interesting collection of finds, mostly excavated in the necropolis of Poggio Pinci, 5km E of Asciano.

The Cassia continues S from Monteroni d'Arbia (see above), and, at 16km, by-passes **Lucignano d'Arbia** (3-star hotel *Grotta Azzurra*), a pretty village on a hill. It has two fine Sienese gates which are joined by the main street, and well preserved medieval and Renaissance houses in brick. In the centre, on a rise, is the Romanesque church of *San Giovanni Battista*, with its impressive bell-tower. Inside is a Crucifixion by Bartolomeo Neroni, called Il Riccio. From the by-pass, a road leads SW to Vescovado and Murlo (8km).

The village of **Vescovado** (3-star hotel *L'Albergo di Murlo*) has some pretty streets with old buildings. The modern parish church contains a *polyptych by Benvenuto di Giovanni of 1475, complete with its painted pinnacles, side-pilasters, and predella, and a small Madonna and Child by Andrea di Niccolò. On a hill to the S is the tiny village of **Murlo** (314m; 3-star camping site *Le Soline* at Casciano di Murlo; trattoria *La Befa*, 8km S), built onto its circle of walls and dominating the surrounding countryside. It has been considerably restored but preserves its medieval character. Next to the church is the former bishop's palace which has been converted into a *MUSEUM (open summer 9.30–12.30, 15.30–19; winter 9.30–12.30, 14–17 except Monday). The small but choice collection includes objects excavated in recent years on the nearby hill of Poggio Civitate. A unique Etruscan architectural complex with a palatial villa has been discovered dating from the 7C and 6C BC. There are extensive remains of walls and roof tiles; small objects in gold, silver, bronze, and ivory; and a vast range of ceramics, all beautifully displayed and labelled. A pretty by-road (12km) leads W from Vescovado via Fontazzi through a varied landscape, passing small villages and ruined castles, to join N223 from Siena to Grosseto, described in Rte 19B.

27km **Buonconvento**, a picturesque fortified village at the confluence of the Arbia and Ombrone. Here Emperor Henry VII, who was planning to lay siege to Siena, died of malaria in 1313. Later, Buonconvento became one of the primary defences of Siena and its fine brick walls and gates are well preserved. On the charming main street are some medieval houses and *Palazzo Pretorio*, with a crenellated tower, all in brick. The church of *Santi Pietro e Paolo*, originally 14C but entirely rebuilt in the 18C, has a *Madonna and Child by Matteo di Giovanni and a *Madonna and Child with saints by Pietro di Francesco Orioli. Opposite is the MUSEO D'ARTE SACRA DELLA VAL D'ARBIA (open Tuesday and Thursday, 10–12; Saturday 10–12, 16–18; Sunday 9–13). The collection includes: Duccio (attributed), *Madonna and Child; Master of the Buonconvento Cross, Crucifix; Luca di Tommé, *Madonna; Andrea di Bartolo, *Annunciation; Sano di Pietro, *Madonna and saints, Coronation of the Virgin; Matteo di Giovanni, *Madonna (a small work), Madonna and Child enthroned; Benvenuto di Giovanni, Annunciation; Pietro di Francesco Orioli, Madonna and Child with saints. There are also some later paintings and some liturgical objects, with a fine early-14C incense-boat and a 15C copper gilt chalice.

From Buonconvento N541 diverges left to the **Abbey of Monte Oliveto Maggiore** (9km), on a promontory in a thick wood of cypresses, one of the best known monasteries in Tuscany. There is a car park outside the gate (and a bar and restaurant). Visitors are admitted daily 9.15–12.15, 15–17 or 18. The convent was founded for hermits by Giovanni Tolomei of Siena (1313), who assumed the religious name of Bernardo and was beatified. The new Olivetan Order, under Benedictine rule, was confirmed by Guido Tarlati, Bishop of Arezzo in 1319. Pius II and Charles V sojourned here, the latter with 2000 followers. The monastery was suppressed by Napoleon in 1810, and after restoration was made a National Monument in 1866. Some monks remain as caretakers and hospitality is available at the guest house.

From the gateway beneath a great tower (1393), decorated with a Della Robbian Madonna and Child crowned by two angels, and a seated figure of St Benedict, a road leads down to the MONASTERY through an avenue of cypresses. The huge brick monastery buildings stand beside the late-Gothic façade of the church (1400–17). In the surrounding cypress woods are small 18C chapels, dedicated to founder members of the Order and to various saints, and a large fish reservoir built by the Sienese architect Giovan Battista Pelori (1533). The GREAT CLOISTER (1426–74), with two storeys of loggias, is famous for its *frescoes illustrating the life of St Benedict, nine of which, those on the W wall, are by Luca Signorelli (1497–98) and the remainder by Sodoma (Giovanni Antonio Bazzi, 1505–08). These are masterpieces of fresco painting and combine a picturesque and lively narrative style with charming naturalistic detail in a variety of landscape and architectural settings. In between the episodes are painted pilasters, several of which are decorated with grisailles and grotesques, also by Sodoma. The scenes follow the account of Benedict's life from the Dialogues of St Gregory the Great.

The cycle begins on the EAST WALL with frescoes by Sodoma. **1.** Benedict departs from his home at Norcia to study in Rome; **2.** Benedict leaves Rome; **3.** Benedict miraculously mends a broken tray (Sodoma painted his own portrait in the richly clad young man with two tame badgers at his feet); **4.** The holy monk Romano gives Benedict a hermit's habit (Subiaco is represented in the background); **5.** Benedict at prayer in front of his cave, with the devil about to break the bell of his bread basket; **6.** A priest is inspired by Christ to take a meal to Benedict on Easter Day; **7.** Benedict instructs a group of peasants; **8.** Benedict overcomes temptation by throwing himself naked into brambles; **9.** Benedict accepts the request of a group of monks to become their abbot; **10.** Benedict with the Sign of the Cross shatters a glass of poisoned wine prepared by the monks who found his rule too strict; **11.** Benedict founds the first twelve communities. SOUTH WALL. Frescoes by Sodoma. **12.** Benedict welcomes into the Order Mauro and Placido; **13.** Benedict chastises a monk tempted by the devil; **14.** Benedict, in answer to the monks' prayers, makes water spring from Monte Oliveto; **15.** Benedict retrieves a scythe which has fallen into a lake; **16.** Mauro is sent to save Placido from drowning; **17.** The miracle of the flask changed into a snake; **18.** Fiorenzo attempts to poison Benedict; **19.** Fiorenzo sends a group of loose women to the monastery. WEST WALL. **20.** (by Bartolomeo Neroni, called il Riccio). Benedict sends Mauro to France and Placido to Sicily. Nos. 21–29 are by Luca Signorelli. **21.** Fiorenzo's death; **22.** Benedict converts the inhabitants of Monte Cassino; **23.** Benedict defeats the devil; **24.** Benedict rescues a young monk from beneath a collapsed wall; **25.** Benedict tells two monks when and where they had dined outside the monastery; **26.** Benedict reproaches Valeriano's brother for breaking the fast; **27.** Benedict unmasks Riggo disguised as Totila; **28.** Benedict recognises and welcomes Totila. The last fresco was destroyed when the door was enlarged. The following frescoes are by Sodoma: **30.** Benedict foretells the destruction of Monte Cassino (by the Lombards in 581). NORTH WALL. **31.** Benedict miraculously obtains flour for his monks; **32.** Benedict appears to two monks in their sleep and instructs them on how to build a church; **33.** Episode of two excommunicated nuns; **34.** Miracle of the monk's burial; **35.** Benedict forgives the monk who had escaped from the monastery; **36.** Benedict releases a bound peasant by merely looking at him.

In the passage leading to the church are two small frescoes of Christ carrying the Cross and Christ at the column, and St Benedict giving the Rule to the founders of Monte Oliveto, all by Sodoma. In the vestibule is a statue of the Madonna and Child by Fra Giovanni da Verona (1490) and a fresco of Hermits in the desert attributed to Giovanni di Paolo. The CHURCH, with a Latin-cross plan, was renovated by Giovanni Antinori in 1772. The magnificent *choir-stalls of inlaid wood are by Giovanni da Verona (1505) and the lectern by Raffaele da Brescia (1520). The Assumption in the cupola is by Jacopo Ligozzi, who also painted the Nativity of the Virgin behind the high altar. Off the N transept is the Chapel of the Holy Sacrament which has a large Crucifix of the late 13C. Opposite is the sacristy with cupboards dated 1417. From the Chiostro Grande is a passageway to the CHIOSTRO DI MEZZO, with a Madonna and Child and angels over the entrance. Leading off the cloister, which is surrounded by a portico, is a vestibule with a 17C lavabo (above which is a fresco by Riccio).

Monte Oliveto, drawn in 1837 by Joseph Pennell

It gives access to the REFECTORY, a large vaulted hall with frescoes by Paolo Novelli (1670). A staircase from the Chiostro di Mezzo gives access to the LIBRARY which is preceded by a vestibule with portraits of Olivetan monks by Antonio Mueller. The door to the library and the Paschal candlestick are by Giovanni da Verona (1515), as are all the carvings in the library itself. A double flight of steps leads to the PHARMACY wih a fine collection of jars. The CHAPTER HOUSE and AULA DI GIUSTIZIA are also richly decorated; the latter has a fresco of Christ and the adulteress by Riccio (1540). The monastery has an important laboratory for the restoration of illuminated manuscripts.

San Giovanni d'Asso lies 8km SE of Monte Oliveto. This village is dominated by its impressive *Castle*, which preserves much of its structure intact, including its wooden doors, some Gothic windows, and a large courtyard with a Renaissance brick portico. The back entrance to the castle gives on to a rectangular piazza from which there is a good view. To the right, opposite an 18C chapel, is the church of *San Giovanni Battista*, which has a Romanesque façade of brick decorated with blocks of travertine and a large oculus over the arched doorway. The interior has been restructured and the Sienese 14C triptych removed to Pienza for safe keeping. A short distance beyond the opposite end of the piazza, surrounded by cypress trees, is the charming little church of *'San Piero in Villore* (11–12C). Its ancient, irregular façade is decorated with blind arches and a doorway with carvings and strange anthropomorphic capitals. The structure, of sandstone and travertine, was restored in the upper part in brick at some later date. Beneath the church is a small crypt. Montisi, 7km E is described in Rte 21.

The Via Cassia continue S from Buonconvento (see above) and at 30km a very pretty road diverges right for Montalcino (14km). On the approach is the church of the *Osservanza*, on a hill to the right, from which there is a good view of the town. The road climbs up steeply passing under the impressive ramparts dominated by the Medici arms. **MONTALCINO** (567m) is a charming little walled town (6300 inhab.), beautifully situated above vines and olive groves, in a panoramic position overlooking the surrounding countryside. It is famed for its red wine, the remarkably long-lived Brunello, one of the choicest Tuscan wines, and considered by some experts to be Italy's finest.

Information Office, 8 Costa del Municipio.

Buses (TRA-IN) from Siena via Buonconvento.

Car Parks outside the fortress or outside the walls.

Hotel. 3-star: *Il Giglio*, 49 Via Soccorso Saloni.

Restaurants. First-class: *Il Moro*, Via Mazzini. Trattoria: *Sciame*, Via Ricasoli. In the environs: first-class: *La Taverna dei Barbi*, località I Barbi; *Poggio Antico* at Poggio Antico; trattoria *Il Pozzo* at Sant'Angelo in Colle.

Annual Festivals. A theatre festival is held here in July, and the *Sagra del Tordo*, on the last Sunday in October, with a bow and arrow competition, dancing, gastronomic specialities, etc.

History. This area was inhabited by the Palaeolithic era and an Etruscan and Roman settlement grew up here. In the Middle Ages Montalcino became a flourishing and independent town, but was repeatedly attacked by Siena and defended by Florence, finally succumbing to Sienese rule after the Battle of Montaperti in 1260. There followed a period of peace and prosperity and in 1462 Montalcino received the title of city from Pius II. After successfully resisting two sieges in 1526 and 1553, the town was forced to capitulate to Florence, despite a heroic defence lasting four years. In 1559 it became part of the Grand Duchy of Tuscany.

Although particularly famous for its *Brunello*, other excellent wines produced locally include the *Rosso di Montalcino*, and *Moscadello*, a sweet fizzy wine. It is also known for its traditional white-and-turquoise coloured pottery, and for its honey.

The town has numerous medieval houses with gardens and orchards, and streets which climb up and down, offering picturesque views. The 14C Sienese ***fortress** (open daily, except Monday, 9–13, 14–18; in summer 9–13, 14–20) was provided with impressive ramparts by Cosimo I in 1571. Inside the courtyard is the nave of a former church and, through an arch, a small garden with ilex trees. On the ground floor of the castle is an Enoteca, where it is possible to taste and buy the local wines. There are fine rooms on the upper floors and steps lead up to the towers and ramparts with a walkway from which there are magnificent views in all directions across the Orcia, Ombrone, and Asso valleys. Via Ricasoli descends from the castle passing (left; No. 44) *Palazzo Pieri Nerli* which has an interesting courtyard with a portico and well. On the right is the monastery of SANT'AGOSTINO, where the Museo Civico e Diocesano (see below) is to open soon. The 14C church has a fine marble doorway and rose-window. The interior preserves many of its original 14C frescoes (very worn); those in the choir of the life of St Augustine are by Bartolo di Fredi. The stained-glass windows are modern. Just beyond the church, at the end of Via Ricasoli, is *Palazzo Vescovile* (No. 4 Via Spagni) where the **Museo Civico e Diocesano** is provisionally installed (open daily except Monday, winter 10–13, 15–17; summer 9.30–13, 15.30–19). It comprises a small archaeological section from local excavations and an important collection of Sienese painting and sculpture of the 12–16C. The works include: a 12C illuminated *Bible in two volumes and a 12C painted *Crucifix from Sant'Antimo; triptych with the Madonna and Child by a follower of Duccio; Luca di Tommé, *Madonna and Child; Bartolo di Fredi, *polyptych, *Coronation of the Virgin; Benvenuto di Giovanni, the Redeemer; Sano di Pietro, *Madonna and Child; Girolamo di Benvenuto, Nativity; and Sodoma, processional banner with the *Crucifixion. The sculpture includes: Della Robbian terracottas; fine polychrome wood statues, including St Peter by Francesco di Valdambrino (1425); Maestro Angelo, Mary and Gabriel; and works by Domenico di

Niccolò dei Cori, Giovanni di Turino, and others. There are also illuminated manuscripts, vestments, liturgical objects, and fine examples of Montalcino pottery.

A steep street leads down from Sant'Agostino to the triangular PIAZZA DEL POPOLO above which looms the tall narrow tower of *Palazzo dei Priori (1292). Numerous coats of arms decorate the front and side of the palace and beneath is a portico with a statue of Cosimo I by Giovanni Berti (1564). In the interior of the palace, which preserves some frescoed and sculpted coats of arms, is an information centre dealing with the local wines (open daily, except Monday, 10–13, 15.30–18.30). Also facing the piazza is the grandiose *LOGGIA, which has the two first bays in stone dating from the 14C; the four larger brick arches were built in the 15C. Opposite the loggia is a café with 19C furnishings. To the right of Palazzo dei Priori, Via del Municipio leads into Piazza Garibaldi at the end of which is the church of *Sant'Egidio*. It contains a frescoed triptych by the school of Luca di Tommé, a Madonna and saints by Francesco Cozza, and a painted Crucifix by Francesco di Valdambrino (c 1420).

Via Spagni leads uphill to the cathedral of **San Salvatore**, situated at the highest point of the town. It was built in 1818–32 by Agostino Fantastici to replace the Romanesque church. It has a grandiose brick portico and a spacious neo-classical interior with Ionic columns. The two altarpieces of the Immaculate Conception and St John the Baptist in the nave are by Francesco Vanni (1588). In the Baptistery Chapel are interesting *reliefs from the Romanesque church representing Christ and the symbols of the Evangelists. In front of the church is a small piazza with a view over the town. Via Spagni continues downhill to the *Madonna del Soccorso*, a sanctuary built in the 17C on the site of an ancient chapel. The elegant travertine façade is by Francesco Paccagnini (1829). The Baroque high altar encloses a venerated image of the Madonna, possibly of the 14C. To the right is an *Assumption of the Virgin by Vincenzo Tamagni. From the terrace next to the sanctuary there is a splendid view towards Siena.

Viale Roma descends along the outside of the walls to Piazza Cavour with a little public garden. Here the former hospital of SANTA MARIA DELLA CROCE founded in the 13C (now the Comune) still preserves parts of its original structure. The old pharmacy, inside the main entrance, has *frescoes of the Madonna enthroned, Saints Jerome and Augustine, figures in niches, and trompe-l'oeil cupboards by Vincenzo Tamagni (1510), visible through a window. Downhill from Piazza Cavour are pretty streets leading to an old mill and wash house and uphill again to the church of *San Francesco*, which preserves its 14C façade and tall square tower. It has been deconsecrated and is now incorporated into the Public Hospital, together with the 16C cloister and the remaining monastic buildings. There are two small chapels frescoed with scenes from the Life of the Virgin by Tamagni (key from the porter). From the terrace in front of the church there is a fine view of the town. From Piazza Cavour the Corso leads back to Piazza del Popolo.

From Montalcino a road leads SE to the picturesque village of *Castelnuovo dell'Abate* (10km), overlooking the *Abbey church of Sant'Antimo (open April–Sept 10.30–12.30, 15–18; winter 11–12.30, 15–17). Gregorian Mass is held here on Sunday at 17.00 (16.00 in winter). One of the finest Romanesque religious buildings in Italy, it is in a delightful setting in the Starcia valley, surrounded by olive groves and hills covered with ilex woods. The original Cistercian abbey is said to have been founded by Charlemagne in 781, and it continued to enjoy the protection of the Holy Roman Emperor,

Sant'Antimo

as well as receiving Papal privileges. A period of decline began in the 13C, and the abbey was suppressed by Pius II in 1462 and placed under the jurisdiction of the bishop of Montalcino. The present church probably dates from the early 12C (the date 1118 is inscribed on a column of the ambulatory). The style combines French and Lombard elements. The simple, lofty FAÇADE was never completed and was probably intended to have a double doorway. Orginally there was a portico supported on two columns resting on lions, which are now inside. The doorway has stylised vine branches in the architrave and other carved decoration. The EXTERIOR of the church has a monumental simplicity, its forms outlined by sequences of pilasters, corbels, and pierced openings. There are blind arches running along the nave under the roof. The prow-like choir gives an impression of compactness with its three beautiful apses. The decoration is subdued: two white columns with fine capitals linked by a row of carved corbels emphasise the curve of each apse. The BELL-TOWER, which is divided into four storeys by a cornice and blind arches, is decorated with some stylised reliefs including a Madonna and Child on the E side. The stone varies in type and colour and the decorative effect is enhanced by some beautifully veined blocks. The older apse of the Carolingian chapel has an oculus at its base through which can be seen the 9C CRYPT, a small vaulted chamber with two apses facing each other and four columns, and a baptismal font let into the ground.

There is a small finely carved doorway on the N side. The doorway on the S side is decorated with palmettes and interlaced bands beneath an architrave carved with eagles, gryphons, and monsters. Above, in the lunette, are the Sergardi arms and corbels with strange heads on either side.

The INTERIOR has a basilican plan: the central nave is supported on columns and four cruciform piers, with an upper gallery and a clerestory above. A timber roof covers the nave, whereas the side aisles are vaulted. The aisles become narrower towards the E end, leading into an ambulatory, with three radiating chapels, a feature which is rarely found in Italian architecture. The interior is built of travertine of a particularly warm tonality, quarried locally. The luminous honey-coloured stone, and the numerous windows combine in creating a wonderful suspended atmosphere. The light changes according to the season and the time of day, and the effect at sunset is particularly beautiful. The sculptural decoration is of exceptionally high quality: the *capitals of the nave present a variety of geometrical and leaf motifs. The finest is that of the second column on the right representing Daniel in the lions' den, which is now attributed to the Master of Cabestany, of French or Spanish origin. The sculptural decoration of the primitive church was subsequently adapted and re-used in some capitals of the ambulatory and gallery, or inserted into the outside walls.

The GALLERY, to which there is access from a spiral staircase next to the sacristy, was partially fitted up with rooms by the Bishop of Montalcino in the 15C and preserves a fireplace and wall paintings. It continues round the entire church. Flanking the entrance to the SACRISTY are carved pilasters of the Carolingian period and a stoup with two superimposed Romanesque capitals with the Piccolomini crescent in each corner. The sacristy occupies the primitive church or so-called CAROLINGIAN CHAPEL, a small rectangular chapel with an apse (the vault was probably added later). It has a 15C cycle of grisaille frescoes of the life of St Benedict by Giovanni di Asciano and two anonymous 16C frescoes of Christ on the Cross between Saints Anthony and Sebastian and a Pietà. The *AMBUL-ATORY, the design of which may have been borrowed from French proto-types, is supremely elegant and refined in every detail. There is great harmony in the play of light created by the columns, windows, vaults, and blind arches. Certain stones and the bases of some columns have been carved in onyx or alabaster instead of travertine and, when sunlight falls directly on them, they take on a translucent glow. Columns surround the high altar, on the steps of which is a long inscription referring to a benef-actor, Count Bernardo, probably dating from the early 12C. Over the altar is an impressive 13C *Crucifix of painted wood. The polychrome wood statue of the *Madonna del Carmine (Umbrian, c 1260) is temporarily exhibited in the Museum of Montalcino. On the right of the altar are steps leading down to a small rectangular CRYPT which has a barrel vault and a frescoed Pietà. At the base of the BELL-TOWER, at the N end of the ambulatory, is an interesting chapel with three niches, tall narrow pilasters in the corners, and three window openings. One of the bells is dated 1219.

Practically nothing remains of the monastic buildings or cloister, except for the well. The fine three-arched window with cushion capitals, suppos-edly belonging to the chapter house, is pre-Romanesque. Organ concerts are given in the church in July and August.

From Sant'Antimo a road (unsurfaced in places) leads W to **Sant'Angelo in Colle** (6km; also reached by a direct road from Montalcino, 9km). An enchanting well-preserved village on the top of a hill (444m), it is contained in its circle of walls. In the piazza at the centre is the Romanesque church of San Michele which has a Madonna of the Rosary by Francesco Rustici, dated 1625. Behind the church, next to the priest's house is a chapel with a Madonna and Child by a follower of Ambrogio Lorenzetti. There is a splendid view from the village across the Orcia valley towards Monte Amiata.

The Cassia continues S from the turning for Montalcino (see above) to (37.5km) *Torrenieri*, a small industrial town important in the past for the production of bricks. It has a 14C polychrome wood statue of the Madonna in the Propositura of Santa Maria Maddalena.

43km **SAN QUIRICO D'ORCIA** (409m; 3-star hotel *Palazzuolo* with restaurant, 43 Via Santa Caterina; first-class restaurant *Vecchio Forno*; information office, 33 Via Dante Alighieri). This little medieval town (2200 inhab.) takes its name from the former church of San Quirico a Osenna, recorded as early as the 8C on the Via Francigena. Little is known of St Quirico (Cyricus) except that he was martyred, allegedly in the 4C. In the 13C the peripheral walls were enlarged and several hospices and hospitals were built here to accommodate pilgrims on their way to Rome. Stretches of the walls survive, as well as some of the former watch-towers, partly incorporated into other buildings. The old Porta Romana was unfortunately destroyed in the Second World War.

From the medieval *Porta Cappuccini*, an unusual polygonal and well preserved gateway, Via Poliziano passes some interesting houses, before reaching Piazza Chigi. The *Chigi Palace* (which has been left to crumble since it was damaged in the war) was built for Cardinal Flavio Chigi by Carlo Fontana in 1679. Immediately on the right is the Romanesque *Collegiata, built in the 12C on the site of an earlier church. The EXTERIOR, built of travertine, has a simple structure, except for the three elaborately decorated doorways, parts of which are in contrasting sandstone. The main entrance, dating from the late-12C, is the finest example of a Lombard portal in Sienese territory. Beneath a large rose-window is a projecting rounded arch resting on strange animal heads, above four slender clustered columns tied together with a loop at their centre. These in turn have Lombard lions at their base. A sequence of inner arches, surrounding the lunette with a seated figure at the centre, are supported on five narrow columns on either side of the door. The architrave is carved with two fighting monsters in sandstone, above which is a frieze of stylised animals and geometrical motifs. The doorway on the S side, with a porch supported on telamons standing on lions, is slightly later in date and is attributed to the school of Giovanni Pisano. It has a fine architrave and is flanked by two elegant Gothic windows; the right window has a kneeling telamon and carved fantastic animals. The smaller doorway, at the end of the S transept, is dated 1298 (both were damaged by shell-fire). The remaining decoration is limited to small blind arches under the roofs. the bell-tower dates from the 18C.

The INTERIOR has a Latin-cross plan, with three arches supported on piers dividing the nave from the short N aisle. The timber ceiling, parts of which preserve the original paint, was discovered under the Baroque vault. The nave and transept chapels are divided from the crossing by arches. In the N transept is a fine *polyptych by Sano di Pietro. The presence in the painting of St Quirico and the red-and-white arms of the town prove that it was painted for this church. The choir was enlarged in the mid-18C to house nine *choir-stalls inlaid with trompe l'oeil scenes and half-length figures by Antonio di Neri Barili (possibly on designs by Signorelli) which originally formed a series of 19 in the Baptist's chapel in Siena cathedral.

The 17C organ is attributed to Cesare Romani of Cortona; it is used for concerts. In the chapel of the Holy Sacrament is a detached fresco of the Madonna and Child, by Girolamo di Benvenuto, known as the Madonna delle Grazie or Madonna del Pomo. On the side wall is a Madonna of the Rosary by Rutilio Manetti. Under the last arch is a marble tombstone of Henry of Nassau, dated 1451 by Urbano da Cortona. To the left of the church is the *Oratory of the Misericordia* which has a Madonna and Child with saints by Riccio.

The principal street, Via Dante Alighieri, traverses the town, with some well-preserved medieval houses and the Renaissance Palazzo Pretorio. In Piazza Libertà is the church of *San Francesco*, also known as the *Chiesa della Madonna* with a (restored) Gothic façade. The interior contains, on the high altar, a Della Robbian Madonna, and polychrome wood figures of the Virgin and Angel Gabriel by Francesco di Valdambrino.

Across the piazza, next to the Porta Nuova, is the entrance to the *HORTI LEONINI (open daily), an Italian Renaissance garden created by Diomede Leoni around 1580. At the centre is a marble statue of Cosimo III by Giuseppe Mazzuoli (1688) which was removed from Palazzo Chigi. The garden, which follows the Renaissance pattern of box hedges in a geometrical design leading to a *boschetto* or ilex wood on a slope, was intended as a resting place for pilgrims. It is surrounded by remains of the old ramparts, above which stood the tall castle tower. Farther along Via Dante is a 14C house (No. 38) where St Catherine of Siena is supposed to have stayed. Towards the end of the street is the charming little church of *Santa Maria Assunta* (11C), built of beautiful stone blocks. It has a fine doorway with a porch (which may originally have been intended for Sant'Antimo). The simple interior is barely lit by small lancet windows. The apse is decorated on the outside with blind arches and zoomorphic heads. Opposite is the *Ospedale della Scala* (which belonged to the eponymous hospital of Siena) dating from the 13C. There are remains of a loggia giving on to the courtyard, which also preserves a 16C well. Pienza, 9km E, is described in Rte 21.

From San Quirico an unsurfaced road leads up through beautiful countryside to the tiny village of *Vignoni* (3km; keep left), now almost totally abandoned. It has a truncated medieval tower, and the little street runs past the 15C Palazzo Amerighi (now Chigi) to the Romanesque church on the edge of the hill. The other fork of the road ends at the restored castle of *Ripa d'Orcia*, dominating the Orcia valley.

From San Quirico, Radicofani can be reached by an alternative (longer) route (34km) along the Val d'Orcia. A by-road branches off the Cassia 4km S of San Quirico along the beautiful Orcia valley. It passes the small fortified granary of Spedaletto and a pretty road for Pienza (see Rte 21). It runs along the stony shallow bed of the river through an interesting landscape with pasturelands and eroded clay slopes, with small sharp ridges, known as *calanchi*. In recent years its wild aspect has been altered by the action of bulldozers which have levelled certain areas to create corn fields. La Foce, described in Rte 21, lies 5km above the valley on the road to Chianciano Terme. The road continues uphill via *Contignano* (481m), a tiny village with a fine castle tower and a 17C church (with a 14C altarpiece of the Coronation of the Virgin), from which there is a splendid panorama embracing Monte Amiata, Radicofani, Monte Cetona, and Pienza across the Val d'Orcia. Radicofani is described below.

The Cassia continues S of San Quirico. 48km. Turning (right) for **Bagno Vignoni**, a tiny medieval thermal station (4-star hotel *Posta Marcucci*, with swimming pool and 3-star hotel *Le Terme*) on a small plateau (threatened with 'development'). The warm sulphurous waters, known since Roman times, bubble up into a large piscina constructed by the Medici in the charming *Piazza.

The Cassia crosses the Orcia and almost immediately afterwards a road (right) leads up to *Castliglione d'Orcia* (540m), another beautifully situated little village, built round a rock with a picturesque ruined castle. It was the birthplace of the painter and sculptor Il Vecchietta (c 1412–80), after whom the piazza is named. In the pieve of Santi Stefano e Degna, a Romanesque church with a Renaissance façade, is a large Crucifixion by Fabrizio Boschi. Three paintings of the Madonna by Pietro Lorenzetti, Vecchietta, and Simone Martini, have been provisionally removed to the museum of Montalcino for safekeeping. The pretty borgo has narrow streets with some medieval houses and a little Romanesque church, the Chiesa delle Sante Marie. There is a fine view over the Orcia valley. Nearby, on the outskirts, is *Rocca d'Orcia*, a particularly well preserved medieval village on a slope, dominated by its spectacular castle, the *Rocca di Tentennano. The piazza has a large octagonal stone well in the centre. The parish church of San Simeone has a fresco of the Madonna of Mercy by a follower of Bartolo di Fredi and a Madonna of the Rosary by Francesco Rustici. There is a long-term plan to install a small museum in one of the other village churches in order to exhibit the Madonna by Giovanni di Paolo which is at present on view in the Pinacoteca of Siena.

59.5km. By-road (right) which leads to *Campiglia d'Orcia* (4km; 811m) in an elevated position on the N slope of Monte Amiata, facing Radicofani. It has picturesque medieval streets and a tall bell-tower built on a rocky spur. In the church of San Biagio is a Madonna and Child with saints attributed to Sebastiano Folli. A road winds S toward Abbadia San Salvatore (see Rte 22) through chestnut woods. 4km SW is *Vivo d'Orcia* (870m; 2-star hotel *Amiata*) reached through oak woods, situated on the torrent Vivo. Near the bridge is the *Eremo del Vivo*, an impressive late-Renaissance building overlooking the valley. A Camaldolese monastery in the early 12C, it became the property of the Cervini of Montepulciano who built a fortified palace here in 1536. The architect is said to have been Antonio da Sangallo the Younger. The church of San Pietro, opposite, has a Romanesque apse. Nearby are *case coloniche*.

At (62km) *La Bisarca* a road to the right leads shortly to **Bagni San Filippo**. Its hot sulphurous springs, known since ancient times, are said to be named after St Filippo Benizzi (1238–85), of the Servite Order. There is a thermal station (2-star hotel *Terme San Filippo*) and beautiful cascades. In the village is the church of San Filippo which has an 18C stucco statue of St Filippo and busts of St Filippo Benizzi and St Filippo Neri.

63km. The main road keeps right, passing through a long tunnel, near Monte Amiata (described in Rte 22), while the old road rises steeply via Le Conie to **Radicofani** (783m; 10km; 2-star hotels), strikingly placed on a basaltic hill, which divides the Orcia and the Paglia valleys. The remains of the *Rocca* dominate the hill. It is associated with the legendary Ghino di Tacco who here imprisoned the Abbot of Cluny, as related by Boccaccio in the *Decameron*. The Rocca was taken in 1469 and rebuilt by the Sienese but was later forced to surrender, together with other Sienese strongholds, to Cosimo dei Medici in 1559. New fortifications of impressive proportions were constructed by the Medici. The castle was devastated by an explosion in the 18C and partly restored in the 1930s (further consolidation of the structure is in progress). The position affords a fine view over the Orcia valley to the N and of Monte Amiata to the W.

Radicofani has pretty medieval streets and is mostly built of grey basaltic stone. In the central piazza is the Romanesque church of *San Pietro* above a flight of steps, with a tall campanile rising from the façade. The fine interior has cross vaults over the transept and an apse supported on transversal arches. There are several good Della Robbia statues and reliefs, a Madonna and Child in polychrome wood by Francesco di Valdambrino and, over the high altar, a glazed terracotta Crucifixion with the Magdalen, by Benedetto and Santi Buglioni. Nearby, in Via Roma, is the Gothic church of *Sant'Agata*, the patron saint of Radicofani. It was rebuilt in the 18C and has a terracotta altarpiece of the Madonna and Child with saints by Andrea Della Robbia. On a road which descends towards the Cassia is a fountain erected by Ferdinando I in 1603 with figures of Justice and Abbundance framing the Medici arms. Opposite is *Palazzo La Posta*, a hunting lodge with arched porticoes on two levels, which was built for the Grand-duke Ferdinando and is attributed to Simone Genga and Bernardo Buontalenti (1584). It later became an inn at which Montaigne, Chateaubriand, and Dickens all stayed. It is now in a sadly neglected state.

72km. The old and new roads rejoin in the Paglia valley which is now followed to the boundary between Tuscany and Lazio, beyond which is Acquapendente, see *Blue Guide Rome and environs*.

21

Pienza and Montepulciano

These two charming small towns lie 12km apart on the N146 above the Val d'Orcia, between the Via Cassia and the Valdichiana. They can be reached from San Quirico d'Orcia (see Rte 20) or from Chiusi (see Rte 29).

Buses (TRA-IN) from Siena.

Information Office. APT *Chianciano Terme-Valdichiana*, 7 Via Sabatini, Chianciano Terme (Tel. 0578/63538).

*PIENZA (491m) is a charming compact little Renaissance town (2400 inhab.), the birthplace in 1405 of Aeneas Silvius Piccolomini, afterwards Pius II. He changed its name from Corsignano by papal bull in 1462 after appointing Bernardo Rossellino to design the monumental main square with its splendid buildings, all built between 1459–62.

Information Office, 59 Corso Rossellino.

Hotel (3-star) *Corsignano*, 11 Via della Madonnina; *Il Chiostro di Pienza Relais*, 26 Corso Rossellino; trattoria *La Buca delle Fate*, 38 Corso Rossellino.

*Piazza Pio II, laid out by Bernardo Rossellino, is a remarkable example of Renaissance town planning. It shows the influence of Leon Battista Alberti, Rossellino's master. On the handsome pavement is an elegant well, also designed by Rossellino, flanked by two slender columns with finely carved capitals and an architrave. The ***Duomo** (open 8–13, 14.30–18.30) has an interesting Classical façade in Istrian stone, divided into three arched bays above which is a pediment with the papal arms of Pius II surrounded by a garland of fruit. The unusual tall and short INTERIOR, with the nave and aisles of equal height, is divided by clustered columns with tall dosserets supporting the vault. The large arched windows, decorated with tracery, continue round the five chapels at the E end, filling the church with light.

The elegant architecture is clearly influenced by Northern European models. The painted ribs of the vault, fanning out from the columns, create a striking effect. The five altarpieces were painted for the cathedral in 1461–63. In the S aisle, Giovanni di Paolo, Madonna and Child with Saints Bernardine, Anthony Abbot, Francis and Sabina (and a Pietà in the lunette). First apse chapel: Matteo di Giovanni, Madonna and Child with Saints Catherine of Alexandria, Matthew, Bartholomew and Lucy (and the Flagellation in the lunette); second apse chapel (of the Holy Sacrament): marble tabernacle attributed to Rossellino, which contains a relic of St Andrew. The E Chapel has fine choir-stalls and a bishop's cathedra of 1462. Fourth apse chapel: Vecchietta, triptych of the Assumption with Saints Agatha, Callistus, Pius I and Catherine of Siena (Ecce Homo in the predella). Fifth apse chapel: Sano di Pietro, Madonna and Child with Saints Mary Magdalen, Philip, James, and Anne (with Ecce Homo in the gable and Annunciation in the predella). In the N aisle, Matteo di Giovanni, Madonna and Child with Saints Jerome, Martin, Nicholas, and Augustine. The tall CAMPANILE (left of the façade) gives access to the CRYPT OF SAN GIOVANNI. The *baptismal font in travertine is by Rossellino; the fragments of Romanesque sculpture displayed here come from the former church of Santa Maria. The whole church has had to be shored up at the E end and the structure is still unstable.

To the right of the Duomo is *Palazzo Piccolomini, begun by Pius II and finished by Pius III, his nephew. It is considered Rossellino's masterpiece, and shows the influence of Alberti's Palazzo Rucellai in Florence. The FAÇADE is built of sandstone with two elegant rows of arched mullioned windows alternating with pilasters, separated by horizontal cornices, and simple doorways. The base becomes a projecting bench on three sides of the palace. The magnificent COURTYARD is surrounded by a portico supported on a splendid Corinthian order, above which are two storeys of square mullioned windows with a glazed loggia on two sides of the upper floor. On the right are stairs leading up to the first floor. Opposite, on the left, is the entrance to the *HANGING GARDEN, facing which is the magnificent garden front of the palace, composed of three superimposed open loggias. The Italian garden of evergreen box hedges and small trees, has remained unchanged. Seen against the backdrop of the Orcia valley, it is a supreme example of the Renaissance idea of the garden as the intermediary between architecture and nature. The main rooms on the FIRST FLOOR are open to the public (guided tours 10–12.30, 15 or 16–18 or 19, except Monday). They were inhabited by the Piccolomini family up until 1962. The SALA DEGLI ANTENATI is hung with family portraits. The DINING ROOM has good furniture and tapestries. In the MUSIC ROOM is a fine scagliola table representing a map of the Sienese State, and Cordova leather hangings. The large SALA D'ARMI has a display of arms and battle paintings by Borgognone. The LOGGIA overlooks the garden and, beyond a beautiful landscape, there is a view of Radicofani with Monte Cetona on the left and Monte Amiata on the right. The BEDROOM has a 17C bed and a fresco over the door with a portrait of Pius II. A passage leads to the LIBRARY, interesting for its furniture, carpets, books, and documents.

Opposite Palazzo Piccolomini is *Palazzo Vescovile*, which was modified and enlarged by Roderigo Borgia, later Pope Alexander VI, whose arms it displays on the corner. It will become the seat of the **Museo della Cattedrale** in 1995 which is at present housed in the nearby *Canonica* (open 10–13, 14.30–16.30, except Tuesday). The contents, assembled from the Duomo and other churches, include: 15C and 16C Flemish tapestries; the early 14C *cope of Pius II in *Opus Anglicanum*, with scenes from the Life of the Virgin, saints and apostles, embroidered in gold and silk; the Pope's silver *crosier and enamelled silver roundels which originally decorated his mitre; 15C illuminated choir-books, with miniatures by Sano di Pietro and other artists; school of Bartolo di Fredi, portable triptych with numerous small scenes of the Life of Christ; Bartolo di Fredi, *Madonna of the Misericordia, signed and dated 1364; Ugolino di Nerio, *polyptych; Sassetta (attributed; or the Master of the Osservanza), portable *triptych; Vecchietta, *polyptych of the Madonna and Child with saints, a lunette with the *Annunciation and a *predella with the Martyrdom of St Biagio, Crucifixion, and a Miracle of St Nicholas; Fra Bartolomeo, *Rest on the Flight into Egypt; Bernardino Fungai, Madonna and Child and a painted *Crucifix by Segna di Bonaventura, both from the church of San Francesco; fine Crucifixes, liturgical objects and vestments, and a small local Etruscan collection. Other important works including a Madonna by Pietro Lorenzetti from Monticchiello and a *tabernacle by Francesco di Giorgio from Montefollonico will also be exhibited here.

Opposite the Duomo is *Palazzo Comunale* with a fine *portico of travertine with Corinthian columns, and double windows on the upper floor, also designed by Rossellino. Corso Rossellino leads out of the piazza along the side of Palazzo Piccolomini, opposite which is *Palazzo Ammannati*, built by Cardinal Ammannati of Pavia. Its top floor loggia is now bricked in. Next to it is the smaller *Palazzo dei Cardinali*. A little further on, to the left, is *San Francesco*, an early Gothic church with some late-14C frescoes. The street ends at the 14C *Porta al Prato* (or Porta al Murello), beyond which on the left is a public garden. The pretty Passeggiata di Santa Caterina leads to the Seminario Vescovile, beyond which is the 18C church of *Santa Caterina*. Also outside Porta al Prato, a charming walk follows Via delle Fonti downhill (600m) to an old fountain. Nearby is the beautiful Romanesque ***Pieve di Corsignano** (or *Santi Vito e Modesto*), in a picturesque setting beside some old farm buildings, with a good view of Pienza. Its unusual circular tower has eight large arched windows. A very ancient church (10–11C), it has a W doorway decorated with reliefs of stylised flowers and palmettes with a strange double-tailed siren in the architrave. Fantastic creatures also decorate the façade which has a two-light window with a female caryatid. The architrave of the S doorway has carvings depicting the Journey of the Magi, and the Nativity, with animals on the jambs. The interior has a basilican plan with piers dividing the nave from the aisles. It still contains the simple baptismal font supported on a Romanesque capital in which Pius II was baptised.

Just inside Porta al Prato, Via Gozzante leads to a delightful raised walkway running along the walls on the S side of the town beside cypresses, and overlooking the valley. It passes beneath the garden of Palazzo Piccolomini and continues from the Canonica to the *Porta al Ciglio*, at the far end of Corso Rossellino. Outside the gate is a fortified palace with two impressive round towers. The old streets of Corsignano are extemely picturesque. Pienza is famed for its sheep's cheese called *pecorino* or *cacio*.

A pretty road leads S from Pienza providing the best view of the garden façade of Palazzo Piccolomini and the great apse of the Duomo to (5km) **Monticchiello** (546m), 4km SE of Pienza, a pretty medieval village with a fine view of Pienza. It preserves its 13C castle, walls and towers, in a relatively good state. The late-13C church of *Santi Leonardo e Cristoforo* has a good doorway and rose window. The interior, rebuilt in the 18C, has 14C and 15C frescoes of the Sienese school. The painting of the Madonna by Pietro Lorenzetti is in Siena but will be exhibited in the new Cathedral Museum in Pienza (see above). The polychrome wood figure of St Leonard is by Domenico di Niccolò dei Cori (c 1420). In the adjacent Piazza San Martino a remarkable local open-air theatre season is held in July. Information from the *Compagnia Popolare Teatro Povero*, Tel. 0578/755118. A by-road leads SE from Monticchiello to Montepulciano (8km; see below).

FROM PIENZA TO TREQUANDA, 28km. This route includes a number of interesting and well preserved small villages in the beautiful *Valdichiana Senese*, with wooded hills (ilexes and oaks) and cultivated fields, to the N of Pienza. N146 leads NE towards Montepulciano. At 6km N327 diverges left. 9km Turn (right) for **Montefollonico** (3km; 567m; Luxury-class restaurant *La Chiusa*), a quiet little fortified village with pretty paved streets and small houses, Sienese in atmosphere. It stands on a ridge between the Orcia and Chiana valleys. Probably of Roman origin, the village developed in the Middle Ages. It preserves parts of its medieval walls with three gates, including the Porta Nuova, a 14–15C double gate through which the road enters the delightful hamlet, with numerous doves and pigeons. The street leads left past the little 13C Palazzo del Comune, with a well-head next to it, to the 13C church of *San Leonardo* (if closed, ring at No. 38, by the E end). The pretty exterior is built of square blocks of local yellow-and-white stone, and is approached by steps on either side of outcrops of rock. The restored interior has a Baroque high altar. In a chapel to the left is a 13C wood Crucifix between two paintings of the Annunciation in stone frames. In the nave are very worn frescoes and paintings of the birth of the Virgin, the Madonna and two saints (by Guidoccio Cozzarelli), and a Circumcision (in a good frame). In the other direction the street leads past the entrance to the little *Chiesa della Compagnia del Corpus Domini* (if closed, ring at No. 5; right bell), recently restored. It is preceded by a tiny courtyard with the bell-tower at one corner. Inside is a Deposition by the school of Signorelli, and interesting 18C frescoed lunettes with amusing details. The street leads on past (right) the roofless church of *San Bartolomeo* to Porta del Triano, bearing the date 1278, and framing a view of Montepulciano on the skyline. Outside the gate is a fine stretch of walls. A footpath continues down to the handsome *Chiesa del Triano* in a group of horse-chestnut trees. Its architectural features in brick and stone stand out against the white intonaco. It has a pretty domed bell-tower. The date 1609 is above the door. The interior has an attractive crossing with an unusual altar screen enclosing a 14C fresco of the Madonna and Child (removed during restoration work along with other important works which will be exhibited in the Museo della Cattedrale in Pienza).

7km N of Montefollonico is the lovely little red-brick village of **Torrita di Siena** (3-star hotel *La Stazione*, 255 Via Mazzini; 2-star hotel *Belevedere*, 31 Via Traversa Valdichiana Ovest. The *Palio dei Somari* is held here on the Sunday following 19 March, with a mule race, flag throwing, etc.). Torrita was an important stronghold of the Sienese Republic until it became part of the Medici grand-duchy of Tuscany in 1554. It preserves parts of its walls and is a particularly well-kept village. It is thought to have been the birthplace of the 13C painter and mosaicist Fra Jacopo da Torrita (or Jacopo Torriti), and of Ghino di Tacco. It has a station on the Chiusi to Siena railway line. In the piazza, with a well, is *Palazzo Comunale* (13C; restored), with a bell-tower. Inside is the restored Teatro degli Oscuri (1824). Next to it is the Romanesque church of *Santa Flora e Lucilla*. In the pleasant brick interior, with some fresco fragments are interesting paintings: on the S altar, triptych with the Crucifixion and saints by the Florentine school (1444). In the sanctuary, school of Sodoma, Madonna in Glory with six saints; N side, Francesco Vanni, Annunciation (1592); (on the altar), Bartolo di Fredi, triptych with the Nativity and Saints Anthony Abbot and Augustine, a charming work; Benvenuto di Giovanni, Madonna and saints, with the Trinity in the lunette above. A painting of the Madonna and Child by the school of Ambrogio Lorenzetti has been removed. Just out of the piazza is the church of *Santa Croce* (1642), with a Baroque interior and stucco statuary on the high altar. Outside *Porta a Sole* (reached along the side of Palazzo Comunale) is the *Madonna delle Nevi*, a little brick chapel erected in 1525. It is preceded by a portico with two Ionic columns. The altar wall has fine *frescoes attributed to Girolamo di Benvenuto. Outside Porta Nuova is the hospital (Spedale Maestri) which owns an interesting small lunette with a bas relief of the Redeemer and angels, attributed to Donatello. Outside Torrita, 2km along the road to Sinalunga (described in Rte 29) is the 16C *Villa La Fratta*, attributed to Baldassare Peruzzi, with a fine garden (admission sometimes on request).

From Montefollonico (see above) a by-road (signposted Trequanda) leads W. At 14km a road diverges left for Petroio through woods past a large terracotta works. The locality has been known since the 18C for its production of vases, pots, etc, using the local ochre coloured calcareous rock. The road descends to (17km) the medieval village of *Petroio* (487m; trattoria *Madonnino dei Monti*), which is built on an interesting circular plan, with a road in the form of a spiral which leads up to the tower of its impressive 13C brick castle, high above its clustered houses. The parish church of San Pietro has a large, but damaged, fresco of the Crucifixion, attributed to Andrea di Niccolò, in the choir. A beautiful fragment of a Madonna and Child by Taddeo di Bartolo also belongs to the church. San Giorgio, an older church, is in need of restoration. Petroio was the birthplace of a famous ascetic, Bartolomeo Carosi, known as Brandano (1483–1554), whose mottoes and prophesies have been handed down to this day. To the N of Petroio (on the road to Sinalunga) is the *Abbadia a Sicille*, a 17C fortified farm on the site of a hospice for pilgrims founded by the Knights Templar in the 11C. The church was built in 1263. The buildings were radically restored in the 19C.

A beautiful road, with wide views of Radicofani, Montepulciano, Pienza, and Monte Amiata, continues from Petroio past fields and olive groves to the village of (20km) **Castelmuzio**, well seen from the approach road. Of Etruscan and Roman foundations, and first mentioned in the 9C, it has simple brick and sandstone houses. It is also built on a circular plan, so that all the streets are curving. In the piazza is the delightful and very unusual *Casa-Torre*, the town hall, reconstructed in the 18C as Palazzo Fratini, and recently restored. Also here is the *Museo della Confraternità della Santa Trinità e di San Bernardino* (opened on request locally). Next to a hospice for pilgrims on the Via Francigena, the Confraternity of Santa Trinità was founded by 1450. The collection contains a Madonna and Child by the school of Duccio; *St Bernardine, by his friend Giovanni di Paolo; and a Madonna and saints, attributed to Matteo di Giovanni or Pietro di Francesco Orioli. In the sacristy and a room on the upper floor is a charming little collection of Crosses, copes, chalices, musical instruments from the local band founded after the First World War (and disbanded in 1950), Etruscan urns, ceramics, etc. Outside the village (well signposted) is the *Pieve di Santo Stefano in Cennano*, founded in 1285 on the site of a Roman building. It stands in a group of olive trees beside a farmhouse, and the key is left in the side door. The impressive large church shows the influence of Lombard architecture, with a fine triple apse at the E end. The W door has an arch carved with animals and human heads. In the interior, which is awaiting restoration, the columns reach up to the roof. It was poorly restored in the last century.

2km S of Castelmuzio is the Olivetan monastery of **Sant'Anna in Camprena** (hospitality available; information from the Curia at Montpulciano), beautifully situated on a hill (422m) which dominates the surrounding countryside. It is approached by a long cypress avenue. It was founded by Bernardo Tolomei in 1324, rebuilt in the 15C, and enlarged in the 17C. The refectory and cloister may be visited (ring for the caretaker). The REFECTORY has very well preserved *frescoes by Sodoma, his earliest works painted in 1503–05, at the age of 25. The splendid colours are extraordinarily vivid, and the landscapes and use of perspective, as well as the expressive figure studies, show remarkable ability. On the entrance wall: Bishop Guido Tarlati approves the Rule of the Olivetan order; the Deposition (a moving scene which includes the figures of St Anna and St Joachim); and St Anna with the Virgin and Child and two Olivetan monks. On the opposite wall: Multiplication of the Loaves and Fishes, divided into three scenes against a background in which the landscape incorporates the Colosseum and the arch of Constantine. The two long walls (the lower parts of which were formerly covered by the refectory benches), bear two frescoed friezes (partially preserved) with roundels of Saints Gregory, Catherine, and Bernardine, alternating with monochrome scenes of the lives of St Anna and the Virgin, and grotesques. Nearby is the old kitchen. From the 16C cloister (which has been partially walled in) is an entrance to the church (open for Mass on Sunday at 16) which was built in the 17C and provided with large paintings of the life of Bernardo Tolomei in the 18C.

A by-road continues N to (23km) **Montisi** (first-class restaurant *La Grancia*, 3 Via Umberto I), a picturesque village on a hill (413m). The castle preserves some Gothic windows. At the top of the hill, beside a clock tower, is the Romanesque church of the *Annunziata* (key with the caretaker at No. 11). The elegant interior has transversal arches supported on travertine columns. In the sanctuary is a large *polyptych of the Madonna and Child with Saints Peter, Louis, James and Paul, signed and dated 1496 by Neroccio di Bartolomeo Landi in a fine frame. The predella is in the Museo della Cattedrale in Pienza. In the N transept chapel is a painted Crucifix attributed to Ugolino di Nerio. Among the numerous medieval buildings is a granary (at the entrance to the village) which belonged to the hospital of Santa Maria della Scala in Siena. San Giovanni d'Asso, 7km W, is described in Rte 20.

28km **Trequanda** (2-star hotel *Casal Mustia*; first-class restaurant *Conte Matto*) is a medieval village which was under the dominion of Siena. There is a car park below the fine round tower of the Castello dei Cacciaconti (restored). The parish church of *Santi Pietro e Andrea* has a delightful façade chequered in brown-and-white stone. The interior contains frescoes by Sodoma and Bartolomeo Miranda and a Triptych of the Madonna and saints by Giovanni di Paolo over the high altar. Also here is the fine gilded wood sculptured coffer of Beata Bonizella (1235–1300). The Palazzo del Comune has a tower reminiscent of a toy castle. Sinalunga, 6km E of Trequanda, is described in Rte 29.

MONTEPULCIANO, 12km E of Pienza, is a dignified and interesting town (14,300 inhab.) on a hilltop (665m) commanding the SE part of Tuscany and Umbria. It is noted for its red wines, the most famous being the *Vino Nobile*.

Information Office, 9 Via Ricci.

Railway Station, *Montepulciano Scalo*, 11km NE, on the Chiusi–Siena line.

Hotels. 2-star *Il Marzocco*, 18 Piazza Savonarola. In the environs, 3km SE on the road to Chianciano: 3-star *Panoramic*, 8 Via di Villa Bianca.

Restaurants (first-class). *Il Cantuccio*, 112 Via delle Cantine; *Porta di Bacco*, Via di Gracciano.

Annual Festivals. The *Bravio delle Botti* is held on the last Sunday of August. Two men from each of the eight quarters of the town compete in rolling uphill, from Piazza Marzocco to Piazza Grande, a barrel weighing 80 kilos. The prize is a painted banner, the *Bravio*, and the privilege of offering the candle to the patron saint of Montepulciano, St Agnes, on her feast day on 1 May, when an annual fair is held. Since 1959 a *Convegno Internazionale di Studi Umanistici* has been held here, devoted to Poliziano, which ends with a concert of Renaissance music in Palazzo Tarugi. During the first half of August, the *Cantiere Internazionale d'Arte* holds a programme of classical and modern music, with performances of plays and dance, and art exhibitions. Throughout August there is a *Mostra Interprovinciale d'Artigianato*, an exhibition of local handicrafts, and on the penultimate Saturday in the month, a gastronomic feast called *il Baccanale* is held here, at which local food and wine may be tasted.

History. After changing hands several times between Siena and Florence, Montepulciano came under permanent Florentine rule in 1511, and its fortifications, including the Porta di Gracciano, were rebuilt by Cosimo I. It was the birthplace of Angelo Ambrogini (1454–94), the great Classical scholar, who adopted the town's late-Latin name Poliziano. Perhaps the most original genius among writers of his period, he was tutor to Lorenzo de Medici's sons. Another distinguished native was Cardinal Roberto Bellarmino (1542–1621), a Jesuit, author of the Catechism of Christian Doctrine, and the bogy of British Protestants in James I's days. Yet another eminent native was Riccardo Cervini (1501–55), later Pope Marcellus II.

Outside Porta al Prato stands the 14C church of SANT'AGNESE, on the site of the convent built by the Dominican abbess, Agnese Segni (1268–1317), canonised as St Agnese of Montepulciano in 1726. The modern FAÇADE incorporates a 14C doorway. The stained-glass rose window, representing St Agnese, is by Bano di Michelangelo da Cortona. The INTERIOR has a single nave; in the first chapel to the right is a fresco of the Madonna attributed to Simone Martini. A door opens into the CAMERA DI SANT'AGNESE, where relics are preserved. Flanking the main altar on which is a marble urn with the body of St Agnese, surmounted by a statue by Mazzuoli, are a Birth of the Virgin by Raffaello Vanni and the martyrdom of San Biagio by Giovanni da San Giovanni. In the chapel on the left is a 13C Crucifix. The CLOISTER, which was begun in the early 14C but only completed in the 17C, has frescoed lunettes with stories from the life of St Agnes, by Ulisse Giocchi, Francesco Nasini, and a certain Marcellino.

Opposite the church is the *Poggiofanti Garden*, dominated by the ramparts built by Antonio da Sangallo il Vecchio, with a fine view over the Val di Chiana. From Porta al Prato, Via di Gracciano del Corso winds up past several 16C palaces including *Palazzo Avignonesi* (No. 91; right), with a rusticated ground floor. Opposite is the Colonna del Marzocco, bearing a copy made in 1856 by Antonio Sarrocchi of the original lion of 1511, now in the museum. On the left is the church of *San Bernardo*, designed by the Baroque architect Padre Andrea Pozzo. The luminous oval interior has a Madonna in Adoration over the altar attributed to Andrea Della Robbia.

The Corso continues past *Palazzo Batignani* (No. 85; right), *Palazzo Tarugi* (No. 84; left), and *Palazzo Cocconi* (No. 70), attributed to Antonio da Sangallo il Vecchio (the top floor was added in the 19C). *Palazzo Bucelli* (No. 73) has Etruscan urns, reliefs, and inscriptions embedded in the lower part of its façade. It housed the Etruscan collection of finds from excavations in the region, created by the 18C scholar and antiquarian Pietro Bucelli, which was donated to Grand-duke Pietro Leopoldo I and is now in the Archaeological Museum in Florence.

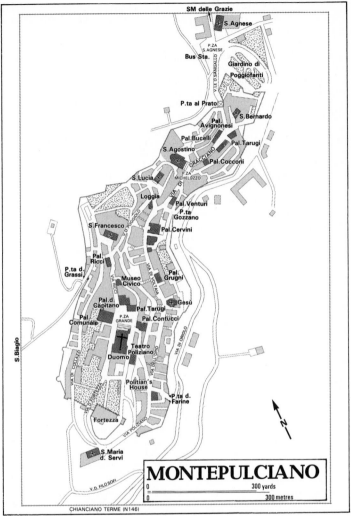

Above a flight of steps on the right is the church of **˙Sant'Agostino**. The fine FAÇADE in Istrian stone, and the doorway with a terracotta high relief of the Madonna and Child with Saints John the Baptist and Augustine, are by Michelozzo. The INTERIOR was redesigned in 1784–91 when the apse and transepts were shortened. On the S side: Raising of Lazarus by Alessandro Allori; St Bernardine signed and dated 1456 by Giovanni di Paolo; and Pietà attributed to Cristoforo Roncalli. On the high altar, poly- chrome wood Crucifix attributed to Donatello. Behind is the CORO VECCHIO of the earlier church, with frescoes and paintings by Bartolomeo Barbiani of Montepulciano, and a Crucifix attributed to Pollaiolo. On the third N altar, Crucifixion by Lorenzo di Credi, and, on the entrance wall, Ascension by Cesare Nebbia (1585), and Madonna della Cintola by Federico Barocci. Facing the church, in Piazza Michelozzo, is an old tower house with a quaint statue of Pulcinella on top which strikes the hours of the clock (the gift of a Neapolitan who settled in the city in the 17C).

Via di Gracciano continues past *Palazzo Buratti-Bellarmino* (No. 28; left), with a 17C doorway and frescoes by Federico Zuccari in the vestibule. To the left, Borgo Buio leads to the Gothic Porta di Gozzano. Via di Gracciano begins to climb steeply uphill through the Arco della Cavina next to the former hospital of Santa Maria della Cavina, to reach Piazza delle Erbe, the market square. Here is the arched *Logge del Grano* (16C), with the Medici arms. Via Voltaia nel Corso continues left past the grandiose *Palazzo Cervini* (No. 21; left), begun by Marcellus II before his pontificate, perhaps by Antonio da Sangallo il Giovane, and *Palazzo Gagnoni-Grugni* (No. 55; left), with a balconied portal by Vignola. Farther on (left), next to the Jesuit College, is the church of the *Gesù*, with a Baroque interior by Andrea Pozzo and illusionistic paintings by his pupil Antonio Colli.

The Corso now becomes Via dell'Opio, lined with several palaces, some of which still reveal their medieval origin. In Piazza dell'Opio, Via del Teatro leads right to Piazza Grande (see below) and Via della Farina leads left to *Porta delle Farine*, a typical example of a Sienese double gate. In Via Poliziano, the continuation of Via dell'Opio, is the 14C house (No. 5; plaque) where Poliziano was born. Outside the town walls is the church of *Santa Maria dei Servi*. The simple Gothic façade with an arched doorway and a rose window, dates from the 14C. The elegant Baroque interior is by Andrea Pozzo. On the N side (second altar) is a 15C fresco of the Madonna della Santoreggia, greatly venerated in the past, and (third altar) a Madonna and Child by the school of Duccio, inserted into a larger painting. The road, from which there is a beautiful view, then skirts the rebuilt *Fortezza* and re-enters the walls by Via della Fortezza to reach *Piazza Grande**, with a pretty well. Here stands the **Duomo** (open 9–18), designed by Ippolito Scalza in 1592–1630. The façade, unlike the sides, is unfinished. The 14C campanile belonged to the earlier church of Santa Maria.

The INTERIOR has a Latin-cross plan with three naves and a cupola over the crossing. The fragments of the *tomb of Bartolomeo Aragazzi, secretary to Pope Martin V, by Michelozzo (1427–36), include the statue of the defunct (right of the W door), two bas-reliefs on the first two nave pilasters, two statues on either side of the high altar, a statue in a niche on the right of the high altar, and the frieze of putti and festoons on the high altar (two kneeling angels from the same tomb are in the British Museum).

SOUTH AISLE. First chapel, polychrome marble altar by Mazzuoli (1683); fourth chapel, two Sienese paintings with gold grounds of the Redeemer and the Assumption; fifth chapel, Assumption by Domenico Manetti and St George by Angelo Righi (1603). On the high altar is a *triptych by Taddeo di Bartolo of 1401, representing the Assumption of the Virgin with saints, predella scenes and pinnacles. In the central nave, on the end piers, are two gilt-wood statues of the Virgin Annunciate and the angel Gabriel attributed to Francesco di Valdambrino. The marble tabernacle on the right pier of the choir is by Vecchietta.

NORTH AISLE. On the pilaster between the fifth and fourth chapels, Madonna and Child by Sano di Pietro; in the Baptistery there is a *font with six bas-reliefs on a base of three caryatid figures by Giovanni d'Agostino, c 1340. On the wall, the so-called *Altare del Gigli*, with Saints Stephen, Bonaventura, Catherine, and Bernardine, by Andrea Della Robbia, enclose a bas-relief of the Madonna and Child attributed to Benedetto da Maiano.

The Duomo of Montepulciano

The statues of Saints Peter and John the Baptist in the side niches are attributed to Tino di Camaino.

The crenellated *Palazzo Comunale* is surmounted by an impressive clock tower. The building dates from the late-14C. The design of the façade, built in travertine with a rusticated ground floor, has recently been attributed to Michelozzo. There is a fine courtyard with a loggia on two sides and another on the upper floor. The tower, which recalls that of Palazzo Vecchio in Florence, may be climbed to enjoy the view which stretches from Monte Amiata to Siena, and E to Lake Trasimene. On the corner of Via Ricci is *Palazzo del Capitano del Popolo*, a Gothic palace considerably rebuilt (with fine Gothic arches on Via Ricci), and a bell-cote on the roof. In front is the elegant *POZZO DE' GRIFFI E DE'LEONI* attributed to Antonio da Sangallo il Vecchio. The well is framed by an architrave resting on two columns, with the Medici arms flanked by the lions of Florence and the griffins of Montepulciano. Next to it is the flank of *Palazzo Tarugi*, with a three arched arcade on the ground floor which continues round in the two left bays of the main front, facing the cathedral. The grandiose travertine façade, which is also attributed to Antonio da Sangallo il Vecchio, has Ionic half-columns on high pedestals supporting a balustrade above the pedimented windows of the main floor. Opposite Palazzo Comunale is *Palazzo Contucci* which was begun for Cardinal Antonio Del Monte (his arms are on the corner) by Antonio da Sangallo il Vecchio. The fine stone façade has five windows on the piano nobile with pediments supported on Ionic columns; the top floor in brick was added later. Inside is an elegant courtyard, and the salone on the first floor is painted with trompe l'oeil frescoes by Andrea Pozzo (1705). The back of the palace rests on the old town walls: the steepness of the site on which the town is built can be appreciated here. To the right of Palazzo Contucci, Via del Teatro leads steeply down and then bends to the right past the *Teatro Poliziano*, built by Giacomo and Sebastiano Barchi and decorated by Giuseppe Castagnoli. It was inaugurated in 1796 by Ferdinando III. The interior is composed of four tiers of boxes.

From Piazza Grande, opposite the Duomo, Via Ricci descends past the 12–13C *Palazzo Sisti*. Opposite on the left is *Palazzo Ricci*, with a simple 16C façade; the back has a loggia and garden with a fine view overlooking San Biagio. On the right is *Palazzo Neri-Orselli* (No. 15), another Gothic palace, modified in later centuries, which now houses the **Museo Civico e Pinacoteca Crociani** (admission April–September, 9–13, 15–18, except Monday and Tuesday; winter on request). The COURTYARD which has a Renaissance loggia and outdoor stairway leading to the upper floors, has sculpture fragments removed from various buildings, the Cocconi and Catenacci arms, the original lion (1511) from the Colonna del Marzocco, and a bust in scagliola of Marcellus II. On the FIRST FLOOR are several Della Robbia works including two altarpieces by Andrea Della Robbia: one with God the Father and angels surrounding a niche with a Nativity and Adoration of the Magi in the predella; and the other with the Madonna and Child between Saints Bartholomew and Longinus and two angels holding a crown. There are also figures of the Virgin Annunciate and angel Gabriel, and of St John the Baptist. The collection of paintings, mostly of the Tuscan and Umbrian schools, is arranged in two large halls. They include: Margaritone d'Arezzo, St Francis; school of Duccio, Madonna and Child with angels; Jacopo di Mino del Pellicciaio, Coronation of the Virgin; Luca di Tommé, Crucifixion; workshop of Filippino Lippi, Crucifixion; Raffaellino del Garbo, Madonna and Child; Girolamo di Benvenuto, Nativity; Giovanni Antonio Lappoli, Immaculate Conception (1545). There are a number of 16C and 17C portraits, including that of Beata Caterina de' Ricci by Giovan Battista Naldini, and several by Florentine artists (Sustermans and Santi di Tito). Among the later paintings: Rutilio Manetti, Holy Family; Anton Domenico Gabbiani, Venus and Cupid; Carlo Cignani, Venus disarming Cupid and Charity; Cristoforo Munari, still life with musical instruments (1712); and Antonio Joli, two views of Arezzo Cathedral. The small 19C collection includes a portrait by Vincenzo Luchini of the tenor Moriani in *Lucia di Lammermoor*, and works by Gazzarrini, Morghen, and Ciseri. On the UPPER FLOOR is a small Etruscan collection.

Farther down Via Ricci, on the left, is the Baroque façade of the *Oratorio dei Cavalieri di Santo Stefano* and *Palazzo Benincasa*, with a bust of Gian Gastone de' Medici over the doorway. Beyond the Porta San Francesco (from which a street leads through the Porta dei Grassi down to San Biagio, see below) is a piazza in the oldest part of the town, with a fine view. Here is the church of *San Francesco* which dates from the 13C. Next to the elegant Gothic doorway are the remains of a pulpit from which St Bernardine of Siena is reputed to have preached. The interior has been heavily restored. Via del Poggiolo passes the Piazzetta degli Archi and leads to the church of *Santa Lucia*, built in 1633, which has an elegant façade. On the high altar is a Crucifix by Giovanni Battista Alessi di Montepulciano. In the first chapel (right) is a fine, but damaged Madonna by Luca Signorelli (locked; light switch behind the grille, operated by a rod).

On the N outskirts of the town, beyond Sant'Agnese (see above), Viale Calamandrei leads to the sanctuary of **Santa Maria delle Grazie**, designed by Ippolito Scalza, with a porticoed façade (1605). The interior was decorated with elegant stuccowork in the mid-18C by Andrea da Cremona. To the right is a Madonna and Child with saints by Niccolò Betti. The second altar has a Della Robbian *tabernacle, framing the Madonna delle Grazie, and two Annunciation figures attributed to Giovanni Della Robbia. In the choir is a Madonna and Child with St Simon Stock by Giovan Battista Ferretti (1766). In the N nave chapels are St Helena adoring the Cross by Bartolomeo Barbiani of Montepulciano (1632), a German Crucifix (16C), with papier-mâché statues of the Virgin and St John (1740), and a Madonna with Carmelite saints by Giuseppe Nicola Nasini. The late-16C *organ is the only example of its kind in Italy (there is a comparable organ at Innsbruck). Its pipes are of cypress wood and produce a particularly soft and gentle sound, which was recommended by Monteverdi for the accompaniment of his *Orfeo*. Since the organ's restoration in 1983, it has been played by organists from all over the world.

From Piazzale Sant'Agnese Via Bernabei leads to Piazza del Mercato, with the 16C Villa La Fantina (unfinished). About 3km from the centre of the town is the *Santuario della Madonna della Quercia*, built in the 18C round an earlier chapel. On the façade are two Della Robbia statues and, inside, an interesting collection of ex-votos.

Just outside Montepulciano, off the road to Pienza, and approached by a noble cypress avenue, is the ***Tempio di San Biagio** (open 9–12, 15–18), one of the great church buildings of the High Renaissance. It was built by Antonio da Sangallo il Vecchio (1518–34) for the Ricci family on the site of an earlier church, also dedicated to St Biagio. It has a Greek-cross plan with a central dome. The EXTERIOR of travertine is of classical sobriety, and the beautifully proportioned design of the façade is repeated on two sides. Only one of the towers was finished, and actually completed in 1545 by Baccio d'Agnolo, who also built the lantern of the dome. The INTERIOR, which is also very beautiful, repeats and elaborates the classical features of the exterior, with sculptural decoration carved in high relief in the yellow sandstone. The marble high altar is by Giannozzo and Lisandro di Pietro Albertini (1584). The statues of Saints John the Baptist, Agnes, Catherine of Siena, and George, are by Ottaviano Lazzari (1617). The venerated 14C fresco in the tabernacle represents the Madonna and Child with St Francis. The lunette fresco is by Antonio Righi (1648), and those in the vault are attributed to Zuccari or Bartolomeo Barbiani. The stained-glass window is by Bano di Michelangelo of Cortona (1568). Behind, in the area corresponding to the apse, is the sacristy, from which a staircase leads to the outside balcony. The Canons' House, nearby, with open loggias on both floors, was built after Sangallo's death.

CHIANCIANO TERME, 9km SE of Montepulciano, reached by N146, is one of the most important spa towns in Italy (455m; 6800 inhab.). It has warm saline and chalybeate waters. With over 200 hotels of all categories, it is given over to the reception of its numerous visitors.

Information Office. APT *Chianciano Terme-Valdichiana*, 7 Via Sabatini (Tel. 0578/63538), 67 Piazza Italia, and in Piazza Gramsci.

Railway station *Chiusi-Chianciano Terme*, 14km E, on the main Florence–Rome line.

Numerous **Hotels** of all categories.

The place was known to the Romans as *Fontes Clusinae*. In the Middle Ages it was contested between Siena and Orvieto. The spa developed in 1915–29, and most of the thermal buildings were rebuilt in the 1950s.

The *Acqua Santa* (open all year round; high season June–September) waters are taken internally for liver complaints. The *Sillene* spring is used for baths. The pleasant old village of **Chianciano Vecchia** adjoins the spa. In the little piazza is Palazzo del Podestà and Palazzo dell'Arcipretura, with a Museo d'Arte Antica (ring on the first floor: 10–12, 15 or 16–17 or 19), where the small collection is well labelled. The large *Crucifix is attributed to the Maestro di San Polo in Rosso (school of Duccio), and the ancona (formerly on the high altar of the church) attributed to the Maestro di Chianciano (early 14C). The Collegiata, beyond, has a detached fresco of the Assunta.

The interesting town of **Chiusi**, 12km E, is described in Rte 29.

A by-road leads W from Chianciano Terme to **La Foce** (5km), on the watershed between the Val d'Orcia and the Val di Chiana, the former home (not open to the public) of Iris Origo (1902–88), historian and biographer, whose life here was described in her autobiography *Images and Shadows* and her war diary *War in Val d'Orcia*. Her book *The Merchant of Prato* about the life of Francesco di Marco Datini, provides a vivid description of life in medieval Italy (see Rte 4). The huge estate (3500 acres) was purchased by Iris and her husband Antonio Origo in 1923 and they spent most of their lives reclaiming the land and bringing it under cultivation. Cecil Pinsent worked on the garden. It includes *Castelluccio Bifolchi*, a small castle. An annual music festival *Incontri in Terra di Siena* is held in summer in the courtyard of the castle, and other localities nearby.

FROM CHIANCIANO TERME TO SARTEANO, CETONA, AND SAN CASCIANO DEI BAGNI, 32km. The pretty road diverges S from the road to Chiusi (N146) just outside Chianciano Terme. 10km **Sarteano** (573m), a medieval village with its streets laid out in a semicircle at the foot of the castle hill. (Pro-Loco information office, Piazza XXIV Giugno; 3-star and 2-star hotels; 4-star camping site *Campeggio delle Piscine*, with hot sulphur swimming pool; first-class restaurant *La Giara*). An Etruscan settlement, it was later con-tested between Perugia, Orvieto, and Siena, until it passed under the dominion of the latter in 1379. At the entrance is the church of *San Francesco* with a fine Renaissance façade of 1480. In Piazza XXIV Giugno above is a war memorial by Arnaldo Zocchi (1923) and the 14C *Palazzo del Comune* (rebuilt in 1845) which contains the *Teatro degli Arrischianti* (1740; being restored). Via Roma goes up past the fine Renaissance *Palazzo Piccolomini*, and then descends through an arch to *San Martino*. In the interior, on the N side, is an *Annunciation by Beccafumi, and a good painting of the Madonna with Saints Roch and Sebastian, complete with its predella, by Andrea di Niccolò. On the S side are two works by Giacomo di Mino del Pellicciaio: Madonna and Child, and a triptych with the Madonna and Saints John and Bartholomew.

From Piazza XXIV Giugno, Corso Garibaldi leads in the other direction past several fine palaces including Palazzo Goti-Fanelli (1535), Palazzo Lichini (14C; enlarged in the 16C), and the 17C Palazzo Forneris to the *Collegiata di San Lorenzo*. In the interior, on the left of the choir, is a chapel with two good paintings of the Virgin Annunciate and Annunciatory angel by Girolamo del Pacchia. In the chapel to the right of the choir is a marble ciborium by Marrina (1514). Opposite is the 15C Palazzo Cennini (rebuilt in the 18C). Outside Porta Monalda, Via della Rocca (right) leads up to the

imposing *Castle*, first built in the 10C. The present bu
by the Sienese in 1467–74.

16km **Cetona**, a beautifully preserved medieval villag
few decades has become a fashionable place to have a c
has fine views of Monte Cetona (see below). Pro-Loco infor
37 Via Roma. 3-star hotel *Belverde*, just outside the town.
luxury-class *Convento di San Francesco*; simple trattorie and p
Osteria Vecchia, and *Da Sacchetta* (just outside the centre).

In the large pleasant Piazza Garibaldi, laid out in the 16C, at the bottom of the hill, is the church of *Sant'Angelo*. In the chapel to the right of the high altar (light by the side door) is a highly venerated seated wooden statue of the Madonna and Child, and on the second altar on the S side, a 16C painting of the Madonna and Child with two saints. At the other end of the piazza is a round tower, near which Via Roma goes up past the 16C ex-Palazzo Cumunale where the MUSEO CIVICO PER LA PREISTORIA DEL MONTE CETONA was opened in 1990 (admission June–mid Oct 9–13, 17–19 except Mon; mid Oct–May Sat 15–17, Sun 9.30–12.30). A delightful little museum, with childrens' corners and modern facilities, it documents the presence of man on Monte Cetona from the Paleolithic era to the Bronze Age. Excavations were carried out in 1927–41 by Umberto Calzoni, and most of his finds are now exhibited in the Archaeological Museum of Perugia. Systematic excavations were resumed in 1984. The most important material dates from the Bronze Age. The first room illustrates the geological formation of the mountain, which was an island in the Pliocene era. R. 2 has remains of a huge bear found in a cave inhabited by Neanderthal man some 50,000 years ago. In R. 3 are Bronze Age finds made since 1984 on the Belverde site. The same ticket allows admission to the archaeological park of Belverde (see below).

Via Roma (attractively paved) continues uphill to the *Collegiata* (closed while the piazza is being restored). It contains a fresco of the Assumption attributed to Pinturicchio. From here there is a view up of the Rocca surrounded by pine trees, and, in the other direction, of Monte Cetona. Farther on, Via della Fortezza leads up to the Rocca (privately owned), and there is a delightful walkway along the walls.

Belverde, 6km from Cetona, is reached by taking the Sarteano road, and, just outside the village, Via di San Francesco. This leads up past the ex-*Convent of San Francesco* (1km), founded in 1212. It has been restored by a community called 'Mondo X' which was founded by Padre Eligio to help young people in need. A member of the community will show visitors the convent including a 14C cloister. There is a well-known restaurant here (see above). The road continues up to another road for Sarteano: the Monte Cetona road instead proceeds downhill to the left through spectacular countryside with the mountain conspicuous on the right. An unsurfaced road (yellow signpost) diverges left downhill to *Belverde* on the side of **Monte Cetona** (1148m), a beautiful wooded mountain (with its summit often hidden by clouds), visible, like Monte Amiata, from miles around. This is the most important Bronze Age site in central Italy. A Cross was placed on the summit in 1968. Delightful walks may be taken on the mountain side. The road passes the *Parco Archeologico Naturalistico di Belverde* (admission with the same ticket as the Museo Archeologico in Cetona; guided tours of c 30 minutes at the same time as the museum; mid-Oct–end of June on request). The interesting vegetation on the cal-careous rock with marine deposits, is pointed out, and a cavern (lit by solar power), formed by the collapse of travertine outcrops, can be visited. Here

Cetona

remains were found of Neanderthal habitation. The cave seems to have been used as a store in the Bronze Age. Below the road is an area (no admission) of excavations begun in 1984, of a Bronze Age settlement.

Just beyond, the road passes the ex-*Convent of Santa Maria a Belverde*, surrounded by lovely old cypresses and ilex trees, with a fine view. A hermitage was founded here in 1367. This is now occupied by a 'Mondo X' community (see above). Visitors are shown the church, preceded by a picturesque portico, divided into three oratories and frescoed in 1380–85. The lower church has a barrel vault and is covered with frescoes including a Crucifixion and St Francis receiving the stigmata attributed, since their restoration in 1973, to Cola Petruccioli. Stairs lead up to the chapel of Santissimo Salvatore with more interesting frescoes of the Life of Christ (including the Resurrection) attributed to Petruccioli and Andrea di Giovanni. A few steps lead up to the adjoining chapel of Santa Maria Maddalena, with scenes from the life of Mary Magdalene, also by Petruccioli. From here an alternative route (4km) may be taken back down to Cetona (signposted).

The road continues from Cetona through lovely countryside with wooded hills and vineyards to (25km) *Piazze* where a road from Città della Pieve in Umbria (11km E; see *Blue Guide Umbria*) comes in on the left. 32km **San Casciano dei Bagni** (582m; 3-star hotel *Terminal* and 2-star hotels) is a little spa town whose hot springs have been known since Roman times. It is situated on the southern slopes of Monte Cetona in woods of oaks, chestnuts, and pines. Mud baths are used here for alleviating rheumatism. The collegiata of San Leonardo has a high altarpiece of the Coronation of the Virgin by Pietro di Francesco Orioli. In the Oratorio della Santissima Concezione is a fresco in a fine tabernacle attributed to Pomarancio. A neo-Gothic castle was built on the site of the Cassero. 1km outside the town are the springs, where the Bagno del Portico was built by Ferdinando II. The Chiesa delle Terme is a primitive building founded in the 11–12C. *Palazzone*, 7km E is known for its wines.

22

Monte Amiata

MONTE AMIATA, the highest mountain in Tuscany (1738m), was originally a volcano. This explains its interesting geological formation, rocky spurs and ravines, mineral deposits, and sulphurous springs. The rich mercury (cinnabar) deposits were known to the Etruscans and they have been systematically mined since 1860. The mountain is covered with woods of chestnuts, beeches, oaks, and fir trees, which are at their most beautiful in autumn. All the roads towards the mountain are inviting and varied: those from the south are perhaps the most spectacular. Picturesque small towns and villages are prettily situated on the slopes. Some modern suburbs, which have developed conspicuously in recent years, testify to the growing importance of the area as a summer and winter resort.

In 1868 David Lazzaretti, the 'Messiah of Monte Amiata', founded a Christian community on Monte Labbro which aimed at instructing and helping the poor. A prophet and visionary, he was regarded with suspicion and condemned by the Church, and his republican ideals were interpreted as a threat by the local authorities. He was shot by carabinieri as he led a throng of followers down from Monte Labbro to Arcidosso in 1878.

Approaches. Monte Amiata is close to the Via Cassia (N2): Abbadia San Salvatore is 7km W of Bagni San Filippo (see Rte 20). It can also be approached from the Siena–Grosseto road at Paganico, described below (Paganico to Castel del Piano, 32km).

Road distances for a round trip of Monte Amiata. **Castel del Piano**— 6.5km *Seggiano*—10km *Pescina*—26km **Abbadia San Salvatore**—30km **Piancastragnaio**—42km **Santa Fiora**—50km **Arcidosso**—54km **Castel del Piano**.

Information Offices. APT *dell'Amiata*, 97 Via Mentana, Abbadia San Salvatore (Tel. 0577/778608). Pro-Loco offices at Santa Fiora, Piancastagnaio,

Arcidosso, and Castel del Piano. *Comunità Montana del Monte Amiata*, località Colonia, Arcidosso and 1 Via Grossetana, Piancastagnaio.

Buses to Abbadia San Salvatore from Siena, Grosseto, Buonconvento, and Chiusi. Abbadia San Salvatore is connected by bus to Santa Fiora and Arcidosso.

Hotels. *Castel del Piano*: 3-star *Impero*, 7 Via Roma; 2-star *Poli*, Piazza Garibaldi. Camping site (3-star) Camping *Amiata*. *Seggiano*: 3-star *Silene* (with restaurant). On *Monte Amiata*: 4-star *Contessa*, Prato della Contessa, Castel del Piano; 3-star *La Capannina*; 2-star *Lo Scoiattolo*, Prato della Contessa and *Le Macinaie*. *Abbadia San Salvatore*: 3-star *Adriana*, 76 Via Serdini, *Giardino*, 63 Via Primo Maggio, and *Kappa Due*, 15 Via del Laghetto. 2-star *San Marco*, 19 Via Matteotti, and numerous others. *Pian-castagnaio*: 3-star *Del Bosco*, 41 Via Grossetana. *Bagnolo*: 2-star hotels including *Il Fungo*, 10 Via dei Minatori. *Santa Fiora*: 2-star *Eden*, 1 Via Roma. *Arcidosso*: 3-star *Toscana*, 39 Via Lazzaretti; 2-star *Gatto d'Oro*, Aia dei Venti, and *Giardino*, 4 Via Risorgimento.

Restaurant (first-class) *Sala Carli*, 46 Via Pinelli, Abbadia San Salvatore.

Winter Sports facilities at Abbadia San Salvatore, Castel del Piano and, località Macinaie, Contessa.

FROM PAGANICO TO CASTEL DEL PIANO, 32km. The road leads through the Orcia valley past (19km) a by-road left for *Montenero*, a village on a hill (338m). Behind the little church of the Madonna, a narrow street leads up through an arched gateway to a piazzetta with a 16C well built by the Medici. Opposite, in the parish church of Santa Lucia, is a large Crucifix by Ambrogio Lorenzetti behind a Baroque altar supporting a graceful glazed terracotta statue of St Lucy. Outside the old walls is a public park from which the view spans westwards. The road continues towards Monte Amiata, and winds round the village of (28km) *Montegiovi*, another typical medieval village built in grey stone, with pretty views on all sides. The church of San Martino has elegant Baroque altars. 30km. The road for Castel del Piano diverges left; just off the Arcidosso road (right) is *Montelaterone* (685m). Perched in a panoramic position, this village is composed of a network of steps and alleys on various levels within its walls, dominated by a castle. The parish church of San Clemente has a medieval portal. The Chiesa della Misericordia, the façade of which was rebuilt in 1907, has frescoes by Francesco Nasini.

32km **Castel del Piano**, one of the largest towns (4600 inhab.) at the foot of Monte Amiata, shares the history of most of the neighbouring towns and villages. In the late medieval period it came under the dominion of Abbadia San Salvatore, and subsequently passed to the Aldobrandeschi and Siena before becoming part of the Grand Duchy of Tuscany under the Medici in the mid-16C. It was the birthplace of the Nasini family which produced three generations of painters, the most important being Francesco (1621–95) and his son Giuseppe Nicola (1657–1736). In the 15C Pope Pius II admired Castel del Piano for its situation and charm. The road enters the town at the main Piazza della Madonna with the church of *Santi Niccolò e Lucia*, with an elegant bell-tower and façade begun in the 18C. Inside are four Baroque altars on either side of the nave. The neo-Gothic ceiling was painted by Francesco Notari, a local 19C artist. The second S altar has a miracle of St Cerbone by Domenico Manetti (c 1642); in the S transept the Cappella del Crocifisso has carved wood figures by Amato and Benedetto Amati of Arcidosso (1670) and a Pietà by Giuseppe Nicola Nasini, who also painted the Agony in the Garden and St Francis receiving the stigmata.

The high altar is attributed to the Mazzuoli brothers of Siena; the Birth of the Virgin is by Giuseppe Nicola Nasini, who also painted the Mystic Marriage of St Catherine of Alexandria and the Martyrdom of St Agnes (second and first N altars).

The *Oratory of the Madonna delle Grazie*, also in the piazza, has a fine stone façade (19C). The altarpiece of the Madonna del Carmine to the right of the nave is by Francesco Nasini (1652). The elaborate Baroque high altar contains a venerated image of the Madonna and Child in the manner of Sano di Pietro. Nearby is the *Town Hall*, in a palace formerly owned by the Gianneschi family, and farther down the main street are some fine houses and the *Oratory of the Misericordia*, which has a Marriage of the Virgin by Francesco Nasini (1664). Beneath the clock-tower a gateway leads into the attractive, walled medieval town. A 16C loggia forms a corner of the Piazzetta degli Ortaggi. There are several Renaissance houses and Via delle Chiese leads from the church of San Leonardo (with a few remains of 15C frescoes inside) to the small church of the *Santissimo Sacramento*. The 18C interior houses a polychrome wood statue of the Madonna of Loreto.

ROUND TRIP OF MONTE AMIATA FROM CASTEL DEL PIANO, 54km. The town is left by Corso Nasini (off which a road is signposted for Prato delle Macinaie, Prato della Contessa, and the summit of Amiata, see below). The road proceeds N, in the direction of Siena, past the cemetery, through chestnut woods and pretty scenery to (6.5km) **Seggiano**. Just before entering the village is (left) the *Santuario della Madonna della Carità*, a small church with a Greek-cross plan crowned by a dome and an elegant façade, which was built by the inhabitants of Seggiano after a terrible famine in 1603. The interior is also simple and elegant. The altarpieces have all been stolen and replaced by modern works. The road winds uphill outside the medieval walls, some built on impressive rocks, to a piazzetta with fine views and the church of Corpus Domini. A street leads downhill from the square to the church of *San Bartolommeo* with a simple Romanesque façade (restored). Inside is a polyptych representing Saints Bartholomew, Michael, and John the Evangelist, attributed to Bartolomeo Bulgarini. On the outskirts of the village, picturesquely situated, is the small *Oratory of San Rocco*, dating from 1486. The choir has frescoes representing the Deposition and the *Madonna enthroned with saints by Girolamo di Domenico (1493).

The pretty road (signposted for Abbadia San Salvatore) passes through chestnut woods to (10km) *Pescina* (747m), a modern resort, with a *Madonna and Child by Luca di Tommé in the parish church. The road continues through a variety of woods, in which beautiful walks can be taken, and at 17km begins to circle round the cone of **MONTE AMIATA**, the summit of which can be approached from the road to Prato delle Macinaie, or from another right turn 1km further on. The peak, marked by an enormous iron Cross by Luciano Zalaffi (1910), can be reached on foot. The view embraces the Orcia, Fiora, and Paglia valleys, and, on a fine day, it is possible to see the Tyrrhenian coast and the islands of Elba and Corsica, as well as the towns of Siena, Cortona, and Orvieto, and the lakes of Trasimene and Bolsena.

The road continues past the church of the Madonna del Castagno which has a simple Renaissance façade (1533), and a 15C tiled floor to (26km) **Abbadia San Salvatore** (812m; 8500 inhab.), on the edge of extensive chestnut woods covering the eastern flank of Monte Amiata. The abbey, which gives its name to the small town, is one of the oldest monasteries in Tuscany. It was an important station in the Middle Ages on the Via

Francigena, the pilgrim route from northern Europe to Rome. The pictur-esque medieval 'borgo' or village preserves intact its outer walls and streets, with medieval and Renaissance houses of local grey stone. *San Leonardo* is a small Gothic church, and *Santa Croce* retains part of its Romanesque façade, although it was rebuilt in the 18C. The modern suburb which has developed round the monastery, has become an important summer and winter resort.

The Benedictine ABBEY, which was immensely rich and powerful, enjoyed numerous privileges under the protection of popes and emperors, and exercised feudal jurisdiction over much of southern Tuscany. It was founded, according to tradition, in 743 by the Lombard king, Ratchis, on the spot where he saw a vision. At the peak of its temporal and spiritual powers in 1035 it was rebuilt and reconsecrated by Abbot Winizzo. There followed a period of decline when it came under the dominion of Siena in 1347, and eventually of the Medici state in 1559. The monastery was suppressed by Grand Duke Leopoldo II in 1783, and most of its treasury and archives were removed to Florence. A Benedictine community was reinstalled here in 1939.

A gateway leads into the piazza, with a fountain at the centre, opposite the abbey CHURCH, restored c 1930, when the Baroque altars were demol-ished, and again in the 1960s and 1980s when an attempt was made to reconstruct its 11C appearance. The narrow FAÇADE, with its three-light window over the arched entrance, is flanked by two towers, a tall square crenallated bell-tower on the left, and an unfinished tower on the right; it is a rare example of Romanesque westwork in Italian architecture. INTERIOR. It is one of the earliest churches to have a Latin-cross plan. The nave has a timber roof and the elevated choir is framed by three rounded arches spanning its entire width. A late-12C carved wood Crucifix (right) shows Christ Triumphant (with open eyes). On the opposite wall is a fresco of the Martyrdom of St Bartholomew by Francesco Nasini (1694). Steps lead up to the choir which was decorated with frescoes in the 17C by Francesco and Antonio Annibale Nasini. The same artists painted the right-hand chapel with frescoes illustrating the legend of King Ratchis and his vision of Christ above fir trees during a hunt, allegorical figures and saints, and the Pietà with angels beneath the altar. The corresponding chapel on the left, dedicated to the Madonna, has stories of the Life of the Virgin and the contiguous chapel has scenes of Christ's Infancy (damaged), also by the Nasini brothers. The *CRYPT, which probably dates from the 10–11C, is one of the largest and earliest in Tuscany. There are 32 columns with beautifully carved capitals supporting a stone vault. The capitals present a variety of leaf, figure, and animal motifs comparable to early Lombard sculpture in Northern Italy.

The monastery, on the left of the church, has a cloister dating from the 16C (restored), with a well. The rich monastic treasury still possesses a tiny 8C Irish reliquary, and a unique 8–9C red silk *cope, probably of Persian origin, woven with a pattern of simurghs (legendary birds) in roundels and once decorated with pearl embroidery. This was for long associated with the cult of the 4C Pope St Mark, but during its restoration in 1991, an inscription relating to Pope John VIII was discovered. The hem was lined with strips of silk, woven in four colours, with roundels containing pairs of ballerinas. This extraordinarily rare work has been reassembled and recent studies date it to the 8C. A copper-gilt *reliquary bust of Pope St Mark (also recently restored), decorated with enamels and dated 1381 is attributed to Mariano d'Agnolo Romanelli.

The road leads S from Abbadia San Salvatore to (30km) **Piancastagnaio** (772m), on the southeastern slopes of the mountain, overlooking the Paglia valley. Before reaching the village, on a hill to the left, is *San Bartolommeo*, a Franciscan church with a simple stone façade and portico. Inside, on the entrance wall, is a fragmentary 14C fresco of the Sienese school, representing the Massacre of the Innocents. The church was refurbished in the 18C. In the chapter house, off the cloister, frescoes of the life of the Virgin have been recently discovered under the whitewash. At the entrance to Piancastagnaio is a fortified gateway beside the impressive Aldobrandeschi *Fortress*, one of the best preserved examples of 14C military architecture in the district. The narrow streets are extremely picturesque. Beyond the Romanesque church of *Santa Maria Assunta*, which contains some 17C paintings, is *Palazzo Bourbon del Monte*, on the main square, built by the Perugian architect Valentino Martelli (1611; in a badly neg-lected state). An annual fair is held in the piazza at the beginning of November coinciding with the chestnut harvest. On the road encircling the village to the left of the gateway is the church of *Santa Maria delle Grazie* with a recently discovered fresco cycle attributed to Nanni di Pietro (15C).

The Santa Fiora road continues past the sanctuary of the *Madonna di San Pietro*, with a 17C façade and bell-tower. The interior, recently restored, is covered with frescoes by Francesco Nasini, illustrating the Four Last Things (1640), in a lively and personal style. The road winds across the southern slopes of Monte Amiata, with splendid views, to (42km) **Santa Fiora**, named after its patron saint. The village, which originally belonged to Abbadia San Salvatore subsequently came under the dominion of the Aldobrandeschi who ruled over much of southern Tuscany. In 1274 their possessions were divided between two branches of the family, that of Santa Fiora (who obtained Monte Amiata and the northern part of the Maremma) and that of Sovana (who controlled southern Maremma and the coastal area). Santa Fiora then passed through the female line to the Sforza Cesarini, until it was incorporated in the Grand Duchy of Tuscany under Pietro Leopoldo. The picturesque and well-preserved village is entered through *Palazzo Sforza Cesarini*, a grandiose late-Renaissance palace (now the town hall) with the family arms showing a lion rampant and a quince tree. Only the clock tower dominating the pretty rectangular piazza survives from the original Aldobrandeschi castle. Via Carolina leads down past the Misericordia to the **Pieve di Santa Fiora e Lucilla**, dedicated to the two saints, whose relics, preserved in a 16C reliquary in the priest's house, were brought here in the 11C. The FAÇADE has a fine rose-window over the entrance. The INTERIOR, divided into three naves by rounded arches, is of great simplicity and elegance; the structure is outlined in grey stone while the sense of luminosity produced by the large Gothic windows is enhanced by the white intonaco. The altarpieces and pulpit in glazed terracotta are by Andrea Della Robbia and his workshop (c 1480–90). On the right wall is a triptych representing the Coronation of the Virgin between St Francis receiving the Stigmata, and the Penitent St Jerome, with a predella showing the Annunciation, the Nativity, and the Adoration of the Magi, in a frame decorated with fruit, flowers, and classical motifs. Beyond a Crucifix in a niche, the pulpit represents the Last Supper, Resurrection, and Ascension. The largest and most elaborate work is the altarpiece, complete with lunette, predella and ornate frame, representing the Assumption of the Virgin with angels and saints, in which the white figures are set against a simple blue ground. In the Baptistery chapel is a lunette representing the Baptism of Christ, and the Last Supper beneath the altar.

A steep road, terminating in steps, leads down to the church of *Sant'Agostino*, with a square bell-tower (closed for restoration) which has a painted wood statue of the *Madonna ad Child by Jacopo della Quercia. The road continues through a gateway, past gardens with vines and roses, to a large public fountain, to the right of which is the little oratory of the *Madonna delle Nevi*. Over the entrance are Della Robbia figures of Fiora and Lucilla. Behind the chapel is the entrance to *La Peschiera (open Saturday and Sunday, 10–12.30, 15.30–18). This delightful garden, created in the 18C, with a fishpond and bubbling rivulets, collects the spring waters of the river Fiora. The river provides the water supply for much of the Grosseto district.

50km **Arcidosso** is situated on a ridge (679m) between Monte Amiata and Monte Labbro. It is now primarily a holiday resort, with a modern suburb surrounding the old walled village at the top of which is the Aldobrandeschi Rocca. On the outskirts, above a flight of steps, is the sanctuary of the *Madonna delle Grazie* (also known as *L'Incoronata*: at present closed), a Renaissance church with a fine façade. To the right is a neo-Gothic fountain in cast iron, made in Follonica in 1833, and transferred here from Piazza del Duomo in Grosseto. *Porta Torre* (heavily restored in the 19C), gives access to the old borgo, with its narrow streets and gloomy fortress. Here the parish church of *San Niccolò* has a Romanesque façade (restored) and, inside, a holy-water stoup, dated 1603, by the local sculptor Pietro Amati. Near the road to Castel del Piano is the 12C church of *San Leonardo*, enlarged in the 16C but preserving its façade. A stone niche by Pietro Amati frames a beheading of the Baptist by Francesco Vanni (1589). The altarpieces, mostly by anonymous 17C artists, include a late-16C Assumption of the Virgin. The two wood statues of Saints Processo and Andrew, by an unknown sculptor, are dated 1617.

On the outskirts of Arcidosso is *Santa Maria ad Lamulas*, recorded since the 9C. Although almost completely rebuilt in imitation Romanesque style, it preserves some fine Lombard capitals and a painted and gilt statue in wood of the Madonna and Child by a mid-15C Sienese sculptor. The road continues towards Castel del Piano past the *Cappuccini* church with a portico, beside its convent. Over the high altar is the *Madonna enthroned with Saints Bernardine, Francis and Leonard by Francesco Vanni (1593), one of the Sienese artist's finest works. The Annunciation is attributed to Giuseppe Nicola Nasini. 54km **Castel del Piano**, see above.

23

Grosseto to Pitigliano

Road, N322, N74, 64km.—29km **Scansano** (for *Roccalbegna*, 30km, and *Magliano in Toscana*, 18km)—40km *Montemerano* (for **Saturnia**, 8km)—46km **Manciano**. N74—64km **Pitigliano** (for **Sovana**, 8km, and **Sorano**, 10km).

Buses from the railway station in Grosseto (run by RAMA) to Scansano, Saturnia, Manciano, Pitigliano, etc.

Information Office. APT of Grosseto (Tel. 0564/454510).

This route passes through an area of great natural beauty. The landscape is immensely varied: at times dramatic and austere, and at others inviting and serene. Thick woods and coppices alternate with rolling hills and fertile valleys. Characteristic are the ruined castles and hill-top villages, built out of the underlying rock or stone, many of them still enclosed in their medieval walls. The countryside has scattered farmhouses. The numerous rivers and streams attracted settlements here long before the Etruscans who arrived in the 7C BC. Necropoli, traces of houses, and remains of walls composed of huge blocks of stone dating from this time are a constant and evocative presence. Following destruction by the Romans, the area came under the dominion of the Aldobrandeschi and other feudal lords, who erected strongholds in defence against attacks mostly from Siena and Orvieto. From the 13C onwards sieges, conflicts, pirate raids, and malaria caused destruction and depopulation until the final capitulation to Sienese rule. When, in 1555, Siena in turn fell to the Medici of Florence and became part of the Grand Duchy of Tuscany, the poverty was such that many villages were all but totally abandoned. Radical reforms did not begin until the 19C under Grand Duke Leopoldo II, who promoted better living conditions and a few industries. However, it has only been in recent years with the disappearance of malaria, the increased ownership of cars and development of tourism, that there has been a real transformation in the standard of living. This explains why so many of these villages survive almost intact and why the landscape preserves its wild and mysterious character.

N322 leads E from Grosseto. 7.5km *Istia d'Ombrone*, a pretty village situated on a bend of the Ombrone river. Parts of its walls survive, and an arched gateway leads to the interesting Romanesque church of San Salvatore. It has a simple brick façade in the Sienese style. The interior contains a late-medieval capital transformed into a holy-water stoup; a 14C fresco fragment of St Anthony Abbot worshipped by three women; Vincenzo Tamagni, *Meeting at the Golden Gate (1528); Giovanni di Paolo, *Madonna and Child; Domenico di Niccolò dei Cori, polychrome wood statue of the *Madonna and Child (c 1445).

The road winds through a hilly landscape passing near (13km) *Montorgiali* (trattoria *Franco e Silvana* on the main road, by the turn), a grey stone village surrounding its Cassero, perched on a hill to the left. It then climbs, with increasingly splendid views, to (20km) *Pancole*. A by-road diverges to the left for the castle of *Montepò* (5km; 451m), an early-16C fortress with four corner towers, much restored (privately owned). The by-road continues for another 2km to the ruined medieval castle of *Cotone*. After a series of bends the main road proceeds towards (29km) **Scansano** (500m; 4-star hotel *Antico Casale*) an agricultural town noted for its red wine called *Morellino di Scansano*. Its streets and houses within the medieval walls (partially intact) are well preserved. The parish church recorded from the 13C was rebuilt in the 17–18C. It contains several minor but attractive altarpieces of the 16C Sienese school. The administrative offices of Grosseto used to be transferred here during the summer months to escape malaria. In the neighbourhood of Scansano (notably at Ghiaccioforte, a hill on the right bank of the Albegna) excavations (unenclosed) have brought to light finds from the Bronze Age, as well as the Etruscan and Roman periods. A small museum in the town hall of Scansano (Via XX Settembre) may be seen mornings on request.

FROM SCANSANO TO ROCCALBEGNA, 30km. N323 leads N passing (5.5km) *Poggioferro*, which has a *Madonna by Giovanni di Paolo in its parish church, and (13.5km) *Murci* (572m), overlooking a vast panorama. There is a striking view of (30km) **Roccalbegna** (522m), perched on the southern slopes of Monte Labbro high above the Albegna valley. It is dominated by a tall, cone-shaped rock 40 metres high, known as *Il Sasso*, on top of which are the remains of an Aldobrandeschi castle. The view from here is worth the climb up the steep steps. Another overgrown rock, on which the former keep stood, was presumably connected to the castle by a stretch of walls which survives in part beside the *Porta di Maremma*. The picturesque and well-preserved village has a regular grid plan with the church of *Santi Pietro e Paolo* at its centre. The simple stone façade has a large oculus over an arched portal, flanked by spiral columns. The interior has been restored to its medieval appearance. On the high altar is a *triptych by Ambrogio Lorenzetti (c 1340), with the Madonna and Child between the two titular saints. The Deposition to the left is attributed to Casolani, and there are a few frescoes and a late-14C Crucifix. Steps lead up to the small *Oratorio del Crocifisso* (opened on request). It has been converted into a museum for liturgical objects, mostly from the parish church, and preserves a large painted *Crucifix by Luca di Tommé (c 1360). Arcidosso, 20km farther N at the foot of Monte Amiata, reached via the village and castle of Triana, is described in Rte 22.

FROM SCANSANO TO MAGLIANO IN TOSCANA, 18km. N323 leads SW passing (10km) *Pereta* (trattoria *Da Wilma*), a charming little medieval hamlet, with a tall tower. 18km **Magliano in Toscana** (first-class restaurant *Da Guido*) with splendid 14C and 15C *FORTIFICATIONS. There was an Etruscan and Roman town here, and a castle was built in the early Middle Ages by the Aldobrandeschi. The Romanesque church of *San Martino* has a fine façade. Next to it is an eccentric building in a medley of styles, built as a centre for the 'colonisation' of the Maremma. From an arch in the walls here there is a beautiful view of the countryside. The Corso continues past the 15C *Town Hall* to the church of *San Giovanni Battista* with a pretty Renaissance façade (1471). Outside the walls is the church of the *Annunziata* which contains frescoes and a *Madonna and Child by Neroccio. In the olive grove beyond the church is the ancient 'witch's olive tree'. Outside the town, just past the cemetery, a by-road (signposted for Sant'Andrea) leads to the imposing ruins of the church of *SAN BRUZIO, built in the 11C, conspicuous among olive trees. The triumphal arch survives before the apse and transepts, but the nave has totally disappeared. It has beautifully carved capitals, lancet windows, and squinches supporting the octagonal drum on which the dome rested. The lonely abandoned ruins are surrounded by spectactular countryside. The main road continues S to join N74 which leads W to the coast near Monte Argentario, see Rte 12.

N322 continues across a number of rivers to (40km) **Montemerano** (303m: trattoria *Podere di Montemerano*), a picturesque village surrounded by its medieval walls on a hill of olive trees. Next to a gateway with beautiful views N is the parish church of *San Giorgio*. It contains a monumental *polyptych by Sano di Pietro; a painted wood statue of *St Peter by Vecchietta; a Virgin of the Annunciation by the Master of Montemerano; a carved relief of the Assumption by Pellegrino di Mariano; and various frescoes by the 15C Sienese school. It is worth exploring the village to enjoy its charming vistas.

From Montemerano a by-road leads N to the **Terme di Saturnia** (6km; 4-star hotel *Terme di Saturnia*), a well-known spa of sulphurous water (37°C), known since remote times. Nearby are the *Cascate del Gorello* next to an old mill, where the hot water falls in cascades over whitened rocks creating natural pools. This uniquely beautiful spot has unfortunately suffered from neglect, and the waters have been partially diverted in recent years. The village of **Saturnia** (3-star hotel *Villa Clodia*; first-class restaurant *I Due Cippi-da Michele*), 2km N, was built on a travertine spur overlooking the valley. It was an Etruscan town of some importance, and there are several necropoli nearby (at Pian di Palma and Puntone). In the 3C BC it became a Roman colony. The Porta Romana, through which ran the Via Clodia, and the adjacent walls are well preserved (the arch is medieval). There are still remains of foundations and floors in the village dating from the 2–1C BC. In the 13C Saturnia was sacked by the Sienese, who then built the fortifications.

The church (of Romanesque origin) has a Madonna and Child by Benvenuto di Giovanni. An antiquarium of excavated Etruscan and Roman objects has been transferred to the Museum of Grosseto.

FROM SATURNIA TO SEMPRONIANO, 15km. The by-road continues N from Saturnia and crosses the Albegna before *Puntone* where there are Etruscan tombs (6–5C BC). Shortly before Semproniano, a by-road leads to *Rocchette di Fazio* (5km), one of the most picturesque and best preserved villages in the area. Built on a rock overhanging the Albegna valley it commands a magnificent view. The small Chiesa della Madonna on the village square has a 14–15C wooden statue of the Madonna. There are a number of interesting medieval buildings including the Ospedale di San Bartolommeo, founded in 1330, the gateway to the 12C castle, and the Palazzo Pretorio. The Romanesque Pieve di Santa Cristina, reached up a flight of steps, has some damaged early-15C frescoes. 15km **Semproniano** (trattoria *la Posta*, 6km S at Catabbio) is a small town situated high up (600m) and clustered round the ruins of its *Castle* built by the Aldobrandeschi. In the nearby Romanesque church of *Santa Croce* is a Renaissance holy- water stoup and a very expressive wooden medieval *Crucifix. In the Borgo is the *Pieve dei Santi Vincenzo e Anastasio* with a tall bell-tower. Among its 17C paintings is the Madonna of the Rosary by Francesco Vanni (1609) originally painted for the cathedral of Pitigliano. The oratory of the *Madonna delle Grazie*, on the outskirts of the town, has been recently restored, and its decorated Baroque interior is typical of this district. Arcidosso, 24km N is described in Rte 22.

The main road winds S of Montemerano through groves of ancient olive trees to (46km) the town of **Manciano** (444m; 3-star and 1-star hotels; trattoria *Da Paolino*), dominating the surrounding countryside. Largely modern in aspect, it nevertheless preserves its picturesque medieval streets and houses. They surround the 15C *Rocca*, which exhibits the Medici and Lorena arms in cast-iron, and houses a collection of paintings by two local artists, Pietro Aldi (1852–88) and Paride Pascucci (1866–1954). The parish church of *San Leonardo* has a modern travertine façade. The rural chapel of *Santissima Annunziata* (16C) contains an Annunciation by Pietro Aldi (1875). At No. 2 Via Corsini an *Archaeological Museum* was opened in 1988 (adm. in winter: 9.30–12.30, 14.30–17.30; in summer: 10–13, 16–19; closed Monday). The exhibits, which belong to the Paleolithic, Neolithic, and Bronze Age eras, were all excavated in the Fiora valley and adjacent areas. They are well labelled, with detailed maps, etc. In the neighbourhood of Manciano are a number of ruined castles (including Pelagone, Scarpena, Castellaccia, and Montauto).

N74 now runs E to (64km) **PITIGLIANO** (4500 inhab; 2-star hotel *Guastini*), spectacularly situated on a rocky spur overlooking on all sides a gorge which has been excavated by three torrents (the Lente, Meleta, and Prochio). Its clustered medieval stone houses, dominated by the cathedral bell-tower and two other towers, give the impression that they are growing out of the rocks and wild vegetation. The area is known for its excellent white wine. On the approach to the town there is a complete view of it from the sanctuary of the *Madonna delle Grazie*, built as an ex-voto after the plague of 1527. Pitigliano's Etruscan origin is apparent in parts of the walls and in the numerous tombs excavated in the vicinity (Poggio Buco, and the Meleta valley). It later came under Roman rule and, after being a feud of the Aldobrandeschi family of Sovana, passed by marriage to the Orsini in 1293. In 1608 it became part of the Grand Duchy of Tuscany. Leopoldo II, commemorated by a bust on an obelisk in the piazza, restored the town and built the church of Santa Maria Assunta and the bridge over the Meleta. The arched aqueduct was built in 1545 by Gian Francesco Orsini, who also commissioned Giuliano da Sangallo to enlarge the 13C *Palace*, which has a fine entrance portal and an elegant courtyard with a well bearing the family arms. It houses a small *Museum* (open 10–13, 15–18; July & Aug 10–13, 15–19.30; closed Monday) of objects from local excavations and paintings by Francesco Zuccarelli (1702–88) who was born here.

Piazza della Repubblica has two modern neo-Baroque fountains. Via Roma leads into the old town whose narrow streets and darkened stone houses, with their outside staircases, well preserve its medieval character. Piazza del Duomo has an impressive monument erected in 1490 celebrating the Orsini family (the bear, or *orso* is the family emblem). The **Cathedral**, medieval in origin, has a Baroque façade, and the interior has been modernised. Two altarpieces (St Michael, and the Redeemer) are by Francesco Zuccarelli. The Madonna of the Rosary is by Francesco Vanni (1609). Two other paintings commemorating Pope Gregory VII are by Pietro Aldi (1885). Next to the sacristy is a *Madonna and Child enthroned with angels and saints by Guidoccio Cozzarelli (1494), originally in Sovana cathedral. The massive bell-tower has a bell weighing three tons.

In Via Orsini is the Renaissance church of *Santa Maria*, built to a strange trapezoidal ground plan. A Romanesque sculptural relief of a figure with two winged animals is inserted in the wall under the tower. A small piazza here has a fine view over the Meleta valley. Steps lead down to the *Porta di Sovana* built into an Etruscan section of the walls (4C BC). Via Zuccarelli leads back to Piazza della Repubblica through the old *Ghetto* with the remains of the former synagogue, which documents the presence in the town of a large Jewish community from the 16C. Outside the town, on the road to Sorano, is a gateway which formed the entrance to *Poggio Sterzoni*, once a famous park created by Niccolò IV Orsini in the 16C. The carved statues, steps, and niches exploit the natural rock formation of the site. It is here that Count Orso Orsini strangled his wife, Isabella degli Atti, in 1575.

Sovana (2-star hotel *Taverna Etrusca* with a restaurant; information office in Palazzo Pretorio), 8km N of Pitigliano, is now a village with little more than a single street running from the castle to the cathedral. It is beautifully situated on a ridge overlooking a wide panorama.

It is traditionally reputed to be the birthplace of Hildebrand, later Pope Gregory VII (1026/8–1085). An important Etruscan settlement and later a Roman municipium, Sovana became a bishopric in the 5C and its period of greatest importance was when it was the seat of the Sovana branch of the Aldobrandeschi family, which separated from the Santa Fiora branch in the 13C. It was then devastated by Sienese troops, who carried off even the cathedral bell. Attempts to repopulate the village under the subsequent Medici rule were doomed on account of malaria.

At the entrance to the village are the impressive ruins of the Aldobrandeschi *Rocca (13–14C), and remains of the Etruscan walls. In the small piazza are *Palazzo Pretorio*, with the arms of the Sienese Podestà and *Palazzo del Comune* with its clock and bell-cote. Also here is the medieval church of SANTA MARIA (open 9–13, 15–19; in winter only at weekends), the interior of which has large round arches dividing the nave from the aisles. Frescoes of the Umbrian or Sienese school of the late 15C or early 16C have recently been discovered under the whitewash. The high altar stands beneath a carved marble *ciborium of the 9C, which was probably removed from the cathedral in the 18C. The workmanship is superb and it is a unique example of its kind in Tuscany: the elegantly carved baldacchino, terminating in an octagonal spire, rests on four slender columns with elaborate capitals.

At the end of the village, in a stone-flagged piazza surrounded by cypresses, is the Romanesque cathedral of SANTI PIETRO E PAOLO (open as for Santa Maria). The original church was probably begun during the papacy of Gregory VII, but its present structure is thought to date from the 12–13C. It has a semicircular apse and a polygonal dome. The doorway on the S side, probably removed from the façade and put together with pre-Romanesque fragments, is decorated with stylised figures, animals, and plants. In the interior, compound piers divide the nave from the aisles and some of the *capitals are finely carved, several of them with Biblical scenes. The martyrdom of St Peter is by Domenico De Manentis, and the 15C urn, possibly Sienese, has a carved image of St Mamiliano, whose body it contains. He was long venerated as the evangeliser of the district in the 6C. There are remains of 15C frescoes in the crossing. The small *crypt has seven rustic columns. The nearby *Canonica* was the bishop's palace until the bishopric was officially transferred to Pitigliano in 1843, together with reliquaries and an altarpiece by Cozzarelli (see above).

Near Sovana are many interesting *necropoli, mostly rock tombs of the 3–2C BC, which were first excavated by George Dennis in 1844. Some, of impressive dimensions among thick vegetation, are visible from the road. Facing Sovana is the vaulted niche of the 'Tomba della Sirena'; other tombs (identifiable with maps obtainable locally) are called 'Tifone', 'Ildebranda' and 'Pola'. To the NW is a typical Etruscan road carved into the rock, known as 'Il Cavone', with wall tombs and inscriptions.

Sorano (374m; trattoria *Fidalma*) is 10km E of Pitigliano, in an area well known for its white wine. This small medieval town, largely derelict but beautiful nonetheless, has a modern suburb. The approach from Sovana, passing Etruscan rock tombs, is particularly spectacular. It is dominated by the old Orsini fortress called the *Masso Leopoldino* (guided tours 9–12, 16–19). An exedra built in 1867 commemorates Garibaldi and Italian Unity. The bell-tower of the church of San Nicola is a neo-classical restoration. Frescoes, close to Sodoma in style, representing scenes from the Aeneid have been detached from a room in the fortress and are now exhibited in the town hall. In the neighbourhood are several ruined castles in panoramic positions, including Montorio and Ottieri, c 10km N. On the road to San Quirico, just S of Sorano, is a ruined 15C Rocca, another stronghold of the Aldobrandeschi and Orsini families.

N74 continues SE from Pitigliano and crosses the Lazio border near the Lago di Bolsena (see *Blue Guide Rome and environs*).

24

The Casentino

The **CASENTINO** is the beautiful wooded upper valley of the Arno in the NE corner of Tuscany. The scenery is superb and it has prosperous and well kept villages. At Camaldoli, on the border with Romagna, is one of the finest forests in Italy. The valley was dominated from the 10C until the middle of the 15C by the Guidi counts whose numerous castles are a feature of the area. Because of its position between Florence and Arezzo, it was for long disputed between the two cities, but Florence remained the dominant force after its victory here on the plain of Campaldino in 1289. High up above the valley are the famous monasteries of La Verna and Camaldoli.

Information Offices. APT of Arezzo (Tel. 0575/377678). Information offices at Bibbiena (Tel. 0575/593098) and at Badia Prataglia (Tel. 0575/559054).

Road. From Florence via (18km) Pontassieve to (34km) the Passo della Consuma, see Rte 3.—51km **Stia**—53km *Pratovecchio* (for **Camaldoli**, 17km)—62km **Poppi**—68km **Bibbiena** (for **La Verna**, 22km, and *Caprese Michelangelo*, 34km).

Buses. SITA bus services (c 8 times daily) follow this route from Florence via the Consuma Pass to Poppi and Bibbiena (to Poppi in 2hrs; to Bibbiena in 2hrs 20mins). SITA buses daily also from Florence to Stia in 1hr 45mins. From Arezzo trains (the line is being renovated) and buses run by LFI to Bibbiena, Poppi, and Stia. Buses (SITA) from Arezzo to Caprese Michelangelo. From Bibbiena buses (LFI) to Camaldoli and La Verna.

Beautiful **walks** can be taken in the Casentino. Information and map from the *Comunità Montana Casentino* at Poppi.

From Florence via (18km) Pontassieve to (34km) the **Passo della Consuma** (*Dal Consumi* has good snacks), see the end of Rte 3. A road from Vallombrosa (see Rte 25) comes in on the right. After the pass (2-star hotel and restaurant *Sbaragli*), the road (N70) traverses bare hills where some replanting is taking place. A pretty by-road on the right offers an alternative approach to Poppi via Montemignaio and Castel San Niccolò (both described below). Just beyond, another attractive road on the left is signposted via Villa to *Castel Castagnaio* (5.5km). The by-road traverses woods and then winds downhill to end a few hundred metres before a little mound on which are the scanty ruins of an 11C castle. It commands splendid views of the wooded hills of the Casentino.

41km. The main road, with a fine distant view in the valley below of the Castle of Poppi with its tall tower, now begins its descent towards the Casentino valley. 44km Scarpaccia. Here a road to Poppi via Borga alla Collina (described below) continues down the valley while this route diverges left for Stia. On the right (47km) the ***Castello di Romena**, perhaps the most important castle in the Casentino, soon comes into view. The 11C castle belonged to the Guidi, the Ghibelline family who dominated the area, with whom the exiled Dante sheltered. Here in 1280 Maestro Adamo, recalled by Dante (*Inferno* XXX, 46–90), forged Florentine florins for the Guidi for which he was later burnt. A short cypress avenue leads up to the impressive and well-kept remains which include the three main towers and traces of three circles of walls. The castle may be visited by booking in advance (Tel. 0575/58633). A room contains suits of armour, as well as a model of the castle. Stairs lead up to a loggia and walkway. The views are splendid.

A road (or path from the villa; c 1km) descends past the *Fonte Branda* (plaque), an overgrown spring, mentioned by Dante (*Inferno*, XXX, 78), to the ***Pieve di Romena**, the most beautiful Romanesque church in the Casentino. It was built in 1152; remains of the 9C church can be seen beneath the building. It has a splendid east end with blind arcading. The lovely interior, with a raised presbytery and fine capitals is opened on request at the second house on the opposite side of the road (No. 7). All the paintings have at present been removed, but they have all been restored and will be returned here. They include: parts of a triptych by Giovanni del Biondo and bottega, a Madonna and Child with two angels by the Master of Varlungo, a 15C Madonna and Child with four saints by the Florentine school (attributed to the Master of San Miniato), and a 16C Madonna of the Rosary.

The main road continues to (51km) **STIA** (first-class restaurant *Filetto*, Piazza Tanucci; trattoria *La Rana (da Filetto)* in woods on the Arno (by the sports stadium); trattoria and pizzeria *La Fattoria*; and trattoria *Loris* at Papiano), a pretty little town (3100 inhab.) on the Arno at the confluence with its first tributary the Staggia. In the Middle Ages it was the residence of the Guidi, and it is noted for its small woollen manufactories (some of the abandoned factories along the river are interesting for their architecture).

On the right bank of the river is the delightful sloping Piazza Tanucci (with a local tourist office) and a well decorated with lions and snakes. Here is the Romanesque church of **Santa Maria Assunta** with an uninteresting façade. The INTERIOR, with fine capitals, is illuminated by a light switch on the W wall. SOUTH AISLE. First chapel, left wall, 16C Nativity, and, on the altar, triptych of the Annunciation and saints with a good predella, by Bicci di Lorenzo. Beneath the altar is a Della Robbian stemma. The marble font dates from 1526. On the right wall is another Annunciaton by the Pistoian school. First altar, Gian Domenico Ferretti, Preaching of St John the Baptist. The quaint wooden pulpit dates from 1584. In the chapel to the right of the high altar, good 16C Florentine painting of Supper in the House of the Pharisee (in very poor condition). On the left is an elaborate (damaged) Della Robbian tabernacle. In the pretty APSE with an ambulatory of four columns is a large 14C wood Crucifix. In the chapel to the left of the high altar, Master of Varlungo, *Madonna and Child, and (on the right wall), Madonna and Child by Andrea Della Robbia. NORTH AISLE. Master of San Miniato, Madonna enthroned with four saints; on the altar, an unusual painting of the Assumption, attributed to the Master of Borgo alla Collina. The 14C fresco of the Madonna and Child was detached from the Pieve of Stia.

On the right of the church is an archway with a fresco of St Francis by Pietro Annigoni (1985). The old streets off the piazza are worth exploring.

On the other side of the river, an avenue ascends past (left) the church of the *Madonna del Ponte* with a terracotta altarpiece by the bottega of the Della Robbia. Opposite is a 16C painting of the Holy Family. The sanctuary is decorated with pretty angels. The avenue continues up to Piazza Mazzini with the modern town hall and a theatre. A road (signposted) leads left for the *Castello di Palagio* reconstructed in 1911 by Giuseppe Castellucci for Carlo Beni, historian of the Casentino. He left it to the Comune and it is open in summer for exhibitions and lectures; the garden, with some statuary, is open daily. A huge vault was built here a few years ago over a spring.

From Stia N556 leads N along the Arno valley via Londa to the Mugello (see Rte 3). Just outside Stia is a by road (signposted) right for **Porciano** (1.5km), approached through pretty meadows. There is a car park below the castle and it is a short way by foot through the hamlet (reconstructed after an earthquake at the beginning of this century) to the massive tall square tower of the CASTLE, privately owned. It was restored in 1964–79 and is open from 15 May–15 October on Sundays, 10–12, 16–19. First mentioned in 1191, this may have been the first Guidi castle in the Casentino. On the ground floor is a small display of agricultural implements and domestic tools, as well as a collection of Red Indian material from North Dakota. The first floor has photographs of the castle before its restoration, and ceramics (including late-13C and early-14C ware) found during restoration work. On the second floor is a hall used for lectures etc. The views are splendid.

The next right turning off the Londa road leads to the church of *Santa Maria delle Grazie* (3km from Stia), in an inconspicuous position above the road. Beside the 15C church is the 'Casa del Pellegrino' with a lovely long loggia and stairs in the centre of the building. The church is only open for services at weekends. It contains a Crucifix attributed to Paolo Schiavo, a 15C Madonna and Child, a pulpit by Mino da Fiesole, and a fresco by Ghirlandaio (1485). A painting of the Madonna and four saints by Niccolò di Lorenzo Gerini was stolen in 1987.

A fine walk of 4hrs leads N from Stia to the source of the Arno and from there to the summit of *Monte Falterona* (1654m), now part of a national park adjoining the Forest of Camaldoli, see below. The adjacent summit of *Monte Falco*, 4m higher, is more easily reached from the *Passo la Calla* (1296m), on the road from Stia into Emilia Romagna via the Bidente valley (see *Blue Guide Northern Italy*). On its slopes, visited by skiers, is the Rifugio La Burraia (1447m).

The road for Poppi and the Casentino leads S from Stia through the large adjoining village of (53km) **Pratovecchio** (trattoria *La Tana degli Orsi*), surrounded by some small factories on the floor of the valley. From Piazza Paolo Uccello (named after the painter who was born here), Via Garibaldi with pretty porticoes leads towards (left) the attractive Piazza Jacopo Landino with a group of lime trees. Here is a fine palace (No. 18) with a coat of arms on the corner dated 1621, and the parish church (undergoing radical restoration). Above the W door is a small Della Robbian relief, otherwise the church is at present empty. To the right of the church, at the end of the piazza, is the entrance (No. 20) to a courtyard in which is the church of *San Giovanni Evangelista* (if closed, ring at the Camaldolese convent). The unusual façade dates from 1909. Over the first left altar is a very well preserved painting of the Assumption, attributed to the Master of Pratovecchio, named from this work. It is very difficult to see as it is inserted behind a larger painting. The high altarpiece of the Coronation of the Virgin dates from the 16C. In Via XX Settembre, off the upper side of the piazza, is a large Della Robbian tabernacle.

On the outskirts of Pratovecchio, just beyond a bridge beside several small factories on the main road to Bibbiena, is the inconspicuous church of *Santa Maria a Poppiena* on the left of the road beside a few cypresses. It is closed while undergoing radical restoration work. An Annunciation attributed to Giovanni del Ponte has been removed.

From Piazza Paolo Uccello a road leads down across the river with some interesting houses, and from the bridge two roads (right and left; 2km) are signposted for the Castello and Pieve di Romena (see above).

FROM PRATOVECCHIO TO THE HERMITAGE AND MONASTERY OF CAMAL-DOLI, 17km. Beyond the railway, this beautiful road (signposted *Santo Eremo*), winds up a wooded valley with a view back of the castle of Romena. A road diverges right for Casalino and the monastery of Camaldoli; this road instead continues left towards Lonnano. It passes close to the little church of *Valiana* (San Romolo), on the right of the road (if closed, ring at No. 1). During restoration work by the local inhabitants in 1984 the original architrave of the door dated 1126 was found beneath the front steps (it is now displayed inside the church). The remarkable painting of *Christ in Pietà with symbols of the Passion (late 14C or early 15C) is attributed to the Master of the Madonna Straus (it was beautifully restored in 1974). From the church there is a delightful distant view of the castle of Romena and the wooded hills of the Casentino. The road continues up through Lonnano, and beyond (10km) Prato alle Cogne (1050m) enters the splendid **Forest of Camaldoli**. Silver firs and beech trees predominate but other trees include sycamore, manna ash, laburnum, ilex, birch, willow, elm, yew, oak, chestnut, alder, poplar and lime. It is part of the forest of the Casentino on the ridge of the Apennines on the border between Tuscany and Romagna, a protected area of some 11,000 hectares which stretches from Monte Falterona (1654m; see above) to the Passo dei Mandrioli (1179m). It is one of the largest areas of forest left in Italy and it became part of the National Park of *Monte Falterona, Campigna e Foreste Casentinesi* in 1991 (see p 110). In 1027 part of the forest was given to the Carthusian monks of

Camaldoli, and in 1866 it became the property of the State. It is traversed by numerous streams and deer run wild here. The road for the hermitage diverges left from the road signposted for Camaldoli.

17km. The **Hermitage of Camaldoli** (1100m) was founded in 1012 by St Romuald in this *campo amabile* (hence the name). The hermits used to live in entire isolation: twelve monks now live here but they no longer choose to live a rigorous hermit's life, and meet for services, meals, and work. The church and cell of St Romuald are open 8.30–11.15, 15–18; fest. 8.30–10.45, 12 or 12.30, 15–18. The CHURCH has a grey and white façade of 1713. In the vestibule is a bas relief of the Madonna and Child attributed to Tommaso Fiamberti. The chapel of St Anthony Abbot, off the transept which precedes the nave has a tabernacle attributed to Andrea Della Robbia and decorations by Adolfo Rollo (1930). The main church has elaborate gilded stucco decoration dating from 1669 and 17C frescoes. The choir stalls date from the 16C and the high altarpiece of the Crucifixion and four saints is attributed to Bronzino. On either side are large marble tabernacles by Gino da Settignano (1531) and in the apse a fresco of the Transfiguration by Ezio Giovannozzi (1937). In the chapter house is a painting of St Romuald and his disciples in the forest by Augusto Mussini (1915). The refectory, which dates from 1679, has a fine wood ceiling.

Outside the church is the gateway into the enclosure (no admission) with the 20 hermits' cells, really a little village of tiny self-contained houses. Opposite the church is the *cell of St Romuald*, which served as a model for the other cells. Above it the library was built in 1622.

A beautiful narrow road descends through the forest to (20km) the **Monastery of Camaldoli** (818m), founded in 1046 which now houses about 40 Carthusian monks. (3-star hotel *Il Rustichello*, 14 Via del Corniolo; 1-star hotel with restaurant *Camaldoli*, and 1-star camping sites open in summer; first-class restaurant *Pucini*). The huge building of the *Foresteria* on the road is used for visitors and meetings. Beyond is a piazza with the main entrance (open daily 6.30–13, 15–20) to the monastery. Steps lead down to the FIRST CLOISTER (*di Maldolo*) dating from 1100 with primitive capitals, but restored. Off it is the ancient CHAPEL OF SANTO SPIRITO with a barrel vault and a large column asymmetrically placed. On the other side of the cloister is the former entrance to the monastery through a tunnel. The SECOND CLOISTER has a portico on three sides with pretty Ionic capitals. It was designed by Ambrogio Traversari (1386–1439), the friend and tutor of Cosimo il Vecchio, who was a monk here. From the piazza another door (No. 14) on the left leads into a small courtyard in which is the CHURCH with an 18C interior. It contains five fine paintings by Vasari, including a Deposition, and a Nativity and Madonna with Saints John the Baptist and Jerome. The REFECTORY has a large painting by Pomarancio, a pulpit in pietra serena, and paintings attributed to Lorenzo Lippi. At the other end of the Foresteria is the entrance to the old PHARMACY (open 9–12.30, 14.30–18.30), with lovely carved wood cupboards and panelling dating from 1543. Products made by the monks are sold here. Another interesting room is arranged as an apothecary's workshop. In a separate building across the road is a private *Ornithological Museum* (No. 19; open on Sunday, or daily in July and August). At the bridge (by a lock) is a road for Bibbiena (another road for Poppi continues beyond the monastic buildings).

The main road from Pratovecchio (see above) to Poppi and Bibbiena reaches a fork at (59km) the plain of *Campaldino* where a column marks the battlefield of 11 June 1289. Here Dante fought as a young man in the

Florentine Guelf army against the Ghibellines of Arezzo, who were defeated, and their leader Bishop Guglielmino Ubertino killed. It has been estimated some 2400 mounted knights and 18,000 foot soldiers took part in the battle which remained for centuries of almost mythical importance in the imagination of the inhabitants of the Casentino.

From here N70 leads back up the valley and runs through a gate beside the tower of the castle of **Borgo alla Collina** (3km), badly damaged in the Second World War. The church of *San Donato* in a piazza with trees contains a fine triptych and predella of the Mystical Marriage of St Catherine, now attributed to the Master of Borgo alla Collina (1408). The tomb of Cristofano Landini, the Dante scholar and tutor of Lorenzo il Magnifico, was erected in 1848 by Lorenzo Bartolini. Landini, as Secretary of the Florentine Republic was given a palace here where he died in 1504.

The main road (N70) continues up towards the Consuma pass (see above) while a by-road (signposted for Strada) descends left for **Castel San Niccolò** (5km) in a lovely position at the foot of the Pratomagno hills. Beyond Strada on low ground to the left of the road by an avenue of lime trees is the *Pieve di San Martino a Vado* (restored in 1968–73). The simple interior thought to date from the 11C has charming historiated and foliated capitals. It contains an interesting font, and detached worn frescoes from the church of San Niccolò beside the castle, which is well seen from outside the church. The road continues through two piazze and then narrows before reaching Piazza Matteotti (or Piazza della Fiera) with an attractive and unusual market building. A medieval paved bridge (reconstructed) leads across the stream and a narrow road (signposted) leads up to the *Castle* (closed during restoration work). It is surrounded by a tiny hamlet and a Gothic postern gate beneath a tower with a huge clock survives on the side of the hill.

The by-road continues and at *Pagliericcio*, with a finely paved street, is a turning left for *Cetica* (9km; keep right and uphill), in another pretty valley. Before the village, near a modern school, is the 13C church of Sant'Angiolo with a low bell tower and steps at one corner of the building. In the wide interior, at the end of the right aisle, is a *Madonna and Child by Francesco Pesellino in a beautiful tabernacle. The E end has lancet windows and a handsome altar table. The road ends at *Bagni di Cetica* (13km), an ancient spa rediscovered in 1686, in a beautiful position.

From Pagliericcio (see above) a road continues up another wooded valley to **Montemignaio** (12km from Borgo alla Collina), an attractive village spread out along the side of the valley, surrounded by numerous trees. On the approach, across the valley can be seen the very tall bell tower of its castle, and then the battlemented tower of the church. The road crosses the bridge: on the right is the PIEVE, probably dating from the 12C with three rose windows above its three doors (restored). The INTERIOR has a deep apse and massive capitals on the two shorter columns at the E end. The two hanging capitals on either side of the presbytery have interesting sculptures representing Life and Death. On the first N altar, Giovanni Toscani, Madonna and Child (fragment of a polyptych). A Madonna enthroned with four doctors of the church by the school of Rodolfo del Ghirlandaio has been removed since 1973 for restoration. In the S aisle is a Della Robbian terracotta of the Madonna and Child with two saints. On the pilasters are scant remains of frescoes. A road leads along the side of the hill for c 1km to the Guidi castle with an oddly-shaped tower. From here there is a distant view of La Verna. A good road leads in 7km back to the Consuma road (see above).

From the fork at the plain of Campaldino the main road continues towards Poppi. Just before (61km) *Ponte a Poppi* is the church of *Certomondo* on the left of the road, approached through an old gate and crumbling courtyard. A convent was founded here in 1262. The church was restored in 1987 when the rose window was exposed. On the right of the presbytery is a fine painting of the Annunciation by Neri di Bicci. On pillars in the nave are fresco fragments of saints in very poor condition. On the right of the façade can be seen scant remains of the cloister (almost totally ruined).

From Ponte a Poppi an avenue (right) leads up past a war memorial to (62km) **POPPI** on a hill, a delightful little town (6000 inhab.). Its splendid

Castle, which dominates the Casentino valley, can be seen from miles around. The hill is very well preserved, especially on its S side. Its streets have a medley of porticoes, some still built in wood.

Car Parking in front of the Castle.

Hotels and Restaurants. 2-star: *Casentino* in front of the Castle. At Ponte a Poppi: 3-star: *Parc Hotel*; 2-star *Campaldino* with restaurant.

Poppi is famous as the residence of the Guidi counts who ruled the Casentino until it succumbed to the Florentine Republic in 1440. The sculptor Mino da Fiesole was born here in 1429.

The approach road passes under a portico into Piazza Amerighi (described below). To the left Via Conte Guidi continues up to the top of the hill with a car park in front of the ***Castello** (open daily 9.30–12.30, 14–17) of the Guidi counts. It was begun in 1274 by Count Simone da Battifolle and is the best preserved castle in the Casentino. Built in two stages, the part on the right of the tower is attributed to Lapo, master of Arnolfo di Cambio, and the wing on the left was probably completed by Arnolfo di Cambio himself. Over the door is a relief of a disgruntled Florentine lion, set up by the local sculptor Jacopo di Baldassarre Torriani in 1477. The *COURTYARD has a delightful staircase with old wooden balconies, and numerous coats of arms, and another Florentine Marzocco. On the left a fine vaulted room with one huge column is used for exhibitions. On the FIRST FLOOR is the well-lit SALONE with a fine floor and painted walls. The *LIBRARY (c 20,000 vols), in two rooms, has a remarkable collection of 519 medieval manuscripts and 780 incunabula (shown in exhibitions every year). Most of the material comes from Fabrizio Rilli-Orsini (1825) and the convent of Camaldoli. At the top of the stairs is a fine stone caryatid representing Count Simone da Battifolle. On the TOP FLOOR beyond a room with a pretty little fireplace is the CHAPEL with good frescoes by Taddeo Gaddi (1330–40), recently restored. The apartment used by the Guidi counts is closed for restoration. Outside the castle is a huge underground cistern.

Behind the castle is the church of the *Agostiniani* which has a terracotta Pietà attributed to the bottega of Andrea Della Robbia above the door. Inside (usually closed) is a Nativity, attributed to Benedetto Buglioni. Opposite Palazzo Pretorio is the ancient *Casa dei Guidi* (with a new outside stair) next to a gate into Villa Rita (ex-Giatteschi) in the garden of which can be seen the *Torre dei Diavoli*.

Below the garden and piazza is Piazza Amerighi with the domed centrally-planned church of the *Madonna del Morbo* begun in 1657 and finished in 1705, dedicated to the Madonna in gratitude for deliverence from the plagues of 1530 and 1631. It is surrounded on three sides by porticoes. Over the high altar is a fine painting of the Madonna and Child with the young St John by Pseudo Pier Francesco Fiorentino. Also in the piazza is the church of *San Marco* which contains a Deposition and a Pentecost (removed for restoration) by Francesco Morandini, named *Il Poppi* from this his native town, and a Raising of Lazarus by Jacopo Ligozzi.

Via Cavour, the main street, entirely lined with picturesque porticoes, ends at the N edge of the hill with the church of **San Fedele** built in 1185–95, one of the most important churches in the Casentino. INTERIOR. On the SOUTH SIDE, Ottavio Vannini, Madonna and Child with saints; first altar, Crucifixion with the Madonna and St John the Baptist and Mary Magdalen (replica of a painting by Maso di San Friano; removed for restoration). NORTH SIDE. First altar, 16C Nativity (being restored); Poppi, Martyrdom of St John; Alessandro Davanzati, Madonna and Child with angels (a very unusual work by a Vallombrosan monk, 1506); Pietro Sorri, Martyrdom of St Laurence, 1596 (being restored); Carlo Portelli, three saints. In the S transept a *Madonna and Child by the Maestro della Maddalena has also been removed for restoration. On the high altar is a 14C painted Cross. In the APSE: Madonna and saints, signed and dated 1527 by Antonio Solosmeo, the only known work by this artist; Passignano, two saints; Jacopo Ligozzi, Assumption and St Benedict. In the CRYPT is buried Beato Torello (1202–82), and here is kept his reliquary bust in gilded bronze (15C). Below San Fedele is Porta a Porrena in the walls which still encircle the town. The other little streets of the town are well worth exploring.

From Ponte a Poppi a road (signposted; left) leads beneath the railway up to the **Zoo** (open daily 8–dusk) of Poppi on a hillside. Pleasantly laid out in 1972 it specializes in European fauna, and includes two bears, buffalo, deer, lynx, llamas, donkeys, and birds. Picnic places are provided.

A by-road (2.5km) leads S from the foot of the hill of Poppi to the pieve of *Santa Maria a Buiano*, one of the oldest churches in the Casentino, built before 1000. It stands beside a farm with round silos (key at the house on the left). It has a charming deep brick apse and crypt. Excavations here in 1977 revealed remains of Roman baths and medieval tombs. This road continues to join another by-road in a pretty, unspoilt valley which traverses fields and woods (right) before reaching *Ortignano*. Outside the village, on a curve of the road, is the church of San Matteo. The road ends at the pretty village of *Raggiolo*, well seen on the side of the valley in chestnut woods beneath its ruined castle. The view to the E back down the valley takes in the headland of La Verna (see below).

68km **BIBBIENA** is the chief town (10,300 inhab.) of the Casentino. Situated on a low hill, it is now surrounded by numerous small factories, especially on the plain to the S.

Information Office, 29 Via Berni (Tel. 0575/593098).

Hotels. 3-star: *Brogi*, with restaurant *Da Marino* and *Giardino*; trattoria and pizzeria *Mon Ami*. **Car Parking** in Piazza Tarlati.

History. One of the oldest towns in the Casentino, the name may be derived from *Vibia*, an Etruscan family. It was first mentioned in the 10C and was destroyed by the Guelfs after their victory at Campaldino. The castle was for long contested between Arezzo and Florence. It was the birthplace of Bernardo Dovizi, called Cardinal Bibbiena (1470–1520), famous statesman and man of letters. He was responsible for the election of Cardinal Giovanni de' Medici to the papal throne as Leo X. He was a friend and patron of Raphael, who painted his portrait (now in the Galleria Palatina in Palazzo Pitti in Florence). He is also well known as author of *Calandra*, a play written in Italian.

The traditional Shrove Tuesday celebrations here (*Bello Ballo*) date from the mid-14C.

The approach road winds up to Via Dovizi, on the left of which is the early-16C *Palazzo Dovizi* (No. 26) opposite the 15C church of *San Lorenzo* (restored in 1917) with two fine enamelled terracotta altarpieces. From Piazza Roma, Via Giuseppe Borghi continues left to *Piazza Tarlati*. Here is a palace with a portico, a clock tower, and a terrace overlooking the valley. Behind the clock tower is another tower, once part of the castle of the Tarlati and on the right is the parish church of **Santi Ippolito e Donato**, usually called *la Pieve*. It was built at the beginning of the 12C as a chapel of the Tarlati castle. The wide INTERIOR, restored in 1972, has four large arches at the crossing. SOUTH SIDE. Maestro di San Polo in Rosso (13C), painted *Crucifix; Jacopo Ligozzi (attributed), Mystical Marriage of St Catherine (restored); seated painted wood statue of the Madonna di Giona, an unusual 12C Tuscan work. SOUTH TRANSEPT. Il Poppi, Annunciation (being restored in situ); Arcangelo di Cola da Camerino, *Madonna and Child enthroned with angels (restored in 1975). Over the high altar, a Crucifix replaces a triptych of the Madonna and Child with saints by Bicci di Lorenzo (temporarily removed). NORTH TRANSEPT. Jacopo Ligozzi, Madonna and Child with saints, signed and dated 1600; organ of 1552 by Onofrio Zeffirini, brought here in 1700 from the abbey of Vallombrosa; 14C frescoed niche with the Crucifixion. NORTH SIDE. Good 14C frescoes by the Florentine school of the Madonna and Child with saints, and, above, Holy Trinity.

Below the piazza (reached by steps) is the *Theatre* (1829), with a neo-classical façade, the Biblioteca Comunale and the 16C Palazzo Comunale. Nearby is the 14C Palazzo della Pretura (later restored).

Just over 1km NE of Bibbiena (reached by a signposted road) is the 15C Dominican convent (closed order) and church of **Santa Maria del Sasso**. It has an attractive portico on the right of the façade with charming frescoed ex-votos in the lunettes (very worn). In the domed INTERIOR is a Renaissance tabernacle by Bartolomeo Bozzolini (of Fiesole) with a Della Robbian frieze. An elaborate silver frame encloses a fresco of the Madonna and Child by Bicci di Lorenzo, and on the back of the tabernacle is an Annunciation by Francesco Brina. SOUTH SIDE. Santi Buglioni, enamelled terracotta of Christ and St John the Baptist. SOUTH TRANSEPT, Jacopo Ligozzi, Birth of the Virgin with saints (signed and dated 1607). Opposite the organ another painting by Ligozzi has been removed for restoration. NORTH TRANSEPT. Lodovico Buti, Madonna with St Giacinto. On the left wall of the church, Paolino da Pistoia, Madonna and saints (1525). Stairs lead down to the lower church and CRYPT, with a highly venerated 15C polychrome wood statue of the *Madonna del Buio. Here can be seen the great rock (*sasso*), around which the sanctuary was built. Legend relates that the Madonna appeared here miraculously in 1347.

FROM BIBBIENA TO BADIA PRATAGLIA, 15km. The road passes (9km) the hamlet of *Serravalle* with views of Bibbiena and Poppi in the far distance. The impressive church was built in full Romanesque style in 1927. Beyond are remains of a castle around a tower (now privately owned). The road continues up the lonely valley to (15km) **Badia Prataglia** (835m), the most important resort in the Casentino, surrounded by fine woods near the border with Romagna. Numerous 2-star hotels, and a 1-star camping site at Capanno. The 11C church, recently well restored, has a Romanesque crypt with interesting worn capitals and primitive reliefs, including one on the left of the altar of a figure in prayer. Fine walks may be taken in the wooded hills which surround the village. The main road continues over the Mandrioli pass (1173m) and descends to Bagno di Romagna in Romagna (see *Blue Guide Northern Italy*).

FROM BIBBIENA TO LA VERNA (22KM) AND CAPRESE MICHELANGELO (34km). The pretty road (N 208) leads up from Bibbiena through woods, with views ahead of the oddly shaped wooded promontory on which the convent of La Verna was built, and views back of Bibbiena and the valley (restaurant *Il Bivio di Querceto* at Querceto). Beyond the village of Dama there is another fine view of La Verna, and in the other direction can be seen the Pratomagno hills. From Case Nuove the panorama takes in the whole of the Casentino. The road continues across a plateau with fewer trees to the little resort of (22km) **Chiusi della Verna** (960m) (2-star and 1-star hotels, and 1-star camping site at Vezzano; first-class restaurant *La Beccia*). Just outside (signposted *Castello del Conti Orlando Cattani*), on the right of the road, is a tiny group of houses with the podesteria and the church of San Michele Arcangelo (1338) below the ruins of a 10C castle, the highest in the Casentino, built on outcrops of rock. A road (3km) diverges left from the Pieve Santo Stefano and Cesena road to climb up through plantations of fir trees to the famous monastery of **La Verna** in a remarkable position on a curiously shaped outcrop of rock (1129m) visible for many miles around. The site was given to St Francis in 1213 by Count

Orlando Cattani and here in 1224 he received the stigmata. It is still a Franciscan convent (c 30 friars) and a retreat. The sanctuary was embellished in 1433 by order of Eugenius IV when a number of altars were commissioned from Andrea Della Robbia, who has here left his masterpieces of enamelled terracotta sculpture.

The monastery is open 6–21.30, and there is a procession of the friars every day at 15 from the monastery to the Cappella delle Stimmate. A cobbled road leads through woods to the entrance arch, beyond which signs indicate the way past the side of the Chiesa Maggiore to the terrace from which the view takes in the Casentino, with Bibbiena in the distance. The CHIESA MAGGIORE was begun in 1348, and continued in 1450–70. On the first S altar, Madonna and Child enthroned between saints, attributed to Andrea Della Robbia. The two pietra serena tabernacles on the right and left of the nave, one with the Adoration of the Child and the other with the *Annunciation, are both by Andrea Della Robbia. In the chapel on the left of the presbytery is an *Ascension surrounded by cherubs and fruit, also by Andrea. At the entrance to the presbytery, the figures of St Anthony Abbot and St Francis are also probably by Andrea. The choir stalls date from 1495.

A covered CORRIDOR with frescoes of the life of St Francis by the 20C Florentine painter Baccio Maria Bacci leads past several sites which recall the life of St Francis here. At the end steps descend to the CELL OF ST FRANCIS with an 18C statue of the saint, beyond which is the tiny CAPPELLA DELLE STIMMATE, above the door of which is a 13C bas relief of the saint receiving the stigmata. This was built by order of Count Simone da Battifolle in 1263 on the spot where the saint received the stigmata, marked by an inscription in the pavement. Over the door, on the inside wall, is a *tondo of the Madonna and Child by Luca Della Robbia. The intarsia stalls date from 1531 (restored in 1906). The large enamelled terracotta Crucifixion (1480–81) is by Andrea Della Robbia (in a delightful frame). From the Chapel of San Bonaventura steps lead up and then down again to the CHAPEL OF ST ANTHONY OF PADUA. From here a door admits to a walkway (temporarily closed) which leads to the PRECIPIZIO, a cave of St Francis. Other holy spots are pointed out by the friars.

A ramp leads down from the terrace to the small church of SANTA MARIA DEGLI ANGELI (or the *Chiesina*, begun in 1216–18) which contains an altarscreen with two polychrome terracotta altars attributed to Andrea or Giovanni Della Robbia, and, beyond, in the earliest church, a blue-and-white altarpiece of the *Assumption of the Virgin, another fine work by Andrea, and Renaissance stalls. Here Count Orlando Cattani is buried. The treasures of the MUSEUM, including reliquaries and choir books, were stolen in 1978. A path leads up to the summit of the rock (La Penna, 1283m).

From Chiusi della Verna a narrow road winds down through lovely scenery to (34km) **Caprese Michelangelo**, a tiny isolated hamlet, with fine views, famous as the birthplace in 1475 of Michelangelo, whose father, Leonardo Buonarroti, was podestà here. Cars should be left outside the gate of the castle (being restored). 2-star hotel and restaurant *Buca di Michelangelo*; 2-star camping site at Zenzano. First-class restaurants *La Faggeta*, *Il Cerro*, and *La Buca di San Francesco*. The Palazzo Pretorio (open 9.30–12.30, 15.30–dusk) is now a (disappointing) museum with some of Michelangelo's works reproduced in photographs or casts. The room where the great artist may have been born is also shown. The castle opposite is being restored. A garden enclosed by the castle walls has been 'decorated' with sculptures (including works by Emilio Greco and Antonio Berti). Michelangelo was christened in the 13C chapel of San Giovanni Battista below the castle.

From Chiusi della Verna the main road continues E to Pieve Santo Stefano (17km; described in Rte 28). A lovely by-road leads SW from Chiusi della Verna through beautiful countryside to Chitignano and Rassina (see below).

FROM BIBBIENA TO AREZZO, 32km. The main road continues S towards Arezzo following the Arno, but soon leaving the Casentino valley. 6km **Rassina**, a busy place with a large gravel works. On the right, on low ground well seen from the road, is **Pieve Socana**. The 11C church has a fine campanile, round below and hexagonal above, beside its lovely apse. The interior (if closed ring at the priest's house on the right) has recently been heavily restored. A gate on the right of the façade admits to a path beneath a vine trellis which leads through an orchard to the E end of the church. Here can be seen a large rectangular Etruscan altar (5C BC) and remains of steps which led up to a temple, excavated in 1969. A by-road (5km) leads from Pieve Socana through a pretty valley up to *Castel Focognano*, a compact little village. Beyond the Torre Grande the road leads up to the church beside the Podesteria (early 15C) decorated with coats of arms. Beyond a narrow archway on the left, beneath the campanile, can be seen its old loggia with a wood roof and more coats of arms, beneath which is an old oven. On the right is a palace with two lions. The road continues up through woods with views ahead of the wooded slopes of the Pratomagno. It then descends into a valley with a stream in which is *Carda* (12km) a quiet well-kept little village. In the old district on a hill (keep left) is the church (ring for the key at the priest's house) which contains a precious triptych attributed to Mariotto di Cristofano (restored in 1974).

Another road from Rassina leads SW to **Talla** (8km; trattoria *L'Orcello*), birthplace of Guido Monaco (990–c 1050). The beautiful carved 16C organ case in San Niccolò has been restored.

Another by-road leads E from Rassina to *Chitignano* (6km), just before which a signpost (right) indicates the castle of the Ubertini counts (now privately owned) above the road on a little hill surrounded by cypresses, with statues high up on its wall. From here Bishop Guglielmino Ubertini, the famous condottiere, set out on 11 June 1289 at the head of the Ghibelline army of Arezzo for the battle of Campaldino, where he lost his life. The scattered village has mineral water springs.

The main road leads S from Rassina through (25km) Giovi, near Pieve a Sietina, a lovely little church, to (32km) Arezzo, see Rte 26.

25

The Valdarno and Pratomagno

The **VALDARNO** lies between Florence and Arezzo, overlooked by the Chianti hills and the western slopes of the **PRATOMAGNO**. In the Pliocene era a huge lake occupied this area and on its shores were tropical forests inhabited by rhinoceros, hippopotamus, and elephants. It later became one of the most fertile areas of Italy, settled by the Etruscans and Romans. The narrow Arno valley has always been an important centre of communications between Florence and the south. In the 14C the Florentine Republic founded *Terre nuove* here at San Giovanni Valdarno, Terranuova Bracciolini, and Castelfranco di Sopra. The Humanists Marsilio Ficino, Poggio Bracciolini, and Benedetto Varchi were all born in the Valdarno. Many of the beautiful works of art in churches here by Florentine masters have been carefully restored in recent years: these include a triptych by Masaccio (born at San Giovanni Valdarno), an Annunciation by Fra Angelico, and numerous Della Robbian works. A fine red Chianti is produced on the *Colle*

Aretine. The hills of the Pratomagno rise to nearly 1000 metres at Vallombrosa, famous for its monastery and forests.

Road (round trip) from Florence.—5km *Bagno a Ripoli*—12km *San Donato in Collina*—23km **Incisa Valdarno**—28km **Figline Valdarno**—36km **San Giovanni Valdarno**—42km *Montevarchi*—51km *Loro Ciuffena*—73km *Reggello*—86km **Vallombrosa**—100km *Pelago*—126km **Florence**.

The A1 **Motorway** from Florence to Arezzo follows the Valdarno with exits at (25km) Incisa (for Figline) and (41km) Valdarno (for San Giovanni Valdarno and Montevarchi).

Railway. The main line from Florence to Rome via Pontassieve has stations at Incisa, Figline, San Giovanni, and Montevarchi (slow trains only).

Buses. Services run by SITA from Florence via San Donato in Collina to Incisa, Figline, San Giovanni, and Montevarchi. CAT services via Pontassieve to the above towns. SITA services via Pontassieve, Pelago and Tosi for Vallombrosa and Saltino.

Information Offices. APT of Florence (Tel. 055/290832) for Incisa Valdarno, Figline Valdarno, Reggello, Vallombrosa, and Pelago. APT of Arezzo (Tel. 0575/377678) for San Giovanni Valdarno and Montevarchi.

Florence is left on the S bank of the Arno at Ponte San Niccolò. The road (signposted) leads past Badia a Ripoli (see Rte 13A) and the residential district of *Sorgane*, much criticised when it was built in 1962–70. 4km *Pieve a Ripoli* (San Pietro), first mentioned in the 8C, has a fine interior. 5km **Bagno a Ripoli** is a large scattered Comune, a pleasant residential area on low hills with fine views. To the N at Quarto is the church of Santa Maria, restored in 1930 by Giuseppe Castellucci. It contains a triptych with a central panel by Bicci di Lorenzo, and side panels by the bottega of Bernardo Daddi, as well as a painting signed and dated 1391 by a certain 'Francesco'. The main road now begins to climb, and on the left, beneath the Arco di Camicia, is the church of *Santo Stefano a Paterno* rebuilt in 1934. It contains a painted *Crucifix by a follower of Cimabue (late 13C). The old road continues left through *L'Apparita* (view of Florence) for Quattro Vie (see below) while the newer road forks right past *San Quirico a Ruballa* (1763) which contains a Madonna and Child with the young St John by Domenico Puligo, a painted Cross of c 1330, and a small wooden 14C statue of the Madonna and Child. Beyond Osteria Nuova, very near the motorway, is the church of *San Giorgio a Ruballa*, restored by Nicolò Matas in 1863. It contains a Madonna and Child with saints dated 1336, and a painted Cross, a late work by Taddeo Gaddi. The two roads rejoin at (10km) *Quattro Vie*. 12km **San Donato in Collina**, in a beautiful position, with fine villas. 1km NE is the splendid 18C *Villa Rinuccini di Torre a Cona* with a medieval tower. It has a cypress avenue and Italianate garden surrounded by a fine park. The road now descends through Palazzolo, with a neo-Gothic church. A road on the right leads to the Romanesque church of *San Lorenzo a Cappiano* (open Sunday morning only) with an 18C interior with a Madonna and Child attributed to the Maestro di Barberino.

The road enters the **VALDARNO** just N of (23km) **Incisa Valdarno**, so called from the deep chalky cutting made by the Arno, through which run the road, motorway, and railway. The conspicuous 14C Torre del Castellano was heavily restored in 1952. On the main road is the Municipio beside the church of *Sant'Alessandro* with three fragments of a polyptych by Andrea di Giusto. In the convent of *Santi Cosma e Damiano* (1538; reconstructed in 1723), preceded by a portico of 1592, are 17C paintings and a polychrome terracotta bas-relief of the Madonna and Child attributed to Buggiano.

A road beyond Sant'Alessandro climbs the hill to the locality known as Castello with a few pine trees on the left of the road. Here is the site of the old town of Ancisa, and the bellcote of the former church above the high pyramidal wall of the ruined castle provides an odd site. In the hamlet on the left is a house (plaques) where Petrarch spent the first seven years of his life. The road continues up to *Loppiano* in beautiful countryside, before which on the left, with a battlemented campanile, is the *Pieve di Santi Vito e Modesto*, of ancient foundation. The exterior is being restored. In the interior (if closed, ring at the house on the right) the painting of the Madonna of the Holy Girdle by Francesco d'Antonio (1427) has still not been returned since its restoration in 1987.

The main road continues S from Incisa. Just before Figline, a by-road right (signposted) leads through pretty countryside to Brollo (4.5km), just beyond which is the tiny hamlet of *San Pietro al Terreno* (unsignposted), with farm buildings beside the church with a bellcote. In the fine 18C interior (if closed, ring on the right) are frescoes in grisaille, stuccoes, and marble confessionals. On the high altar, *Madonna and Child with four saints by an early-16C Florentine master (attributed to Giuliano Bugiardini, perhaps in collaboration with Mariotto Albertinelli; restored in 1985). In the choir, detached 14C fresco of the Madonna and saints. On the left altar, 17C painting of the Madonna of the Rosary. The painting of the Holy Trinity by Agostino Melissi was removed many years ago for restoration.

28km **FIGLINE VALDARNO** has been an important market town (13,600 inhab.) since the 12C.

The castle of Fegghine was first mentioned in 1008, but the town on this site was laid out on a regular plan in 1259 by the Florentines, who also built its walls in 1356. **Hotels**. 3-star: *Antica Taverna Casa Grande* (with restaurant), 84 Via Castelguinelli, and *Torricelli*, 2 Via San Biagio. First-class **Restaurant** *Papillon*, 83 Piazza Ficino. 4-star camping site *Norcenni Girasole Club*.

The lovely large PIAZZA (market on Tuesdays) is named after the great Humanist scholar Marsilio Ficino (1433–99) who was born here. It has porticoes and balconies, and a medley of houses. At one end is the 17C *Spedale Serristori* with a loggia. This was founded in 1399 by Ser Ristoro Serristori, and the hospital was transferred to Villa di San Cerbone (see below) in 1890. Four very worn frescoes beneath the loggia are by Niccolò Lapi (late 17C). At the other end of the piazza is the COLLEGIATA DI SANTA MARIA, founded in 1257, with a dark INTERIOR heavily restored in this century. SOUTH WALL. Madonna and Child with saints (including St Romulus holding a model of Figline), attributed to Giovanni Andrea De Magistris (1593; restored in 1991). The pretty circular CHAPEL OF THE HOLY SACRAMENT, with a colonnade of columns and a lantern above the cupola dates from the 19C. The seated statue of St Joseph in polychrome terracotta (temporarily removed for restoration) is attributed to Andrea or Luca Della Robbia (c 1505–10). The *Maestà is ascribed to the Maestro di Figline, named from this work. It was restored in 1975 and is remarkable for its subtle colouring. NORTH WALL. The 16C font has been placed by a worn fresco of the Annunciation. Beyond a niche with a damaged fresco of the Crucifixion is a painting of the transition of St Joseph by the local painter Egisto Sarri (late 19C). A small MUSEUM (admission on request) has been arranged in two rooms beyond the sacristy. It contains a painting of the Martyrdom of St Lawrence by Lodovico Cigoli; two charming angels painted by Domenico Ghirlandaio in 1480 which formerly surrounded the Maestà in the church; and church silver, chalices, vestments, illuminated choirbooks, etc.

The narrow Vicolo Libri leads out of the square beside the Collegiata to the 14C *Palazzo Pretorio*, over-restored in 1931, next to a leaning bell tower at the foot of which is a little open chapel which contains a Madonna enthroned with saints in polychrome terracotta by Benedetto Buglioni (the garland, angels, and some details were added in 1930 by the Cantagalli workshop). In the piazza is the church of **San Francesco**, founded in 1229 and preceded by an attractive portico beneath which, on the left, is a 14C statuette of the Madonna in a tabernacle. The INTERIOR was over restored at the beginning of this century. The *frescoes on the WEST WALL (restored in 1984–90) are fine works by Francesco d'Antonio (Crucifixion and saints, Annunciation, and Coronation of the Virgin, and St Francis). On the SOUTH WALL has been placed a frescoed lunette of the Madonna and Child with two saints attributed to Pier Francesco Fiorentino (detached from the cloister). In the NORTH TRANSEPT are 14C frescoes of Christ in Pietà between saints and a Crucifixion above. On the altar on the NORTH WALL of the church is a late 15C fresco of the Madonna of the Holy Girdle between Saints John the Baptist and Julian, attributed to the school of Botticelli. A door leads into the CLOISTER with very worn frescoes of the early 17C, off which is the CHAPTER HOUSE (opened on request) which has a 14C fresco of the Crucifixion and a painting of the Madonna and Child signed and dated 1392 by Giovanni del Biondo. On the opposite side of Piazza San Francesco is *Santa Croce* (entrance on Via Santa Croce), next to a convent (closed order). In the 18C interior is a 16C painting of the Crucifixion and a wood Crucifix by a Tuscan sculptor of the late 15C or early 16C (restored 1991).

A road leads out of Piazza Ficino on the right of the Collegiata to Via Castelguinelli where at No. 86 (marked by two pine trees) is the *Casagrande dei Serristori*, now a hotel and restaurant. The Renaissance loggia and Italianate garden (as well as part of the old walls) can be seen on request at the restaurant. Corso Matteotti leads out of the other end of Piazza Ficino beside the Spedale Serristori. It ends in Piazza Serristori with the *Teatro Garibaldi* (being restored), built in 1868–70 by the local architect Andrea Pierallini and decorated by Egisto Sarri. A fine stretch of town walls (1356–75) and the Cassero can be seen here. On the outskirts of the town (reached from Piazza Serristori by Via Vittorio Veneto; c 500 metres), beyond the neo-classical cemetery, and next to a palace of 1570, is the sanctuary of *Santa Maria al Ponterosso*, with a fine fresco of the Madonna and Child over the high altar by a follower of Perugino.

At the S end of the town (to the right off the main road) is the 17C **Villa di San Cerbone**, seat of the Ospedale Serristori since 1890 (admission on request at the convent). The chapel has an Annunciation by Lodovico Cigoli and paintings by Niccolò Lapi. Off the 15C courtyard is the refectory with a Last Supper attributed to Giorgio Vasari. The pharmacy, founded in 1399, has interesting 16–19C majolica vases and glass, a painting of the Madonna enthroned with angels attributed to the Maestro del 1399, and the head of the Redeemer by Matteo Rosselli. This road (signposted Cesto and Gaville) continues past the inconspicuous church of **San Bartolomeo a Scampata**, refounded in a farm building on the left of the road in 1970, when the old church on the hill above to the right was abandoned. It contains (right wall) a *Madonna and Child by Ugolino di Nerio (restored in 1985). The pretty road continues up to *Gaville* where the Ubertini castle was destroyed by the Florentines in 1252. A road (signposted for the Museo della Civiltà Contadina) continues up to the ancient **Pieve di San Romolo**, in a beautiful position, with a fine apse and campanile of 11–12C. It contains an Annunciation by the Florentine school (c 1500). A painting of St Christopher by Bicci di Lorenzo has not yet been returned here since its restoration in 1988. Next door is a local *Ethnographical Museum* illustrating peasant life in the area (open Saturday 16–18, Sunday 15–19; or by appointment). The wide view takes in the lignite mines and blast furnaces on the plain (see below).

The main road (N 69) continues towards San Giovanni and near the locality of *Restone* is the church of *Sant'Andrea a Ripalta*, above the road on the right. It is usually locked but has an 18C stuccoed interior and a triptych with a fine predella dated 1436 by Andrea di Giusto. 36km **SAN GIOVANNI VALDARNO**, the most industrialised town of the Valdarno (19,000 inhab.), built after 1296 as one of the *Terre nuove* of the Florentine Republic. It is laid out with rectilinear streets on either side of the two central piazze (closed to through traffic). Some streets have narrow porticoes.

Hotels. 3-star: *La Bianca*, 38 Viale Don Minzoni, and *River*, 10 Via Fratelli Cervi. **Restaurants** (first-class): *Adriano VII*, 16 Piazza Masaccio, *Castellucci*, 44 Corso Italia.

San Giovanni was the birthplace of the painters Masaccio (Tommaso Guido or Tommaso di Giovanni Cassai, 1401–c 1428), Mariotto di Cristofano, 1393–1457, and Giovanni di San Giovanni (Giovanni Mannozzi, 1592–1636).

In the centre of the two main squares, Piazza Cavour and Piazza Masaccio, is the *PALAZZO PRETORIO (restored in 1991), with a tall central tower (restored in the 19C), and surrounded on four sides by porticoes. It is covered with coats of arms dating from the 15C to the 18C, some in enamelled terracotta by the Della Robbia workshop. The palace was attributed by Vasari to Arnolfo di Cambio. A museum is to be opened here to display finds from excavations during restoration work which include medieval ceramics, 15C majolica, 16C–18C local ware, and coins. Outside is a copy of the Florentine Marzocco (the original has been placed in the atrium). In Piazza Cavour, with a monument to Garibaldi by Pietro Guerri (1902) is the 14C *Pieve di San Giovanni Battista* (restored in 1920; often closed), preceded by a portico. It contains a 17C sculpted Pietà and a 15C painting of the Madonna and Child. In the same square (at No. 12) is the convent of the *Agostiniani* (now a school; admission on request). In the oratory are good works by Antonio Puglieschi (the ceiling fresco, side altarpiece, and high altarpiece of the Annunciation, c 1685). On the left altar is a tender *Madonna and Child on a gold ground by the Maestro della Natività di Castello. In the corridor is a relief of the Madonna and Child derived from a prototype by Ghiberti.

In Corso Italia there is a plaque on a house supposed to have belonged to Masaccio. In Piazza Masaccio, beyond the *Palazzaccio* (or Palazzetto Ricorboli) with three pretty loggias, is *San Lorenzo*, with a plain Gothic façade. The interior has been over restored. On the high altar, Giovanni del Biondo, polyptych of the Coronation of the Virgin. In the right aisle, remains of frescoes (very ruined) include a fragment of the martyrdom of St Sebastian, the only known signed work by Scheggia (1457), and St Anthony Abbot with stories from his life (almost illegible) attributed to Mariotto di Cristofano.

The **Basilica of Santa Maria delle Grazie**, begun in 1484, has a façade of 1856–85, with an unusual portico and double staircase. The E end, with a dome, was rebuilt in the 1950s after severe war damage. At the foot of the staircase is a colourful lunette of the Assumption of the Virgin with saints by Giovanni Della Robbia (1515). The church is entered at the top of the right staircase. In the first part, dating from the 18C, with painted vaults, the elaborate high altar has 18C paintings of angels surrounding a venerated image of the Madonna and Child. On the altar wall, fresco of the plague of 1479 in the town. Over a side altar, Domenico di Michelino, Madonna enthroned with six saints. The sacristy is lined with wooden cupboards and benches. The unattractive rotonda (in very poor repair) dates from the 1950s. Here is a fresco of the Marriage of the Virgin by Giovanni di San Giovanni, detached from the exterior of the church. The MUSEO DELLA BASILICA is entered from a door beside the high altar (open 15–18 except Monday). It is arranged in three rooms above the portico overlooking the piazza. R. 1: Mariotto di Nardo, triptych with the Trinity and four saints; Paolo Schiavo, St Ansano, St Biagio, chorus of angel musicians; works by Lo Scheggia, including a chorus of angels; Giovanni da Piamonte, Tobias and the archangel Raphael (also attributed to Bartolomeo della Gatta); Jacopo del Sellaio, Annunciation; and works by Mariotto di Cristofano, including Christ in Pietà between the Virgin and St Lucy. In the room to the right, a beautiful painting of the *Annunciation, from the convent of Montecarlo. This is generally attributed to the hand of Fra Angelico and dated c 1431 since its restoration in 1984. It is another version of the painting of the same subject by Angelico in the Museo Diocesano in Cortona. In the room to the left, Gregorio Pagani, St John the Baptist, St Lawrence; Giovanni di San Giovanni, beheading of St John the Baptist.

From San Giovanni a by-road leads W through *Santa Barbara* (5km) laid out in the 1930s next to the open lignite mines and huge blast furnaces (visible from miles around) of an ENEL plant. From *Castelnuovo dei Sabbioni* (10km) a road continues up through Massa Sabbioni to the PARCO NATURALE DI CAVRIGLIA (15km; poorly signposted) on the wooded Chianti hills (800m) overlooking the Valdarno. This is a protected area created in 1978 with a well laid out zoo (open daily 8–21) with bears, buffalo, wolves, llama, deer, wild fowl, etc. There is a car park outside (if cars are driven into the zoo enclosure a fee is charged), and sports facilities, refreshments, and marked nature trails (wild deer can often be seen in the vicinity).

From Castelnuovo dei Sabbioni a road leads SE to *Cavriglia* (2-star camping site and Youth Hostel at Cafaggiolo), with a lot of new building, above which is a pieve with a square tower with unusual crenellations. It is preceded by a garden of lime trees. The lunette over the church door of St John the Baptist in the desert is by Benedetto Buglioni. The interior (if closed, ring at the priest's house on the right) is being restored. It has fine Baroque side aisles. A 14C bronze Crucifix, and three white enamelled terracotta busts of angels by Benedetto Buglioni are kept locked for safety. Cavriglia is on the road (N408) between Montevarchi and Gaiole and Siena (see Rte 13A).

2km SW of San Giovanni is *Montecarlo*, a Franciscan convent founded in 1429, and now a religious community. An Annunciation by Fra Angelico formerly in the church is now in the Museum of San Giovanni Valdarno (see above).

42km **MONTEVARCHI** was also laid out in the early 14C by the Florentine Republic. (3-star hotel *Delta*, 137 Viale Diaz). It has an interesting oval plan with two outer streets, slightly curved, parallel to the two main streets which pass through the central piazza. It is now an important market town (22,700 inhab.) with new suburbs. It is worth exploring for its Art Nouveau and Art Deco buildings. In the central Piazza, named after the Humanist Benedetto Varchi who was born here (1503–68), is the **Collegiata di San Lorenzo**, with an unusual façade dating partly from the 18C and partly from 1932 (when the bas-relief of the Martyrdom of St Lawrence was placed high up on the façade). The campanile (1440) was completed in 1560, and the statue of St Lawrence was added by Pietro Guerri in 1894. The sober INTERIOR was redesigned in 1706–09 by the local architect and sculptor Massimiliano Soldani Benzi. Pretty stucco frames surround paintings by Giovanni and Camillo Sagrestani and Matteo Bonechi (some have been removed for restoration). The two altarpieces (recently restored) on the right and left side of the Madonna in glory with saints are by Giovanni Balducci (Il Cosci) and Carlo Maratta (1611). In the chapel on the right of the high altar, the dome paintings are attributed to the Sagrestani and Bonechi. The E end is covered for restoration: above the high altar, with the reliquary of the Madonna del Latte, by Gherardo Silvani are stuccoes of the Madonna in Glory by Giovanni Baratta. The terracotta bust of the Madonna and Child dates from the 15C and the bronze statue of the Madonna is by Soldani. In the chapel on the left of the high altar, Matteo Rosselli, Adoration of the Magi.

The MUSEO DELLA COLLEGIATA (admission by appointment; enquire at the door on the right of the façade) is entered off the right side of the church. It is beautifully arranged in two rooms. R. I: large wood 17C Crucifix; three 14C illuminated manuscripts; 16C reliquary bust of one of the Virgins of St Orsola, by Simone di Antonio Pignoni; Cross with reliefs by Piero di Martino Spigliati, a pupil of Cellini; a reliquary in the form of a ciborium with 16C paintings by Giovanni Del Brina; detached frescoes from the church of Cennano by Roberto (or Luberto) da Montevarchi (an assistant of Perugino). In the second room is the beautiful *TEMPIETTO ROBBIANO. This was formerly the Cappella di Santa Maria del Latte, and it was partly destroyed when it was removed from the church in the 18C. It was reconstructed here in 1973. It was designed to contain a venerated reliquary given to the church in the 13C by Conte Guidoguerra dei Guidi (who had obtained it from Charles of Anjou in gratitude for his valour in a victorious battle in 1266). The enamelled terracottas are by Andrea Della Robbia: above the altar are reliefs of St John the Baptist and St Sebastian in niches on either side of a copy of a terracotta Madonna and Child now on the high altar of the church. Below are four angels protecting the reliquary and a beautiful Pietà. The ceiling of the chapel and friezes of cherubs are also by Andrea. On the wall is a fine Della Robbian frieze, also attributed to Andrea, formerly on the façade of the church, showing the reliquary being presented to the church. Also here are two Della Robbian *stemme*, fragments of ceramic oriental draperies, and a stone bas relief dated 1283.

Via Bracciolini, in front of the church, leads left past Palazzo del Podestà, a house with a portico, and Palazzo Carapelli with reliefs by Romano Romanelli (early 20C). The church of the *Ges* has a 19C façade. It contains 18C wooden benches and a large wood statue of Christ. Beside it is the church of *Cennano* with frescoes by Vasarri. At No. 36 is the *Accademia Valdarnese del Poggio*, founded in 1804, in an old monastery with a fine courtyard. It has a libarary and an important PALEONTOLOGICAL MUSEUM (open Tuesday–Saturday, 9–12, 16–19; Sunday 10–12; closed Monday). In the showcases of 1870 are rock, vegetable and animal fossils found in the Valdarno, including the *canis etruscus* studied by Professor F. Major of Glasgow. Georges Cuvier, the great French naturalist came here in 1810 to study the collection.

At the N end of the town, near the railway, is the church of the *Madonna del Giglio* with a handsome cupola attributed to Matteo Nigetti (1607–15) and a portico, and a fresco fragment over the altar. In an unattractive part of the town to the S, also near the railway, at La Ginestra is the church of *Santa Croce* on a little hill. Thought to have been founded in 614–20, the Benedictine monastery beside it was transformed into a factory in the 19C (being restored). Beyond a door on the right of the church can be seen a fresco of St Benedict and St Scholastica. A huge building, once a hat factory, below the hill is being restored and beyond it can be seen the monumental *Palazzo Masini*, an extremely ornate Art Nouveau building with a tower (1924–27).

The main road continues S from Montevarchi towards Arezzo. At Levane (5km) a by-road diverges right for Bucine (9km), just beyond which, after Pogi, a narrow (signposted) road leads past several farms and up through woods (with a view right of the castle of Lupinari, with a red tower) to **Cennina** (15km) a peaceful little village with beautiful views, where a number of houses have recently been restored. The remains of its 12–13C castle include an isolated gateway. In the attractive little piazza at the top of the hill with a well and houses covered with creepers, is the Sala d'Armi (enquire locally for the key) where concerts are held in August.

Another road (8km) leads S from Montevarchi to *Galatrona* with a Romanesque church which contains important works by Giovanni Della Robbia (1510–21; key at the priest's house in Mercatale).

FROM MONTEVARCHI TO AREZZO, N69, 32km. This hilly road passes 6km S of *Laterina* where in 1973 were unearthed long and almost intact streches of the Via Cassia Vetus. After crossing beneath the motorway and just before *Indicatore* station N69 passes, on the S, *Arezzo British Military Cemetery*, with 1267 graves. The road now descends into the Valdichiana for Arezzo, see Rte 26.

From Montevarchi a road leads across the Arno and motorway to (46km) *Terranuova Bracciolini*, now surrounded by ugly new buildings (3-star and 2-star hotels, and restaurant open at weekends of the *Cooperativa Agricola Valdarnese*, at Paterna, booking necessary). This was another *Terra nuova* of the Florentine Republic, founded in 1337. The Humanist Poggio Bracciolini (1380–1459) was born here. The road continues up to (51km) *Loro Ciuffena*, also now surrounded by new buildings (2-star hotels with restaurants). The old medieval village is in a fine position on rocks above the Ciuffena river. The church of Santa Maria Assunta has 16C paintings by Carlo Portelli who was born here. **Gropina**, 2km S, reached through pine woods, is a charming medieval hamlet built around a Romanesque *PIEVE (open 8–12, 15–19; or ring at the priest's house in front of the side door). The bare interior built in pietra serena has delightful carved capitals and a primitive pulpit. Beneath the right aisle, stairs lead down to remains of earlier buildings on this site (Roman and Palaeochristian finds). A secondary road continues to Arezzo via *San Giustino Valdarno*, with another Romanesque pieve.

From Loro Ciuffena a beautiful road (the *Strada dei Sette Ponti*), roughly on the line of the Roman Cassia Vetus, leads along the side of the **PRATOMAGNO** hills back towards Florence. It passes the sanctuary of the *Madonna delle Grazie di Montemarciano*, built in 1532 and surrounded by a portico of the early 17C. It contains a fresco attributed to Francesco d'Antonio. A by-road left leads to the village of *Montemarciano* with remains of its castle destroyed by the Florentines in 1288. 61km *Castelfranco di Sopra*, founded by the Florentines in 1299, and laid out on a circular plan perhaps to a design by Arnolfo di Cambio. Outside the village on the left is the Vallombrosan *Badia di San Salvatore a Soffena*, rebuilt in 1394 (and restored in 1966). It contains interesting early 14C frescoes including works by Bicci di Lorenzo, Paolo Schiavo, the Maestro del Cassone Adimari, Mariotto di Cristofano, and Liberato da Rieti. The road continues with a fine view of the valley to (66km) *Pian di Scò*. Here the Romanesque pieve of Santa Maria (11–12C), with interesting capitals, has a fresco attributed to Paolo Schiavo. 73km **Reggello** (4-star hotel *Villa Rigacci* in the country at Vaggio). 1km outside the town (on the Figline Valdarno road) is CASCIA, birthplace in the 14C of the musicians Giovanni and Donato da Cascia. Here is the Romanesque pieve of *San Pietro*, marked by its tall bell-tower, and preceded by a 13C portico. It is traditionally thought to have been founded by Countess Matilda. It is open 7.30–12, 15–19; if closed ring at No. 1 in the piazza). At the end of the left aisle (light) is a beautiful small *triptych of the Madonna and Child with Saints Bartolomeo, Biagio, Giovenale, and Antonio Abate. Dated 1422, this is the first known work by Masaccio. It was rediscovered in 1961 in the nearby church of San Giovenale, restored in 1984, and installed here in 1988. The church also contains interesting capitals, an ancient Crucifix in the apse, an Annunciation on the left wall by Mariotto di Cristofano, brother-in-law of Masaccio, and a Pietà signed and dated 1601 by Santi di Tito.

Near Montanino, below Cascia, are *Calanchi*, yellow sandy hills which have been eroded into strange forms. From Reggello the road continues to

(76km) *Pietrapiana* (3-star hotel *Archimede*, with restaurant) where the road forks.

FROM PIETRAPIANA TO RIGNANO, 11km. A road (signposted) descends left to the Romanesque church of *Sant'Agata in Acerfoli* on the left of the road (yellow sign) beside a cedar of Lebanon. There is a splendid view from the terrace. The porch was added in 1928. The 13C cloister is interesting. In the interior (if closed ring at the house on the right) is a tomb with carved decoration opposite a medieval carved pluteus and a fresco of the Madonna and saints with the Pietà surrounded by grottesques, by Raffaellino del Garbo. The fine presbytery was designed in 1928 using old columns and pilasters. The pretty road continues down between old walls and past vineyards to (3km) the hamlet of *Cancelli* with (right) the church of Santa Margherita. It contains a fresco of the Crucifixion and, on the left, a fragmentary fresco of good quality by the bottega of Paolo Schiavo. The road continues down past (8km) the entrance to the *Castello di Sammezzano* (now a 4-star hotel). A drive, 2km long, leads up through splendid woods, including numerous sequoia trees, to the 'castle' built by Ferdinando Panciatichi Ximenes d'Aragona in 1813–53, which is a remarkable sight. The exterior has elements which recall the Taj Mahal, and the colourful interior has some splendidly decorated rooms on the piano nobile, some of them modelled on the Alhambra of Granada.

The main road along the Arno from Incisa to Pontassieve passes the church of *San Clemente a Sociano* (on a curve of the road above to the right), preceded by a portico. In the interior (if closed, ring at the house on the right) there are two lovely marble candle-bearing angels in the sanctuary by Mino da Fiesole, and, in the left transept a marble •bas-relief of the Madonna and Child by Antonio Rossellino. The two altar-pieces are in poor condition: on the left, St Michael and saints attributed to Giovanni Battista Naldini, and on the right, Madonna and saints by the bottega of Santi di Tito. Across the Arno is (11km) *Rignano*, an unattractive place on the railway on flat ground surrounded by factories. The new church in the centre contains an Assumption by Matteo Confortini (1623), and (at the end of the left aisle) a hexagonal font in enamelled terracotta by Benedetto Buglioni. In a chapel off the left side is a polychrome terracotta relief of the Birth of the Virgin, and a 16C Crucifix and painting of St Roch. The Romanesque pieve di San Leolino, N of the town, is being restored.

From Pietrapiana another road (signposted Donnini) continues along the side of the hill with views of the valley to *San Donato in Fronzano* (if closed ring at the door on the right) with a 17C façade, and an interesting interior. Beyond is the *Pieve a Pitiano* (being restored) with an 11–12C campanile (if closed ring at the door on the left). Over the high altar is an Annunciation by Ridolfo del Ghirlandaio. From Donnini (6km) another road, lined with cypresses and olives, leads up towards Tosi (see below) climbing round the Villa Pitiana with a 19C yellow façade (and 14C and 16C elements).

From Pietrapiana the direct road for Vallombrosa winds up through **Saltino** (970m) with wide views, an old-fashioned resort with large hotels (including *Grand Hotel*, 3-star, and *Croce di Savoia* and *Villino Medici*, 2-star), some of them built at the end of the 19C or early 20C (open only in summer). 86km **Vallombrosa** (997m) is surrounded by a thick forest of pines, firs and beeches, which has been owned by the State since 1866. Cool in summer and conveniently close to Florence, it has a number of restaurants. It is famous for its monastery founded by St John Gualberto in 1040, the first home of the Vallombrosan order. The monastery was suppressed in 1866 but reinstated in 1963 and some 20 monks now live here. An avenue precedes the MONASTERY with a lawn and fish pond on the left. Beyond a walled garden is the splendid façade with numerous small windows by Gherardo Silvani (1610–40). The CHURCH has a a façade of 1644. Beneath the portico is a Madonna and Child by the bottega of Ghiberti and a statue of St John Gualberto by Giovanni Battista Caccini. The interior contains 18C frescoes and paintings. On the high altar, Assumption by Volterrano and 15C carved wooden choir stalls. In the S transept, Sigismondo Cocca-pani, martyrdom of St Sebastian, and in the N transept, Lorenzo Lippi, Trinity. The chapel in the N transept has a fine ceiling with frescoes and stuccoes by Alessandro Gherardini. In the sacristy, Madonna and saints with donors by Andrea Della Robbia and paintings by Raffaellino del Garbo (St John Gualberto and saints), and Giuseppe Sabatelli. The MONASTERY (closed for restoration, but usually shown on guided tours) has an 18C refectory with paintings by Ignazio Hugford and an enamelled terracotta by Santi Buglioni, and a fine kitchen. In the guest house known as the *Paradisino* Milton is supposed to have stayed in 1638 (plaque): 'Thick as autumnal leaves that strow the brooks/ In Vallombrosa, where the Etrurian shades,/ High over-arch'd imbower;' (*Paradise Lost*). Fine walks can be taken in the forest, and a road (9km) leads up to *Monte Secchieta* (1450m), which has winter sports facilities.

A road from Vallombrosa leads to the Passo della Consuma (see Rte 24), while the direct road to Florence descends steeply through woods past several streams to Pian di Melosa, where the main road commemorates Bernard Berenson who often stayed nearby at San Miniato in Alpe. *Tosi* is known for its furniture makers. Beyond (100km) **Pelago**, described in Rte 3, a lovely hilly road continues down past open fields to Pontassieve and the main road (N70) for (126km) **Florence**.

26

Arezzo

AREZZO is pleasantly situated on a low hillside (296m) about 5km S of the Arno, but now surrounded to the S by industrial suburbs. It is a lively agricultural provincial town (87,300 inhab.), with several notable churches and interesting museums. In the church of San Francesco is the famous fresco cycle painted by Piero della Francesca.

Tourist Offices. APT, 116 Piazza Risorgimento (Tel. 0575/23952); Information Office (IAT), 22 Piazza della Repubblica (outside the railway station), Tel. 0575/377678.

Railway Station, Piazza della Repubblica, about 500m SW of San Francesco, on the main Florence–Rome line. Some fast 'Intercity' trains stop here (from Florence in 45mins); otherwise slower trains (frequent service) in c 1hr. Local trains to Sinalunga via Monte San Savino, and (every hour) via Bibbiena and Poppi to Pratovecchio-Stia.

Country Buses. Services run by SITA from Piazza Stazione to Florence (in 1hr 20mins–2hrs); to Sansepolcro (via Monterchi and Anghiari) in c 1hr; to Città di Castello (in 1hr 30mins); to Caprese Michelangelo (in 1hr 30mins–2hrs). Services run by LFI to Siena (in c 1hr 30mins); to Cortona (via Castiglion Fiorentino) in c 1hr; and to Urbino (in c 3hrs).

A **town mini-bus** service (ATAM) from outside the railway station traverses the town, otherwise closed to traffic.

Car Parking near the centre of the town (closed to traffic) is difficult, and most car parks (in Via Niccolò Aretino, Via Alberti, Via Pietro Aretino, etc.) charge an hourly tariff. Free parking in Via Mecenate, and caravan park outside Porta San Clemente.

Hotels. 3-star: *Continentale*, 7 Piazza Guido Monaco (Pl. 1); *Europa*, 43 Via Spinello (Pl. 2). On the outskirts (towards the motorway): *Minerva*, 4 Via Fiorentina (3-star); *Etrusco*, 39 Via Fleming (4-star). 2-star: *Astoria*, 54 Via Guido Monaco (Pl. 3); *Cecco*, 215 Corso Italia (Pl. 4). *Youth Hostel*, *Villa Severi*, Via Redi (beyond Borgo Santa Croce; Bus No. 4 from Piazza Guido Monaco).

Restaurants. Luxury-class: *La Buca di San Francesco*, 1 Via San Francesco (Piazza San Francesco); *Le Tastevin*, 9 Via dei Cenci (off Corso Italia). First-class restaurants: *La Lancia d'oro*, Piazza Grande; *Continentale*, 7 Piazza Guido Monaco; *Minerva*, 2 Via Fiorentina (on the outskirts towards the motorway). Trattorie: *L'Agana*, 10 Via Mazzini; *Il Saraceno*, 6A Via Mazzini; *Cecco*, 215 Corso Italia; *La Vigna*, Via Spinello; *Loggie Vasari*, Piazza Grande; *Il Cantuccio*, 78 Via Madonna del Prato.

A popular **antiques fair** is held in Piazza Grande and the surrounding streets on the first Sunday of every month (and the day before). **Annual Festivals**. A famous international choral festival (*Corso Polifonico Internazionale Guido d'Arezzo*) is held in the city in late August. The *Giostra del Saracino*, a tournament held twice annually in the Piazza Grande on the last Sunday of August and the first Sunday in September at 17 has an origin going back to the 13C. Two competitors from each of the four quarters of the town, mounted and armed with lances, charge in turn across the piazza at a pivoting quintain called *Buratto Re delle Indie* which holds the target in its left hand and in its right a whip, ending in three wooden balls. Points are awarded (from 1–5) for aim, with bonus points for a broken lance, and penalties if the horseman is struck by the wooden balls as the figure turns on its pivot. Each of the four ancient quarters of the town enters a team under a captain, with standard-bearers, foot-soldiers, bowmen, and a band, which plays the Saracino hymn. The four quarters have their own colours: Porta Sant'Andrea, white and green; Porta Crucifera, red and green; Porta del Foro, yellow and crimson; Porta Santo Spirito, yellow and blue. The team (not the individual) scoring the most marks is declared the winner. Tickets are available in advance (information from the Tourist Office); standing room only on the day.

History. *Arretium* was one of the more important of the 12 cities of the Etruscan Confederation. The bronze statues of Minerva and the famous Chimera (c 380 BC) found here in the 16C (now exhibited in the Archaeological Museum in Florence) testify to the quality of the work of local Etruscan artists. Arezzo was originally the enemy and later the faithful ally of Rome. It emerged as a free republic in the 10C. Generally supporting the Ghibelline party it was frequently at odds with Florence; it shared in the defeat at Campaldino in 1289 and submitted to Florence in 1384. As a road junction the town had tactical importance in the Second World War when nearly every important building was harmed to some extent by bombing.

Ever since the Etruscan period Arezzo has produced notable artists and craftsmen. The famous Arretine pottery, with a bright red glossy finish, was first produced here c 50 BC, and was later mass produced and exported all over the world by some 90 firms working in Arezzo. Among its eminent citizens were C. Cilnius Maecenas (died 8 BC), the friend of Augustus and the patron of Virgil and Horace; Guido d'Arezzo (c 995–1050), the inventor of the musical scale; Margaritone, the painter (1216–93); Petrarch, the poet (1304–74); Spinello Aretino, the painter (c 1350–1410); Aretino (1492–1566), the most outspoken writer of the late Renaissance; and Giorgio Vasari (1512–74), the architect, painter, and art historian.

The pleasantest approach from the station is by *Corso Italia*, the main street of the medieval town, which leads gently uphill. Via Cavour diverges left for Piazza San Francesco, a small square created in the 19C (the monument to Vittorio Fossombroni is by Pasquale Romanelli, 1863) in front of *San Francesco. The church was built by Fra Giovanni da Pistoia in 1322. At the foot of the rough-hewn front is part of the facing which was never finished.

The bright Franciscan INTERIOR (open 8–12.30, 14–18.30; on Sunday visitors are asked to visit the church 10–11, 14.30–18.30) contains the world-famous frescoes by Piero della Francesca in the choir, but also numerous other frescoes (mostly fragments) in the nave, many of them showing his influence on the local school. The interior and Piero's frescoes are being restored. WEST WALL. The rose window has *stained glass by Guglielmo di Marcillat (William of Marseille, 1520) showing St Francis before Honorius III. The frescoes include: Supper in the house of the Pharisee by Giovanni di Balduccio, and the Mystical Marriage of St Catherine of Alexandria, an unusual scene with the figure of St Christopher attributed to Paolo Schiavo. SOUTH WALL. First chapel, frescoes, dated 1463, showing St Bernardine of Siena leading the Aretines from the church of San Francesco to destroy the Fons Tecta (connected with a pagan cult), by Lorentino d'Andrea, an assistant of Piero della Francesca. On the wall, Niccolò Soggi, Sacred Conversation. Second altar, frescoes with scenes from the life of St Bartholomew by a follower of Piero della Francesca. On the wall, fresco of the Crucifixion, and, above an unusual fresco of two figures in monochrome guarding a door closed with chains (from the family name *Catenacci*). Surrounded by a tabernacle in pietra serena, 14C wood Crucifix, and a fresco fragment by Antonio d'Anghiari, master of Piero. Beyond the third altar, with ruined frescoes attributed to Parri Spinelli, in a finely carved tabernacle, is a Roman sarcophagus, the tomb of Beato Benedetto Sinigardi (died 1282), friend of St Francis. At the end of this wall, Annunciation by Spinello Aretino. The chapel to the right of the sanctuary also has damaged frescoes (restored) by Spinello Aretino: right, deeds of St Michael; left, Legend of St Giles. The triptych of the Madonna of the Holy Girdle is by Niccolò di Pietro Gerini.

In the SANCTUARY hangs a huge painted *Crucifix, with St Francis at the foot of the Cross, attributed from this work to the Master of San Francesco (1250). On the walls of the choir is the **LEGEND OF THE TRUE CROSS (light; offering) by Piero della Francesca (finished in 1466), his masterpiece, and one of the greatest fresco cycles ever produced in Italian painting. The Bacci, a rich Aretine family commissioned Bicci di Lorenzo to paint the sanctuary: he had only painted the four Evangelists on the vault and the Last Judgement (restored in 1987) on the triumphal arch before he left Arezzo in 1448 (he died in 1452). Piero della Francesca was called to complete the frescoes, possibly in 1448. He may have interrupted work on them during a stay in Rimini in 1451, and another in Rome in 1459. The frescoes illustrate the Legend of the True Cross, taken from the *Legenda Aurea* by Fra Jacopo Voragine (13C), and the time span runs from the Death of Adam to the Battle of Chosroes in the 7C AD. Studies and tests are being carried out as part of a lengthy and extremely complicated restoration programme (1985–1993) of the frescoes. They have deteriorated alarmingly for a number of reasons: the wall is particularly thin, the circulation of air in the church was altered when the roof was rebuilt and central heating was installed, and the delicate frescoes were damaged by poor restorations in the past. At present only the right wall can be seen.

The chronological order of the scenes, as they illustrate the story is as follows: *right wall (lunette)*, Death of Adam. On the right, Adam seated on the ground, announces his imminent death from old age to his family; on the left is the dead figure of Adam, and Seth planting a tree on his grave (from which the Cross on which Christ is Crucified will be made). *Right wall (middle band)*, The Queen of Sheba recognises the sacred wood (used as a bridge over the Siloam river) and kneels in adoration before it, and (on the right) she is received by Solomon. *Right of the window (middle panel)*, the beam is buried deep in the ground by three men, by order of Solomon. *Right of the window (lower panel)*, Constantine's Dream in 313 AD. The Emperor, asleep in his tent the night before battle, dreams that an angel shows him the Cross and announces 'By this sign, you shall conquer'. *Right wall (lower band)*, Constantine's bloodless victory over Maxentius early the next morning. *Left of the window (middle panel)*, Torture of a Jew named Judas. He is kept in a dry well until he reveals the secret hiding place of the Cross, stolen after the Crucifixion. *Left wall (middle band)*, Discovery and Proof of the Cross. Judas digs up the Cross before St Helena and her courtiers, and on the right, in a scene in front of a church, its authenticity is demonstrated by the raising from the dead of a young man, while Helena kneels in wonder. *Left wall (lower band)*, Battle scene showing the victory of Heraclius over Chosroes in the 7C AD, after Chosroes, king of the Persians, had seized the Cross and placed it near his throne (shown to the right). After his defeat he kneels awaiting execution. *Left wall (lunette)*, Heraclius restores the Cross to Jerusalem. Also by Piero are the two figures of Prophets on the window wall, and the Annunciation (thought by some scholars to be St Helena receiving the news of her death and thus connected to the main cycle).

In the chapel to the left of the sanctuary is a fine painting of the Annunciation by Neri di Bicci, and a damaged fresco of the Annunciation attributed to Luca Signorelli or Bartolomeo della Gatta. NORTH WALL. In the last chapel, terracotta funerary monument to Francesco Rosselli, attributed to Michele da Firenze (1439; being restored), and, in a 17C altar, Bernardino Santini, Ecstasy of St Francis. On a pilaster, fine fresco of St Elizabeth of Hungary, by the school of Spinello Aretino. In the middle of this wall is a chapel with *frescoes (recently restored) of St Anthony of Padua and stories from his life, and a lunette of the Visitation, by Lorentino d'Andrea, showing the influence of Piero della Francesca (and possibly on a cartoon by him). Beyond are remains of a fresco of St Francis and Pope Honorius III by Parri Spinello. The LOWER CHURCH (13–14C) has been restored, but is open only for exhibitions.

The ***Pieve di Santa Maria**, at the end of Corso Italia (see above; closed 13–15) is a 12C church replacing an earlier edifice, sacked in 1111. It is one of the most beautiful Romanesque churches in Tuscany. The superbly conceived *FAÇADE has a deep central portal flanked by blind arcades which support three tiers of colonnades, the intercolumnations of which diminish towards the top. The 68 diverse pillars include a human figure. The portal (covered for restoration) bears reliefs of 1216 and the months are illustrated in the intrados. The beautiful tall *INTERIOR has clustered pillars with good capitals and arches showing the transition to Gothic. The mullioned windows provide a diffused light on the mellow sandstone. The drum was to have supported a dome which was never built. In the raised presbytery is the *polyptych by Pietro Lorenzetti commissioned for the church by Bishop Guido Tarlati in 1320. The crypt below has good capitals, and a reliquary *bust of St Donato (1346) by a local goldsmith. In a chapel off the left side of the nave is a polychrome statue of the Madonna and Child by the 15C Florentine school.

The arcaded apse of the Pieve and its original *campanile* (1330) with its 40 mullioned windows are best seen from the steeply-sloping ***Piazza Grande**, behind the church (reached by Via di Seteria which skirts the interesting flank of the church opposite medieval shop-fronts). The piazza was laid out c 1200 (some medieval houses and towers survive here). It is still the centre of city life, and the scene of the *Giostra del Saracino* in summer and of a monthly antiques fair. Beside the apse of the Pieve is the *Palazzo del Tribunale* (17–18C) preceded by a circular stair, and the elaborate little *Palazzo della Fraternità dei Laici* in a mixture of Gothic and Renaissance styles. The lower part dates from 1377 (with a detached fresco of Christ in Pietà by Spinello Aretino), and in 1434 Bernardo Rossellino added the relief of the Madonna of the Misericordia in the lunette above and two statues in niches on either side. The delicate cornice and loggia above were designed in 1460 by Giuliano da Settignano. The bellcote and clock date from 1552. One whole side of the square is occupied by Vasari's handsome *Palazzo delle Logge* (1573). The long portico continues NW back to Corso Italia in which is *Palazzo Camaiani* (16C), with a tower of 1351, now housing the Provincial Archives. Via dei Pileati continues uphill past the 14C *Palazzo Pretorio*, its façade decorated with the armorial bearings of many podestà; it is occupied by the Public Library. The road curves uphill to the left, and at No. 28 Via dell'Orto is the *Casa Petrarca* (admission on request here or at the Accademia Petrarca, Via degli Alberghetti, 10–12, 15–16 or 16–17; closed Saturday afternoon and fest.), the supposed house of Petrarch reconstructed (after its destruction in the Second World War) as an academy and library for Petrarchian studies. Visitors are shown the library with MSS and an autograph letter of the poet (1370). A huge monument to Petrarch (by Alessandro Lazzerini, 1928) stands in the *Parco il Prato*, an attractive large park with pine trees, lawns and pretty views of the Tuscan countryside. The 14–16C *Fortezza* (admission daily), also in a park, was rebuilt by Antonio da Sangallo the Younger (and partly dismantled in 1800).

The **•Duomo** (closed 12.30–15) was begun in 1278 and continued until 1510, with a campanile added at the E end in 1859 and a façade completed in 1914. Fine travertine steps (1525–29) surround the exterior. The handsome S flank incorporates a good portal (1320–40), with worn reliefs, and terracotta statues of the Madonna and Child between St Donato and Gregory X, attributed to Niccolò di Luca Spinelli. The beautiful Gothic •INTERIOR has a nave, tribune, and aisles, with clustered columns and pointed arches. The splendid stained glass •windows are by Guglielmo di Marcillat (1519–23), a French artist who lived in Arezzo. He also painted the first three vaults of the nave and the first of the N aisle (light at the W end, but extremely difficult to see as they are so high up) in 1521–27. The remaining vaults of the nave were painted in 1661 by Salvi Castellucci. SOUTH AISLE. Funerary monument to Cardinal Stefano Bonucci (died 1589), with a fine bust. The stained glass window by Marcillat illustrates the calling of St Matthew. The sepulchral monument (1320–30) of Gregory X who died at Arezzo in 1276 is a fine Gothic work. The second window by Marcillat shows the Baptism of Christ. To the left of the altar, fragment of a 14C fresco of the Madonna enthroned with saints, and a lunette of the Risen Christ, by Buffalmacco. The window by Marcillat shows the Expulsion of the Merchants from the Temple. On the third altar are 14C frescoes. The window of the •Woman taken in Adultery is the last work in the Duomo by Marcillat. The medieval Tarlati Chapel has a beautiful sculptured canopy by Giovanni d'Agostino. The fresco of the Crucifix and saints is attributed to a local painter known as the Maestro del Vescovado (mid-14C). The fine 4C Paleochristian sarcophagus rests on a marble tomb with a bas-relief of a bishop saint, and three inscriptions. The window by Marcillat shows the •Raising of Lazarus. The 18C Maurizi monument has two busts.

In the chapel to the right of the apse, marble ciborium of 1783 and a stained glass window of 1477. The Gothic sculptured •HIGH ALTAR, by many 14C artists including Giovanni di Francesco and Betto di Giovanni, encloses the body of St Donato (martyred in 361), the patron saint of the city. The two lateral stained glass lancet windows in the tribune are by Domenico Pecori (16C); the central one dates from 1953.

NORTH AISLE. On the left of the sacristy door is a beautiful fresco of •St Mary Magdalene, by Piero della Francesca (inconspicuous light on the nave pillar). Next to it is the unusual •tomb of Bishop Guido Tarlati, by Agostino di Giovanni and Agnolo di Ventura, with panels representing the

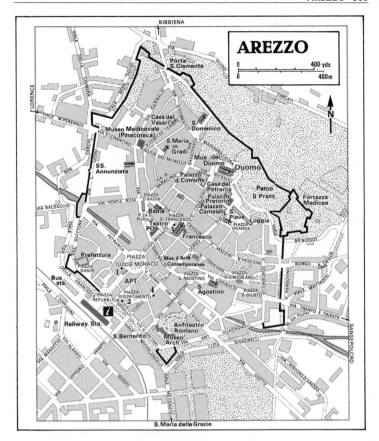

S.Maria delle Grazie

warlike life of this zealous Ghibelline (died 1327). The small funerary monument of Girolamo Borro (died 1592) bears a bust. The cantoria is the first architectural work of Vasari (1535); the organ dates from 1534 (by Luca Boni da Cortona). Beneath it is a 13C wood statue of the Madonna and Child, and 14C fresco fragments. Beyond an altarpiece of the Martyrdom of St Donato by Pietro Benvenuti (1794) is a little fresco by Luigi Ademollo of the Aretines receiving the body of St Donato. The large LADY CHAPEL (closed for restoration), preceded by a pretty wrought-iron screen, was added in 1796. On the right, above a funerary monument to Bishop Albergotti (died 1825), with reliefs by Odoardo Baratta, is an Assumption by Andrea Della Robbia. On the right wall, large painting of Judith (1804) by Pietro Benvenuti, much admired by Canova. In the chapel to the right of the main altar, Andrea Della Robbia, Crucifix (right wall). The main altar was designed by Giuseppe Valadier (1823). In the chapel to the left of the main altar, statue of Bishop Marcacci by Stefano Ricci and on the left wall, a polychrome terracotta attributed to Giovanni Della Robbia. On the left wall, large painting of David and Abigail by Luigi Sabatelli. On the wall near the entrance to the chapel, *Madonna and Child, by Andrea Della

Robbia. In the north aisle, funerary monument of Francesco Redi (died 1697). At the W end of the aisle opens the Baptistery. The three beautiful *schiacciato* reliefs on the font are attributed to Donatello or his school.

It is necessary to return round the exterior of the E end of the Duomo to the Piazzetta dietro il Duomo to visit the **Museo del Duomo** (open Easter–September, weekdays 9–12; winter: Thursday, Friday and Saturday only, 9–12). R. 1 contains three wood *Crucifixes of the 12–13C: the oldest one is on the left of the entrance (it was painted in 1264 by Margaritone di Arezzo). The tabernacle with a terracotta bas-relief of the Annunciation is attributed to Bernardo Rossellino (1434). The frescoes include an Annunciation by Spinello Aretino, a tabernacle, also with an Annunciation, by Parri di Spinello, and a Madonna and Child with Saints James and Anthony Abbot by Spinello Aretino. The painting of the Annunciation is by Andrea di Nerio, master of Spinello. The cases of church silver include the Pax of Siena, in the base of a neo-classical reliquary. It is a 15C Flemish work in enamel surrounded by precious stones depicting Christ supported by an angel, and the Madonna supported by an angel. R. 2: Bartolomeo della Gatta, *St Jerome in the desert, a fresco and its sinopia; detached fresco of the Madonna and Child by Lorentino d'Andrea; Della Robbian polychrome bust of St Donato; Bartolomeo della Gatta and Domenico Pecori, Madonna and Child with Saints Fabiano and Sebastian; Domenico Pecori, Madonna in glory with saints; Niccolò Soggi, Founding of the Basilica Liberiana; Luca Signorelli, panels from a predella. R. 3: Vasari, Preaching of the Baptist, Baptism of Christ, and tondo of the Madonna della Misericordia (a processional standard); Santi di Tito, Christ in the house of Martha. The last room displays church vestments.

On the cathedral steps stands a statue of Ferdinando I, by Francavilla, after a design by Giambologna. It was erected by the Aretines in 1594 in gratitude for the grand-duke's agricultural reforms and land reclamation in the Valdichiana. Across Piazza della Libertà is the *Palazzo del Comune* of 1333. The old Via Sassoverde descends right from Via Ricasoli to **San Domenico** in a square of lime trees. The church, founded in 1275, has a Romanesque portal with a lunette frescoed by Angelo di Lorentino, and a Gothic campanile.

The bright INTERIOR has a miscellany of fresco fragments of particularly high quality. On the WEST WALL, Parri di Spinello, Crucifixion and saints and (in the lunette) two scenes from the life of St Nicholas of Bari. On the SOUTH WALL, in a Gothic canopied altar by Giovanni di Francesco, Christ with the doctors in the temple by Luca di Tomm. Above, between the windows, Madonna and Child by the school of Duccio. In a pretty carved polychrome niche, St Peter Martyr by the Della Robbian school. The large detached fresco of a triptych with St Catherine of Alexandria is by the school of Spinello. Above an 18C wall monument, fragment of a fresco by Parri with angel musicians. Beside the steps, damaged fresco of Christ blessing the faithful. EAST END. In the chapel to the right of the main altar, a fine stone 14C statue of the Madonna and Child and a fresco of the *Annunciation by Spinello Aretino. The *Crucifix in the main apse is by Cimabue (light). In the chapel to the left of the apse, Giovanni d'Agnolo, triptych with St Domenic, Archangel Michael, and St Paul. On the NORTH WALL of the church are frescoes by Giovanni d'Agnolo, Parri di Spinello (Marriage of St Catherine), and Jacopo di Landino (stories of St Christopher). Vasari records that the last fresco on this wall of St Vincent Ferrer is the only known work by his great-grandfather Lazzaro Taldi Vasari. On the W wall is a large frescoed composition by Spinello Aretino.

At No. 55 in Via XX Settembre is **Vasari's House** (open 9–19; ring). Giorgio Vasari, the famous art historian, painter, and architect, finished building the house after he purchased it in 1540, and then carried out the painted decorations, with the help of assistants (restored in the 19C). It was acquired by the State in 1911 and contains a collection of 16–17C paintings, many of them by artists in the circle of Vasari.

In the HALL is a late-16C bust of Vasari. The SALA has ceiling paintings by Vasari of Virtue, Envy, and Fortune, the Four Seasons, the Four Ages of Man, and allegorical figures and landscapes. The CAMERA D'ABRAMO, with a ceiling painted by Vasari in 1548, contains paintings by Vasari (Deposition), Aurelio Lomi (Ecce Homo), Francesco Vanni (Flagellation), Perin del Vaga and Giovanni Stradano. Beyond a corridor (with Ceres in the vault) which gives access to the garden, is a room which was the kitchen (the frescoes by Raimondo Zaballi date from 1827). Here are hung portraits by Giovanni Maria Butteri and Scipione Pulzone, and two 16C marble bas-reliefs of Aristotle and Plato. The CAMERA D'APOLLO has the best ceiling by Vasari. The paintings include works by Alessandro Allori, Jacopo Ligozzi, Maso di San Friano, Paolo Farinati and Il Poppi. The painting in a pretty frame of Prudence (which may have belonged to Vasari) is attributed to Il Doceno. The CAMERA DELLA FAMA has another good ceiling and portraits in the lunettes of Lazzaro Vasari, Giorgio Vasari, Luca Signorelli, Spinello Aretino, Bartolomeo della Gatta, Michelangelo, and Andrea del Sarto. The paintings include works by Giovanni Stradano, Girolamo Macchietti, Carlo Portelli, and Giovanni Maria Butteri. The majolica head of Galba is by Andrea Sansovino (purchased by Vasari). The last room has a wood model by Vasari of the Logge in Piazza Grande, and works by Maso di San Friano. The precious family archives include letters of Michelangelo.

The church of **Santa Maria in Gradi**, farther on (left), has a fine interior rebuilt in 1592 by Bartolomeo Ammannati. 17C frescoes of the Apostles have been uncovered and restored. On the first altar on the left, *Madonna del Soccorso by Andrea Della Robbia. A staircase leads down to the remains of an earlier church or crypt (probably 10C) with a 13C wood Crucifix. The two decorative cantorie (and chapels below) are by Salvi Castellucci (1633) and Bernardino Santini (1629).

At the corner of Via Garibaldi is the **Galleria e Museo Medioevale e Moderno**, housed in the fine 15C *Palazzo Bruni* (admission every day 9–19). Off the courtyard which has fragments from the Pieve are two rooms with medieval sculptures and 14C Madonnas from gates in the walls, an early 14C statue of St Michael Archangel, a late 13C statue of a King(?) and a seated statue of St Anthony Abbot by Michele da Firenze. FIRST FLOOR. R. I: Margaritone, St Francis, Madonna, and Crucifix; school of Guido da Siena, Madonna; circle of the Maestro della Maddalena, Madonna and Child. Sculpture: Agostino di Giovanni, head of a warrior (1330); 13C portrait head; in cases, Romanesque Crosses and Crucifixes. R. II: 15C frescoes by Giovanni d'Agnolo di Balduccio (c 1370–1452), pupil of Spinello Aretino. R. III: Frescoes by Spinello Aretino and his son Parri di Spinello, and a *Madonna of the Misericordia by Parri; painting of St Michael Archangel by Giovanni d'Agnolo di Balduccio. RR. IV and V: Early Renaissance. The chimneypiece is by Simone Mosca, and tournament armour and coins are displayed in cases. Also here: Bartolomeo della Gatta, two paintings of St Roch, the smaller painting including a view of medieval Arezzo. On the opposite wall, Lorentino d'Arezzo, Madonna and saints. R. V contains frescoes, some attributed to Signorelli and cases of small bronzes. The next five small rooms contain a magnificent *collection of majolica from Faenza, Gubbio, Deruta, Castel Durante, and Urbino (13–18C), and terracottas by Andrea Della Robbia, a bas relief by Michele da Firenze, and a statuette of St Luke by Vincenzo Danti. In two rooms the MARIO SALMI BEQUEST has been arranged which includes small works by Il Poppi, Empoli, Agostino Ciampelli, Arcangiolo Salimbeni, Franciabigio, Francesco Granacci, Alessandro Magnasco, Ludovico Carracci, and Adriano Cecioni. In the gallery is the Banquet of Ester and Assuero, Vasari's largest painting (1548). SECOND FLOOR. In the first room are 19C works and paintings by the Macchiaioli school. The second room has works by Gaspare Dughet, Salvator Rosa, etc. RR. 3 & 4. 16C and 17C works (Jacopo Bassano, Carlo Dolci, Vasari, Alessandro Allori, Cigoli, and Jacopo Vignali), and 16C–19C glass. The Salone has more 16C works (Vasari, Domenico Pecori, and Poccetti).

On the opposite side of Via Garibaldi is the Renaissance church of the **Santissima Annunziata**, with an Annunciation by Spinello Aretino on the outside. The beautiful Renaissance grey-and-white *INTERIOR is by Bartolomeo della Gatta (1491) and Giuliano and Antonio da Sangallo the Elder (c 1517). The interesting plan includes a columned atrium and a dome over the crossing; the capitals of the columns and pilasters are superbly carved. The stained glass tondo in the atrium is by Guglielmo di Marcillat. There is a light on the right of the S aisle for the altarpieces. In the chapel to the right of the high altar, Madonna and St Francis by Pietro da Cortona, and a 16C terracotta Madonna and Child with saints, and a relief of God the Father above. The 17C high altar incorporates Renaissance statues in silver and a venerated statue of the Madonna attributed to Michele da Firenze. The chapel on the left of the high altar has an Annunciation by Matteo Rosselli and a Nativity by Niccolò Soggi (1522). On the third N altar is a 14C Crucifix, and on the first altar is a good painting of the Deposition painted by Vasari at the age of 18 on a cartoon by Rosso Fiorentino.

On the left, farther on, is the **Badia** or abbey church of Santi Fiora e Lucilla, built by the Benedictines in 1278, and transformed by Vasari in 1565. The octagonal campanile dates from 1650. The INTERIOR is an interesting architectural work by Vasari. On the W wall is a delightful *fresco of St Lawrence, by Bartolomeo della Gatta (1476). SOUTH SIDE. Second altar, Baccio da Montelupo, wood Crucifix; beyond the third altar, large painted Crucifix by Segna di Bonaventura (1320). In the sacristy is furniture decorated with intarsia attributed to Giuliano da Maiano. The HIGH ALTAR has good paintings by Vasari, including the Calling of the Apostles, intended for his own tomb. On the right wall of the choir, Assumption, also by Vasari. The cantoria of the fine organ dates from 1651 and bears two paintings by Raffaello Vanni. The cupola has a trompe l'oeil fresco by Andrea Pozzo (1702). On the wall of the N side, exquisite marble tabernacle attributed to Benedetto da Maiano (the bronze door was stolen in 1978). The former monastery preserves a fine 15C cloister.

Via Garibaldi continues SE, crossing the broad Via Guido Monaco to Piazza Sant'Agostino (scene of a daily market, threatened with 'development', despite local protest). The church has a 13C campanile. On Corso Italia is a local Museum of Contemporary Art, containing works mostly dating from the 1960s. From here Via Margaritone leads to the *Convento di San Bernardo* whose rebuilt double loggie follow the curve of the *Roman Amphitheatre* (117–138 AD; the well-kept ruins are entered from Via Crispi, 8–19.30, or from the archaeological museum). The charming rooms of the convent, overlooking the amphitheatre, now house the **Museo Archeologico Mecenate** (admission 9–14; fest. 9–13). Other parts of the amphitheatre are visible in the museum rooms. GROUND FLOOR. R. 1: Archaic finds from Arezzo: architectural fragments and small bronzes. R. 2: Hellenistic finds from Arezzo, including terracotta heads. R. 3: (right) displays a krater by the potter and vase painter Euphronios (c 510–500 BC). RR. 4 & 5 contain material from the Valdichiana, including a fine red-figure amphora (420–410 BC) and kraters and stamnoi of the 5C BC. RR. 6 & 7 (right) have an excellent display of the famous Arretine vases mass-produced in Arezzo from 50 BC to 60–70 AD, in a shiny red glaze, usually decorated with exquisite bas-reliefs. Moulds and instruments are displayed as well as the production of individual workshops. R. 8 continues the display with superb works from the Ateius pottery (which had branch workshops in Pisa and Lyon). R. 9: collection of grave-goods from the tomb of a young girl from Apulia (1C BC). RR. 12–16 (temporarily closed) display Roman mosaics and bronzes, statues, sculpture, urns, a marble altar of the Augustan period, with the legend of Romulus and Remus, and the portrait of a woman of the Augustan period.

UPPER FLOOR. To the left are three rooms of vases: a curious urn with a human head and arms from Chiusi (7C BC), good red-figure Greek vases (5C BC), bucchero ware, etc. Two rooms to the left off a corridor display: Roman glass and a *portrait of a man moulded in gold (Aretine, 1C BC); small bronzes; and the Ceccatelli collection acquired in 1988 with finds from Vulci (7C–6C BC). Off the left side of the long corridor: the Gamurrini collection (small bronzes) and the Vincenzo Funghini (1828–96) collection (mostly 4C–3C BC). Off the opposite side of the corridor are the Palaeolithic and Neolithic collections from the territory of Arezzo.

To the SE of the station, reached through an ugly part of the town (an unpleasant walk from the station of c 15mins) is the church of **Santa Maria delle Grazie** (1449), enclosed in a walled garden. The graceful *loggia (covered for restoration) is by Benedetto da Maiano. It contains a beautiful marble and terracotta *high altar by Andrea Della Robbia which encloses a fresco of the Madonna of the Misericordia by Parri di Spinello. On the right wall is a very ruined fresco by Lorentino d'Arezzo. The adjacent oratory of St Bernardine (1450–56) has a pretty vault.

27

Cortona

CORTONA (22,600 inhab.) is a delightful, peaceful little town, particularly well preserved, with olive groves and vineyards reaching up to its walls. It is built on a long hillside with narrow winding medieval streets covering the steep slopes. It has numerous interesting churches (including Santa Maria del Calcinaio, a famous Renaissance building), and two fine museums. Its works of art include paintings by Luca Signorelli who was born here. There are magnificent views over the wide agricultural plain which provides the main source of its economy.

Tourist Information Office (IAT), 42 Via Nazionale (Tel. 0575/630352).

Railway Stations. Camucia, 5km from Cortona, is the nearest station on the Florence–Rome secondary line; a few trains a day from Florence in 1hr 15mins. Bus from Camucia c every 30mins in 10mins to Piazza Garibaldi. *Terontola*, 11km from

Cortona, is on the main line between Florence and Rome, but no fast 'Intercity' trains stop here; local trains in c 1hr 30mins from Florence. Bus from Terontola c every hour in 25mins to Piazza Garibaldi.

Car Parking (the centre is closed to traffic). Free car parks in Piazza del Mercato, Porta Colonia, Porta Santa Maria, or Via Gino Severini.

Country Buses (LFI) from Piazza Garibaldi to Camucia, Terontola, Castel Fiorentino, and Arezzo.

Hotels. 4-star: *San Michele*, 15 Via Guelfa (Pl. 1). 3-star: *San Luca*, 2 Piazza Garibaldi (Pl. 2); *Sabrina*, 37 Via Roma (Pl. 3). 2-star: *Italia*, 5 Via Ghibellina (Pl. 4). The beautiful private *Villa il Bacchino*, Via Bobolino, 126 Torreone (above S. Maria Nuova) takes in guests. *Youth Hostel Ostello per la Gioventù San Marco*, 57 Via Maffei.

Restaurants. Luxury-class: *Il Falconiere*, in the countryside at the bottom of the hill, off the road to Castiglion Fiorentino (località San Martino a Bocena). First-class restaurant: *Il Cacciatore*, 11 Via Roma; *La Loggetta*, Piazza Comunale. Simple trattorie: *La Grotta*, 3 Piazzetta Baldelli; *Dardano*, 19 Via Dardano; *Dell'Amico*, 12 Via Dardano; *Taccone*, 46 Via Dardano; *La Casina dei Tigli*, in the public gardens near San Domenico is open in summer. Outside the centre at Ossaia *La Tufa* (also pizzeria). **Picnic places** on the hillside off Via Santa Margherita.

An **antiques fair** is held in September, and on the third weekend of every month.

History. The origins of Cortona, in an excellent strategic and commercial position dominating the Valdichiana, are uncertain. It was one of the twelve cities of the Etruscan Confederation in the 4C BC when it is thought the first walls were built (some 3km in circumference). By the end of the century it had come under Roman influence. In the 13C and 14C Cortona was a flourishing commune, ruled after 1325 by the Casali family. In the 15C and 16C it was a dominion of the Florentine Republic.

During the 14C and early 15C many Sienese artists were working in the town, including Sassetta. Fra Angelico lived and worked here c 1408–18, but most of his paintings have been destroyed. The most famous painter born in Cortona was Luca Signorelli (1441–1523), the great precursor of Michelangelo, a number of whose paintings survive here. Another outstanding native painter (and architect) was Pietro Berrettini (1596–1669), called Pietro da Cortona. Gino Severini (1883–1966), the painter was also born here.

Half-way up to the town is the church of •**Santa Maria del Calcinaio**, a masterpiece of Renaissance architecture. It is difficult to reach without a car; but there is a request stop outside the church served by buses to Camucia. Otherwise it is a walk of several kilometres (partly on the main road) from Porta Sant'Agostino. It is one of the few works to have survived certainly by Francesco di Giorgio Martini (1485). It is built on a Latin-cross plan with an octagonal cupola. It had been completed only as far as the drum of the cupola at the death of Francesco di Giorgio in 1501. The building was completed under the direction of Pietro di Norbo in 1508–14, almost certainly following the design of Francesco di Giorgio. Set into the hillside, its beautiful form can be fully appreciated as it is approached from above along a short road with a few ancient cypresses. The exterior is being restored. It was built on the site of a tannery (called a *calcinaio* from the use of lime), on the wall of which a miraculous image of the Madonna appeared. The Arte dei Calzolai (guild of shoe-makers) commissioned the church to house the venerated Madonna from Francesco di Giorgio, on the advice of Signorelli.

The beautiful light grey-and-white INTERIOR (open 15–17; summer 16–19; fest. 10–12.30), with clean architectural lines, has a handsome high altar of 1519 by Bernardino Covatti which encloses the devotional image of the Madonna del Calcinaio (14C or 15C). The stained glass in the rose window is by Guglielmo di Marcillat, and the two smaller windows are by his pupils. On the right side, the first and third altars have an Annunciation and

Assumption by the local painter, Tommaso Bernabei, called Papacello (1527 and 1526). The Madonna and Child with saints by Alessandro Allori, in the right transept, has been removed for restoration for years. Left side: third altar, Madonna and saints (including Thomas Becket), a good Florentine Mannerist painting by Jacopo di Giovanni di Sandro, called Jacone; second and first altars, Immaculate Conception, and Epiphany, both attributed to Papacello.

The road continues up towards the centre (car parks signposted): to the right, near the main entrance to the town, is the early-15C church of **San Domenico**. Over the portal is a worn fresco by Fra Angelico. The pleasant INTERIOR has 17C side altars designed by Ascanio Covatti. The detached fresco on the W wall of St Roch is by Bartolomeo della Gatta. On the S side, first altar, wood Crucifix of uncertain date, and, in the chapel to the right of the high altar, *Madonna and saints by Luca Signorelli (1515; removed for restoration). The bright *ancona on the high altar of the Coronation of the Virgin is signed by Lorenzo di Nicolò Gerini (1402). North side, third altar, Palma Giovane, Assumption; second altar, Passignano, Circumcision.

The *Passeggiata* along the hillside behind the church through public gardens has fine views. In Via Santa Margherita is the façade of the lower church of **San Marco**, with a mosaic of St Mark by Gino Severini (1961). The frescoes on the vault of the oratory date from 1665. A staircase leads to the upper church with a 17C high altar sculpted by Andrea Sellari, and an altarpiece (on the right) by Andrea Commodi. Via Santa Margherita continues uphill to the church of the same name (described below).

At the entrance to the town *Piazza Garibaldi* has a superb view of Santa Maria del Calcinaio and Lake Trasimene. In **Via Nazionale**, popularly *Rugapiana*, the main and only level street of the town, are several fine 16C palaces, and *Palazzo Ferretti* (No. 45; now the Pretura) built in 1738 by Marco Tuscher. Via Nazionale ends at **Piazza della Repubblica**, the centre of the town. The 13C *Palazzo Comunale* was enlarged in the 16C and extends to Piazza Signorelli, where the façade has a worn *Marzocco* (the Florentine lion) of 1508. Here is **Palazzo Casali** (or *Palazzo Pretorio*), the handsome 13C mansion of the Casali who became governors of the city. The Renaissance façade was added by Filippo Berrettini in 1613. The 13C flank, on Via Casali, has numerous coats of arms of the governors of the city. It houses the *Museo dell'Accademia Etrusca** (admission 10–13, 16–19; winter 9–13, 15–17; closed Monday). The palace is the seat of the *Accademia Etrusca*, a learned society founded in 1727 for historical and archaeological research. Famous throughout Europe in the 18C, Montesquieu and Voltaire were both early members. The important *library* has c 30,000 vols, and 620 codices.

The MUSEUM is entered from the outside staircase in the courtyard. The splendid MAIN HALL (2) has a fine display of small bronzes. On the platform to the right is an Etruscan *chandelier, a very unusual work probably dating from the late 4C BC. It is decorated on the underside with intricate allegorical carved decorations between the 16 little oil lamps, surrounding a gorgon's head. Also here is an inscription of 2C BC, formerly attached to the chandelier. On the platform to the left are eight fine wooden show cases: in the first, Attic amphora of the mid-6C BC with Hercules and the Nemean lion and two lions in an heraldic pose, and an amphora in grey bucchero of the mid-6C BC. In the first case on the right: statuette of Zeus (6C BC) and a bronze plaque with Etruscan letters, divinities, and figures of Hercules. 2nd case: statuettes of athletes, Kourai, votive figures, animals and warriors. 3rd case: 16–17C bronzes including a statuette of Marsyas (perhaps derived from a

Città di Castello

CORTONA

0 — 200 yards
0 — 200 metres

AREZZO PERUGIA & Rly Station

work by Antonio Pollaiolo), and N Italian ivories of the early 15C. In the double case at the end: Christ crucified (French or German, 12–13C), Paleochristian glass chalice and a globe of 1710 with the constellations. In the cases on the left: 18C and 19C bronzes in imitation of Antique works, alabaster statuette of Hecate (with 3 bodies) of 1C AD; two votive statuettes (with inscriptions on their legs) of 3C–2C BC; and (last case) Italic and Etruscan votive statuettes. In the small case opposite the entrance: the famous *Musa Polimnia* an encaustic painting for long thought to be a Roman work of the 1–2C AD, but now considered an excellent fake of c 1740. Other paintings displayed around the walls include: a tondo by Francesco Signorelli; Luca Signorelli, Adoration of the Shepherds; Pinturicchio, tondo of the Madonna and Child; works by Piazzetta, Pietro da Cortona (including a Madonna and saints from the church of Sant'Agostino), Ciro Ferri, Cristofano Allori (self-portrait with Ludovico Cigoli), Empoli, and Santi di Tito, as well as two 18C self-portraits by Zoffany and James Northcote.

In a room (3), off the right end of the hall, is an interesting and representative Egyptian collection made by Monsignor Corbelli, Papal delegate in Egypt in 1891–96. It includes a rare wood model of a funerary boat (2060–1785 BC), statuettes, mummies, canopic vases, papyri, etc. In the other room (4), off the hall, Niccolò Gerini, four saints; Bicci di Lorenzo, triptych; 12–13C Tuscan mosaic of the Madonna in prayer. The small rooms (5–7) to the right contain furniture, material relating to the military architect Francesco Laparelli (1521–70), born in Cortona, who designed La Valletta in Malta, fans, ivories, miniatures, swords, 18–19C livery, and the portrait of an old lady by Bartolomeo Passarotti. Beyond the hall (8) with a good ceiling and two 18C globes, is a room (9) with an elaborate porcelain *tempietto* presented by Carlo Ginori to the Accademia in 1756, and seals including works by Pisanello and Matteo de' Pasti, and jewellery. R. 10 (left) contains the numismatic collection, including rare Etruscan coins. The ceramics include Ginori, Delft, Deruta, and Gubbio ware. R. 11: Roman and Etruscan bronzes and terracottas and votive statuettes. R. 12 contains Etruscan cinerary urns, Bucchero ware, and Attic vases. A door leads out onto a walkway above the courtyard which leads back into the main hall. The last room, next to the ticket office, has a representative display of works by Gino Severini (1883–1966), born in Cortona.

Via Casali descends to the **Duomo** (closed 12.30 or 13–15 or 15.30) on the site of an earlier church. It was rebuilt in the 16C probably by a local architect, a follower of Giuliano da Sangallo (but was later much modified). Remains of the Romanesque church can be seen in the façade (including a large capital with human heads). The campanile (1566) is by Francesco Laparelli. There is a fine view of the countryside from the terrace here. The entrance is on the S side beneath a pretty 16C portico through a delightful *doorway by Cristofanello (1550).

The striking INTERIOR, with a barrel vault, has capitals similar to those in San Lorenzo in Florence. On the W wall is the impressive neo-classical funerary monument of Giovanni Battista Tommasi, by Romualdo Galli (1806). SOUTH AISLE. Second altar, Raffaello Vanni, Transfiguration; fourth altar, Lorenzo Berrettini, St Joseph. In the chapel to the right of the sanctuary, 13C terracotta Pietà (removed for restoration). The HIGH ALTAR, with four carved angels, is a fine work by the local sculptor Francesco Mazzuoli (1664). In the CHOIR (light) are some good paintings (right to left): Cigoli, Madonna of the Rosary; Andrea Commodi, Consecration of the church of San Salvatore; 16C Florentine school, Descent of the Holy Spirit; Luca Signorelli (attributed), Crucifixion; Francesco Signorelli, Incredulity of St Thomas; Alessandro Allori (attributed), Madonna of the Holy Girdle; Giovanni Morandi, Madonna and saints; Andrea del Sarto (or his school), Assumption. At the end of the N aisle, carved ciborium dated 1491 attributed to Cuccio di Nuccio or Urbano da Cortona. NORTH AISLE. On the wall: fifth altar, Lorenzo Berrettini, Madonna and saints; fourth altar, Andrea Sellari, wood Crucifix; third altar, Pietro da Cortona, Adoration of the Shepherds; second altar, Lorenzo Baldi, St Sebastian; first altar, 15C terracotta statue of the Madonna and Child (heavily decorated and repainted). On the W wall, fine funerary monument of Giovanni Alberti attributed to Santi di Tito.

Opposite the façade of the cathedral is the *Museo Diocesano (admission 9–13, 15–18.30; winter 9–13, 15–17; closed Monday), which incorporates the former church of the Gesù, and contains some beautiful paintings. The room (2) to the right of the entrance has a Roman sarcophagus (end of the 2C) with the battle of the amazons and centaurs, admired by Donatello and Brunelleschi. Fresco fragments here include the Way to Calvary by Pietro Lorenzetti. The former CHURCH OF THE GESÙ (3) has a fine wooden ceiling by Michelangelo Leggi (1536). Here are displayed: Sassetta, Madonna and Child with four saints; Pietro Lorenzetti, large painted *Crucifix; Fra Angelico, *Madonna enthroned with saints, with a fine predella, *Annunciation (1428–30), one of his most beautiful works; baptismal font by Ciuccio di Nuccio; Bartolomeo della Gatta, *Assumption of the Virgin. In the room

(4) behind the font, Maestro della Madonna di Lucignano (school of Duccio), *Madonna and Child; Pietro Lorenzetti, Madonna enthroned with four angels, signed and dated 1320; Giusto da Firenze, Vagnucci reliquary, signed and dated 1458; 13C Aretine master, St Margaret and stories from her life (very damaged); and the Passerini church vestments of 1515, including a cope made for Leo X's visit to the town, embroidered on designs by Andrea del Sarto and Raffaellino del Garbo. A case of church silver includes a chalice by Michele di Tommaso da Siena (late 14C). In R. 5 (at the end of R. 1): Luca Signorelli, *Deposition, with a fine predella; *Communion of the Apostles, signed and dated 1512; and four works by his bottega. R. 6: bottega of Signorelli, Assumption. At the bottom of the stairs leading to the LOWER CHURCH, Pietro Lorenzetti, painted Crucifix. The vault of the lower church was painted by Giorgio Vasari, and (lunettes) Cristoforo Gherardi (Il Doceno). The plain stalls are by Vincenzo da Cortona (1517), and the terracotta Deposition group is a 15C Florentine work.

From Piazza Signorelli, beyond the *Teatro Signorelli* (1854), the pretty old VIA DARDANO leads uphill before descending to the simple *Porta Colonia* (which preserves its wooden doors). Here are the most considerable relics of the ETRUSCAN WALLS, the huge blocks conspicuous below Roman and medieval masonry above. The walls stretch away up the hill towards the Fortezza Medicea, above the church of Santa Margherita, the top of which can just be seen in the woods (both described below). Outside the gate (reached by a pretty road), in beautiful countryside on the hillside below the town, the fine centrally-planned church of **Santa Maria Nuova** is well seen. It is known that both Cristofanello (in 1550–54) and Vasari were involved in the construction of the church, which was not finished until 1600 when the cupola was built. It contains altarpieces by Alessandro Allori and Empoli, and a 16C organ by Onofrio Zefferini. From the gate Via delle Mura del Duomo, a charming little lane with acacia trees, leads back along the top of the walls to the Duomo.

From Piazza della Repubblica three narrow old roads descend to gates in the walls. VIA ROMA passes beneath an archway of Palazzo Comunale and ends at the medieval Porta Santa Maria. On the left is the entrance to the church of *San Filippo* with a cupola, a fine work by Antonio Iannelli (1720). It contains altarpieces by Camillo Sagrestani (high altar) and Giovanni Battista Piazzetta (second altar on the left). Beside the church is the little *Porta del Morto* of *Palazzo Cinaglia* (No. 25), with a worn carved architrave. Many old houses in Cortona have a second small doorway usually raised above the level of the street (and now often used as a window). This was known as the *Porta del Morto* as it was popularly supposed that it was used only to carry out the coffin when an inhabitant of the house died. Instead it is now thought to have been used as the usual door of the house (which could easily be defended in times of trouble when the larger doorways were barred). On the right (No. 26) is the fine medieval *Palazzo Quintani*. Just before the gate is the pretty Via Jannelli (right) with medieval houses and wooden *sporti*.

VIA GUELFA leads S from Piazza della Repubblica steeply down to Porta Sant'Agostino. At the beginning on the right is **Palazzo Mancini-Sernini** (No. 4) with an unusual tall *facade incorporating a loggia on the top storey. It was designed by Cristofanello for the Laparelli in 1533. Lower down is the church and convent of *Sant'Agostino* with a Gothic exterior and a 17C interior (side altars by Filippo Berrettini, 1613). It contains an altarpiece by Empoli. Behind the church (reached by Via del Marzocco) is the unusual exterior of the church of *San Benedetto* (closed) built in 1722 on an elliptical plan. It contains an interesting wood statue of Christ at the Column. Nearby is a medieval house with wooden *sporti* and a 13C public fountain. Outside Porta Sant'Agostino is the church of the *Spirito Santo* (closed) built in 1637 by Filippo Berrettini with a cupola of 1751. It contains an 18C Madonna and Child with saints by Giuseppe Angeli, and a wood statue of the Dead Christ by Fabbrucci (1687–1767).

Via Ghibellina leads down from Piazza della Repubblica to the walls where the Etruscan Porta Ghibellina has been partially excavated. There is a pleasant walk from here back to Porta Sant'Agostino along the top of the walls.

The stepped Via Santucci mounts through the *Palazzo del Popolo* in Piazza della Repubblica to the church of **San Francesco**, the first church to be built outside of Assisi by the Franciscans after the death of St Francis. The architect was Brother Elias, friend and disciple of St Francis, who died in the convent of the church in 1253. It preserves a worn Gothic portal.

In the altered INTERIOR (being restored; entrance through the courtyard), with 17C side altars, there are attractive pews. On the W wall are interesting remains of frescoes. South side, first altar, Niccolò Monti, St Francis before the Sultan (1842); second altar, Orazio Fidani, Meeting at Porta Aurea; fourth altar, Cigoli, Miracle of St Anthony of Padua. In the chapel to the right of the main altar, Gothic tomb of Ranieri Ubertini by Angelo and Francesco di Pietro (1360). On the left wall of the chapel, Madonna and saints by Ciro Ferri. The 17C marble tabernacle by Bernardino Radi on the HIGH ALTAR, encloses a precious Byzantine ivory reliquary of the Holy Cross. Behind the altar is buried Brother Elias. It is thought that Luca Signorelli was buried in the crypt below. NORTH SIDE, third altar, *Annunciation, the last work (left unfinished) by Pietro da Cortona; second altar, Camillo Sagrestani, Martyrdom of St Lucy; first altar, Raffaello Vanni, Nativity (in very poor condition). On the wall, 15C fresco fragment.

Beneath the steps of the church is a 13C public fountain. Opposite the high wall of the church and convent in Via Maffei is the pretty Renaissance portico of the *Ospedale di Santa Maria della Misericordia*. Via Berrettini, a very steep road, leads up from San Francesco through a delightful quiet residential part of the town, with bright gardens and plants around the well-kept houses. Beyond a large circular water cistern is the *birthplace of Pietro da Cortona* (No. 33; plaque). The road follows the high convent wall of *Santa Chiara*. The convent and church were built in 1555 by Vasari. In underground rooms are remains of a huge Roman cistern, and the church contains an Immaculate Conception by Andrea Commodi, and a Deposition attributed as an early work to Pietro da Cortona. The small triangular Piazza della Pescaia is beautifully planted with ilex trees. The road continues to ascend (keep left) towards the charming little Romanesque bellcote of *San Cristoforo* (entered to the left). It contains damaged detached frescoes by the 13C Umbrian school. Beside a large square water cistern a road (right) descends shortly to **San Niccolò**, a 15C church approached through a peaceful walled garden with cypresses. The wooden porch with Ionic capitals was added in 1930. The church is opened by the custodian who lives here (ring at the door on the left). Over the altar is a standard painted on both sides by Luca Signorelli with a *Deposition (in excellent condition) and a Madonna and Child (shown by the custodian). On the N wall is a votive fresco of the Madonna and saints by Signorelli or his school.

Via Santo Stefano continues uphill; on the left Via Porta Montanina leads to the edge of the hillside planted with pine trees beside the charming *Porta*

Montanina, decorated with four arches, with its doors still intact. Remains of the Etruscan walls, and of a second fortified gate can be seen here. A fine stretch of walls leads steeply down the hillside beside orchards, and uphill to the Fortezza Medicea. Outside the gate there is a view of Santa Maria Nuova and the pretty countryside below the town.

From Via Santo Stefano, Via Santa Croce (signposted for Santa Margherita), a stepped lane with gardens on either side, continues uphill. It traverses cypress woods before reaching the sanctuary of SANTA MARGHERITA, rebuilt in 1856–97 in the Romanesque-Gothic style, and preserving a single rose window of its predecessor. The *sarcophagus of St Margaret of Laviano (1247–97) is probably by the native artists Angiolo and Francesco di Pietro (1362; also attributed to Giovanni Pisano). Below the church, Via Santa Margherita descends to the public gardens (see above), past a Via Crucis in mosaic by Gino Severini. A road continues up to the **Fortezza Medicea** or *Girfalco* in a splendid position dominating the town (651m). There is a magnificent view of Lake Trasimene, and part of the outer circle of walls built by the Etruscans can be seen from here. The castle was built by order of Cosimo I in 1556, and was once thought to be the work of Francesco Laparelli, but is now considered to be by his friend Gabrio Serbelloni. At present the interior is open only for exhibitions in July–September (10–13, 15–19). Outside is a stone bench carved by Joe Tilson in 1990.

The environs of Cortona

On the plain at the foot of the hill are a number of interesting Etruscan tombs. From the road junction, known as the Cinque Vie, near Santa Maria del Calcinaio (see above), a road (signposted for Sodo) leads to the *Tanella di Pitagora* (ring for the custodian), a vaulted circular Etruscan tomb, probably formerly covered by a tumulus. Restored in the 19C, it is now surrounded by cypresses. Despite its name, it has nothing to do with Pythagoras (who lived at Crotone in southern Italy). It had been discovered by the 16C when Vasari visited it, calling it the tomb of Archimedes. Formerly thought to date from the 4C BC, it may have been built in the 3C or even the 2C BC. Nearby, in Località Piaggette, is the *Tanella Angori*, similar in form, but less well preserved, discovered in 1949.

Near the railway station (entrance on Via Lauretana) is the *Melone di Camucia*, an Etruscan tumulus tomb excavated in 1842 by Alessandro François. It has a perimeter of 200 metres, and was in use from the 7C BC to the 4C BC. Finds from the two burial chambers are in the Archaeological Museum in Florence.

In the locality of Sodo, at the foot of the hill, off the road to Castiglion Fiorentino, are two more tumulus tombs. They are on either side of the road to Foiano. The *Primo Melone del Sodo* (ring for the custodian) was discovered in 1909 and is marked by a pine tree on top of the mound. It has a circumference of 185m, and was in use from the early 6C BC to the 3C BC. Inside is an inscription dating from the 4C BC. On the left of the Foiano road is the *Secondo Melone del Sodo* discovered in 1927. Excavations have been in progress here since 1990 beside the tumulus, which has proved to be one of the largest ever discovered in Etruria. A monumental stairway has been uncovered, on either side of which are two large carved sphynxes with warriors.

Outside Porta Colonia (see above) the Città di Castello road climbs NE. After c 1.5km a by-road (left) leads shortly to the picturesque *Convento delle Celle*, in a beautiful position on the lower slopes of Monte Egidio. The pretty stone buildings, immaculately kept, are grouped beside a river torrent. A hermitage on this site was probably occupied by the Franciscans c 1214–17, who were visited by St Francis in 1226. The convent has been occupied by the Cappuccini since 1537. The hillside has had to be shored up above the convent to prevent landslides. Visitors can see various chapels including the cell of St Francis. The road continues up through *Torreone*, at the watershed between the Valdichiana and Val Tiberina. From here a road leads to Santa Margherita (described above). The road continues up to *Castel Gilardi* (trattoria; a cool place to eat in summer). From here a rough road leads N along the wooded slopes of *Monte Egidio* (1056m) where Villa del Seminario is on the site of the Hermitage of St Egidio. There are particularly beautiful views from this road (of Cortona) and from the Città di Castello road (of Lake Trasimene). From Castel Gilardi a road (29km) leads over the Umbrian border to descend into the Tiber valley, joining the road from Umbertide to Città di Castello, see *Blue Guide Umbria*.

Below the Public Gardens (see above) Via delle Contesse and Via del Palazzone (left) lead to *Villa Passerini*, known as *Il Palazzone*, built for Cardinal Silvio Passerini by Giovanni Battista Caporali (1521), and now used in the summer by the Scuola Normale di Pisa. The salone has frescoes by Papacello and a chapel is frescoed by Signorelli and his pupils. Nearby, at *Metelliano*, is the 11C church of *Sant'Angelo*.

A road leads SW from Cortona towards Mercatale via the *Rocca di Pierle* (16km) an impressive large square castle dating from before 1098, surrounded by a little hamlet. Mercatale is in Umbria (see *Blue Guide Umbria*).

A road leads across the plain from Camucia to the ABBAZIA DI FARNETA (15km), probably founded in the 8C. The interesting Romanesque building has a beautiful 10C triple apse and *crypt, restored since 1940. In the priest's house (admission on request) is a local paleontological collection.

FROM CORTONA TO AREZZO, 33km, N71. A pretty by-road descends from Porta Colonia through beautiful countryside, with retrospective views of Cortona and its monuments strung out along the skyline of the long sloping hillside. At the foot of the hill it joins N71. 9km A narrow road (signposted on the right) winds through charming countryside up a hill to the castle of *Montecchio Vesponi, which was for long contested for its strategic position, given to the condottiere Sir John Hawkwood (c 1320–94) by grateful Florentines c 1381. Born at Sible Hedingham in Essex, Hawkwood came to Italy as a mercenary in 1362, married the daughter of Bernabò Visconti, and captained the Florentine army from 1377. The splendid 13C walls (the crenellations were added in the 19C) enclosed a village up to the end of the 17C, but now only a tower and 16C house remain. It is shown usually 11–13 on Monday (in winter and other times, by appointment, Tel. 0575/651272). (3-star hotel *Villa Schiatti*, 131 Via Montecchio).

The main road continues (good view back of the castle) to (12km) **Castiglion Fiorentino**, a walled agricultural market town on a hill dominated by the oddly-shaped Torre del Cassero. From the Porta Fiorentina the Corso leads up past the church of *San Francesco*, in a piazza to the left. It has been in restoration for many years (the entrance is at present through the cloister) and the paintings have nearly all been removed to the museum (see below). In *Piazza Municipio* there is a pretty 16C loggia with some arcades open to provide a view of the valley (the Collegiata is conspicuous on the side of the hill). Opposite is Palazzo Comunale. On the hillside above, built into the rock, is the ancient *Cassero*, with the church of Sant'Angelo, founded in the 11C, restored to house the PINACOTECA COMUNALE, instituted at the beginning of this century and reopened here in 1991 (admission 10–12.30, 15–17 except Monday). In this delightful little museum, the works of art are well labelled. Visitors first enter the church of *Sant'Angelo*, with a high altar by Filippo Berrettini. Here is displayed a painted Cross by the late-13C Umbrian school (from the church of San Francesco). On the left wall is a painting of the Madonna and Child with Pope St Silvester and St Anthony (also from San Francesco), by Vasari. In the *Sacristy* are exhibited two *Crosses in gilded copper, one dating from the end of the 12C or beginning of the 13C showing northern European influence, and the other an exquisite work of 13C French manufacture. The silver gilt reliquary *bust of Sant'Orsola dates from the 14C and is attributed to a French master. Stairs lead up to the Pinacoteca in the *Coro delle Monache*. In the first part of the room: painted *Cross by an Aretine master of the 13C; bottega of Margarito di Arezzo, St Francis; Taddeo Gaddi, Madonna and Child (fragment); Pseudo Pier Francesco Fiorentino, Adoration of the Child; Bartolomeo della Gatta, St Michael Archangel, and *St Francis receiving the stigmata; Giovanni di Paolo, St Catherine of Alexandria, and Madonna and Child. Also here is a case of church silver. In the second part of the room: Iacopo del Sellaio, Pool of Bethesda; Gian Domenico Ferretti, St Teresa (1723); Antonio di Donnino del Mazziere, Adoration of the Shepherds (1538); Papacello, *Madonna and Child with St Anne. Another flight of stairs leads up to the *Saletta della Torre*, decorated with 13–16C coats of arms, with a fine view.

On the top of the hill is the *Torre del Cassero*. From Piazza Municipio, Via San Michele continues downhill to Piazza Verdi, and by a pretty little Mannerist doorway, Vicolo dei Signori leads steeply down to a piazza with three churches, with a good view of the countryside. The neo-classical *Collegiata* contains a Della Robbian terracotta of St Anthony Abbot (first S altar); Bartolomeo della Gatta, Madonna enthroned with saints (recently harshly restored; third S altar); (altar in the S transept), Annunciation, another Della Robbian relief; (chapel to the right of the main altar), Lorenzo di Credi, Adoration of the Child. In the N transept is a large *Maestà signed by Segna di Bonaventura. The *Pieve* (deconsecrated), next to the church (half of which was demolished) is entered from the right side of the Collegiata (unlocked on request). Near the 15C font is a Deposition by the school of Signorelli and a Della Robbian Baptism of Christ. Behind the Pieve is the *Gesù* with a portico. Via San Giuliano leads downhill to the Porta Romana, outside which is the octagonal *Madonna della Consolazione*. Nearby is the ex-church of *San Lazzaro*, now a small museum of frescoes (Crucifixion by the school of Giotto).

The road continues, skirting the Valdichiana, with low hills on the right, some of them planted with olives and vines, into (33km) **Arezzo**, see Rte 26.

28

Arezzo to Sansepolcro

Road, N73, 45km.—28km *Le Ville*. Turning for **Monterchi** (4km)—35km *San Leo*—37km **Anghiari**—45km **Sansepolcro**.
An alternative, shorter route (35km) runs N from Arezzo and then E across the Valico di Scheggia to Anghiari. This is a slower road, but it also traverses beautiful countryside. It has the disadvantage of not passing close to Monterchi.

Bus Services run by SITA from Arezzo follow the main road to Anghiari, Le Ville, Monterchi, and Sansepolcro.

Information Office. APT Arezzo, 22 Piazza della Repubblica (Tel. 0575/377678).

N73 leaves Arezzo to the S (well signposted for Città di Castello and Sansepolcro). It leads through pretty, wooded countryside, with remarkably few houses, and vineyards on the hills. At (10km) the *Foce di Scopetone* (526m) a by-road comes in on the left from Arezzo. 14km *Palazzo del Pero* (405m). Here a secondary road leads S through a beautiful wooded valley to Castiglion Fiorentino (14km; see Rte 27). The road now becomes windier, although it is well engineered, as it follows the valley of the Cerfone. 23km *Pieve a Ranco* (blue signpost on the right). Approached over a very narrow bridge, the church of *Santi Lorentino e Pergentino* (if closed, ring at the priest's house beside the E end of the church) was damaged by earthquake in 1916. It contains a beautiful polychrome wood 14C seated statue of the Madonna and Child at the E end. 28km *Le Ville*. Here the Città di Castello road (N221) forks right for Monterchi (4km), well seen on a hill ahead.

Monterchi is a quiet little fortified village, damaged by earthquakes in the past, the birthplace of the mother of Piero della Francesca. Here, since its restoration in 1993, has been kept the famous *MADONNA DEL PARTO by Piero in an old school building in Via della Reglia (open 9–13, 14–18 or 19 except Monday). It was formerly in the church of Momentana, partially demolished in 1785, and was then included in a chapel in the cemetery at the foot of the hill, just outside the village. It was detached in 1910, and in 1956–69 the chapel was transformed to isolate it from the cemetery. It has not been decided whether the fresco should be returned to the little chapel. It was painted c 1460 and shows the pregnant Madonna revealed by two angels pulling back the curtains of a pavilion. It is thought that Piero's mother was buried in the cemetery and this work was intended as a memorial to her.

At the top of the hill, near a piazza with lime trees, is the *Pieve di San Simone*, rebuilt in 1966. Its works of art are in poor condition. South Side, first chapel, 16C detached fresco of the Madonna of the Misericordia; second chapel, 14C fresco fragment of the Madonna and Child, found beneath the Madonna del Parto (see below), and a little polychrome terracotta ciborium (damaged but preserving its original painted wood door). Between the second and third chapels are three interesting 15C bas reliefs of the Pietà. On the 3rd N altar, 15C wood Crucifix. Behind the church is a lovely old medieval passageway.

At the foot of the hill, the main road to Città di Castello passes the cemetery and the avenue which leads (left) to the chapel which formerly contained the Madonna del Parto. A by-road continues from the chapel over the hill to (2km) the interesting little town of Citerna in Umbria, described in *Blue Guide Umbria*. N221 continues across the Umbrian border to Città di Castello (17km; see *Blue Guide Umbria)*.

The main road (N 73; see above) continues N towards Sansepolcro. Two by-roads diverge left for Anghiari: at (35km) San Leo, the second turning, can be seen the unusual campanile of *Santa Maria a Corsano*, dating from around 1000, next to an abandoned farm house. The direct road for Sansepolcro (6km) continues from this crossroads, but the more interesting route via Anghiari, well seen on top of its hill, diverges left.

37km **ANGHIARI** (6000 inhab.), once *Castrum Angulare* in a spectacular position (430m) above a plain, has a well-preserved old centre, typical of a medieval walled town. It was the scene in 1440 of a victory of the Florentines led by Francesco Sforza over the Visconti of Milan (the subject of a fresco commissioned from Leonardo da Vinci for Palazzo Vecchio in Florence, the completed fragment of which has been lost), and in 1796 of a French defeat of the Austrians.

Information Office Pro Loco, Piazza Baldaccio (next to the post office). **Buses** (CAT) from Sansepolcro and Arezzo.

Car Park off Via Matteotti below Piazza Baldaccio, with a pretty walk (signposted; keep left) up to an old gate in the walls, which provides an entrance to the medieval town, near Palazzo Pubblico.

Hotels. 3-star: *Oliver*, 16 Via della Battaglia and *La Meridiana*, 8 Piazza IV Novembre. **Restaurants** (first-class) *La Nena*, 12 Via Gramsci; trattoria *Da Alighiero*, 8 Via Garibaldi. In the environs: *Castello di Sorci* at Sorci, and *Antico Posto di Ristoro*, 10km W at Scheggia (a cool place in summer).

Local artisans are particularly skilled cabinet makers, and there is an institute here for the restoration of antique furniture.

In **Piazza Baldaccio**, the old market-place, with a statue of Garibaldi, is a monumental arcade, the *Galleria Magi* (1889), an unexpected sight. Beyond it, in Piazza IV Novembre, is the neo-classical *Teatro dei Ricomposti*, with a façade (recently restored) crowned by statues. Nearby is an Art Nouveau villa. On the other side of Piazza Baldaccio is the unspoilt walled medieval town. From the piazza, the higher road (right) leads to the scenographic Via Trieste, which ascends steeply to **Santa Maria delle Grazie** (the Propositura) at the top. It has an 18C neo-classical interior with a barrel vault. In the N transept are two charming paintings in their original frames by Sogliani: *Last Supper, and Christ washing the disciples' feet. The high altar and tabernacle are Della Robbian. On the right of the high altar is a Madonna and Child with four saints and two angels by Matteo di Giovanni (recently restored; from the church of Sant'Agostino), and a painted wood high relief of the seated *Madonna, with the standing Child by Tino da Camaino (c 1316; also recently restored). This is the only wood sculpture known by Tino di Camaino. In the right transept is a Deposition by Domenico Puligo. Beside the church can be seen the walls and a clock tower.

The lower road out of Piazza Baldaccio leads shortly to Piazza Mameli which has a number of old houses including the fine Renaissance **Palazzo Taglieschi** (open every day 9–19), which contains the **Museo dell'alta Valle del Tevere**, a good local museum, well maintained and carefully labelled. In the basement are architectural fragments, and in the entrance hall an enamelled terracotta lunette by Benedetto and Santi Buglioni. On the upper floor: Andrea Della Robbia, Nativity and saints (from the church of the Badia); a 16C organ from Santo Stefano; Giovanni di Turino, seated statue of St Anthony Abbot; and (in a separate room) *Madonna in polychrome wood, well preserved and one of the best works of Jacopo della Quercia (c 1420), purchased by the State in 1977. The Child, formerly on the Madonna's knee, has been exhibited separately since its restoration. It is not known if it was sculpted at the same time, nor whether it was intended as part of this group. The 17C paintings include works by Matteo Rosselli. The collection also includes dolls, statuettes, ecclesiastical objects, copes, furniture, household objects, etc.

The church of *Sant'Agostino*, also in the piazza, has been closed for many years during excavation work on an earlier church below the foundations. St Thomas Becket is supposed to have stayed here. Beside it a tunnel (signposted) leads down to Porta Sant'Angelo and the walls. A road continues up left from the piazza to a fork. Uphill to the right (beneath an archway) is *Palazzo Pubblico*, with coats of arms on its façade, while to the left a street leads to the inconspicuous church of the *Badia*, with an unusual asymmetrical interior, which contains (left) a carved dossal attributed to Desiderio da Settignano. Around the high altar are four 18C statues. In the little piazza here is the former headquarters (with an interesting old window) of the *Misericordia*, now a delightful little museum (for admission, ring at No. 13 Via Nenci) illustrating the history of this charitable institution, still very active all over Tuscany. In the hall, dating from the early 16C, are displayed a carriage (1861) and a litter (1909), surgical instruments, costumes worn by members of the brotherhood, etc. In a room with traces of 15C frescoes, are the archives.

Via Matteotti leads straight downhill from the 16C church of Santa Croce, preceded by a portico, through Piazza Baldaccio, and, near the bottom, right past the church of SANTO STEFANO (ring at No. 13), with its little bellcote. This is a remarkable church on a Byzantine Greek-cross plan, thought to date from the 7–8C, partly enclosed in a later building. It is one of the earliest buildings to have survived in the upper Tiber valley.

From Anghiari a pretty secondary road for Arezzo (20km) winds around the hill with wonderful views of Anghiari to the left. It follows an undulating ridge of hills planted with trees and passes a turn (yellow signpost) left for *Pieve a Sovara*, reached in less than 1km along an unsurfaced road, isolated beside a group of farm buildings. The church, with a prominent campanile, was founded in the 9C but mostly rebuilt in 1480. It contains a 15C font. The Arezzo road continues to Tavernelle where a castellated villa, with a tall central tower, called *La Barbolana* is conspicuous on a hill to the right. The valley now narrows and the road climbs gently uphill past thick woods (and few houses) to a summit level of 575m at Scheggia (restaurant, see above). It then descends past cypresses, pines, and chestnuts to join N71 which continues due S into Arezzo.

3km N of Anghiari is the church of *Santa Maria a Micciano*, of ancient foundation. It contains a 15C altarpiece of the Madonna and two saints.

From Anghiari a remarkably long and straight road descends to cross the plain, site of the famous battle of Anghiari (see above) for (45km) **SANSEPOLCRO** (properly *Borgo San Sepolcro*), an attractive little town (15,500 inhab.) in a plain (335m) in the upper Tiber valley, where tobacco is grown. Most of its buildings date from the 15C, and it is famous as the birthplace of Piero della Francesca (1416–92).

Tourist Office, 5 Via della Fonte (Tel. 0575/740536). *Comunità Montana Valtiberina Toscana*, 32 Via San Giuseppe.

Railway. *Ferrovia Centrale Umbra* from Perugia (see *Blue Guide Umbria*) via Città di Castello to Sansepolcro.

Buses SITA from Porta Fiorentina, and *Baschetti* from Viale Vittorio Veneto for Arezzo, Anghiari, Città di Castello, Pieve Santo Stefano, Rimini, Caprese Michelangelo, and Badia Tedalda.

Car Parking outside Porta Fiorentina or Porta del Castello.

Hotels. 3-star *Fiorentino*, 60 Via Luca Pacioli; 2-star: *Da Ventura*, 30 Via Niccolò Aggiunti. Outside the centre: 3-star *Oroscopo*, 66 Piazza Togliatti, località Pieve Vecchia.

Restaurants. Luxury-class: *Oroscopo*, 66 Via Togliatti; first-class: *Da Ventura*, 30 Via Niccolò Agguinti; *Fiorentino*, 60 Via Luca Pacioli; pizzeria *Da Antonio*, Via XX Settembre.

History. According to an ancient tradition Sansepolcro is named in honour of relics brought back from the Holy Sepulchre in Jerusalem by two pilgrims named Arcano and Egidio who settled here on their return. In 1012 an abbey was built here which was granted privileges by popes and emperors and held sway over the town, which became seat of a bishopric in 1520. The town was contested between Perugia, Milan, Città di Castello, Rimini, and the Pontifical States, until it came under Florentine dominion in 1441. It was severely damaged by earthquake in 1351–52, and was again damaged in the Second World War. Here in 1827 the Buitoni family began their pasta business. The painters Matteo di Giovanni (c 1430–95), Raffaellino del Colle (1490–1566) and Santi di Tito (1538–1603) were born here.

Annual Festivals. The *Palio della Balestra* is held on the second Sunday in September, with a crossbow contest in medieval costume against Gubbio. The town is famous for the skill of its flag-throwers, the 'Sbandieratori'. A large fair, the *Mezza Quaresima* is held after the fourth Sunday in Lent, and on 16 August, the *Festa Popolare di San Rocco*, there are various festivities.

The centre of the city is *Piazza Torre di Berta*, named after a tower, destroyed in 1944, through which runs the main street of the town, Via XX Settembre (usually called the *Corso*). Palazzo Pichi-Sermolli has a fine 16C façade with handsome windows and a central balcony. On the corner of the Corso is another palace with two balconies. The wide Via Matteotti leads out of the piazza past the **Duomo** which has an imposing Romanesque INTERIOR (13–14C) with Gothic elements (restored). On the W wall are two high reliefs of St Benedict and Romuald by the Della Robbian school. SOUTH WALL. Fine fresco of the Madonna with Saints Catherine of Alexandria and Thomas Becket by the Riminese school (1383); first altar: Santi di Tito, incredulity of St Thomas (1575); fresco of the Crucifixion by Bartolomeo della Gatta; second altar: Durante Alberti, Nativity. At the end of the aisle is a delightful Baroque altar, lit from above by a little oval dome decorated with cherubs. In the SANCTUARY, Niccolò di Segna (attributed), polyptych with the Resurrection of Christ, which influenced Piero della Francesca (see below). The organ was built by Tamburini. In the chapel to the left of the high altar, *Volto Santo, a huge wood Crucifix, probably dating from the 10C or earlier (restored in 1989). NORTH SIDE. On the right of the sacristy door, polychrome statue of the Madonna and Child (14C or 15C), and on the left of the door, Della Robbian tabernacle. Second altar, Palma Giovane, Assumption (signed and dated 1602); Perugino (attributed, or Gerino da Pistoia on a cartoon by Perugino), Ascension. Beyond the wall monument to Simone Graziani (1509), Raffaellino del Colle, Resurrection; first altar: Romano Alberti (16C), Crucifixion.

On the right of the façade, at No. 3, is a covered way which leads past part of the cloister with fine capitals towards Via Piero della Francesca. On the wall is a Roman cippus. On the right is the *Cappella del Monacato* or *di San Leonardo*, of ancient foundation. It contains a 17C altar and a fresco attributed to Cherubino Alberti around a 15C sculpted Crucifix. It is thought that Piero della Francesca is buried here. Opposite the Duomo is Palazzo Gherardi with two 12C towers. Next to the Duomo is Palazzo delle Laudi (1592–1609) by Alberto Alberti and Antonio Cantagallina, with a monumental portico. It is now the town hall. Opposite is the 16C Palazzo Aggiunti. In Piazza Garibaldi is *Palazzo Pretorio*, decorated with Della Robbian coats of arms. First built in the 14C it was restored in 1843. The Gothic hall on the ground floor with a 16C fresco is used for exhibitions. The fine Gothic windows at the W end are best seen from the museum (see below). The Arco della Pesa connects Palazzo Pretorio with the ex-Palazzo Comunale, which has an outside stair. It is now the seat of the **Museo Civico** (entered around the corner at No. 65 Via Aggiunti), famous for its masterpieces by Piero della Francesca. Admission every day 9.30–13, 14.30–18; summer 9–13.30, 14.30–19.30; closed 1 Jan, 15 Aug, Christmas Day, and Easter Sunday afternoon.

R. 1: church vestments and ecclesiastical objects belonging to Bishop Costaguti (18C). On the end wall, Last Supper by Antonio and Remigio Cantagallina (1604). **R. 2**: the crown and vestments (mid-14C) used to adorn the Volto Santo in the cathedral (see above). **R. 3**: triptych by Matteo di Giovanni (removed from the Duomo); the central panel, with the Baptism of Christ, by Piero della Francesca, is now in the National Gallery of London. **R. 4**: tabernacle in terracotta of the Nativity, by the school of Giovanni Della Robbia; Luca Signorelli, *standard painted on both sides (Crucifixion and saints); Gerino da Pistoia, Saints Peter and Paul. **R. 5** contains the masterpieces of the gallery by Piero della Francesca. The *RESURRECTION was brought to the attention of a new generation of art historians after it had been described by Aldous Huxley in 1925 as the 'best picture in the world' in his *Notes and Essays of a Tourist* (*Along the Road*). Justly one of his most famous works, it was frescoed in another room of the palace in 1463, and moved here in 1480. The *polyptych of the Madonna of the Misericordia was commissioned from Piero by the local confraternity of the Misericordia (1445–62). Also here are two frescoes: fragment of the bust of a *saint (St Julian?), found in the former church of Santa Chiara, and St Louis of Toulouse (recently attributed to a follower of Piero known as Lorentino). **R. 6**: Raffaellino del Colle, Assumption (in a beautiful frame), St Leo, and Annunciation; Pontormo, Martyrdom of St Quinten. **R. 7**: Giovanni de' Vecchi, Presentation of the Virgin in the Temple, and Birth of the Virgin; Santi di Tito, St Nicholas of Tolentino, Pope St Clement among the faithful, and Pietà. **R. 8**: Agostino Ciampelli, Destruction of the idols; Leandro Bassano, Adoration of the Magi. Stairs mount to rooms with 14C (detached) frescoes, and a view of the two Gothic windows of Palazzo Pretorio (see above), and another flight of stairs leads up to a local archaeological collection with prehistoric material found locally, displayed in three rooms.

In the tree-planted Piazza San Francesco are two churches. **San Francesco** was founded in 1285, but transformed in 1752. INTERIOR. SOUTH SIDE, second altar, Giovanni de' Vecchi, St Francis receiving the stigmata (1614), and, to the right, a profile in marble of Cristoforo Gherardi, the native painter (c 1556). The altar table (1304) in sandstone has reliefs and is surrounded by little Gothic arches. NORTH SIDE. Second altar, Francesco Curradi (attributed), Eternal Father and saints; first altar, Passignano, Christ among the Doctors in the Temple (in very poor condition). In the adjoining cloister are lunette frescoes (1681–83) of the Life of St Anthony (also in very poor condition).

Fresco fragment of the bust of a saint by Piero della Francesca, Museo Civico, Sansepolcro

On the other side of the piazza is the church of **Santa Maria delle Grazie**, with a pretty double loggia (1518). The interior has fine carved altars. The high altar has a delightful decorated niche around the Madonna in Prayer by Raffaellino del Colle, flanked by two marble angels. The carved wood ceiling is by Alberto Alberti. On the S altar is a wood Crucifix and on the N altar a painting of saints by Francesco Gambacciani. The organ dates from the 17C. An interesting (but damaged) detached fresco of St Lucy with two saints also belongs to the church. Beneath the loggia beside the church is a pretty *oratory* (now used for exhibitions) with a vault and 15 frescoed lunettes attributed to Giovanni Alberti and Raffaello Schiaminossi. The Assumption in the centre of the ceiling is by Federico Zoi.

In Via Niccolò Aggiunti are a number of interesting palaces: at No. 47 is a very unusual brick building (17C), and at No. 57 a 16C palace with graffiti decoration. On the opposite side is a 15C palace (No. 84). At No. 71 is the *Casa di Piero della Francesca*, a large palace which was probably designed by the famous artist (restored in the mid-16C). It has a fine row of windows high up on the façade. It has been restored as a study centre. In the garden opposite is a monument to the painter by Arnaldo Zocchi (1892). Just beyond, next to the headquarters of the Misericordia is the church of *San Rocco* (ring for admission), the contents of which were restored in 1988. It contains two angels attributed to Alessandro and Giovanni Alberti, and St Sebastian attributed to Leonardo Cungi (died 1569). On the left side is an 18C painting of three saints. Behind the carved and gilded altar is a statue of the Dead Christ. The oratory beneath the church (also shown on request; ring in Via della Fonte), has frescoed lunettes by the Alberti and a replica of the Resurrection of Christ by Raffaelle dal Colle in the Duomo. Behind is a copy of the Holy Sepulchre in Jerusalem, an imitation of a work by Leon Battista Alberti in Florence.

Via XX Settembre (the Corso), which traverses the town from the 16C Porta Fiorentina, in a fine stretch of walls through Piazza Torre di Berta to the site of Porta Romana, is well worth exploring, especially at the E end. At the W end is the church of *Sant'Agostino*, rebuilt in 1771 by Vincenzo Righi with a bright interior decorated with white stuccoes. South side, second altar, Annibale Lancisi, Annunciation (1762); third altar, 14C Crucifix. In front of the high altar, painted wood sarcophagus of 1230, and in the apse, Madonna della Cintola by Giovanni Cimica. North side, third altar, 17C Florentine school, Birth of the Virgin; first altar, Giovanni Cimica, Madonna in glory with St Nicholas of Tolentino.

At No. 46 Via XX Settembre is the 18C Palazzo Alberti with a bust of Cosimo II. Beyond Piazza Torre di Berta, Via XX Settembre passes (right) Palazzo Graziani, a handsome early-17C palace. Across Via del Buon Umore, with four flying arches, is the 16C Palazzo Ducci Del Rossi (No. 131; covered for restoration), seat of the town library. On the left is Teatro Dante (now a cinema) built in 1835, and (No. 139) Palazzo Turini with an old tower. The last part of the Corso, with numerous shops, has small side streets, many with arches.

In the S part of the town (reached from Piazza Torre di Berta by the pretty Via della Fraternità) is the church of *Santa Maria dei Servi*. On the right of the high altar, Matteo di Giovanni (attributed), Madonna in Glory, a fine but damaged painting. On either side are two paintings of four saints (with the Annunciation in tondoes above), part of one painting by Matteo di Giovanni. In Via Santa Croce is the deconsecrated church of *San Lorenzo*, with a Renaissance loggia on one corner. It contains a *Deposition by Rosso Fiorentino (1528), a dark and crowded composition (for admission, apply at the Tourist Information Office or the Museo Civico).

The *Fortezza Medicea* (in urgent need of restoration), at the NE corner of the old town (no admission) was built for Cosimo I in 1561–63 by Alberto Alberti on a design by Giuliano da Sangallo; at the NW corner is the *Cannoniere del Buontalenti*, a bastion erected in the walls by Bernardo Buontalenti. Other pretty steets in the town include Via San Giuseppe, Via Sant'Antonio, Via Piero della Francesca, and Via Luca Pacioli. To the N of Piazza San Francesco is the old Buitoni factory (being restored); a new factory has been erected on the S outskirts of the town.

16km N of Sansepolcro, reached by N3bis (a new fast road between Perugia in Umbria and Cesena in Emilia-Romagna) is **Pieve Santo Stefano** (433m), which was systematically mined in the Second World War when the Collegiata was left standing almost alone amid ruins. The church, rebuilt in 1844–81 in neo-classical style, contains a

Martyrdom of St Stephen, attributed to Spagnoletto, a dossal in enamelled terracotta with the Assumption (1514; attributed to Andrea Della Robbia), and a 16C polychrome Madonna. The church of the Madonna dei Lumi, on a domed Greek-cross plan, dates from 1590–1625. In Palazzo Comunale is a fine terracotta of the Good Samaritan (1511). The Loggia del Grano is an old covered marketplace. The main road continues N to cross the border into Emilia Romagna (see *Blue Guide Northern Italy*). A windy by-road from Pieve Santo Stefano leads W via La Verna to Bibbiena in the Casentino, described in Rte 24. 10km SW of Pieve Santo Stefano is Caprese Michelangelo, also described in Rte 24.

From Sansepolcro another road lead N across the Passo di Viamaggio (983m). Here a rough road leads W to the hermitage of *Cerbaiolo*, founded in 722 by the Benedictines and owned by the Franciscans since 1216. The 13C church and cloister survive, in beautiful countryside. The main road continues to **Badia Tedalda** (30km), a little hill resort (756m) with 2-star hotels, and a 2-star camping site. The parish church contains enamelled terracotta altarpieces by the Buglioni, including the high altarpiece of the Madonna and four saints commissioned in 1516 from Benedetto Buglioni, a Madonna of the holy Girdle (1521), and Saints Julian, Sebastian, and Anthony (1522), by Santi Buglioni. The road continues to **Sestino** (44km; 2-star hotel *Villa Rosa* at Ponte Presale), an ancient Roman municipium, in the E corner of Tuscany, on the border with the Marches. An Antiquarium (temporarily closed) founded here in 1930–36 displays local Roman finds including statues of the Imperial era. The ancient Pieve of San Pancrazio contains a huge painted Cross by the 14C Riminese school. The primitive crypt is also interesting.

Another by-road leads NE from Sansepolcro past the 14C church of *Santa Maria* near Montagna, where local 14C frescoes have recently been restored. The rough road continues up to the convent of *Montecasale*, surrounded by fine woods and cypresses. A hermitage was built here by St Francis (now occupied by Cappuchin fathers). The church contains a 12C wood statue of the Madonna and Child.

On the left bank of the Tiber, 5km W of Sansepolcro is the church of *San Martino di Montedoglio*, restored in 1981. The first church here was probably founded before 1000. It contains a fresco of St Martin attributed to the school of Piero della Francesca or to Gerino da Pistoia, and a 15C terracotta statue of St Sebastian.

N3 bis leads S from Sansepolcro across the Umbrian border towards Città di Castello (described in *Blue Guide Umbria*).

29

Arezzo to Chiusi (the Valdichiana)

The **VALDICHIANA** is the plain lying between the upper basins of the Arno and the Tiber. In prehistoric times this valley was the bed of the Arno, which flowed not into the Tyrrhenian Sea but into the Tiber. The unhealthy marshes left behind when it took its new direction were first drained by the efforts of Cosimo de Medici, and draining and irrigation operations have gone on almost continuously since. The waters of the valley are carried off N to the Arno by the *Canale Maestro della Chiana* (begun in 1551) and S to the Tiber by the much smaller *Chianetta*.

Road, 70km. N73.—11km turning for *Civitella in Val di Chiana* (8km)—22km **Monte San Savino**—30km **Lucignano** (*Foiano della Chiana*, 8km)—38km **Sinalunga**. N326—70km **Chiusi**.

This route takes in the main places of interest, but the most direct road (N327, 56km) diverges S from N73 and follows the Chiana valley via Foiano della Chiana to Chiusi.

The A1 MOTORWAY from Florence to Rome also follows this route, with exits at Monte San Savino, *Valdichiana* (for Sinalunga) and Chiusi.

Railway. A secondary line from Arezzo has stations at Monte San Savino, Lucignano, Foiano, and Sinalunga. Sinalunga is also on the Siena–Chiusi line. Chiusi can be reached direct from Arezzo in 50 minutes on the main line from Florence to Rome.

Information Offices. *APT Arezzo* (Tel. 0575/377678) for Monte San Savino and Lucignano, and *APT Chianciano Terme-Valdichiana* (Tel. 0578/63538) for Sinalunga and Chiusi.

N73 runs SW from the centre of Arezzo (see Rte 26), and crosses the *Canale Maestro della Chiana* on the plain. 11km. Turning (right) for *Civitella in Val di Chiana* (8km). This delightful little hamlet lies in a beautiful position on a wooded ridge with fine views. The road leads through Porta Senese beside the Cassero (open daily 8–20), an impressive 13C castle with high ruined walls. The main street, with pretty brick paving and delightful arcades, continues past Palazzo del Podestà with coats of arms and a characteristic portico, the lines of which are repeated in the other buildings nearby. The rebuilt parish church in the piazza stands beside an inscription and bronze relief commemorating the inhabitants who lost their lives here in a brutal act of retaliation during the Second World War. An unsurfaced by-road leads downhill to the S through spectacular countryside via Ciggiano to Gargonza (11km; described below).

22km **MONTE SAN SAVINO** (330m; 7500 inhab.) was the birthplace of the sculptor and architect Andrea Contucci, called Sansovino (1460–1529), and preserves a number of works by him.

Hotel (3-star) *San Gallo*, 16 Piazza Vittorio Veneto. An annual **fair** (*Fiera dell'equino e dello scaldino col fischio*) is held on 24–25 November.

History. Of Roman foundation, Monte San Savino is named after a church dedicated to the 5C bishop of Chiusi, San Savino. For long hostile to Arezzo, in 1325 it was destroyed by the Aretine bishop Guido Tarlati. Members of the local Di Monte family (who became counts of the town in the 16C) included Cardinal Antonio (friend and adviser of Julius II), and Pope Julius III. The town has been known since ancient times for its production of ceramics and Andrea Sansovino began his artistic life here as a ceramist.

The town is entered by *Porta Fiorentina* built c 1550 by Nanni di Baccio Bigio Bigio (on a design by Giorgio Vasari). Here begins Corso Sangallo which traverses the small town past several fine palaces. In the first piazza the interesting palaces include one at the far end with an unusual ground floor window with two carved herms. The obelisk was set up in honour of Mattias De' Medici who became ruler of the Principality in 1644. The *Cassero* (open for exhibitions in summer, when it is also the seat of a tourist information office) is attributed to the Sienese architect Bartolo di Bartolo (1383; restored). The exterior is now hidden by 17C houses. It contains a small collection of local ceramics. The church of *Santa Chiara*, built in 1652, is privately owned and usually kept locked. In the interior are two paintings of saints by Guidoccio Cozzarelli (probably on a cartoon by Matteo di Giovanni); a splendid *altarpiece of the Madonna and Child with four saints by Andrea Sansovino (c 1490), glazed by Andrea or Giovanni Della Robbia; an unglazed terracotta altarpiece of St Laurence between Saints Roch and Sebastian (1486), also by Andrea Sansovino; a polychrome terracotta altarpiece of the Nativity, attributed to Giovanni Della Robbia; and a statue of St Anthony Abbot, attributed to the Della Robbia or to Sansovino.

Farther on in Corso Sangallo is the handsome ***Loggia dei Mercanti**, built in 1518–20 by Andrea Sansovino for Cardinal Antonio Di Monte. The high arcade is borne on Corinthian columns and pilasters (in poor repair). Opposite it is the town hall in *Palazzo Di Monte* built in 1515 by Antonio da Sangallo the Elder, also for the Cardinal. It has a fine courtyard with two rectangular wells, beyond which is a hanging garden designed by Nanni di Baccio Bigio. The **Pieve** was built c 1100 and the interior remodelled in the mid-18C with stuccoes and marbling. On the left of the W door is the recomposed sarcophagus of Fabiano Di Monte (father of Cardinal Antonio), an early work by Andrea Sansovino (1498). Above the benches towards the E end are two small square reliefs, possibly also early works by Sansovino. On the right of the high altar is a fresco fragment with two angels. The organ dates from the 17C.

On the other side of the Corso is the 14C tower, decorated with coats of arms, of *Palazzo Pretorio*. Beyond is Piazza Di Monte, laid out by Andrea Sansovino in front of his house (plaque). Above the public fountain is a Marzocco lion. The interior of the church of **Sant'Agostino** has a delightful double loggia with Ionic columns at the W end by Andrea Sansovino. The altars date from 1710, and it has an interesting pavement. On the W wall are good frescoes of the Crucifixion, Adoration of the Magi, and Presentation in the Temple by Giovanni d'Agnolo di Balduccio (1370–1452). Above is a rose window by Guglielmo di Marcillat. On the right wall, St Lawrence with stories from his life. The high altarpiece of the Assumption is signed and dated 1539 by Vasari. It is flanked by a Nativity and Adoration of the Magi by Orazio Porta. On the left wall is a Resurrection, also by Porta (in very poor condition). Below the little pulpit is the worn tomb slab of Sansovino, found in 1969 beneath the pavement of the church. The damaged fresco of the Pietà, with five saints below, is by Paolo Schiavo. There is a fine cloister next to the church, perhaps designed by Sansovino (1528). The church of *San Giovanni*, which has a door by Sansovino, is usually closed.

2km E of Monte San Savino (towards the motorway) is the sanctuary of **Santa Maria delle Vertighe**, with a campanile attributed to Sansovino. In the primitive apse is a copy of an *altarpiece by Margaritone d'Arezzo (which has been removed for safety to Arezzo). When a security system has been installed, it should be returned here, together with the contents of the museum (admission on request at the monastery), which include two saints by Ridolfo del Ghirlandaio, and a painted Crucifix by Lorenzo Monaco.

The road continues beneath the motorway, and a by-road diverges right for *Marciano della Chiana* (8km) which has scant remains of its walls and towers (being restored). The altarpieces in the church are in very poor condition: the interesting trompe l'oeil frescoes at the E end date from 1750. A road leads S to *Pozzo*, beyond which, by the cemetery, is SANTA VITTORIA, an octagonal chapel with a cupola and lantern thought to have been designed by Ammannati or Vasari in 1572. It was commissioned by Cosimo I to commemorate the battle here of Scannagallo in 1554 in which the Florentines were victorious over the Sienese and French. It is an unusual, but well-proportioned building in brick and pietra serena (locked, and in poor repair).

N73 winds W from Monte San Savino towards Siena. The road becomes prettier as it climbs into woods and a by-road (right; signposted) leads down to **Gargonza** (8km), a beautiful little circular medieval hamlet surrounded by wooded hills. An Ubertini castle in the 13C, it was sold to Siena in 1381, but its possession was subsequently contested by Florence, who ordered the destruction of its walls in 1433. It has been carefully restored as a 'Residence' where houses can be rented.

A by-road continues S from Monte San Savino towards Sinalunga. 30km **Lucignano** (3-star hotel, with restaurant, *Da Totò*, 6 Piazza del Tribunale) is a delightful, cheerful little medieval village laid out on an elliptical form, and well preserved. It has some interesting works of art, and fine views. Above the 14C *Cassero*, with a tall tower, is the large *Collegiata*, approached by a pretty flight of curving steps. The campanile is covered for restoration. The interior by Orazio Porta, dates from 1594. The gilded wood angels were installed in 1706. In the S transept, Giacinto Gemignani, St Charles Borromeo. The high altar is by Andrea Pozzo. In the N transept, Matteo Rosselli, Visitation. On the N side is a 16C Crucifix (third altar) and a martyrdom of St Lucy by Gemignani.

Beyond the Collegiata is the 14C *Palazzo Comunale*, recently restored. It houses the MUSEO COMUNALE (open 9.30–13, 15–18.30; closed Monday), which was reopened in 1982. In the entrance is a 16C fresco of the Pietà. In the entrance corridor is church silver of 1628, and a small painting of the Madonna enthroned with saints attributed to Lippo Vanni. The vaulted *Sala del Tribunale* has delightful frescoes dating from 1438–65 of illustrious people from the Bible and Classical heroes, and a huge gold *reliquary (over 2.5 metres high) known as the TREE OF LUCIGNANO made in 1350–1471 and decorated with coral and exquisite miniatures. R. 3: lunette by Luca Signorelli of St Francis receiving the stigmata (with a lovely landscape), and a Madonna and Child attributed to him. R. 4: Madonna and Child enthroned by the Sienese school (c 1320); *triptych of the Madonna with Saints John the Baptist and John the Evangelist by Bartolo di Fredi; *St Bernardine (1448) by Pietro di Giovanni Ambrogio; small *Crucifixion by the 13C Sienese school.

Beside Palazzo Comunale is the church of *San Francesco* (1248), with a Romanesque façade, also recently restored. It has numerous fresco fragments of great interest, attributed to Bartolo di Fredi, Taddeo di Bartolo, and others. On the last altar on the S side is a painted polychrome wood statue of the Madonna and Child by Mariano di Angelo Romanelli (1380–90; restored in 1983). Behind the high altar, polyptych of the Madonna with four saints by Luca di Tommé. The organ dates from the 16C. Other churches of interest (usually closed) include the *Santissimo Crocifisso* and the *Oratorio della Misericordia*, with two Della Robbian statues.

The church of the *Madonna della Quercia* is c 1km outside the village (indicated by yellow signs). The road passes the ruins of the old Medici fortress built by Cosimo I on a hill, and the cemetery. The church (in poor condition), next to a farm house, is only open for services at weekends. It was built in the late-16C perhaps on a design by Vasari, and the fine interior is attributed to Giuliano da Sangallo.

A road leads across the motorway to **Foiano della Chiana** (8km), a small agricultural town, with some industries, near the plain of the Chiana. From the gate a road leads up to Piazza Cavour where the Palazzo Comunale faces Palazzo Monte Pio, well restored. It was built by Ferdinando II as a hunting lodge and used as such up to 1670 when it became the Monte di Pietà. It now contains offices of the Comune. A modern flight of steps leads down to the left and across Corso Vittorio Emanuele (which has an 18C loggia) to the church of *San Michele Arcangelo*, with a pretty exterior and campanile. It contains fine carved confessionals and benches dating from the 17C, and 15C choir stalls. On the second S altar is a Madonna of the Rosary by Lorenzo Lippi, and on the third N altar, a Della Robbian terracotta of the Ascension. Off the S side is an oratory with elaborate stuccoes in the vault and lunettes. The Corso continues to Piazza della Collegiata with a well and imposing brick fortifications (a round tower is being restored) and a row of houses above brick bastions on either side of Porta Castello. The *Collegiata* has a Baroque façade. On the third S altar is a Madonna della

Cintola (1502) attributed to Andrea Della Robbia, and on the second N altar, a Coronation of the Virgin, a late work by Luca Signorelli and his school. Steps lead up through Porta Castello, a double brick gate, to the church of *Santa Maria della Fraternità* (not open regularly; ask at the Comune for the key) which contains a 17C ceiling, cantoria, benches, and organ. Four paintings are attributed to Giovanni Camillo Sagrestani, and a Madonna and Child shows the influence of Andrea Della Robbia. A 17C gilded wood coffer is being restored. On the outskirts of the town, by the hospital, and preceded by a portico, is the church of *San Francesco* (usually open in the afternoon). It contains 16C terracotta statuary, and a large Della Robbian altarpiece of Christ in Glory with saints.

From Foiano a road leads over the Chiana via the Abbazia di Farneta to Cortona (12km), both described in Rte 27.

From Lucignano a secondary road continue S to (38km) **Sinalunga** (4-star hotel *Locanda dell'Amorosa*, with luxury-class restaurant, 2km S), now a small industrial town. From the 12C up until 1864 it was known as *Asinalunga*. Here the Sienese defeated the English mercenaries of Niccolò da Montefeltro in 1363; here also Garibaldi was arrested in 1867 by Victor Emanuel II, to prevent an ill-timed descent on Rome. In the ugly large Piazza Garibaldi is the COLLEGIATA (San Martino). In the interior are large white stucco statues of saints. On the S side, the third chapel contains a 16C Crucifix. In the S transept is a Deposition by Francesco Vanni (called 'il Pacchia, 1563–1610) with a predella (in a good frame). On the S wall of the sanctuary, Madonna and saints by Benvenuto di Giovanni (1509) with another good predella and frame. On the N wall of the sanctuary a tondo by Pseudo Pier Francesco Fiorentino has been removed. In the N transept, *Madonna and the standing Child by Sodoma above Christ supported by two angels flanked by Saints Bernardine and Catherine.

To the right of the church is *Santa Croce* with an 18C façade. In the pretty interior is (right altar) a Marriage of the Virgin by the school of Luca Signorelli. Also in the piazza is the church of *Santa Maria delle Nevi* with a painting attributed to Benvenuto di Giovanni. On the right of the façade of the Collegiata Via Mazzini winds round to *Palazzo Pretorio*, in an unusual site, between two streets. It is built in brick, with coats of arms and a tower. In front of the palace a road continues down to *Santa Lucia* (deconsecrated; used by a musical society), which contains a fresco attributed to Benvenuto di Giovanni. Beyond is a view over the Valdichiana. Near Palazzo Pretorio is a *Theatre* (1797–1807), with an inconspicuous exterior (No. 17). It is named after Ciro Pinsuti (1824–88), born in Sinalunga.

Outside the town is the Franciscan convent of *San Bernardino* (or the *Madonna del Riposo*; yellow signposts), approached by a short avenue. Off the 18C church (shown by a nun) is an octagonal chapel with some fine paintings: Guidoccio Cozzarelli, Baptism of Christ (1470); Benvenuto di Giovanni, Annunciation (1470); Guidoccio Cozzarelli, Madonna and Child with saints (1486). A Madonna and Child by Sano di Pietro, stolen in 1971, is to be replaced by a copy. Over the high altar is a copy (the original has been removed for safekeeping) of a Madonna and Child known as the Madonna del Rifugio, attributed to Sano di Pietro.

Sinalunga is just S of a main road (N 326) to Siena, which passes close to *Rapolano Terme* (16km from Sinalunga), a medieval town with spa waters and travertine quarries.

The road for Chiusi (N 326) continues S from Sinalunga through Torrita di Siena, described, together with the interesting little towns to the W (including Montefollonico, Trequanda, Montisi and Castelmuzio) in the *Valdichiana Senese*, in Rte 21. This route soon joins a road from Montepulciano (also described in Rte 21) for (70km) **CHIUSI**, a little hill-top town of 8700 inhabitants. It was an Etruscan town of great importance, as can be seen from the finds in its interesting museum, and the vast Etruscan necropolis which surrounds the town.

Information office, Pro-Loco, 61 Via Porsenna.

Railway Station on the main line between Florence and Rome. Services from Arezzo in 40mins.

Buses every half hour to the railway station. Bus services to Lago di Chiusi, and to Montepulciano via Chianciano Terme.

Car Parking off Via Pietriccia and Via dei Longobardi.

Hotels at Querce al Pino, 4km W: *Il Patriarca* (4-star), *Ismaele*, and *Rosati* (both 3-star). 1-star camping site near Lago di Chiusi.

History. Chiusi was called *Chamars* by Livy, but is thought instead to have been the Etruscan *Clevsins*. One of the twelve cities of the Etruscan Confederation, it reached its greatest splendour around the 7C or 6C BC. The Latin authors often referred to the fertility of the surrounding countryside, which produced oil, wine, and wheat in abundance. Strabo described how the Lago di Chiusi could be reached by river from Rome up the Tiber and Chiana. Lars Porsena, the *Lucumo* or king, attacked Rome in 507–06 BC (see Macaulay's *Horatius*), but the town became subject to Rome after 296 BC and took the Roman name of *Clusium*. It continued to flourish in the Augustan era, and was then occupied by the Goths from 540 probably up until the 10C, when it became part of the Lombard duchy. The neighbourhood of the unhealthy marshes of the Valdichiana brought about the decline of Chiusi, but the drainage works begun by Cosimo de' Medici restored some degree of prosperity. Under the streets runs a labyrinth of Etruscan galleries.

The Duomo and Etruscan Museum (well signposted) are close together. The **Duomo** (San Secondiano) was founded in the 6C and rebuilt in the 12C, but heavily restored in 1887–94. In the INTERIOR the splendid *columns and capitals, including one in breccia marble at the W end, come from various local Roman edifices. The nave and apses were painted by Arturo Viligiardi in 1887 in imitation of antique mosaics. In the S aisle is an alabaster font in the style of Andrea Sansovino. Off the left aisle is an Adoration of the Child by Bernardino Fungai. At the W end of the N aisle is a monument to San Mustiola of 1785. A tall fortified tower was transformed into the CAMPANILE in 1585. It covers a huge cistern of the 1C BC (apply for admission to the Museo Nazionale Etrusco, see below).

Under the portico to the right of the façade is the **Museo della Cattedrale**, founded in 1932 and reopened in 1984. It is well-arranged and labelled (open daily 1 June–15 October, 9.30–12.45, 16.30–19.30; fest. 16.30–19.30; winter 9.30–12.45). R. I contains finds including tombstones and inscriptions from the local catacombs of Santa Mustiola and Santa Caterina. Also here are Roman fragments from the Duomo, as well as Lombard and late medieval material. In the GARDEN, reached by a steep flight of steps cut into the walls in the last century, are remains of Etruscan fortifications which have been in the process of excavation since 1985. These include walls of the 3C BC with a square tower, on top of an Etruscan building. Nearby is the entrance to a remarkable long Etruscan gallery, which may have served as a water channel, or as part of a defensive system, and which has been opened to the public. Inside the museum building, at the top of the stairs, R. II contains: Girolamo da Benvenuto, Madonna and Child with saints (very ruined; recently restored); church silver and vestments; and 15C ivories by the bottega degli Embriachi. Stairs continue up to a long passage above the portico with a fine display of 21 antiphonals from the abbey of Monte Oliveto Maggiore dating from the second half of the 15C, illuminated by Liberale da Verona, Sano di Pietro, Lorenzo Rosselli di Bindo, and others.

The *Catacombs of Santa Caterina*, near the station, can be seen on a guided tour at 11 on request at the museum (a custodian accompanies visitors in their car). They date from the mid-3C AD and have been lit. The *Catacombs of Santa Mustiola*, dedicated to the Roman saint, beneath a farm house, and in use from the 3C to the 5C can also be visited (as for Santa Caterina).

The *Museo Nazionale Etrusco* (admission daily 8–14; fest. 8–13) was founded in 1871 and opened in this fitting neo-classical building by Partini in 1901. Chiusi was one of the first Etruscan cities to be explored, as early as the 15C, but unsystematic excavations, especially in the 19C, led to the dispersal of much of the material, and most of the objects in the museum are of unknown provenence and some have been poorly or incorrectly restored. A great number of inscriptions were found in and near Chiusi, but they are now in other museums.

The display is divided into three sections; the first illustrating the history of archaeological research in the area; the second showing the chronological development of local products, and the third with finds arranged topographically. In the centre of the hall is prehistoric and Villanovian material, with finds dating from the 9–8C BC, including canopic vases of the 7–6C BC. In a small room are displayed Archaic reliefs (late 6C BC), showing Greek influence, and five sculptures of the 6–5C BC. At the end of the hall are cases of Bucchero ware and 5C Attic black-figure and red-figure vases, terracotta architectural fragments, and 5–4C bronzes. In the outer corridor: Etruscan vases and sarcophaghi and cinerary urns (4–2C BC) in alabaster and terracotta, including the sarcophagus depicting the deceased Lars Sentinates. The Roman material includes a head of Augustus, architectural and votive terracottas (3–2C BC) and Hellenistic bronzes, ceramics and sarcophaghi.

The narrow Via della Misericordia leads to the 13C church of *Santa Maria della Morte*, with a very unusual tower. In the pleasant Piazza XX Settembre, with a clock tower and 14C loggia (altered) is the town hall (enlarged in the 19C) and a 19C fountain. At the bottom of Via Lavinia can be seen Porta Lavinia, and the countryside beyond. Near the clock tower is the church of *San Francesco*, founded in the 13C, with an ancient portal. The interior dates from the 18C; the stained glass windows at the E end were made in 1944 in Florence. Via Paolozzi leads to Piazza Vittorio Veneto, with a panoramic view. In the garden are Etruscan and Roman fragments. Via Arunte descends to a column of 1581 in Piazza Graziani, and then Via Porsenna continues up past several handsome palaces back to Piazza Duomo.

On the outskirts of the town, in Via della Violella, off the Chianciano Terme road, part of the Etruscan walls of the city can be seen.

The ETRUSCAN TOMBS in the neighbourhood have all been closed for conservation reasons, except for the Tomba della Pellegrina and Tomba del Leone, which can be visited by appointment at the Museo Archeologico. There are long-term plans to reopen the others. They are approached by pretty country lanes, most of which can be negotiated by car. Just outside the town, on the road to Chianciano Terme, Via delle Tombe Etrusche diverges right for (3km) the *Tomba della Pellegrina*, with several urns and sarcophagi. The *Tomba della Scimmia* (of the Ape) has important wall-paintings, and the *Tomba del Leone* has recently been restored. The *Tomba del Granduca*, has eight cinerary urns remaining on their stone benches. Another itinerary leaves the city beyond the Cimitero Nuovo, and includes the *Tomba Casuccini* (or *del Colle*), with a fine doorway (now visible through a glass door) and wall-paintings of sports and games, and the *Tomba delle Tassinaie*, the only painted tomb from the Hellenistic period. The *Poggio Gaiella*, a tufa hill 4km N, has three storeys of passages and galleries; according to tradition, it is the mausoleum of Lars Porsenna.

To the N of Chiusi are two small picturesque lakes, with reedy shores, the LAGO DI CHIUSI (387 hectares) and the LAGO DI MONTEPULCIANO (188 hectares), surrounded by cultivated fields and poplars. They are remnants of the huge marsh which once occupied this area. The interesting vegetation includes numerous varieties of aquatic plants, including water lilies. On the shores of Lago di Montepulciano is the Museo Naturalistico del Lago (the lake can be visited by appointment, Tel. 0578/767518). Fishing is carried out by the local inhabitants.

From Chiusi N146 leads W to Chianciano Terme, Montepulciano, and Pienza, all described in Rte 21. Città della Pieve, 11km S of Chiusi in Umbria is described, together with Lake Trasimene to the E of Chiusi, in *Blue Guide Umbria*. Cetona and Sarteano, interesting little towns SW of Chiusi are described in Rte 21.

30

The Islands of Elba and Capraia

ELBA (29,000 inhab.), is the largest island in the Tuscan archipelago, and is only 10km from Piombino on the mainland. It has an area of 223 sq km, and is 27km long and 18km across at its broadest. The climate is mild and sunny and the sea bathing good, and it is crowded with visitors in summer. It is popular as a holiday place with Germans, particuarly in September. Its geological formation, with numerous varieties of different minerals, is of the highest interest. The Greek *Aethalia* and the Roman *Ilva*, it has been known since ancient times for its iron ore, which has been mined here for centuries. It became famous in 1814–15 as Napoleon's place of exile. The inhabited part of the island has pretty hills covered with the *macchia*, low vegetation typical of the Mediterranean, while other parts are barren and deserted. The beautiful Monte Capanna (1019m) is covered with woods of chestnuts, oaks, and ilexes. The English have been coming here since the 17C, and Joseph Conrad based his last unfinished novel *Suspense* (begun in 1905) on Elba, although he never visited the island. The beauty of the island has been threatened in recent years by forest fires. The excellent red and white wines once produced here are now difficult to find, although the sweet desert wines *Aleatico* and *Moscato* are still sold on the island.

Information Offices. *APT dell'Arcipelago Toscano*, 26 Calata Italia, Portoferraio, Elba (Tel. 0565/914671). *Comunità Montana dell'Elba e Capraia*, Viale Manzoni, Portoferraio (who publish a map of the numerous footpaths on the island).

Approaches. The port for Elba is Piombino, see Rte 12. Maritime services are run by *Toremar*, *Navarma*, and *Elba Ferries*. It is always advisable to book the return trip for cars in advance, especially on holidays and in summer. *Toremar*: Piombino office, 13 Piazzale Premuda (Tel. 0565/31100); Portoferraio office, 22 Calata Italia (Tel. 0565/918080). *Navarma*: Piombino office, 13 Piazzale Premuda (Tel. 0565/221212); Portoferraio office, 4 Viale Elba (Tel. 0565/914133). Frequent car ferries and hydrofoils (much more expensive) run to Portoferraio on the N coast in c 1hr (hydrofoils in 30mins). Another boat serves Porto Azzurro and Rio Marino on the E coast. Hydrofoil to Cavo.

By rail, the slower trains on the main line from Pisa and Livorno to Rome stop at Campiglia Marittima, where there are frequent services to Piombino Marittima for the ferry. In summer there is one return train a day from Florence direct to Piombino Marittima (the *Freccia dell'Elba*) in c 2hrs 15mins in connection with the ferry.

Accommodation. There are some 200 hotels and residences of all categories on the island, and only a very small selection is given below. Near Portoferraio: 4-star *Villa Ottone*, località Ottone, and *Picchiaie Residence*, località Picchiaie. 3-star Residence *Acquabona Golf Hotel*, località Acquabona. At Biodola: 4-star *Hermitage* and *Biodola*. Near Capoliveri: 3-star *Capo Sud*, località Lacona, and Residence *Costa dei Gabbiani*, località Ripalte. Rio Marina: 3-star *Rio*, 31 Via Palestro. There are numerous Camping Sites all over the island. These include the 3-star *Rosselba Le Palme* at località Ottone, E of Portoferraio. Others on the S coast, particularly near Lacona.

Restaurants. Portoferraio: First-class restaurant *La Ferrigna*, Piazza della Repubblica; trattoria *Da Elbano Benassi*, località Casaccia. Capoliveri: first-class restaurant *Il Chiasso*. Rio Marina: trattoria *La Canocchia*. Poggio: first-class restaurant *Publius*. Marciana Marina: first-class restaurant *Rendez-vous da Marcello*.

Bus services from near the ferry quay at Portoferraio to Procchio and Marciana, to Cavo via Porto Azzurro and Rio Marina, to Capoliveri via Porto Azzurro, and to Marina di Campo.

Car and bicycle hire available at Portoferraio.

The chief town and port is **Portoferraio** (10,600 inhab.), with the great *Ilva* blast furnaces. It was founded in 1548 by the Medici Grand Duke Cosimo I when the remarkable fortifications were begun by Giovanni Battista Bellucci and Giovanni Camerini. The modern seafront, where the ferries dock, is unattractive; the old port, now used by private boats, is at the end of the promontory. It was occupied by the British fleet in 1795–97. The fortified Porta a Mare (1637) leads into the old district, still the centre of the town, with a covered market. The *Museo Archeologico della Linguella*, in the old salt warehouses, was opened in 1988 (open 9.30–12.30, 16–19; summer 9–12, 16–19; closed fest.). It contains late Bronze Age finds from Santa Lucia; a Punic amphora (7–6C BC); Etruscan material from the fortresses of Monte Castello (above Procchio) and Castiglione di San Martino (5–2C BC). The exhibits relating to shipwrecked boats found offshore include huge anchors. There are also Etruscan and Roman finds from the necropolis of Profico at Capoliveri, and mosaics from Villa Le Grotte.

A road (or steps) lead up from the main Piazza della Repubblica to the Medici *Forte Stella* (recently restored) which dominates the port and from which there is a good view. Napoleon's principal residence was the *Villetta dei Mulini*, overlooking the sea. The modest house (open 9–13.30; summer 9–19) contains Napoleonic souvenirs. The main defensive system is to the W around *Forte Falcone*; this can be visited on the descent to the *Porta a Terra* on the sea front. In the Caserma de Laugier is the *Pinacoteca Foresiana* (open 9.30–12.30; closed fest.), with Tuscan works of the 16–19C.

A road leads along the coast W from Portoferraio to *Capo d'Enfola* (7km), on a rocky promontory with beaches and hotels.

Another road runs SW from Portoferraio for Marciana. Beyond the junction with the road for Porto Azzurro (see below) is (2.5km) the fork left for the VILLA SAN MARTINO (admission as for the Villetta dei Mulini), in a fertile

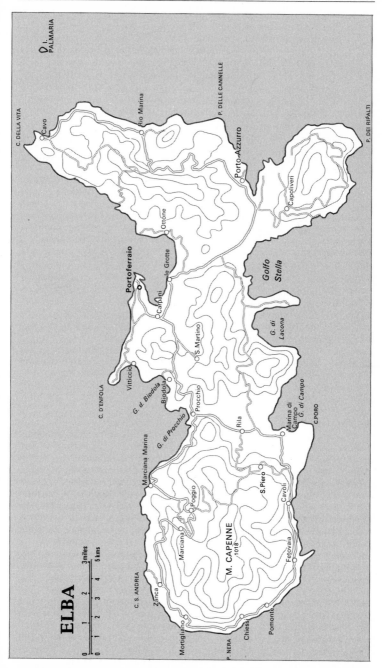

ELBA

C. DELLA VITA
Cavo
I. PALMARIA
Rio Marina
P. DELLE CANNELLE
Porto-Azzurro
Capoliveri
P. DEI RIFALTI
Ottóne
Golfo Stella
le Grotte
Portoferraio
Capôliri
G. di Lacona
S. Martino
Viticcio
C. D'ENFOLA
G. d. Biodola
Biodola
Procchio
Rila
Marina di Campo
G. di Campo
C. PORO
Marciana Marina
G. di Procchio
Poggio
S. Piero
Marciana
Cavoli
M. CAPENNE
1018
Fetovaia
C. S. ANDREA
Zinca
Mortigliano
Chiessi
Pomonte
P. NERA

3miles
5kms
0 1 2 3 4
0 1 2 3

valley, Napoleon's summer residence. The large one-storey neo-classical edifice was built in front of Napoleon's house by Prince Demidoff in 1851 as a memorial to him. The Galleria Demidoff, with a collection of engravings was opened here in 1987. The Pinacoteca Foresiana has been moved to Portoferraio (see above). Napoleon's simple house above is reached by a path on the left. It is charmingly decorated in the style known as *retour d'Egypte* with frescoes commemorating Napoleon's Egyptian campaign in 1798–1800. They were painted by his official court painter, Vincenzo Antonio Revelli in 1814.

The main road continues above the pretty little bay and sandy beach of (6km) *Biodola* (by-road right), with a small bunglaow colony and camping site. 11.5km *Procchio*, a busy resort, with a good beach. A road leads from here past a little airport on a plain to *Marina di Campo*, an attractive bathing resort on the coast, with perhaps the best beach on the island, and numerous hotels. It also has a fishing fleet. A windy road continues from Procchio along the N coast where access to the sea is limited. 19km **Marciana Marina**, a pretty little port with sardine fisheries. The cylindrical tower on the mole was built by the Pisans in the 12C. There are long-term plans to expand the harbour. From here the road runs uphill through chestnut woods to the most beautiful part of the island around (21km) *Poggio* (330m) and (27km) *Marciana Alta*, both delightful little villages. The Museo Civico Archeologico (open in summer 9–13, 16–19; fest. closed) was opened here in 1968. It contains prehistoric material found on the island, including vases of the Rinaldone culture; Etruscan and Hellenistic finds; and amphora found offshore. A cable-car (open from May to September 10–12, 14.30–18) ascends to the summit of *Monte Capanne* (1018m), which can also be climbed by marked paths in c 2hrs. The road continues around the W shore of the island which has splendid views and wild scenery. A by-road (right) leads to *Sant'Andrea*, an elegant resort. Farther on the main road passes the pretty village of *Chiessi* amidst vineyards, before reaching Marina di Campo (see above).

The main town in the E part of the island is **Porto Azzurro**, a fashionable resort overlooking a beautiful bay. With its great Spanish fort of 1602 (now a prison), it was formerly called *Porto Longone*. It is reached by a road (15.5km) from Portoferraio which passes the *Terme di San Giovanni*, a small spa, with mud baths rich in sulphur (used to help alleviate rheumatism). Nearby, on the shore, are the remains of *Villa Le Grotte*, a Roman villa of the Imperial era, excavated in 1960. Its swimming pool is one of the largest ever discovered. A by-road right just before Porto Azzurro leads to **Capoliveri**, a delightful little old miners' town in a charming position. 12km N of Porto Azzurro, reached by an inland road, is **Rio Marina**, interesting as the chief ore-port and centre of the mining area, with tall grim houses. The local Mineral Museum is open April–Sept 9–12, 15–18; fest. 9–12. A road continues along the E coast to (7.5km) *Cavo* at the northernmost point of the island.

Some of the most beautiful scenery on the island can be seen on the unsurfaced road from Bagnaia (10km E of Portoferraio) to Rio nell'Elba. Another fine road the *Volterraio* leads from Ottone to Rio nell'Elba.

To the N of Elba, 55km from the mainland at Piombino is the mountainous volcanic islet of **CAPRAIA** (20 sq km). It is reached by ferry (*Toremar*) in 2hr 30mins from Livorno once a day (sometimes via Gorgona). At some periods of the year there is also a service once a week from Portoferraio (in 2hrs). Information from the *Cooperativa Parco Naturale Isola di Capraia*

(Tel. 0586/905071), and Pro-Loco (Tel. 0586/905171). 4-star hotel *Il Saracino* and a number of residences, and rooms to let. 3-star camping site *Le Sughere*.

The prison here was closed in 1986. The only settlement is Capraia (300 inhabitants), beneath Forte San Giorgio, reached from the port by the only road (c 1km) on the island. From here paths lead over the wild countryside of volcanic origin, with beautiful vegetation, where cormorants nest. The highest hills reach a level of 400 metres above sea level, and there is a little inland lake. The island was named Capraia by navigators of ancient Greece who found numerous goats here. The rocky shore, with caves, is frequented by skin divers.

The tiny island of **Gorgona** (2.2 sq km), is the northernmost island in the archipelago, 44km N of Capraia, and 37km off the mainland at Livorno. It is still used as a prison. It is also a beautiful wild place, with numerous pine trees and interesting bird life, but can only be visited by booking one month in advance at *Tecatravel*, 60 Corso Amadeo, Livorno (Tel. 0586/897621).

14km S of Elba is the low-lying islet of **Pianosa**, also used as a prison. With an area of 10 sq km, it rises to a maximum of 29 metres above sea level, and has a particularly mild climate. Some 90 amphorae were discovered in 1991 offshore: they have probably remained here exactly as they fell from a Roman shipwreck.

The most isolated of the islands in the Tuscan archipelago is **Montecristo**, 40km S of Elba, and 63km W of the Argentario. It has an area of 10 sq km. This romantic island, now deserted and declared a European nature reserve in 1988, cannot normally be visited. It is formed of a granite mass covered with woods, rising in the centre to Monte Fortezza (645m). Here are the ruins of the Benedictine monastery of San Salvatore and San Mamiliano, devastated by the pirate Dragut in 1553. A legend that the monks had buried their treasure here before abandoning the island gave inspiration to Alexandre Dumas for his historical novel *The Count of Montecristo*. The island was acquired by George Watson Taylor in 1852, who built a villa at Cala Maestra (the only port of the island), later used as a hunting lodge by Victor Emmanuel III, and surrounded by a luxuriant garden.

The islands of Giglio and Giannutri, reached from Monte Argentario, are both described in Rte 12.

INDEX TO ARTISTS

INDEX TO PEOPLE

INDEX TO PLACES

The largest or most important places are highlighted in bold. Florence and Siena have
sub-indexes to streets, squares, museums and monuments.

If you would like more information about
Blue Guides please complete the form below
and
return it to

Blue Guides
A&C Black
Freepost
Cambridgeshire
PE19 3BR
or fax it to us on
0171-831 8478

Name..

....

Address...

....

....

....

....

....